CONGRESS INVESTIGATES
1792–1974

CONGRESS INVESTIGATES
1792–1974

EDITORS

Arthur M. Schlesinger, jr.

Albert Schweitzer Professor in the Humanities
City University of New York

Roger Bruns

National Historical Publications Commission

with an introductory essay by
Arthur M. Schlesinger, jr.

New York
CHELSEA HOUSE PUBLISHERS

in association with

R. R. BOWKER COMPANY
New York and London
1975

Project Editor: Kathryn Hammell
Managing Editor: Roberta Morgan
Assistant Editor: Deborah Weiss

Published by Chelsea House Publishers in association with R. R. Bowker Company (a Xerox Education Company)

Printed and Bound in the United States of America
by Quinn & Boden Company, Inc.

Schlesinger, Arthur Meier, 1917– comp.
Congress investigates.

1. Governmental investigations—United States.
I. Bruns, Roger. II. Title.
JK1123.A2S34 1975b 328.73'07'452 75-28106

ISBN 87754-032-2 (Chelsea House)
0-8352-0864-8 (R. R. Bowker)

PREFACE

When the House of Representatives, on March 27, 1792, established a committee to investigate the ignominious defeat of General Arthur St. Clair at the hands of Indian warriors in the Ohio country, Congress entered for the first time a new and controversial area of activity. From the St. Clair disaster to the Watergate imbroglio, congressional committees have investigated a succession of critical events. This series of essays, selected from the twenty-eight essays which appeared in the five-volume Chelsea House–R. R. Bowker Company documentary publication, *Congress Investigates; A Documented History, 1792–1974,* examines the political controversies and constitutional questions surrounding selected investigating committees throughout the history of the United States Congress.

Attorney General Harry Daugherty, refusing in 1924 to testify before a select Senate committee probing bribery charges against the attorney general, claimed that the committee was conducting a vindictive trial and engaging in character assassination. Daugherty was raising only one of many pivotal questions that have surrounded congressional investigations. Do congressional investigating committees infringe upon powers specifically delegated to the judiciary and therefore violate the doctrine of separation of powers? Does the power to subpoena witnesses fall within the right of Congress to acquire information for purposes of legislation? Are such investigations consistent with the spirit of the general legislative power granted by the Constitution? Does the interrogation of witnesses by some congressional committees constitute a violation of personal liberties? Are committee investigations motivated in most cases by legislative intent or are they largely forums for partisan rancor and political pressure? The sixteen investigations included in this series were selected with respect not only to their historical significance but for their appropriateness in illustrating these legal and constitutional problems. This study graphically illustrates the controversies surrounding the struggles of congressional committees to exercise inquisitorial power.

There has been a notable lack of secondary historical literature on the individual committees represented in the series. With a few exceptions, such as the Teapot Dome investigation and the McCarthy hearings, one looks in vain for adequate secondary accounts. Even such obviously prominent committees as the Joint Committee on Reconstruction following the Civil War and the Pecora Securities investigation of 1932 have had limited treatment. Considering the enormous amount of newspaper space allotted to these investigations and the importance of the investigations in their own contemporary settings, this series represents work in a field of historical inquiry generally ignored by scholars. Or perhaps, as one embattled historian in the series remarked after wrestling with many volumes of testimony, "the source material scared them off."

The congressional inquisitorial hand has touched subjects of great interest to scholars, students, and laymen, and an illuminating political, military, and social history is reflected in the work of the committees examined in this series. The study represents a tool not only for academicians or other individuals seeking information relating specifically to a particular committee; it is of interest to those interested in American history in general and to those studying the personalities and events surrounding these committees. The work of the Committee on the Conduct of the War, for example, had ramifications in the Civil War period far beyond the specific problems encountered by the committee's members. The study of the Pujo Committee of 1912 is of interest to both economic historians and those examining the Progressive movement. Similarly, the explosive McCarthy hearings have much to say about life in this country in the 1950s.

Because of the disparate nature of the source material and the research problems unique to each of the investigations, the authors were free, within general limits of space, to produce interpretative historical essays and to select the type of bibliography or "bibliographical essay" best suited to the documentation. Appended to each bibliography is a list of documents which were presented in the five-volume series.

If the contributors have waded into an area where few have trod, the effort has been rewarding. From the often massive amounts of printed congressional documents, from private manuscript collections, material from previously unpublished records of Congress, and contemporary newspapers and articles, they have studied and analyzed a mine rich in the substance of the investigatory power of Congress. Indeed, several contributors to the series uncovered documents never before used in any study of the respective investigations. The essay on the St. Clair inquiry, for example, was written largely from previously obscure manuscript materials in the National Archives. The study of the investigation of Douglas MacArthur's removal involved the use of committee documents only recently declassified. The author of the Nye investigation essay used many letters from actual participants in and figures surrounding the proceeding.

The work of the contributors and the editors has been greatly facilitated by the generous assistance of manuscript curators, librarians, and archivists in numerous repositories. The editors especially acknowledge the assistance of Mary Giunta and Sara D. Jackson, National Historical Publications and Records Commission; Jane Lange, National Archives Library; George Perros, Legislative, Judicial, and Fiscal Branch, National Archives; and David Rudgers, Records Declassification Division, National Archives and Records Service.

Roger A. Bruns

CONTENTS

CONTRIBUTORS

Michael Les Benedict—Assistant Professor of History, Ohio State University.

Roger A. Bruns—Assistant Executive Director, National Historical Publications and Records Commission.

George C. Chalou—Archivist, Center for the Documentary Study of the American Revolution, National Archives.

Hasia Diner—Lecturer, University of Maryland and Federal City College.

Elisabeth Joan Doyle—Professor of History, St. John's University.

Philip Kurland—Professor of Law, University of Chicago; Consultant, Senate Watergate Committee.

Donald Ritchie—Graduate Student, University of Maryland.

Richard N. Sheldon—Archivist, National Historical Publications and Records Commission.

Herman J. Viola—Director, National Anthropological Archives, Smithsonian Institution.

H. Lew Wallace—Chairman, Department of History, Northern Kentucky State College.

W. Allan Wilbur—Assistant Professor of History, Purdue University.

Theodore Wilson—Professor of History, University of Kansas.

John Wiltz—Associate Professor of History, Indiana University.

Michael Wreszin—Instructor of History, Queens College, City University of New York.

INTRODUCTION

A republic that has suffered the gross abuse of Executive power is well advised to reexamine the fundamental problem of representative democracy—the problem of control. That problem received its classical American formulation in the 51st Federalist Paper. "In framing a government which is to be administered by men over men," the authors of the Federalist wrote, "the great difficulty lies in this: you must first enable the government to control the governed; and in the next place oblige it to control itself."

The American Constitution was an ingenious effort to resolve this difficulty. It established a government with power to govern—i.e., to control the governed. At the same time it sought to establish a political order that would contain and limit the governing power. Dependence on the people, the 51st Federalist said, was doubtless the ultimate restraint. The Constitution thus provided that the new government be elected by the people or their representatives and be in a variety of ways accountable to them. But experience, the Federalist added with a certain irony, "has taught mankind the necessity of auxiliary precautions."

How in particular to oblige government to control itself? The great auxiliary precaution in the Constitution was the idea, novel then and still rare now, of dividing the powers of government among three branches in such a way that each branch could become a check on the other. The separation of powers, in the words of the Federalist, was the "policy of supplying, by opposite and rival interests, the defect of better motives." The Founding Fathers supposed that the Legislative branch would play its part in preserving the balance of the Constitution through its possession of three vital powers: the power to authorize war; the power of the purse; and the power of investigation.

This system of control through representative institutions and the separation of powers worked well enough in domestic matters. It proved less successful in foreign affairs. Here Presidents often felt impelled to take action on their own in order to meet threats, real, contrived, or imagined, to the safety of the nation; and here the check-and-balance instrumentalities—not only Congress and the courts but the press and public opinion—were generally less sure of their ground, less confident of their information and judgment, and therefore more inclined to defer to the Executive.

It was the erosion of the system of control under the pressure of international crisis that, after thirty years of war, hot and cold, created the Imperial Presidency. The Executive emerged as not simply the salient but, for a moment, the supreme branch of the government. This process, in its earlier stages at least, was no doubt as much a result of congressional abdication as of presidential usurpation. By 1950 Congress had relinquished the war-making power. As the cold war continued, congressional deference to the Executive in foreign affairs became a way of life. In time a President came to office determined to apply at home the powers his predecessors had received to meet crises abroad.

For five years the Nixon Administration strove to carry the logic of Executive supremacy to its conclusion. It moved systematically and, until Watergate, without serious congressional or public resistance, to expropriate the two vital powers still remaining in Congress. Against the congressional power of the purse Nixon invoked a doctrine of unlimited Executive impoundment. Against the congressional power to investigate the Executive branch, Nixon invoked a doctrine of unreviewable Executive privilege. Had Nixon succeeded in imposing his two doctrines in the absolute form in which he propounded them, he would have effectively ended Congress as a serious partner in the constitutional order.

Watergate terminated this extraordinary adventure in Executive usurpation. It also revived interest in the problem of rehabilitating the "auxiliary precautions" defended in the Federalist Papers. Congress, recovering a little from its failure of nerve, began to consider anew how it might oblige the Executive to control itself. An essential legislative weapon was, of course, legislation. The courts, by invalidating the Nixon doctrine of Executive impoundment, soon restored the congressional power of the purse; and the Congressional Budget and Impoundment Control Act of 1974 sought to make that restoration permanent. The War Powers Act of 1974 represented an effort, perhaps somewhat ill-conceived, to reclaim the war-making power.

There remained the third vital power—the power of investigation. In 1974 the Supreme Court admitted the doctrine of Executive privilege to explicit constitutional status, at least in relationship to judicial process, while rejecting the use Nixon had made of it to save himself from impeachment. But the Senate Select Committee on Presidential Campaign Activities (the Ervin Committee) had already vindicated once again the role of the investigative power, and no one can doubt that it will be used a good deal in the future. While the conventional assumption is that the strength of legislative bodies lies in the power to legislate, a respectable tradition has long argued that it lies as much or more in the power to investigate. The investigative power may indeed be the sharpest legislative weapon against Executive aggrandizement.

The duty of the legislature, John Stuart Mill thus wrote in *Consideration on Representative Government,* is "to watch and control the government; to throw the light of publicity on its acts; to compel a full exposition and justification of all of them which any one considers questionable; to censure them if found condemnable." Mill had the parliamentary system in mind, but his argument applies equally to a system based on the separation of powers. Woodrow Wilson made this point in *Congressional Government.* "Quite as important as legislation," he said in a memorable phrase, "is vigilant oversight of administration." Indeed, since free government required an informed electorate, the education the nation received from legislative revelations of Executive performance made oversight "even more important than legislation."

> Unless Congress have and use every means of acquainting itself with the acts and the disposition of the administrative agents of

> the government . . . the country must remain in embarrassing, crippling ignorance of the very affairs which it is most important that it should understand and direct.

Because Wilson believed that "the only really self-governing people is that people which discusses and interrogates its administration," he concluded that "the informing function [of Congress] should be preferred even to its legislative function."

Wilson did not draw the distinction, later common in discussions of the investigative power, between Congress informing itself in the furtherance of a congressional task and Congress informing the public for its general delectation and edification. He saw Congress as "the eyes and the voice" of the nation and evidently felt that the investigative power was ultimately justified by its contribution to public instruction and guidance.

> The chief use of such inquisition is, not the direction of those affairs in a way with which the country will be satisfied (though that itself is of course all-important), but the enlightenment of the people.

This was an exceedingly broad case for congressional investigations. Whether Wilson would have modified it if later distinctions were pressed upon him, no one can say. As Justice Frankfurter declared for the Supreme Court nearly seventy years after the publication of *Congressional Government*, "Wilson did not write in light of the history of events since he wrote; more particularly he did not write of the investigative power of Congress in the context of the First Amendment."

The Mill-Wilson argument for parliamentary oversight had ample historical sanction in the Anglo-American legislative experience. It is true that no provision in the American Constitution gave Congress express authority to conduct investigations and compel testimony. But it was not considered necessary to make an explicit grant of such authority. The power to make laws implied the power to see whether they were faithfully executed. The right to secure needed information had long been deemed by both the British Parliament and the colonial assemblies as a necessary and appropriate attribute of the power to legislate.

"We are called the Grand Inquest of the Nation," William Pitt the Elder had told the House of Commons in 1742, "and as such it is our duty to inquire into every Step of publick management, either Abroad or at Home, in order to see that nothing has been done amiss." James Wilson, next to Madison the dominating figure in the Constitutional Convention and later one of Washington's first appointees to the Supreme Court, repeated the idea in the American context a half century later when he called the House of Representatives "the grand inquest of the state" and said that its members must "diligently inquire into grievances, arising both from men and things." As the Supreme Court put it in 1957, "The power of the Congress to conduct investigations is inherent in the legislative process."

So, when General St. Clair led his disastrous expedition along the Wabash River in 1791 and suffered a humiliating defeat by a numerically inferior band of Indians, a congressional investigation was a natural recourse. In the early republic such investigations were directed toward misconduct or maladministration in the Executive branch. Then in 1827 the

House of Representatives gave its Committee on Manufactures "the power to send for persons and papers" in order to discover information that might be of use in tariff legislation; thereafter Congress began to assert the right to summon private persons and to inquire into private situations when the result might be to enlighten congressional judgment in law-making.

Ordinarily congressional investigations were authorized by special resolutions and conducted by select committees equipped with subpoena powers. They thus differed in procedure and in intensity from the hearings routinely held by standing committees. In 1798, in the first of a number of laws developing the investigative power, Congress provided for testimony under oath and punishment for perjury. The title of a statute passed in 1857 after nearly three-quarters of a century's experience with congressional investigations expressed the hardening investigative purpose: "An Act More Effectually to Enforce the Attendance of Witnesses on the Summons of Either House of Congress, and to Compel Them to Discover Testimony." The legislative record demonstrates, as the Supreme Court observed in 1927, the clear and consistent congressional intention to institute inquiries, to exact evidence, and to subject contumacious witnesses to indictment and punishment in the courts.

The history of congressional investigations, authoritatively set forth in the essays that follow, has been picturesque and turbulent. Legislative inquiries have informed, enlightened, entertained, confused, divided, and at times even demoralized the republic. The reputation of the investigative power has fluctuated wildly among both contemporaries and historians. For legislative passions, like Executive passions, are liable to abuse. The problem has been to encourage Congress to serve as the grand inquest of the nation without permitting it to become the grand inquisitor.

There have been two special threats to the responsible use of the investigative power. One has come from the Executive, the other from the legislature itself. From time to time the Executive branch has tried to block or frustrate congressional investigations that promised to result in political damage to an administration. Nixon's invocation of Executive privilege in order to conceal criminality in his White House represented a notorious effort to hamstring the investigative power. From time to time Congress on its side has conducted investigations so arbitrary and reckless as to bring the whole process into disrepute. As early as 1820 Andrew Jackson, the subject of a congressional investigation, complained (he was writing in the third person) that "he was deprived, of the privilege of confronting his accusers, and of interrogating and cross-examining witnesses summoned for his conviction." And from time to time lawsuits produced either by resistance to or abuse of the investigative power have risen for decision to the Supreme Court. Three decisions in particular define the rights and limits of congressional investigation.

One decision resulted from Senate inquiries into the scandals of the Harding Administration. Even before these inquiries began, the investigative power had fallen to low repute. Walter Lippmann, in *Public Opinion* (1922), spoke of "that legalized atrocity, the Congressional investigation, in which congressmen, starved of their legitimate food for thought, go on a wild and feverish manhunt, and do not stop at cannibalism." The inquiries into the Harding scandals by committees headed by Senators Thomas J. Walsh and Burton K. Wheeler, though widely praised in retrospect, were severely condemned at the time. Dean John H. Wigmore, the famous specialist on the law of evidence, denounced "the Senatorial debauch of investigation—poking into political garbage cans and dragging the sewers of political intrigue." Respectable newspapers like the *New York Times* and the *Washington Post* joined the outcry. In a famous article in 1924 called "Hands Off the Investigations," Felix Frankfurter of Harvard defended the committees: "Nothing in the experience of the Walsh and Wheeler investigations reveals the need of changing the process or confining the limits of congressional investigations." (Frankfurter added, "Of course the essential decencies must be observed, namely, the opportunity for cross-examination must be afforded to those who are investigated.")

The Wheeler Committee was looking into the affairs of Harry M. Daugherty, who had been Harding's attorney general. In pursuit of the inquiry the committee subpoenaed Daugherty's brother Mally, an Ohio banker. Mally Daugherty refused to comply with the subpoena. The Senate, thereupon, had John J. McGrain, the deputy sergeant-at-arms, take Mally Daugherty into custody. Daugherty sought a writ of habeas corpus, and a federal district court ordered his release. The attempt to compel his testimony, the lower court found, was unconstitutional since it was not in aid of the legislative function.

The Supreme Court reversed the lower court in 1927 by an 8 to 0 vote. Harlan Stone, who as attorney general had argued for McGrain, was now on the Court himself and did not take part in the decision, but had the pleasure of seeing his brethren adopt his argument. The Court was unimpressed by the district judge's contention that the Senate investigation had been judicial in character and therefore not an exercise of a legislative function. "Plainly the subject was one on which legislation could be had," Justice Van Devanter declared for the Court, "and would be materially aided by the information which the investigation was calculated to elicit. . . . The only legitimate object the Senate could have had in ordering the investigation was to aid it in legislating; and we think the subject-matter was such that the presumption should be indulged that this was the real object."

The decision did not distinguish clearly between oversight of administration and inquiry into private matters. Though Harry Daugherty had been a federal official, Mally was a private citizen; and his case, it could be argued, raised somewhat different questions. The Court, however, simply concluded that anything necessary to the efficient exercise of a legislative function belonging to Congress under the Constitution was permissible. What *McGrain* v. *Daugherty* did was to make it clear that the investigative power applied to *all* persons, private citizens as well as public officials, if they possessed information relating to a conceivable legislative purpose and if the questions put were pertinent to the matter under inquiry. The Court further said that, so long as the subject-matter of the investigation was within the scope of legislation, even if no direct law-framing purpose was avowed, the investigation must be *assumed* to be in aid of the legislative function.

Under the charter of *McGrain* v. *Daugherty* Congress swept ahead to undertake the celebrated investigations of the 1930s and 1940s. Public attitudes toward the investigative power remained mixed, depending in great part on whose ox was gored. Senator Hugo Black of Alabama was one of the ablest of the congressional investigators; and his investigation of the utility lobby provoked criticism as angry as that experienced by Walsh and Wheeler a decade before. Black replied:

> There is no power on earth that can tear away the veil behind which powerful and audacious and unscrupulous groups operate save the sovereign legislative power armed with the right of subpoena and search. . . . This power of the probe is one of the most powerful weapons in the hands of the people to restrain the activities of powerful groups who can defy every other power.

Robert Luce, a conservative congressman from Massachusetts and author of several books on legislative procedures, offered the opposite view:

> Prosecution turned into persecution, the ruthless sacrifice of reputation, the vindictive display of prejudice, the mean debasement of partnership, the advancement of personal fortunes through the use of scurrilous publicity—these are some of the features that make the whole thing a stench in the nostrils of decent men.

Liberals who scorned this view when Congress was investigating government corruption or business malfeasance began to see merit in it when legislators like Martin Dies and Joseph R. McCarthy used the investigating committee as a vehicle for ideological discipline and personal abuse. In 1953 a new case testing the reach of the investigative power reached the Supreme Court. A right-wing agitator named Edward A. Rumely was protesting his conviction for contempt of Congress after he refused to disclose the names of those who had made bulk purchases of his political tracts. The Court, which now included both Frankfurter and Black among its members, unanimously reversed Rumely's conviction.

Speaking for the Court, Frankfurter was prepared, thirty years after Teapot Dome, to lay at least one hand on the investigations. The investigative power, he now declared, had to be considered "in the context of the First Amendment." The problem was that of accommodating contending principles—"the one underlying the power of Congress to investigate, the other at the basis of the limitation imposed by the First Amendment." Determined as always to avoid unnecessary constitutional questions, Frankfurter concluded simply that the resolution establishing the inquiry did not authorize the committee to seek the names from Rumely and declined to go into the larger question whether, had the resolution authorized the questions, it would have been valid. Black, however, joined Douglas in a concurrent opinion that faced this question and argued that, if the enabling resolution had been broader, it would have violated the First Amendment.

> Once the government can demand of a publisher the names of the purchasers of his publication, the free press as we know it disappears. . . . Through the harassment of hearings, investigations, reports, and subpoenas government will hold a club over speech and over the press. Congress could not do this by law. The power of investigation is also limited. Inquiry into personal and private affairs is precluded. . . . And so is any matter in respect to which now valid legislation could be had. . . . Since Congress could not by law require of a respondent what the House demanded, it may not take the first step in an inquiry ending in fine or imprisonment.

These were the McCarthy years, and concern was growing about the collision between the investigative power and the Bill of Rights. In 1954 a labor organizer named John T. Watkins testified before the House Committee on Un-American Activities. Watkins, as he freely admitted, had been a close collaborator of the Communist party. He told the committee he would answer any questions put to him about himself or about persons he believed still to be party members. But he declined to talk about people who had long since left the Communist movement on the ground that such inquiries were not relevant to the work of the committee and beyond its constitutional authority. Watkins's refusal led to a contempt citation and conviction. In 1957 the Supreme Court, by a 6 to 1 vote, dismissed the indictment and freed Watkins.

The Court decided the case on a relatively narrow issue; but along the way Chief Justice Warren made the most comprehensive judicial definition of the powers and limitations of congressional investigations. The Court was not concerned in this case, he said, "with the power of the Congress to inquire into and publicize corruption, maladministration or inefficiency in agencies of the Government." This was what Woodrow Wilson had meant by "the informing function," and it had been discharged by Congress from its earliest history. In general the Court said, the investigative power was broad:

> It encompasses inquiries concerning the administration of existing laws as well as proposed or possibly needed statutes. It includes surveys of defects in our social, economic or political system for the purpose of enabling Congress to remedy them. It comprehends probes into departments of the Federal Government to expose corruption, inefficiency or waste.

But, the Court continued, "broad as is this power of inquiry, it is not unlimited."

What were the limits? First the Court restated and somewhat enlarged the test of legislative purpose laid down in the *McGrain* decision. There was, the Court said, no general authority to expose the private affairs of individuals without justification in terms of the functions of Congress. "No inquiry is an end in itself; it must be related to and in furtherance of a legitimate task of the Congress." Where Van Devanter in *McGrain* had said that the only legitimate congressional task was legislation, Warren's broader language in *Watkins* left room for other legitimate congressional tasks, such as the oversight of administration. In addition, *Watkins* said far more clearly than *McGrain* that the investigative power, as much as other forms of governmental action, was subject to the restraints of the Bill of Rights. "Witnesses cannot be compelled to give evidence against themselves. They cannot be subjected to unreasonable search and seizure. Nor can the First Amendment freedoms of Speech, press, religion, or political belief and association be abridged."

What this meant was that "investigations conducted solely for the personal aggrandizement of the investigators or to 'punish' those investigated are indefensible." If no proper congressional purpose was served, if the *only* purpose of the inquiry was to inform the public, then the investigation would be constitutionally invalid; and even the pursuit of a proper congressional purpose had to defer to the Bill of Rights. As the Court summed it up, "There is no congressional power to expose for the sake of exposure. The public is, of course, entitled to be informed concerning the workings of its government. That cannot be inflated into a general power to expose where the predominant result can only be an invasion of the private rights of individuals."

Watkins confirmed the rather spacious charter laid down in the *McGrain* case. But it also reemphasized the test of legitimate congressional purpose and went beyond *McGrain* in making the Bill of Rights itself an explicit restraint on the investigative power. It further established the principle that, when a witness thought a congressional inquiry was violating his constitutional rights, he could appeal to the courts for final judgment. This resolution of the dilemmas of the investigative power was entirely in the spirit of the Founding Fathers. The "true meaning" of the separation of powers, said the 66th Federalist, was not rigid separation; rather "a partial intermixture of those departments for special purposes" was "not only proper but necessary to the mutual defence of the several members of the government against each other."

Watkins, it later developed, contained a hidden ambiguity. One paragraph spoke of the problem of accommodating "the congressional need for particular information with the individual and personal interest in privacy," adding: "The critical element is the existence of, and the weight to be ascribed to, the interest of the Congress in demanding disclosures from an unwilling witness." Half the justices who supported the *Watkins* decision thought that this paragraph prescribed a general balancing test: that is, a balancing by the courts of the competing private and public interests at stake in a particular case. The other half, including Warren, who wrote the opinion, construed this paragraph narrowly and denied that it called for a general balancing process (see Justice Black's dissent, joined by Warren, in *Barenblatt* v. *United States*). The *Watkins* majority subsequently fell apart over this issue.

The argument over balancing registered a grave practical disagreement, though less perhaps of a philosophical disagreement than the terms of the argument suggested. Even Black could not escape the balancing argument in certain cases, as he acknowledged in his *Barenblatt* dissent; even the 'balancers'—preeminently Frankfurter and Harlan—accepted a presumption in favor of the First Amendment. The argument in consequence affected the application of the *Watkins* principles rather than the principles themselves. And these principles, even when the judicial result was less solicitous of individual liberties and more favorable to the investigative power than *Watkins,* remained generally intact for almost twenty years. Then in 1975, in the case of *Eastland* v. *United States Servicemen's Fund,* the Court beat what appeared to be a considerable retreat from the *Watkins* position that the First Amendment was a fundamental restraint on the investigative power and that the courts had the last word when witnesses claimed that congressional committees were violating their constitutional rights.

The new case involved the validity of a subpoena issued by a Senate committee requiring a New York bank to produce the list of financial contributors to an anti-Vietnam War organization. Had the subpoena been served directly on the Servicemen's Fund, then the Fund could have refused compliance and tested the constitutional issues in a contempt proceeding, as had happened in *Watkins.* But, by serving the subpoena on the bank, an indifferent third party not likely to refuse compliance, the Senate committee created a new legal situation. When the Fund sued the committee and the bank in order to enjoin the execution of the subpoena, Chief Justice Burger, speaking for four of his colleagues, ruled that the Fund had no remedy "even though compliance with subpoena may infringe upon First Amendment rights."

Burger's argument was that the Speech or Debates clause of the Constitution—the clause (Article I, Section 6) providing that "for any Speech or Debate in either House, [legislators] shall not be questioned in any other place"—was an "absolute bar" to judicial interference when legislators were acting within the legitimate legislative sphere. Therefore, the uninterested third party had to obey the subpoena and the interested second party could do nothing about it. Three more justices, speaking through Justice Marshall, agreed with the particular result but were disturbed by Burger's bleak conclusion. Marshall insisted that the Speech or Debate clause was designed to give legislators personal protection against suits, not to "immunize congressional action against judicial review." However, the Marshall three avoided the question of the proper procedure and the proper defendants when a witness tries to bring a constitutional challenge to a third-party subpoena.

Given the obscurity of both opinions and the division among those upholding the subpoena, it is hard to assess the inroads made by the *Servicemen's Fund* decision upon *Watkins.* It seems plain, however, that the Bill of Rights may no longer be a restraint on the investigative power when a congressional committee serves its subpoena on an indifferent third party—a point that, one imagines, will not be altogether lost on future committees.

The 1975 decision plunged the investigative power into a new situation of uncertainty. Apparently only the test of legislative purpose remained as an effective restraint—until at least a recalcitrant witness was cited for contempt and haled into criminal court. The result was to make the point that ultimately Congress and not the courts would determine whether the investigative power was to be used responsibly or irresponsibly. This generation of Americans had seen the investigative process both at its worst and at its best. As the McCarthy hearings illustrated the gross abuse of that power, so the Ervin hearings twenty years later demonstrated the indispensability of that power to a free state. The future of congressional investigations rest only secondarily with the courts. It rests primarily with Congress itself.

When Harry S. Truman resigned in 1944 as chairman of one of the exemplary investigating committees in American history, he told the Senate: "In my opinion, the power of investigation is one of the most important powers of Congress. The manner in which the power is exercised will largely determine the position and prestige of the Congress in the future." He could have gone further. The manner in which Congress exercises the investigative power will do much to determine in years to come whether the problem posed in the 51st Federalist can be satisfactorily answered—whether the constitutional order will in the end oblige the American government to control itself.

Arthur M. Schlesinger, jr.

St. Clair's Defeat
1792

General Arthur St. Clair lost more than half of his 1400-man troop when Indians attacked his fort in the Northwest Territory, and became the target of the first congressional investigation in 1792.

St. Clair's Defeat, 1792

by George C. Chalou

Late Friday afternoon, March 30, 1792, Secretary of War Henry Knox was busy at his desk drafting a letter to President Washington. Normally at this time of the day, and especially on Fridays, Knox could be seen propelling his asymmetrical 280-pound frame down Chestnut Street in Philadelphia toward home. But Mrs. Knox and her social schedule for that evening would have to wait until her husband had informed Washington that a select congressional investigating committee had that day requested papers and records from his office. "I have the honor to submit to you," wrote Knox, "an order of a Committee to inquire into the failure of the late expedition. As I do not conceive myself authorized to deliver these papers of myself, I beg your permission that they may be laid before the Committee." With careful deference he added, ". . . if you should see no impropriety therein." Knox gave the letter to his messenger and sent him to the President.

Three days earlier, for the first time in the history of the infant republic, the House of Representatives had voted to investigate a co-equal branch of the federal government. "Resolved, That a committee be appointed to inquire into the causes of the failure of the late expedition under Major General St. Clair; and that the said committee be empowered to call for such persons, papers, and records, as may be necessary to assist their inquiries."

Did the Constitution grant such power to the Legislative branch? Was the

Army of the United States under the control of the President? What would the House do if Secretary of War Knox simply refused to turn over the records and papers? Could a committee steer its way past these and other sharp reefs that crested just below the surface? On this voyage the captains of the House faced the President and his cabinet—Thomas Jefferson, secretary of state; Alexander Hamilton, secretary of the treasury; Henry Knox, secretary of war; and Edmund Randolph, attorney general.

Washington seldom called the department heads together, but they met on Saturday, March 31. The private notes of Jefferson disclosed: "A meeting at the P's present Th. J, AH, K, & ER." According to Jefferson, the President prefaced the discussion by emphasizing that he had made no decision about the request but called the cabinet together because this was the first example of the House's investigation power. Since his response to the committee would become a precedent, "it should be rightly conducted." Despite Washington's plea of absolute openness, he conceded that there might be papers of "so secret a nature" that they ought not be surrendered. Because they were called together—an unusual happening—and because of the grave constitutional issue of separate but equal branches of the federal government, his counselors requested more time to reflect.

Sunday was a day of rest and contemplation, but on Monday the department heads "met again at P's on same subject." Jefferson noted that the group reached unanimity on the essential points: the House could conduct an inquest, institute inquiries, and call for papers. The President, however, could release such papers as the "public good would permit and ought to refuse those the disclosure of which would injure the public." Jefferson wrote that neither the House nor the committee had a right to call on department heads to release records. Requests for Executive records were to be made directly to the President.

Near the end of the department heads' meeting, Washington decided to honor the committee's request but announced that the original records would stay in the physical custody of the department. It was agreed that the House of Representatives could send a clerk to check that the copies prepared for the committee were accurate and complete. The department heads—or cabinet officers as they came to be called—also agreed to speak privately with the committee members and endeavor to bring "them by persuasion into the right channel."

Thus on April 2, 1792, Congress had initiated its first investigation. Two days later President Washington ordered Knox and Hamilton to turn over copies of the pertinent records to the committee.

The first congressional investigation was inspired by the greatest Indian victory in American history. The smashing defeat of the U.S. Army—dwarfing even Custer's extermination at the Little Big Horn—has received scant attention in history textbooks. But the white survivors' recollections of the scene on the headwater of the Wabash River on November 4, 1791, were as clear and sharp as if a master engraver had made plates of the scene. The warriors of the Ohio country had killed more than 600 "long knives," as white soldiers were called.

Since the Treaty of Paris in 1783, certifying the nation's independence,

Indian tribes residing west of the Allegheny Mountains and north of the Ohio River had repeatedly raided white settlements along the Ohio River. More daring war parties struck deep into what is now Kentucky. These raids brought forth the militia. Indian treaties were made at Fort McIntosh in 1786 and Fort Harmar in 1789, but neither the militia nor the treaties pacified the warriors of the Shawnee, Wyandot, Ottawa, Miami, Potawatomi, and Kickapoo tribes residing in the Northwest Territory—present-day Ohio, Indiana, Illinois, and Michigan. Within a cycle of the moon, over 2,000 warriors would converge on Kekionga, the capital of the Wabash Confederacy (now Fort Wayne, Indiana).

Following two futile peacemaking efforts in 1789 and 1790, the governor of the Northwest Territory, Arthur St. Clair, informed Washington and Knox that a major thrust into the heart of the Indian country was needed. In the early autumn of 1790, Brig. Gen. Josiah Harmar started north from recently constructed Fort Washington (Cincinnati). Arriving south of Kekionga, Harmar divided his force into three columns, while the observant Indian spies accepted his invitation to disaster. Led by the Miami war chief, Little Turtle, the warriors attacked quickly and killed 183 U.S. soldiers.

St. Clair, Knox, and Washington, all former Continental army officers, prescribed more of the same medicine—a larger and better American army. Planning started immediately, but only after considerable debate did Congress pass a new military bill which permitted the raising of two regiments of short-term regular troops, called levies, and a second U.S. regiment. Concurrently, Governor St. Clair was appointed major general of the American army. During March 1791, he traveled to Philadelphia and consulted with the Administration on expedition operations. The army was to be recruited in the East, sent to the West, and supplied, equipped, and trained within three months. The President wanted St. Clair and his new army tramping down the shoulder-high grass lacing the feeder streams of the Great Miami River in Ohio as soon as possible. In addition, the Administration ordered a series of supply forts constructed while the army moved northward toward the Miami Indian town of Kekionga. There the army was to construct a large fort capable of quartering at least 1,000 troops. These demands called for more than good luck and heroics, for the President gave St. Clair just five months to accomplish his mission.

Arthur St. Clair had considerable military experience. He was born in Scotland and at the age of twenty-three obtained a commission as ensign in the British army. It was his good fortune to assist Jeffrey Amherst before Louisburg in 1758, then to join General Wolfe on the Plains of Abraham during the struggle for Quebec. Following the end of fighting in the French and Indian War, St. Clair soon tired of the military and resigned. His new interest was Phoebe Bayard, a young belle from a prominent Massachusetts family. According to St. Clair's nineteenth-century biographer, Henry Smith, the tall, graceful, dignified St. Clair—with chestnut hair, handsome blue-gray eyes, and fair complexion—had no trouble winning the hand of Miss Bayard.

With his wife's dowry and his own modest fortune, St. Clair purchased land at Ligonier in central Pennsylvania. From 1763, until the outbreak of the War for Independence, Arthur St. Clair was content with raising a family and growing crops. As the fires of the patriots grew hotter, St. Clair warmed to their cause and accepted a commission as colonel in the Continental army. In those days, the government issued commissions and then had the officers raise their own troops. During the spring of 1776, St. Clair proved an able recruiter; he raised six companies of troops and marched them to Canada. Throughout the war, St. Clair remained a steady but unspectacular general officer in the Continental army. He was promoted to brigadier general, survived a storm over his relinquishing of Fort Ticonderoga, and served at Brandywine, Valley Forge, and Yorktown.

Because of his long experience as a military officer and his popularity in Pennsylvania, St. Clair was appointed to the Confederation Congress in 1786. Almost at once his fellow delegates elected him president of the Congress. During his tenure, the Ordinance of 1787 was passed, creating the Northwest Territory and establishing a blueprint of government for the nation's western lands. His resignation from Congress and acceptance of governorship of the new territory—a decision he later regretted—was never explained. Not until July 1787 did St. Clair arrive in the territory northwest of the River Ohio and assume his new duties. The governor was in his mid-fifties when he accepted the military commission as major general in 1791. Both Washington and Knox believed that St. Clair was the logical choice to command the new Indian expedition.

After meeting with Washington and Knox, St. Clair placed his second in command, Brig. Gen. Richard Butler, in charge of recruiting and moving the soldiers toward Fort Washington on the Ohio River. Quartermaster General Samuel Hodgdon was responsible for procuring equipment and making certain the contracts for supplies and provisions were honored. These three key army officers were to be in Fort Washington on July 15, ready to move north.

Only eighty-five privates and noncommissioned officers welcomed St. Clair's May 15 arrival. Additional troops scattered at Forts Harmar, Knox, and Steuben added another 189 men to his western army. The general could also count on the taverns and jails of the East to supply another 2,000 regulars and levies.

St. Clair was also faced with many other problems. The supply contractor, William Duer, failed to secure all the necessary provisions. Quartermaster Hodgdon (a subordinate of Knox) and his assistant failed to hire enough flatboats to take the troops down the Ohio River. Low water on the Ohio delayed the few boats that were available. Nevertheless, by the end of July, St. Clair had managed to gather 427 rank-and-file troops at the new post on the Ohio. His departure goal already past, the commander crossed the Ohio to obtain militia from Kentucky.

Growing impatient, St. Clair started north on August 7 with a mixed assortment of regulars and levies numbering 1,500. Heat and gout wore on the fifty-seven-year-old commander, and the absence of Butler and Hodgdon added to his burden. The season for the expedition was rapidly passing, yet the army moved like a debilitated animal groping toward its burial place. During September, Butler and Hodgdon arrived with additional troops and Kentucky militia units. The construction of Forts Hamilton and Jefferson along the way took longer than expected because what few axes the quartermaster supplied had blades that "bent like dumplings."

Not knowing that General Butler had descended the Ohio the last of

August, Knox informed the second in command, ". . . it is the decided orders of the President of the United States that you repair to headquarters with all possible dispatch." Washington considered the status of the troops "an unhappy omen." By August 25, Knox informed his generals that Washington "laments exceedingly" the delays in troop deployment and that if the "highest exertions" were not made "to repair the loss of the season" all the expense and efforts of the government would be lost, "and that the measures from which so much has been expected will issue in disgrace."

Before dawn on the morning of November 4, the President's prophecy was realized. The 1,400 ill-equipped troops near the heart of the Indian confederacy were struck by about 1,000 greased and painted warriors who totally encircled the large camp. While the troops were preparing breakfast, screaming and shooting began on the perimeter of the camp. The militia fled headlong into the regulars' camp with the commander on their heels screaming at them to halt. Finally, in anger and frustration, St. Clair started shouting "cowards, cowards, cowards." Later, a wagoner recalled that the start of the battle was "like a thunderstorm that came up quickly and rapidly."

Arthur St. Clair had faults, but cowardice was not one of them. The commander was so sick with gout that he was unable to mount his horse. As four men pushed him into the saddle, the horse was shot. St. Clair was brought another horse, and immediately it too was shot. Finally, on a third horse, he began to direct the troops. The regulars made a determined stand and pushed the braves back with bayonets. The three and six pounders were belching away but the Indians, mostly behind trees, were well directed by the Shawnee chief Blue Jacket and the Miami chief Little Turtle.

Within an hour the sounds were frightening and the sights horrifying. Death was everywhere. Among the more than 100 camp followers were wives, prostitutes, and children. Some of the women grabbed branding irons from the still glowing fire and drove skulking, fear-glazed soldiers out from under wagons and hiding places.

After two hours of desperate struggle, the perimeter of the camp was much smaller. St. Clair realized that retreat to Fort Jefferson, a new supply post, was the only rational decision. About 8:30 A.M. the commander gathered some soldiers and broke through the ranks of the warriors, and what remained of an army followed. St. Clair later informed Knox that the retreat "you may be sure, [was] a very precipitate one, it was in fact, a flight." The flight continued all the way to Fort Jefferson, twenty-nine miles to the south. Camp equipment, artillery, and wagons were abandoned. Men dropped their arms and accouterments to run faster; red and blue haversacks dotted the path. Fortunately for the Americans, most of the warriors were enamored with their booty and did not pursue the white survivors.

At sunrise on November 5, the survivors struggled into Fort Jefferson. By marching day and night the remnants of the United States Army arrived at Fort Washington on the afternoon of November 8. Of the original 1,400 troops, 657 were killed, including General Butler, and 271 were wounded. Adding the casualties of camp followers and authorized wives, there were more than 1,000 casualties. The warriors of the Ohio country had destroyed the United States Army.

Reluctantly, St. Clair informed the war secretary of the defeat. The dejection of St. Clair was evident in his first line: "Yesterday afternoon the remains of my army got back to this place, and I now have the painful task to give you an account." Then, in several pages, the commander laid down his story of the defeat. He knew the hopes and expectations of the Washington Administration would be shattered when his letter reached Philadelphia.

On the evening of November 9, the President and Martha were giving a dinner party when a messenger arrived bearing news of the western defeat. According to the most reliable accounts, Washington took the note in private and returned to the table without comment. When the last guest had gone, the President vented his anger and frustration. He exclaimed that the Indian surprise was the very thing he had warned St. Clair about in March when he had sent the general his instructions. "Oh God! Oh God!" Washington shouted as he paced his library. "How can he answer to his country?"

The next day the story broke in the Philadelphia *Gazette of the United States,* but St. Clair's letters were not printed until the following Wednesday, December 12. Meanwhile, the President sent his personal secretary, Tobias Lear, to Congress with a short message announcing the defeat and instructed Knox to begin drafting another plan for dealing with the Indian situation. Knox's report to Congress declared that a "deficient number of good troops" and the lateness of the season caused the defeat.

General St. Clair came to Philadelphia late in December to meet with Washington and Knox. Observing that some sectors of the public and press had blamed him for the disaster, he asked for a court of inquiry or a court-martial to clear his name—during the Revolution St. Clair's evacuation of Fort Ticonderoga had brought public censure upon him and a court of inquiry had exonerated him. He argued that after the inquiry "I may hope to be permitted to resign." On March 26, 1792, he pledged to Washington that if it were found that he had neglected his duties as commander of the expedition, he would "patiently submit to the merited censure."

The President's polite refusal came two days later. St. Clair's court of inquiry proposal was "highly laudable," wrote Washington, but the lack of officers of "competent rank to form a court" made it impracticable. The President thanked St. Clair for his offer of affording "your successor all the information of which you are capable," and to make certain his message was understood, added a private message, ". . . while I accept your resignation for the cause you state, I sincerely regret the occasion."

St. Clair replied that his intention to retire was conditioned on the conclusion of an inquiry or court-martial. The Pennsylvanian wished to retain his commission; if misconduct were indicated, a court-martial was in order. By this time, St. Clair had learned of the House inquiry. "Should the public service require it," he wrote Washington, "I am ready to make the resignation forthwith," but he pleaded that the President not demand his resignation because it would appear to validate public rumors.

Washington, however, had made up his mind. On April 4 he wrote St. Clair: "The reasons you offer for retaining your commission—would be conclusive with me under any other circumstances than the present." The President indicated that the public service of the nation required that the commanding general be with his troops on the frontier, and this demanded that a successor be immediately appointed. Washington added that he hoped St.

Clair could clear himself through the inquiry about to start in the House of Representatives.

The President had given his general no option, and St. Clair's reply of April 7 evidences his extreme disappointment. "Although I was very desirous, sir, to hold my commission, I do now formally resign the appointment of Major-General." He told Washington that he welcomed the inquiry and hoped public vindication would be the result.

At the same time that St. Clair was urging Washington to institute a court of inquiry, he was also persuading friends and congressmen that a full airing of the defeat was necessary. As early as February 2, a motion had been made in the House that a committee investigate the causes of St. Clair's defeat. The motion had died quickly, and nothing decisive had happened in the House until March 27 when the brash thirty-year-old congressman from Virginia, William Branch Giles, stirred up feelings by introducing a motion requesting President Washington to institute an inquiry into the causes of the western disaster.

As the debate opened, John Vining of Delaware asked Giles why he desired the President to carry out the investigation. Arguing that passage of the motion would only embarrass the President without producing the desired effect, Vining urged a full and complete inquiry by the House, and if deficiencies of conduct were uncovered, "let those who are to blame be impeached." Because the impeachment power rested with the House, he continued, so did the investigating power.

William Smith of South Carolina replied that this would be the first instance in the nation's history of the House investigating the conduct of officers "immediately under the control of the Executive" and would be considered as an impeachment of the President. He reminded his listeners that the Constitution provided for three distinct and separate branches of government and that responsibility for execution of laws rested with the President. The South Carolinian, a close associate of the secretary of the treasury, questioned the wisdom of the House conducting a "grand inquest of the nation." He said that the National Assembly of France had recently wasted an entire night examining a drum major and he hoped the House would not resort to such minor operations.

Smith's strict constructionist interpretation of the Constitution and his argument against the British system—wherein the House of Commons investigated the policies of the British ministry—swayed few members. Many remembered that colonial assemblies had exercised investigatory powers during the past century. As the debate continued, it became clear that what concerned many congressmen was whether Washington would view such a motion as an insult to his conduct and his prerogative as President, particularly since it was widely known that he had refused to authorize an inquiry despite St. Clair's persistent appeals.

John Steele of North Carolina stated that he did not care who carried out the investigation, the House or the President, as long as there was one. He desired justice for the public, the officers, and men, and had no doubt that an inquiry would lead to impeachment.

Thomas Fitzsimons of Philadelphia, an Irish-born Revolutionary War veteran and an influential member of Pennsylvania's large delegation, believed it out of order to request Washington to institute a court of inquiry or court-martial. He favored a committee inquiry into the expenditures of public money for the expedition because that aspect properly came "under the cognizance" of the House. James Madison opposed holding a court of inquiry or court-martial because high-ranking officers were not available to testify.

At this point in the debate a vote was taken on Giles's motion: "That the President of the United States be requested to institute an inquiry into the causes of the late defeat of the Army under the command of Major General St. Clair." The motion was defeated 35 to 21. The two emerging political parties —Federalists and Jeffersonian Republicans—were still in the gestation stage and no clear ideological pattern was discernible in the vote.

It was apparent that some congressmen desired to know more about the disaster but were unwilling to risk the displeasure of the President. Fitzsimons therefore moved that the House appoint its own committee of inquiry. Most members of the House were aware of the precedent-setting aspects of the proposal, but they also believed the virtual destruction of the nation's military force and the huge expenditure of funds demanded a public accounting. The motion passed on a vote of 44 to 10.

Fitzsimons was appointed chairman with Giles, Steele, Vining, John F. Mercer of Maryland, Theodore Sedgwick of Massachusetts, and Abraham Clark of New Jersey constituting the committee.

In order to placate the President, the House passed a resolution on April 5, requesting Washington to have the proper officers "lay before this House such papers of a public nature" as might enable it to investigate the causes of St. Clair's defeat. A committee of Fitzsimons, Giles, and Steele was appointed to present the President with the resolution. On April 9 Knox turned over copies of War Department records to the House. While the new resolution had added the term "public" papers because Washington and his cabinet declared that the President had power to refuse to give up papers which would "injure the public," in this case no records were withheld. A clerk from the House was allowed to watch the copying from the originals to make sure the transcripts were full and accurate.

The committee, anxious to begin work, started the investigation before the pertinent records of the War Department and Treasury Department were turned over to the House. Although no records of the committee proceedings are extant, bits of information appear in the correspondence of participants. On April 4, St. Clair wrote his assistant, Winthrop Sargent, secretary of the Northwest Territory, that this letter was "being scribbled in the Committee with a crowd about me and questions and answers that I am obliged to attend to." The former general believed that the committee's motive was to discover some cause of complaint against Knox. "The investigation would, nevertheless, answer the purposes of the inquiry into my conduct," concluded St. Clair.

The committee sessions were public, and the principal parties were notified in advance of the time and place. St. Clair made his personal papers available to the committee and attended most of its sessions, Knox testified before the committee, and Hamilton appeared before the Senate to present his papers. Giles complained later that the secretaries, when attending the sessions, appeared extremely anxious to get away to their offices. At the

business." This led, the committee reported, to the loss of many horses and thus slowed the expedition.

In addition to Knox's handling of his subordinate, Hodgdon, the secretary came in for criticism on his own account. At several stages in the preparation of the campaign, the lack of funds either hindered or retarded the expedition. During 1791 the federal government borrowed over 20 percent of the War Department's appropriation to wage war on tribal America. The committee expressed surprise that the secretary of war had expended only $575,906 rather than the authorized amount of $652,761. Many times St. Clair, Butler, Hodgdon, or the contractors complained that supplies could not be obtained because they had no funds. The committee also injured Knox's pride when they suggested that the "orders to the recruiting officers appear not to have been sufficiently explicit" on when enlistment of the levies started. Also, Knox was reminded that the pay for the levies did not leave Philadelphia until December 3, 1791, and arrived at Fort Washington in January 1792, "sometime after the last enlisted levies were known to be entitled to their discharges." The emphasis on these points, plus the barrage of evidence against Hodgdon, who was responsible to Knox, lent weight to St. Clair's comment at the beginning of the proceedings that the committee seemed determined to "discover some cause of complaint against General Knox."

The committee also reminded Congress and the Washington Administration that the act for raising St. Clair's army was not passed until March 1791, yet the expedition was to have begun July 10. This tight scheduling contributed to the "lack of discipline and experience in the troops." The committee did not, however, recommend censure or court-martial for civil or military officers of the federal government.

According to Arthur St. Clair, the committee unanimously agreed on the findings of the report. The last day of the first session of the Second Congress was hectic, but Chairman Fitzsimons presented the report to the House. It was read, but action was delayed until the start of the second session in November.

While the committee hurried to complete its work, other steps were taken by the House and the Executive branch to avoid future military disasters. Congress authorized Secretary of the Treasury Hamilton to take over responsibility for the procurement of army supplies—a slap at Knox. Three weeks before this proposal was authorized the secretary had dumped Hodgdon. During April, Knox had obtained a copy of a James Wilkinson letter which heaped abuse on Hodgdon. "The more I reflect on the state of the Quartermaster's Department," Knox wrote Washington, "the more anxious I am that a successor to Hodgdon be immediately appointed." The following day the President informed his secretary of war that the Senate had concurred in naming a new quartermaster general.

Knox and St. Clair met accidentally after the adjournment of Congress and talked about the committee's report. St. Clair remarked that the public mind had at last calmed over the military debacle in the Ohio country, and he expressed his hope that the report of the committee would be adopted without opposition in the next session of Congress. Knox looked St. Clair in the eye, hesitated, and then exclaimed, "No sir, that must be rejected."

When the second session of the Second Congress opened in November 1792, Territorial Governor St. Clair was not on the Ohio River tending his duties. The vindicated general had stayed in Philadelphia, hoping to pick up the latest gossip and political currents. He expected Knox would maneuver to block House approval of the committee report and was on the scene to protect his newly won vindication. On November 13, a motion was introduced in the House calling on Knox and Hamilton to attend its session the next day, when debate on the report was to take place. The secretaries were then to "furnish such information as may be conducive to the due investigation of the matters stated in the said report." Supporters of Hamilton and Knox urged adoption of the resolution because the committee report implicated them in the causes of the failure of the expedition. Only upon their statements to the House, argued William Smith of South Carolina, would they have an opportunity of "exculpating themselves." Fisher Ames of Massachusetts, a superb orator by contemporary standards, believed Knox and Hamilton should address the House because they were "so intimately implicated in the matter" and because the public wanted further investigation of the late defeat. It was "to justice, to truth, and to the national honor" that a thorough investigation was in order. This inquiry, announced Ames, "appears to be the beginning of an arrangement preparatory to an impeachment." Although the anti-Hamilton chorus in the House was increasing and becoming more vocal, Knox and Hodgdon were subjected to much more opprobrium than Hamilton.

Jonathan Dayton of New Jersey wished more testimony. He held that St. Clair was "highly culpable" in several instances: "the slowness of his movements, his dilatoriness in constructing forts, and his being surprised by the enemy." This oratorical stoning by Dayton brought forth no defenders of St. Clair, but Giles objected to the resolution. He preferred a thorough discussion of the report, and then, if necessary, the request for additional information.

Madison suggested either the taking up of the report or a new inquiry by the entire House. He opposed the pending resolution on constitutional grounds and because it was contrary to customary practice of the House. Instead of calling on Knox and Hamilton to testify, Madison urged that the two secretaries submit written answers to questions supplied by the House or the committee. The fate of the proposal was totally doomed when Fitzsimons announced his intention to vote against the resolution. He stressed, as had Madison, that calling Knox and Hamilton would be improper. "No person," claimed Fitzsimons, "had applied to the House for redress of any supposed injury received by the report." Even a weaker resolution that simply notified the two secretaries of the taking up of the report met defeat.

The next day, however, it became obvious that a powerful figure outside the Legislative branch did object to the committee report. Speaker of the House Jonathan Trumbull laid before his fellow congressmen a written request from the secretary of war that he be allowed to attend, supply evidence, and furnish explanations to the House when the committee's report was taken up. Because the report, "founded upon *ex parte* investigation," was prematurely printed and circulated in newspapers around the country, Knox asserted, conclusions "very injurious to my reputation" have formed. Knox appealed to the House that he be allowed to attend the debate on the committee report. In addition, the secretary believed information and explanations from him would refute several allegations against him and "might conduce to a right understanding of facts, in which I am so materially implicated."

Knox was appealing for a chance to explain his case just as St. Clair had appealed to Washington nine months earlier. During the past summer, the secretary had written that the committee report was "full of injustice. I presume it will not be accepted" by the House. But now Knox was not sure. His usual good nature and optimism were subdued. Serious setbacks had struck the former artillery officer. He had lost a child that year, a land speculation scheme with Duer had crashed, and now voices were heard challenging his competency as secretary of war. News that the House refused to reopen the investigation "has added to my solicitude and regret." Accompanying the Knox appeal was a long memorial written by Samuel Hodgdon, his former quartermaster general, seeking to restore Knox's tarnished reputation.

The Knox appeal and Hodgdon memorial heightened debate on what to do with the committee report. Madison suggested that the House recommit the report to the committee along with the appeals of Knox and Hodgdon. Ames wanted the whole committee to hear Knox and others make their "defence in the face of the world." Justice to them and to the public required it, warned the Massachusetts congressman. "Will not precluding them look like a wish to smother all further inquiry into the matter?" Debate seemed evenly divided on whether to send the report back to the committee along with the new evidence or to act as a committee of the whole.

The suggestions of unfair treatment of Knox irked Giles. He reminded the House that the committee sessions were public and that "the Secretaries could have attended all the time had they seen proper." They came but once, declared Giles, although the committee would have been "extremely glad to have had those gentlemen present oftener, and to receive all the information they could give, and supposed they had done it."

Only former Quartermaster General Hodgdon escaped Giles's censure because his absence in Europe, following dismissal from office, had not given him an opportunity to present documentation in his favor. Steele of North Carolina and William Findley of Pennsylvania suggested that the new evidence provided by Knox and Hodgdon be committed to the committee of the previous spring. The House then voted 30 to 22 to reopen the investigation and send the new documents to a committee of Fitzsimons, Giles, Steele, Findley, and Clark. This was almost the same personnel as the first committee, with the addition of Findley and the omission of Vining, Mercer, and Sedgwick. Upon this crucial point the congressional friends of Hamilton, Knox, and Hodgdon had won a victory.

One task confronting this revised congressional committee was the examination of Hodgdon's thirty-five-page memorial and twenty-five depositions. The former quartermaster general wrote that to his "astonishment" it was his "lot to be classed among the victims then offered to appease the Public indignation." In the memorial, Hodgdon maintained that what he had suffered could not be recompensed. The committee might, however, "repair, as far as is in their power, the wrong my reputation has sustained by the exparte investigation which the business has undergone." The War Department official, reduced to the status of agent for the quartermaster general, predicted that with the additional documents the committee would see how far they had been "drawn aside" from the truth.

The committee held hearings for Knox, Hodgdon, and St. Clair to question witnesses and be questioned by the committee, if it chose.

Inspector of the Army Francis Mentges—whose duty it was to inspect the men, arms, and clothing and to report the state of discipline, posts, hospitals, and treatment of the sick—was an important witness. If blame was to be apportioned, Mentges's testimony would be critical. Of the twenty-four questions asked the inspector, the committee posted fourteen, Knox five, St. Clair three, and Hodgdon one. The congressmen wanted to know the nature of his official duties and the quality of the recruits. Knox wanted Mentges to state that the delay in the expedition and the reason for the defeat had nothing to do with the quality or quantity of arms and supplies. St. Clair wanted it on record that Hodgdon's lateness in reaching the army had forced other officers to perform his functions to the neglect of some of their own responsibilities. Hodgdon asked only one question: "Do you know of any complaint of the powder?" The inspector did not. Mentges was asked about the recruits and replied that they "were a bad set of men, not fit to be soldiers; a number of them with rotten legs. . . . They had no discipline at all." The officer distributed the blame; he did not seem to be under the spell of his superior, Secretary of War Knox.

In addition, the committee, St. Clair, Knox, and Hodgdon questioned Brig. Gen. Josiah Harmar and Maj. David Zeigler. Both found complaint with Hodgdon's conduct and Zeigler termed the army clothing infamous as many soldiers arrived at Fort Washington "almost naked." Zeigler, known for his direct and crude manner, wasted no time attacking Hodgdon. "I think, from my own experience," he testified, "I never saw such a degree of trouble thrown on the shoulders of any other general that I have served with, as upon General St. Clair, from the absence of the quartermaster." Although Knox and Hodgdon were present, it appears that neither cross-examined Major Zeigler. Later, other officers were questioned, but Knox and Hodgdon did not attend.

In general, the officer cadre testified that the quartermaster's inefficiency had delayed the entire expedition and that the levies were unprepared to meet the Indian warriors. Of all the troops, only the first regiment was capable of fighting the enemy, and on the eve of the battle, St. Clair had sent it pursuing deserters forty miles to the rear.

During the proceedings of the second committee, the secretary of war submitted a 125-page report to the Congress defending the conduct of himself and his subordinate, Hodgdon (no text of this report has been located). St. Clair prepared a long rebuttal to it as well as to Hodgdon's memorial to Congress. He prefaced his written statement by declaring that if his observations cast blame on the secretary of war and quartermaster, "they have themselves to thank for it." Believing that Knox had influenced the House to reject the first committee report, St. Clair was in no mood to be courteous, and methodically attacked the many contentions of the secretary of war. Discussing Hodgdon's memorial, the former general wrote that Hodgdon's "communications are so replete with insolence and folly that "it would serve little purpose to respond in full. Nevertheless, St. Clair responded. Of the many affidavits produced by Hodgdon, St. Clair remarked that most of them came from the contractors' men who would naturally support Hodgdon's claim of high-quality products. "Besides," wrote St. Clair "the affidavits are all in the handwriting of Mr. Hodgdon's clerk, [and all the] questions and answers, except two." He implied that only the favorable questions and answers were submitted as all of the original affidavits were never furnished to the committee.

It was not until February 15, 1793, that William Giles submitted the revised report to the House. It contained additions and corrections to the original report, plus explanatory information which bordered on excuse making. The committee adopted this reporting mode "because the original report is thereby preserved, mistakes existing in the same, and which are now corrected."

Hodgdon was afforded some relief by the committee. The revised statement declared that the arms and powder were in good order before their distribution to the troops, and that some of the pack saddles were of the right size and of good quality. The question of . . . the troop's payroll was never resolved. The committee noted, however, that there was no good reason why Hodgdon had delayed moving from Pittsburgh to Fort Washington. The quartermaster had been at Fort Pitt from June 10 to August 26, 1791. During this time the "presence of the Quartermaster General was necessary at the army." Some of the censure was shifted from Hodgdon to Knox. Knox was blamed for not devising a system to recruit levies, not designating a paymaster for the army until after the expedition was over and not stopping some improper contracting procedures during the spring of 1791. William Duer, Knox's partner in a land speculation scheme, had not given a security bond to Knox or Hamilton for the performance of his contract. Despite the mismanagement mentioned in the report, the committee did not recommend that the House take specific action against any government official.

Between the end of the committee sessions and the presentation of the report to the House, Hodgdon wrote to several congressmen hoping to influence their views on the investigation. Possibly this maneuver may have been effective, for on February 26, 1793, the committee of the whole took into consideration the reports of the select committee and ordered that the committee be discharged from any further consideration of the reports.

St. Clair, more than anyone else, felt his reputation damaged by the lack of action in the House. The former general did succeed in having a resolution passed on March 2, 1793, allowing all principals in the proceeding to have copies of documents made at public expense. For more than a year St. Clair wrote to the House seeking some action on the tabled report, but to no avail. The revised report was never taken up by the House of Representatives. St. Clair then asked the House to order the report printed. The House refused. In 1812, the old and penniless St. Clair wrote, "And now I am obliged to do it myself . . . in vindication of my old reputation, in which, if the public have no interest, now that I am past service, my children have a great one." St. Clair, who had sacrificed "a very liberal fortune in public service," could offer his children only a vindicated reputation. He emerged neither victor nor victim in the first congressional inquest.

There is no documentation of the investigation in the House of Representatives' records. What happened to them or where they are remains a mystery, but on March 27, 1792, the House of Representatives had taken a step on the long march toward full utilization of the investigatory power of the Legislative branch. The strength of that power remains part of the present drama of the American political arena.

BIBLIOGRAPHY

Because of a fire in the building housing War Department records in 1800, and the British burning of the Capitol in August 1814, some documentation essential for a complete study of the St. Clair defeat is missing. However, James Ripley Jacobs, *The Beginnings of the U.S. Army, 1783-1812* (Princeton, 1947), places the military defeat and investigation in perspective. In 1812, Arthur St. Clair was determined to tell his side of the story in *A Narrative of the Campaign Against the Indians Under the Command of Major General St. Clair* (Philadelphia, 1812). The debates and proceedings relating to the investigations can be found in the *Annals of Congress*, 2nd. Cong., 1, 2 Sess.; the committee reports are in the *American State Papers, Military Affairs*, vol. 1.

Unpublished materials, pertinent to the investigation and never fully utilized, are in the records of the adjutant general's office in the National Archives. Additional material relating to the campaign is in the *American State Papers, Indian Affairs*, vol. 1. A detailed study of the first three Congresses might reveal that the Legislative branch, at the outset, was very eager to define the Constitution at the expense of the Executive branch of the government. In this context, the *Annals of Congress* may be examined to develop a more detailed account of the St. Clair inquiry.

PERTINENT DOCUMENTS

House Debate over Resolution Establishing Investigating Committee, March 27, 1792

Report of Arthur St. Clair to Committee, May 1792

Committee Report, May 8, 1792

House Debate over Committee Report, November 13 and 14, 1792

Memorial of Samuel Hodgdon, November 1792

Extracts from the Minutes of the Committee, December 1792–January 1793

"Observations" by Arthur St. Clair, February 1793

Committee Report, February 15, 1793

Indian Rations and Sam Houston's Trial 1832

U.S. Signal Corps photo (Brady Collection)

Sam Houston's beating of Representative William Stanberry, for remarks concerning Houston's attempt to secure a lucrative government contract, presented the House with novel issues concerning its responsibilities and powers.

Indian Rations and Sam Houston's Trial 1832

by Herman J. Viola

"MOST DARING OUTRAGE AND ASSAULT," ran the storyline in the *U.S. Telegraph*. Another newspaper called it an "UNPRECEDENTED OUTRAGE." Normally, a mugging on Pennsylvania Avenue would not arouse such journalistic indignation, but the one that occurred on the evening of April 13, 1832, was no ordinary street crime. The victim was William Stanberry, a congressman from Ohio; and his assailant was Sam Houston, no ordinary hooligan. Indeed, the entire affair is one of the most bizarre episodes in the history of Congress. Because of it, the House of Representatives tried Houston for violating the privileges of the House; he was tried in the U.S. Circuit Court of the District of Columbia for assault and battery; and a special House committee investigated his role in the controversy that surrounded a contract for feeding emigrating Indians that the War Department planned to award in 1830. Although Houston emerged from all this with only a reprimand, his trial in the House did establish the precedent that Congress could punish an assault committed on one of its members for words spoken in debate.

The roots of this affair went back to the spring of 1830, when Congress was embroiled in discussions over the controversial Indian Removal bill. Enacted in late May of that year, the bill provided for the resettlement of Eastern Indian tribes located west of the Mississippi River. It also authorized ". . . such aid and assistance as may be necessary for their support and subsistence for the first year after their removal." The contract for feeding 80,000 Indians would be lucrative. Even modest estimates indicated it would be worth millions. Sam Houston wanted that contract.

At thirty-seven, Houston had already accomplished more than most men in the proverbial four score and ten. An ensign in the War of 1812, he had served under Andrew Jackson at the Battle of Horseshoe Bend, which had destroyed the powerful Creek confederacy. The young officer had come away from that terrible fight with three wounds that had left him near death. He had recovered, but surgery to remove a musket ball from his right shoulder had maimed him for life. Yet his audacity under fire had earned him Old Hickory's admiration and friendship. Because of that friendship, Houston moved rapidly up the political ladder. His fellow officers in the Tennessee state militia made him a major general. After a brief stint as attorney general of the Nashville district, he served four years in Congress as a representative from Tennessee, followed by two years as the state governor. His rise to prominence had been so phenomenal that some political analysts considered Houston a likely prospect to succeed Jackson in the presidency.

Inexplicably, Houston's star faded. On January 22, 1829, he married eighteen-year-old Eliza Allen, daughter of a prominent middle-Tennessee family. According to Marquis James, Houston's biographer, ". . . no other woman by such womanly means, or by any other means, has so changed the face of American history." The marriage lasted less than three months; the reason for its failure remains a mystery. Regardless, Houston immediately resigned the Tennessee governorship and went into self-imposed exile, joining a band of Cherokee Indians with whom he had spent much of his youth. He may have been a general, a congressman, a governor, but the Cherokees knew him as the Raven or Big Drunk. Houston couldn't have cared less. Gone were his stylish clothes; in their place were beaded buckskins, feathered turbans, and brightly colored blankets that scarcely concealed his massive six-foot-two-inch frame.

Even among Indians, Houston could be no ordinary citizen. These were difficult times for the Cherokees, who needed every potential resource they could find. Who better to defend their interests in Washington than a former congressman and a close friend of President Jackson? Accordingly, in mid-January 1830, the Raven returned to the Capitol, this time as a representative of tribal constituents. In his buckskins and blanket, he created a mild sensation as he went about his business. One item on his agenda was garnering the contract for feeding the emigrating Indians for himself and John Van Fossen, a New York financier with whom Houston had visited on his way to Washington.

Old Hickory may have been puzzled by his protégé's erratic behavior, but their friendship remained strong, as shown by the Raven's conspicuous presence at White House parties. However, the old comrades did not spend all their time drinking and swapping yarns. Houston, armed with Van Fossen's solid financial support, convinced the President that by giving him the rations contract, Jackson could help both the Indians and the public treasury. The government was currently paying roughly twenty-two cents a day to feed each Indian; Houston would provide top quality rations for eighteen cents, thereby saving the country thousands of dollars daily. This sounded good to Jackson and to fellow Tennessean John H. Eaton who as secretary of war had administrative responsibility for the nation's Indian affairs. Eaton balked at only one thing: the contract could not be given outright to Houston; it must be done through competitive bidding. As the secretary of war confided in a note to the President, "Public men must act, not merely [not] to deserve; but also not even to seem to deserve censure. Accordingly, I have said to Gen. S. Houston, that we cannot make a *private contract* with him; but must advertise for proposals. He is quite satisfied with the course. I propose therefore *if* you approve it, to advertise say 30 days for proposals for supplying the Indians who may emigrate during this year; or, may, for the next also. I submit it for your consideration." Jackson jotted his concurrence on the same sheet of paper: "The president, with respects to the Secretary of War, approves the within. February 16, 1830."

Meanwhile, trusting nothing to chance, Houston also approached Thomas L. McKenney, superintendent of Indian Affairs. His office, conveniently, was just a few steps down the hall from Eaton's, on the second floor of the War Department building, two hundred feet west of the White House. Houston exchanged pleasantries, then came straight to the point. If the Indian removal bill passed, the contract for furnishing rations to the emigrating Indians would be awarded to a private firm. "It is my intention to make an attempt to engage in this business; I wish you to aid me; you can do much in accomplishing my intentions. Everybody knows your acquaintance with this business, and you can have the matter attended to, pretty much as you please. If I succeed, as I am sure I can by your aid, you shall lose nothing by it."

"General Houston," McKenney replied, "I regret the mode of approaching this subject, and the terms you have employed in presenting it. I have no power whatever over the subject."

Houston assured McKenney he had meant nothing offensive in his remarks. As he left the office, he invited the superintendent to drop by his hotel to chat in less formal surroundings.

The next morning Houston returned. "Have you seen Eaton?" he asked McKenney. When McKenney said yes, Houston asked what had been said about the rations contract.

"Nothing," came the superintendent's prompt response.

"It is damned queer," Houston muttered as he turned to leave. He returned at least twice more that day, but McKenney had nothing to tell the impatient visitor. Houston found the delay difficult to believe; the secretary of war had promised him that the notice soliciting bids for the rations contract would appear in that day's issue of the *Telegraph*.

The next day Houston again returned. He asked McKenney to remind Eaton about the rations business. McKenney refused, insisting it was not his affair. Houston was not one to take no for an answer—he pulled up a chair and sat down next to McKenney. It had been agreed that the contract would go to the lowest bidder. Since meat was cheaper in the West, suppliers there would be more competitive than Eastern firms. Houston wanted McKenney to ensure that the advertisements announcing the bidding would specify a thirty-day limit in which to submit bids to the War Department. Such a limit would effectively prevent Western contractors from bidding. When McKenney persisted in his refusals to help, Houston drew his chair closer. "There's $50,000 in it for you, if I get the contract," he whispered.

"Get out of my office," McKenney ordered. "From this hour, I never want you to speak to me again upon any matter, official or otherwise."

Houston then threatened to reveal that McKenney had given a fifteen-hundred-dollar bribe to a delegation of Cherokee Indians.

"I have about as much authority as my doorkeeper to issue that sum to anyone," McKenney retorted.

Houston stormed from the room, turned, shook his finger at McKenney, and said: "You shall suffer for this."

Later that day, Eaton called McKenney to his office. "Have you seen Houston?" he asked.

"Indeed, I have," McKenney replied, "and my interviews have not been of the most agreeable sort."

Eaton let McKenney's response pass. Pulling a crumpled sheet of paper from a pocket, he said, "I have forgotten for some days to hand you this paper. It contains proposals for rations for Indians, written by Houston. Take it, and examine it, and if it is correct have it copied, and sign it, and let it appear in the *Telegraph* of the morning."

McKenney scanned the note hurriedly and immediately objected to some of the terms. "It is late now," Eaton answered. "Take it home with you and examine it, and draft one that you think more appropriate."

The next morning McKenney hurried into Eaton's office with Houston's suggested advertisement and one of his own composition entitled "Proposals for Supplying Emigrant Indians with Rations, West of the Mississippi." It read as follows:

> Sealed proposals, and to be endorsed "proposals for rations" will be received by the Secretary of War until for supplying rations to such Indians as may emigrate to their lands West of Arkansas and Missouri—said rations to consist of one pound and a quarter of fresh beef, or one pound of fresh pork; with two quarts of salt to every hundred of these; or if salted meat is issued, one pound of beef and three quarters of a pound of pork, with a quart of corn, or corn meal to each ration of meat, whether fresh or salt, or Eighteen ounces of flour.
>
> The entire expense, whether of transportation, or issuing, or of building houses for the preservation of the supplies, or any other, to be borne by the Contractor.
>
> Bonds with approved security will be required for the faithful fulfilment of the contracts. No advances will be made.

Eaton looked the drafts over carefully. "You have left blank the date by which bids are to be received," he noted.

"It is my object to call your attention to this," McKenney replied. "Perhaps you would like to reconsider this part of the proposals. My opinion is, those supplies can be furnished in Arkansas upon cheaper terms, and with greater readiness, than on this side of the Mississippi." By limiting the bidding to thirty days the government would eliminate Western contractors, McKenney explained.

"I do not think it is of much importance," Eaton said sharply, "for it is my opinion the supplies will come chiefly from Ohio and Kentucky; thirty days will be long enough for the proposals to circulate through that district of country. Besides," he added, "Houston is waiting."

"As you wish," McKenney replied.

On the afternoon of February 18, 1830, McKenney sent the proposal, including Eaton's alterations, to the editors of the *Richmond Enquirer,* the *Baltimore Republican,* the *Philadelphia Gazette,* the *Cincinnati Republican,* the *National Intelligencer,* the *Ohio State Bulletin,* and the *Louisville Advertiser.* He asked the editors to run the notice three times a week until five days before the March 20 deadline.

The War Department received about a dozen replies. The bids ranged from eight to twenty cents per ration; Houston came in at eighteen cents. Figuring that some eighty thousand Indians had to be fed enroute to the West and supported for a year after their arrival, McKenney knew that the difference of a few cents per ration was important and emphasized this point in a report to Eaton on April 7. At ten cents a ration, removal would cost the government fifty-five dollars per Indian—more than four million dollars for all of them. Reducing the cost of the ration to six cents, a price McKenney considered reasonable, would keep the overall cost under three million dollars.

The March 20 deadline passed, but the War Department failed to announce the recipient of the contract. Several bidders asked McKenney why, and he, in turn, asked Eaton. The secretary said an announcement was unnecessary. Only one bid had been submitted—from Houston, in the name of Ben Hawkins, a mixed-blooded Cherokee Indian. When McKenney insisted he had given several bids to Randolph, Eaton claimed these bids had arrived too late for consideration.

Nevertheless, Houston did not receive the contract. He had been less than discreet in his efforts to get it, and had approached several others besides McKenney on the subject. One of these was Duff Green, editor of the *U.S. Telegraph.* The prominent journalist had long been a friend of the Administration and a trusted member of Jackson's Kitchen Cabinet. Lately, however, he had fallen from favor because of the notorious Peggy O'Neale affair. John Eaton had married the former bar maid, scandalizing the ladies of Washington, especially several wives of Jackson's cabinet members. The sharpest critic was Mrs. John C. Calhoun, one of the city's social lionesses. Duff Green, whose son was married to a Calhoun daughter, found himself forced to side with his son-in-law against Jackson. Nevertheless, Green at this point still had the President's ear; and many people, including Green, believed Jackson owed the presidency to him.

About the time the advertisements were sent to the newspapers, Green, while in the White House, surprised Eaton, Houston, and Jackson, in earnest conversation. Eaton called the editor over to the table. "Duff, what time should an ad for the next day's edition be sent to the *Telegraph* office?"

"Anytime before ten."

"I will send you one tomorrow," Eaton said.

"No!" Houston interrupted. "I will call and take it."

A month later, Eaton met Green and told him the War Department was about to award Houston the important contract for feeding the emigrating Indians. Eaton said his figures indicated rations had been costing the government twenty-two cents each; Houston would take the contract for eighteen cents a ration. "Imagine the savings," Eaton beamed, "at least twelve thousand dollars daily."

The arithmetic did not impress the editor, who suspected the secretary of war was fishing for a favorable editorial about the award in the *Telegraph*. Instead, Green tried to convince Eaton he was making a mistake. Like McKenney, he pointed out that the government stood to save still more money by giving the contract to a Westerner.

"I know beef can be purchased in Missouri and Illinois, on foot, at from one dollar to one dollar and fifty cents per hundred pounds, and that, without further inquiry, I should suppose that the ration ought not to cost more than six cents."

When Eaton refused to reopen the bidding to give Westerners a crack at the contract, the editor sought out John Shackford, a wealthy Missouri merchant. Green told Shackford he suspected a conspiracy to give Houston the contract at an inflated price and urged his friend to submit a low bid, force the contract down to an honest price, and save the Jackson Administration from a black eye. Shackford was sympathetic, but he claimed his funds were tied up in the construction of the Louisville and Portland Canal.

Undaunted, Green decided to confront Jackson himself. The next morning, March 19, found him in the President's office expressing concern over the apparent decision to give Houston the rations contract. Jackson was a sick man, but the old fire remained. He could see nothing wrong with the arrangement. At eighteen cents, Houston would be saving public money. Still more would be saved if the contract were awarded at six cents, Green replied.

"Will *you* take it at *ten?*" Jackson asked.

"No."

"Will *you* take it at twelve cents? If you will, you shall have it at that."

"I am not a bidder," Green answered. He had come to Jackson only to save the Administration from censure, not to speculate. With the interview over, the editor left the Executive mansion convinced the decision had been made to give Houston the contract. Returning to his office, he wrote a short letter appealing to Eaton's sense of integrity. "I should be unfaithful to the administration, to Gen. Jackson, and to myself," Green declared, "if I did not bring the subject before you in such a shape as to guard against the consequences which I foresee will follow any such contract as the one he [Jackson] contemplates. Such a contract may enrich a few who are concerned in it, but will destroy the confidence of the public, I fear, in the administration, and impair the fair fame of the President, which it is your duty and mine to guard. Will it not be well to extend the time, so as to enable the people of Missouri and Arkansas to bid?"

That evening Green again sought out Shackford. Telling him of his fruitless conversation with the President and unaware that others had already submitted lower bids than Houston's, he prevailed on the St. Louis merchant to submit a bid before the deadline, thereby thwarting Houston's plans. Shackford, realizing he stood to profit immensely should his bid be accepted, submitted one for seventeen cents. The next day, March 20, the deadline, Shackford changed his bid to fifteen cents.

Meanwhile, still another person was muddying the waters for Houston. This was William Prentiss, a Washington merchant, who submitted a bid for nine cents. The only lower bid came from Luther Blake, who was legally disqualified because of his position as a subagent in the Indian Service. By rights, then, Prentiss should have received the contract. But on March 21, he was visited by Houston and Van Fossen, who urged him to withdraw his bid, join their partnership, and make more money from half the profits at *their* price than he could make alone. Prentiss turned them down, although the fact that Houston and Van Fossen knew the amount of his bid convinced him that a conspiracy existed in favor of Houston.

Prentiss then spent almost a month pestering the War Department for a decision on the proposals. Eaton tried to stall him with several ploys. He left notes with his clerk; he solicitously wondered how Prentiss could make money at such a low price; he said Jackson would have to be consulted before the contract was awarded; he refused to tell Prentiss the amounts of the other bids; he admitted that Prentiss had the lowest allowable bid, but then denied this required the contract be given to him; and finally he claimed ". . . circumstances . . . impose the necessity of advertising new bids."

Eaton was trying to give the contract to one of his "bosom friends," the bitter merchant wrote. "During the days of Bargain, Sale, and Corruption, I have no recollection of any such unfair method of transacting business—little right had I to expect it in these days of reformation." Eaton ignored this angry letter, but replied immediately when the persistent Prentiss asked again for a decision six months later. No Indians are emigrating at present. Until some decide to remove, Eaton wrote, "no mode will be agreed upon, or considered of, as to their removal and support."

This brought to a close the exchange of correspondence between the disappointed bidder and the secretary of war. It also ended public debate about the rations contract. Houston returned to the Indian country and again dropped from sight. Eaton left the cabinet as a result of the Peggy O'Neale business and became governor of Florida. Most people turned their attention to other matters. The request for bids was quietly withdrawn, and the chore of feeding the Indians went to the Commissary Department of the Army. Houston did salvage one satisfaction from the tempest, however: McKenney was removed from office.

Almost two years passed before the scandal was revived. Political rhetoric for fall elections had already begun when, on March 31, 1832, speaking on the floor of the House, Ohio Congressman William Stanberry, during a sweeping criticism of the Jackson Administration, declared: "Was not the late Secretary of War removed in consequence of his attempt, fraudulently, to give to Governor Houston the contract for Indian rations?" Moreover, Stanberry continued, President Jackson ". . . had full knowledge of the business, and . . . it did not meet with his disapprobation." Two days later Stanberry's remarks were printed in Washington's *National Intelligencer*.

Meanwhile, unknown to Stanberry, the Raven had returned to Washington. He had escorted a group of Cherokee on business with the "Great

Father." Although not officially a member of the delegation, Houston had drafted the four-page petition to Jackson that the Indians brought with them. Houston was still wearing his Indian garb, which now included a large knife and an attractive buckskin coat with a beaver collar, gifts from Opothle Yoholo, chief of the Creeks. Enroute to Washington, Houston had treated the delegation to a guided tour of the Hermitage, Jackson's plantation a few miles from Nashville. While tramping across the grounds of the magnificent estate, Houston had used his new knife to cut a walking stick, later given to a friend in Georgetown from a hickory sapling. The party reached the capital in late January and took lodgings at Jesse Brown's Indian Queen Hotel, the city's best, at Tenth and Pennsylvania Avenue.

The delegation had almost completed its business when Houston read Stanberry's remarks in the newspaper. Immediately, he rushed to the Capitol Building in search of the unsuspecting Stanberry. When fellow Tennessean James K. Polk, later to be President of the United States but now holder of Houston's former House seat, saw him lurking behind the Speaker's chair, he ushered him from the chamber. Polk warned the angry Houston that his friends could do nothing for him if he assaulted Stanberry in the Capitol. Houston then decided to seek satisfaction by the *code duello.* Accordingly, Congressman Cave Johnson of Kentucky agreed to take a note to Stanberry, who still had no idea of the storm that was about to engulf him. The note, dated April 3, but not delivered until the following morning read:

> Sir, I have seen some remarks in the National Intelligencer of the 2nd Instant, in which you are represented to have said, "Was the late Secretary of War removed in consequence of his attempt, fraudulently, to give to Governor Houston the contract for Indian rations?"
>
> The object of this note is to ascertain whether my name was used by [you] in debate, and, if so, whether your remarks have been correctly reported.

Stanberry, who viewed the note as a formal inquiry that etiquette required to precede a challenge to a duel, refused to reply to Houston. Instead, he sent a note to Johnson:

> I received, this morning, by your hands, a note signed Samuel Houston, quoting . . . a remark made by me in the House. The object of this note is "to ascertain whether Mr. Houston's name was used by me in debate, and whether my remarks were correctly quoted." I cannot recognize the right of Mr. Houston to make the request.

When Johnson delivered the letter to Houston, in a lobby of the House of Representatives, he muttered, "I'll introduce myself to the damned rascal. I'll whip the damned rascal before he leaves the House."

"You can't do that," Johnson answered. "It would be a contempt to the House."

Houston met this objection with a string of curses and then snarled, "I right wrongs wherever they are given, even were it in the court of Heaven." By now he had worked himself into a frenzy, and it was all his friends could do to get him away from the Capitol Building.

For the next two weeks Stanberry did his best to avoid Houston, whom he saw almost every day stalking the halls of Congress, the hickory cane, retrieved from his Georgetown friend, tucked under one arm and a pair of pistols protruding from the buckskin coat. As Stanberry claimed later, "I expected he would attack me with the bludgeon, and that, if I made any resistance, he would resort to pistols and a dirk."

When the two finally met on the evening of April 13, it was by accident. Houston had been chatting with several friends in Senator Felix Grundy's Capitol Hill boarding house. About 7:30 P.M., Houston took leave. Senator Buckner of Missouri and Congressman Blair of Tennessee rose with him, and the trio strolled leisurely along Pennsylvania Avenue towards the Indian Queen. About halfway, they paused. As they stood talking, Blair suddenly turned on his heels and walked briskly away.

"Now why would he do that?" Buckner asked Houston. Instead of answering, the Raven took a firm grip on his hickory cane and stepped in the path of a man crossing the avenue towards them. Because of the dim lamplight, Buckner at first did not recognize the pedestrian. But as the man stepped up onto the curbstone, he realized who it was.

"Are you Mr. Stanberry?" Houston challenged.

"Yes, sir," the Ohioan replied politely, bowing slightly.

"Then you are the damned rascal," Houston roared, breaking his cane over Stanberry's head.

"Oh, don't," Stanberry groaned as he stumbled backwards into the street. He tried to shield his head with his arms as Houston flailed away at him with the splintered cane, held in his left hand, his right arm hanging loosely, still crippled from old war wounds. When Stanberry turned to run, Houston grabbed him. They wrestled a few moments, and Stanberry fell on his back. Houston lunged. Stanberry pulled a pistol from his pocket and fired it into Houston's chest. The flintlock flashed but misfired, and Houston ripped it from Stanberry's grasp. The congressman lifted his legs to ward off the continued assault, giving Houston the opportunity "to strike him elsewhere," Buckner delicately reported later. Stanberry finally stopped hollering and lay still. Buckner thought he was dead. But when Houston returned to the sidewalk, the pistol jammed in his belt, Stanberry rose shakily to his feet.

"Why did you try to assassinate me in the night?" he cried.

"I did not try to assassinate you," Houston retorted. "I only intended to chastise you for defaming me."

When someone in the gathering crowd questioned Houston further, he growled, "I attend to my own business. The damned scoundrel deserved his beating. If I've broken the law, I'll answer for it." With that, he pushed his way through the spectators and disappeared. Buckner then walked off in another direction, leaving the dazed Stanberry standing in the street.

The congressman did not take his seat the next day. Instead, writing from his bed, he penned a formal protest to Speaker of the House Andrew Stevenson. "I was waylaid in the street near to my boarding house last night . . . and attacked, knocked down by a bludgeon, and severely bruised and wounded by Samuel Houston, late of Tennessee, for words spoken in my place in the House of Representatives; by reason of which I am confined to my bed and unable to discharge my duties in the House, and attend to the interests of my constituents. I communicate this information to you," he wrote, "and request that you will lay it before the House." When Stevenson finished reading the letter to the assembly, one of Stanberry's colleagues from Ohio introduced a resolution calling for Houston's arrest by the sergeant-at-arms. Polk, the spokesman for Jackson in the House, tried to block this move, contending that Congress would be establishing a dangerous precedent for violating the rights of private citizens if it interfered in the affair, but the vote calling for the arrest carried 145 to 25.

Two days later the sergeant-at-arms informed Stevenson that he had Houston in custody. The Speaker then asked the House what he should do. After considerable debate, the House passed a resolution ordering Houston to be brought before the bar to answer the charge that he had assaulted a member of the House for words spoken in debate. Houston, still adorned in his buckskins, walked down the aisle of the chamber, stopped before the Speaker's chair, and bowed. Stevenson read the formal arraignment. "If you desire the aid of counsel, the testimony of witnesses, time to prepare for your defence, or have any other request to make in relation to this subject, your request will now be received."

"I wish no counsel," the defendant responded. He did wish to summon witnesses, and he asked for twenty-four hours to prepare his case—the House gave him forty-eight.

After Houston left, the House adopted a resolution providing for the appointment of a committee of privileges to report a mode of proceedings. The committee reported the next day. Houston would be asked whether the charges against him were true. If he admitted assaulting Stanberry for words spoken in debate, the House would "proceed to judgment thereon." If Houston denied the charges, Stanberry would be called to testify, after which Houston could introduce any "competent" evidence in his defense. A committee would examine the witnesses. All questions were to be in writing, as would be all answers. Any member of the House could submit written questions to a witness through the Speaker. Any member of the House could challenge questions or testimony. After all evidence had been presented, Houston could be heard by himself or through his counsel. The House would then consider the subject and ". . . take such order thereon as may seem just and proper."

The trial opened on April 18, to packed galleries. "It must have been the novelty of the occasion that drew so great a crowd," noted Gales and Seaton, editors of the *National Intelligencer*. Between the arraignment and the beginning of the trial, Houston had reconsidered the need for a counsel and had selected Francis Scott Key, author of the National Anthem. Together they marched through the crowded House chamber and stood before the Speaker's table.

"Samuel Houston," Stevenson asked, "have you any request to make of the House before you are put upon your trial?"

Houston protested the legality of the entire proceeding, but he agreed to submit to whatever the House considered proper. He also asked, through his counsel, that the House remove a member who had publicly expressed an opinion on the case. In effect, he challenged the jury. This sparked a lively debate, prompting Key to remove the request.

Stevenson read the charges, which Houston denied in general terms. True, he had assaulted Stanberry, but not for words spoken in debate on the House floor. His indignation had risen from reading the remarks in the public prints; his reputation had been besmirched throughout the nation. The attack occurred because of a chance meeting at night. Houston's only weapon had been a common walking stick, which he later introduced as evidence. Stanberry had carried a pistol. In chastising the Ohio congressman, Houston had meant no disrespect to the House of Representatives or its privileges.

The trial dragged on for more than a month, attracting unprecedented crowds and publicity. *Niles' Weekly Register,* pointing to the historic implications of the affair, preempted normal congressional coverage to give readers the daily proceedings of the trial. "Let the truth of these charges be what they may," wrote Hezikiah Niles, ". . . *it is impossible to admit the right of individuals thus to punish representatives of the people, for words spoken in debate*. What one man may do to another man, fifty may do to fifty men."

President Jackson, on the other hand, considered the trial "the greatest act of tyranny and corruption ever attempted under our government." A week into the trial, he wrote to his daughter-in-law, Sarah, "Congress is still in excitement. Much to do, & nothing done. When it will rise, the Lord only knows, for it is beyond mortal men." That Jackson considered the proceedings little more than a farce is indicated by the fact that he enclosed for his son Andrew's "amusement" a cartoon of Houston beating Stanberry. ". . . [It was] taken from the real facts and deposed to by Senator Buckner a witness who was present. preserve it."

Old Hickory obviously came from the same bolt of cloth as his protégé, and his approval of Houston's caning Stanberry was well-known. Indeed, several newspapers quoted the President to the effect that, if five or six other congressmen had received the same treatment, "it would have a salutary effect upon the proceedings of both the Senate and the House." These remarks, calculated to encourage other assaults on members of Congress, were greeted with approval in some quarters. "We have read the president's Conversation with his friends in Genl. Houston's affair and [we are] happy to inform you that it meets with the general approbation of his friends and the principle [is] approved of by many of his opposers," wrote one of Senator John Tipton's constituents in Indiana. Another Hoosier wrote, ". . . it appears to us rediculous [*sic*] in the extreme that congress should squander so much time and money debating upon a subject of so little importance as that Stanberry business. The people of all parties in this quarter are completely incensed at the proceedings particularly while so much important business is pending."

Nevertheless, the trial consumed almost six weeks, demonstrating the remarkable inability of the House to conduct such an investigation according to any recognized system of procedure. John Quincy Adams tried to persuade the House to appoint a select committee "to examine the precedents in cases of contempt and breaches of privilege," but his resolution was tabled. Actually, there were no real precedents. The House had never had a similar case, and had to feel its way. As a result, Key, as counsel to the accused, tried his best to get the case thrown out on constitutional grounds.

Houston, all the while, insisted his fracas with Stanberry had been a private affair and attributed the hullabaloo to politics. Certainly he felt no alarm. "My trial progresses slowly," he wrote a friend on May 1, "and tho I play the part of a *patient man*, I do not feel precisely so composed,—I apprehend no difficulty, beyond the trial, & discussion upon the subject. Congress can do nothing with me, and of this they are satisfied, as I believe. It is the test of a great principle, in which the liberty & reputation of every American Citizen is involved, and I am proud to be its representative on the present occasion."

Jackson also considered the trial a cheap political ploy to embarrass him and the Administration. Before Houston was to speak in his own defense, the old general summoned his former comrade-in-arms to the Executive Mansion. Houston had never before seen him so angry.

"Are those the only clothes you have?" Jackson asked, referring to Houston's buckskins.

"Yes."

"Then take this money and buy some clothes befitting a gentleman," the President ordered, tossing a clinking purse across his desk. "Sam, you must take this money and when you make your defense tell those infernal bank thieves, who talk about privileges, that when an American citizen is insulted by one of them, he also has some privileges." Houston took the money and ordered a suit of the latest cut, complete with satin vest, silk hat, and leather boots.

The tailor delivered the clothes the afternoon before Houston was to speak. That evening, a number of his friends gathered in his room at the Indian Queen, where they toasted his new wardrobe and forthcoming defense. As Houston later recalled, "You may guess how we drank when I tell you that Stevenson [the Speaker of the House] at midnight was sleeping on a lounge in the room. Bailey Peyton was out of commission and had gone to his room, and Felix Grundy had ceased to be interesting. Polk rarely indulged and left us early." No wonder Houston had nothing to fear.

At noon the next day, after washing away his headache with coffee and donning his splendid outfit, Houston presented himself at the bar of the House. His lengthy and passionate speech brought bouquets from the packed galleries. Immediately a resolution calling for dismissal of the charges was amended by another declaring Houston "guilty of a contempt in violation of the privileges of the House." The amendment sparked four days of debate before it passed by a vote of 106 to 89. The sentence was a reprimand from the Speaker. Polk beat back an attempt by Stanberry's friends to deny Houston his House privileges, which he still enjoyed as a former member of Congress.

Stevenson delivered the reprimand on May 14. It reads more like a compliment than a rebuff. "When addressing a citizen of your character and intelligence, and one who has himself been honored by the people with a seat in this House," Stevenson informed his friend, "it cannot be necessary that I should add to the duty enjoined upon me, by dwelling upon the character of consequences of the offense with which you have been charged and found guilty!" Stevenson continued briefly in this vein, then concluded by saying:

"I forebear to say more than to pronounce the judgment of the House, which is, that you have been guilty of a high breach of its privileges, and that you be reprimanded therefor, at its bar, by the Speaker; and, in obedience to the order of the House, I do reprimand you accordingly." He then ordered Houston released from the custody of the sergeant-at-arms.

The results of the trial did not meet with universal approval. "Oh! most lame and impotent conclusion!" wailed an editorial in the Richmond *Whig*. "We had supposed that the members of . . . [the House] would have rated their dignity and privileges a little higher, but they certainly ought to be the best judges of their own consequence, when they rate themselves so humbly. *The House has committed a much greater contempt upon itself than Houston did*, and should he presume to pull the Speaker's nose in reply to his reprimand, *the House, we suppose, would re-reprimand him*." Andrew Jackson, on the other hand, was outraged that the House had taken even a limited action against his friend. "Those high dignitaries and would be privileged order, has voted their power to punish a citizen for whipping a member of Congress distant from the Congress Hall," he fumed in a letter to his son, "and when it was not in session by a majority of seventeen. The people will inquire into this act of usurpation," he vowed, "and make those little Tyrants who have thus voted feel the power of the people."

Most indignant of all was Stanberry. He could not let Houston off so lightly. The same day Stevenson issued the reprimand, the Ohio congressman went to the U.S. Circuit Court for the District of Columbia where he obtained a bench warrant from Judge William Cranch for Houston's arrest "for a violent assault and battery with an intent to kill." He also introduced a resolution in the House calling for the appointment of a select committee "to inquire whether an attempt was made by the late Secretary of War John H. Eaton, fradulently [*sic*], to give Samuel Houston, a contract for rations to such Indians as might emigrate to their lands west of Arkansas and Missouri, and whether said Houston made a fradulent [*sic*] attempt to obtain said contract; and that said committee be further instructed to inquire whether the President of the United States had any knowledge of such attempted fraud, and whether he disapproved or approved of the same; and that said committee have power to send for persons and papers."

Interestingly, Houston's civil suit received almost no public attention. He regarded it as little more than another annoyance. "My trial is to take place on . . . [June] 12th," he wrote a friend, "and will be ended in one day, I hope." His hopes for speedy justice were not realized, however. A week later, on June 16, he wrote: "I do hope my trial will end to day. The court have had it before them for two days, on the Constitutionality of a second trial—no argument upon it, but the point made to the court—it will be settled to day, and the trial finished I hope." The next day he again wrote his friend: "My trial in court is not [*sic*] thro, but is in the situation as when I wrote you last." Not, in fact, for another two weeks did the trial end, and the results were not to his liking. "My trial took place to day, at One oclock," he informed his friend on June 28, "and the Honble I [*sic*] Cranch the old sinner fined me $500.00 with costs of suit! This is *tough* enough, in my opinion. It is not necessary to pay it until next winter, so that I will not be detained, in consequence of the Judgment of the court. It was made solely on party grounds, and I will bear it, for the sake of *Party!*" Although the jury had found no evidence that Houston intended to kill Stanberry, it did find him guilty of assaulting ". . . said William Stanberry with the walking cane . . . as also with the fists and feet . . . [and] did then and there beat, kick, wound and ill treat [him]."

Houston never paid a cent. After nearly two years, he petitioned President Jackson to remit the fine. "The expenses incurred, while, upon trial before the H. [*sic*] of Representatives, as well, as before the court were very considerable and oppressive to your memorialist," he explained in his memorial of April 20, 1834. "For these reasons set forth, as well, as the sincere belief that your memorialist, from the nature of the injury which he had received, could not have, done less in vindication of his feelings and character. He prays that the *fine and costs of suit,* may be remitted by *your Pardon.*" To Jackson the request seemed quite reasonable, and he asked Benjamin F. Butler, the attorney general, for a ruling, claiming that Houston had been tried twice for the same crime. Not so, Butler replied. "The act committed by . . . [Houston] constituted but one indictable offense, and he was therefore liable to only one conviction on *indictment,* but if this act was also a breach of the privileges of the House of Representatives, and a contempt of that House, they had the right to punish him for the contempt, independently of the action of the Criminal Courts and *so vice versa.*" This was not the decision Jackson wanted. "It appears [to me]," he grumbled, "that for the same act he was indicted and fined $500. Under the circumstances of the case I regard his fine as excessive and therefore remit it."

Stanberry drew even less satisfaction from the House investigation of the intrigues surrounding the 1830 rations contract, although he chaired the seven-member select committee. Stevenson also appointed to the committee Isaac Chapman Bates of Massachusetts and John Leeds Kerr of Maryland, both Whigs; and Jacksonian Democrats William Drayton of South Carolina, James Moore Wayne of Georgia, Henry A. P. Muhlenberg of Pennsylvania, and Henry Hubbard of New Hampshire. Although Stanberry professed to be a Jacksonian Democrat, he had no intention of letting party loyalty deter his determination to even the score with Houston and his cohorts, whoever they might be. But he should have realized he had embarked on a fool's errand, for Stevenson had stacked the committee. Wayne and Hubbard were numbered among the most zealous and able supporters of Jackson in the House. For his loyalty to the Administration Wayne later received an appointment to the Supreme Court, while Hubbard secured a seat on the important and powerful House Ways and Means Committee. Of William Drayton, a former Federalist, the President once commented, "I like the man but I fear his politics." Nonetheless, only a few months before the investigation he had offered him a cabinet post as secretary of war, following Eaton's resignation. Muhlenberg, another party dependable, represented a Pennsylvania county noted as the tenth legion of democracy.

Houston knew he was safe in the hands of this group. "All will be right, you may rest easy," he confided to a friend on June 17, midway through the hearings. "The *fraud* committee, . . . [has] been at work for some days, or weeks, and I had not looked at the testimony until yesterday, and today —hence I have been very busy. I looked over it and fo[und] with all the inclinations which some w[it]nesses had to lie, they could show noth[ing] wrong, either with the President, Secy of War, or even the 'Man of Broken fortune, and blasted reputation.' "

The hearings ran from May 18 to July 2, 1832, and the committee met twenty-six times in that period, although all members were seldom present. Drayton, leader of the Jacksonian Democrats on the committee, skipped half the sessions; Stanberry missed only one.

Although Stanberry may have been the only member who took the hearing seriously, the committee conducted a thorough investigation, issuing subpoenas for scores of documents and a dozen witnesses. Lewis Cass, who replaced Eaton, and Elbert Herring, who replaced McKenney, had to ransack their files to answer the committee's requests for copies of the original bids, the advertisements written by Houston and McKenney, and ". . . all other papers relating to the subject matter of the inquiry before this committee; also, of the decision and doings of the late Secretary of War thereon." The committee wished particularly to see any correspondence between Houston and his partner, Van Fossen. Although Van Fossen had several letters touching their business relationship, he objected to presenting them to the committee, thereby making them part of the public record, "because they contained matters not relating to the contract aforesaid." Hubbard, Wayne, and Kerr were appointed a subcommittee to screen the correspondence, deleting the private material, before entering the letters into the record, and Van Fossen withdrew his objection.

Houston also gave his approval to the subcommittee arrangement, but not before establishing his right to withhold the letters if he so desired. "The letters have all been placed in my possession by General Van Fossen, and are fully within my control," he informed the committee on June 12. "They are *private personal* property, to which the committee have no claim, and, however inquisitorial the course of the proceedings may be, I am determined not to withhold them, although my absolute right to do so must be admitted." The contents of the letters must have disappointed Stanberry; they contained little new information and nothing to implicate either Eaton or Jackson.

The testimony of the witnesses proved far more interesting. Auguste Choteau, summoned from his Arkansas trading post for a very brief appearance, had come the greatest distance; McKenney, who answered two subpoenas, proved to be the star witness, however, testifying six times between May 28 and June 2, and then again on June 18.

"Were you an officer of the Government in the War Department in the year 1830?" Stanberry asked to open the questioning.

"I was an officer in the War Department in 1830, and had charge of the Bureau of Indian Affairs."

His response to a question about conversations with Houston or Eaton on the subject of the proposals and the newspaper advertisement took up the better part of five consecutive sessions. As McKenney's story unfolded, it became apparent that Houston had been the favored bidder and that Eaton had done his best to accommodate his friend.

"Have you ever said to any one that Major Eaton had attempted to give a fradulent [*sic*] contract to Governor Houston . . . for the supply of Indian rations?" asked Wayne.

"I have no recollection of ever having expressed myself in such terms,"

McKenney answered. He did admit discussing the affair with numerous individuals since then, however, because ". . . the subject has been made one of general notoriety." He also had obtained considerable additional information from the newspapers and from other persons involved. Luther Blake, for instance, had told him much. "I confess, putting the whole together, I have thought inferences grew out of it which go far to implicate the parties, and I have said this much, and that the aspect of the case was an ugly one."

Summoned a second time from his Philadelphia home, McKenney was asked how it had been possible for Houston to receive access to official records of the Indian Office at the time of the rations controversy. The former superintendent recalled a complaint from his chief clerk that Houston had been rummaging through the office files. McKenney immediately ordered his staff to keep him out of the files. When the clerk tried to enforce the regulation, Houston went into a rage, forcing McKenney to bring the matter to Eaton's attention. The secretary of war at first remained silent. Then, pointing to a sofa in his office, he said, "There are some papers, and, I think, a letter book. You had better take them." The chief clerk later confirmed that Houston had removed the documents from the files.

Following McKenney's second appearance at the hearings, the committee called on Van Fossen to testify. The New York financier claimed he had been present at one of the meetings between his partner and McKenney. Houston had raised very serious charges against members of the Indian Service. McKenney at first tried to defend them and then "begged off." Van Fossen's testimony, which Stanberry transmitted to Philadelphia, enraged the ex-superintendent. "I have never 'begged off' or shrunk from any charge," he retorted, firing back an eleven-page rebuttal. "I stand ready at any moment to account for every action of my official life, & I hurl an indignant defiance at the author of this insinuation." McKenney then proceeded to relate additional information he had not provided in his previous testimony. He admitted Houston had made sweeping charges against members of the Indian Department, especially against those residing west of the Mississippi. He called them "*base—dishonest—and corrupt!*" At first McKenney had believed them, but then he heard rumors that Jackson planned to reorganize the Indian Department, to carve a new district out of Missouri and Arkansas, and eliminate the existing St. Louis superintendency under William Clark, the venerable veteran of the Lewis and Clark expedition. The superintendent of this new Western district would have been responsible, among other things, for regulating the resettlement of the Eastern tribes. "I had no *official* evidence of this design," McKenney admitted, but how else explain Houston's determined efforts to discredit the Indian agents in that area, including "the pure & unimpeachable" Clark? Moreover, "I was convinced that Gl. Houston had the ear, & the confidence of both the President and Secretary of War; and that the mode he had adopted was the most likely to ensure the dismissal of these officers, and thus open the way for new appointments—and I could not give to Gl. Houston the credit of searching so diligently after corruption; and travelling so far to reveal it, *purely* to serve the public interests, or to protect the Indians."

Interestingly, McKenney never revealed to the committee the $50,000 bribe Houston had offered for his cooperation. Believing that he would eventually be recalled to the Indian Office he had created, McKenney had no intention of unduly antagonizing the powerful figures concerned in the affair. He kept the confidence until November 1841, when he finally realized he had no hope of being returned to office, either by a Democratic or Whig administration. Angry and despondent, he revealed the bribe attempt in letters to the secretary of war and to other influential members of the Tyler Administration, who he thought had blocked his reappointment. For his honesty in 1830, McKenney wrote, "I was *marked* as one of Gl. Jackson's 'enemies.' His motto was—'I reward my friends and *punish* my enemies.' His enemies were all those who dared to have any *conscience* or *will*, that did not square with his own. I know of no case of conflict between us, except this ration case, and no cause for my removal, if it be not that." Unfortunately, this bit of information came too late to do McKenney or Stanberry any good.

Even if McKenney had revealed the attempted bribery to the "fraud committee," the outcome probably would have been no different. He was not the only one who could speak firsthand of the machinations of Houston and Eaton. Duff Green, Luther Blake, William Prentiss, and others fully informed the committee of their roles in the affair. Blake testified that Houston had also offered him a partnership if he would withdraw his lower bid. Prentiss provided copies of his extensive correspondence with Eaton and related Van Fossen's efforts to persuade him to withdraw his bid, all to no avail. On July 3, the committee held a closed session and two days later Drayton presented the findings to the House of Representatives. The majority of the committee —Drayton, Wayne, Muhlenberg, and Hubbard—had discovered nothing to indicate Eaton attempted "fradulently" to give Houston or anyone else the rations contract. Therefore, they introduced the following resolution:

> That John H. Eaton, the late Secretary of War, and Samuel Houston, do stand entirely acquitted, in the judgment of this House, from all imputation of fraud, either committed or attempted to be committed, by them, or either of them, in any matter relating to or connected with the premises.

Stanberry, Bates, and Kerr did not concur in this report, however. In their dissenting statement, Stanberry and Bates claimed they had tried to have the evidence submitted to the entire House. Overruled by the others, they felt obliged to declare that in their opinion "Houston did attempt, wrongfully, to obtain the contract . . . for the supply of rations to the emigrating Indians. That the late secretary of war did attempt, wrongfully, to give said contract to Samuel Houston, and that this was known by the President. As an official transaction," Stanberry and Bates viewed ". . . it as extraordinary and unjustifiable throughout."

Kerr, in a very reasoned and dispassionate statement, also presented a dissenting opinion:

> What should be deemed "fradulent" conduct in men invested with the power to confer public offices and contracts upon individuals coming in competition for them, admits, perhaps, of some difference of opinion . . . and how far it is politically just, in such

> cases, to prefer favorites and friends, is a topic of frequent controversy amongst political partisans; but, in any case, to prefer a favorite or a friend to the obvious or to the slightest detriment of the public, certainly cannot be justified by any mode of reasoning.

To Kerr, the evidence showed that Houston had used strong endeavors to obtain the rations contract and that "other persons, at diverse times," joined him in that attempt. The evidence also proved that Eaton manifested ". . . a strong desire to prefer" Houston in his application. All that prevented the consummation of this arrangement were ". . . the remonstrance and interference of others, . . . the glaring difference in the lower terms offered and pressed upon the [war] department, and, it is but just and charitable to add, . . . a final conviction of error in calculations assumed." The President certainly knew the terms of Houston's proposal and at one time approved his having the contract ". . . on the highest terms proposed by him," but Kerr would not "undertake to impute to him a *consciousness* of the existence of 'fradulent' practices, and an approbation of them."

The dissenting opinions mattered little. Houston had been vindicated and restored to prominence. He shed his beads and buckskins. Gone was Big Drunk; in his place was the empire builder history remembers. Years later Houston reflected on that painful episode in his life. "I was dying out," he said, "and had they taken me before a Justice of the Peace and fined me ten dollars for assault and battery, they would have killed me. But they gave me a national tribunal for a theatre, and that set me up again."

Before leaving, Houston could not resist a parting shot at Stanberry. On July 9, the Washington *Globe* published "To the Public," a lengthy statement in which Houston denied all charges and attributed his recent difficulties to the depravity of the Honorable Stanberry. "Nothing but the blackest malignity can justify the perverseness and vindictiveness of this man!" Houston wrote. "Insensible to every manly emotion, he is incapable of an attempt to rise in the scale of being, and seeks only to drag others to his own loathsome degradation. His vices are too odious to merit pity, and his spirit too mean to deserve contempt."

Needless to say, Stanberry's public humiliation did little for his political career. Less than four months later his Ohio constituents voted him out of office, news which Polk gleefully relayed to his cronies: "The elections in Ohio you see have terminated favorably . . . Stanberry [is] beaten." The unfortunate congressman was left only with the dubious distinction of being the instrument for settling the question whether Congress can recognize an assault committed elsewhere by third parties on members of Congress for opinions expressed from the floor.

BIBLIOGRAPHY

Bassett, John Spencer. *The Life of Andrew Jackson.* New York, 1916.

Houston, Sam. *The Writings of Sam Houston, 1813–1863.* Edited by Amelia W. Williams and Eugene C. Barker. Austin, 1938–1943.

McKenney, Thomas L. *Memoirs, Official and Personal.* Lincoln, Neb., 1973.

Sellers, Charles G. *James K. Polk, Jacksonian.* Princeton, 1957.

Viola, Herman J. *Thomas L. McKenney, Architect of America's Early Indian Policy, 1816–1830.* Chicago, 1974.

PERTINENT DOCUMENTS

Debate over Resolution to Serve Warrant on Sam Houston, April 14, 1832
United States' Telegraph Report, April 16, 1832
Sam Houston Trial Proceedings, April 18, 1832
Niles' Weekly Register Report, April 21, 1832
Niles' Weekly Register Report, April 28, 1832
Sam Houston's Defense in House Trial, May 7, 1832
End of Houston Trial and Stanberry Resolution for Select Committee, May 14, 1832
Testimony of Thomas L. McKenney before Fraud Committee, May 28–June 4, 1832
Testimony of General John Van Fossen, June 11–14 and 21, 1832
Thomas L. McKenney to William Stanberry, June 23, 1832
Majority Report of Fraud Committee and Dissenting Opinions, July 5, 1832
Washington Globe Report, July 9, 1832
Sam Houston Petition, Washington *Globe*, July 10, 1832
Sam Houston Petition to Andrew Jackson, April 20, 1834
Benjamin F. Butler to Andrew Jackson, June 25, 1834
Jackson Remission of Houston Fine, July 3, 1834

The Covode Committee
1860

U.S. Signal Corps photo (Brady Collection)

On March 5, 1860, John Covode launched his crusade against the Democrats by calling for a House committee to investigate President Buchanan's conduct in office.

The Covode Committee 1860

By Roger A. Bruns

"Honest John" Covode was out to get the President. The Pennsylvania congressman was determined to prove that James Buchanan was a corrupt, groveling politician, if not a common criminal. Bribery, fraud, political payoffs, and numerous other charges were laid by Covode at the White House door in the early months of 1860. Covode's forum for exposing this presidential arrogance of power, was a House investigating committee. The possible result, impeachment. For nearly three months the committee would interrogate over 100 witnesses, probing the inner workings and machinations of the Buchanan Administration. The beleaguered Democratic President assailed what he considered a foul, partisan campaign, not only by the Congress, but by the press, to smear his good name and the office of the President. He attacked the House committee's work as a violation of the doctrine of separation of powers and as an unconstitutional assault on the Executive branch of government. The Covode Investigation of Buchanan's Administration would provoke a bitter, violent confrontation between the President of the United States and the Congress.

When John Covote stood in Pittsburgh's Lafayette Hall on October 8, 1859, exciting a screaming crowd of 500 abolitionist Republicans with a virulent attack on the Buchanan "sink of corruption" few individuals could have known that his fervent campaign against the Democrats had only just begun. He was not an influential congressman. The financially comfortable, heavy-set, Pennsylvania-German grandson of an indentured servant, had worked hard in the House but had suffered from anonymity—a condition especially aggravated by the fame of his Pennsylvania colleague, Thaddeus Stevens. Although not one of the shining intellectual lights ever to grace the halls of Congress, Covode was, nevertheless, a dogged, combative, political fighter. The sobriquet "Honest John," gained during his first political campaign for justice of the peace nearly thirty years before, would, he imagined, stand him in good stead in a battle against the graft and iniquity infecting the Washington political scene. And such a battle would certainly thrust the obscure Covode prominently onto the political stage.

In the view of Republicans generally, an exposé of administrative corruption would provide much aid and comfort to party campaigners in the imminent 1860 elections. The Democrats, although badly divided over the slavery issue, were amassing political capital by invoking the spectre of John Brown and by attempting to link every politician under the Republican banner to the Harper's Ferry invasion. Indeed, with James Murray Mason's investigating committee dragging numerous Republican politicians and abolitionists into his Senate lair, Republican election prospects were diminishing.

On March 5, 1860, John Covode, to the general delight of Republicans, launched his crusade, submitting an explosive resolution calling for a House committee to investigate the President of the United States. Covode had been on the scent for months, eagerly digesting rumors floating in the Washington atmosphere of Administration bribes to pass the Lecompton Bill which would have foisted slavery upon the territory of Kansas; of Administration money parceled out to newspapers to influence editorial policy (especially on the Kansas question); of illegal uses of the patronage in extending government contracts to political cronies; of gross funds in the election of 1856; of the use of government employees to "electioneer"; and of the expenditure of government money in the political campaign itself. Covode was convinced that this corruption had not merely eaten away at the fringes of the Administration, but that the rot had burrowed deeply into the White House itself. He was convinced that Buchanan was not ignorant of the sordid mess under him, but, on the contrary, was a central figure *in* it.

Covode's resolution itself was clumsily conceived. It called for a committee to investigate whether the President or other officers of the government had by improper means "sought to influence the action of Congress . . . for or against the passage of any law appertaining to the rights of any state or territory." It sought also to determine whether the President had attempted to subvert the laws of the United States, and whether corruption existed in the post offices, navy yards, and "other public works of the United States." It also called for an inquiry into the illegal employment of money to carry elections "in Pennsylvania, and any other State or States."

The sweeping investigative authority granted by the resolution and the ill-defined charges supporting the authority were seized upon by Covode's enemies to prove that a veritable inquisition had been created. Reaction in the White House itself on March 5, 1860 was swift and violent. Representative John Underwood of Georgia, striking a chord that the President would later echo, claimed that the House of Representatives had no business creating an investigative committee upon "vague, loose, and indefinite charges." Representative John Ashmore of South Carolina lashed out, "I will not vote for an investigation merely upon insinuations and imputations. . . ." Underwood and Ashmore notwithstanding, John Covode's resolution passed by a sizable, partisan vote, and his investigating committee became a reality.

The Republican press was ecstatic. Portraying Buchanan as a shifty-eyed, devious politician who had attained the presidency through subterfuge and wile rather than ability, the *New York Times* welcomed the investigation. "Mr. Buchanan has shown himself simply a cunning intriguer," the *Times* charged, "without any broad principles of public action, without faith either in measures or men. . . . He has carried into the Presidential office all the little arts and tricks by which sharp wire-pullers secure for themselves a local and temporary ascendancy." Horace Greeley's *New York Tribune* urged the committee to expose the "rascality and roguery, public and private, which have gangrened every department of the Administration." It was these fraternal devils—the Congress and the press—which the President feared, attempting to drown him and his colleagues in scandal and resounding disgrace. And he was determined to vindicate himself and his Administration.

It had been a stormy three years in office for James Buchanan. Turmoil and unrest had haunted him almost from the moment that he, as the fifteenth President, stepped confidently through the White House door. Two days after he took the oath of office the Supreme Court laid down the Dred Scott decision protecting slavery under the constitutional guarantees of property. Later that year, the Panic of 1857 upset the economy. "Bleeding Kansas," the raid on Harper's Ferry, a rising crescendo of disunionist sentiment and sectional hatred—an ugly national malaise—had begun to overwhelm the confidence of the Chief Executive. The former secretary of state's plans of making significant progress in the realm of foreign affairs, of extending United States possessions in Latin America, of sweeping European influence from the Caribbean, had been deluged by civil strife. Buchanan's hopes of conciliating the country, of playing the umpire in its divisions, had evaporated. And now John Covode was challenging his honesty and integrity.

On March 22 the secret hearings of the Committee to Investigate the Buchanan Administration were launched. The five members included three Republicans—Covode, Abram Olin of New York, and Charles Train of Massachusetts; and two Democrats—James Robinson of Illinois and Warren Winslow of North Carolina. Their first witness was Cornelius Wendell. Printer by trade, political gadfly by reputation, Wendell had been the financial manager of the *Union,* the Administration's sheet in Washington. Wendell was also the holder of a very lucrative government printing contract. Wendell, in the course of the hearings, became a star witness called on numerous times to give insights—as few in the nation's capital could—into the peculiar machinations in Democratic political circles. In the eyes of the Administration, he was a profligate traitor. A close confidant of Buchanan and others in the White House inner sanctum, and privy to the Administration's most intimate secrets, he was considered to have become a seedy informer by agreeing to testify before Covode.

On this first day of his interrogation, Wendell began to spin his absorbing accounts of life with the Buchanan Administration. Wendell, a conduit for large sums of political cash, disclosed that he had, out of his own pocket, contributed upwards of one hundred thousand dollars for the benefit of the Democratic party within a period of four years. It had been through his industrious efforts that money had been funneled in rather questionable ways to newspapers, lobbyists, and campaign workers. Not an independently wealthy man, Wendell had passed out money, on the "authority of the President," in astonishing amounts. Where did he get it, if not directly from government funds? Wendell led the committee through a bewildering maze of financial maneuverings, including the following: ". . . I would draw a check for a given amount of money and take it with me when I went to Philadelphia, or I would draw my check in Philadelphia and swap checks with friends in Philadelphia who would give me the money for my draft on my banker here. And I would divide the money up and give it out to different parties. I would, perhaps, make a bet of $500, and give from $500 to $1,000 in different districts. But this was all mixed up so that I really could not tell exactly how it was done, as I did not keep a minute of the details. . . ."

Did Buchanan himself give Wendell instructions as to the fortunate recipients of these cash gifts? Not exactly. "He never went into details," Wendell remarked, "but we were to make satisfactory arrangements, and not bother him about it." Covode dismissed this democratic "bagman" for the moment, but Wendell would return later.

The committee pressed for additional information about Democratic campaign finances. On March 28, Augustus Schell, collector of customs for New York and a large contributor to Democratic causes, appeared before the committee to describe his service in a fund-raising organization called the "New York Hotel Fund." This subterranean enterprise, according to Schell, distributed nearly $40,000 during the election of 1856 to needy Pennsylvania politicians and additional cash to Democratic hopefuls in other states. Covode wanted to see a list of the private financial contributors to this fund. After discussing the committee's request with an increasingly nervous Buchanan, Schell refused to turn over the list, declaring that . . . such production, without the authority of the persons whose names may be connected with it, would involve a breach of the implied confidence recognized as existing in such cases . . . I think the Committee have no power to order the production of it, if it is in my possession." Schell was supported by Warren Winslow, Buchanan's staunch defender on the committee, who argued that the committee had no constitutional authority to impugn the names of private citizens across the land in a scurrilous witchhunt. Even the *New York Tribune*, Horace Greeley's Republican sheet, attacked efforts to secure Schell's list. "If the object is to fish out evidence on which to base a prosecution, we object that the mode is illegal, unconstitutional, and the whole procedure fraught with danger to the rights of every citizen." The *Tribune* concluded, ". . . dragging private citizens . . . before Investigating Committees, to be catechised in secret, under circumstances which secure them no protection against insult, nor against the most inquisitorial and impertinent peering and prying into their private concerns, will not answer. It must either be strictly limited or utterly stopped."

Against such opposition, Covode's effort to force Schell to comply with the committee's demand was blocked. He briefly attempted to force the issue on the House floor, but with no success. Even with this minor defeat, however, John Covode was making the President of the United States exceedingly worried and angry.

Seeing a pack of political wolves at his heels, Buchanan on March 28 responded to the committee's work with a formal protest addressed to the House of Representatives. Buchanan had decided to strike at what he regarded as character assassins skulking behind anonymous tips and lolling in political mud.

Buchanan's protest was a kind of jeremiad pleading for the rights of the presidency. Bitter and vindictive, the message assailed the Covode Committee as an unconstitutional affront to the authority and dignity of the presidency. Declaring that there was no act in his public life which would not bear scrutiny, the President then proceeded to argue against legislative scrutiny. He charged that the field of inquiry laid out in the resolution establishing the committee was immense, and gave *carte blanche* authority to subject the Executive to an unlawful inquisition. Although admitting that Congress technically had the right to investigate specific charges of corruption, Buchanan denounced efforts to ransack government records and badger government officials to explore rumors and insinuations. An investigation into charges leading to impeachment, he insisted, should be referred to the House Judiciary Committee, not to a prejudiced and partisan select committee chaired by the President's chief accuser. "The trial of an impeachment," Buchanan warned, "would be an imposing spectacle for the world." In the event of a president's removal from office, "his character, both in the eyes of the present and of future generations, might possibly be tarnished. This disgrace cast upon him would in some degree be reflected upon the character of the American people who elected him." With such national humiliation at stake the President, Buchanan declared, must be accorded a fair hearing. The House, in establishing this proceeding, was denying the President his basic right to justice and was charging hell-bent down a road of despotism. The committee was created only to embarrass the President, Buchanan insisted, and "to foster a band of interested parasites and informers," a group of revengeful, frustrated, office-seeking vermin. The committee was determined to render Buchanan subservient to the Congress. If unresisted, it would establish a dangerous precedent and would weaken the presidency.

Much of the force of Buchanan's arguments rested on the wording of the resolution itself. If Covode had more narrowly defined the bounds of the investigation in the original resolution, Buchanan's charges that the committee was an inquisition bent on persecuting and defiling the President would have seemed hollow. As it was, Buchanan gained a measure of public sympathy—he was an oppressed figure hounded unjustly by his critics.

Buchanan's protest, not unexpectedly, touched off a virulent debate among inflamed members of the House. John Sherman, Republican of Ohio, charged that the President, in objecting to the investigation, had expressed a doctrine that had gone out when Charles I lost his head on the block—that the King is not accountable for his actions. "This doctrine set up by the President," Sherman declared, "is, in my judgement, the very worst that has been enunciated since the foundation of this Republic." F. Burton Craige,

Democrat of North Carolina, interrupted the excited Ohioan to inform him that he had missed Buchanan's point entirely. Buchanan was not denying the power of impeachment, Craige insisted, but was asserting that impeachment procedures must be prompted by specific charges.

While the debate continued amidst shouting and confusion, one member was lying in wait with a bombshell. If the members of the House wanted specific grounds for the investigation, Covode would give it to them. The committee, Covode asserted, had heard testimony that the President of the United States was privy to the illegal use of money in influencing elections, and that there were documents to prove it. The chairman was undoubtedly aware that any attempt to reveal on the House floor evidence taken before a secret committee would be scuttled. It was Lawrence Branch of North Carolina who stopped the chairman on this point of order. ". . . the Chairman of the select Committee," he charged, "has not a right to divulge upon the floor any *ex parte* statement of the testimony that has been taken before the Committee." Covode accepted the obvious. He could not reveal the vile, incriminating evidence against Buchanan just yet. He had, however, cleverly left tantalizing suggestions of corruption to fester in the minds of the congressmen and the general public.

The rancorous debate continued, the members finally deciding to send Buchanan's message to the Judiciary Committee and await its report. President Buchanan, on the other hand, was more anxious to learn of the impact the message had generated among the public, and how it had played in the hinterlands. The first returns were encouraging.

On April 4 an "Indignation Meeting," under the auspices of the Young Men's National Democratic Association, was held in Cincinnati. The speeches at that meeting vilified the House for a fishing expedition designed to embarrass the noble President and his party. A "mean, sneaking attack," one inflamed speaker lamented. In addition to this numerous letters arrived at the White House. One admirer wrote that the protest had done more for Buchanan's reputation than any other single act of his career. Another declared that the protest was popular with the Party and "surprised the enemy." One ecstatic observer called it "apples of gold in pictures of silver."

As could be expected, the *New York Times* saw no "golden apples" in the presidential message, only sour grapes. Calling the protest "a deplorable exhibition of feminine indignation," the *Times* continued to pummel the President as a conniving demagogue. The public and the Congress would not fall for such a tactic as this contemptible message, the *Times* reported. Of the investigation, the *Times* exclaimed, "Let it, by all means, go on."

On April 9, the Judiciary Committee submitted its report on Buchanan's protest. Dwelling upon the dangers of a president who had begun to assume a "kingly prerogative," the Judiciary Committee report declared that the President possessed no privileges or immunities beyond those of any other citizen. It asserted that the conduct of a president was constitutionally subject to the investigation, supervision, and judgment of Congress. Deriding Buchanan's claims that the committee had specifically accused him of crimes, the report emphasized that the committee was only making an inquiry. An inquiry, the report continued, was preliminary to accusation, trial, and judgment; and, in such an inquiry, the procedures for the investigation were determined by the House, not by the President. The Congress had a right to conduct this inquiry without specifically defining charges or accusations. Should Congress yield to presidential demands in this case, the immense power of the Executive would be even more oppressive. "In the case of an office controlling millions of dollars of patronage," the report concluded, "and an influence penetrating every city, town, and hamlet of a vast country, it would be unsafe to assume informers and witnesses would volunteer against him, especially as favorites and beneficiaries would be the most likely to possess the knowledge needed in the ascertainment of the truth. For Congress to reach the conclusion to which the President would lead them, would be to practically settle forever that impeachments are obsolete, and that officers had the immunity of perfect irresponsibility." The majority recommended a resolution, later adopted by an overwhelming vote, affirming the right of the House to conduct the investigation.

Two members of the Judiciary Committee disagreed with their counterparts and each submitted a minority report. George Houston, quoting Washington's farewell address, warned about the encroachment of the Legislative branch against the Executive branch, and suggested that the entire Covode proceeding had originated from street rumor and a vile newspaper assault against the President. Houston charged the committee with parading disappointed, office-seeking dregs of society to vent their grievances against Buchanan, and of attempting to dignify lies by making them part of the records of Congress.

Miles Taylor of Louisiana also had some unkind words for "Honest John" and his committee. Suggesting that the chairman was instituting a "roving Commission" to rake around sewers of rumor, Taylor challenged the committee to come forth with facts to substantiate the claim that Buchanan had violated his public trust and had committed any acts of treason, bribery, or other high crimes and misdemeanors. "Why," Taylor asked, "has an inquisition into the whole official life of the President been authorized without any foundation for it on legal or constitutional grounds, and in palpable violation of the principles of common justice?" The Covode Committee, Taylor continued, was "a secret Star Chamber."

Bolstered by the Judiciary Committee's report and encouraged by what he considered a desperate reaction by the President, the determined chairman paraded many witnesses through a great morass of political skullduggery. They told of thousands of forged naturalization papers ("sick papers") distributed among the German and Irish working population to enable them to vote for the Democratic party. They told of a Democratic "taxing system" on employees of the Philadelphia custom-house and other government agencies—compulsory political contributions backed up by undisguised threats. They told of temporary workers, or "floating" work forces, being added to government payrolls immediately prior to elections, the only function of the employees being to campaign for Democratic candidates. They told of political cronies, one of whom was related to Buchanan, receiving lucrative government positions and performing absolutely no work. They told of newspaper reporters paid weekly donations to write stories favorable to the Administration. They even told of government money being used to hire several mediums to communicate with and to elicit favorable influence for the Democratic party from the spirit world. With this kind of "heavenly" support, Covode thought, no wonder the Democrats had fared so well in recent years.

The significant question implicit in all of these revelations was just how much the President of the United States knew of this sordid business and how actively involved he was in it. Buchanan's defenders claimed that the President, absorbed in matters of critical national significance, was aloof from petty political struggles. Covode's witnesses, thus far, they claimed, had not directly implicated the President himself in any criminal activities.

The opposition press was out to destroy this administration posture. The *New York Times* claimed that Mr. Buchanan had sleazily meddled throughout his career in local elections and was deeply involved with political payoffs and influence peddling. The *Times* reported on April 12 that the net was closing in on the beleaguered President. His credibility destroyed, Buchanan was a pathetic figure, turning up his eyes "in holy indignation" against the committee, reduced to preaching sermons on respect for the office of the presidency. The more he ranted, the *Times* declared, the more he revealed of himself. And as the investigation itself progressed the *Tribune* asserted, the disgusting facts of Buchanan's years in office would be revealed.

On April 17, as Robert Walker of Mississippi strode into the committee room, the members prepared to hear evidence about the struggle between pro-slavery and anti-slavery elements in and especially about Buchanan's support of the Lecompton "Constitution." Former secretary of the treasury and territorial governor of Kansas, the diminutive Walker, whom one detractor had once called "pigmy" to his face, was, if not large in physical presence, of considerable political stature, and certainly not one of those frustrated "office-seeking vermin" represented in Buchanan's general categorization of the Covode Committee witnesses.

Robert Walker had been drafted by the President in 1857 as the man most competent to deal with the perplexing Kansas problem. Buchanan had earnestly appealed to the Mississippian to accept the critical governorship as a solemn duty, and Walker had reluctantly agreed. On March 15, 1857, however, Walker had written to the President: "I understand that you and all the Cabinet cordially concur in the opinion expressed by me, that the *bona fide* residents of the territory, by a fair and regular vote, unaffected by fraud or violence, must be permitted in adopting their state constitution to decide for themselves what shall be their social institutions." Walker ardently supported popular sovereignty; a new constitution; a slavery vote by the people in the Kansas Territory. His price for taking the governorship—at least in his own mind—was Buchanan's assurances that the President would stand behind him on these issues.

On July 12, 1857 Buchanan had written a letter to Walker purportedly supporting Walker's contention that a new constitution for Kansas had to be submitted to the people. In October 1857 a pro-slavery convention at Kansas adopted a pro-slavery constitution. Although the constitution was rejected overwhelmingly, Buchanan, against the policy of Governor Walker, in February 1858 submitted the rejected Lecompton Constitution to Congress and asked that Kansas be granted statehood. Buchanan's support of the Lecompton Constitution was denounced by free-state Republicans, by Democrats, and by those who favored popular sovereignty, as a capitulation to slavocracy. The bill died in the House. A compromise measure, the English Bill, eventually passed the Congress, providing simply that Kansas be given statehood under the Lecompton Constitution if a majority of the voters approved the document. Later, the Lecompton Constitution was again rejected by the voters of Kansas. Buchanan's efforts to obtain support in the press and in Congress for the English Bill and for the Lecompton Constitution prompted Walker's resignation as governor. It was also these efforts which spurred the alleged fraud, influence-peddling, and bribery which John Covode was two years later trying to reveal.

Covode first wanted to see that July 12, 1857, letter written by Buchanan addressed to Walker. Warren Winslow objected. The committee, Winslow declared, had no right to ask for personal correspondence between the President and an officer of the government. Abram Olin interrupted Winslow to assert that subpoenaing such evidence was perfectly within the province of the committee. Winslow, waving the banner of Executive privilege, shot back that only the President had the right to determine whether the committee should see such correspondence and that only the President had a right to determine whether it was compatible with public interest to introduce it as evidence.

The debate over Executive privilege continued as follows:

> Mr. Olin: I had supposed that the power of Congress was sufficiently adequate to call for the production of even a private and confidential communication or a communication of any character made by an officer like the President of the United States, whose conduct in the discharge of his duties is always given to inquiry; and that the merely private nature of such a correspondence, its confidential character, would not put it beyond the power of the House or exempt it from examination.
>
> Mr. Winslow: I think there is not a single administration of the government in which it will not be found that the President has refused to communicate to Congress some papers called for . . . I hold that the power of the House, and of a committee acting under authority of this House, is not sufficient to enable them to call for any letter from the President of the United States to any officer of the government where it is official, or what is sometimes called private, where it touches the public policy of the government.

As would be the case for the remainder of the hearings, Warren Winslow, the jaunty, sarcastically witty North Carolinian, was a lonely voice for Buchanan. Robert Walker was instructed to turn over the letter. The former governor rose, and to a hushed committee room recited the contents of the notable Buchanan communication to him of July 12, 1857. "The point on which your and our success depends is the submission of the Constitution to the people of Kansas," Buchanan had written. "On the question of submitting the Constitution to the *bona-fide* resident settlers of Kansas, I am willing to stand or fall." It was one of those statements that politicians live to regret—one destined to haunt James Buchanan. The President's retreat from his support of popular sovereignty in 1857, Walker's testimony suggested, was a cowardly sell-out to Southern slave interests, a surrender to threats of secession by Southern fire-eaters.

Although not implicating Buchanan in a criminal act, Robert Walker's testimony, Covode felt, confirmed Buchanan's penchant for deceit and treachery; and with this groundwork carefully laid, Covode was now bent on establishing Buchanan's penchant for common corruption. What better witness was there to explore this area than Cornelius Wendell? Wendell, the government printer who in 1858 passed around huge expenditure of money (close to $40,000, by his figures) for the purpose of "carrying the Lecompton Bill," was on May 2 grilled vigorously by the chairman. Covode eagerly examined the unfortunate Wendell's bank books. Covode wanted to discover whether "carrying the Lecompton Bill" meant, in some instances, actual payoffs to congressmen and whether, indeed, Wendell had received his orders from the President of the United States. The industrious Covode rattled off lists of checks from Wendell's books, asking for the reasons behind the drafts.

Wendell's memory, unfortunately, was not equipped for such sport, and in the middle of the interrogation he declared in frustration, "Sometimes checks would be drawn and I would get the money and put it in my pocket, and then the devil himself could not tell what became of it." Asked if all these financial transactions to influence the Lecompton Bill had passed through a bank, Wendell replied, "No sir. I frequently had a great deal of money about my person. I have had $8,000 or $10,000 in my tobacco box at one time. If I had any money about me, it was almost certain to be in my tobacco box." Wendell's testimony about tobacco boxes full of cash, about money fed to men controlling newspapers, and about funds parceled out to political cronies with close government ties, ground to a close with the printer denying he had bribed anyone, especially congressmen. He passed these gifts to lobbyists, "not knowing or caring how the money was to be expended." And the President himself? Wendell had not taken specific instructions from Buchanan. Mr. Buchanan, Wendell declared, was only "aware" of the printer's magnanimous financial gestures for the good of the party. And was Wendell given his government contracts by Buchanan because of these gestures? "No sir. I had no understanding of that sort." As Wendell left the witness chair, John Covode was still looking for that one incriminating document or that one witness who could drive a spike deeply into the President.

As Covode's quest for this damaging information progressed, his committee was becoming a major news happening. Buchanan and his friends almost daily condemned the newspapers which, as one Administration supporter noted, "always exaggerate." The leaks from the Covode Committee room to the anti-Buchanan sheets in New York had swelled into a flood, with testimony appearing in public print almost as quickly as the words were uttered in the committee room. Warren Winslow was especially upset over garbled testimony against Buchanan printed daily in the *New York Times* and the *New York Tribune*. Every particle of evidence, he felt, injurious to the President, whether rumor or hearsay, was splashed across anti-Buchanan papers day after day, inundating the public with a distorted slant on the progress of the Covode dragnet.

On April 23 Winslow rose, in the House, to protest that letters which had not even been introduced before the committee had appeared in a New York paper, represented by the editors as evidence taken in the interrogation.

He termed their publication slander against the President. Winslow, in a light vein not usual for those tense days, declared, "I was early taught that there are three classes with whom I never should get into controversy. One is the preachers, for they have pulpits and I have not in which to answer them. And then editors, for they have journals and I have not in which to answer them. And the other is women, because they always will have the last word." With such egregious violations of journalistic ethics by the anti-Buchanan press, Winslow had decided to violate his cautious principles and speak out. As for the leaks, he remarked, there must have been three or four "black cats" in the committee room.

Ironically, it was Covode who decided to take forceful action, but his ire was not directed at the *Times* or the *Tribune*. On May 17, George Bowman, the editor of the *Constitution*, the Administration paper in Washington, was summoned by the chairman to explain where he had unearthed information with which to insult and berate the committee. This was an unusual move—for a committee chairman to drag an editor before Congress. Perhaps Covode had thoughts of charging Bowman with slander. At any rate, the chairman launched into a diatribe against this "cad" who dared challenge the investigation. Especially loathsome to Covode's thinking was a recent article under the *Constitution's* banner, accusing the committee of aiding witnesses to commit perjury against Buchanan; or, as the *Constitution* phrased it, "if they [witnesses] stumble in the slippery path of perjury they are kindly placed on their feet again, instead of being pinned down by cross-examination . . ."

> Question (by Mr. Olin): From what . . . sources have you gained any information in regard to this matter except the statements in the newspaper?
>
> Answer: I suppose it is known to every gentleman that it is common talk about the streets, in every barroom, in the halls of Congress, in the passages about the Capitol . . .

It was general knowledge, Bowman claimed, that the Covode Committee was an infamous inquisition. Obviously, Covode did not think so. At least in the barrooms and streets through which *he* and *his* friends traveled, there was no such talk. Olin did not think so either, and called the *Constitution* a "scurrilous sheet." Bowman was dismissed. The editor had been shaken, but the *Constitution* would continue vigorously to attack the committee. In addition, Covode's ill-advised impulsive move in bringing Bowman before the committee appeared as an attempt to intimidate the press and gave additional ammunition to attackers of his committee.

But John Covode's battle with the *Washington Constitution* had not ended. On May 16, Ellis B. Schnable, an intimate of leading Democratic politicians, testified that the *Constitution* was ruled by the iron fist of Buchanan's Attorney General, Jeremiah Black, who, especially with regard to the Lecompton question, dictated editorial policy. The *Constitution's* attacks on the committee, Schnable suggested, had been specifically directed by the Administration. Black, who had been advised that Schnable was to testify, was sitting in the committee room, angrily passing notes to Warren Winslow. Winslow, in turn, peppered the agitated Schnable with leading questions; and, at one point, the infuriated witness labelled Black a "liar and scoundrel." When Schnable later strutted out of the committee room he was closely followed by Black, the two gentlemen screaming at each other and exchanging threats and expletives. John Covode was pleased with the testimony. He was certain he had proven that the major press opposition to the committee had originated from the Administration itself.

On May 30 one of Buchanan's worried political advisers wrote to the President warning of future bombshells from the Covode witness chair. ". . . if this thing goes on," William Bartlett intimated, "you will be more surprised by subsequent disclosures." This gentleman and others in Buchanan's White House inner circle were especially apprehensive over the imminent testimony of John W. Forney. A newspaper editor and former close Buchanan lieutenant, the passionate and irascible John Forney, had broken with his mentor in 1857 over Buchanan's refusal, apparently on the demands of Southerners angered by Forney's support of popular sovereignty, to appoint him to a prestigious patronage position in Washington.

Forney, now clerk of the House of Representatives and a Republican, knew well the inside of the Buchanan Administration and was seething with contempt for Buchanan. Earlier in the year, Forney, in a Washington speech dripping with malice, called his former chieftain a "despot," claimed that Buchanan had, crouched in fear on his knees, sold out to Southern slave interests, and accused the President of perpetrating acts of tyranny which, if performed in France, would have stirred a revolution. Forney declared that he had come to Washington to resolve his feud with "Old Buck." "If he is now sitting in his easy chair at home," Forney swelled in anger, "he must hear our loud and hearty cheers, and they will remind him that his old friend, Forney, has come back to settle the old debt with him." No wonder Forney created nervous tremors at the White House, with Buchanan himself writing to a friend that Forney's examination would be critical. Naturally, Covode looked forward to Forney's appearance.

On June 11 John Forney began to gain revenge on his despised adversary. He testified that Buchanan, intimidated by Southern Democrats, had refused to appoint him to a position in Washington, and instead had offered him the Liverpool Consulate. To encourage Forney to accept his exile, the Administration dispatched "bagman" Cornelius Wendell to offer him an additional inducement of $10,000 which Forney saw as a bribe. Forney instead started a newspaper in Philadelphia, flaunted the cause of popular sovereignty, and broke irrevocably from the camp of James Buchanan.

Forney also on June 11 claimed that Buchanan had manipulated the patronage to silence opposition newspapers. He disclosed that Attorney General Black had dispatched an agent in 1858 to Philadelphia to offer Forney (then editor of the *Philadelphia Press*) $80,000 worth of printing contracts if Forney would silence his guns on the Lecompton question. "You can get all that Post Office printing," the emissary promised, "if you will write an editorial article as long as your hand" (favoring the Lecompton Constitution). Although Buchanan's defenders maintained that John Forney's open hostility and resentment toward the President made his credibility highly suspect, Forney's testimony had been destructive. When David Webster, lawyer and Pennsylvania bureaucrat, admitted that he was the agent who offered the $80,000 contract to Forney and when Cornelius Wendell on June 12 corroborated the story that he offered $10,000 to Forney to accept the Liverpool Consulate, John Covode felt that the President of the United States had been gloriously skewered. The chairman, on June 12, persuaded the committee to close the hearings.

The long, gruelling interrogation of over 100 witnesses was now complete. The Republican members of the committee now wrote a Majority Report, a document which would, Covode hoped, effectively expose the arrogant abuse of power by the President. Covode did not write the report himself. He delegated that responsibility to Charles Train, a lawyer. But the report itself reflected the sentiments of the chairman. On June 16 the report was read on the floor of the House. Signed only by the Republican members, Covode, Train, and Olin, the report accused Buchanan of attempting, through "forgeries, frauds, and force," to make Kansas a slave state. It also charged Buchanan with illegally employing, through such agents as Cornelius Wendell, enormous sums of money to influence passage of the Lecompton and English Bills. It charged the President with attempting to crush and bribe newspaper editors who opposed his policies. It charged Buchanan with illegally dispensing lucrative government patronage to cronies in return for political favors and contributions. It accused Buchanan of encouraging election frauds and countenancing such crimes as the distribution of forged naturalization papers. The document was a devastating catalogue of presidential abuses of power—a remarkable series of charges, impeachable in character. *But the report did not call for impeachment.*

Republican members candidly remarked that they would not press for impeachment proceedings. The Senate, more pro-Administration than the House, would be unlikely to vote for conviction in a Senate trial of the President. Also, Buchanan would be an enormous liability to the Democrats. Republican candidates would run in the fall elections against a Democratic party with the Buchanan albatross around its neck. So Covode rested his case with the report and with the voters who, the chairman trusted, would "impeach" James Buchanan and the Democrats at the polls. And to spread the word of Buchanan's infamy the Republicans printed thousands of copies of the committee report as campaign ammunition.

Warren Winslow submitted a minority report on June 16, which could well have been entitled "Ode to a President Abused." Elegantly portraying the work of the committee as an exercise "for the gratification of passion, spleen, and malignity," the indomitable North Carolinian suggested that the whole investigation had been concocted solely as an election tactic. A "pack of slanderers, jackalls of society" had been set loose, Winslow continued, to raise suspicions against the President. Damaging evidence, whatever its distorted character, had been telegraphed to Northern papers. Private presidential correspondence had been maliciously and indiscriminately waved in front of the American people in violation of confidentiality. "And when the records of this committee shall become known," Winslow remarked, "this systematic violation of the plainest principles of common justice will be condemned by the American people."

Buchanan himself had private doubts. Although the President was relieved that the committee had not recommended articles of impeachment and although he felt the evidence against him was generally weak, the President worried about public reaction. On June 18 Buchanan, who had throughout the hearings been assailing the gentlemen of the press, looked for help from the Third Estate in the person of James Gordon Bennett of the *New York Herald.* In a desperate attempt to blunt the effects of the committee report, the President, writing to Bennett, denounced the "secret conclave" which had sat for months compiling filth from disappointed office seekers. He claimed that a careful reading of the report would demonstrate his innocence. Buchanan also sent his political ally, William Bartlett, to the offices of the *Herald Tribune* on June 19 to assure Bennett that any rumors filtering up to New York, injurious to the Administration, were exaggerated. The dutiful Bartlett even carried the message to the *New York Tribune,* engaging Horace Greeley in something of a debate over the work of the Covode Committee. The staunchly Republican Greeley must have been thoroughly amused.

Buchanan, with newspapers across the country now spreading the Majority Report over their pages, decided on June 25 to address another formal protest to the House of Representatives. Charging the Covode Committee with assault of the constitutional prerogatives and attempting to degrade the office of the President, Buchanan declared that the "beautiful symmetry" of the Constitution had been under grave attack by a band of inquisitors reminiscent of the days of Robespierre. "Should the proceedings of the Covode Committee become a precedent," Buchanan warned, "both the letter and spirit of the Constitution will be violated. One of the three massive columns on which the whole superstructure rests will be broken down. Instead of the Executive branch being a coordinate, it will become a subordinate branch of the government. The presidential office will be dragged into the dust."

Buchanan looked to past impeachment proceedings and saw nothing like the Covode Committee. "At the commencement of each judicial investigation which might lead to an impeachment," he asserted, "specific charges were always preferred; the accused had an opportunity of cross-examining the witnesses, and he was placed in full possession of the precise nature of the offences which he had to meet . . ." The Covode Committee, he charged, had violated all of these precepts. Wild, vague charges; no cross-examination; a special committee run by a zealot who had manufactured the "lies" in the first place; a procession of vindictive, disappointed politicians given a forum for their frustration—the Covode Committee was a brutal outrage against Buchanan himself, and against the integrity of the presidency. Such committees, dissecting every word and action of the President, were a distinct threat to the nation's very form of government.

Buchanan's message was conveniently timed. Congress was preparing to recess. Republican John Sherman noted that the protest, had it been submitted earlier in the month, would have been the subject of heated debate on the floor of the House. As it was, Benjamin Stanton of Ohio, whose name had not been associated with the Covode Committee, declared Buchanan's missive ill-founded and astonishing. "I did suppose," Stanton continued, that the President was "responsible to the people; that it was essential, to make that responsibility worth anything, to enable the people to pass upon the action of the President as well as of Congresses, that there should be somewhere a power to investigate the official conduct of the President as well as of Congress. The people have the right to know the action, secret and public, of all public functionaries, that they may hold them responsible . . . for the manner in which they discharge their official duties." Stanton called for a select committee to examine the constitutional questions surrounding Buchanan's document and to report at the next session of the Congress. A committee of five was appointed, including Stanton and Charles Francis Adams of Massachusetts.

William Barksdale of Mississippi made one last defense of his President: "He has come out of the fiery ordeal unscathed; and he stands before the country today without fear and without reproach, occupying a prouder, loftier, nobler position than ever before, illustrious as ever been his services to the country." Few members accepted Barksdale's oratorical flourishes. The business of the first session of the Thirty-Sixth Congress was now concluded, and Speaker Pennington, declaring the House of Representatives adjourned, bid the members "an affectionate farewell." As most of the House members left behind the heat of the Washington summer, James Buchanan declared he had been vindicated. But vindication from the issue of impeachment in his case was not necessarily vindication from all the charges of corruption directed at the Buchanan White House during his "fiery ordeal."

During the summer of 1860, Charles Francis Adams, with suggestions from Stanton, composed a long, plodding defense of the Covode Committee and the authority of the House to conduct such investigations of the Executive branch. The notable document, something of a civics lesson directed to the President of the United States, was never presented, as it was intended, as a report of the House. By the time the second session of the Thirty-Sixth Congress convened in September, the nation and its legislators had critical questions of secession and the possibility of war with which to grapple. As Adams wrote, "Nothing is talked about but the actions of the slaveholding states." But Adams's document, although never officially submitted to the Congress, illustrates dramatically the constitutional struggle that had occurred in the Covode investigation.

Adams claimed that the Covode Committee had not infringed upon a coordinate branch of government, had not violated the doctrine of separation of powers, and was perfectly within the constitutional prerogatives of the Legislative branch. Buchanan's radical error, Adams asserted, was his confusion of an inquiry with an accusation. The Massachusetts congressman declared: "As he [Buchanan] truly remarks there is but one accusing body designated in the Constitution to act against the President, and that is the collective body called the House of Representatives. The form of accusation is also provided, which is impeachment before the Senate who are the sole judges. But it does not at all follow from this that because the House possesses the sole power to accuse, it is therefore debarred from pursuing any form of preliminary inquiry it may think proper in order to obtain the information necessary to determine the question whether it should accuse or not. On the contrary this power seems necessarily to belong to it as an incident to the full execution of the other and the greater one."

On this question of impeachment, Adams admitted that the offenses for which a president can be held accountable were only vaguely defined by the Constitution—"treason, bribery or other high crimes and misdemeanors." But Adams rejected the notion that only criminally indictable acts as defined in the courts constitute impeachable offenses. Because the power of impeachment has been historically instituted to curb abuses of power and because there are innumerable offenses, criminal or otherwise, by which a President can abuse his power, it is the role of the House of Representatives to affix the precise meaning to the general term "high crimes and misdemeanors." An impeachable offense, therefore, is what the House of Representatives decides is an impeachable offense. Adams asserted that the House, with such solemn responsibility, must be granted the widest latitude in obtaining information relative to possible impeachment proceedings, and such latitude includes investigations such as that conducted by the Covode Committee.

Charles Francis Adams, a dedicated Republican, despised James Buchanan. His paper in some ways reflected these prejudices. But his remarks vividly illustrate the critical issues raised in the Covode investigation, some of which remained unresolved in later years. In adversary confrontations between the Executive and the Congress such as that in 1860, the ill-defined concepts of separation of powers and Executive privilege remain matters of great contention, the two branches defiantly defending what they consider their respective constitutional prerogatives.

The Covode investigation had been an extraordinary inquiry into a variety of issues surrounding the Buchanan Administration. Although the committee had marshalled little substantive evidence that Buchanan was himself directly implicated in criminal activities, the inquiry had demonstrated that the President had presided over an Administration mired in corruption. The list of tainted Administration practices—from bribery, to influence peddling, to illegal manipulation of patronage, to election fraud—was a jaundiced testiment to Executive abuse of power. At least under Charles Francis Adams's broad definition of "impeachable" offenses, Buchanan had been clearly in violation. And although the President did not suffer the final ignominy of impeachment, Covode's brazen challenge of the President aggressively asserted the power of the House to investigate and to act as a check on the Executive branch. As James Buchanan, then a young member of the House of Representatives, had declared in March 1828, "It is a maxim of despots that the people should never inquire into the concerns of government."

Buchanan was a lonely figure in the election campaign. In a summer speech in Washington, his voice whispering and weakening, to shouts from the crowd of "Go it, old man," he was a pathetic figure. He remarked during the campaign, "The duties of the presidency are severe and incessant. I shall soon retire from them; and if my successor shall be as happy in coming in as I will be in going out, he will be one of the happiest men in the world." Charles Francis Adams had told a friend, in the summer of 1860, that Buchanan's star had so fallen that it was no longer worth the effort to attack him. The ball and chain of Administration corruption, Adams had predicted, would drag the Democratic party down to ignominious defeat. And although the question of slavery and the crisis of secession unquestionably had more impact on the election than Democratic corruption, it is ironic that the new President carried into the White House the sobriquet "Honest Abe."

As for "Honest John" Covode—he would be heard from again. On February 21, 1868, Covode rose on the House floor and offered the following resolution:

> *Resolved,* That Andrew Johnson, President of the United States, be impeached for high crimes and misdemeanors.

BIBLIOGRAPHY

The paucity of secondary literature on the Covode Committee is regrettable. The most helpful source for a study of the committee is Edward W. Chester, "The Impact of the Covode Congressional Investigation," *Western Pennsylvania Historical Magazine*, 42 (December 1959), 343–50. This article is based on Chester's M.A. Thesis, "The Covode Committee and the Election of 1860," submitted in 1958 at the University of Pittsburgh. Another M.A. Thesis at the University of Pittsburgh, Archibald J. Dodds, "Honest John Covode," submitted in 1933, provides useful background information on the career of John Covode.

The general survey literature is predictably divided on the significance and legitimacy of the investigation. Philip S. Klein's biography, *President James Buchanan* (University Park, Pa., 1962), dismisses the inquiry in two pages as a political witchhunt and hatchet job on the Chief Executive. Roy F. Nichols, in *The Disruption of American Democracy* (New York, 1948), calls the committee's work a "bad precedent . . . which sought to reduce the executive to subservience." In the same mold is the venerable biography of Buchanan by George Ticknor Curtis, *Life of James Buchanan* (New York, 1883), which laments that Buchanan had been subjected to the worst political attack on a president in the history of the Union.

A most valuable secondary discussion of the committee appears in Emerson D. Fite's *The Presidential Campaign of 1860* (New York, 1911) which attempts to place the proceedings of the committee in the context of the political campaign. Contrary to Messrs. Klein, Nichols, and Curtis, Fite asserts that most of the charges against the administration were substantially true. Allan Nevins in *The Emergence of Lincoln* (New York, 1950) agrees with Fite. He remarks that "Seldom in our history has a Congressional investigation furnished material more damaging to a President and his coadjutors."

The committee hearings, the *Congressional Globe*, and the contemporary newspaper accounts remain the vital source of information on the Covode proceedings. As is the case with most of the congressional investigations in this series, the work of the Covode Committee—whether witchhunt or substantive inquiry—remains relatively unexplored in secondary historical literature.

PERTINENT DOCUMENTS

First Protest by President Buchanan and House Debate, March 29, 1860

New York Times Report, March 30, 1860

New York Times Report, March 31, 1860

New York Daily Tribune Report, March 31, 1860

Report of the House Committee on the Judiciary on the Protest of the President, April 9, 1860

New York Times Report, April 12, 1860

Testimony of Robert J. Walker, April 17–18, 1860

Testimony of Cornelius Wendell, May 3, 1860

Testimony of John W. Forney, June 11, 1860

Extracts from Majority and Minority Reports of Covode Committee, June 16, 1860

Second Buchanan Protest and House Debate, June 25, 1860

Extracts of Draft Report of Charles Francis Adams on Buchanan's Protest

The Conduct of the War
1861

U.S. Signal Corps photo (Brady Collection)

As chairman of the Committee on the Conduct of the War, Benjamin Wade defended Congress' retention of its full range of powers despite the Civil War crisis.

The Conduct of the War 1861

by Elisabeth Joan Doyle

It was the end of July 1861, and the North was still reeling from the defeat administered to its forces by the Confederate Army at Bull Run. Young James Wade, the elder son of Senator Benjamin F. Wade of Ohio, wrote to his mother that he had seen "by the papers that Pa was in the battle. . . ." James, who was on recruiting duty in Columbus, felt distinctly left out. "I am always out of the way when there is anything going on," he mourned.

Certainly that could not be said about his father, who did indeed participate in the First Battle of Bull Run. He and his friends Senator Zachariah Chandler of Michigan, Congressman Albert G. Riddle of Ohio, and several visiting civilians—who had driven out from Washington in their open carriage to watch the fight—had been so shocked by the disorderly rout of Union troops that they had moved to stop it. Parking their carriage across the road near Centreville, Virginia, the group, armed with navy revolvers and Maynard rifles (except for Senator Wade, who had brought his squirrel rifle), had blocked the retreat and had threatened to shoot any Union soldier who did not turn around and return to the fight. The incident was characteristic of Wade, and the feelings it evoked in both Wade and Chandler would provide the seed for the plant of indignation against the Lincoln Administration's "bungling" which they grew to feel. Describing it as "the gloomiest hour in my life" and the Union officers' behavior as "very stupid," Wade nevertheless assured his wife that "we can & will retrieve the honor of the North."

The special session of the Thirty-Seventh Congress which President Lincoln had called to approve funds for his response to the Confederate attack on Fort Sumter ended on August 6, and there was little Wade and Chandler could do between then and the opening of the regular session on December 2, 1861, aside from seething at the way affairs were going. But the origins of the Joint Select Committee on the Conduct of the War unquestionably lay in their brief (indeed, it was the closest either man would ever come to military combat in his life) encounter with the fleeing troops of Major General Irwin McDowell.

During the interval between the special and regular sessions, Senator Chandler traveled to St. Louis to look into the affairs of Major General John C. Frémont, who was in command there. Frémont, the first Republican presidential candidate, a former Indian scout, and son-in-law of the leading Missouri politician Thomas Hart Benton, was a favorite of such Radical politicians as Wade and Chandler. But Frémont was being criticized not only for having contributed to the death of Union General Nathaniel Lyons at the Battle of Wilson's Creek on August 10, but also for unilaterally proclaiming the emancipation of the Missouri slaves, whom he regarded as the property of traitors, and therefore "contraband of war." The President had asked him to withdraw the proclamation; when Frémont had refused, Lincoln had revoked it himself. Chandler went West to see if Frémont was being persecuted.

Chandler soon found this was not the case at all. Indeed, on October 12, 1861, he reported to his wife in a letter marked *"Confidential—not to be talked about at all"* that affairs in St. Louis were in terrible shape. "Frémont is a failure," he wrote. "Imbecility, banality & an informal court seems to have been the rule."

Developments in Missouri were certainly bad enough, but even from that distance Chandler was getting negative reports on McDowell's replacement as commander of the Army of the Potomac in the East. "I am greatly dissatisfied with General McClellan," he told his wife. "He seems to be devoting himself to parades and military shows instead of clearing the country of Rebels."

From Ohio, in the meantime, Chandler's friend Wade, who had not had the sobering experience of viewing firsthand Frémont's mistakes in Missouri, wrote gloomily about the country's prospects. On October 8, Wade told Chandler that he despaired "of ever putting down this rebellion through the instrumentality of this administration. They are blundering, cowardly, and inefficient." Traitors lurked, he said, "in all their offices and are in high favor with them in every department." Meanwhile, he said, the only worthwhile fighting soldiers came from the Old Northwest, and it was they who made it "possible for Mr. Lincoln & his Cabinet [to] breathe freely and eat their dinner in peace, and . . . Mrs. Lincoln without interruption [to] pursue her French and *dancing*." It was all too outrageous to be borne.

Finally, neither Wade nor Chandler could stay around their Midwestern homes any longer. In late October, accompanied by their fellow Midwesterner Senator Lyman Trumbull of Illinois, they returned to Washington and, inspired by deep messianic complexes, began a series of hortatory visits to the Administration's political and military leaders. "We are not here a moment too soon," Chandler wrote his wife on October 27. "If Wade & I fail in our mission the end is at hand . . . in fact, I told Mr. Lincoln last night that I was in favor of sending for Jeff Davis *at once* if their [Lincoln's cabinet] views are carried out."

Chandler, Wade, and Trumbull wanted the President to use his constitutional powers to order the Union military to attack the Confederate lines in nearby Virginia immediately. But they found themselves battling against the determination of the army's new commander, Major General George B. McClellan, to go into winter quarters until he had retrained the disorderly horde which had fled Bull Run, and until the unpaved roads of northern Virginia—turned into muddy tracks by the autumn rains—were hard enough for artillery to pass over. No matter how fervently the self-appointed saviors argued for movement, the three legislators found themselves thwarted by a general who also thought of himself as the nation's last hope and who possessed, to that point, the support of his political superior.

When McClellan had first been brought East to replace McDowell, it had been at the urging of old General Winfield Scott, who then held the rank of lieutenant general and general in chief of all the Federal armies. As a young lieutenant McClellan had served under Scott in Mexico as, indeed, had such Confederate commanders as Beauregard and Lee; and he was at first very deferential to the old soldier. But as the autumn wore on, McClellan became convinced that Scott stood in the way of his achieving some significant goal, though it is difficult to say what he thought it was. He later complained first that the Lincoln Administration was demanding that he move before he was ready, and then that when he *was* ready, the government was refusing to give him enough men to do the job. What old General Scott's role in these complaints could have been is not easy to discern.

Nevertheless, McClellan did not hesitate to use Wade, Chandler, and Trumbull to push the old general out. "For the last three hours," he wrote his wife at 1:15 A.M. on October 26, "I have been at Montgomery Blair's, talking with Senators Wade, Trumbull, and Chandler about war matters. They will make a desperate effort tomorrow to have Gen. Scott retired at once; until that is accomplished I can affect but little good. He is ever in my way, and I'm sure does not desire effective action."

On November 1, McClellan got his wish, and Scott was placed (by his own request, so the President told McClellan) on the retirement list. In Scott's place—and with the entire cabinet concurring—the President told McClellan in a private letter, that he had decided to name McClellan "to command the whole army." The order was effective at once.

Whether or not this development grew out of the urging of the Radical senators is hard to say, though Chandler wrote to his wife on October 27 of the October 26 meeting with McClellan, and of another meeting with Lincoln which lasted until midnight the following night. Chandler's estimate of McClellan at that point was not flattering: McClellan had "accomplished *nothing* with ten times the amount" given to Frémont, whose "operations were bad enough in all conscience, but as compared with McClellan's they were splendid."

Apparently Wade, Chandler, and Trumbull were willing to wait to see if the removal of Scott would result in movement on the part of the Army of the Potomac. But Chandler added, "If we fail in getting a battle *now*, all is lost & up to this time, a fight is scarcely contemplated."

I. Formation of the Committee

It was in this atmosphere of winter gloom and mounting dissatisfaction within the President's own party that the Thirty-Seventh Congress convened on December 2, 1861, for the opening of its first regular session. At last Wade and Chandler, in whom mounting frustration was fostering some rather extreme theories of constitutional interpretation, had an arena in which they could act, not simply as concerned busybodies, but as they truly saw themselves—the elected guardians of the best interests of the American people and the nation's first line of defense against treason. The Congress, as the chosen representatives of the loyal people of the United States, could move even if General McClellan and all his armies refused to.

On December 5, Chandler, who had become chairman of the important Senate Commerce Committee in this new Republican-dominated Congress, rose to propose the formation of a committee of three senators to "inquire into the disasters of Bull Run and Edwards' Ferry, with power to send for persons and papers." Though he had indicated that he would like quick action on his motion, there was some delaying discussion. Senator James Lane of Kansas wanted to amend the resolution so as to include the disasters at Wilson's Creek and Lexington in Missouri; and Senator James W. Grimes of Iowa wanted to add the eastern engagements at Belmont and Big Bethel in Maryland. Chandler objected that adding the other topics would require a committee to travel all over the country, whereas the two he had proposed were close at hand; but Grimes persisted. His attempt to amend Chandler's motion, to make the investigatory unit a joint House-Senate body of two senators and three representatives to inquire "into the causes of the disasters that have attended the public arms," was postponed until the next day.

On December 9, Grimes introduced a different and substantially broadened version of Chandler's original motion, asking that "a joint committee of three members of the Senate and four members of the House of Representatives be appointed to inquire into the conduct of the present war, and that they have power to send for persons and papers, and to sit during the sessions of either House of Congress." Senator John P. Hale of New Hampshire, whose son was married to Chandler's daughter, objected that the charge to such a committee would be too broad, but Chandler declared himself satisfied with it. When the motion was voted on, only three of the ten Democrats still in the Senate (Carlile of western Virginia, Latham of California, and Rice of Minnesota) voted against it, while thirty-three of the thirty-nine other senators approved it.

Though both the Senate and the House were relatively small groups in 1861, it still took a certain amount of time for the machinery of setting up a joint committee to grind through the two houses. It was not until December 17, therefore, that, on Chandler's motion, Vice President Hannibal Hamlin named as the Senate members Chandler, his friend Wade, and Andrew Johnson of Tennessee, who had remained in his seat despite his state's secession the preceding June. The House having concurred in the resolution, Speaker Galusha Grow of Pennsylvania—apparently with a few hints from Chandler—on December 20 named George Washington Julian of Indiana, Daniel W. Gooch of Massachusetts, Moses Odell of New York and John Covode of Pennsylvania as the House members.

II. Membership of the Committee

Almost everything written about the Joint Select Committee on the Conduct of the Present War has pointed out that its membership was heavily weighted in favor of the Radical Republican point of view, despite the presence of such Democrats as Johnson and Odell. Even the pre-Sumter party affiliation of these two seems to have had very little effect on their views once the committee began its investigations. It has also been suggested that the committee's Democratic members, whose party was so badly outnumbered in both houses for the first time since 1845, never had more than a lukewarm interest in the goals of the committee, and quickly began to ignore its meetings. This is not borne out by the journal of the committee in the case of either Johnson or Odell. Only Johnson's replacement, Senator Benjamin F. Harding of Oregon, appears significantly to have slighted his responsibilities as a committee member.

Over the three-and-one-half years of the committee's life, it held 272 meetings: 164 during the Thirty-Seventh Congress and 108 during the Thirty-Eighth. Of these, the full membership attended, according to the journal of the committee, forty-four meetings during the Thirty-Seventh Congress and thirteen meetings during the Thirty-Eighth; but these figures do not tell the entire story, for two or more members were frequently absent on committee business, taking testimony in areas outside Washington—often from military men whose responsibilities made it impossible for them to leave the field long enough to come to Washington. Indeed, if demerits were to be passed out for absenteeism, one very black mark would have to be lodged against the name of John Covode, reputed to be a Radical, who missed 44 of the 164 meetings during the Thirty-Seventh Congress. Illness was given as a reason at times, and Covode was not re-elected to the Thirty-Eighth Congress. Even the ardent—and often vehement—George W. Julian missed twenty-three meetings in the Thirty-Seventh Congress, and a whopping forty-three in the Thirty-Eighth. It could scarcely be argued, however, that Julian was cool to the committee's work.

All in all, previous political affiliation does not seem to have affected the enthusiasm or the vigor for investigation of most of the members of the Joint Committee on the Conduct of the War. Individual members of the public, or the press, might occasionally suggest that some members were less committed to their work than they should have been; but there is no evidence that either Wade or Chandler were dissatisfied with any individual member of the group.

A glance at the membership of the committee does, however, suggest one or two points of common interest among the membership: With the exception of Andrew Johnson and Benjamin F. Loan of Missouri (who was to replace Covode as a House member), all came from north of the Mason-Dixon Line; and when Johnson resigned his Senate seat to become the first military governor of Tennessee, no other loyal Southerners were left in Congress to replace him. Four of the committee members hailed from what had been the old Northwest Territory, and they seemed to share a strong conviction that this endowed them with moral superiority. Three members had been born in Pennsylvania, while only one was a New Englander. Almost to a man, the members of the Joint Committee on the Conduct of the War shared a total ignorance of military affairs at the time the war broke out. Not one among the original committee had ever served even one day in any branch of the armed services; and taking their cue, perhaps, from their outspoken chairman none ever had a good word for either the United States Military Academy at West Point nor for its graduates, Union or Confederate. Indeed, among the membership of the committee, there was a shared distrust of the professional military that was almost a caricature of this traditional American attitude.

The original membership of the Joint Committee on the Conduct of the War was selected officially by the Speaker of the House, and by the vice president acting as president of the Senate. But the wishes of Senator Zachariah Chandler, who had moved the initial resolution calling for an investigative committee, apparently were heeded in its formation. A wealthy Detroit merchant and former mayor of that city, Chandler had been one of the founders of the Republican Party at its Jackson, Michigan, meeting in 1854 and would for many years enjoy an eminent position in the party's councils. As such, he saw to it that the committee's membership clearly reflected his own strong commitment to the Radical anti-slavery cause.

All in all, eleven different senators and representatives served on the committee during the life of the Thirty-Seventh and Thirty-Eighth Congresses, between 1861 and 1865. Seven were lawyers prior to their election to Congress. Most were middle-aged: one was only thirty-eight years old when the Civil War broke out; six were in their forties; three were in their early fifties; and one—Wade—was a feisty sixty-one years old.

The original group consisted of Chandler, an impassioned foe of slavery and the South, who could carry a grudge with the tenacity of a bulldog, and who could—by custom—have claimed the chairmanship of the committee for himself; Wade, an attorney and former Ohio judge to whom Chandler deferred on this because he felt the chairmanship ought to go to a lawyer; and Andrew Johnson, who was Chandler's safe concession to bipartisanship among the Senate members of the committee.

Wade, whose grimly sardonic mien disguised an often violent temper and a talent for expletive that left opponents breathless, had early become known as an opponent not to be trifled with. Johnson, fifty-three years old when the Civil War began, had attracted immediate national attention when, alone among the Southern senators, he had remained in his seat after his state had seceded from the Union. A resident of strongly Unionist eastern Tennessee, Johnson was an early War Democrat. Though he served barely four months on the committee before being named military governor of his home state by President Lincoln, he was an active and enthusiastic committee member.

Johnson was replaced in 1862 by Senator Joseph A. Wright of Indiana, who had been nominated by Governor Oliver P. Morton to replace Senator Jesse Bright, whom the Senate expelled on February 5, 1862, for having addressed a letter to Jefferson Davis as "President of the Confederate States of America." Like Johnson, Wright was regarded as a safe Democrat by the Radicals on the committee; but, as a former Indiana governor and United States Minister to Prussia (who had apparently greatly relished his post at Berlin) Wright did not share Johnson's active anti-slavery views and did not seek election to his Senate seat after January 14, 1863.

In the Thirty-Eighth Congress Wright's place on the committee was taken first by Oregon Senator Benjamin F. Harding, who was least in sympathy with the committee's goals, and who amassed the highest absentee record of all the committee members. Later Harding's committee seat was occupied by Pennsylvanian Charles R. Buckalew. Neither Harding nor Buckalew contributed much to the committee's actual work.

Committee members from the House of Representatives demonstrated only slightly more permanence than their senatorial colleagues. The choice of Indiana's George Washington Julian, whose credentials as a *bona fide* Radical abolitionist were well-known, was no surprise. A protégé of the Quaker anti-slavery protagonist Joshua Giddings, Julian not only reflected his mentor's views but subsequently married his daughter.

Daniel Gooch of Massachusetts, a fine lawyer who had already served two terms in the House, was also considered a reliable Republican, and he worked extremely conscientiously on the committee. John Covode of Pennsylvania, the third House member, enjoyed a not entirely deserved reputation as a Radical Republican as a result of having conducted the vigorous investigation of corruption in the administration of Democratic President James Buchanan. Covode's principal contribution seems to have been obtaining the services of a stenographer for the committee. Defeated for re-election in 1864, he was replaced by Missourian Benjamin F. Loan, who had been recently elected from that border state as an "emancipationist" candidate. Loan was the only member of the committee ever to have had any military experience. From 1861 to 1863 he had served with the Missouri militia as a brigadier general of volunteers and, as a volunteer officer untainted by West Point training, must have been most acceptable to Wade and Chandler.

The bipartisan note from the House was struck by the inclusion of "War Democrat" Moses Odell of Brooklyn, New York. Though Odell was essentially a political "hack" left over from the preceding administration, he became a surprisingly hard-working member of the Joint Committee on the Conduct of the War.

Despite this broad range of membership, the bulk of the committee's work—including all of its investigative duties and the writing of its reports—was done by a relative few. Indeed, almost all of the voluminous 2,000 pages of reports were written by Wade, who was also the only member to miss scarcely a meeting. On December 27, 1861, early in the committee's life, Chandler had moved that a quorum not be required for taking testimony. After that it was not unusual for substantially less than the full membership to be present, even for the testimony of high-ranking military witnesses. On three occasions, for example, Major General George G. Meade was summoned to appear and found himself testifying only to Wade.

III. Method of Operation

The Joint Committee on the Conduct of the War actually operated on two levels: as an investigatory body with wide powers and broad interests; and as the visible, vocal manifestation of a group new to national power and deeply imbued with a sense of mission as to what ought to be accomplished with that power. The committee may not have consciously set out to bring on a revolution in the government of the United States, but some facets of the constitutional philosophy of its leaders would certainly have accomplished that if they had been followed to their logical conclusions.

These particular aspects of constitutional philosophy are especially apparent in the committee's *modus operandi,* and fall into at least two significant categories.

The first of these was the relative position of the Executive branch vis-à-vis the Legislative branch. The second concerned the constitutional rights of witnesses appearing before the committee. In each case the philosophical position of the committee's leadership can be regarded as essentially identical with that of all the Radicals in the two houses of Congress, though at times, certain members such as Senators Wade and Chandler seemed to be well in advance of their own party in the extremity of their views. In either case the development of these aspects of Radical constitutional philosophy can be observed in the manner in which the committee conducted its business almost from its first meeting.

Chairman Wade had succeeded Stephen A. Douglas as chairman of the Senate Committee on Territories after the Republican triumph in the election of 1860, and so, in a national capital painfully short of office space, Wade ordained that the new committee would share the room of the Committee on Territories in the basement of the Capitol Building.

The Congress customarily began its sittings at noon daily in order to allow its members to attend to such business as patronage appointments (which took up an inordinate amount of time in a new, pre-civil service administration), committee meetings, or—as was too often the case in those hard drinking days—just getting over the night before. It was decided that the new committee should meet at 10 A.M. on Friday, December 20, 1861. At that first meeting Wade was formally elected chairman, and it would be he who would set the times and dates of meetings from that day forward.

At its first meeting the committee decreed that its deliberations should "as a matter of honor" be secret, though this would later be amended to allow members to use portions of the testimony they heard in arguments on the floor of Congress. There were no public hearings, and none were ever covered by members of the press. The subjects of inquiry referred to the committee for investigation were, however, mentioned in the record of debates printed in the *Congressional Globe* so that the press and the general public soon became aware of the committee's work.

In a great many instances the committee would vote to meet in "executive session," and such meetings were so secret that even the committee's stenographer was excluded. Thus, historians have only the "official" reports and the word of the witnesses of what went on in these secret sessions. Relatively few of the latter actually recorded their experiences; and the reports, extensive as they are, contain no record *at all* of many of these secret sessions.

The witnesses who appeared before the committee were largely military men whose oath of silence could be enforced by military as well as civil sanctions. Thus, it is not surprising that so few of these witnesses confided, either in letters to their wives or in personal diaries, what occurred in the sessions to which they were summoned. Indeed, considering the rigid limitations imposed on their civil rights the surprise is that we can know anything at all of what happened there.

Thanks to legislation already on the books before 1861, any witness *summoned* to testify before a committee of either house of Congress was compelled to *appear* and, indeed, to *testify*. And, though an act of 1857 had forbidden the use of evidence developed in a congressional investigation for the purpose of obtaining a civil conviction, the Republican leadership, mindful that former Secretary of War John B. Floyd had escaped prosecution on graft charges under the Buchanan Administration, moved early in 1862 to close that loophole. H.R. 219 and S.R. 161 were both reported out of the respective Judiciary Committees in January 1862. The House bill was quickly adopted in place of the Senate version and, despite the opposition of some Senate Republicans and Democrats, was passed by a vote of 21 to 19. President Lincoln signed the bill into law on January 21, 1862.

Though this legislation was not the work of the Joint Committee on the Conduct of the War, Wade as chairman was very active in pushing its passage. Reminded by Senators Isham G. Harris of New York and James Bayard of Delaware that, in closing the loophole, Congress might be tampering with the Fifth Amendment rights of witnesses, Wade made it very clear that he did not consider the Fifth Amendment valid when it came to testimony before a congressional committee. "I am entirely unwilling," he declared, "that this rule [the Fifth Amendment] shall be extended to investigations before the Congress. I think it is impolitic. [The rule] is not broad enough for the great issues involved in investigations before your committees affecting millions [of dollars in] property and hundreds of men combined. It is better that the rule be reversed, that you may inquire of the party all he knows, and give him immunity against making what he says evidence against him in a court of justice. . . . That is all a rascal ought to have at the hands of justice, and even more than he ought to have."

With the chairman espousing such a position, it is not surprising, therefore, that no witness who appeared before the committee attempted to invoke the Fifth Amendment. No witness, furthermore, was represented by counsel; nor was anyone accused of a serious act ever allowed to face his accusers. In the notorious case of General Charles P. Stone, it was nearly two years (including more than six months he spent in jail) before Stone even saw the testimony against him. Witnesses regarded as recalcitrant were simply remanded to jail (as was one Francis Waldron in March 1864, until it was decided his reputation for truthfulness was not sufficient to warrant forcing testimony from him). No effort was ever made to sift out the bias of a witness; and hearsay evidence was not only accepted, but frequently solicited. Witnesses were asked leading questions, sometimes in fields in which they had no direct knowledge.

Indeed, so flagrant were the abuses of the civil rights of the objects of the committee's wrath (selective vendettas were carried on against a number of military officers) that one can only conclude that in the mid-nineteenth century most of the Republican majority in Congress agreed with Wade and Congressman Thaddeus Stevens that, in wartime, there could be neither a Constitution nor a Bill of Rights. Certainly the fact that the chairman and most of the membership of the Joint Committee on the Conduct of the War were trained attorneys, and that the chairman had been a judge, did nothing to assure a legalistic regard for the rights of witnesses subpoenaed to appear before them.

In selecting the topics to be investigated by the committee it is clear from the resolution creating the group that Wade and Chandler had a hand in deciding on the initial investigation of the First Battle of Bull Run. That choice proceeded directly out of their experience as spectator participants in the engagement. Later, other events, such as the disasters that attended the Army of the Potomac under its first four or five commanders, provided more grist for the committee's mill. Between the meetings in which it addressed itself to such major topics as the operations of the Army of the Potomac the committee was routinely asked to investigate series of newspaper stories and rumors which had reached the ears of other members of Congress. In addition, once it became known that the committee was engaged in investigating aspects of the conduct of the war, private citizens regularly addressed Wade, as the committee's chairman, or other members of Congress, to suggest that the committee check into what the writers regarded as abuses.

The search for material to complete these investigations invariably led the committee into contact with the Executive branch; and it was in this contact that evidence of the committee's rather revolutionary view of the relationship between the two branches appears. Though Wade and Chandler were probably the most articulate and vocal members of the committee in their constitutional philosophy on the relationship, their views seem to have been shared by all the Republican members, and even by one or two Democrats. During the summer of 1862, in the course of a debate on legislation concerning pardon and amnesty for rebels which, it was feared, the President might veto, Wade clearly set forth his conviction that the Legislative branch was superior to the Executive and was intended to be so by the Founding Fathers. It was, he asserted, "the constitutional right" of Congress "to pass all such laws as we believe ought to be passed." And no one, he thundered, ought to "go mousing around the President to see if there is any little difficulty that may be removed. . . . Sir, it is disgraceful!"

Similarly, on the question of the powers of the President as Commander in Chief of the armed forces, Wade assailed Senator James Dixon of Connecticut during the debate on the First Confiscation Act. When Dixon argued that the power of Congress "to legislate as a Legislature was not increased by war," but that the powers of the President were, in that, as Commander in Chief he could order the confiscation of enemy property as a war measure, Wade was furious. What Dixon was preaching was the surrender of congressional power to the Executive, and his "arm would fall off before [he would] surrender one jot or tittle of that power. . . . I cannot bear to hear with complacency the doctrine urged that Congress has no power to regulate these rights of war, that the moment war is declared . . . Congress loses all power to regulate the rights of war, and they are devolved by the Constitution, *ipso facto,* in all their breadth and depth upon the Chief Magistrate of the nation, and we cannot modify or control them." That, he fumed, was "a slavish doctrine." The President might be Commander in Chief; "but Congress, the legislative power sitting superior to him or any other magistrate in the nation, may regulate, modify, and direct whatever principles they please [that] their chief commander shall act upon and execute."

Furthermore, Wade asserted, Congress could, if it wished, even end the war and make peace, simply by enacting a law disbanding the army. Senator

Fessenden tried to offer a mild objection to this constitutional interpretation but was rudely silenced by Wade. If Congress were to pass a law "that our armies shall be disbanded, and that there shall be peace, would it not be a good law so far as we are concerned?" he asked. Perhaps the Confederates would not pay much attention to it; "but the enactment of our law would stand against the world, against the President, and everybody else."

So too with congressional investigations, as Wade indicated to General William B. Franklin when that unfortunate officer was summoned before the committee on December 26, 1861. "We are here armed with the whole power of both houses of Congress," he told McClellan's protégé. "They have made it our duty to inquire into the whole conduct of the war; into every department of it. We do not want to do anything that will result in harm or wrong. But we do want to know, and we must know if we can, what is to be done, for the country is in jeopardy."

The possibility that the Executive branch might be equally aware of the dangers the nation faced was one that Wade and the Joint Committee on the Conduct of the War simply denied. Seeing themselves as the country's saviors, the members of the committee were convinced that they, and *only* they, had a clear view of the direction in which salvation lay; and to question the clarity of their vision in so serious a matter as the nation's survival was not just heresy, it was treason. Indeed, the words "treason" and "traitors" were so widely applied by various members of the committee as to suggest a nearly psychotic irresponsibility. Anyone who was not *with* them was *against* not only them but, by extension, God, the nation, and the flag.

Needless to say, such convictions were to make relations between the committee (as the self-designated overseer in the Legislative branch) and the Executive branch (which it saw itself as overseeing) increasingly difficult as the war went on. Despite open hostility between these two bodies, however, members of the committee enjoyed an access to and cooperation from the Executive branch that, a century later, seems remarkable.

As has been noted, even before the formation of the committee, Wade, Chandler and Trumbull had hurried to Washington weeks in advance of the opening of Congress and had asked for, and gotten, meetings with such presidential advisers as Montgomery Blair and Simon Cameron, with General McClellan, and several times with Lincoln himself. After the committee had been organized in December 1861 such meetings continued.

Though full records of all the encounters between the committee and the President and his cabinet have not survived, in a few instances some of the participants did record their impressions. Had these thoughts been published at the time rather than confided to wives and diaries, the writers might have been surprised indeed to learn who among them shared the others' usually unflattering views of the entire group.

Of the meeting on January 6, 1892, for example, the committee's journal states simply that "the full committee met the President and his whole cabinet at 7½ P.M. yesterday, according to previous arrangement." Secretary of the Treasury Salmon P. Chase recorded in his diary that the committee members, "especially Messrs. Chandler, Wade, Johnson, Odell, and Covode were very earnest in urging the vigorous prosecution of the War, and in recommending the appointment of Genl. McDowell as Major-General, to command the Army of the Potomac." Committee members also pushed the idea of dividing the army into *corps d'armée* after the style of Napoléon, and Chase recorded that he had supported this idea while at the same time defending McClellan.

Representative George W. Julian, a committee member who was present, reported that the committee had met with Lincoln and his cabinet at the President's request (the committee journal said it had been suggested by Cameron). Julian had found the meeting extremely disconcerting. "The most striking fact revealed by the discussion which took place was that neither the President nor his advisors seemed to have any definite information respecting the management of the war, or the failure of our forces to make any forward movement," he recorded in his own journal.

Furthermore, not only did no one have any idea of McClellan's plans, but the President seemed to feel that, as a layman, he had no right to question the general about them. Except for Chase, who seemed to Julian to be sympathetic to the committee's views on the army's inaction, the cabinet generally defended McClellan. This had enraged Wade, Julian reported, and the chairman had set forth the views of the committee "in a remarkably bold and vigorous speech, in which he gave a summary of the principal facts which had come to the knowledge of the Committee, arraigned General McClellan for the tardiness of his movements, and urged upon the Administration, in the most undiplomatic plainness of speech, an immediate and radical change in the policy of the war. But," Julian concluded, "the President and his advisors could not be disenchanted, and the conference ended without results."

Though we have no record of Lincoln's feelings about this particular meeting (his friend Ward H. Lamon later recorded that criticism by the Joint Committee annoyed and depressed the President), he had written reassuringly about the committee to McClellan, who had been ill at his home at the time. He had heard, wrote the President, that the "doings" of the committee had given the general "some uneasiness" (which was certainly quite true), and he wanted McClellan to "be entirely relieved on this point. The gentlemen of the Committee were with me an hour and a half last night [December 31, 1861], and I found them in a perfectly good mood. As their investigation brings them acquainted with the facts, they are rapidly coming to think of the whole case as all sensible men would."

On the day after the meeting of January 6—and possibly as a result of Wade's harangue urging movement on the part of the army—Lincoln wrote to Halleck in St. Louis, asking him to name "as early a day as you safely can, on, or before which you can be ready to move southward in concert with General Buell. Delay is ruining us; and it is indispensable for me to have something definite." Two days later the President wrote a note to McClellan, urging that the general appear before the committee at "the earliest moment your health will permit—today, if possible."

According to the committee's journal there were at least eight occasions during the Thirty-Seventh Congress on which Lincoln was asked to meet either alone or with such members of his cabinet as Cameron, Stanton or Seward, or with the full cabinet, with members of the committee, coming in a body, or with its representatives. The smaller representations almost always included Wade. Soon after the opening of the Thirty-Eighth Congress a perfunctory letter was sent to Lincoln, requesting a meeting with the committee.

The President agreed, but no meeting took place because Lincoln's note setting a time was said to have arrived too late to notify the membership. Since the members were all in Washington and lived within a short distance of both the Capitol and the White House, this may have been a studied rebuff by the busy President, whom Wade and Chandler were already planning to replace with a more militant candidate on the Republican ticket in the Fall.

A month or so after this incident, Wade and Chandler, angered at General George Meade for not having followed up his victory at Gettysburg the previous July, met with Lincoln to demand Meade's removal. Lincoln had already decided to appoint Grant commanding general of all Union armies, however. The Senators' efforts were, therefore, needless efforts and Meade was temporarily retained.

There seems to have been no time when any individual member of the Joint Committee on the Conduct of the War requested an interview with the President and was denied it. Equally impressive was the record of cooperation on the part of the cabinet departments. Like many individuals in Washington, the committee disliked and distrusted Secretary of State William H. Seward. Chandler was delighted to learn, during the course of a White House dinner in 1864, that Mrs. Lincoln shared his dislike for the New Yorker; and Secretary of the Navy Gideon Welles reported several attempts by the Radicals to force Seward out of the cabinet. No one, however, was able to convince the President that his trust in Seward was misplaced. Indeed, one of the major political efforts made by the committee in the spring of 1864 was a fresh attempt to compel Lincoln to dismiss Seward and Blair, a goal that became an issue in the presidential campaign of that year. Blair went in the autumn of 1864, but Seward remained; and Lincoln even gained a point on his Radical critics by accepting Salmon P. Chase's resignation while rejecting Seward's.

Despite all this hostile maneuvering, however, not even Seward ever refused a committee request for documents concerning any topic under its consideration. From the secretary of war—whether it was Cameron, who remained at that post for only a brief time after the committee began its investigations—or from Stanton, who committee members felt was sympathetic to their aims, full cooperation was the rule. At times there may have been misunderstandings or delays, as was the case with Major General William T. Sherman at the end of the war. But the witnesses invariably appeared, or were somehow made available to those committee members who traveled to the battlefields to question them.

Secretary of War Stanton, especially, proved readily accessible to committee members, both in person and to their written communications; and he was so amiable in his relations with them as to lay himself open to charges of being the Radicals' representative in meetings of the cabinet. During the year 1862 alone he met with committee members on eight recorded occasions, sometimes in the evening at his home on K Street, as on February 20, or in his office. The secretary was a welcome visitor at meetings of the committee —even at those executive sessions from which the stenographer was barred. Indeed, Stanton's biographers suggest that the secretary's cooperation with the committee secured him the occasional use of its subpoena power to get information not otherwise available to him.

According to Ward Hill Lamon, Lincoln complained of this "improvised vigilant[e] committee," termed it "a marplot," and charged that "its greatest purpose seems to be to hamper my action and obstruct the military operations." In point of fact, however, Lincoln never committed such thoughts to paper himself, nor does he ever seem to have allowed the committee to usurp his constitutional powers as Commander in Chief.

Probably more indicative of Lincoln's attitude toward the committee and its frequently gratuitous advice was the ironic note expressed in his November 20, 1863, letter to Chandler. In this brief but classic Lincoln missive, marked "Private" in response to Chandler's "Private" letter of November 15, the President told Chandler that he was "very glad to hear [that] the elections of this autumn have gone favorably and that I have not by native depravity, or under evil influences, done anything bad enough to prevent the good result." To Chandler's warnings about listening to the advice of Thurlow Weed and Montgomery Blair (who, Chandler had read in the papers, were urging a "conservative" course on Lincoln), the President replied that he hoped "to 'stand firm' enough not to go backward, and yet not go forward fast enough to wreck the country's cause."

It was probably this typical light irony which angered the Wades, Chandlers, and Julians in Congress more than anything else Lincoln did. For, to these essentially humorless men, it must have been clear by the fall of 1863 that Lincoln was not going to take seriously the advice they kept urging on him. To self-appointed saviors there could scarcely be any more aggravating attitude for a President to take.

IV. The Committee During the Thirty-Seventh Congress

No sooner had the Joint Committee on the Conduct of the War met for the first time on December 20, 1861, and elected Wade chairman than it entertained its first motion. Chandler moved—and the committee agreed—that it should "proceed to investigate the disaster to our arms at Bull Run, Virginia, in July last." This, of course, had been uppermost in his and Wade's minds ever since they had returned from that battlefield themselves.

Of almost equal importance to the Radicals of the committee was the fate of General John C. Frémont, now relieved of his command in Missouri and transferred to Wheeling in western Virginia—a move which he, his wife, the fiery Jessie Benton Frémont, and the Radicals considered demotion to a military backwater. The committee, therefore, next instructed Wade to make inquiries at the War Department as to what proceedings were being carried on against Frémont. He was somewhat mollified on being told there were none, but the committee's decision to investigate affairs in Missouri was not rescinded.

On the following day, December 21, the committee began to broaden the scope of its inquiry to include the Army of the Potomac and *its* inaction. Chandler and Odell were appointed a subcommittee to obtain information that certainly would be regarded as "Classified" in the twentieth century, but to which the committee, despite its rather loose security precautions, seemed to feel perfectly confident it had a right. The subcommittee was instructed to find out "the number of men accepted by the government; also the number of men now actually in the field, their character, and where located; also the number of officers of each grade now in service; also the number of regiments in process of formation, accepted, but not yet mustered into the service." In addition, Congressman Gooch moved that a note be sent to McClellan expressing the unanimous desire of the committee for an interview with him in their meeting room. Another motion was passed to summon Frémont from his eyrie in Wheeling to come on January 6, 1862, to ". . . testify to the conduct of the war in the department of the west."

In all, the Joint Committee on the Conduct of the War would issue three reports during the Thirty-Seventh Congress: *Senate Reports* Number(s) 41, 71, and 108. The first two dealt respectively with the treatment by the rebels of Union officers' remains after the Battle of Bull Run in 1861, and with the Battle of Fredericksburg in 1862; these were published on April 30 and December 23, 1862. The third—one of the longest ever produced by the committee—appeared in three thick parts on March 2, 1863, and covered not only the first Battle of Bull Run; the incident at Ball's Bluff; the administration of the Western—or Missouri—Department under Frémont; a number of miscellaneous topics, such as the Port Royal and Burnside expeditions, the fall of Fort Donelson, the capture of New Orleans, "rebel barbarities," trade across the lines, and the method of "communicating the countersign"; and, finally, the wordiest section of all: that on the Army of the Potomac. This last proved to be such a *chef d'oeuvre* that the committee put it aside from time to time in favor of the other investigations and submitted its reports on those prior to publishing *Senate Report* Number 108.

The decision to investigate the engagement at Ball's Bluff was based on a suggestion from the Senate floor. Though the affair was minor as a military engagement, one of its casualties had been President Lincoln's friend and the senators' old colleague, Colonel (formerly Senator) Edward Baker. During the special session of the previous summer Baker had caused a sensation when he had swept into the Senate chamber, magnificently clad in the well-fitted uniform of a brigadier general of volunteers, and had attacked Kentucky Senator (and former vice president) John C. Breckenridge as a traitor. Now Baker was gone, and his colleagues wanted to know on whom to pin the blame for his death.

Though in fact the responsibility probably belonged to Baker himself, who had engaged in an act of needless bravado, the committee soon received information from other volunteer officers that Baker's death had resulted from orders issued to him by his superior, Brigadier General Charles P. Stone, a West Point graduate. The manner in which the committee handled the case of General Stone has often been cited as typical of the committee's unwarranted and unprofessional trampling of the civil rights of military officers. As an example of the worst in investigatory techniques and of character assassination, the handling of General Stone has seldom been equaled. Malicious, slanderous and hearsay evidence against him was accepted and printed without challenge. Stone himself was never allowed to face his accusers nor, indeed, even allowed to see their testimony until 1863. On the committee's orders, with the cooperation of McClellan and Stanton (and certainly with no interference from Lincoln), Stone was arrested and held in a military prison in Washington and then at Fort Hamilton, New York, for more than six months.

Responsibility for his treatment by the committee lay partly, however, with General Stone himself, for he adopted a reserved and lofty tone toward the committee at first and then, when it was suggested he might be disloyal because of family connections in Virginia, became testy. His demeanor, of course, would not excuse the illegal course of action pursued against him, nor the fact that, though essentially a good officer, his services were lost to the nation and his career utterly shattered by the affair. Probably the most important result of the Ball's Bluff investigation, however, was its effect on subsequent military witnesses: almost all writers on the period agree that it forced the officers to treat the committee with extreme deference.

The investigation of the "treatment by the Rebels at Manassas of the remains of U.S. officers and soldiers" and of reported "employment of Indians by the rebels" was undertaken on the motion of Senator Charles Sumner of Massachusetts, who introduced his resolution in the Senate on April 1, 1862. The committee, which by that time had already looked rather closely into the Battle of Bull Run, complied with alacrity. Its report on the "atrocities"—some of which should have surpassed the credibilities of rational men—was published on April 30, 1862.

Even more prompt was the committee's response to the suggestion, made on December 18 by Senator J. M. Wilkinson of Minnesota, that it investigate the recent military disaster at Fredericksburg. But the committee spent more than a year preparing its voluminous report on the Army of the Potomac. Here, the original question seems to have been why this force was making no movement against an enemy encamped scarcely more than twenty-five miles from the Capitol. The committee hoped to learn this from McClellan when, on December 22, 1861, he accepted its invitation to appear before it. But the general did not appear at the room of the Committee on Territories at 10 A.M. on December 23 as he had written he would, and the committee did not receive word until Christmas Eve that he was "so unwell" that he would be "unable to leave his house at all."

McClellan's illness was later said to have been typhoid—always a threat in those days of uncertain water supplies. But the authenticity of the diagnosis was, apparently, open to doubt, and McClellan himself remained silent on the subject aside from describing himself as "sick." Whatever its nature, McClellan's illness evoked little sympathy from members of the committee. Deprived of the witness himself, they elected to move along to the questioning of his subordinates and anyone else, such as Quartermaster General Montgomery Meigs (whose appointment McClellan was known to have opposed), who might enlighten them about the army's lack of action. In trooped a collection of lesser military commanders, a few of them McClellan's friends but a more substantial number officers who held general's rank only as volunteers and who were inclined to be critical of the imperious young man who had been jumped over them to the top command.

Of the nineteen generals interviewed up to the time of the stormy meeting of January 6 between the committee, the President, and his cabinet, few held high rank in the regular army, most having been promoted or appointed to the rank of brigadier general of volunteers at the outbreak of the war. All were asked essentially the same questions, as would be those who were interviewed later in the year as well, dealing with the readiness to fight of the Army of the Potomac: What is your position? How is the health of your men? Are your officers competent? Will your men improve as soldiers after spending a long time in camp? Would not experience under fire make them better? How are the roads now? What do you think of the organization of the army? Would it be better organized by corps? What do you think of the cavalry? Are you oversupplied with cavalry? (This was Wade's hobby horse—he was convinced that cavalry units were unnecessarily expensive.) The question about organizing the army into corps, which would result in some delegation —and therefore a subdivision—of McClellan's authority, was introduced by General Irwin McDowell during his testimony, and this question, asked of all succeeding witnesses, became a second obsession of the committee.

The responses to this catechism divided more or less along lines related to the respondent's closeness to the General-in-Chief. Chandler's constituent Israel B. Richardson, who had served in the Mexican War and who had started the Civil War as a colonel in command of the Second Michigan Volunteers, forthrightly opined that a large number of cavalry was not necessary; that McClellan had never sought the advice of his general officers in any sort of council of war; that the roads of northern Virginia were in good enough condition for an army to move over them; that he did not think a general—not even the General-in-Chief—required a large staff; that the Army of the Potomac already was large enough to undertake an attack; that the condition, discipline and morale of the troops were excellent; that their condition would not be improved by staying in camp but probably would be better for, as Wade put it, "smelling a little powder"; and that he thought that capturing such ports as Charleston, Savannah, and New Orleans would be "worth more than the whole state of Virginia."

Somewhat less confident was the testimony of General W. F. ("Baldy") Smith, who at the time war broke out had been a captain of topographical engineers and an instructor in mathematics at the hated Military Academy at West Point. He reported that many of his men had typhoid and he himself had been on sick leave for the preceding five weeks. Some of his officers, he said, were good, some were not. While he had all the cavalry he needed, he did not think the cavalry of the Army of the Potomac as a whole met the textbook standard of one-sixth the size of the infantry. Asked if he knew of "any military obstacle, any particular reason . . . any good reason whatever, why we should act entirely on the defensive in regard to this army of the Potomac," Smith answered defensively that he knew "nothing about the army's strength or condition." Nor was he any better informed about the strength of the enemy, other than what he could read in the newspapers.

Most irritating to the committee, however, was the testimony of William B. Franklin and Fitzjohn Porter. These two McClellan intimates made it clear that they looked only to the General-in-Chief as their authority and refused to say anything to which they thought McClellan might object. The two young generals—Franklin immediately followed Porter on the Army list, and both had been appointed brigadier generals on May 17, 1861—followed a policy of extreme circumspection on what would today be regarded as "classified" material. Franklin admitted he had had "private, confidential" talks with McClellan. On December 26, Franklin was asked by Wade, "Are you willing to disclose what you know to the Committee? You know we are all sworn to secrecy. We want to know what the plans of the commanding general are."

Before telling the committee of McClellan's plans, Franklin replied, "I would prefer, if the committee will permit me, to see General McClellan on the subject because I do not think he has made known his plans to anybody. . . . And he gave us these plans with the understanding that we were to see him before saying anything to anybody about it."

From this point on the questioning seemed to get more testy and more angry. Did Franklin know "any insurmountable obstacle to a proper movement of the Army now as well as at any other time?" That depended on what sort of movement Wade was referring to. "I am not now inquiring where you should go," the Chairman shot back. "I want to know if any advantageous movement could be made to rid this capital of this siege now as well as at any other time." But Franklin was still evasive. He said he could only speak for his own division. "Well speak of that," snapped Wade. After still more discussion the chairman forced a conclusion from the witness that "really, the non-movement of the army [was] not occasioned by any want of transportation or provisions."

Franklin was finally excused after admitting that he agreed it might be better if McClellan had sought the counsel of his generals. In turn he had to listen to a stern lecture from Wade, who reminded him, "This nation is making an extraordinary effort. Next March we shall be $600,000,000 in debt for what we have already done. And nothing has yet been done that seems to be at all commensurate with the exertions the nation has made. . . . All this is hanging upon one man who keeps his counsels entirely to himself. If he was an old veteran who had fought a hundred battles, or we knew him as well as Bonaparte or Wellington was known, then we could repose upon him with confidence. But how can this nation abide the secret counsels that one man carries in his head, when we have no evidence that he is the wisest man in the world?"

Young General Fitzjohn Porter was, in the view of the committee, just as unsatisfactory in evading questions whose answers he had not cleared with McClellan. "You can qualify your answers as you please," Wade told him sharply. "We are here clothed with authority and of course we have duties to perform. Congress has enjoined it upon us to make these inquiries, and of course it will be our duty to use our information as carefully as would the officers of the army themselves." Wade continued to ask Porter specific questions about the strength of his division, with Johnson interposing that Porter need not worry about giving out secret information as the committee had "a full report from the War Department of the numbers of the Army of the Potomac"; but Porter was not persuaded. Those figures, he said, gave only *numerical* strength; they did not indicate how many effectives there were.

Wade moved on from that to the Army's general policy. "You have had this matter under consideration for a great while no doubt. . . . We are endeavoring to ascertain of military gentlemen what disposition they think should be made now in relation to the army. Should it retire into winter quarters, or should it attempt . . . to dislodge the enemy?"

Back came the maddening reply, "That is a question I cannot answer."

"I merely ask your military opinion," rejoined Wade. But Porter was firm. He "decline[d] to give a military opinion on that point."

Could Congress, then, do *anything to help* the army get ready to move? "Not that I am aware of," came the lofty answer. "I believe that General McClellan is carrying out his plans as rapidly as he possibly can. What those plans are is not for me to say—that is, I think it is better for you to get them from him."

Later in 1862 Franklin—whom McClellan always addressed as "Dear Frank"—was deprived of his command in the Army of the Potomac and sent off to Louisiana, where he fought bravely and was wounded at Pleasant Hill in the Red River campaign. Porter was still less fortunate. Court-martialed for failing to follow the orders of Radical favorite General John Pope at the Second Battle of Bull Run, Porter was convicted and cashiered from the army. Though the Joint Committee on the Conduct of the War cannot be said to have authored this disposal of two uncooperative witnesses, the members drew a grim satisfaction from their fate, especially that of Porter who, according to Chandler, "ought to have been shot."

While these interrogations proceeded, the Army of the Potomac did not move, and the committee's members found their irritation mounting with each day. Finally they had the stormy meeting with Lincoln and the full cabinet which resulted in Lincoln's plea to Halleck to get moving, and his hint to McClellan to get out of bed and over to the committee room as soon as possible.

On January 14, 1862, McClellan finally wrote to Wade, "The condition of my health is now such that I can appear before your committee when you wish." Morning would suit him best, he indicated, and Wade obliged him by responding that the Committee would be meeting the following day at 10:30 A.M., and would "be pleased to see" him then or at any other time convenient to him.

McClellan wrote the President that he was going, adding, "If I escape alive I will report when I get through." That the interview was an unpleasant experience for McClellan may be inferred from his subsequent references to the committee as "the rascals," and "these treacherous hounds" and—more simply—"my enemies."

A later entry in the journal of the committee noted that, on January 19, "the President of the United States, as commander in chief of the army and navy, issued orders for a general movement of all the armies of the United States. . . ." Lincoln's next step was the issuance of the "President's Special War Order No. 1," dated January 31, in which he ordered McClellan to seize and occupy a point on the railroad southwest of Manassas and to start this movement on or before February 22. Still, McClellan dawdled. Without moving a single soldier he haggled with the President over which route the army should use to get at Richmond: one involving a direct overland march against Confederate forces encamped around Manassas, or a more circuitous one, favored by McClellan and approved by a bare majority of his generals, which required transporting the army by water to the tip of the peninsula between the York and the James rivers.

The choice of the peninsular route to Richmond and the subsequent disasters that attended it meant that the investigation by the Joint Committee on the Conduct of the War would concern itself not only with the initial delays in the movement of the Army of the Potomac but be subsequently broadened to include the Second Battle of Bull Run, the Peninsula campaign, and the Battle of Antietam. This investigation covered in detail the rest of McClellan's military career and shone a merciless spotlight on him.

On March 10, the Confederates withdrew from in front of Manassas. For months McClellan had objected that he dared not move the Army of the Potomac overland because of the fearsome strength of the Rebel position there. With the Confederate evacuation, Federal forces and, worse still, Federal civilian visitors (including committee members Julian, Gooch, and Odell) flocked to see the enemy's former works. They found that the "terrifying" Confederate artillery against which McClellan had dared not move was a collection of logs painted black to look like gun barrels.

So far as the committee was concerned, this was conclusive evidence not just of stupidity but of McClellan's treachery. "A majority of the committee at this time strongly suspected that General McClellan was a traitor," recalled George W. Julian, who said he had found the visit "full of interest and excitement." Though there is no evidence that Lincoln ever came to so extreme a conclusion about his General-in-Chief, he did use the incident as an excuse for relieving McClellan of overall command, leaving him as head only of the Army of the Potomac.

During May and June, while McClellan and the Army of the Potomac blundered their way up the Virginia peninsula, the Joint Committee on the Conduct of the War continued to examine witnesses on a variety of lesser subjects, while still keeping a supercritical eye on military developments. The second session of the Thirty-Seventh Congress would meet until mid-summer —long enough for the committee and all the world to learn of the string of military disasters through which the detested McClellan was to lead the Army of the Potomac.

The committee continued its meetings through July 16, 1892. Certainly by summer there was no doubt in the minds of such leaders as Wade and Chandler that McClellan was a "traitorous cuss,"and "an awful humbug [who] deserves to be shot," and "an imbecile if not a traitor."

Between the end of the second session of the Thirty-Seventh Congress on July 17 and the opening of the third session on December 1, 1862, both Chandler and Wade were up for re-election. Wade faced an uphill fight in his home state of Ohio, as Democrats picked up House seats throughout the Midwest and a Senate seat in Illinois. It seemed touch-and-go for a time, and the Ohio legislature did not re-elect Wade to the Senate until the following spring. But friends such as Stanton and Chandler let it be known that, despite Wade's critical attitudes, his re-election was considered essential to the Republican cause. Chandler, meanwhile, won re-election in Michigan with only minor opposition.

When the third session of Congress opened, the committee held its first meeting on Wade's call four days later. It had received on December 4, from the House of Representatives, a request that it investigate conditions at "Camp Convalescent," a medical facility for Union soldiers in nearby Alexandria, Virginia. Gooch, Covode, and Odell had promptly visited the camp and found much "needed there in the way of reform." Chandler moved that they visit Secretary Stanton as soon as possible in order to present their recommendations.

The Battle of Fredericksburg took place a few days later, and, though the committee no longer could aim recriminations at their favorite target, McClellan (Lincoln had relieved him on November 5, 1862), they clearly had another case of administrative error to explain to the nation. They hurried off to Falmouth, Virginia, to get the story straight from the lips of the new commander, Major General Ambrose E. Burnside.

The battle had been fought on December 13. The committee made its on-site inspection of the battlefield on December 19 and 20 and published a forty-page report by December 23. The visit to the battlefield so soon after the action proved almost traumatic for some of the members. Chandler reported to his wife that the "sights here were awfull [*sic*]. Arms, legs piled up in banks around hospitals & dead men buried in Trenches each morning at 5." The committee had wisely taken their "own provisions [and] blankets & slept on the floor . . . & barring the cold had a good time." Then, apparently lest he seem to be taking too frivolous a view of the whole subject, Chandler added, "Our poor wounded men are suffering there but they are being brought away rapidly."

Congressman George W. Julian, too, had his initial experience with the horrors of war at Fredericksburg. He was so moved by the committee's visit to the camp hospital at Falmouth, in which he found some of the wounded "too far gone to speak," that he later recalled that he could "not forget the impression it made."

When Congress had adjourned the previous July the committee's report on the Army of the Potomac had not yet been completed. As a result, after the report on the Battle of Fredericksburg was rushed to the government printer on December 23, the membership once more addressed itself to completing the major report on the failure of McClellan's leadership.

"McClellan is as dead as a herring," Chandler reported to his wife after returning from the Christmas recess on January 22, 1863. "Our Committee will soon report & when it does he will receive his *eternal quietus*." Cheering as this thought should have been, "I am more discouraged at this time than I like to admit even to myself," Chandler continued. "Our Generals don't improove [*sic*] at all. Burnside is a slow coach & will do nothing effective." He thought General Joseph Hooker, who would soon replace Burnside, would "fight if he could have a chance but that he cannot have at present as the McClellan men in the Army are down *upon him* & they are today too powerful for him. This we shall soon change."

The third session of the Thirty-Seventh Congress expired on March 3, and the committee's report on the Army of the Potomac consumed most of the members' time in the two months between their return from the Christmas recess and adjournment. Both the House and the Senate, however, continued to pass along resolutions for new investigations of lesser importance. Examples of these were the motion by Representative C. A. White of Ohio that the committee investigate the death of Union Captain John Elwood in the Old Capitol Prison; the motion of Representative John B. Alley of Massachusetts that they "inquire what rules or restrictions, if any, are applied to trade in those portions of the country now under military occupation, and whether any officers in the service of the government are, or have been, engaged in trade or speculation, or affording special privileges or facilities to other persons to do so . . ."; or the lengthy resolution of Senator James Harlan of Iowa that the committee "inquire whether vessels and other means of transportation, under the control of the War Department, have been used to convey disloyal women, or other disloyal persons, from places under the control of the rebels to places within the Union lines . . ."; and that of Senator Henry Wilson of Massachusetts that the committee "inquire whether Major General A. E. Burnside has, since the battle of Fredericksburg, formed any plans for the movement of the Army of the Potomac . . . and, if so, whether any subordinate generals of said army have written or visited Washington to oppose or interfere with the execution of such movements . . . and if so by what authority."

The committee did make an effort to find out what had happened to Captain Elwood, but Julian reported on February 7 that he had been "unable to learn any facts concerning it." No effort at all was made to follow up on Senator Harlan's rambling resolution, and consideration of it was postponed immediately upon its being read. But Representative Alley's resolution for investigating the subject of trade in the occupied areas would be followed up later by the committee and also by a special military inquiry conducted under the leadership of Major General Irwin McDowell, under a presidential order.

The life of the Joint Select Committee on the Conduct of the War, like the life of the Thirty-Seventh Congress, was now fast running out, and committee members were beginning to fear there would not be enough time to complete their investigations and write up their reports. General Charles P. Stone, probably the only innocent "victim" of the committee's investigation, was finally allowed to examine the testimony that had been given against him and, on the evening of February 27, 1863, so effectively rebutted it that the committee finally desisted in its campaign against him, though it made no apology for injury done.

Not so fortunate was General George McClellan, who, after being relieved from his command of the Army of the Potomac, had been ordered to his home in Trenton, New Jersey, to await further orders—orders that did not come. On February 19, the committee notified him that it desired to take his testimony. When McClellan wired back on February 23, asking to be told "upon what points the committee desire my testimony" so that he could "greatly facilitate their objects and save much time by refreshing my memory by consulting papers before starting," Wade responded that the committee wanted "information generally of your military administration. It is impossible to state all the points to which we may wish to call your attention in connexion with the testimony we now have."

When McClellan arrived on February 26, Wade and Odell were both absent, and, after some conversation among the rest of the committee, it was agreed to postpone McClellan's examination until February 27 to allow him to prepare a written submission. When he was again examined in person on February 28, and on March 2, Gooch served as the sole inquisitor as McClellan, hazy on the precise numbers of men involved, nevertheless crisply defended his command tactics. His testimony was printed with the report but not released to the press. Indeed, more space in the summary report was given to analysis of McClellan's errors by his subordinate, General John G. Barnard, who started with McClellan's long delay in moving the Army of the Potomac during the winter and spring of 1861–62. Having damned McClellan in the words of his subordinate, the summary report concluded that it was not necessary "to devote so much space to the campaign in Maryland. The same mind that controlled the movements upon the Peninsula controlled those in Maryland, and the same general features characterize the one campaign that characterize the other . . . unreadiness to move promptly and act vigorously; the same desire for more troops before advancing; and the same references to the great superiority of numbers on the part of the enemy."

In the closing days of the session, the committee chose to deal with the resolution of Senator Henry Wilson concerning Burnside, his plans, and the possibility of interference from his subordinates. That Burnside was having trouble with his subordinates, and especially with General Joseph Hooker and a group of his supporters, was obvious shortly after the new year had opened. Determined to cashier all his critics with one blow, Burnside had prepared dismissal orders for Generals Hooker, W. H. T. Brooks, John Newton, John Cochrane (for having gone over his head to complain directly to Lincoln), William B. Franklin, William F. ("Baldy") Smith, Samuel D. Sturgis and Edward Ferrero (whom he deemed "of no further service to this army").

When he had showed this order to Lincoln during a midnight visit to Washington on January 23-24, however, Lincoln had refused to approve it. Instead, on January 25 the President relieved Generals Edwin V. Sumner, W. B. Franklin, *and* Ambrose E. Burnside and transferred the command of the Army of the Potomac to the Radicals' "white hope," General Joseph E. Hooker. When this news was announced the committee promptly called for testimony from Burnside, Newton and Cochrane, as well as from Quartermaster General Montgomery Meigs, Major Generals Samuel P. Heintzelman and E. V. Sumner and Brigadier General W. W. Averill.

The brouhaha among the military was briefly summarized by the committee in its report. In his testimony before them Burnside complained that he had asked the President to accept his resignation from the Army if the President would not approve his order removing the offending subordinates; but Lincoln had refused to accept the resignation, though disapproving the order. Burnside was especially upset that, in issuing the order relieving him, Lincoln had stated that it was being done "at his own request," which, Burnside argued, was unjust to him and "unfounded in fact; but upon the representation that any other order would do injury to the cause, he consented to let it remain as it then read."

Seeing that they could not complete their work before March 3, on February 28 the committee instructed Chandler to introduce a concurrent resolution in the Senate, calling for the extension of the committee's duration and powers for thirty days beyond adjournment. The two houses approved the resolution on March 3, and it was agreed that the Senate members (consisting by this time only of Wade and Chandler) would complete the taking of testimony and write the final report. The House members announced that they would "be absent at their homes for two weeks."

Wade and Chandler worked until March 19, and between then and March 31 they, too, went home on vacation. The committee continued to meet in abbreviated form until April 1, then with all members present until its life expired on April 3. The report on Frémont's administration of the department of the west was finished and read to the entire group, but Gooch and Odell declined to sign it on the grounds that it was based on incomplete evidence. They did sign a statement which was attached to the report, however, saying that they preferred to submit the testimony "without any report thereon." It was one of the rare instances in which all the members were not in agreement on a report.

Having completed this work, the committee concluded its summary report with a review of all the Union triumphs which they felt had occurred since the fall of Fort Sumter: victories such as Grant's capture of Fort Donelson and Fort Henry, the fall of Memphis and New Orleans, the capture of Hatteras and Port Royal , the success of the blockade and of the government's efforts at raising money to cover war expenses. It was all whistling in the dark, but the committee thought these were hopeful signs. The report ended on an upbeat, if militant, note of praise for the army and a declaration of the national determination not to entertain "for a moment . . . the idea of a partition of our territory or . . . any base compromise with rebels."

V. The Committee During the Thirty-Eighth Congress

During the Thirty-Seventh Congress the committee was more or less trying its wings, its momentum provided largely by the personal indignation of Wade and Chandler at the way the early military engagements were fought and lost, and fueled by their personal animus toward General George B. McClellan. Thus, the topics of the investigations between 1861 and 1863 were fairly limited in scope, if not in words.

But when the Thirty-Eighth Congress met for its first session on December 7, 1863, the make-up of the House of Representatives had been markedly changed and reflected a mounting dissatisfaction with the war policies of the Administration. In the previous Congress there had been 43 Democrats and 30 representatives of smaller parties in opposition to 105 Republicans. Now the figures stood at 75 Democrats, only 9 members of smaller parties, and 102 Republicans.

The change in the Senate, where the number of Democrats fell from 10 to 9 and the number of Republicans increased to 36, suggested that a comfortable majority for the Administration party had survived. Despite the figures, the Administration was not assured of the support of *all* Republicans at *all* times, and this certainly would be true of the membership of the Joint Committee on the Conduct of the War. Though the House elections demonstrated that not everyone in the North was enchanted with the work of the Thirty-Seventh Congress, the demand for copies of the committee's reports required additional printings.

On Wednesday, January 13, 1864, therefore, Wade introduced—and asked for immediate consideration of—a concurrent resolution to reconstitute the Joint Committee on the Conduct of the War. Though Senator Solomon Foot of Vermont, the president *pro tem* of the Senate, tried to use parliamentary tactics to show its consideration, Vice President Hannibal Hamlin overruled him, and the resolution was sent to the House for approval.

The House returned the resolution a week later, on January 20, with an amendment, proposed by former Union General Robert Schenck of Ohio, that broadened Wade's original wording considerably. In addition to its charge "to inquire into the conduct and expenditures of the present war," the committee was now also to investigate "all the facts and circumstances of contracts and agreements already made, or that may be made" up to the time of the committee's final report. Further, the subpoena power to "send for persons and papers" which had been granted to the original committee was expanded to specify that the sergeant-at-arms of the Senate or House attend all committee meetings and "serve all subpoenas put in his hands by the committee, pay the fees of all witnesses, and the necessary and proper expenses of the committee." Furthermore, the subpoena power was not to be limited to times during which Congress was sitting but was to be vested in the Speaker of the House or the Vice President and President of the Senate so that they might "issue subpoenas to witnesses during the recess of Congress, upon the request of the committee, in the same manner as during the sessions of Congress"; and the Committee was to have the authority ". . . to report in either branch of Congress at any time."

On January 21, 1864, Vice President Hamlin reappointed Wade and Chandler to the committee and named Senator Benjamin F. Harding, an Oregon Democrat, to replace Indiana Senator Wright, who had earlier replaced Andrew Johnson. Speaker Schuyler Colfax of Indiana renominated Gooch, Julian and Odell and added Missouri emancipationist Benjamin F. Loan, as the representatives of the lower house.

During the course of the Thirty-Eighth Congress the committee addressed itself to an amazing miscellany of topics and published eight different reports, of which the longest—*Senate Report* Number 142—was itself divided into parts and covered a number of topics. Some idea of how varied and far-reaching was the scope of the committee's supervision of governmental affairs can be gained from a glance at a few of these topics.

First to appear, on April 11, 1864, was *Senate Report* Number 47, "On the Origin, Progess, and Results of the Late Expedition into Florida." This was followed on April 20 by *Senate Report* Number 54, "On the Military Administration of Alexandria, Va." ; on May 5 by *Senate Report* Number 63, "On the Fort Pillow Massacre" ; on May 9 by *Senate Report* Number 68, "On the Condition of Returned Union Prisoners" ; on December 15 by *Senate Report* Number 114, "On the Explosion of the Mine Before Petersburg" ; on February 11, 1865, by *Senate Report* Number 119, "On the Exchange of Prisoners" ; on February 13 by *Senate Report* Number 121, "On Heavy Ordnance" ; and the lengthy and varied *Senate Report* Number 142, which covered everything from ice contracts for Union military hospitals, to the expedition against Fort Fisher, to Banks's disastrous Red River campaign, to the treatment of rebel prisoners.

Some of these reports were extremely brief, running no more than a single page and simply indicating that the committee had followed up a congressional resolution calling for some investigation. Others, such as the reports on the Fort Pillow massacre and the treatment of returned Union prisoners, were lengthy and rather lurid, and their prompt publication and wide distribution were essentially propaganda activities in a presidential election year. For the leadership of the Joint Committee on the Conduct of the War not only found its old adversary George B. McClellan running for President on the Democratic ticket, it was also unhappy with the renomination of President Abraham Lincoln by the Republican Party. Chandler in particular—but Wade as well—worked hard to dump Lincoln after the President pocket-vetoed the stringent Reconstruction proposals endorsed by Wade and Radical Representative Henry Winter Davis—the Wade-Davis Bill of 1864.

All these political activities lay ahead, however, when the reconstituted committee accepted Stanton's invitation to meet with him at 8 P.M. on January 27, 1864. None of the participants left a record of this meeting, but the committee clerk was instructed to note that the group had met with the secretary of war "and had a very satisfactory interview with him, and agreed upon certain principles to govern the committee in their investigations." In the meantime, the first investigation of the new Congress had already been outlined in the January 25 motion of Massachusetts Senator Henry Wilson, who wanted to know what kind of heavy ordnance the government was buying and why delivery on contracts was so slow. On January 27 Congressman Gooch moved that the committee ask the Patent Office for information concerning "all patents for ordnance . . . now in use by the government, such information to embrace the dates of patents, subjects of patents, names of patentees, assignees &c." Wade was instructed to obtain this material.

Other congressional resolutions quickly stimulated committee interest in still more diverse avenues of inquiry. On February 2 Senator Wilson moved that the committee be instructed to inquire into the military administration of Alexandria, across the Potomac River from the Capitol, to see whether or not a "cruel and unusual character" of punishments was being inflicted on prisoners held in that place, and what happened to fines levied and collected there. Ten days later Chandler, Harding, Julian, Odell, and Loan traveled to Alexandria to see for themselves. The result was included in *Senate Report* Number 54, a four-page document issued on April 20, which concluded that the stories of cruel and unusual punishment were unfounded. Indeed, reported the committee, "the administration of General [John P.] Slough has been characterized by energy, discretion, and a careful regard for the peace and good order of the community over which he was appointed. . . ." General Slough deserved not criticism, the report concluded, but "the commendation of the military and civil authorities of our government."

Soon resolutions were offered for a dizzying variety of subjects: the ice contracts, as well as the operation of military hospitals, beginning on February 3; a request from Stanton for the committee to "investigate the operations of the quartermaster's department in the cities of New York and Philadelphia"; the February 29 resolution of Congressman Isaac N. Arnold of Illinois that the committee check on the possibility of using Confederate prisoners of war on public works so that "they may earn an honest livelihood while in our hands"; Congressman James Garfield's motion of the same day that the committee "inquire into and report on the practical operation of the trade regulations of September 11, 1863"—a suggestion to which Representative Frank Blair jr. of Missouri objected and on which he then demanded the "Yeas" and "Nays" because, as he heatedly put it, "I want to see how many there are in the House who wish to whitewash Mr. Chase." The vote showed that seventy-five members did, while only forty-three did not. In due time—but rather more time than was customary for more headline-grabbing topics—such a report was published.

On February 22 Congressman Gooch moved that a three-man subcommittee, which was to include Wade, be named to visit New York and Philadelphia to follow up Stanton's request for an investigation of the quartermaster's operations there. Though Wade begged off because of his wife's "sudden illness," Gooch and Odell were appointed. Wade suggested they all meet with Stanton at the War Department next day to go over the subject.

Meanwhile, the committee continued the examination of a variety of witnesses. Major General Dan Sickles, who felt he had been displaced when General George G. Meade was named commander of the Army of the Potomac the previous year and had been retained in that post despite his lack of follow-up action after Gettysburg, was a willing volunteer witness on February 25 and 26. Meade himself, who tended to look on the investigation as an imposition, appeared on March 5 amidst a string of subordinate generals from the Army of the Potomac.

While these witnesses were being heard, Senator Thomas Hendricks of Indiana had moved that the committee "inquire into the causes of, and circumstances attending, the recent military expedition into Florida. . . ."—a reference to the less than brilliant military maneuver against Olustee on February 20, in which Union forces had suffered a total of 1,828 casualties. The committee decided to ask Stanton and Halleck for details on this, and subsequently published a report.

Other requests for committee inquiries were apparently regarded as too time-consuming and of less pressing importance. Thus, consideration of Congressman Loan's motion that the committee investigate rumors of abuses in his home state of Missouri and a request from Pension Commissioner J. W. Edmunds "relative to the administration of affairs in Arkansas" were postponed. When word reached the committee, however, that the Reverend Henry Ward Beecher (who usually championed the committee in his weekly journal, the New York *Independent*), had, in a speech in London, charged that General Hooker "had been under the influence of intoxicating liquor" at the Battle of Chancellorsville, Wade was immediately directed to contact Beecher to ask the source of his information. Beecher later said he had made the statement in confidence to a temperance group on the authority of a source whose identity he was not free to reveal.

In the meantime, Hooker himself, apparently fearful that other generals of the Army of the Potomac might be maligning him in their testimony, wrote from east Tennessee (where he had been assigned after being relieved from his Potomac command), pleading that the committee call him as a witness. Chandler subsequently moved that Stanton be asked to order Hooker to Washington, but the secretary demurred.

The two most sensational investigations to be made by the committee still lay ahead. On April 18 the group was advised of a Senate resolution that they investigate "the truth of the rumored slaughter of the Union troops after their surrender at the recent attack of rebel forces upon Fort Pillow, Tennessee; and also whether Fort Pillow could have been evacuated or sufficiently reinforced; and, if so, why it was not done. . . ." After some discussion it was decided that Wade and Gooch would be appointed a subcommittee ". . . with authority to proceed to such place or places as they may deem necessary . . . and to take the stenographer of the committee with them, or employ one in his stead."

Wade and Gooch forthwith set out by train for Tennessee, stopping enroute to inspect the military hospital at Cairo, Illinois, to which some of the Fort Pillow survivors had been evacuated. That Wade's son James was serving with a unit then on duty in the Department of the Gulf was perhaps an added incentive for the chairman to undertake such a long investigative journey, but it is clear from the report that the fact that the slaughtered Union troops at Fort Pillow had been Black appealed to his deep-rooted sense of racial injustice.

In the chairman's absence (Wade and Gooch were gone until May 4), Chandler presided over two committee meetings. Wade was back in time to receive the communication of Brigadier General Henry C. Hoffman, the commissary of prisoners, urging the committee to hurry over to Annapolis to observe "the condition of prisoners recently returned from Richmond." The group resolved to go on Friday, May 6. On May 5 Wade and Gooch presented their report on the Fort Pillow affair. Seething with indignation over the barbarities reported by the team, the committee ordered that 60,000 copies of the report be printed—20,000 for members of the Senate and 40,000 for the members of the House to distribute to their constituents.

What the committee saw in Annapolis (Loan and Chandler had to be excused for reasons of official business, but the others all went) left them, if possible, even more outraged than had the events at Fort Pillow. In interviewing the survivors of that affair while he was in Cairo, Illinois, Wade had asked an artist to sketch some of the victims. Apparently feeling that there might be charges that such pictorial representations could be doctored to look worse than the victims actually did, in Annapolis Wade saw to it that a photographer took pictures of six very emaciated, obviously ill men who, his report would later state, had just been returned from a Richmond prison on one of the first flag-of-truce boats to operate since the breakdown of the prisoner cartel in 1862. Several of the photographs identified the unfortunate men, and each carried a caption noting that the victim had died within a few days after being photographed.

The effect that propping up desperately ill, near-nude patients long enough to be photographed by a mid-nineteenth century photographer may have had on their physical well-being weighed little in the balance against the propaganda possibilities of both the Annapolis and Fort Pillow reports in an election year. At one of the committee's last meetings before adjournment of the first session of the Thirty-Eighth Congress, it was moved that copies of the two reports be bound together for distribution to the public. Both reports charged the Confederates with unspeakable atrocities, and Wade wanted to repay such cruelties in kind to Confederate officer prisoners of the North. To his disgust, Senator Charles Sumner objected.

During the summer of 1864, the Joint Committee on the Conduct of the War met only once: on July 2, just before the session ended on July 4. At that time it was decided that "any two members of the committee shall be empowered to take testimony during the recess of Congress: *Provided*, That before doing so they shall notify in writing the other members of the committee of the time and place, when and where, they propose to take such testimony." Wade also laid before the group a Senate resolution of June 29, calling for the committee to "inquire what progress has been made in the construction of iron-clad steam gunboats contracted for in the year 1862. . . ." But no immediate action on this was called for. With this the committee adjourned until after the November elections, and its members scattered to participate in the campaign.

During this period Chandler worked so hard to block Lincoln's renomination and to substitute the old Radical hero Frémont as the Republican nominee that he seriously undermined his own health. Always a heavy drinker, apparently, Chandler must have imbibed to excess in those months for, on his return to Washington in November 1864 he was confined to his room under the care of a physician and he confided to his wife that the doctor recommended total abstinence, a course he said he would try to follow until the end of the second session.

When Congress returned to Washington on December 2 for the "Lame Duck" session of the Thirty-Eighth Congress, Wade called the committee into session again on December 13 in order to resume its investigations of a host of topics left over from the second session, as well as of some new subjects. Gooch and Odell were promptly appointed to a subcommittee to go to New York and Boston to follow up on the Senate's June 29 resolution concerning the gunboat contracts. Major General N. P. Banks, who had been ordered to Washington following his disastrous defeat in the Red River campaign in Louisiana, was summoned to appear before the committee at 10 A.M. on December 14 if he was still in town and "not otherwise occupied." From the Senate came two more resolutions calling for still other inquiries—one into charges that "large numbers of disloyal persons" were holding jobs in navy yards, quartermaster departments, and ordnance offices "throughout the country, to the exclusion of loyal men"; another into "the facts concerning the attack on Petersburg on the 30th day of July, 1864."

Apparently shelving permanently the resolution concerning disloyal employees, the committee joyfully returned to the scent of military mismanagement in the Army of the Potomac. On December 18, Chandler, Harding, Julian, Loan and the stenographer left Washington aboard the naval steamer *Baltimore* for City Point, Virginia. There they set up shop to take the on-the-spot testimony of Generals Meade, Franklin, O. B. Wilcox, G. K. Warren, Robert B. Potter, H. J. Hunt, E. O. C. Ord, and Edward Ferrero, and even that of Lieutenant General Ulysses S. Grant himself. The result of their efforts was *Senate Report* Number 114, in which they tried to assign the blame for the inopportune explosion of a huge mine in front of the town of Petersburg at the end of the preceding July. This affair had been part of an attempt to tunnel under the Confederate lines defending Richmond and to plant explosives that would blow up the Confederate forces. But the army engineers had miscalculated, and their mine had blown a huge crater *between* the lines of the Union and Confederate forces.

Inasmuch as Meade was still the commander of the Army of the Potomac, the committee was anxious to pin the blame for this fiasco on him—to Meade's considerable annoyance. A military court of inquiry, the findings of which were incorporated into *Senate Report* Number 114, had convened on August 2, 1864, on orders of Adjutant General E. D. Townsend, for the purpose of finding out if any officer had been to blame for the disaster. It had named no one. Now the politicians were reopening the investigation, and had come to the front lines to do it.

In the end Grant absolved Meade of all responsibility; but a number of junior officers were only too glad to tell the committee that they still felt the responsibility lay with the army commander. The committee's investigation had no effect on the command arrangements set up by Grant, however.

With the opening of 1865, the Joint Committee on the Conduct of the War was busy in almost every direction. Wade, Gooch, and Odell had gone to Boston, New York, and Philadelphia on December 17, 1864, to investigate naval contracts; but Wade reported on January 11 that, though they had interviewed eleven witnesses, they needed to take further testimony on the subject. At the same time, members of the committee continued to hear the testimony of General Banks and his aides about the Red River campaign; and on January 13, they resolved to follow up the Senate's January 12 resolution that they investigate the unsuccessful Union attempts, begun on Christmas Day, to capture Fort Fisher, near Wilmington, North Carolina.

On January 13 the committee concluded its examination of General Banks, and though criticism of the Red River campaign had been extremely hostile in the press and within the ranks of the army's officers, Banks was let off relatively lightly by a split report. The majority concluded that the Red River campaign was undertaken "without the direction of anyone," and without hope even by Banks that it would succeed; that it was attended by disaster and "conducted without capacity or discipline"; and that Banks's allowing cotton speculators to accompany the expedition and his conducting state elections in the Army's camps was "clearly a usurpation on the part of the military authorities . . . ." Gooch, in his minority report, nevertheless exonerated his fellow Bay Stater. The holding of elections, Gooch argued, had not "caused the slightest delay to the movements of the army or navy, or influenced or controlled the expedition in the slightest degree." Banks himself felt he had come through the ordeal safely and eagerly awaited his reassignment to Louisiana.

His predecessor in the post of commander of the Department of the Gulf, Major General Benjamin F. Butler, had been the leader of the equally ill-fated expedition against Fort Fisher. When he was asked to appear before the committee on January 17, Butler arrived with a massive stack of documents and put on a dazzling performance that left the committee not only convinced of his innocence in the Fort Fisher attack but even impressed by his presumed military brilliance.

Throughout the rest of January and into February the committee's investigations pushed on. As the life of the Thirty-Eighth Congress ebbed, its members began to hold night sessions as well as the usual afternoon ones, a practice which Chandler, still weak and underweight from his illness, found very tiring. Finally the extra session of the Senate, necessary for the upper house to complete action on last-minute legislation sent up from the House of Representatives, came to an end, and the Senate adjourned *sine die*.

Prior to adjournment, both houses had approved a concurrent resolution extending the life of the Joint Committee on the Conduct of the War for ninety days in order that the committee could "complete their investigation of certain important matters now before them, and which they have not been able to complete, by reason of inability to obtain important witnesses. . . . " Thus, the committee would continue to meet and to examine witnesses through the rest of March.

On March 27, on Julian's motion, the sergeant-at-arms of the Senate was instructed to make arrangements for the committee to go to North Carolina "or wherever they may deem necessary, to take the testimony of officers in the field." The members had been discussing this trip since early March, but had encountered difficulty in getting transportation for themselves from the Navy Department. The war was winding down by this time, and the members looked forward to the trip almost as an excursion. Those whose wives were with them in Washington were to be allowed to bring the ladies along, and all concerned anticipated a bracing sea voyage, a restful change and plenty of interesting sights. By April 6 Chandler, who had made a hurried trip home to Detroit but was unable to persuade his wife to return with him to Washington, was reporting to her that the plans had been altered so that the group would go south by way of Richmond, which had been occupied by the troops of Major General Godfrey Weitzel on April 3.

The committee finally left Washington at 2 P.M. on Tuesday, April 11. Lee had surrendered to Grant at Appomattox two days before, but there had been no word of other surrenders yet. So the sergeant-at-arms had equipped each of the members "with a fine Spencer rifle, with belt, rigging, ammunition etc. and a Colt's navy revolver"—equipment which George W. Julian felt would assure his going home "bristling with war and glory!" The group reached Fortress Monroe at 6 A.M. on April 12, and there learned that the naval vessel *Alabama* would not be ready to take them on to Charleston for twenty hours while it took on coal. But they were told by Admiral David Dixon Porter that they could proceed upriver to Richmond if they were willing to risk what Julian referred to as "the torpedoes," by which he probably meant mines. The group apparently agreed cheerfully to the risk in exchange for the opportunity to sightsee in the capital of the defeated enemy.

That night they slept on the boat, "lulled by the music of the guitar and the singing of the negroes below," reported Julian, who also said he had "slept sweetly [on his] first night in Richmond." The next day at 8 A.M. the group, including the ladies, set out in carriages and on horseback to see the city, guided by a personal orderly for each of them. They visited Weitzel's headquarters (in the house just vacated by Jefferson Davis), the Confederate Capitol, Libby Prison (Julian could not bring himself to inspect the "dungeons" there "where our poor boys suffered so much," which were then occupied by Confederate prisoners), and the rebel fortifications around the city. Julian certainly—and presumably the others on the committee, too—found it all fascinating.

A note of annoyance was introduced just as the group returned to their ship when they read in the Richmond *Whig* that General Weitzel had invited the original pre-secession Virginia legislature to meet in Richmond on April 25 "to confer with us on the restoration of peace. . . ." The committee, reported Julian, was "thunderstruck," and he added, "I never before saw such force and fitness in Ben Wade's swearing. Curses loud and deep were uttered by more than one at this infamous proposition to treat with leading rebels."

By Friday morning, April 14, the group had reassembled at Fortress Monroe, still aboard their original vessel, the *Baltimore*. Enroute down the river they had decided not to go on to Charleston after all, but to return to Washington. "Wade would not go. Chandler refused and, in fact, never intended to go, doing all he could to prevent the trip," Julian recounted.

"Gooch would not go without Wade, and so the thing was given up, much to the chagrin of our party, who had set their hearts upon seeing Charleston." Presumably the "party" to whom he referred consisted of Julian and the ladies.

The members of the committee were very tired when they returned to the capital that night, and Julian went to bed at 10:30. Almost immediately he was aroused by a housemate who told him that "Lincoln was murdered, and Seward and son probably, and that assassins were about to take the town."

The assassination of President Lincoln caused a major shift in emphasis in the investigations and activities of the Joint Committee on the Conduct of the War. Though the committee still had another six weeks of life, and though it did sternly quiz General Weitzel on his "infamous order" and demanded an explanation from Major General William T. Sherman of the generous surrender terms he had granted to Confederate General Joseph E. Johnston, it was clear that all the members now had other things on their minds.

Most reassuring as the life of the committee ran out was the succession of their old colleague, Andrew Johnson of Tennessee, to the presidency. Though Chandler had told his wife with disgust that, at the Inauguration of Lincoln, Johnson had been "too drunk to perform his duties and had disgraced himself & the Senate by making a drunken foolish speech . . ." even he joined Wade and the other leading Radicals in rejoicing that Johnson was now in the White House. With the fighting over, Radical interest shifted from military campaigns and contracts to the question of Reconstruction. Lincoln had appeared to be an obstacle to Radical plans while he was alive; Wade and his friends were sure that Johnson would not be. After all, when he had served with them on the committee during the Thirty-Seventh Congress he had been the most militant and critical of the War Democrats.

Cheered by this thought, the committee wrote the new President, assuring him of their friendship, inviting him to their remaining meetings, and requesting—and getting—an early interview with him. The business of the committee was now wound up quickly. Officers whom they had not been able to interview in person were asked to fill out written interrogatories. Sherman appeared on May 22, and satisfied them that he had not done anything to help the detested rebels in his agreement with Johnston. When Sherman concluded his testimony, the Joint Committee on the Conduct of the War—by this time consisting only of Wade and Loan—declared its business concluded.

VI. The Committee and the Public

During the more than three years in which the committee had met, heard testimony, and written up its reports, only a few members of the general public had actually had firsthand information on what it had been doing. The fact that its meetings were held in secrecy and that witnesses were forbidden to discuss their testimony with the press had kept all but a few scraps of news from reaching the public unless Wade and his colleagues chose that they should have it. As a result, congressional correspondents of newspapers such as the *New York Tribune* could discover little but the general nature of the topics referred to the committee for investigation. The conclusions of such major reports as *Senate Report* Number 108 (on the Army of the Potomac) were now published so that the public could learn what the gist of the inquiry had been and, depending on the political bias of a particular newspaper, what its editors thought of the committee's work. If the public wished to know more, they could address a request to their senator or representative for copies of the reports, and many individuals apparently did so.

Readers of the *New York Tribune*, which was extremely sympathetic to the Radical viewpoint, were able to read the entire "Summary Report on the Army of the Potomac in 1863." The *Tribune* devoted most of its available columns for several days to this report, and even offered inexpensive reprints to its readers. But the Washington *National Intelligencer*, a journal of more Democratic leanings, chose merely to summarize the report's findings on the grounds that the whole thing would take up too much room. Its editor also made sharply critical comments on the validity of some of the testimony summarized in the report. But the testimony itself was not released to the press, so that editors could only express in print their regret at not being able to see it.

Generalized and sketchy as all this information was, the electorate seems to have been aware of the overall responsibilities of the committee. Wade especially, but Chandler too, received numerous letters, both from approving constituents and from citizens in the nation at large, urging continued vigorous prosecution of the committee's investigations. Many correspondents suggested new avenues of investigation, but once *Senate Report* Number 108 had appeared at the end of the Thirty-Seventh Congress, other members of Congress kept the committee busy following up leads they sent along in resolution form, and tips from citizens assumed little importance.

Not all Americans approved of what the committee was doing—certainly not the 1,805,063 who voted for McClellan in the presidential election of 1864—44.9 percent of all the votes cast, and probably not all of the 2,219,362 who voted for Lincoln. But a sufficiently large percentage of the population clearly did approve and apparently told their legislators so, for the Joint Committee on the War to enjoy a remarkably long life for a controversial investigative committee.

If the general public's attitudes were based on limited access to information about the committee, a smaller but still substantial group derived very decided opinions about the committee's activities from direct contact. These were the military men who appeared before it as witnesses. Given Wade's ruthless disregard for the Fifth Amendment, it is surprising that any supporters of the committee could be found among these officers; but some of them, such as Hooker, Sickles, Butterfield, Butler, and Doubleday, were willing witnesses and looked to the committee to redress whatever grievances they harbored. Most of the military, however, bitterly resented the committee's investigations as unwarranted and totally undeserved interference. Of these, perhaps the reactions expressed by General George Meade were among the mildest. Certainly McClellan's were the strongest.

When Meade was called to testify concerning the Battle of Fredericksburg in March 1863, he wrote his wife, "I am very sorry I have been called, because my relations and feelings toward all parties have been of the most friendly character, and I shall be sorry to become involved in any way in the controversies growing out of this affair." Later, after he had been interrogated by "old

Ben Wade," Meade told his wife he thought the committee was determined to pin the blame for the defeat at Fredericksburg on Franklin and that they were "seeking all the testimony they can procure to substantiate this theory of theirs." That Meade had not tried to dissuade them from attacking Franklin is clear, as is his reason for not trying. "I sometimes feel very nervous about my position, they are knocking over generals at such a rate," he wrote, adding that Major General Horatio G. Wright, whom he had "picked out as the most rising man," had been forced out of the army because he had tried to steer a middle course between "the extremists of Ohio (anti-slavery) and those of Kentucky (pro-slavery). . . ." Later, he said he had tried to put in a good word for Franklin with Lincoln; but he did not argue with the committee.

When Meade was called to appear before the committee a second time in 1864, to testify on the Petersburg mine incident, he again found himself alone with Wade, who "was very civil, denied there were any charges against me, but said the committee was making up a sort of history of the war. . . ." Meade spent three hours outlining his actions at Gettysburg, and then saw Stanton, who hinted that Chandler really wanted to see Hooker put back in command. Meade consoled himself with the thought that this move would not succeed. "The only evil that will result is the spreading over the country [of] certain mysterious whisperings of dreadful deficiencies on my part, the truth concerning which will never reach the thousandth part of those who hear the lies."

Meade, like McClellan and Franklin, was a Democrat, and he did get the sympathy of Senator B. F. Harding, the one Democratic senator on the committee at that time. Meade regarded the efforts to have him relieved of the command of the Army of the Potomac as "nothing less than a conspiracy, in which the Committee on the Conduct of the War, with Generals Doubleday and Sickles, are the agents."

Later Meade reported more favorably on the committee, with some exceptions, telling his wife on March 14, 1864, that he had had another interview with Wade about Gettysburg, and that the Senator had taken "great pains to endeavor to convince me that the committee were not responsible for the newspaper attacks on me, and I might rest assured there was no disposition on their part to do me injustice." He added that he had learned it was Senators Chandler and Wilkinson who were his foes, that Wade was "rather friendly, and that Harding of the Senate, Gooch and Odell of the House, were my warm friends."

Meade was remarkably explicit in telling his wife of his experiences before the committee, and probably violated the secrecy agreement to which witnesses were expected to subscribe. He was fortunate at the time, however: of all the correspondents to whom he wrote in any way about his appearances before the group, only Democratic Senator Reverdy Johnson of Maryland violated his confidence by showing his letter to a newsman, who subsequently published portions of it.

Of the other officers who were called as witnesses, most were careful to print no details of their testimony while the war was going on, and many never did afterward. McClellan consistently referred to the Radicals in general and committee members in particular as "those hounds," or worse. But he did not speak of individuals, even though he must have known that Chandler was carrying on a vendetta against him.

Franklin, who was also an object of Chandler's hatred, wrote bitterly of what must have been a distressing experience. But Banks, who skinned by in accounting for his failure along Red River, assured his wife that he felt he had done very well in his appearance before the committee.

VII. Conclusion

Was the committee as bad as the press it has had since the Civil War period? Did it help or hinder the war effort? Did it produce any legislation —always the ostensible purpose of congressional investigations?

To the first of these questions, it would be safe to answer that, despite its often outrageous treatment of witnesses and its partisan disregard for the constitutional rights of many military men, the faults displayed by the Joint Committee on the Conduct of the War were no worse than those of some other congressional investigations. The personal animus toward such generals as McClellan, Franklin, and Porter was not consonant with the view of statesmanlike conduct accepted either at the time or now; but there is no evidence that it impeded the war effort or resulted in the removal from national service of any military commander of such surpassing brilliance that the war would have ended sooner had he been kept in command.

Generals such as McClellan, Franklin, and Porter were treated very unfairly. But McClellan had a personality flawed by traits that were disastrous in a military commander. Franklin and Porter were brave and honest officers, but neither had displayed unusual talents. The often-recalled injustice to General Charles Stone was, of course, an unforgivable trampling of his civil, constitutional, and personal rights; but it would be hard to make the point that this in any way prolonged the war, or even that it did irreparable damage to the morale of any of the military or civilians who were misled by the charges. The Executive branch played at least as large a role as did the committee in the perpetration of injustice in that it made no serious effort to exonerate Stone, or even to free him from harassment by the committee.

If the committee did little damage to the war effort by attacking truly competent generals, its support of less-than-able generals such as Butler, Frémont, Pope, and Hooker did very little to help. Indeed, its partisanship for generals willing to join the Radical chorus seems to have encouraged a natural tendency to factionalism and divisiveness that often characterizes the military in areas affected by the political arm.

As to positive results of its investigations, especially in the way of new legislation, the Joint Committee on the Conduct of the War was truly a "mountain which labored and delivered a mouse." After meeting 272 times over a period of three-and-one-half years, it produced only one piece of legislation—a bill allowing President Lincoln to take over the operation of the railroads for government needs. This was proposed and passed early in the war. No other legislation came out of the hours of interrogation and the reams of reports.

Yet the Joint Committee on the Conduct of the War was a significant example of Congress sincerely trying to oversee the actions of the general government during an important crisis. That this turned into an attempt by one branch of a government to dominate the others was in all probability not intentional from the start. And if the members of the committee were too careless in brushing aside individual constitutional rights as not allowable in wartime, they could look to the Executive branch which, in suspending the writ of *habeas corpus,* certainly endorsed the validity of such a view.

Insofar as Lincoln's reaction to the committee was concerned, in fact, though he may have found its actions annoying after a while, he was blessed with a sense of humor certain members of the committee lacked, and kept his perspective. Nowhere did he complain of any infringement on the rights of the office of the President. Nowhere did he attempt to lecture the committee and, through it the Congress, on the limits of its power—though the Radical leaders were more than willing to tell him how weak they considered him to be.

In the end, aside from reaffirming the right of Congress, as the elected representatives of the American people, to supervise expenditures by the Executive branch of the people's tax monies—and aside, perhaps, from establishing the outer limits to which a congressional investigation might go in trampling individual civil rights—the Joint Committee on the Conduct of the War accomplished nothing either of immediate good or of lasting significance.

BIBLIOGRAPHY

The most detailed and comprehensive study of the work of the Joint Committee on the Conduct of the War can be found in T. Harry Williams, *Lincoln and the Radicals* (Madison, Wis., 1941). Though this work examines the entire relationship between Lincoln and the Radical leaders, its principal focus is on their activities in the committee.

An excellent picture of the activities of the group's chairman is to be found in Hans L. Tréfousse, *Benjamin Franklin Wade* (New York, 1963). Sister Mary Karl George also devotes extensive coverage to Chandler's role in the committee in her *Zachariah Chandler: A Political Biography* (East Lansing, Mich., 1971).

PERTINENT DOCUMENTS

Debate on Resolution to Establish Committee on the Conduct of the War, December 5 and 9, 1861

Testimony of General William B. Franklin, December 26, 1861

Testimony of General Fitz-John Porter, December 28, 1861

Report on Treatment by Rebels of the Remains of the Union Troops at Manassas, April 30, 1862

E. B. Ward to Benjamin F. Wade, February 7, 1863

Testimony of Major-General George B. McClellan, February 28 and March 2, 1863

Testimony of General Joseph Hooker, March 11, 1863

Report of the Joint Committee on the Conduct of the War (Army of the Potomac), April 6, 1863

Report on the Fort Pillow Massacre, May 5, 1864

Testimony of Ulysses S. Grant on Petersburg Disaster, December 20, 1864

Report on Explosion of the Mine before Petersburg, February 10, 1865

Report on Exchange of Prisoners (Testimony of Ulysses S. Grant), February 11, 1865

Joint Committee on Reconstruction
1865

U.S. Signal Corps photo (Brady Collection)

Thaddeus Stevens fought to make the defeated South pay the cost of the Civil War.

Joint Committee on Reconstruction 1865

by W. Allan Wilbur

Few investigating committees played as important a role in determining the political and economic relationship between the Executive branch of government and the United States Congress as did the Joint Committee on Reconstruction. That committee wrote the Fourteenth Amendment to the Constitution of the United States as part of the first congressional attempt to reconstruct the Union after the Civil War. In one of those curious tricks often played in human events, the Fourteenth Amendment became the constitutional shield of industrial capitalism against effective economic regulation in the years following its ratification. The due process and equal protection clauses of the Fourteenth Amendment did not protect those it was originally intended to protect until nearly a century later.

The forces and motivations that lay behind the Amendment are inextricably intertwined in the history of the committee itself and in the background of the Reconstruction era. It is to the latter story that one must turn first to comprehend the purpose of the Joint Committee on Reconstruction and its handiwork—the Fourteenth Amendment.

I

The reconstruction of the Union in 1865 would have been a difficult task for any President. While the Civil War had secured the abolition of slavery, guaranteed the triumph of nationalism, and ensured the supremacy of the modern industrial order, the armed conflict created as many difficulties as it had resolved.

The abolition of slavery and the emancipation of four million human beings resulted in a tremendous social upheaval in the South. Lacking formal education, having no material resources, and facing endemic racial prejudice—in the North as well as in the South—the freedman was the pawn in an economic, social, and political dilemma. Neither the Congress nor the Chief Executive was adequately prepared to face the vital matter of how to implement the guarantees of citizenship to the ex-slave.

The triumph of nationalism spawned disagreement over the readmission of the seceded states. With Lee's surrender on April 9 and the final capitulation of all Confederate forces on May 29, civilian government ceased to exist in a large portion of the South. Lincoln had stated that the war had been waged to preserve the Union and to vindicate the supremacy of the federal government—in a word, to prove the impossibility of secession. Radical Republicans in Congress, seeking a more thoroughgoing social revolution in Southern society, disagreed with the President's definition of the purpose of the war. Thus, a political controversy exploded over the status of the Confederate states and raised important constitutional questions. If states could not secede under the Constitution, were they not still part of the Union? And if the states were in the Union, what was the proper method to restore normal relations with the federal government? The gap between the views of President Lincoln and members of Congress over reconstruction widened during the course of the war, but in the spring of 1865 it was not an unbridgeable chasm.

Tragedy intervened on April 14. The assassination of Lincoln removed the one man capable of managing the factions within the Republican party. Lincoln's own plans for reconstruction had remained vague, but his skill in party management, his wartime leadership, and his popularity in Unionist circles at the close of the war would have been invaluable assets in the resolution of the emerging conflict between the President and a restless Congress determined to reduce Executive power and play a larger role in reconstruction. The elevation of Andrew Johnson to the presidency sharply reduced prospects for an amicable mediation of the differences between Congress and the Executive.

Other circumstances prevented an easy settlement of the reconstruction program along the lines Lincoln expounded. The problem of reconstruction did not receive the nation's full attention until after 1865. Had the Congress and the President cooperated and compromised fully with one another, the difficulties inherent in securing the freedman his rights and in restoring the rebel states to the Union were, even under the best circumstances, nearly insurmountable. But, despite a plethora of congressional oratory, reconstruction was not the singular concern of the nation. The mood of the nation was discerned in other events, particularly the rapid demobilization of military forces after the war. Southern forces disbanded immediately, the Northern armies demobilized nearly as rapidly. By September 1867, the Union army had a total strength of 56,875 officers and men. Peace was welcomed by nearly everyone, North and South.

Exhausted by the war, most Americans set about the business of making a living. The energies of the nation concentrated not so much upon the problem of reconstruction as they did upon the search for, and enjoyment of, prosperity. The economic cycles of boom and depression in the years between 1865 and 1877 absorbed the nation's attention. Moreover, the dilemma of reconstruction occurred in a time of rapid industrial expansion and consolidation. In oil, steel, railroads, meat packing, flour milling industries, and in finance capitalism itself, business moved toward consolidation.

Political collisions between farmers, labor, and business during the era of Reconstruction did not lead to the formation of stable and cohesive political interest blocs. On many issues (and some non-issues) the various interest groups exhibited a diversity of views, motives, and intentions that belied any cohesive expression of their purposes. The economic dimension of the reconstruction conflict was not a clear-cut sectional or class struggle. It was a contest between opposing groups of bankers, farmers, investors, industrialists, and labor fought out on both intra- and inter-sectional lines. The changes which took place during reconstruction, as David Donald and James G. Randall have observed, "affected Northern views of the Southern question and kept the best brains in the nation from squarely facing the problem of reconstruction."

The South was devastated by the war—plantations wrecked, billions of dollars invested in slave property wiped out by emancipation, banks shattered and without investment capital, factories in ruin, the transportation network devastated, and the great cities, Atlanta, Columbia, Mobile, and Richmond in shambles. Veterans returned to find their homesteads destroyed and their families impoverished. The harsh reality of defeat, coupled with the elevation of the black man to a freed status, presented enormous social and economic difficulties south of the Mason-Dixon. But while the outlook was grim, Southerners began a difficult but steady adjustment to new conditions. Both races set about rebuilding the region with impressive alacrity.

Reconstruction cannot be understood wholly in terms of legal and constitutional issues. Contemporaries made ambiguous and often contradictory statements about their purposes. The South fought heroically for independence; yet with defeat Southern men claimed they had never been legally apart from the Union. On the other hand, Radical Republicans, who had tried to prevent secession, now announced that the Southern states had seceded and thereby abrogated their rights. They became conquered provinces to be treated as Congress saw fit. As the disagreement between the President and the Congress grew more intense, the principal spokesmen wrapped themselves in the mantle of the Constitution to give legal justification to their respective positions. Both the President and the Congress found solace there, but the truth of the matter was that both branches had employed extra-constitutional means—the President by appointing military governors for the Southern states and the Congress by imposing conditions upon suffrage in the South.

The roots of Lincoln's reconstruction proposals began in the midst of war, when federal troops overran the South and it became necessary to reestablish civil government. However, Lincoln's reconstruction programs were stopgap measures and the President kept an open mind on the subject, constantly refining his views on the matter. These views were the result of the exigency of wartime. In Maryland and Kentucky federal troops upheld the Unionist government. In Missouri Lincoln approved the policy followed by the Union military commanders who reassembled a Missouri convention, declared all state offices vacant, and then appointed Hamilton R. Gamble to the governor's post. A further adaptation came in 1862 when Lincoln appointed Andrew Johnson governor of Tennessee and gave him "such powers as may be necessary and proper to enable the loyal people of Tennessee to present such a republican form of State government, as will entitle the State to the guaranty of the United States therefore, and be protected under such State government, by the United States against invasion and domestic violence."

The ten percent plan proclaimed on December 8, 1863 was a more general formulation of reconstruction procedures. The President offered pardon, with some exceptions, to those Confederate supporters who would swear an oath to the Constitution of the United States and renounce disunion sentiments. Where a sufficient member of citizens of a state (equal to one-tenth of the popular votes cast in the presidential election of 1860) qualified by taking the oath and, in establishing a state government, agreed to abolish slavery, Lincoln promised Executive recognition of the government.

Opposition to Lincoln's program of easy restoration among Radical Republicans led to the passage of the Wade-Davis Bill (July 2, 1864). Led by Henry Winter Davis, Benjamin Wade, Zachariah Chandler, George W. Julian, Thaddeus Stevens, and Charles Sumner, the Radical Republicans proposed a harsher measure than Lincoln's ten percent plan. The Wade-Davis Bill stipulated that under the authority of the provisional governor an enrollment of white male citizens was to be made. If a majority of white citizens enrolled took an oath to support the Constitution, the loyalists were then to select members for a constitutional convention to launch a new state government. All Confederates who had held office in the state or the Confederate government, or who had served in the armed forces of the Confederacy, were not permitted to be delegates to the convention.

The bill called for the repudiation of the rebel debt and prohibited slavery in the states. It ensured that power in the former Confederacy was entrusted to a majority whose loyalty was a matter of record, while the Lincoln plan pledged support to a minority ready for future loyalty. In either case power remained in the hands of a relatively few persons, supported by the Union army.

Lincoln and the Congress locked horns on the Wade-Davis Bill. The differences between the President and the Congress were so fundamental that Lincoln pocket vetoed the legislation. To placate Radical opposition, the President issued a proclamation announcing his disapproval of the Wade-Davis Bill, but iterated that any state wishing to adopt the provisions of the bill was at liberty to do so. He also agreed to direct provisional governors to implement the recommendations of the Wade-Davis Bill in any state which might adopt them.

Lincoln's proclamation—signalling his readiness to give effect to a bill that never became law—left the South with two alternatives: they could adopt the ten percent plan, which rejected the idea of disenfranchisement of leading citizens, or the Radical program, which advocated disenfranchisement and included other obnoxious features. Reconstruction under Lincoln's plan was carried forward in Tennessee, Arkansas, Louisiana, and Virginia, but it did not successfully resolve the dilemma of how to maintain a loyal Union government and win the confidence of the population in any of those states.

Louisiana produced a constitution that prohibited slavery by a popular vote of 6,836 to 1,566—more than ten percent of the voters in 1860 had accepted the document. Lincoln extended support to the new government and treated it as if it were restored to the Union. The validity of its elections to state and federal offices was challenged, however, and the issue of Louisiana's representation in the federal Congress remained unsettled at Lincoln's death.

The ten percent plan proved unworkable in Arkansas. In March 1864 a pro-Union constitution was adopted by a vote of 12,177 to 266, drawn from a total of 54,000 eligible voters in 1860. The election and the convention were irregular proceedings and the election results never proved satisfactory to Congress, even though Arkansas abolished slavery. On June 29, 1864 the United States Senate denied seats to the two Arkansas senators, claiming Arkansas was not as yet entitled to representation.

Tennessee had been under the rule of military governor Andrew Johnson since 1862. Although one faction in the state claimed that the measures taken by him to ensure compliance and loyalty were irregular, Johnson performed the tasks of governor throughout the remainder of the war. In September 1864 and again in January 1865, a state convention met to draw up a constitution, but a significant proportion of the states' electorate denied its authority to create a constitution for the whole state. Nevertheless, the convention members recommended amendments to abolish slavery and repudiate the secession resolutions. On February 12, 1865 the amendments were ratified and on March 4, W. G. ("Parson") Brownlow was chosen governor. Prior to his assumption of the vice presidency, Johnson issued a proclamation claiming that Tennessee had acted in accordance with the President's reconstruction program.

However, because of irregularities in choosing presidential electors in 1864, the electoral votes of Tennessee were not tabulated in 1865. The situation in Tennessee remained confused at the time of Lincoln's death. The state had delegates in the House of Representatives in the Thirty-Seventh Congress (1861–1863), but had neither congressmen nor senators in the Thirty-Eighth (1863–1865). Lincoln had planned to have Johnson appoint the United States senators but the proposition was never carried out. In early December 1865, when the Thirty-Ninth Congress assembled, Tennessee was denied representation, even though one of its citizens was President of the United States.

Conditions in Virginia led to the creation of a "restored government" with its capital in Alexandria. The government established a state constitution which abolished slavery and altered the franchise to ensure the election of loyal citizens. Virginia sought full recognition towards the end of the war, but representation in the government at Washington was denied. In the Thirty-Eighth Congress Virginia had no representation in the House and in the two succeeding Congresses it went unrepresented in both houses of Congress. When reconstruction finally came in Virginia, the restored government under Francis H. Pierpoint was ignored, despite the fact that the Pierpoint government had negotiated the separation of the western part of the state to create West Virginia and had been considered competent to perform other such tasks.

Lincoln's plan for reconstruction never went into full effect in any state.

Indeed, the concessions to the Radicals in Congress undoubtedly underscored Lincoln's apprehension about the effectiveness of his ideas. The partial recognition of the Wade-Davis proposal in 1864 and his decision to sign, under protest, the joint resolution excluding the electoral count from all eleven states of the former Confederacy, including those states he regarded as having fulfilled the requirements of his own program, were two indications of the President's anxiety and uncertainty about the future of reconstruction.

It was clear that Lincoln sought a "proper, practical relation with the Union" for the South. His course was a pragmatic one, preferring to work with Unionist elements in the states, tolerate irregularities, and try to improve the state governments, rather than reject them and dishearten Union sympathizers there. Lincoln sacrificed legal perfection to practicality, and his program rested upon the exercise of Executive and military power in the South, a power the President hoped would soon be replaced by home rule. He overlooked imperfections in the name of a rapid and benevolent reconstruction.

But wartime reconstruction failed to achieve restoration and it failed to clarify the guiding principles for the Administration. The Chief Executive and the Congress worked at cross-purposes and the subject remained deadlocked in April 1865. The effort to restore the states rapidly, while sentiment for such an event was strong among both the victors and the vanquished, was lost.

II

Andrew Johnson became President with less rancor than one might have expected in those times. He retained Lincoln's cabinet, perhaps in retrospect an error in judgment, as at least two of its members were sympathetic to the Radicals. Johnson had begun as an impoverished, orphaned and self-educated man in Greenville, Tennessee. Soon the lure of politics attracted him and he had risen rapidly in state politics as alderman, mayor, state legislator, state senator, congressman, governor, and United States senator. An ardent Jacksonian, Johnson's democracy was consistent with the social and racial thinking of his time. To his mind, Negroes formed no part of the body politic; he condoned slavery and acquired several servants. When the Civil War and secession crisis arose in Tennessee, the state was split. The middle and western sections favored the retention of slavery while the eastern portion of the state opposed it.

When Tennessee seceded after the firing on Sumter, Johnson was the only senator from a disloyal state to declare his loyalty to the Union. Upon the expiration of his term as senator in 1862, Lincoln appointed him military governor of Tennessee. Two years later the Republican party, seeking to emphasize its Unionist character and to ward off an internal schism, nominated Johnson for the vice presidency. Lincoln's election victory in 1864 made Andrew Johnson, a Tennessee Union Democrat, Vice President of the United States. Six months later, an assassin's bullet made him President.

It was Andrew Johnson's character and personality which brought him into collision with the Radicals. As a backwoods stump politician, Johnson made a poor start when, as the vice president elect, he delivered a rambling, incoherent, harangue at Lincoln's second inaugural. It was evident to all that Johnson was intoxicated, although he was not normally a heavy drinker.

When party struggles over reconstruction became heated, the President's opponents revived and embellished the incident, falsely labelling him a drunkard. Moreover, Johnson sought the counsel of Montgomery Blair, Lincoln's former postmaster general, whose conservative views on reconstruction were well known and despised by the Radicals. Johnson soon became a President without a party.

Lincoln had had the support of a significant proportion of the Republican party and had enjoyed popular prestige as Commander in Chief of the victorious Union cause. He had maneuvered his political enemies with adroitness, patience, and skill. Johnson, on the other hand, did not possess the same political acumen. He lacked patience and flexibility; he tended to be both stubborn and blunt with his political contemporaries. In the wake of the assassination, the new President obviously felt compelled to act more deliberately and forcefully, as if to emphasize the continuity of government and demonstrate his own capacity to govern.

Johnson's first statements on reconstruction sounded radical. He told a New Hampshire delegation shortly after taking office that "treason is a crime . . . and must be punished as a crime. . . . It must not be excused as an unsuccessful rebellion to be . . . forgiven." As a former member of the Radical-controlled Joint Committee on the Conduct of the War, he was expected to inaugurate a firmer policy toward the South. When Johnson took over the presidential duties, Benjamin F. Wade, chairman of the committee remarked, "By the gods, there will be no trouble now in running the government."

The President's initial comments were misleading, for Andrew Johnson considered the preservation of the Union the cardinal purpose of reconstruction. He believed the continued occupation of the South by Union forces an unwise policy because it divided the people and engendered hatreds, all at a considerable expense to the national government. And while the war had ended slavery, unlike some Radicals who saw in victory an opportunity to obtain social and political equality for the black man, Johnson remained unsympathetic to the cause of civil rights for the freedmen.

There were substantial political questions involved as well. Radicals considered the question of Southern representation in Congress an important issue touching upon the political future of the Republican party. The readmission of Southern representatives to Congress would soon augment Democratic strength and give the "party of rebellion" a majority in the national government. Radicals could not be expected to permit themselves to be turned out of power or to allow the wartime gains of the North to be undone. The fear of the loss of political and economic power, coupled with the idea that the defeated section could regain in Congress what it had lost on the battlefield, was at the root of the disagreement over reconstruction policy. Moreover, with the lapse of the Three-Fifths Compromise (in which three-fifths of the slaves had been counted as population in the determination of representation to Congress), all ex-slaves would be tabulated, thus affording the South greater political leverage than before the war. Radical Republicans and their moderate colleagues in both houses resisted any policy amounting to political suicide, but they wished to compromise with the Chief Executive rather than become embroiled and deadlocked on reconstruction. President

Johnson considered restoration an Executive, not a legislative, function, and he minimized the significance of the fact of political survival facing the Republican party.

Was responsibility for the reconstruction of the Southern states a presidential or a congressional function? Put succinctly, did Congress or the President have greater legal basis to control the reconstruction program? Many historians have attempted to answer the question by assigning responsibility for reconstruction to one branch or the other. A sounder view of the matter suggests that both the President and Congress were responsible and should have cooperated. Indeed, a source of considerable difficulty lay in the lack of coordination between the Executive and Legislative departments. The confusion of authority was a key factor in the deadlock.

The President could have called a special session of Congress in April 1865, but Johnson seemed intent on completing the presidential reconstruction process prior to the first meeting of the Thirty-Ninth Congress in December 1865, thereby presenting Congress with a completed act. By the time Congress met in December, antagonism among the members of the Legislative branch ran high, and the struggle over the reconstruction program was joined as one between the President and the Congress in an atmosphere of mutual hostility and suspicion.

The President's first steps in 1865 were to continue Lincoln's plan of reconstruction, along with some features of the Wade-Davis Bill. By December every state except Texas had fulfilled the President's requirements and had elected federal senators and representatives, many of whom had travelled to Washington to await recognition in the Thirty-Ninth Congress.

On May 9, Johnson had issued a proclamation that declared rebel authority null in Virginia and called for the reestablishment of federal authority, pledging aid to the government of Francis H. Pierpoint in accomplishing the task. On the twenty-ninth, after consulting with his cabinet, Johnson proclaimed amnesty and pardon to all former insurgents, except fourteen special classes of citizens who required only an oath of allegiance in return.

The proclamation also appointed W. W. Holden provisional governor of North Carolina and outlined the President's reconstruction plan. A convention to be chosen by the "loyal" people of the state was to prepare a constitution. All the delegates to the convention and the electorate were required to take the amnesty oath declaring their support of the Constitution and they were then to determine the permanent voting and office holding qualifications for the state. For a brief period of time the civil government was to be administered under the authority of the provisional governor. This plan was fully discussed in the cabinet and none of the members voiced reservations about the power of the President to reorganize state governments.

The state conventions repealed or nullified the ordinances of secession, repudiated the portion of the state debt that related to the prosecution of the war, and abolished slavery. After each state had complied with the provisions outlined above, ratified the Thirteenth Amendment to the Constitution, and had elected officials to state offices, Secretary of State William Seward retired the provisional governor by proclamation and the powers of the office were vested in the regularly elected governor chosen by the "loyal" citizens.

Johnson's program did not disenfranchise the ex-Confederates and it did not concern itself with Negro suffrage. The process was an Executive one, involving direct personal cooperation between the President and the leaders of the state reorganization efforts in the South.

Congressional leaders, already uneasy with the two proclamations of Johnson's program, cautioned the President not to proceed too hastily without consulting Congress. To many Radicals in the North, the conventions seemed reluctant to dissolve their attachments to the secession cause. Many Southern state conventions had balked at debt repudiation and refused to consider extending suffrage to the freedman. Johnson himself, growing impatient with the delay and the discontent of the Radicals, counseled Governor William L. Sharkey of Mississippi to extend suffrage to all freedmen who could read the Constitution, write their names, and who paid taxes on real estate valued at $250. It was, as Johnson candidly admitted, a token gesture to silence Radical critics.

It was not the process, but the result, which created further suspicion and distrust of Johnson and the governments he helped to create in the South. The Southern states denied blacks equal rights with whites. Mississippi, South Carolina, and Louisiana passed severe "Black Codes" which reduced the freedman to second-class status. Moreover, the restored state legislatures unwisely elected several former Confederate leaders to the United States Senate. Among them were Alexander H. Stephens, the vice president of the Confederacy, and Herschel V. Johnson and William A. Graham, who had been senators in the Confederate Congress.

Conflicting reports on conditions in the South filtered into Washington in the months prior to the convening of Congress. General Ulysses Grant toured the South in November-December 1865 and reported that the Southern states accepted the present state of affairs and wished to return to self-government within the Union as soon as possible. A newspaper correspondent, Benjamin C. Truman, observed that the South was more loyal in early 1866 than it had been at the conclusion of hostilities. Those two reports contradicted the conclusions of Carl Schurz, whom President Johnson sent to view the situation. Schurz reported that he had found no influential class in the South whose loyalty could be counted upon or who could be depended upon to conduct their state governments in a manner in accordance with the national spirit. Freedmen and white Unionists in the South were the victims of a brutal hatred levelled at them by Southern whites, Schurz recounted, and their safety and protection required the continued presence of a military force in the region. He was convinced that Southern whites would keep the freedmen in a state of economic and social servitude, and he urged that the extension of suffrage to the freedmen was the only means of preventing their further relegation to an inferior status.

The Schurz report was well known among the Radicals with whom he kept council. When Congress convened, the Senate called for the report and used Schurz's findings as evidence against the President's reconstruction policy. Johnson, in turn, submitted Grant's brief report, and in April 1866 he transmitted Truman's report to Congress to refute Schurz's findings. Though contradictory, each report was partially correct. Southern society did not react in a monolithic fashion to the surrender at Appomattox. Most Southern whites conceded, however, that further efforts at armed resistance in defense of the doctrine of states' rights or the reestablishment of slavery were futile.

If the North required some gesture on the part of the former Confederacy to signify total capitulation and the acceptance of military occupation, it was not forthcoming. Southerners did not repudiate their past, nor did they change their attitude toward the present. They remained defiant and contemptuous of their conquerors, at least in the minds of many prominent members of the Republican party, and that condition alone justified stronger and more thorough reconstruction measures.

III

As the date for the opening session of Congress drew nearer, the Radical Republicans became more dissatisfied with the President's reconstruction policy. Five days before Congress convened, Thaddeus Stevens of Pennsylvania, a leading Radical in the House of Representatives, met with President Johnson and expressed his opposition to the wholesale pardoning of rebels. Stevens urged an alteration in presidential policy to gain the support of the Republican majority in Congress. Two days after the interview Stevens and twenty-five or thirty Radical congressmen caucused to find some basis for party unity on the reconstruction question. In caucus Stevens related the substance of his conversation with Johnson and offered his opinion that the President, while urging conciliation, was unalterably attached to his own plan for the restoration of the Southern states. A careful canvass of the Senate led Stevens to the conclusion that the senators were inclined to be more conservative than members of the House and would allow properly qualified members from the "rebel" states to take their seats. Such action would prevent the adoption of any alterations in the President's reconstruction plan; to prevent it, Stevens argued forcefully for the creation of a joint committee to which all questions relating to the Southern delegations and the restoration of the rebel states would be referred. The enabling resolution appointing the committee was to be so worded as to prevent one house from admitting Southern representatives until the other had reached the same conclusion. The ostensible purpose of this action was to force a delay which would prevent the Senate from admitting Southerners until that body had more Radical sympathizers. To impress upon the Senate the gravity of the issue, the caucus urged that the Radical members of the House act in an undivided unity. The proposal was agreed upon and Stevens presented it to the full party caucus held on Saturday, December 2.

In the Republican caucus a committee of seven was appointed to consider the question of Southern representation, with Thaddeus Stevens named as its chairman. Henry J. Raymond of New York, a prominent conservative member of the committee, failed to comprehend the significance of the resolution and it passed without a dissenting vote. The nucleus of an opposition to the President's reconstruction program had formed, but the aggregate of the Thirty-Ninth Congress was not committed to the Radical program. An analysis of the relative strength of the factions within the Republican party has shown that the Congress was a divided one at the outset and did not have any organized plan of opposition to the President. The Democrats and a few conservative Republicans were prepared to admit the Southern representatives immediately. Senator John C. TenEyck of New Jersey, Leven W. Powell and Henry Grider of Kentucky, and Thomas A. Hendricks of Indiana opposed placing any further conditions upon the South. They urged support of Johnson's program, considering it the fulfillment of Lincoln's plan. The representatives from the reorganized states were to be seated in Congress, the states readmitted to the electoral college, and normal federal-state relations resumed.

This view either misunderstood or ignored the dominant view north and west of the Mason-Dixon line, however. Hatred of the South had increased as battle casualties mounted during four years of bitter warfare. Sentiment grew in the North in favor of imposing terms and demanding guarantees of concessions from the defeated South. But Republicans were not in agreement when they discussed the specific terms they desired. Republican Senators Edgar Cowan and J. R. Doolittle joined with the Democrats in calling for immediate and unconditional restoration, but their views were not representative of their party and they lacked influence in party counsel.

The large majority of congressmen were moderate men who favored speedy readmission with rigid conditions imposed to prevent future treason. It was not their purpose to bring about a social revolution in the South; their intent was to keep the former leaders of the Confederacy from regaining power. They did, however, feel some obligation toward the freedman, and they wished to guarantee his physical security and prevent his economic reenslavement.

Fewer in number, though articulate and influential, the Radical Republicans had hoped to cooperate fully with President Johnson. But, the appeal of Johnson's plan among ex-Confederates and the President's apparent disregard for the status of the freedman disappointed the Radicals. They commanded much influence because their number included such prominent men as Charles Sumner, Zachariah Chandler, James Ashley, George Boutwell, George Julian, Benjamin Butler, Levi P. Morton, Henry Wilson, Richard Yates, and Thaddeus Stevens.

At seventy-five Stevens was the leader of the Radical coterie in the House. He was determined to make the Southerners pay the cost of the war. The Pennsylvanian abhorred the leniency of the President's amnesty plan and he recommended that all rebel property and public lands be confiscated and redistributed among the freedmen, in order to prevent the former slaveholders from gaining economic ascendency over the ex-slaves. Stevens openly admitted that his view of Southern reconstruction had a partisan motive. Granting suffrage to the freedman in the South, he reasoned, insured the continued domination of the Republican party in the national Congress. If excluded from the franchise, the Southern states, in the hands of white ex-rebels, would send Southern Democrats to Congress, who, when allied with their Northern counterparts, would soon gain control of the presidency and Congress. Stevens—and perhaps the majority of his Republican contemporaries in the North—assumed that there was an integral nexus between the welfare of the Republican party and that of the nation.

The most distinguished Radical in the Senate was Charles Sumner of Massachusetts. Educated at Harvard, Sumner was a polished speaker and had devoted a major portion of his career to the cause of the black man. Sumner's motives were sincere. Unlike some of his Radical friends, he was free of racist sentiments and enjoyed a reputation for integrity. As the collision between the President and Congress became imminent during the winter and spring of 1865–1866, many of Sumner's colleagues came to detest him because of his intransigent position, erudite mannerisms, and self-righteous attitude toward his colleagues, whom he considered less principled than himself.

Neither Sumner in the Senate, nor Stevens in the House worked in a united way to consolidate Radical opposition to the President, nor did they control the membership of the Republican party. The two men came to dislike one another intensely during the ensuring struggle. The parliamentary maneuvers of Stevens in the House and the oratory of Sumner in the Senate were aimed at persuading moderate Republicans to reject or revise presidential reconstruction. If they failed in their objective, Stevens counseled delay until Congress became more Radical. In all of the political maneuvers during the winter of 1865–1866, no one with the exception of Stevens had a clear-cut idea of what Radical reconstruction entailed, or how long it would take to accomplish its goals.

In no case was the above more clearly illustrated than in the history of the Joint Committee of Fifteen on Reconstruction. At the opening of Congress a clever parliamentary maneuver, engineered by Thaddeus Stevens, excluded all Southern representatives from their seats in the House. The clerk of the House, Edward McPherson of Pennsylvania, legally the presiding officer until the election of a Speaker, omitted calling the names of the members-elect from the Southern states. Despite protests by Democrat James Brooks from New York and member-elect Horace Maynard of Tennessee, the action was sustained. Ignoring the uproar, the House proceeded to elect Schuyler Colfax Speaker of the House. Thereupon Thaddeus Stevens asked unanimous consent to introduce a resolution calling for the creation of a joint committee of fifteen members, nine from the House and six from the Senate, to inquire into the condition of the "so-called Confederate States of America" and report whether they were entitled to representation in Congress. The resolution stipulated that the committee would have leave to report to the Congress at any time, "by bill or otherwise." Until such a report was made and acted on by Congress, the resolution continued, no member was to be seated in either house of Congress from the Southern states. Finally, it declared that all papers relating to the representation question were to be referred to the committee without debate.

Stevens's resolution failed to secure unanimous consent. He then moved a suspension of the rules, which was carried, and by moving the previous question, debate was shut off and the resolution passed. As Benjamin Kendrick has pointed out, in every test vote Stevens was sustained by the entire Republican party. The vote represented both their dissatisfaction with presidential policy and their lack of any clear-cut conception of the proper reconstruction policy. While Democrats considered the Joint Committee a "revolutionary tribunal" or "star chamber," Stevens's motion had been endorsed by moderates and Radicals alike. Senator William Pitt Fessenden of Maine, the moderate Republican selected to become chairman of the committee, defended it:

> This question of the readmission . . . I conceived to be of infinite importance, requiring calm and serious consideration, and I be-

> lieved that the appointment of a committee, carefully selected by the two Houses, . . . was not only wise . . . but an imperative duty resting upon the representatives of the people in the two branches of Congress.

The resolution submitted by Stevens was a joint, rather than a concurrent, one. The Pennsylvanian was aware that a joint resolution required the signature and approval of the President, while a concurrent resolution was a legislative document where Executive scrutiny was not necessary. Stevens planned to force the issue with the President immediately, but the Senate was more conservative than the House.

The Radicals in the Senate who would have joined with Stevens were led by Sumner, Wade, and Horne of Wisconsin. The moderate Republicans under the leadership of Fessenden, Grimes of Iowa, and Lyman Trumbull of Illinois, while convinced that the President's policy had not gone far enough, were unwilling to break with him. They hoped that by making mutual concessions and adopting an attitude of mutual respect they could work in harmony with the President.

The Administration Republicans in the Senate who supported the President were Doolittle of Wisconsin, Cowan of Pennsylvania, and Dixon of Connecticut. The most prominent Democrats were Reverdy Johnson of Maryland, Guthrie of Kentucky, and Hendricks of Indiana. Gradually, the Democrats joined with the Republicans who supported Johnson's policies, but, in the Senate and the House, no clear-cut majority supported the Radicals or the President. A majority of members of both houses, though inclined to believe the President had been too lenient, preferred to delay commitment to any policy and await the outcome of events. In the first session of the Thirty-Ninth Congress Radicals and supporters of the Administration worked diligently to gather political allies and convince the moderates that theirs was the proper attitude on the reconstruction question. It was in this spirit that the Senate considered the House resolution sponsored by Thaddeus Stevens.

The Senate at first postponed consideration of the resolution to create the Joint Committee on December 5 and 6. On the eleventh Republican senators caucused and, by a vote of 16 to 14, changed the wording of the resolution to read:

> Resolved by the House of Representatives, (the Senate concurring) that a joint committee of fifteen members shall be appointed, nine of whom shall be members of the House, and six members of the Senate, who shall inquire into the condition of the states which formed the so-called Confederate States of America, and report whether they, or any of them, are entitled to be represented in either House of Congress, with leave to report at any time, by bill or other wise.

The Senate resolution differed from the original House resolution in three ways. The House resolution was joint; the Senate's was concurrent in form and did not require presidential approval. In the House version the members pledged themselves to receive no member from the Southern states until the committee had reported; the senators did not bind themselves to that clause.

On the question of the judging of the election returns and qualifications of its own members, the House had agreed to divest itself of the prerogative and place the power in the hands of the Joint Committee; the Senate was unwilling to give up the power to determine its own membership. The Senate passed its version of the resolution on December 12, 1865.

The public considered the passage of the concurrent resolution an indication that Congress intended to demand further conditions before admitting the representatives and senators from the former Confederate states. Democratic sentiment, expressed in the *New York World,* bitterly attacked the Radicals for their attempt to obstruct the President's restoration plan. The *New York Tribune* had supported Johnson, but preferred some guarantee of Negro suffrage in the South, and therefore favored the appointment of the committee; it saw no reason to consider the committee hostile to the President.

IV

The amendment to Stevens's resolution by the moderate Republicans in the Senate demonstrated that they held the balance of power between the Democrats and Administration Republicans on the one hand, and the Radical Republicans on the other. By retaining the right to reconsider the admission of Southern senators at any time, the moderates were in a position to support Radical demands should relations with the President reach the breaking point by the latter's refusal to compromise. It was not Stevens and Sumner who held Congress in check; it was the moderates who hoped to reach an amicable compromise with the President.

Eric McKitrick has offered an accurate assessment of the significance of the appointment of the Joint Committee:

> The manipulations of Thaddeus Stevens thus seemed to set the whole tone of the first day of the first session of the first reconstruction Congress, and indeed, the man's work and the notoriety of his name were to cast shadows over the entire history of reconstruction. But it would be wrong to suppose, from this, that Congress in December, 1865, was abandoned to radical madness. The formation of the committee was actually a more routine decision, less of an extreme step, than was implied in the flamboyant circumstances amid which it was done. The trappings of intrigue and wirepulling, though certainly there, would hardly have made the difference between doing it and not doing it. In all likelihood the business would have been transacted anyway; the same essential project, a day or so later, might just as plausibly been fathered by almost any Republican in the House as by Thaddeus Stevens. Conflict with the President was not, so far as most men were concerned, implied in the existence of such a committee. Even here a strong moderate balance prevailed.

The House appointed its nine members on December 14 and the Senate announced its six nominees seven days later.

Thaddeus Stevens was chairman of the Joint Committee in the House of Representatives. Thoroughly a Radical, Stevens had enunciated his "conquered provinces" theory defining the relationship of the states of the former

Confederacy to the Union as early as August 1861. In a speech in the House made on December 18, 1865, Stevens reiterated his belief that the Confederacy had waged war on the Union and that it was proper for the Union to treat them as conquered belligerents, severed from the Union.

In sharp contrast to Stevens was William Pitt Fessenden, senator from Maine. A Whig who had served one term in Congress in the 1840s, Fessenden had opposed the expansion of slavery. Coming to the Senate in 1854, elected by anti-slavery Democrats and Whigs, he allied with the Republican party (after the dissolution of the Whigs) and took an active part in the campaigns of 1856 and 1860. During the war, Fessenden served as secretary of the treasury after Salmon P. Chase resigned. He returned to the Senate at the expiration of Lincoln's first term and served until his death in 1869.

Fessenden believed Johnson had made a strategic error in not consulting the Congress on reconstruction, but when Congress met he was not among those disposed to provoke a breach with the President. He felt that additional guarantees should be demanded—he was unwilling to consider Johnson's state governments the final act of reconstruction—however, he was equally opposed to allowing reconstruction policy to fall into the hands of the Radicals. Fessenden accepted the post as chairman of the Joint Committee reluctantly because of ill-health, but he felt strongly that the chairmanship be kept from the Radicals. Aware of the political responsibility of his new job, he wrote to his cousin shortly after his appointment:

> Mr. Sumner was very anxious for the place, but standing as he does before the country, and committed to the most ultra views, even his friends declined to support him, and almost to a man fixed upon me. Luckily I had marked out my line, and everybody understands where I am. I think I can see my way through, and if Sumner and Stevens, and a few other such men do not embroil us with the President, matters can be satisfactorily arranged—satisfactorily, I mean, to the great bulk of Union men throughout the states.

Other members of the committee for the Senate were James W. Grimes (R.–Iowa), a moderate Republican supporter of Fessenden; Ira Harris (R.–New York), who contributed little to the committee, but supported the Radicals on reconstruction; Jacob M. Howard (R.–Michigan), a colleague of Radical Zachariah Chandler who had helped draw up the first Republican party platform; George H. Williams (R.–Oregon), characterized unflatteringly as a "time server and office seeker" who nevertheless voted with the Radicals and later became attorney general during the second Administration of Ulysses S. Grant; and Reverdy Johnson (D.–Maryland), previously a United States senator (1845-1849) and had served as attorney general to President Taylor. As a Democrat, Johnson's influence on the committee was limited, but his attempts to moderate the harsher measures proposed by the Republican majority, rather than categorically rejecting them, were invaluable to the committee. With the exception of Fessenden and Johnson, the Senate members of the Joint Committee were not a distinguished group, and three of the least distinguished were Radical Republicans.

The House of Representatives appointed, in addition to Stevens, Elihu B. Washburne (R.–Illinois), an extreme Radical who later became secretary of state under Grant and subsequently United States' minister to France; Justin

S. Morrill (R.–Vermont), who had served in Congress continuously for forty-three years and attended committee meetings religiously, usually voting with the Radicals; John A. Bingham (R.–Ohio), closer to Fessenden than to Stevens in his view on reconstruction, he worked successfully to incorporate a federal guarantee of civil rights for the freedman into the committee's recommendations; Roscoe Conkling (R.–New York), a protégé of Thaddeus Stevens who supported the Pennsylvanian on reconstruction; George S. Boutwell (R.–Massachusetts, an ultra-Radical who urged the wholesale disenfranchisement of rebels and advocated a broad enfranchisement of former slaves; and Henry T. Blow (R.–Missouri), a Virginian by birth who had opposed secession, he worked for the Union cause in Missouri and was rewarded by Lincoln with an appointment as minister to Venezuela. A two-term congressman by 1865, Blow at first voted with the Radicals, but supported Bingham's resolution in the committee. Other members of the committee were Andrew J. Rogers (D.–New Jersey), a "Copperhead" who was a violent racist opposed to all Republican measures seeking the improvement of the freedman; and Henry Grider (D.–Kentucky), who entered Congress for the second time in 1861, having served two terms in the mid-forties. As Democrats, neither Rogers nor Grider had any influence in the decisions of the committee.

V

The Joint Committee met on January 6, 1866 and appointed a subcommittee composed of Fessenden, Johnson, and Washburne to confer with the President, hoping to obtain assurances that he would defer all action on reconstruction until the committee had reviewed the subject. On Tuesday, January 9, after voting to make committee sessions confidential business, Fessenden reported on the interview with the President. They reported that they had stressed their desire to "avoid all possible collision or misconstruction" between the Executive and the Congress. For his part, President Johnson had stated that reconstruction should be advanced as rapidly as possible, but, in the interests of harmony, he assured them that he did not intend to do more than had been done.

The Joint Committee arranged itself into four subcommittees to hear testimony and examine papers to "inquire into the condition" of the Southern states. Conflicting reports by individual travellers, correspondents, and public officials, the committee contended, had not provided the President with an accurate estimate of conditions in the South when he authorized the governments created under the revised ten percent plan. The committee appointed Grimes, Bingham, and Grider to hear testimony from residents of Tennessee. Howard, Conkling, and Blow examined citizens from the states of Virginia and North and South Carolina. Georgia, Alabama, Mississippi, and Arkansas residents testified before Harris, Boutwell, and Morrill. Louisiana, Florida, and Texas citizens were examined by Williams, Washburne, and Rogers. These subcommittees spent approximately five months, from January to May, hearing witnesses and in addition to public hearings, the full committee met in secret sessions to consider appropriate measures on the representation question, the guarantee of civil rights to freedmen, and the readmission of Tennessee.

The first formal inquiry by a congressional committee into conditions in the South after the Civil War, it was not the last. Whenever an event of political significance occurred in any of the Southern states from that time until the end of Reconstruction in 1877, Congress appointed an investigating committee to examine the event. The reports served a double purpose. Each investigation was usually an excuse for some legislative proposal, and the reports served to illustrate that Southern "rebels" continued to engage in disloyal activities. The publication of investigative reports put Northern voters on their guard and warned them to vote with care for loyal guardians of the Union—all of whom were presumably Republicans. So it was with the testimony taken by the Joint Committee on Reconstruction. Their investigation delayed approval of the presidential policy of restoration and it justified the adoption of the Fourteenth Amendment, the major recommendation of the committee. The testimony before the committee served Radicals well as a political campaign document in the congressional elections of 1866.

The report of the Joint Committee on Reconstruction was a biased document that reflected how little each section really knew about the other, and how eagerly the North had sought information about conditions in the South. Congress printed 100,000 copies of the report, which senators and representatives distributed among their constituents. Newspapers published copious extracts from the testimony, together with editorial comments. Howard K. Beale has calculated that of the 144 witnesses called by the committee, 114 were men whose interests and prejudices biased them against Southerners, while perhaps only 39 had an interest in restoration. Seventy-seven of the witnesses were Northerners living in the South. Many of the sixty-seven Southerners called held personal grievances against the governments of the rebel states. All who favored the continuation of military rule in the South were classified as follows: ten were Northern officeholders in the South, ten were Northern travellers in the South, thirty-eight were Northern army officers, fifteen were Northern Freedmen's Bureau officers, three were Northerners living in the South, twenty-one were Southern white loyalists, and eight were Negro loyalists. The thirty who were not anti-Southern included sixteen white citizens of the South, ex-Confederates like Robert E. Lee; two provisional governors; one governor; and seven Southern state officers, four of whom, among them Alexander H. Stephens, the former vice president of the Confederacy, were members-elect of Congress.

The procedure of each subcommittee had been to ask specific questions phrased to elicit a desired answer, many commencing with the phrase, "Is it not true . . . ?" On the face of it, the Joint Committee asked questions that could only be used to discredit President Johnson's restoration plan. The pattern of the inquiry was shaped to allow witnesses to respond to a set of stock questions that were asked repeatedly throughout the hearings. The testimony of military officers stationed in the South left the impression that the army was not welcome and that its personnel were ignored by Southern rebels. They expressed the opinion that neither the loyal Unionist nor the Negro would be safe without the continued presence of the army. It was their considered military opinion that if a vacillating President, such as James Buchanan, ever again became President, Southerners would reconsider secession. They testified that Southern loyalty to the Union was of such an ephemeral quality that if the nation went to war with France or England, the South would join with the enemy. While testimony such as this reappeared throughout the hearings, the committee did not attempt to obtain specific evidence, but was satisfied with a general impression that, on the whole, presented a portrait of a disloyal, secessionist-minded South prevented only from repeating the steps of 1860–1861 by the presence of Union military forces. Obviously, it was a distorted picture.

This procedure changed in the cases of the few Southerners interrogated by the committee. Each witness was questioned about the present feelings of the people toward the events of the war, and each was asked his opinion of the federal troops stationed among them. General questions preceded a series of rebuttal questions phrased in the following manner: "Is there or not a bitter feeling between those who supported the rebellion and those who supported the general government during the war? Are these Union men safe without army protection, or do they enjoy social intercourse and business relations with former rebels?" Under such questioning procedures, there was little that Southerners could do to correct the opinion solicited by the committee.

Among other queries, Southerners were also asked about their loyalty in the event of a foreign war. The committee asked if Southerners expected indemnities to be paid for slaves lost and whether they preferred seeing ex-rebels or Union men in public office. In the matter of the freedmen, the committee sought to discover their attitude toward the Freedmen's Bureau and their willingness, without coercion, to grant suffrage to the Negro and provide for his public education. High-ranking ex-Confederates such as Stephens and Robert E. Lee were asked a series of loaded questions phrased to raise doubts about their responses and the sincerity of their answers. The committee raised questions about Lee's loyalty, his acceptance of defeat, his willingness to pay federal taxes, his attitude toward the Negro, and his future conduct in case of a foreign war.

Seeking evidence of brutality and disloyalty, they found it. A substantial portion of the testimony received was true with respect to the South—so far as it went—but it was not the entire truth. The fault of the report was not that it was inaccurate, but that it lacked the balance necessary to insure intelligent action with respect to reconstruction.

The committee report submitted to Congress on June 6, 1866 by Fessenden and Stevens was offered as an accurate picture of Southern attitudes and conditions. The report began with a definition of the constitutional status of the former Confederate states: The former states were, in effect, outside the Union, without civil government, commercial connections, national or international relations, and subject to martial law. The committee concluded that the Southern states were not "entitled to representation in the Congress of the United States; that, before allowing such representation, adequate security for future peace and safety should be required; . . ." President Johnson had merely acted in an emergency manner in creating governments in the conquered South, the committee declared, because the President did not have the appropriate information to act in any other way.

Accusing the South of responsibility for the war and rebellion against the United States Government, the report warned that the Johnson government had failed to provide adequate guarantees against future treason. It was absurd to think that "treason defeated in the field, has only to take possession of Congress and the Cabinet." Moreover, the committee demanded further proof that the South had rejected secession and disloyalty. In effect, it was a condition of reconstruction that the South exhibit a change of heart, a spirit of repentance, to act out their defeat in the terms laid down by the North.

With the evidence the committee gathered, they summarily rejected the validity of the state governments, refused to recognize the results of their recent elections, and set aside the new governments until they met the contitins set forth in a new plan recommended by the Joint Committee. Reconstruction was no longer a constitutional problem concerning the respective powers and duties of the Executive or the Legislative branch. It was a political issue, where constitutional arguments became useful reference points to substantiate one's position.

In a region ravaged by war and occupied by a victorious army, where civil government had been reestablished as a makeshift arrangement and where economic, political, and racial dislocations affected everyday life, it was possible to find whatever anyone, for whatever purpose, sought. There, President Johnson found a basis for support of his program for restoration. There, too, the Joint Committee on Reconstruction located the conditions they wished to see—conditions that justified the repudiation of the President's program.

Reverdy Johnson attempted to introduce a minority report drawn up by the Democrats on the committee. After a two week delay because of objections by Lyman Trumbull, who urged that the submission of a minority report was bad precedent, the Senate accepted the document as a statement of the opinion of the minority, but would not accept it as a basis for any future recommendations to the Congress.

The Democrats stated clearly that their legal presumption rested on the belief that the Union was permanent and indestructible, regardless of the treason committed by parts of its citizensry. Citizens could be punished for treason, the document declared, but states could not. Contradicting the view of the majority, the Democrats challenged the conclusion that evidence had shown the presence of continued disloyalty in the South. The South might be willing to repudiate the Confederate debt and the unnecessary guarantee of federal obligations, the minority document reasoned, but they would not approve the representation scheme outlined in the Fourteenth Amendment nor the wholesale disqualification of ex-Confederates. The minority recommended the rapid recognition of the Southern states as a measure that would serve national unity better than ratification of the Fourteenth Amendment. Supporting the general outline of Johnson's restoration plan, the document had no effect on the members of the Joint Committee or the Republican-dominated Congress, however. It served those representatives and senators from Democratic districts or states as a counterargument to the findings of the committee majority in the elections of 1866.

VI

It would be a distorted view of the work of the Joint Committee if one failed to notice the process by which gradual deterioration in the spirit of cooperation between Congress and the Executive occurred. Both Congress and the President had expressed, repeatedly, their wish to compromise. But political events between December 1865 and June 1866 brought about an open rupture in the relations between the President and the Congress.

Both branches of government were at fault. Andrew Johnson failed to understand the changing and more Radical-minded mood of the North with respect to their requirements for Southern reconstruction. The Congress was at fault because ultra-Radicals attempted to force a breach between the two branches of government by inflammatory public statements and their insistent doctrinaire characterizations of the South and Southerners as disingenuous traitors masking their real sentiments, awaiting the opportunity to reestablish their former leaders in power.

The President's Annual Message to Congress in December 1865, prepared for him by historian George Bancroft, justified the creation of restored governments during the previous six months. Johnson, aware of the resolution establishing the Joint Committee on Reconstruction, spoke with pride and dignity when he noted that warfare had ceased and civilian government had been restored in the former Confederate states. These states, Johnson emphasized, had never left the Union and had thus been restored. He observed the happy result of the Southern states' participation in the process of ratifying the Thirteenth Amendment, and he counseled for a patient consideration of the plight of the freedmen. The President had decided against insisting on suffrage for the freedmen, he remarked, because the Constitution plainly left determination of the franchise to the individual states. Emphasizing peace and harmony, the message called upon Congress to judge the qualifications of the new members.

While the President's message exuded confidence and optimism, the Congress was not ready to follow the President's lead. On December 18, Thaddeus Stevens rephrased his "conquered provinces" theory in Congress, declaring that the insurgents had forfeited all their rights and were in the condition of a subdued region placed under military rule. Until the ratification of amendments to the Constitution that based representation on the voting population, Stevens proclaimed, he would not consider readmitting them. He stressed the one theme that unified Radicals and moderate Republicans—the fear of the loss of political power in the event the Southern states were readmitted to the Union without the basis of representation having been altered.

The breakdown in relations between the two branches was the result of the failure of adamant men to reach a compromise program gaining the broad support of moderate men. Johnson erred when he failed to reach a compromise with the moderate Senator Lyman Trumbull of Illinois—a valuable political ally who had broken with the Radicals during the war. Trumbull had sponsored a bill extending the life of the Freedmen's Bureau, first created by Congress on March 3, 1865. The Bureau offices in the South fed white and black refugees, found employment for former slaves, supervised labor contracts entered into by freedmen, established schools and medical services, and protected the civil rights of the freedmen from vigilante terrorist groups in the South. To moderate Republicans the Bureau was an ideal agency to protect the rights of blacks in the South without antagonizing the President. Sponsored by Trumbull and endorsed by Fessenden, the bill provided protection for freedmen against the "Black Codes" and authorized the Bureau to extend its protection and jurisdiction to cover all cases of discrimination based on race or color. Any person found guilty of violating the antidiscrimination clause was subject to imprisonment and a fine.

Passed by overwhelming majorities in both houses, the bill went to the President in early February. To his credit, Johnson sought advice on the legislation from his friends and his foes alike. Apparently undecided on the matter, but with the proponents of the bill under the impression they had secured the President's assent to the measure, Johnson withheld action on the legislation. Cautioned by his advisers not to resist the act, Johnson ignored their advice. Prior to his veto message on February 19, the President had learned that a harsh substitute resolution on the readmission of Tennessee had been submitted by the Radical subcommittee composed of Williams, Boutwell, and Conkling to the Joint Committee on Reconstruction. Angered by the more stringent recommendations made by the Joint Committee and convinced that a compromise with Congress was useless, the President vetoed the Freedmen's Bureau bill on the grounds that it was an unconstitutional continuance of the war power in time of peace. The bill, Johnson declared, invaded both the legal and the judicial power of the states. Aroused by the President's adherence to the states' rights doctrine in the veto message, the Senate, nonetheless, failed to muster the two-thirds majority required to override the veto.

Three days after Johnson vetoed the Freedmen's Bureau bill, Johnson, speaking to a crowd and carried away with his own oratory and prodding by the assembled audience, linked the names of Thaddeus Stevens, Charles Sumner, and the abolitionist Wendell Phillips with those of the Confederacy, "the Davises, the Tombses, the Slidells." He labelled them all men who were "opposed to the Union," men whom the President considered "opposed to the fundamental principles of this government, and as now laboring to destroy them." Johnson's remarks were foolish and in bad taste—hardly the kind of words that gained the President congressional allies. Thaddeus Stevens responded to the President's remarks with a speech in the House of Representatives that was as adroit as it was sarcastic. An old newspaper recounting Johnson's state of inebriation at Lincoln's second inaugural was read to the assembled members, at Stevens's insistence.

Neither the President's remarks, nor Stevens's reply, enhanced the reputation of the President or Congress. But even the veto message and the indecorous public performances did not entirely rule out a compromise with Congress. Hoping that Johnson would approve some measure to extend a federal guarantee of protection of civil rights to the freedman, the moderates in Congress joined with the Radicals to back a civil rights bill introduced by Lyman Trumbull. The Joint Committee on Reconstruction had yet to make any recommendations to Congress. Lyman Trumbull introduced a bill which defined citizenship and extended its provisions to persons of every race and color, except native Indians. Offenders who denied the guarantees contained in the bill faced imprisonment and fines. Federal courts were given exclusive jurisdiction in the enforcement of the act, and final appeal of all questions arising from interpretation of the bill might be taken to the United States Supreme Court.

Only three Republicans voted against the bill in the Senate. The Civil

Rights Act of 1866 had the approval of the whole Republican party. The opportunity to reach a compromise with moderate Republicans lay with President Johnson, yet against the advice of his political friends, the President vetoed the bill on March 22. In the veto message Johnson asserted that relations between the races was a matter for the states to decide. He questioned the authority of Congress to legislate civil guarantees for ex-slaves when it had never done so for whites. He doubted the wisdom of granting citizenship to four million Negroes while foreigners waited five years before obtaining citizenship. The President concluded with another appeal for cooperation, but the message left no doubt that conciliation would have to be on presidential terms.

Unlike the Freedmen's Bureau bill, Congress had a two-thirds majority to override the President's veto, and the civil rights bill was enacted into law. The action was a firm repudiation of the President's views on reconstruction. Further evidence of the willingness of moderates to cooperate more fully with the Radicals was indicated when the Senate unseated Democrat John Stockton of New Jersey, because of alleged improprieties in the method of his election by the state legislature. The extreme partisanship exhibited in the Stockton matter carried over into the Senate's vote on the decision to override the President's veto of the civil rights bill. It was on the day of the arrival of the veto message on the civil rights bill that the Senate voted to unseat Stockton. When, shortly afterwards, the veto message came up for consideration, a sufficient number of moderates joined with the Radicals to override the veto by a vote of 33 to 15. Three days later on April 9, 1866, the House followed suit by a margin of 122 to 41.

VII

It had become clear by mid-April that whatever good will existed between the President and the Republican party had been exhausted. The Southern state governments created by Johnson's restoration were in the hands of leaders opposed to Republican leadership, and many Southerners were already making overtures to Northern Democrats. Under the grip of wartime hysteria and fearful that Southerners, with their Nothern allies, would repeal the Civil Rights Act, end the Freedmen's Bureau, and return the Negroes to a condition of virtual slavery, Northern legislators demanded additional safeguards before readmission. Nearly everyone in Congress agreed that any amendment proposed had to protect the rights of the freedmen and prevent ex-Confederates from holding office. Immediate and impartial suffrage was recommended by some Radicals. Salmon P. Chase and Thaddeus Stevens favored the idea and Charles Sumner, initially doubtful about the merits of immediate enfranchisement, concluded that without the franchise the Negro remained helpless and unprotected in the South.

Generally, moderate Republicans doubted the wisdom of the enfranchisement propositions. They feared that a proposal for the extension of suffrage to former slaves would have adverse political repercussions in Northern states where state laws restricted the Negro's right to vote. The moderates backed a plan which reduced the representation of the ex-Confederate states until the states were safely under Republican control.

These political pressures forced the Joint Committee on Reconstruction to produce an amendment acceptable to the majority of Republicans in Congress. The creation of the Fourteenth Amendment should then be properly regarded as a compromise measure. It did not wholly satisfy the desires of either the Radicals or the moderates, but the wording was sufficiently ambiguous to permit each faction to support it. The drafting of the amendment involved a complex and elaborate series of negotiations stretching over five months in 1866. While space does not permit a detailed analysis of the drafting process, a general picture of the means and the manner by which the Joint Committee arrived at the document presented to Congress for adoption sheds light upon the inner workings of the committee and the political forces that lay behind the compromise amendment.

On March 16, Senator William Stewart of Nevada had introduced into Congress a series of resolutions that caused a considerable stir in Washington because of the simplicity and fairness with which they treated the most difficult questions the Joint Committee considered—the matter of representation, the issue of the disqualification of Confederates from state offices, and the guarantee of civil rights for Negroes. Stewart's plan called for universal amnesty and universal suffrage. Not intending the resolutions to become an amendment to the Constitution, he proposed them as the basis for legislation that would promise restoration to the Southern states after they amended their state constitutions to eliminate discrimination in civil rights, repudiated the Confederate debt, renounced all claims to compensation for emancipated slaves, and eradicated suffrage discrimination on the basis of color and prior servitude. Amnesty would follow after the ratification of the above conditions by a popular vote.

On April 12, Stewart introduced a resolution amending the Constitution on the basis of his plan. The excitement Stewart's plan stirred galvanized the Joint Committee into action. Four days later the committee met with Stewart to discuss his plan, but it failed to gain their approval. The Radicals reasoned that if the Negroes gained suffrage and Southern whites obtained amnesty, it would not be long before the imposition of educational and property qualifications for voting could disenfranchise sufficient numbers of freedmen to give Southern white leaders control of the state governments and an even greater proportion of national power than they had enjoyed under the Three-Fifths Compromise. The Stewart plan did not diminish the number of Southern representatives, nor did it guarantee that the increased representation would be sufficiently radical in its politics. The plan failed to be adopted by the Joint Committee because it was *politically* unsuitable to the Radical Republicans.

The pressure of public opinion brought a new sense of urgency to the task of resolving the reconstruction quagmire. The President, in his civil rights bill veto message, had unequivocally expressed his intention to oppose any major legislation concerning the Southern states so long as those states remained unrepresented. But public opinion now ran against the President, and the Joint Committee, under pressure to propose an alternative, turned to another set of resolutions proposed by Robert Dale Owen, the Indiana reformer and humanitarian.

Owen, the son of Robert Owen, one of the great English Radicals in the

19th century, had come to Washington in the latter part of March with his own plan for reconstruction. He outlined his plan to Senator Oliver P. Morton of Indiana who listened with apparent approval. Owen then called upon Thaddeus Stevens and read the plan to him. Stevens liked it, although he told Owen plainly, "We haven't a majority, either in our committee or in Congress, for immediate suffrage; and I don't believe the States have yet advanced so far that they would be willing to ratify it." Nevertheless, Stevens promised to put the resolution before the Joint Committee. Fessenden thought the plan the best yet presented, and there was at least a guarded approval of it by every Republican member of the committee. It was a compromise plan that met all of their requirements, yet recognized the political limitations extant in the committee and the Congress.

The Owen plan, introduced in committee by Stevens on April 21, was a five-part amendment to the Constitution. The first part provided for equal civil rights, the second required impartial suffrage in all states after 1876, with the stipulation in the third part that representation would be restricted until 1876 in those states that denied freedmen the right to vote. The fourth section prohibited the payment of the rebel debt or compensation for emancipated slaves, and the fifth clause gave Congress the power to enforce the previous four sections by appropriate legislation.

The Joint Committee rejected Owen's plan because they did not wish to confront the troublesome issue of the Negro suffrage requirement. Perhaps the knowledge that several large Northern states had held congressional caucuses during the week also influenced the committee's judgment, for several Republicans on the committee had concluded that a direct Negro suffrage provision would be a political hardship in the upcoming elections in 1866. Another explanation is simpler. Many prominent Republicans reasoned that the South would give the Negro the vote without coercion rather than suffer reduction in representation; and Stevens, impressed as always by the gravity of the requirements for victory at the polls, moved to strike the suffrage section from Owen's plan.

The Joint Committee added a comprehensive definition of civil rights to the first section of Owen's amendment. On the recommendation of John A. Bingham, the committee incorporated the "due process" and "equal protection" principles into the amendment and changed the word "citizen" to "person." A disenfranchisement section was also added, disqualifying those who had voluntarily participated in the rebellion from participating in federal elections until 1870. As for readmitting Southern states upon ratification of the amendment, Fessenden softened Owen's resolution by changing the word "shall" to "may" [be admitted].

These alternatives became the Joint Committee's plan of reconstruction, reported on April 30 by Fessenden and Stevens to their respective branches of Congress. It consisted of a five-part amendment to the Constitution and two bills. One bill was the enabling act for readmission; a second defined those persons disqualified from holding federal office.

The committee had completed its work, but there was little enthusiasm for the fruits of its labor. The public recognized it as a compromise proposal that faced an uncertain future in both the House and Senate, because the document represented neither the wishes of the Radicals nor the moderate view implicitly. President Johnson made his position clear. He disavowed the document, preferring to trust the people for vindication of his principles in the fall elections. A press release from the White House to the newspapers gave the President's opinion:

> The President was earnest in his opposition to the report of the Committee, and declared himself against all conditions precedent to the admission of loyal representatives from the Southern States in the shape of amendments to the Constitution, or by the passage of laws. He insisted that under the Constitution no State could be deprived of its equal suffrage in the Senate, and that Senators and Representatives ought to be at once admitted into the respective houses as presented by law and the Constitution. . . . He remarked, in general terms, that if the organic law is to be changed at all, it should be at a time when all the States and all the people can participate in the alteration.

With the President unequivocally opposed to the handiwork of the Joint Committee, the Republicans concentrated upon passing an amendment to promote party unity in the face of presidential opposition.

The Fourteenth Amendment passed the House on May 10. Consideration of the enabling bill awaited the action of the Senate on the amendment. On May 23 the Senate considered the amendment and debate centered upon the disenfranchisement section. It was soon clear that the section had no support and a substitute proposal would have to be written. Senator Clark of New Hampshire introduced a disqualification section to replace the disenfranchisement clause. Henry Wilson of Massachusetts recommended extending Clark's substitute to include disqualification from state officeholding in addition to disqualification from federal office. Senator Wade sought an explicit definition of the word "citizen" in section one and suggested that a federal debt guarantee clause be added to the section on the repudiation of Confederate debts.

These changes met with the general approval of the senators. The direct Negro suffrage proposal died on the floor of the Senate, although Stewart had attempted to revive it and rally support for general amnesty. Representation based on voters was reintroduced by Senator Sherman, but the proposition failed. Republican senators caucused over the weekend of May 26 and 27 to iron out the conflicting points and put the amendment into final form. When two caucus sessions produced no agreement, the senators appointed a five-man committee chaired by Fessenden and composed of the Republican members of the Joint Committee to draft a conclusive resolution. What emerged was a measure that substantially altered the committee's report in the following manner: (1) to the first section had been added a definition of citizenship; (2) the disenfranchisement section had been eliminated; (3) a new disqualification section was added and it was incorporated into the revised amendment, with the disabilities capable of being removed by a two-thirds vote of Congress; (4) a federal debt guarantee clause was added to Section 4; (5) the enabling act was altered to allow readmission as soon as the states ratified the amendment; (6) perhaps in a gesture of compromise, based on the testimony gathered by the most moderate subcommittee, Tennessee was to be readmitted at once, having already complied with the requirements set forth in the amendment. The Fourteenth Amendment, introduced in revised form on May 29, passed the Senate on June 8, and the House concurred in the Senate version on June 13.

Reaction to the amendment was lukewarm. It was a compromise measure that most Unionist journals thought weighted on the moderate side. The amendment was vague enough in its wording and intention to allow Republicans to go into the fall elections without fear of repudiation by the voters, although Congress adjourned without passing the enabling legislation. What Congress intended to do about future readmissions, apart from the Tennessee case, was left deliberately ambiguous and it failed to make clear whether ratification of the Fourteenth Amendment promised an end to reconstruction.

Several questions concerning the motives of the framers and the adoption of the Fourteenth Amendment have troubled historians. Was the amendment framed in such a way as to guarantee its nonacceptance in order to prepare the way for military rule in the South? The question presumes the existence of a plot, a presumption that cannot be sustained in light of the complex political forces at work in both the committee and the Congress. It was a process of accommodation, with some measures made harsher and others toned down, to gain the acceptance of Congress. Having rejected the President's restoration procedure, the Republican majority in Congress, all factions included, felt obligated to create an alternative plan.

However, it may generally be assumed that the Fourteenth Amendment was never intended to signal an end to reconstruction. When the Republican party failed to agree on a definitive arrangement on the details of reconstruction, they went to the people in the fall elections and asked them to choose between the President's plan and the congressional amendment. Republican strategy was to get the amendment passed, leave the restoration question open, and readmit Tennessee as a gesture of good faith. Joseph B. James, in his study *The Planning of the Fourteenth Amendment* (Urbana, Illinois, 1956), has concluded:

> The most important purpose in the minds of most framers and members of the Republican party in the summer of 1866 was undoubtedly that the amendment might furnish a popular platform in the political campaign. This was the immediate aim, and politicians traditionally have been willing to sacrifice ultimate hopes for present success.

Events after June 1866 are more properly left to the history of Radical reconstruction which followed in the wake of the rejection of the Fourteenth Amendment by the remaining ten former Confederate States.

Certain constitutional ambiguities arising out of Reconstruction illustrate the legal confusion that existed throughout the era. One of the ambiguities was the mode of ratifying the Fourteenth Amendment. The Congress is limited either to the legislative or the convention procedure. The Southern states, considered out of the Union in actual practice, were required to ratify the Fourteenth Amendment as a condition for readmittance and they had to accept whatever definition Congress decided upon for the terms of "immunities" and "privileges." The amendment excluded ex-Confederates from the ratification process, thus applying the effects of the amendment prior to ratification. In the final analysis the Fourteenth Amendment, though it was not the deliberate intention of the framers as some writers have charged, served the business corporation better than it served the cause of civil rights for freedmen in the forty years after 1866. Of the 604 cases before the Court under the Fourteenth Amendment, only 28, or 5 percent, dealt with the Negro and his rights. The remainder of the cases treated such matters as eminent domain, taxation, procedure, and especially police powers. The Negro, in the days ahead, discovered the reality of the Jim Crow era and the denial of federal protection of rights as matters for the state to decide. It would not be amiss to conclude that the nation, and especially the freedmen, paid a heavy price for the failure of the Congress and the President to achieve some measure of effective cooperation in enacting a just and comprehensive reconstruction program.

The Joint Committee on Reconstruction had completed its work. The committee met on June 6, 1866 to approve the written report prepared and submitted by Fessenden. It was reappointed for the second session of the Thirty-Ninth Congress, but it met only twice, on February 4, 1867 and again on February 6. At the first meeting the committee discussed Stevens's reconstruction bill, but there were no conclusive results of that meeting or the one two days later.

What had been the purpose of the Joint Committee? On the face of it, the committee had been a natural outgrowth of a standard congressional procedure. Prior to the recommendation of legislation acceptable to a majority of conservative and moderate Republicans who, though opposed to the President's restoration program, were in disagreement among themselves on the matter, an investigation was necessary to reach a compromise. In practice, the Joint Committee was at the center of a political struggle with the President for control of reconstruction policies and programs. The report of the committee was an anti-Johnson campaign document and the testimony elicited by the committee did not result in an impartial investigation into conditions in the South at the end of the war. It was an indictment of the South and the Johnson-authorized state governments. As an investigatory agency, the Joint Committee on Reconstruction left a great deal to be desired. As a political maneuver setting the stage for a more Radical reconstruction policy, it was entirely successful.

BIBLIOGRAPHY

The revision in Reconstruction historiography in the last fifteen years has produced a number of important new studies. James G. Randall and David Donald's *The Civil War and Reconstruction* (Boston, 1961) is a valuable introduction. Eric McKitrick, *Andrew Johnson and Reconstruction* (Chicago, 1960), revises Johnson's role in Reconstruction. W. R. Brock, *The American Crisis: Congress and Reconstruction, 1865–1877* (London, 1963); LaWanda and John H. Cox, *Politics, Principle and Prejudice, 1865–1866: Dilemma of Reconstruction America* (New York, 1963); Kenneth M. Stampp, *The Era of Reconstruction, 1865–1867* (New York, 1965); David Donald, *The Politics of Reconstruction* (Baton Rouge, 1965); James H. McPherson, *The Struggle for Equality: Abolitionists and the Negro in the Civil War and Reconstruction* (Princeton, 1964); Martin E. Mantell, *Johnson, Grant and the Politics of Reconstruction* (New York, 1973); and Hans L. Trefousse, *The Radical Republicans: Lincoln's Vanguard for Racial Justice* (New York, 1969) reflect the revisionist viewpoint on Reconstruction. Attempts to synthesize the older view with the new are Avery Craven, *Reconstruction, The Ending of the Civil War* (New York, 1969); and Rembert W. Patrick, *The Reconstruction of the Nation* (New York, 1967). Two valuable collections of essays reflecting recent scholarship are Harold Hyman, ed., *New Frontiers of the American Reconstruction* (Urbana, 1966); Kenneth M. Stampp and Leon F. Litwack, eds., *Reconstruction, An Anthology of Revisionist Writings* (Baton Rouge, 1969).

Two older studies, still useful, are William A. Dunning, *Reconstruction, Political and Economic, 1865–1877* (New York, 1907, 1962) and Howard K. Beale, *The Critical Year, A Study of Andrew Johnson and Reconstruction* (New York, 1930, 1958). A useful documentary history of Reconstruction is Walter L. Fleming, ed., *Documentary History of Reconstruction* (New York, 1906, 1950).

Biographies of major and secondary figures of the Reconstruction era abound. Among the most important ones are the studies by Fawn Brodie, *Thaddeus Stevens, Scourge of the South* (New York, 1959); David Donald, *Charles Sumner and the Rights of Man* (New York, 1970); Charles A. Jellison, *Fessenden of Maine* (Syracuse, 1962); Mark M. Krug, *Lyman Trumbull, Conservative Radical* (New York and London, 1965), and Benjamin P. Thomas, *Abraham Lincoln* (New York, 1952).

Studies of the congressional investigating process, helpful in a general way, are Marshall Edward Dimock, *Congressional Investigating Committees* (Baltimore, 1929); Ernest J. Eberling, *Congressional Investigations* (New York, 1928); Joseph P. Harris, *Congressional Control of Administration* (Washington, D.C., 1964).

Two important studies of the Fourteenth Amendment are Horace E. Flack, *Adoption of the Fourteenth Amendment* (Baltimore, 1908), and Joseph B. James, *The Framing of the Fourteenth Amendment* (Urbana, 1956).

PERTINENT DOCUMENTS

Abraham Lincoln's Proclamation on Reconstruction, December 8, 1863

The Wade-Davis Bill, July 8, 1864

Extract of Andrew Johnson's First Annual Message to Congress, December 4, 1865

Senate Debate on House Resolution to Appoint Committee on Reconstruction, December 12, 1865

Speech of Thaddeus Stevens on Reconstruction, December 18, 1865

Report of Lieutenant-General U. S. Grant on Conditions in the South, December 18, 1865

Conclusion of Carl Schurz's Report on Conditions in the South, December 18, 1865

Testimony of Robert E. Lee on Conditions in Virginia, February 17, 1866

Testimony of Clara Barton, February 21, 1866

Robert Dale Owen on Proposed Fourteenth Amendment, June 1875

Resolutions of William Stewart on Representatives of Southern States, March 16, 1866

Thaddeus Stevens Introduces "Owen Plan" in Committee, April 21, 1866

Joint Committee's Recommendations, April 28, 1866

Report of the Joint Committee on Reconstruction, June 6, 1866

Speech of Andrew J. Rogers, June 13, 1866

Minority Report, June 20, 1866

Message of Andrew Johnson to Congress on Fourteenth Amendment, June 22, 1866

Andrew Johnson's Impeachment
1867

U.S. Signal Corps photo (Brady Collection)

National Archives

top: *A ticket to Andrew Johnson's impeachment trial.* bottom: *The Senate Impeachment Committee (l. to r.)—Benjamin Butler, James Wilson, Thaddeus Stevens, George Boutwell, Thomas Williams, John Logan, John Bingham.*

Andrew Johnson's Impeachment 1867

by Michael Les Benedict

Today, Americans can hardly appreciate the reality of civil war. It is something that happens in other, less stable lands, to be read about in newspapers. But to the generation that lived through it, the American civil war was tragically real. More than anything, the American civil war was a social revolution—not on the part of white Southerners who committed treason to preserve their economic and social system, but on the part of Northerners, who in the course of the war decided that the only way to secure permanent union was to destroy that system. If the stakes of the American civil war had been less, there never would have been a struggle over the terms of reunion, because white Southerners were willing, in fact anxious, to resume their places in the government. They were even reconciled to the elimination of slavery as an economic system, if only they could retain its social component—the total subordination of the black race to the white. But the victorious Northerners were not willing to make concessions. The war to preserve the Union had become a war to extirpate the barbaric system that precipitated it, and for the majority of Northerners that meant not only slavery, but its "incidents." So even after the armies disbanded, the most divisive issue of the war remained to be settled—the terms of racial and social adjustment in the South. It would be decided, moreover, through political institutions designed primarily for peacetime government.

This was a dangerous, bold decision. A period of civil war—when there are real traitors about, not just phantoms conjured by designing politicians and their paranoid supporters—generally causes a drastic restriction in civil liberties. People who have risked their lives or have seen loved ones sacrificed are rarely willing to return to peacetime politics until the issues that precipitated war are irrevocably settled.

If the American civil war had followed the general pattern, with democratic procedures suspended and wartime issues completely settled by the sword, there never would have been an investigation, impeachment, or trial of Andrew Johnson, the seventeenth President of the United States. But throughout the struggle Americans had been warned that civil war might precipitate military dictatorship. Americans chose, however, to subject their democratic institutions to the strain of settling bitter wartime differences rather than to risk losing those institutions by turning to alternative solutions. Even during the war the Republicans and war Democrats who had formed the Union party (a party formed by Democrats and Republicans whose sole purpose was to save the country) did little to limit electoral freedom. When the war ended, even the minor interferences it justified ceased.

The elections of 1864 insured that reconstruction policy would be set by the Republican-dominated Union party. President Abraham Lincoln had been elected on the Union ticket, and so had three-quarters of the members of the new Congress scheduled to meet in December 1865. After hard-fought campaigns centering on war issues—especially the abolition of slavery and prosecution of the war to total victory—the people of the North had entrusted the government to them, and although a minority, so-called radical wing of the party in Congress, favored a more extreme restoration program than did Lincoln, there was every reason to suppose that the Republican President and the Republican Congress would agree on a policy. If the Democrats challenged it, the people would then be the judges in the congressional elections of 1866.

The assassination of Lincoln and Vice President Andrew Johnson's elevation to the presidency did not disturb that expectation. Within a year Johnson deserted his party, allied himself with the Democrats, and tried to enforce a reconstruction program that alienated even the most conservative of his former allies. What had promised to be a rather straightforward if hard-fought struggle between Democrats and Republicans over reconstruction became a constitutional crisis when each side gained control of a coordinate branch of the government. After all, the issues had precipitated a war; the combatants knew that they were fighting to determine the future of the nation. With the stakes so high, both the Republican Congress and the suddenly anti-Republican President were willing to go the limits of their constitutional powers in the struggle. At their extremities those powers overlapped, and inevitably each side accused the other of usurpation.

The United States Constitution provides remedies for congressional and presidential usurpation. One method is the appeal to the Supreme Court against unconstitutional action, and in recent times Americans have grown accustomed to traversing that route when challenging government activities.

In the years following the civil war, that habit was not yet fixed. The Supreme Court had regularly reviewed the constitutionality of *state* laws, but only twice had it overturned national enactments.

This was first done in 1803 and then a second time in 1857, when in the *Dred Scott* case the majority ruled that the Congress could not prohibit the expansion of slavery into the territories. That decision had shaken the court's prestige to its foundation and helped to tumble the nation into war. The issues that divided the President and Congress were political—indeed, many of the same issues underlay the *Dred Scott* case. The people, consequently, were reluctant to permit eight judges to decide the case, and the justices were understandably chary of making the attempt.

A President has yet another recourse against a Congress that he believes is exceeding its powers; he may veto its legislation. Johnson did this, but in every case except the first his vetoes were overturned. If these recourses are unavailing, the President has only one other alternative, to appeal to the people to elect new congressmen. Congress, however, is more suitably armed to deal with presidential excesses; it may impeach the President.

When Andrew Johnson became President, he inherited Lincoln's wartime reconstruction program. In areas conquered by Union forces, Lincoln had instructed his military commanders to encourage the formation of new, loyal state governments. Whenever a number of state citizens equalling one-tenth of those who had voted in the 1860 presidential elections took an oath promising future loyalty to the United States Government and support of emancipation (the so-called amnesty oath), the commanders were ordered to organize elections for a state constitutional convention. Only citizens who had taken the oath could participate and the resulting constitution had to be consistent with the oath. (That is, it had to provide for the abolition of slavery.) Once the new constitution was framed, elections would be held for state officers and congressional representatives. At that point, the state would resume normal relations with the national government, so far as Lincoln was concerned, although he specifically conceded that Congress had the sole right to determine whether to seat the newly-elected representatives and senators.

New state governments had been formed in Arkansas, Louisiana, and Tennessee under Lincoln's program. (In fact, Johnson had served as military governor in Tennessee, the only state where Lincoln had put a civilian in charge of the restoration process.) Lincoln had also nurtured a loyal, skeleton government in Virginia. Congressional Republicans had been reluctant to accept his policy completely, however, worrying that emancipation based on oaths alone might not be secure. In 1865 after Congress proposed the Thirteenth Amendment freeing the slaves, resistance seemed to diminish and Senate Republicans, with the exception of a handful of radicals, were willing to recognize the restoration of Louisiana, a test case for other states.

As Lincoln had fashioned a reconstruction policy based primarily on Executive action, congressional Republicans passed laws with important implications for peacetime adjustment. The Confiscation Act permitted the government to sell rebel property for the lifetime of the rebel, with the proceeds going to the United States Treasury. Strong pressure was developing in Congress to make the Confiscation Act permanent and both the House and

Senate had gone on record favoring such a change. A Test Oath Act required all national government officers and congressmen to swear they had never aided the rebellion, and the Freedmen's Bureau Act created a federal bureaucracy designed to protect Southern blacks in the transition from slave to free labor. The bureau commissioner was given control over Southern property abandoned by Confederate owners in the path of Union advances and confiscated property not yet sold. That property was to be used for the freedmen's benefit and perhaps ultimately divided among them. Although Congress had no reconstruction policy of its own, when the war ended the combined Lincoln-congressional Republican policy provided for the quick reconstruction of loyal state governments through a process administered by the army or civilians who would take the test oath, with national political offices in the South going only to those who had never aided the rebellion. A Freedmen's Bureau was responsible for protecting blacks' civil rights and economic interests. Most likely, rebels' property would be redistributed among landless black and white farmers.

After the last Confederate armies surrendered, Johnson adopted the mechanics of Lincoln's program with few modifications. He confirmed Lincoln's offer of amnesty to all who would swear an oath of future loyalty to the Union, with the exception of Confederate civil, military, and economic leaders, who would have to seek pardons; he appointed civilian provisional governors to oversee the reconstruction process; he required the number of citizens taking the amnesty oath to equal fifty percent of the voters in the 1860 elections, instead of ten percent, before the process could begin; he explicitly required provisions in the new constitutions abolishing slavery and repudiating the rebel war debt; and he insisted that either the state conventions or the new state legislatures pronounce secession null and void and ratify the Thirteenth Amendment. The restoration process proceeded rapidly from June to December 1865. By the time Congress convened, every Southern state except Texas had framed its constitution, held elections for state officers and congressmen, and met the President's conditions.

Ignoring the congressional elements of the evolving Republican reconstruction program, many historians have written that Johnson's policy was merely an extension of Lincoln's and that Republican opposition to it after 1866 was a repudiation of the martyred wartime leader's programs. But Republicans did not perceive their position this way. Not only did Johnson ignore congressional enactments, Congress soon suspected that, even while he adopted the mechanics of Lincoln's restoration program, he was abandoning its spirit. Despite misgivings, most Republicans had accepted Lincoln's program because they knew what many Americans have today forgotten, that Lincoln was a politician as well as a statesman. Lincoln saw reconstruction in political as well as patriotic terms; he intended to strengthen the Republican party as well as the nation. His policy was designed to put Southern government in the hands of men most of whom had never aided the rebellion or who had repented their treason while the war continued, while there was still a chance for Southern success. He expected these loyalists to gravitate to the Union-Republican party, spreading the Republican organization southwards, where it would appeal to voters on economic issues and eventually as an alternative to the discredited Democratic party that had led the South to war and ruin. While he must not have envisioned such racial egalitarianism as would alienate the Southern electorate, Lincoln anticipated that Southern loyalists would afford freedmen protection in their basic rights. (Under radical pressures Lincoln, in 1865, suggested the enfranchisement of literate blacks and the nearly two hundred thousand black veterans.) He always insisted that the establishment of such loyalty was more important than the means through which it was done. Throughout the war he affirmed his willingness to allow Southerners to restore their governments by procedures different from his, and in his last public address conceded that the exigencies of peace might "require some new announcement to the people of the South." He would "not fail to act," Lincoln assured his audience, "when satisfied that action will be proper."

Johnson's goal seemed to be different. As concerned with the political consequences of reconstruction as Lincoln, Johnson had never considered himself a Republican. A passionate Jacksonian Democrat before the war, Johnson thought of himself as a Democratic member of the Union party. He listened willingly to the blandishments of his former friends, who promised political support in return for a reconstruction policy that would quickly restore their Southern allies' political rights, enabling the reunited Democratic party to wrest power from its Republican adversary. Ultimately, Johnson hoped that his program of speedy reconstruction would place him at the head of a great, conservative party made up of former Democrats and those Republicans who believed quick restoration of fraternal loyalty was more important than proscription of rebels or protection for former slaves. Radical, Negrophile Republicans on one hand, and die-hard rebels on the other, would be left to make what ineffectual political opposition they could.

As he pursued his program, Johnson ignored, in fact subverted, the congressional component of the wartime reconstruction policy. In the process he virtually nullified several laws. With few exceptions his provisional governors would not take the test oath required of national officers; he did not submit their names to the Senate for confirmation, as his had been submitted by Lincoln; he authorized his cabinet to fill national offices in the South with men who could not even qualify to take the required oath. With Johnson's encouragement, the attorney general instructed United States district attorneys to drop confiscation proceedings. In a controversial decision, Johnson ordered the Freedmen's Bureau to return all abandoned property and all confiscated property not yet sold to the Confederates taking the amnesty oath or getting pardons directly from him.

Slowly, the implications of these actions became apparent. Some radical Republicans were convinced from the beginning that Johnson intended to betray them. Other Republicans grew nervous as they witnessed ex-Confederates gaining control of the new governments created under Johnson's supervision. In most of the Southern states outright rebels were elected to the state offices in the elections that followed modification of their old state constitutions. In Louisiana, and to some extent Virginia and Arkansas, where reconstruction had already begun under Lincoln, loyalist officeholders were removed. Confederate army officers and political leaders were elected to Congress (among them four generals and Alexander H. Stephens, the vice president of the Confederacy). Each state legislature except that of North Carolina passed restrictive laws governing the conduct, rights, and economic possibilities of the newly freed slaves.

Despite their uneasiness, only a few Republicans openly challenged Johnson's activities in 1865. Political reasons and honest concern for the nation's future caused the vast majority of Republicans to refuse to risk alienating the President. They knew that the Democrats were wooing Johnson; they did not yet know for certain how receptive he was. They dared not push him into their enemies' embrace. His desertion would undoubtedly divide the Union party and restore the Democrats to power, bringing a return to the prewar political situation—when Southerners dominated the national government in the interest of slavery through their control of the Democratic party.

When Congress met in December 1865, only the most radical Republican congressmen—Representatives Thaddeus Stevens, George S. Boutwell, James M. Ashley, Senators Charles Sumner, Benjamin F. Wade, Zachariah Chandler, and others—urged their colleagues to repudiate Johnson's policy and organize new, territorial governments in the South, with territorial legislatures and governors under direct national control, elected by Southern blacks and whites alike. Republican congressmen listened to the more conservative counsel of moderate leaders such as Senators William P. Fessenden, Lyman Trumbull, and John Sherman, and Representative John A. Bingham. They could not bring themselves to abandon the freedmen to Southern whites without any national protection, but they would not permit a confrontation with the President. Merely postponing recognition of Johnson's new Southern state governments rather than replacing them, Republican congressmen in 1866 almost unanimously passed legislation protecting freedmen's civil rights and economic interests and proposed that certain safeguards be written into the national Constitution. That done, conservative and middle-of-the-road Republicans expected to recognize the restoration of the state governments erected at the President's initiative, and Johnson would be satisfied. If the radicals refused to go along, insisting on the imposition of black suffrage or territorialization, the conservatives and centrists would rally to the President's side.

But the strong-willed Johnson refused to cooperate. Encouraged by the Democrats, the President denied Congress's power to postpone recognition of his state governments. The states had never been out of the Union, he insisted; they had never lost their rights as states. Their *officials* had committed treason, leaving the state governments without legal officeholders. He had merely initiated the process to refill those offices after the Confederate surrender. The state governments were operating once more and Congress had no power to deny their representation in the national legislature.

As he denied congressional Republicans a voice in the restoration process, Johnson also argued that the legislation proposed by the nonradicals to protect the freedmen was an unconstitutional invasion of state jurisdiction. In February and March of 1866, he vetoed the Freedmen's Bureau and civil rights bills and openly attacked the Republicans in Congress, believing that they were all radicals. Stunned, nonradicals joined radicals in challenging Johnson's arguments. Johnson had never before indicated that the Southern states had retained all their rights, despite the rebellion. And he certainly had done more than merely set the state governments going again; he had required changes in their constitutions, the ratification of the Thirteenth Amendment, and nullification of the secession ordinances. Even as he vetoed the Freedmen's Bureau and civil rights bills, the army, under his orders, retained authority to intervene in Southern state affairs.

Republicans maintained that a state of war existed and would continue to exist until Southern states were given civil, territorial governments or were restored to the Union as states. Until peace was officially proclaimed the national government could administer the South under its war powers. This was what Johnson really had done after Appomattox as Commander in Chief, Republicans insisted. His assertion that the rebel states had never forfeited their rights seemed to deny Congress the opportunity to use the same powers he had exercised. However, the Constitution charged Congress, not the President, with making the laws. Perhaps the President had been justified in beginning the reconstruction process after the Confederate surrender, while Congress was in recess, but ultimately restoration was a question of law and required the sanction of the people's legislators. As for the Freedmen's Bureau and civil rights bills, the first was justified as wartime legislation and both were legitimate efforts to give effect to the Thirteenth Amendment to the Constitution.

If Johnson expected large numbers of Republicans to follow him into an alliance with the pro-Southern, anti-Negro Democrats, he was disappointed. Only a small number of Republican congressmen sustained him and an even smaller proportion of the party rank-and-file. The stakes were too high to permit faltering, no matter the temptation of presidential patronage or fear of a party split. After a short, fruitless effort at accommodation, Republican congressmen passed the civil rights bill and a new Freedmen's Bureau bill over Johnson's vetoes and sent another constitutional amendment to the states for ratification. It guaranteed citizens' civil rights, changed the system of parceling out seats in the House of Representatives to compare more closely to the number of voters in each state, disqualified leading Confederates from holding national office, and guaranteed the national debt while repudiating the Confederate debt. In essence, this was the same program with which conservative and moderate Republicans had hoped Johnson would cooperate. Despite the President's desertion, radicals had been unable to force more extreme measures. Most Republicans agreed that the Johnson-created Southern state governments would be restored to normal relations in the Union when they ratified the amendment.

With the passage of the Fourteenth Amendment, the struggle between Johnson and congressional Republicans began in earnest in the congressional elections of 1866. As Republican candidates defended the congressional program as just and moderate, Johnson's advisers sought to bring his few Republican supporters, Northern Democrats, and white Southerners, together in a grand alliance. At a "national union" convention in Philadelphia, Northern and Southern delegates entered arm-in-arm, swore renewed loyalty, and denounced Republican radicalism. Pro-Johnson Republicans and Democrats fused at the local level to support single candidates for Congress. They ran on Johnson's platform—the restoration process was complete; Southern states were entitled to all their rights in the Union; Congress had no power to interfere with state regulation of black citizens; the Fourteenth Amendment was unnecessary insofar as it guaranteed the national debt and wrong insofar as it mandated racial legal equality and limited ex-Confederates' political privileges. If elected, the coalition candidates would simply vote to admit Southern congressmen-elect to their seats, thus recognizing the return of normal American government relationships.

In the battle, Johnson used all the powers of the presidency. He had already vetoed Republican legislation, using his veto messages as sounding boards for his position, buttressing his constitutional justifications with blatant appeals to racial prejudice. He sent friendly military officers on fact-finding investigations designed to discredit the Freedmen's Bureau. In September he seized on an invitation to lay a wreath at the newly-erected Stephen A. Douglas memorial in Chicago to launch an unprecedented campaign swing through the North in support of the pro-Johnson congressional candidates. (Since no President had ever made such a campaign tour before, Americans did not know how to react. Military officers like General Grant and Admiral Farragut felt obligated to accompany the President when he asked them to join him, despite their reluctance to endorse his program. Leading Republicans joined in offering the formal welcomes traditionally reserved for Presidents visiting in their official capacity, only to be subjected to campaign speeches. From whistlestops and hotel balconies, the barnstorming President launched very bitter invective at his Republican opponents from which even his supporters urged him to desist.)

As the 1866 campaign wore on, Johnson used his power over the patronage to force national civil servants to endorse his policies. Over thirteen hundred staunchly Republican postmasters, about one-tenth the total number, were removed and replaced by Democrats or pro-Johnson Republicans; the remainder prudently kept silent or went to work for Republican opponents. Many Republicans were critical of Johnson's use of the patronage whip. Like most Americans, they believed that to the political victors belonged the political spoils; what they objected to was giving the spoils to the *losers*. So long as the people freely elected an administration, the distribution of patronage remained the result of democratic decision. Johnson disregarded that decision, in an effort not only to sustain his deeply held constitutional convictions but to amass political power. If he was not checked, Republicans feared, he would set a precedent through which future Presidents might turn the national civil service into personal political machines.

Wherever the opportunity offered itself, Johnson sustained his supporters in less savory ways. In Maryland, the pro-Johnson governor, Thomas Swann, determined to insure Johnson's success, abrogated the registry law passed in 1864 to prevent Confederates from voting. Fearing that the Baltimore election judges appointed by the Republican police commissioners would throw out rebels' votes, Swann replaced the commissioners with Conservatives (as the anti-Republicans were called in Maryland). When the Republican commissioners refused to vacate their offices and appealed to a state judge, who sustained them, Swann prepared to use force and secured a commitment from Johnson to supply him with federal troops, if necessary. Only quick action by Grant, who fashioned a compromise that ultimately guaranteed a Conservative victory, avoided bloodshed.

New Orleans was not so lucky. There Johnson encouraged local, pro-Johnson officials to disperse an unauthorized convention called by Republicans to amend the Louisiana constitution. Assured by the President that the army would not intervene except to help, New Orleans officials presided over the massacre of over forty delegates and observers. At the same time, Grant and Secretary of War Edwin M. Stanton had to engage in bureaucratic delay maneuvers to prevent Johnson from turning national armaments over to the newly forming, ex-Confederate-dominated Southern state militias.

Despite the efforts of Johnson and his allies, it soon became apparent that Republicans would retain at least a majority in both branches of Congress. Johnson's appeals to conservative constitutionalism, to racial prejudice, and for a return to "normalcy" simply could not overcome the majority of Northerners' fears of renewed Southern power and desires for a commitment to at least some protection for Southern blacks. But as the tide turned to the Republicans, Johnson's friends hinted that he might not acquiesce in the popular verdict. If enough pro-Johnson candidates were elected in the North so that they and the excluded Southern congressmen-elect outnumbered the Republicans, Johnson might recognize his allies as the lawful Congress of the United States instead of the Republican-dominated body. Johnson's supporters asked, "Is the Rump a Congress?" and referred to "the illegal constitution of the two Houses of Congress." As Johnson himself called Congress a body "hanging upon the verge of the Government . . . which assumes to be . . . the Congress of the United States," Republicans began to fear that the President was seriously contemplating a *coup d' etat*. Since a majority of the House consisted of 121 members, Republicans anxiously appealed to Northern voters to "secure the all-important point, *the election of at least 122 Republicans to the next House of Representatives*, the only way . . . by which the country can be saved from an outbreak of violence." In the end, the Northern electorate responded, overwhelmingly repudiating Johnson and his reconstruction policy by returning a Congress that was three-quarters Republican.

Republican congressional leaders, returning to Washington for the second session of the Thirty-Ninth Congress in December 1866, anticipated that the elections of 1866 had settled the reconstruction question. They expected that the Johnson-created Southern state legislatures would see the futility of continued resistance and ratify the Fourteenth Amendment, meeting the congressional Republican condition for restoration to normal relations. But as ratification movements developed in Virginia and Alabama and threatened to spread elsewhere, Johnson personally intervened. "What good can be obtained by reconsidering the constitutional amendment?" he telegraphed Alabama's ex-Governor Lewis E. Parsons, who had asked his advice on behalf of the state legislature. If Southerners remained firm in their rejection of congressional overtures, the people of the North would eventually turn against the Republicans, Johnson and his allies assured the ex-Confederates. White Southerners heeded the advice and adopted a policy Johnson's friends called "masterly inactivity." "Time . . . will gradually teach the masses of the North the necessity of redeeming the republicanism of the country," they assured each other. "There is much virtue in passive resistance, when the influence of time is on the side of those who passively resist."

Johnson-supporting Southern state legislatures one by one rejected the

Fourteenth Amendment. Almost two years had passed since Lee's surrender, and the Union still was not restored. How long would Northerners sustain Congress in such a deadlock? Fearful of further drift and angry at Southern intransigence, from January to March 1867 congressional Republicans finally framed and passed two reconstruction bills over Johnson's veto. Declaring Johnson's governments provisional, the law authorized military commanders to protect life and property where necessary, to supersede local legislation and promulgate their own regulations, to replace local officials (ultimately, the commanders used these powers sparingly), and to require them to organize new state constitutional conventions whose delegates were elected by whites and blacks alike. The Southern states would be restored to normal relations in the Union when they framed new constitutions eliminating racial discrimination in civil rights and voting and ratified the Fourteenth Amendment.

Many of the more radical Republicans were dismayed at the limitations of the new congressional policy. They had wanted to treat the South as United States territories, with blacks and whites governing together under ultimate congressional supervision until they learned to respect each other's rights. Many of them had hoped to require the establishment of free public schools; others wanted to break up the large plantations and redistribute the land in an effort to replace the Southern aristocracy with independent yeoman farmers.

But most of all, radicals had opposed turning reconstruction over to the army, in part because they feared the military's inate conservatism, but primarily because, as President, Andrew Johnson was Commander in Chief of the Armed Forces. Johnson had already displayed his willingness to ignore the test oath and confiscation laws. The Freedmen's Bureau commissioner was already privately complaining of Johnson's interference, and national law officers had done nothing to enforce the Civil Rights Act. What likelihood was there that Johnson would fairly administer the reconstruction laws? "As well commission a lunatic to superintend a lunatic asylum, or a thief to govern a penitentiary!" exclaimed one radical newspaper.

Impelled by the conviction that Johnson would subvert any congressional reconstruction program, radical Republicans worked for the President's impeachment at the same time Congress hammered out the reconstruction bills. But more conservative Republicans acted to check them. The party caucus resolved, over radical objections, that no resolution of impeachment might be brought to the floor of the House without prior caucus approval. Further, the Republicans agreed that the caucus should sanction no impeachment resolution unless it was first approved by the House Judiciary Committee.

Impeachment was far too radical a step for Republican conservatives and moderates. Instead they determined to remedy presidential abuses by legislation. They made certain that General Grant remained a buffer between the President and the army by creating a new headquarters of the army, requiring all presidential orders to pass through it and forbidding Grant's assignment elsewhere without his approval. (Earlier, Johnson had tried to get Grant out of Washington by ordering him to Mexico on a diplomatic mission; Grant flatly refused to go.) To limit Johnson's control of patronage, they passed the Tenure of Office Act, which required senatorial consent for removal in the case of all officers below cabinet rank whose appointment required senatorial confirmation. Officers might be suspended temporarily during congressional recesses, but the President would have to send reasons for the removal to the Senate when it convened, and if the Senate refused to agree, the officer would have to be restored. Members of the cabinet were to be protected this way only for one month after the term of the President who appointed them, so that senators would not be tempted to keep a retiring President's cabinet in office against the will of his successor, a danger when the new Chief Executive belonged to the party opposing the old President and the Senate majority.

But such measures did not reassure the radicals. On January 7, 1867, Representative James M. Ashley proposed an impeachment resolution with the caucus-required proviso that it be referred to the House Judiciary Committee with instructions to commence an investigation of the President. After some conservative Republicans failed to prevent a vote, the House passed the resolution, and the tedious job of taking testimony and searching through documents began.

In the 1860s House committees did not have the resources that are now at their disposal. The Judiciary Committee had one staff secretary. The nine members had to go through the published record, assess congressional documents that indicated possible presidential abuses, turn up new lines of inquiry, and take testimony. In this they were helped, at first, by a few zealous representatives who indicated that they already had important information.

Three Republicans, committee chairman James F. Wilson, George S. Boutwell, and Thomas Williams, assumed the brunt of the burden, each devoting himself to a particular area of interest. Wilson inquired into the connection between Johnson and his White House staff and the pardon brokers who for a fee sought to acquire Executive pardons for those ex-Confederates excluded from the benefits of the amnesty proclamation. He delved into the relation between Johnson and the rumors of *coup d' etat* in the summer of 1866, and into charges that Johnson bartered government positions for promises of political support. Boutwell investigated the Administration's return of confiscated and abandoned property to former rebels, its suspension of the test oath law in the Treasury Department, Johnson's involvement in aborting Southern ratification of the Fourteenth Amendment, hints of personal corruption, and allegations that Johnson ordered charges of desertion dropped in exchange for votes for a congressional candidate pledged to him. Williams tried to determine if the President had improperly delayed the trial of Jefferson Davis and to secure evidence that the President had usurped the powers of Congress when he set the reconstruction process in motion in 1865. The two Democrats specialized in defending the President in often incisive cross-examinations of witnesses.

As the investigation got under way early in February, the committee concentrated on charges that involved clear-cut corruption. Ashley suggested that he had information that would tie Johnson to Lincoln's assassination. Ashley was permitted to examine one of his principal sources, Lafayette C. Baker, who testified that he had seen an 1864 letter from Johnson to Jefferson Davis in which Johnson described the distribution of United States Armed Forces. Baker also insisted that he knew of correspondence between Davis and John Wilkes Booth and that entries implicating others in the assassination conspiracy had been cut from the diary found on Booth's body. Prodded by his interrogators, Baker told the committee where he learned of the damning material and who might know where it could be found. Questioned by

Chairman Wilson, Baker also claimed that he had trapped two women who obtained pardons on commission, indicating that they derived their influence (and thus their incomes) from a too familiar acquaintance with the President.

As Wilson searched into the business of selling pardons, he also investigated the efforts of Edward R. Phelps and Thomas J. Barr to acquire part of the lucrative "general order" business in New York. If they acquired the franchise, which was under the control of the port customs collector, Phelps and Barr would be paid for hauling and storing goods not going immediately through the customhouse for taxation. In his questioning of Phelps, Wilson learned that the two entrepreneurs had offered one-quarter of their profits to another of Johnson's friends, Mrs. Perry, in exchange for her influence. Phelps testified that Mrs. Perry arranged an interview with Johnson, where the President agreed to order the New York collector to give them what they desired because he wanted to "benefit" Mrs. Perry.

In other early meetings, Boutwell plumbed the relationship between Johnson and his friend, Michael Burns, the Confederate-sympathizing president of the Nashville and Chattanooga Railroad. The Massachusetts radical developed leads showing that as military governor of Tennessee Johnson had persuaded the government to complete the Nashville and Northwestern Railroad. After becoming President, he personally ordered that the new line be turned over to its former owners, Burns's Nashville and Chattanooga Railroad, free of charge, with Burns having to pay only for the new, government-supplied locomotives, cars, and other rolling stock. At the same time it appeared that Johnson had taken out two $20,000 loans, one of them from a bank of which Burns was a director. Johnson used the money to meet military expenses, but when the government forwarded him $40,000 to repay the loans, Johnson failed to do so. In November 1866, when the now bankrupt banks pressed him for repayment, Johnson hired Burns to negotiate a settlement which resulted in the repayment of only $30,000. Shortly before Burns arranged the compromise, Johnson authorized Burns's railroad to delay payment of the first installment on the $1,500,000 it owed the government for the rolling stock. As Burns completed his testimony on February 28, 1867, swearing that the two matters were unrelated (but admitting that he hired Johnson's son-in-law, Tennessee Senator David T. Patterson, to help get control of the Nashville and Northwestern), Boutwell prepared to subpoena Johnson's bank records to find out if the $30,000 had come from him or whether Burns might have provided it.

At the same time both Boutwell and Wilson moved into more nebulous areas. Wilson educed testimony that Johnson had offered government positions to obtain support for his reconstruction policy and that he offered to sign a bill granting statehood to Colorado if its senators-elect would promise to support him. (After they hedged, he vetoed the bill.) Boutwell sought to link Johnson to Treasury Secretary McCulloch's decision to appoint treasury agents who could not take the test oath in the South and began to investigate the Administration's failure to enforce the Confiscation Act.

Meeting on fourteen separate days from February 6 to the close of the second session of the Thirty-Ninth Congress on March 2, the Judiciary Committee had barely gotten into its investigation, cautiously taking testimony on facts already in the public record and clearly proposing to call Johnson's defenders to explain them. As the Judiciary Committee's caution became manifest, frustrated radicals tried to hurry the investigation's pace. When the Republican committee members unanimously asked more time on February 28 (the Democrats urged that the investigation simply be dropped), grumbling radicals decided to put the question out of their hands. In a caucus held March 6, Benjamin F. Butler, Stevens, and John Covode proposed transferring the investigation to a special committee made up of the Judiciary Committee plus six new appointees. But committee Chairman Wilson, James G. Blaine, and some radicals urged patience. The debate grew testy. Butler angrily queried whether conservative defenders of the committee, like Bingham, would ever favor impeachment; Bingham answered acidly that he was not "like some gentlemen, in favor of preferring articles of impeachment and hearing the testimony afterward." But when Wilson made the motion an outright test of confidence in the Judiciary Committee, insisting that it be replaced completely or not at all, the radicals backed down and joined in authorizing the committee to continue its work through the upcoming congressional recess.

Failing to remodel the investigating committee, radicals pressed for an early report. Stevens moved that the caucus commit Republicans to reconvening Congress on May 8, 1867, to deal with impeachment. Chairman Wilson, sustained by Blaine and Bingham, urged October 20 instead. As Butler attacked Wilson, arguing that to postpone impeachment so long was to abandon it, Bingham angrily denounced Butler's "arrogance and presumption in attempting to dictate to an independent body of his peers on a grave question like this." But on this issue the House radicals won, defeating Wilson's proposal 80-37 and carrying Stevens's. A middle-of-the-road Republican, who explained that "I always like to vote . . . so as to not be called upon to explain too much at home," worried, "Matters look gloomy to me here now. I fear impracticable men will have the ascendency in the House."

Senate Republicans were even less enthusiastic. In their caucus only Zachariah Chandler called for the President's impeachment, and on the Senate floor conservative Republicans and Democrats passed a resolution to adjourn as usual to the following December, over the objections of radicals, who were not so much in favor of pressing impeachment as they were afraid of leaving Johnson unchecked while the Reconstruction Acts were being carried (or not carried) into effect. After days of wrangling, the radicals and nonradicals compromised, but only after it became apparent that there could be no impeachment under the present circumstances. The House and Senate agreed that Congress might reconvene on the first Wednesday of July if a quorum were present. If not, it would reconvene early in November. Behind the scenes, radical Representative Robert C. Schenck and conservative Senator Edwin D. Morgan, the co-chairmen of the Congressional Campaign Committee, were delegated the responsibility of consulting with colleagues and determining if it would be necessary to meet. All agreed that a July meeting was unlikely. Conservative Republican Senator James W. Grimes wrote his wife that the impeachment movement was subsiding. "We have very successfully and thoroughly tied his [Johnson's] hands, and, if we had not, we had better submit to two years of misrule . . . than subject the country, its institutions, and its credit, to the shock of an impeachment," he wrote. "I have always thought so, and everybody is now apparently coming to my conclusion."

To the dismay of the radical members, as the Judiciary Committee returned to its investigation towards the end of March, the case that had been developing against the President began to unravel. Witness after witness swore that John Wilkes Booth's diary was now in the same condition as when removed from his body; pages had not been removed, as Baker had implied, to shield a wider conspiracy. Baker seemed unable to locate the missing Johnson-Davis and Davis-Booth correspondence, or even find the people who told him of it. War Department officials (including Judge Joseph Holt, no friend of the President's reconstruction policy) told the committee that they had sent detectives on the case and they were convinced the papers never existed.

Baker's testimony on Johnson's role in the pardon broker scandals proved no firmer. The women he had trapped swore they had obtained only a handful of pardons, and both claimed unlawful entrapment by Baker's agents. The clerks accused of cooperating in plans to secure pardons for money denied the charges. The ladies turned out to have no special access to Johnson; they saw him during his regular visitation hours, waiting in the antechambers like the rest of the public. Most important, clerks and the President's secretaries testified that Johnson had specifically ordered them to accept no commissions or gratuities for making out pardon papers and announced his intention to give no pardon where money had been involved. Although much of the testimony was self-serving and there could be no doubt that one of the ladies had obtained a pardon for one of Baker's men in exchange for money, the committee could not link the President directly to the offense.

The investigation of Johnson's link to Burns and the Nashville and Chattanooga Railroad did not bear the expected fruit either. Secretary of War Stanton had already testified in February that he and his aides agreed that Southern railroads, even those built or expanded by the government, should be transferred to private hands as quickly as possible, without requiring reimbursement for the government work. "They were constructed under the pressure of war, and for temporary purposes," Stanton insisted. "The object of arriving at the actual cash or money value or equivalent for the roads was not only impracticable, but really of but very little practical interest in comparison with the great end of having the channels of commerce in the rebel States opened and carried on." Stanton presented the committee with a mass of documents showing that the Nashville and Northwestern Railroad was but one of many turned back to civilians in the South after the war, although he conceded that in this case Johnson had issued special orders. Moreover, about half the Southern railroads that owed the government money had been excused from their first payments.

When the cashier of the First National Bank of Washington gave the committee the President's financial account with the bank, it learned that the $30,000 settlement had been paid for out of Johnson's funds after all. (When the cashier told Johnson he would have to comply with the committee's demand, the President told him he did not object.) The worst that could be said was that Burns might have used his good offices to reduce Johnson's debt in exchange for preferential treatment for his railroad (and treatment not too preferential, at that); Johnson had not repaid the loans as soon as he received the $40,000 from the War Department, thus gaining about two years' interest on the $40,000 at seven percent and finally retaining the difference between the $40,000 and the $30,000 settlement; and his decisions might have been influenced by the fact that he possessed state-guaranteed Nashville and Northwestern bonds. Boutwell, who had concentrated on this charge, could provide no evidence that Burns had given Johnson the $30,000 to pay off the loan.

Finally, Wilson was unable to link Johnson directly to a promise to sign the Colorado statehood bill in exchange for its senators' support for his reconstruction policy. The President's private secretary testified that it was his idea, not Johnson's, to try to commit the senators-elect. He had tried to get their promises of support because he favored Colorado statehood and wanted to strengthen his argument when he tried to persuade the President.

Only one more instance of possible outright corruption came to light after most of the earlier charges tottered. Butler learned that Johnson had ordered charges of desertion dropped against nearly two hundred disfranchised West Virginia soldiers after a pro-Johnson congressional candidate had written that he needed their votes to win a close election. Again the committee radicals —Boutwell once more taking the lead—had difficulty connecting Johnson directly to the decision. The question of whether Johnson had ever seen the letter hung until the last minute, when in November 1867 new evidence finally indicated (though not conclusively) that he had. But the offense, if offense there was, was minimal; a War Department investigation of the case had delayed the pardons until after the election, and Johnson's candidate had lost.

As the charges of personal corruption collapsed, Republican committee members reevaluated their positions. If an impeachment were to be brought against the President, it would have to be for *abuse of power* rather than for corruption. From late March through July, the more radical members of the committee—Boutwell, William Lawrence, and Thomas Williams —concentrated on the President's refusal to enforce the Confiscation and Test Oath Acts, his decisions to return confiscated and abandoned property to pardoned rebels and to begin the reconstruction process without involving Congress, and the seemingly endless delay of the Jefferson Davis treason trial.

The facts in most of these areas were clear: Southern United States district attorneys, former Attorney General James Speed, and Attorney General Henry Stanbery conceded that treason and confiscation proceedings in the South had been halted. Freedmen's Bureau Commissioner Oliver Otis Howard and former Assistant Commissioner for South Carolina Rufus Saxton testified that Johnson had ordered a change in Freedmen's Bureau instructions that required immediate restoration of confiscated property to pardoned Confederates—Saxton was replaced when he refused to comply. Documents showed that forty-five Southern railroads captured and operated by the government during the war, worth about $73,000,000, had been returned to their pro-rebel owners. About 400,000 acres of the 800,000 acres held by the Freedmen's Bureau at the end of the war had been returned to pardoned owners by April 1866. The President had not reconvened Congress in the summer of 1865, when he began the reconstruction process; he had appointed civilian provisional governors who did not take the test oath; he paid them out of contingency funds of the War Department; and he turned confiscated cotton, rosin, and other products over to them to help defray the operating costs of their provisional governments in the absence of a congressional appropriation. Finally, Davis's trial had been put off for two years, and in May 1867, the government did not challenge a defense motion for his release on bail, which was granted.

But the testimony of both present and former officials—including that of Secretary of War Stanton and former Attorney General Speed, both of whom had remained loyal, if conservative, Republicans after Johnson's defection—demonstrated that they and the rest of the cabinet had endorsed Johnson's 1865 decisions on confiscation, the test oath, and reconstruction. General Grant, whose support both Democrats and Republicans claimed, suggested that he might have played an important role in committing the President to a lenient restoration policy. Stanton told the investigators that Saxton had been removed from South Carolina not at the President's order because he obstructed the return of rebel property, but at the request of Freedmen's Bureau Commissioner Howard, who had worried about the deteriorating relations between Saxton and white South Carolinians.

Speed and the district attorney who had direct responsibility for the Davis trial testified that the proceedings were delayed because they wanted Supreme Court Chief Justice Salmon P. Chase to preside. Chase refused to do so until Johnson withdrew the military's authority to interfere with the courts in the South. The President had played no part in the decision to seek Chase's participation in the case and insisted that he *had* withdrawn the military's right to interfere with the courts; ironically, it was Congress that argued that the South was not yet restored to normal relations in the Union, that it was still under military control. It was less clear why the government had not opposed Davis's release on bond, but the committee could not trace this decision to Johnson either.

By May and July 1867, it became clear that Johnson had not personally imposed a pro-Southern reconstruction policy on resisting aides, or even that he was the program's chief instigator. His had been the policy of an entire administration, undertaken in good faith. Except for the vague Tennessee Railroad affair and the dropping of the desertion charges, there was no hint of personal corruption in the policy's execution. But the evidence also showed that in carrying it out, Johnson had, with the consent and help of his subordinates, many of whom were still loyal Republicans, systematically nullified congressional legislation and violated its spirit, interpreting his presidential powers more broadly than any President before Lincoln. And modern America's love for the martyred President must not blind us to the fact that his view of Executive power far exceeded that expounded by accepted prewar authorities.

But the question remained as to whether these decisions amounted to impeachable offenses. As the Judiciary Committee collected testimony and documentary evidence, Americans arrived at two opposite concepts of the law of impeachment. Ultimately, these differing opinions were expounded primarily through three discussions: an indirect exchange in the American Law Register of March and September 1867, between Professor Theodore M. Dwight of Columbia College Law School and Judiciary Committee member

William Lawrence, who participated only rarely in the questioning of witnesses; the majority and minority reports on impeachment delivered by the House Judiciary Committee in November; and the speeches delivered by Boutwell and Wilson in the House defending the majority and minority reports in December.

The Constitution permits the impeachment of United States officers for "treason, bribery, or other high crimes and misdemeanors." Dwight, Judiciary Committee Chairman Wilson, Bingham, and most of the more conservative Republicans and Democrats concluded that this meant that President Johnson could be impeached only for an actual crime, a violation of law for which he might be indicted before a court of law. They pointed to the manifest similarities between impeachment and trial before the Senate and indictment and trial before a court. They noted that the Constitution often mentioned impeachment in conjunction with ordinary criminal process. ("The trial of all crimes, except in cases of impeachment, shall be by jury"; the President "shall have power to grant reprieves and pardons for offences against the United States, except in cases of impeachment.") They interpreted the English precedents as requiring indictable crimes, and they emphasized that the United States Senate had refused to convict defendants in two earlier impeachment trials which turned at least in part on whether the alleged, *nonindictable* offenses were impeachable.

For many years historians accepted the conservatives' view as correct, suggesting that the radicals' insistence on a broader definition was based on partisanship and vindictiveness. But recently, opinion has shifted towards the radical position. The more radical Republicans—including Boutwell, Williams, and Lawrence on the Judiciary Committee—argued that the framers of the Constitution had intended impeachment to be a remedy for noncriminal *abuses of power*. The Constitution vests the President and judges with broad, easily abused discretionary powers. Congress cannot pass laws making it illegal to use those powers; Americans must rely on their officers to use them in good faith. But if that faith is misplaced, impeachment must be the remedy. Otherwise, there is no remedy. To buttress their argument, some of the radicals also turned to the English precedents, insisting that, contrary to the conservatives' interpretation, those precedents demonstrated that indictability was not a prerequisite for impeachment (other radicals conceded that the English impeachments required indictable crimes but emphasized differences between English and American experience). They pointed out that every impeachment by the House of Representatives involved at least some nonindictable offenses; they stressed the convictions of Judges John Pickering and West H. Humphries by the Senate for nonindictable offenses in 1804 and 1862; and they quoted the opinions of the eminent constitutional authorities of the late eighteenth and early nineteenth centuries—Madison, Hamilton, Story, Kent, and Rawle.

Like other Americans, the committee members divided over the issue. In discussions held in late May and early June, the Republicans Wilson, Frederick E. Woodbridge, and John C. Churchill, sustained by Democrats Samuel S. Marshall and Charles A. Eldridge, concluded that Johnson's activities did not amount to the "high crimes and misdemeanors" the Constitution held impeachable. Boutwell, Williams, Lawrence, and Francis Thomas disagreed, and on a preliminary vote taken June 2, the committee voted 5 to 4 against reporting an impeachment resolution.

As the disagreement grew, Wilson withdrew more and more from active pursuit of evidence damaging to the President, maintaining a certain detachment. His occasional questions tended to exonerate Johnson from individual responsibility for decisions. Boutwell and Williams bore the brunt of the investigation in May and July when the Democrats began to counterattack more vigorously. The impeachment movement seemed to sputter.

While the more radical Republicans concluded that President Johnson was impeachable for his abuses of discretionary power, Johnson himself provided more ammunition by fulfilling radicals' fears that he would interfere with the military's administration of the Reconstruction Acts. Johnson did appoint military commanders to execute the laws, as the acts required, but when they began to order the removal of particularly obstructive and violent officers of the Johnsonian provisional governments, the President ordered the removals deferred and asked his attorney general for an official opinion on the commanders' powers. Read to the cabinet in May and appearing officially on June 12, 1867, Stanbery's opinion virtually emasculated the Reconstruction Acts. Declaring that all new laws should be narrowly construed, the attorney general held that the military commanders had power only to keep the peace and punish criminal acts. The provisional governments and federal courts retained all other jurisdictions, therefore the military authorities could not intervene to enforce the Civil Rights Act, had no jurisdiction over crimes committed before Congress passed the Reconstruction Acts, and had no authority over acts not in violation of state or national law. Commanders could not remove the officials of the provisional governments. Although the Reconstruction Acts disqualified many former Confederate civil and military officers from voting or running for office while the states remained under military control, Stanbery determined that registration boards had to accept Southerners' oaths that they did not fall within the proscribed group, as the boards had no power to investigate whether the swearer had perjured himself. Finally, Stanbery affirmed that the President retained supervisory power over the enforcement of the Reconstruction Acts, "to see that all 'the laws are faithfully executed.' "

Stanbery's opinion shocked the Republicans and the military commanders. The commander in the Carolinas, General Sickles, wrote Washington headquarters that it "prevents the execution of the Reconstruction acts, disarms me of means to protect life, property, or the rights of citizens and menaces all interests in these States with ruin." Other commanders asked Grant whether they must consider the circular a direct order. Grant told them to enforce their own constructions of the law until ordered otherwise.

As rumors circulated that Johnson would order the commanders in the South to restore to office all officials they had removed, even conservative Republican congressmen concluded that a July session of Congress would be necessary. But as soon as it convened, a bitter struggle developed over what to do and how long to stay. Aided by Washington's intolerable summer heat and humidity, conservatives rammed through a resolution to limit the session to the repair of the damage to the Reconstruction Acts. Impeachment resolutions would be ruled out of order.

Unable to force an impeachment report from the Judiciary Committee during the July session, radicals urged their colleagues to return to Washington early in October to take up the question. But as Boutwell pressed the radical proposal, Wilson opposed it and congressmen learned of the division of opinion within the Judiciary Committee. Assured that Johnson intended no more interference with the law, Republicans once again rejected the radicals' importunings. As they passed a new, supplementary Reconstruction Act to repair the damage done by the attorney general's opinion, the two houses voted to adjourn until November 21.

But Johnson's assurances proved illusory. On August 5 he asked for the resignation of Secretary of War Stanton, the last loyal Republican in his cabinet and the buffer between Johnson and the army. Encouraged by Republican friends, Stanton refused to resign; Johnson ordered his suspension and appointed Grant secretary of war *ad interim*, apparently following the procedure outlined in the Tenure of Office Act. Johnson countered by ordering the replacement of Sheridan in his Southern command and Sickles in the Carolinas. Grant warned General Pope, commander in Georgia, Alabama, and Florida, that he would probably be next. Republicans reacted with stunned outrage. The conservative publisher of the Boston *Advertiser* wrote to Sumner, "Is the President crazy, or only drunk? I am afraid his doings will make us all favor impeachment." Throughout the country Republican demands for impeachment grew, and leaders began to endorse the idea.

The Judiciary Committee took no new evidence on the President's alleged obstruction of the law. The lines were already drawn. Boutwell, Lawrence, Williams, and Francis Thomas favored impeachment for abuse of power. They already had evidence of Johnson's disregard of the Confiscation, Test Oath, and Freedmen's Bureau Acts and his "usurpation of power" in 1865 when he proceeded with reconstruction without congressional involvement or authorization. His subversion of the Reconstruction Acts was frosting on the cake; the impeachment managers could gather new evidence and frame new articles on that charge after the House voted an impeachment resolution. The one Republican and two Democratic members, Churchill, Wilson, and Woodbridge, opposed impeachment for anything less than an indictable violation of the law, and no evidence existed to show Johnson had committed such a violation. (Actually, Churchill would surprise the radicals and change his mind; Johnson's new offensive persuaded him to vote for impeachment.)

If Johnson's summer and fall offensives drove more Republicans to endorse impeachment, other factors continued to hold many back. Many Republicans preferred that Johnson remain President rather than elevating Benjamin F. Wade, who, as president *pro tempore* of the Senate, was next in succession. Wade had not only made bitter enemies of such influential colleagues as Fessenden and Grimes, but he believed in high protective tariffs on imported goods and favored a large money supply including paper currency not tied directly to gold. Many Republicans opposed those policies on principle; others feared that a Wade administration would divide the party on fiscal and revenue issues, destroying the unity born of the reconstruction crisis.

Presidential politics also played a role. Wade himself was a candidate for the Republican nomination, supported by many radicals who agreed with his economic ideas. Supreme Court Justice Salmon P. Chase, a radical, also was in the running, but was supported by powerful, fiscally conservative allies in the financial community. Both candidates had many enemies in the party; each was firmly identified with radicalism and economic ideas which would alienate many voters. Those Republicans who thought maximum Republican strength could be obtained only by muting these issues turned more and more to General Grant as a safe, conservative candidate. The successful impeachment of Johnson would place Wade in the presidency, making certain the nomination of a radical candidate and, cautious Republicans believed, ultimately weakening the party.

The elections of fall 1867 seemed to confirm the conservatives' fears. In the midst of calls for impeachment and demands for new, more stringent reconstruction measures, the voters seemed to rebuke Republican radicalism. Fortunately for the Republicans, few important officers were involved, but in every Northern state but one, Republican candidates for local office lost ground. In Ohio, Republicans lost control of the state legislature, dooming Wade's chances for reelection to the Senate (and for the Republican presidential nomination, as well). The results firmed conservative Republicans' resolve to resist impeachment, as sobered congressmen gathered that November in Washington.

On November 15 the Judiciary Committee met to take some last minute evidence, and then debated the implications of what they had found. To everyone's surprise, Churchill shifted. On November 20 he, Boutwell, Lawrence, Williams, and Thomas voted to recommend an impeachment resolution to the House; Wilson, Woodbridge, Marshall, and Eldridge recorded their opposition.

The members of the Judiciary Committee offered their conclusions to the House on November 25, 1867 in three separate reports. The majority report—written by Williams and signed by Boutwell, Lawrence, Thomas, and Churchill—endorsed the President's removal. Without specifying articles (that would be left to a special committee if the House endorsed an impeachment resolution), the majority proposed to impeach the President for abuse of his powers. "The great salient point of accusation . . . is *usurpation of power,*" Williams's report asserted, for the "purpose of reconstructing the shattered governments of the rebel States in accordance with his own will, in the interests of the great criminals who carried them into the rebellion, and in such a way as to deprive the people of the local States of all chances of indemnity for the past or security for the future . . . by hurrying them back . . . into a condition where they could once more embarrass and defy, if not absolutely rule the government which they had vainly endeavored to destroy. It is around this point, and as auxiliary to this great central idea, that all the special acts of mal-administration we have witnessed, will be found to gravitate. . . ." To achieve his illicit objective, Johnson issued "his imperial proclamations" setting the restoration process in motion, "creating, under the denomination of provisional governors, civil offices unknown to law; appointing to those offices men who were notoriously disqualified by reason of their participation in the rebellion. . . ." Unable to support the governors and their administration with congressionally appropriated funds, the President "not only directs the payment of a portion of them out of the contingent fund of the War Department, but with a boldness unequalled even by Charles

I, when he, too, undertook to reign without a Parliament, provides for a deficit by authorizing the seizure of property and the appropriation of moneys belonging to the government. . . ."

With this inflammatory language Williams detailed "other measures of state, of less publicity, perhaps, but equally arbitrary and lawless of themselves, which . . . were . . . a part of the same great conspiracy . . ."—the return of rebel property (emphasizing especially the Nashville and Northwestern Railroad), the subversion of the Confiscation and Freedmen's Bureau Acts, the refusal to punish the leading rebels, and abuse of the appointing and pardon powers. Acknowledging that the President's constitutional authority in some of these areas is "without apparent limitation upon its exercise," the report went to the heart of the congressmen's interpretation of the law of impeachment: "It would [be] a false logic, and a poor statesmanship . . . to infer that [such powers are] . . . without reasonable limitations altogether, and may be exercised without discrimination, to the great damage, and possibly to the entire destruction of the government. Every power granted by the Constitution is subject to such a qualification, and if susceptible of abuse, is only to be checked and controlled by the remedy of impeachment."

Listing seventeen presidential acts "involving undoubted usurpation of power, and repeated violations of law," Williams's report became grounds for the impeachment. Citing the most venerated English and American constitutional authorities, Williams concluded that impeachment lay for high crimes and misdemeanors *against the state* and demonstrated the inconsistency of the narrower view with past practice and interpretation.

The dissenting Republicans, Wilson and Woodbridge, offered one of the two minority reports. While Williams's report was an incitive, partisan indictment of the President, Wilson correctly divined the wish of most Republicans to project the appearance of fairness. He appealed to the lawyers' commitment to strict forms and common law procedures. Arguing that crimes must consist of infractions of known laws, Wilson insisted that only indictable offenses against the United States were impeachable. He cited the language of the Constitution, traversed Senate decisions in previous impeachments, and insisted that as a rule the English precedents sustained his position.

Turning to the evidence, Wilson quoted the testimony of Johnson's cabinet members, demonstrating the unanimity with which they had endorsed his policies. He reminded the House that the Joint Committee on Reconstruction, which had investigated Johnson's policy and recommended the Fourteenth Amendment, had not accused him of wrongdoing. Indeed, congressional Republicans themselves had been willing to recognize the legitimacy of the Johnson-sanctioned state governments if they ratified the Fourteenth Amendment.

Wilson quickly disposed of abuse of discretionary power charges. Johnson was following long-standing custom in appointing political supporters and removing opponents from the civil service. Testimony showed that the decision to appoint officers who could not take the test oath was made on the advice of the cabinet, limited to one department, and done to improve the administration of the government rather than to promote rebel control in the South. In the case of the pardoned deserters, rules of criminal evidence precluded the determination that the President ever saw the letter promising their political support, and even if he had, the act of pardon itself was lawful. "For what, then, is he to be impeached—the bad motive or the good deed?" The testimony did not sustain charges of personal corruption in the granting of pardons; the general policy of leniency had the endorsement of the cabinet, including the members now arrayed with the Republican party against the President; so did the decision to restore confiscated railroads to civilian control and to return property to pardoned rebels. The Nashville and Northwestern case was but a specific instance of the general policy.

Assuming the calm, judicious tone of nonpartisanship, Wilson's report clearly impressed conservative and centrist Republicans. Since Wilson and Woodbridge were defending a political enemy, their colleagues credited their views as neutral evaluations of the case. A more careful investigation might indicate that their arguments based on the language of the Constitution were fallacious, that they had carefully culled inappropriate citations from the English and American precedents, and had been forced to deny the validity of most of the English ones (indeed, recent scholars have concluded that Wilson and Woodbridge's legal arguments were wrong), but the dissenters had struck a responsive chord. Unwilling to impeach the President for political reasons, hoping that he would cease his attacks on the Reconstruction Acts with his latest removals, most Republicans happily accepted Wilson and Woodbridge's conclusions. The Democrats, of course, endorsed Marshall and Eldridge's view that the President's activities were not only unimpeachable but praiseworthy.

On December 5, 1865, more than nine months after Ashley had moved his impeachment resolution, the House finally began its impeachment debate. As the senior signer of the Judiciary Committee's majority report, Boutwell spoke first, offering the most convincing argument yet made for the President's removal. Arguing in the same calm but earnest tone Wilson had adopted in the minority report, Boutwell sympathized with those Republicans who feared that the remedy of impeachment might be worse than the abuses of Johnson's Administration. He admitted that he too might have been willing to drop the matter if he was not even more afraid of the consequences.

Recognizing that Wilson's report had convinced most Republicans that Johnson's course did not constitute an impeachable offense, Boutwell turned to Wilson's legal argument first. "If the theory of the law submitted by the minority of the committee be in the judgment of this House a true theory, then the majority have no case whatever," he admitted. His job was to demonstrate its fallaciousness. Deftly, Boutwell responded to Wilson's argument that the language of the Constitution implied that impeachment lay only for indictable offenses. Certainly, as Wilson had emphasized, the Constitution provided that an impeached offender could later be indicted and tried in a regular court; of course, the Constitution had specifically prohibited a President from pardoning an impeached defendant. (Wilson argued that this linked impeachment to the kinds of criminal offenses for which a pardon was appropriate.) Thus, in a specific case, an officer *might* be impeached for an indictable crime, and if he was, he could not claim immunity from a regular court trial afterwards or receive a pardon. The fallacy in Wilson's argument lay in his assumption that because an impeachable offense *might* be indictable, it *must*, therefore, be indictable.

English precedents cited by Wilson were irrelevant, Boutwell continued. The framers of the Constitution had adopted the impeachment proceeding developed in England and put it to a new, limited use. In England its purpose was to punish crime; removal from office was merely the side effect. In America impeachment was designed *solely* to remove government officials; any criminal punishment had to be preceded by a courtroom trial. "It follows naturally and necessarily from the distinction stated that in this country a proceeding by impeachment is not a criminal proceeding," Boutwell concluded.

He pointed out that the framers of the Constitution could not have intended impeachment to lie only for indictable crimes against the United States. The government was in existence for over a year before Congress passed a crimes act "and during that time neither treason nor bribery was indictable by law in any court of the United States. . . . Will anybody say in view of this provision of the Constitution that our fathers would have sat silently and submitted to the administration of a man who was elected by bribery, but whose offense was by no law of the land indictable?" Moreover, Boutwell added, murder, arson, and most other crimes are within *state* jurisdiction, and Congress could not pass laws against them. Under the minority theory, "a civil officer might be guilty of murder within the jurisdiction of a State where the crime is not and cannot be punishable by any law of Congress, and the House and Senate would have no power to arraign, try, and remove him from office." Finally, it would be impossible to anticipate by specific criminal laws all the possible types of misconduct. "At the present moment we have no law which declares that it shall be a high crime or misdemeanor for the President to decline to recognize the Congress of the United States, and yet, should he deny its lawful and constitutional existence and authority, and thus virtually dissolve the Government, would the House and Senate be impotent and unable to proceed by process of impeachment to secure his removal from office?" Congress could not be expected to anticipate all the ways in which government officers might abuse their trusts. The minority theory "offers substantially free license to executive and judicial officers," Boutwell insisted. Turning to the great English and American legal authorities, and the course of past American impeachments, Boutwell demonstrated that the precedents corresponded to his logic.

Only after establishing his legal argument did Boutwell turn to the facts of the particular case. Johnson's offense was in using his discretionary powers for the purpose of reconstructing this Government in the interest of the rebellion . . . ." True, standing alone his acts might not be impeachable.

> It was only by a series of acts, . . . by participation direct or indirect in numerous transactions, some of them open and some of them secret, that this great scheme was carried on. . . . When you bring all these acts together; when you consider what he has said; when you consider what he has done; when you consider that he has appropriated the public property for the benefit of rebels; when you consider that in every public act . . . from May, 1865, to the present time, all has tended to this great result, the restoration of the rebels to power under and in the Government of the

> country . . . , can there be any doubt as to his purpose, or doubt as to the criminality of his purpose and his responsibility under the Constitution?

And if Congress did not act in the face of assertions of presidential power to dispense with laws, what lay in the future? Would congressional timidity bring on an even greater crisis by encouraging Johnson to abrogate the reconstruction laws in 1868, insisting that Southern whites (and Southern whites alone) had the right to vote in the presidential election? Would Congress accept Southern electoral votes in those circumstances? If not, would Johnson acquiesce? "If that logic be followed, the next presidential election will be heralded by civil war. . . ."

Boutwell's attack upon the minority theory of the impeachment law was so powerful that Wilson immediately retreated from it as he began his rejoinder on December 6. "No member of the minority of the committee regards the doctrine that only crimes and misdemeanors indictable under the statutes of the United States will justify an impeachment of a civil officer of the slightest importance so far as a correct determination of this case is concerned," he announced. Nonetheless, he devoted nearly his entire speech to defending the proposition, drawing blood by emphasizing the differences between Boutwell's persuasive speech and Williams's mediocre report. Once again he appealed to the lawyers' distaste of unlimited power. Boutwell had argued that the impeachment power "is subject to no revision or control, and that its exercise is to be guided solely by the conscience of the House," Wilson said.

> Correctly interpreted, this doctrine, as it seems to me, comes to this: that whatever this House may declare on its conscience to be an impeachable offense, reduce to the form of articles, and carry to the Senate for trial, that body is only to be allowed to declare whether the officer impeached is guilty of the facts presented against him, but is not to be permitted to say that such facts do or do not constitute a crime or a misdemeanor. Does he desire to intrust the character, extent, and uses of this power to the shifting fortunes of political parties? What could be more dangerous to the peace and safety of the Government than this?

Wilson then turned for a few moments to the facts, but he abruptly dropped them to return to the legal issue. "Sir, we must be guided by some rule in this grave proceeding. . . . If we cannot arraign the President for a specific crime, for what are we to proceed against him? For a bundle of generalities such as we have in the volume of testimony reported by the committee to the House in this case?" So despite his disclaimer, Wilson relied, after all, on his legal objections, and then he moved to lay the resolution on the table.

An intense struggle followed. Over forty pro-impeachment Republicans had prepared speeches, many of them bitterly critical of their more cautious colleagues. But by moving to table the resolution, Wilson precluded debate. The radicals and those centrists who intended to vote with them tried to filibuster the House in an attempt to open the floor, but the anti-impeachment Republican and Democratic coalition held firm. The radicals won their opponents' consent only to vote directly on the impeachment resolution instead of the motion to table it; and on December 7, 1867, without further debate, the Judiciary Committee impeachment resolution was defeated 57 to 108. Sixty-six Republicans voted against it; the radicals had not carried even a majority of their own party. The acrimony was so bitter that many Republicans predicted an open rupture in the party.

Buoyed by the impeachment vote, Johnson and his supporters renewed their attacks on the congressional reconstruction program. General Winfield S. Hancock, whom Johnson had named to replace Sheridan in Louisiana, began to reverse his predecessor's decisions by restoring the pro-Confederate officials Sheridan had replaced. In Virginia, the conservative military commander, John M. Schofield, cooperated with conservative white Southerners against radical Republicans and blacks. On December 28 Johnson removed Pope, General Edward O. C. Ord, commander in Arkansas and Mississippi, and Ord's subordinate, Wager Swayne, commander in Alabama. Desperately, Southern Republicans pleaded with Congress to intervene. Alabama, the first state to make a decision, rejected the proposed new state constitution framed to meet the requirements of the Reconstruction Acts. If other states did the same, Republicans would face impatient Northern voters in the 1868 presidential and congressional elections without having made headway in restoring the Union.

Ominously, Johnson continued his effort to gain complete mastery of the War Department. On December 12 he sent to the Senate his reasons for suspending Stanton the preceding August, urging the senators to sanction Stanton's ouster as required by the Tenure of Office Act. But he did not intend to abide by the Senate's decision. He secured Grant's promise not to return the secretary of war office to Stanton if the Senate refused to endorse his removal. Possibly, Johnson hoped Stanton would go to the Supreme Court, a majority of whose justices reputedly agreed with the President's reconstruction policy, to get back his office. But Grant, faced with a fine and imprisonment for violating the tenure law if Stanton was upheld, changed his mind. When the Senate rejected Johnson's reasons for Stanton's removal, the general returned the office to him.

Furious, Johnson accused Grant of double-dealing, publicly admitting his intention to disregard the Senate decision. Seizing the opportunity, Stevens persuaded the House to transfer the impeachment question to the Reconstruction Committee, where he proposed a new impeachment resolution based on Johnson's conspiracy to violate the Tenure of Office Act. But there too a Democratic-Republican coalition, led by Bingham, defeated the measure.

Having alienated Grant, who later openly allied with the Republicans, the President turned to the popular war hero, General William "Tecumseh" Sherman, who still sympathized with his policy. But when Johnson moved to promote Sherman to Grant's rank and ordered the creation of a new military department headquartered in Washington, with Sherman in command, the general balked. "The President would make use of me to beget violence . . . ," he wired his brother, Senator John Sherman. He would resign rather than accept the new commission. Johnson had to abandon his plan.

But Johnson would not give up. Despite the collapse of his schemes, on February 21, in apparent violation of the Tenure of Office Act, he ordered Stanton's removal from the War Department.

Johnson's final act of defiance infuriated not only the radical Republicans, but the conservative and moderate Republicans who had opposed the earlier impeachment efforts. They could bear no more. As one senator explained, "I have been among those who have hesitated long before resorting to this measure. I thought it better . . . that we should bear much and suffer very much rather than resort to this extreme measure. I had constantly hoped that we had got to the end of the usurpations and the defiances which have been hurled at Congress from time to time by the President of the United States; but at last I am convinced, as I believe all at least upon this side are, that there is to be no end to this course of conduct." Without dissent, Republicans referred another impeachment resolution to the Reconstruction Committee.

After only one day's consideration, the Reconstruction Committee favorably reported the resolution back to the floor. The report consisted of only a few sentences and copies of Johnson's letter dismissing Stanton and appointing General Lorenzo Thomas as his replacement. Moving quickly, Stevens and Bingham arranged two days of debate. One after another, Republicans rose to denounce the President—those who had opposed the December 1867 impeachment resolution expressing dismay at Johnson's continued intransigence and satisfaction that his culpability was now clear. Finally, on February 24, the House passed the committee's simple resolution: "*Resolved,* that Andrew Johnson, President of the United States, be impeached of high crimes and misdemeanors in office." Stevens and Bingham, symbolizing the harmony between the conservative and radical wings of the party, were appointed to inform the Senate of the decision, and a seven-man committee —including Stevens, Bingham, Boutwell, and Wilson—was named to frame the actual articles of impeachment.

As the committee set to work, the argument over the nature of an impeachable offense broke out again. Boutwell and Stevens urged broad articles; Bingham and Wilson pressed for narrowly conceived charges that would approximate the specifications of an indictment. Although Speaker of the House Colfax had appointed a clear majority of radicals to the committee, they knew that the President could not be convicted in the Senate without the firm support of the conservatives. The fiery Stevens, growing ever more feeble (he died six months later), no longer had the strength to sway his colleagues by the brute force of his will. Exhausted, he scrawled a note to Butler, complaining that "the Committee [is] likely to present no articles having any real vigor in them" and urging Butler to offer a few more on the floor of the House which would be "worth convicting on."

The committee reported nine impeachment articles to the House on February 29. Each alleged a different and narrow facet of Johnson's effort to oust Stanton: the President was charged with violating the tenure law and the Constitution by commissioning General Thomas without first obtaining Senate confirmation; violating the 1861 law against conspiracies to obstruct United States officers in their official duties; unlawfully attempting to control the disbursements of the Department of War; and attempting to coerce the military commander of the district of Washington to accept military orders outside the channels established by law. Operating under a resolution presented by the House leadership limiting debate to two days and speeches to fifteen minutes each, the House accepted the committee's suggestions, rejected another proposed by Butler, and then elected seven representatives to manage the House's case. Bingham received the most votes, followed by Boutwell, Wilson, Butler, Williams, John A. Logan, and Stevens. Five of the managers had favored impeachment in December, but Republicans also had made sure to include its two most influential opponents.

Even as the managers met, the wrangling between radicals and conservatives continued. Boutwell was elected chairman, with the support of most of the radicals; Wilson and Williams supported Bingham, who was so disappointed that he announced his intent to resign from the case. Careful to avoid a radical-conservative split, Boutwell withdrew at the next meeting and nominated Bingham. But, in return, the managers agreed to report (and the House then passed) two new impeachment articles, one by Butler charging Johnson with seeking to bring Congress into disrepute and citing as evidence some of Johnson's inflammatory, threatening speeches of 1866, and another by Stevens, which revived some of the spirit of the December impeachment effort, charging that Johnson's violation of the Tenure of Office Act was part of a long conspiracy to subvert the reconstruction legislation of Congress.

In the two weeks between the passage of the impeachment articles in the House and the March 5 scheduled opening of the Senate trial, the managers interrogated key witnesses and sent requests for important documents to the department heads. The case seemed simple. Witnesses would testify that General Thomas had gone to the secretary of war's office pursuant to the President's instructions and ordered Stanton to leave. Others would swear that Thomas had told them that he ultimately intended to use force if necessary. William H. Emory, overall commander of United States troops in Washington, and George W. Wallace, commander of the local garrison, told the managers that Johnson had asked them about troop placements the day Thomas presented his ultimatum to Stanton. He had remonstrated against Emory's adhering to the law requiring military officers to obey orders from the President only if they passed through Grant's headquarters. Still other witnesses would swear to the accuracy of newspaper accounts of Johnson's inflammatory 1866 speeches, the basis for the tenth article.

The managers assigned Butler, the most experienced and capable trial lawyer among them, to prepare the managers' opening statement and examine and cross-examine witnesses, placing the major burden of the prosecution upon the man most disliked by Senate conservative Republicans Fessenden and Trumbull. Wilson presented documentary evidence. All the managers attended the Senate trial, sitting at the managers' table, helping Butler with notes and advice, occasionally joining him in arguing the admissibility of evidence challenged by Johnson's counsel or in objecting to evidence submitted by them.

Republicans felt sure of success, their case was open-and-shut. Forty-two of the fifty-four senators were political allies. Republicans had regularly amassed the two-thirds of the Senate vote needed to pass legislation over presidential vetoes. Conviction in an impeachment trial required the same support. There was no reason to suppose it would not be forthcoming now that their dangerous enemy had openly defied their legal authority over appointments and removals.

Although the trial did not go well from the beginning, it took several weeks for the managers to realize that they might lose the case. At the start, over the managers' vehement objections articulated by Butler, Bingham, and Wilson, the Senate permitted Johnson's lawyers extra time to prepare his defense. Then the senators implicitly rejected Butler's argument that the impeachment trial did not require strict courtroom standards of procedure, evidence, and proof by their modification of the original rules given to Chief Justice Chase, who was required by the Constitution to preside over the trial of a President. He was granted the right to make decisions of law (subject to Senate reversal) and to cast votes in the case of ties. In fact, the Senate began to call itself the "high court of impeachment" (again changing its original rules). The House managers continued to address Chase as "Mr. President of the Senate" long after defense counsel and most senators conceded his judicial capacity by calling him "Mr. Chief Justice."

As Butler presented the House's witnesses, the case seemed to hold up well enough on the charges of violation of the Tenure of Office Act, but when he tried to prove the articles alleging conspiracy to use force, several senators objected to the evidence's admissibility. Evidence supporting Article Nine seemed fatally weak but still, Republicans remained confident.

When Johnson's lawyers presented the President's defense, the simplicity of the House's case proved illusory. With the consummate skill through which they had earned their towering reputations, former Supreme Court Justice Benjamin R. Curtis, former Attorney General Henry Stanbery, legal giants William M. Evarts and William S. Groesbeck, and the less eminent Thomas A. R. Nelson peppered the prosecution's case. They appealed to the senators' conservatism, emphasized the political nature of the conflict, and minimized the seriousness of Johnson's offense. After arguing that a President had the right to refuse to enforce laws he thought unconstitutional (two of Johnson's lawyers, Curtis and Groesbeck, made the more limited—and better received—assertion that the President could disobey a law trenching on executive power in order to raise a test case), they adroitly concentrated on the question of the President's intent when he violated the law. He believed the law unconstitutional, they insisted; he violated it only to force a court test. Alternatively, they pointed to the law's vague wording; the President had not believed that the law applied to department heads such as Stanton. (The inconsistency of the two arguments did not faze the President's lawyers, although it is difficult to explain how the President intended to test the constitutionality of the Tenure of Office Act by removing an officer he did not believe covered by it.) Over the managers' repeated objections, senators agreed to hear testimony from cabinet members, General Sherman, General Thomas, and others who agreed that Johnson had endeavored to get a court decision on the constitutionality of the Tenure of Office Act.

The managers had argued that irrespective of the Tenure of Office Act, the President could not legally replace Stanton with an *ad interim* appointment while the Senate was in session; while the Senate sat, a government officer could be replaced only by the confirmation of a successor by that body. In response, Johnson's lawyers offered long lists of *ad interim* appointments of government officers removed without waiting for a successor's confirmation. The managers objected that the lists could be misleading and demanded that the defense counsel provide detailed accounts of how and why each appointment and removal was made. Again the senators rejected the objections and admitted the evidence. (The managers' fears were well founded. The lists contained only a handful of cases which bore directly on Stanton's. Most were easily distinguishable, and some did not belong in the lists at all.)

Despite these defeats, the managers did prevent the presentation of some evidence they thought inadmissible. But even when the Senate sustained their objections, more than the one-third of the Senate required to acquit the President often voted against them.

Not only did the President's counsel erect a formidable defense, but Johnson's conduct mellowed. As his interference in the South ceased, most of the ex-Confederate states met the conditions set out by the Reconstruction Acts for restoration, and elected Republican state governments. By May, as senators prepared to vote on impeachment, legislation restoring seven of the states to normal relations in the Union was before Congress, and was certain to pass. At the same time, Johnson made overtures to conservative Republicans by naming General Schofield secretary of war and promised to cease his resistance in the South. Johnson's new restraint made the prospect of a divisive Wade administration even less palatable to conservative Republicans, causing them to weigh the risks of leaving Johnson in place against the risks to American governmental institutions by removing the President for essentially political offenses. They were encouraged by Evarts's brilliant final argument for the defense—a direct appeal to conservative Republicans to acquit Johnson in order to maintain the constitutional balance between Congress and the Executive.

As the trial drew to a close early in May, Republicans knew that they faced defeat. Acquittal was certain on several of the articles. The votes of at least ten Republicans—including Fessenden, Trumbull, and Sherman—were doubtful even on the strongest articles, and these were more than enough to acquit Johnson when combined with his twelve Democratic stalwarts. In the crisis, all the managers but one (Wilson), who had remained in the background while Butler presented their case, prepared eloquent, impassioned final arguments for conviction. Bingham accepted the task of preparing the managers' final rebuttal to the defense arguments, and he delivered a masterful address, holding the senators' rapt attention. Still the result remained uncertain.

In the eyes of most Republicans, the consequences of failure loomed disastrously. Johnson's lawyers had argued—without much emphasis before the unsympathetic body—that a President could refuse to execute laws he believed unconstitutional. What if, freed from the threat of impeachment, Johnson acted on that conviction and refused to recognize the new, Republican Southern state governments? If the soon-to-be-replaced pro-Johnson governments, recognized by the President as legitimate, refused to disband, violence almost certainly would result. How would United States troops react with Johnson in reconfirmed command?

Finally, the defeat of impeachment could demoralize the Republican rank and file and rejuvenate the Democrats, already encouraged by their 1867 victories. It seemed to Republicans that the struggles of four bloody years of war and three more of reconstruction might end in a Democratic and Southern victory. Throughout the country, Republicans threatened wavering Republican senators with political reprisals. As they did, other Republicans —especially influential Republican newspapers—rallied to the dissidents' side. In the trial's final days, the great pressure exerted upon the undecided Republicans and those who were gravitating towards acquittal provided the real source of the antipathy lawyers and historians have since displayed toward the Johnson impeachment.

Although the last-minute effort to force conviction ruined the historical reputations of the Republican impeachers, the action itself did not succeed. The undecided Republicans were evenly divided. Sherman, Henry B. Anthony, Waitman T. Willey, and others voted for conviction; Fessenden, Trumbull, and five other Republicans dissented, motivated especially by a desire to protect the institution of the presidency. On May 16 the Senate voted on Stevens's eleventh article. Thirty-five senators found the President guilty of high crimes and misdemeanors; nineteen found him not guilty. Ten days later the senators voted on articles two and three with the same result. Knowing that there was even less support for conviction on the articles, the Republicans gave up, and the Senate court of impeachment adjourned *sine die*.

The impeachment and trial of Andrew Johnson have been described by historians as a travesty of justice, essentially a political trial. It *was* a political trial, but that does not mean it was unjustified. Despite the recent trauma of the American presidency, presidents have been rarely tempted to abuse their power for criminal ends. The danger of great, concentrated power is that it can be channelled into efforts to sustain political policies and maintain political power. The framers of our Constitution feared this, and that is what the radical Republicans of 1867–1868 believed they faced. Unable to impeach the President for usurpation of power in 1867, they joined conservative and moderate Republicans in impeaching him for violating the law in 1868. The charge was too narrow, the law too vague, and the fear of disrupting the constitutional system too great to secure a conviction. But the tradition of our revolutionary ancestors was not defied when they used the older, parliamentary recourse against expanding Executive power; they were within that tradition, a tradition perhaps no longer viable in our president-oriented political system.

BIBLIOGRAPHY

One cannot assess the impeachment and trial of Andrew Johnson without a full understanding of the controversy over Reconstruction that precipitated it. Historians' evaluations of that controversy have differed widely since the 1890s when the first studies appeared, and the historical reputation of the President who presided over it has risen and fallen accordingly. Evaluations of the stage and actors involved in the drama of the impeachment and trial of Andrew Johnson have therefore been tempered by the political, social and psychological, and economic factors influencing these interpreters of history.

There are now three monographic studies of the Johnson impeachment —Hans L. Trefousse's *The Impeachment of a President* (Nashville, 1975), my recent book entitled *The Impeachment and Trial of Andrew Johnson* (New York, 1973), and David Miller Dewitt's *The Impeachment and Trial of Andrew Johnson, Seventeenth President of the United States: A History* (New York and London, 1903), written much earlier. The pro-Johnson histories—such as George F. Milton's *Age of Hate: Andrew Johnson and the Radicals* (New York, 1930), Milton Lomask, *Andrew Johnson: President on Trial* (New York, 1960), Robert W. Winston's *Andrew Johnson: Plebian and Patriot* (New York, 1928), Lloyd Paul Stryker's *Andrew Johnson: Profile in Courage* (New York, 1929), and Paul G. Bowers, *The Tragic Era, The Revolution after Lincoln* (Cambridge, Mass., 1929)—go further than DeWitt in establishing virtually a "devil" theory of impeachment, with Radical Republicans cast as the devils. The only historian among the early writers to offer a more considered view of impeachment was William A. Dunning. His "The Impeachment and Trial of President Johnson," in his *Essays on the Civil War and Reconstruction*, remains the best essay on the subject. Without judging the case, Dunning clearly recognized the weakness of many of the arguments presented by Johnson's lawyers and discussed the points of law with a fuller understanding and deeper insight than any historian since.

As historians have become more sympathetic to the Radical Republicans in recent decades, they have moderated the harshness of their judgments of the barely aborted attempt to remove the President. David Donald, Eric L. McKitrick, and Hans L. Trefousse have all described the mitigating circumstances surrounding impeachment, but they continue to argue the flimsiness of the case and disparage its political motivation. Only Harold M. Hyman and I have implied that the events that preceded impeachment may have justified it. For Donald's, McKitrick's, and Hyman's analyses, see Donald, "Why They Impeached Andrew Johnson," *American Heritage*, VIII (December 1956), 21–25; McKitrick, *Andrew Johnson and Reconstruction* (Chicago, 1960); and Hyman, "Johnson, Stanton and Grant: A Reconsideration of the Army's Role in the Events Leading to Impeachment;" *American Historical Review*, LXVI (October 1960), 85–100. Hyman carried his suggestions further in *Stanton: The Life and Times of Lincoln's Secretary of War* (New York, 1962), coauthored with Benjamin Thomas. For a complete historiography of impeachment, see James E. Sefton, "The Impeachment of Andrew Johnson: A Century of Writing," *Civil War History*, XIV (June 1968), 120–47.

Much of the prejudicial view of impeachment adopted by many historians is based upon the mistaken notion that government officials can be impeached only for actual criminal offenses indictable in civil courts. However, numerous studies have contradicted this conviction and sustained the position adopted by the Radical Republicans at the time of the Johnson impeachment crisis. Among analyses of impeachment published by lawyers and political scientists are David Y. Thomas, "The Law of Impeachment in the United States," *American Political Science Review*, II (May 1908), 378–95; Paul S. Fenton, "The Scope of the Impeachment Power," *Northwestern University Law Review*, LXV (November-December 1970), 719–47; and Raoul Berger, "Impeachment for 'High Crimes and Misdemeanors,'" *Southern California Law Review*, XLV (1971), 395–460. Two recently published books, Raoul Berger's *Impeachment* (Cambridge, Mass., 1973) and Irving Brant's *Impeachment: Trials and Errors* (New York, 1972), are interesting and conflicting additions to impeachment historiography.

For the student who wishes to delve into the primary materials, the most important source is, of course, the published record of the impeachment trial, *The Trial of Andrew Johnson, President of the United States, Before the Senate of the United States, on Impeachment by the House of Representatives, for High Crimes and Misdemeanors*, 3 vols. (Washington, 1868). The *Congressional Globe* offers the record of congressional infighting over the impeachment-connected issue of adjournment as well as both the December 1867 and February 1868 battles over impeachment itself. Representative William Lawrence's analysis of impeachment, "The Law of Impeachment," which represented the views of the more Radical Republicans, was published in the *American Law Register*, XV, o.s. (September 1867), 641–80. Theodore Dwight defended the more conservative view that the President could be removed only for indictable crime in "Trial by Impeachment," *American Law Register*, XV, o.s. (March 1867), 257–83. The majority and minority reports on impeachment by the House Judiciary Committee and testimony given to the committee are published in *House Report No. 7*, 40th Congress, 1st session.

The foregoing delineation of sources is by no means complete. The student who wishes to undertake further primary and secondary research into both the impeachment proceedings and the era itself will have to be willing to embark on the "literature search," that frustrating, exhausting, and tedious job, hoping that along the way he will find one of the many keys which unlock the gates of the garden of history.

PERTINENT DOCUMENTS

Impeachment Resolution of Representative James M. Ashley, January 7, 1867

Testimony of Postmaster General Alexander W. Randall before House Judiciary Committee, May 13, 1867

Testimony of Secretary of War Edwin Stanton before House Judiciary Committee, May 18, 1867

Testimony of Attorney General Henry Stanbery before House Judiciary Committee, May 20, 1867

Testimony of Virginia District Attorney Lucius H. Chandler before House Judiciary Committee, May 24, 1867

Testimony of Chief Justice of the Supreme Court Salmon P. Chase before House Judiciary Committee, May 25, 1867

Testimony of District Judge of Eastern Virginia John C. Underwood before House Judiciary Committee, May 25, 1867

Testimony of Secretary of the Treasury Hugh McCulloch before House Judiciary Committee, May 28, 1867

Testimony of Ex-Attorney General James Speed before House Judiciary Committee, July 2, 1867

Excerpts of Majority Report of House Judiciary Committee, November 25, 1867

Excerpts of Minority Report of House Judiciary Committee, November 25, 1867

Address of Representative George Boutwell on Judiciary Committee Impeachment Resolution, December 5 and 6, 1867

Speech of Representative James F. Wilson on Judiciary Committee Impeachment Resolution, December 6, 1867

Impeachment Report and Documents from House Reconstruction Committee, February 22, 1868

The Articles of Impeachment, March 4, 1868

Testimony of Representative James K. Moorhead in Senate Trial, March 21, 1868

Testimony of Delegate Walter A. Burleigh in Senate Trial, April 1, 1868

Testimony of William H. Emory in Senate Trial, April 2, 1868

Testimony of Secretary of the Navy Gideon Welles in Senate Trial, April 17 and 18, 1868

Final Argument for the Defense by William M. Evarts, April 28, 1868

Argument of John A. Bingham, May 4 and 6, 1868

Opinion of Senator William Fessenden, May 1868

The Pujo Committee
1912

Banker J. P. Morgan testified to a standing-room-only crowd of spectators and reporters as the House inquired into the growing concentration of economic power.

The Pujo Committee 1912

by Richard N. Sheldon

Dressed in hunting clothes and carrying shotguns, five men set out in late November 1910 for Jekyl Island, a secluded millionaires' retreat off the coast of Georgia. The men were Nelson Aldrich, Republican senator from Rhode Island, and representatives from the largest banking houses in New York: Henry P. Davison of the House of Morgan, Frank A. Vanderlip of Rockefeller's National City Bank, and Paul Warburg of Kuhn, Loeb and Company. Accompanying them was Harvard economist A. Piatt Andrew. They were on their way, not to hunt ducks as they so ostentatiously claimed, but to draft a new national banking and currency bill. The masquerade was dreamed up by Davison, the most active, and certainly one of the most imaginative, of the Morgan partners. The idea was to conceal their real purpose from prying reporters and forestall accusations of undue Wall Street influence. After all, Congress had passed legislation designating eighteen of its members as a National Monetary Commission, headed by Aldrich, for the specific purpose of drafting a new banking bill. And now, nearly three years later, Aldrich had suddenly decided it was time to act. The subsequent failure of his efforts, and the failure of the commission, opened the way for more radical solutions. The National Monetary Commission was scrapped, and the ominous Pujo money trust investigation rose in its place.

The origins of the Aldrich Commission, and the Pujo hearings, went back to the chaotic course of nineteenth century industrial finance and banking in America. A growing consolidation and combination of industry found expression in the formation of trusts, and these, with their demands for huge amounts of capital, gradually came under the general domination of bankers. Financiers had become so powerful by the end of the century that during the severe depression of the 1890s the federal government, facing bankruptcy, went for help to J. Pierpont Morgan. For a substantial commission, Morgan advised government leaders and restored their faith in free enterprise so they would take no actions to avoid such embarrassment in the future. Morgan and members of his banking house were directors in many important—often competing—companies and, as a railroad president once expressed it, "wherever Morgan sits on a board is the head of the table even if he has but one share." It was obvious that Morgan and a few other titans of Wall Street held power and influence far transcending their awesome personal wealth and stock holdings.

The country's rapid industrial growth was achieved despite the antiquated and inadequate national banking system established by the Lincoln Administration during the Civil War. Chronic deflation and tight money plagued small businessmen and farmers, and their demands for reform began finding organized support from concerned bankers by the end of the century. Then in 1907 a catastrophic financial panic swept Wall Street, ruining many banks and investors. The House of Morgan was credited with averting even greater disaster through selfless actions, and several of the largest banking houses emerged with their holdings not only intact but enhanced. Nonetheless, the experience was so harrowing that the Republican Congress enacted the Aldrich-Vreeland bill, a stop-gap measure designed to increase the supply of currency during emergencies. More importantly, the act established the National Monetary Commission, and assigned it the task of drafting a comprehensive long-term proposal to deal with the banking and currency problem. Nelson Aldrich, as the senior Republican on the commission, was named chairman.

The commission produced over twenty lengthy reports, but draft legislation was not forthcoming until a Democratic House of Representatives was elected in November 1910. Jolted into action by this disturbing event, Aldrich quickly arranged his secret meeting with Wall Street leaders and commission economist Andrew. After arriving at Jekyl Island and throwing aside their costumes, the five conspirators hammered out a draft proposal in ten days. The Aldrich plan, unveiled the following month, provided for a new central bank controlled by bankers. For a year its details were discussed and polished, and in January 1912, the bill was offered to Congress.

It was too late. Despite support from bankers, the United States Chamber of Commerce, and a National Citizens League, the Aldrich bill languished in committee. Most Democrats, traditionally suspicious of a central bank, preferred a decentralized system with local control. Radical Democrats, and a few progressive Republicans, denounced the plan as a Wall Street scheme to keep the money power in the hands of Eastern financiers. They renewed their charge that the panic of 1907 had been planned and executed by Morgan and a few others for their own gain, and clamored for a full-scale investigation of the money trust. This chorus was soon swelled by the voices of a number of prominent Democrats, including New Jersey Governor Woodrow Wilson.

Conservative congressional Democrats, wary of any currency issue since the disastrous silver campaign of 1896, sought to restrain the zeal of their colleagues. But a progressive Republican, Representative Charles A. Lindbergh of Minnesota, father of the famous aviator, succeeded with the help of radical Democrats in introducing a provocatively worded resolution calling for a congressional investigation. In a stormy Democratic caucus, conservatives succeeded in breaking the measure into three harmless resolutions. These were duly passed by the House, and two were sent to the Banking and Currency Committee, chaired by Arsene P. Pujo of Louisiana. Pujo took half the members as a subcommittee to investigate the money trust, while the remaining members, under the second-ranking Democrat, Carter Glass of Virginia, were given the task of drafting a substitute for the Aldrich Bill.

The Pujo Subcommittee began by mailing questionnaires to 30,000 banks and trust companies around the country, but only 12,000 responded and these were mainly smaller banks. Most of the national banks contested the committee's authority to pry into their affairs, claiming that the National Banking Act gave visitorial powers only to the Comptroller of the Currency. Faced with this possibly fatal impasse, the committee engaged legal counsel; Samuel Untermyer of New York and Judge Edgar H. Farrar from Pujo's home state were finally chosen.

Untermyer was particularly well qualified for this job. In the words of the inimitable stock broker and author, Thomas W. Lawson, Untermyer "has either prosecuted, defended, or had an inquisitorial finger in every sword-swallowing, dissolving-view, frenzied finance game that has been born or naturalized in Wall Street within the decade." In middle age, Untermyer had become interested in reform, and had helped precipitate the great insurance investigation that made Charles Evans Hughes famous. He also championed the rights of corporate stockholders who management had been systematically fleecing for decades. He joined the growing chorus of money trust critics and spoke out for regulatory legislation. His speech before the Finance Forum in December 1911 was credited with spurring Congress into action and getting the Pujo investigation underway. Dapper in appearance, he always kept an orchid from his own hothouse in his buttonhole, and carried a supply of these flowers in a damp paper bag so he could change to fresh ones during the day.

Untermyer proceeded to take over the work of the committee with such energy and expertise it is doubtful the investigation would have amounted to much without him. Objecting that the resolution authorizing the investigation was too narrow, he proceeded to resurrect the more powerful one thrown out earlier by the Democratic caucus. Its scope had to be comprehensive, he insisted, because it was not a question simply of banks and currency, but of a concentration of control over the great interstate corporations as well as financial institutions. He was accused of trying to get the investigation transferred to the Rules Committee, where greater scope was possible, and whose chairman, the radical Robert Lee Henry of Texas, seemed more sympathetic to his own views than the usually conservative Pujo. The House balked at the transfer, but obligingly passed the more comprehensive resoluton after a brief debate in which the Democrats found it difficult to go on public record as opposing an effective investigation. House Republicans enjoyed the spectacle of their confused and embarrassed opponents voting on the floor in favor of a measure they had voted down in caucus. Oscar Underwood of Alabama, conservative House Democratic leader, insisted that the Pujo resolution could have been defeated easily.

The resolution authorizing the investigation asserted there was reason to believe that "the management of the finances of many of the great industrial and railroad corporations of the country . . . is rapidly concentrating in the hands of a few groups of financiers" who had increasingly gained control over the funds of these great corporations to stifle the competition. While harmful to interstate commerce and the general public, the resolution continued, such practices had moreover brought these financial leaders the power to "create, avert, and compose panics," a power "that is despotic and perilous and is daily becoming more perilous to the public welfare." The committee was authorized to hold hearings to determine whether and to what extent these conditions actually existed, and to recommend remedial legislation. It was not alleged by the resolution, and in fact was repeatedly denied by Untermyer, that the money trust was a trust in the statutory sense of the term—that is, an illegal combination in restraint of trade. The investigation was not designed to discover whether laws had been broken but whether new laws should be written.

It was also decided at this time that all the questioning of witnesses should be done by Untermyer, although committee members could submit questions to him. This procedure was criticized by some members of the House, but was ably defended by young committee member James F. Byrnes of South Carolina, then serving his first term in Congress. He pointed out that it allowed a single line of questioning to be pursued, a much more effective method than the usual free-for-all among committee members which left many important follow-up questions unasked.

Untermyer decided against fighting (in court) for the right to examine national bank records. It was already late April 1912, and the current Congress expired on March 4, 1913. Instead Pujo introduced a bill granting the necessary authority to examine bank records to any congressional committee. Although quickly passed by the House, the bill met powerful opposition in the Republican-controlled Senate. Untermyer promised to resign if the committee were denied the authority contained in the Pujo bill, as he believed failure of the inquiry was certain without it. Hope for passage continued as late as December 1912, and in the meantime Untermyer found that impressive progress could be made without the additional power.

In any event, the hearings had to be postponed to allow time to collect and digest information from cooperating banks. Since it was a presidential election year, the committee also decided to delay the hearings until after the election to avoid the appearance of manipulating the investigation for partisan political purposes. Unfortunately such a delay would leave the expiring Congress little time to act on committee recommendations, and a delay on legislation could lead to vitiating compromises, thus nullifying the work of the committee. This was a risk that had to be taken.

The committee soon ruled, however, to take immediate testimony on "certain collatoral subjects," such as securities exchanges and clearing houses, and six days of hearings were accordingly scheduled in May and June 1912. Some stock exchange abuses were common knowledge to anyone familiar with Wall Street in those days, but the Pujo Committee revelations were certain to bring cries of outrage from average investors around the country.

Run like a private club, the New York Stock Exchange had largely escaped governmental regulation since it was founded shortly after the Civil War. Following the panic of 1907, a special investigating committee appointed by New York Governor Charles Evans Hughes had concluded that "only a small part" of Exchange transactions represented genuine investments, while the great majority were characterized by the Hughes Committee as "virtually gambling." Indeed, the Exchange was famous for swindles of every description—matched orders, wash sales, short-selling, pools, ring settlements—every kind of "frenzied finance" by which optimistic bulls and short-selling bears sheared the lambs; and fortunes were made and lost daily.

Price manipulation, witnesses told the Pujo Committee, was often managed by a pool of investors who, by simultaneously buying and selling approximately equal amounts of the same stock, gave the investing public a false impression of activity. The price could be forced up or down in this manner until the desired point was reached for either selling out at an artificially high price, or buying all available stock at a low price. This kind of price-rigging could be combined with other tricks, such as short-selling, by which stocks not owned were sold at a high price, the seller counting on a price drop before delivery so he could then purchase what he had already sold. The manipulators often had to be fast on their feet to avoid being crushed by their own financial maneuvers, and their anguished cries could occasionally be heard above the normal din of the Stock Exchange floor or "pit."

Officials of the Exchange thought these activities were perfectly legitimate, and said so on the witness stand. Whether they were ethical or not was another matter, as former New York Stock Exchange president Frank K. Sturgis testified. Untermyer asked if he approved of someone manipulating the price of a stock through simultaneous buy and sell orders.

"I approve of transactions," Sturgis replied, "that pay their proper commissions and are properly transacted. You are asking me a moral question, and I am answering you a stock-exchange question."

"What is the difference?" Untermyer persisted.

"They are very different things."

"I thought so. There is no relation between a moral question, then, and a stock-exchange question?"

"Sometimes."

Sturgis and other representatives of the Exchange were quick to point out, however, that there were strictly enforced rules against such practices as charging a customer less than the rate of commission fixed by the Exchange or communicating with a member of the competing but much smaller Consolidated Exchange. For such activities, which might encourage competition, a member faced a one-year suspension or permanent expulsion. Getting caught by one's own manipulative schemes was also a cause for expulsion, as in the Columbus and Hocking Coal and Iron pool. In that case, two of ten brokerage firms failed to withstand an unexpected price break, and were expelled from membership in the Exchange while the remaining eight firms were allowed to stay on. For this type of offense, it was clearly not a matter of how you played the game, but whether you won or lost.

The extent of gambling on the Exchange could be gleaned from figures prepared by the committee comparing the number of stocks sold with the number actually transferred on a corporation's books, representing investment purchases. These ranged from the Reading Company, whose stock transfers between 1906 and 1912 amounted to only 8.6 percent of the number of stocks sold, to the comparatively stable 40 percent of the Consolidated Gas Company. During the same period, the entire common stock of the Reading Company was sold at least twenty times a year, and in one year the stocks were sold forty-three times.

The committee concluded that stock exchange gambling not only deceived the public as to the real value of securities and encouraged speculation, but siphoned millions of dollars away from legitimate business. In its report, the committee recommended legislation which would strike at the worst abuses of stock exchanges through their dependence on interstate communications. The report advised Congress: to prohibit all exchange messages from being transmitted across state lines by telephone, telegraph, or mail unless the exchange was incorporated; to require public notice of a corporation's financial affairs whose securities it listed; to raise the margin requirement (the initial stock purchase installment) from ten to twenty percent; to prohibit simultaneous buy and sell orders; and to adopt certain other reforms.

Untouched by these recommendations, the Board of Governors of the New York Stock Exchange refused to list, or remove from the list, any stock at any time. This practice often played into the hands of manipulators since removal from the list meant an almost automatic drop in price. It also left intact the power of the Exchange to ignore the interests of the public in its effort to wage war against the smaller Consolidated Exchange. The president of the New York Stock Exchange, James B. Mabon, testified that if a member of the Consolidated Exchange owned stock listed only on the New York Exchange, he would have no way of marketing it except privately, because of the NYSE's noncommunication rule regarding the other Exchange. In other words, the NYSE would turn away business to hurt its weaker competitor.

Of less renown than the NYSE, but no less significant in its impact on the nation's finances, was the New York Clearing House Association. The Association's function was a simple one: to provide a place for representatives of member banks to meet once a day and charge off the checks drawn against each other, thus obviating the constant and dangerous traffic of large amounts of money between banks. Ruled by a five-man committee, representing five member banks, the New York Clearing House became an instrument of oppression, usurping the policymaking functions of member banks for the purpose of destroying competition and imposing exorbitant charges upon bank users.

To allow or refuse membership in the association could make or break a bank. As a matter of practice, only large banks, those with a capitalization of at least one million dollars, were allowed membership in the New York Clearing House, but certain other banks were permitted to clear through member banks. Withdrawal of membership was equivalent to a death warrant, and in the wake of the 1907 panic, the New York Clearing House wielded this weapon to destroy several banks. These banks were technically in sound financial condition and could withstand the demand for retiring all their outstanding clearing house loan certificates. But the publicity of losing their membership effectively killed public confidence, and the ensuing run on the banks quickly led to their ruin. This tyranny of membership kept competition under a tight rein while aiding consolidation.

Competition between banks was stifled and the public gouged because of the imposition on member banks by the New York Clearing House to devise a uniform commission on clearing out-of-town checks. A transaction which did not involve the clearing house at all (since the clearing house was concerned only with clearing the checks of local banks), the clearance of out-of-town checks had once been handled individually by the banks, and competition had kept commissions relatively low. The New York Clearing House had eventually muscled in on this potentially lucrative area, forcing its members to charge the same uniformly high commission for this service.

It was alleged by Untermyer that the power behind the New York Clearing House was J. P. Morgan, whose company, ironically, was not even a member. Morgan's general dominance, at least during the panic of 1907, was acknowledged by several witnesses, including George B. Cortelyou. While secretary of the treasury in 1907, Cortelyou had spent considerable time in New York during the worst period of the panic, consulting with Morgan and other leading financiers. Appearing before the committee, he admitted lending New York national banks $42 million in government funds without interest to help relieve the money shortage, and acknowledged that Morgan had more or less directed the whole operation. Did Cortelyou know, asked Untermyer, that the government money had gone straight into the Stock Exchange? He had heard later, Cortelyou allowed, that a large amount of the money had found its way there. Exactly which banks were granted this free bounty, counsel wanted to know, and how much was each given? Cortelyou said it was in the book he held in his hand, and the information was, he claimed, in all sorts of government records. But he could not, when asked, find it in the book, and suggested that the committee members could find it easily enough. Untermyer realized the former cabinet member was being less than honest, however, since he knew that the requested data had never been published. Yet Cortelyou's performance on the witness stand was a masterpiece of evasion, and the most he would finally admit was that he could not recall if the government had actually published the information.

It was not surprising that the Roosevelt Administration had attempted to conceal the details of its assistance during the panic. Call money at the Stock Exchange, normally lent at 6 percent, was commanding between 100 and 120 percent interest on October 24, 1907, the day Cortelyou opened the United States Treasury to Morgan and his friends.

Cortelyou's testimony ended the preliminary hearings, and the committee recessed for the summer. Although Untermyer left for his annual European vacation, there was little rest for politicians, as both parties held their presidential nominating conventions. The Republicans were divided; Theodore Roosevelt finally bolted the convention to form the Bull Moose party. The Democrats suffered serious divisions as well, but after forty-six ballots agreed to support the nomination of Woodrow Wilson. William Jennings Bryan had promised to get a plank adopted in the Democratic platform assailing the money trust, but had to settle for one condemning, in true Jacksonian fashion, the establishment of a central bank such as that proposed by the Aldrich bill. Wilson, however, compensated for this omission in his acceptance speech. While denying that there was anything conspiratorial or illegal about them, the Democratic nominee warned against the growth of "vast confederacies" in business and industry, and the "concentration of the control of credit which may at any time become infinitely dangerous to free enterprise." Only time would tell whether such campaign oratory was to be taken seriously.

Wilson's nomination was welcome news for reformers and helped persuade Untermyer to continue as committee counsel, despite serious setbacks during the summer and fall recess. The main problem was the impasse over the Pujo bill which had quickly passed the House but was defeated in the Senate Finance Committee by a 7 to 6 vote. Untermyer was encouraged by the closeness of the vote, and hoped passage might still be possible. He noted with satisfaction that Morgan had returned to New York from Europe, apparently in the belief that the inquisitorial dragon had been mortally wounded, if not slain, by the Senate Finance Committee action. He sent orders to have Morgan and other Wall Street tycoons subpoenaed while they were still available. A few, however, such as National City Bank Chairman James Stillman, who had resided in Europe since 1910, never appeared before the committee.

With the Pujo bill foundering, Untermyer sought the aid of the Executive branch of government. This would prove to be a tug-of-war in which the President, 320-pound William Howard Taft, could hardly be budged. Taft's attitude toward the money trust issue could be predicted from his response to questionable practices of certain national banks. In evading the National Banking Act's prohibition against holding bank stocks and other securities, these banks had created dummy security companies. The stock certificates of the security companies were printed on the back of the stock certificates of the parent national bank so that ownership was identical and proportional. The bank's directors and officers were appointed to positions in the security company, whose quarters, naturally, were in the same building. In 1911 Attorney General George Wickersham wrote an opinion holding this tactic illegal, but Treasury Secretary Franklin MacVeagh promptly issued a contrary opinion. The papers were turned over to the placid Taft, who laid the matter aside.

The President showed the same lack of interest toward Untermyer's requests for cooperation. In June 1912, Untermyer approached the Comptroller of the Currency, the only person explicitly authorized by law to enter national banks and inspect their books. The Comptroller simply referred committee counsel to the President for a decision, and Taft delayed making a decision until September.

Untermyer's request was two-fold. He asked, first, that the relevant records already on file in the Comptroller's office be turned over, particularly those records on which the Comptroller had based the statement in his 1911 Annual Report that "dishonest practices by officers of National Banks, of receiving personal compensation for loans made by the Bank, call for criminal legislation." Untermyer's follow-up letter of September 24 made clear that this information was obviously in the Comptroller's files. Second, he requested that the Comptroller conduct examinations of the national banks to obtain certain additional information deemed important by the committee.

Attorney General Wickersham, in his opinion of November 9, came to the strange conclusion that "it would appear from the letter of Mr. Untermyer that but little, if any, of this information is now in the Comptroller's possession." Taft, in his letter to Untermyer on November 21, carried this interesting process of diminution one step further:

> The statement of fact and the [attorney general's] opinion both show that the Comptroller is not now in possession of the information which you seek, but that it will be necessary for him to make an independent investigation for the purpose. . . . Were the evidence which you seek in the actual possession of the Comptroller, I should not feel like withholding it from your committee, but should exercise my discretion and direct its being turned over to you.

With a final flourish of ambiguity, Taft concluded that he "must decline to direct that the Comptroller shall give to the committee any other evidence than that which he has on file in his own office."

Did the President mean that he was, after all, going to turn over the information already on file, even though he somehow believed, on the basis of Untermyer's letter and Wickersham's opinion, that such information did not exist? Or was he going to "decline to direct" the Comptroller to do anything, and simply let time run out on the Sixty-Second Congress and its unpleasant money trust inquiry?

No information was forthcoming from the Comptroller, as it took four more weeks of urgings and clarifications from Untermyer for the President to take action and issue the promised order. By then it was December 17, and the hearings were scheduled to end in January. Needless to say, the committee in its report characterized the information furnished as "only a fraction of the required data."

The President had succeeded in keeping the Comptroller's files out of the committee's hands for several months without invoking Executive privilege, and yet had shown a spirit of conciliation by finally releasing the records. At that time, it was too late to use the information and the President did not turn over all the requested information in the files. He held certain important papers sent to him by the Comptroller, and refused to turn those over to Untermyer. These papers referred to the security companies set up by some of the national banks. Ironically, one of the witnesses, George F. Baker, after admitting (on the stand) that the security companies were designed to evade the law, agreed to submit information from his own files equivalent to that withheld by the President.

The full irony of this episode, however, was not revealed until Comptroller of the Currency Laurence Murray took the witness stand three weeks later and testified that his closely guarded files were routinely opened to examiners from the various clearing house associations. Moreover, the national banks, concealing from the committee their records behind the statutory provision giving only the Comptroller visitorial rights, had all along been allowing free access to clearing house examiners.

The election in November 1912 of a Democratic President, House, and Senate, set off a newspaper campaign to discredit the Pujo investigation. The New York *Sun*, for example, ran an editorial criticizing Untermyer's methods of questioning witnesses, even though no testimony had been taken for five months. A few days later assistant counsel Edgar Farrar resigned, due to pressing business commitments at home, causing rumors of friction with Untermyer and sympathy with Wall Street. Yet Farrar's resignation letter to Pujo had anticipated and denied such charges, indeed going so far as to urge that "you must impress on them [the committee members] the acrid and almost venomous hostility this investigation is exciting among the interests affected, [and] the support these interests are getting from their subsidized friends the press." The letter was carefully edited by the New York News Bureau, deleting this and other explanatory sentences from their news ticker.

The hearings were resumed on December 9, when a large number of witnesses began testifying during the few days available before the Christmas recess. Several days were taken up with testimony explaining the clearing house and stock exchange matters. Untermyer had carefully scheduled the proceedings to climax on December 18 and 19 with evidence from the committee's accountants and investigators documenting the extent of the concentration and control of money and credit, to be immediately followed by the appearance of the star witness, J. Pierpont Morgan. The Christmas recess would then provide time for the public to absorb these revelations and begin, Untermyer hoped, their clamor for remedial legislation.

During this period, the committee's power to elicit testimony was first challenged. Frederick Lewisohn, involved in a recent promotion of the California Petroleum Company, adamantly refused to give details of the scheme. After being warned of the seriousness of his refusal, he returned the following day, reluctantly offering the requested information. A later witness, however, being questioned on the same subject, proved more stubborn. George G. Henry of Salomon and Company refused to divulge the names of national bank officers involved in the stock promotion syndicate. He refused on the advice of ex-Senator John C. Spooner, who appeared as counsel to several of the most important witnesses. The committee immediately voted to bring contempt charges against Henry; the House of Representatives concurred without a dissenting vote, and a month later a federal grand jury issued an indictment. An abortive legal battle then ensued, with Henry first appealing a *habeas corpus* ruling. This appeal took two years to reach the United States Supreme Court, where it was dismissed. The Court disappointed observers by refusing to rule specifically on the power of Congress to elicit testimony from witnesses, but its action nonetheless cleared the way for Henry's trial to proceed. The defendant's legal resources were vast, however, and two and a half years later the trial was still pending while Henry remained at large. At that time, on July 6, 1917, Henry died of injuries received while playing polo.

J. P. Morgan had been subpoenaed to appear on December 19, the last day before the recess, but, anxious to go abroad and hoping to get through the ordeal earlier, he had gone to Washington on December 17. The titan of Wall

Street was seventy-five-years-old and within five months of his death. Washington reporters noticed that his appearance had deteriorated since two months earlier when he had testified before the Clapp Committee on campaign financing. He had wanted to go to Washington alone, but his advisers would not hear of it, and he arrived with a party of sixteen, including seven lawyers and five business partners. In the early afternoon of December 18, Morgan and several members of his party appeared unexpectedly at the large marble committee room. They watched the committee statistician explain how the House of Morgan, as shown by the elaborate charts and tables, dominated the control of money and credit in the United States.

Morgan seemed to be alone, however, indifferent to the testimony describing how he and his ten partners held seventy-two directorships in forty-seven corporations with resources or capitalization totaling over $10 billion. The so-called inner group, consisting of the House of Morgan, the directors of George F. Baker's First National Bank of New York, and Rockefeller's National City Bank of New York, held 341 directorships in 112 corporations controlling over $22 billion. As Louis Brandeis later explained, $22 billion had little meaning to the average person until it was pointed out that it amounted to "more than three times the assessed value of all the property, real and personal, in all New England." Kuhn, Loeb and Company of New York, Kidder, Peabody and Company of Boston and New York, and Lee Higginson and Company of Boston and New York saw the committee present charts showing an elaborate network of interlocking directorates connecting the great railway systems and the largest corporations, as well as the most important financial institutions.

When the committee statistician finished his testimony the proceedings seemed to take on the air of a court trial where the prosecution had just rested its case. The intimidated defendants would now be asked to explain their crimes as best they could. When called to take the stand, Morgan stood and turned about in confusion, uncertain where to go. The most powerful man on Wall Street gave every appearance of being no more than someone's benign old grandfather.

Untermyer went through some preliminary questioning, then called for adjournment until the next day, as originally planned. Pleased with the brevity and superficiality of the proceedings, Morgan happily shook hands with committee members, and asked to go home. His partners, he insisted, could furnish any information needed. But the key witness and star of the show could not be dismissed; the following day he appeared again, to a standing room only crowd of spectators and reporters. The witness seemed to have recovered from the strain of anxiety displayed the previous day, and was alert and animate throughout four hours of testimony.

During the committee's questioning, Morgan denied that he had any financial power. "You and Mr. Baker dominate the anthracite coalroad situation, do you not, together?

"No, we do not."

"Do you not?"

"I do not think we do. At least, if we do, I do not know it."

"Your power in any direction is entirely unconscious to you, is it not?"

"It is, sir, if that is the case."

"You do not think you have any power in any department of industry in this country, do you?"

"I do not."

"Not the slightest?"

"Not the slightest."

"And you are not looking for any?"

"I am not seeking it, either."

Morgan denied that company directors could be controlled by the trustees who annually appointed them. Again, he seemed to prefer appearing foolish to admitting anything that might advance his adversary's argument.

"You think, therefore, that where you name a board of directors that is to remain in existence only a year and you have the power to name another board the next year, that this board so named is in an independent position to deal with your banking house as would be a board named by the stockholders themselves?"

"I think it would be better."

"You think it is a great deal better?"

"Yes, sir."

"More independent?"

"Better."

"Will you tell us why?"

"Simply because we select the best people that we can find for the positions."

"Is it your experience, then, that the people who name a board of directors and have the right to rename them, or to drop them, have less power with them than people who have no concern in naming them?"

"Very much so, sir."

Morgan's desperate attempts led him into strange contradictions; when he denied that bank directors knew what was going on in their own banks, Untermyer worked around to the same question from another angle, and then Morgan was emphatically of the opposite view.

The witness's opinions concerning competition proved self-contradictory and seemed composed more to avoid suspected traps in the questioning than to express any coherent position on the subject. When first asked, Morgan said he favored cooperation and combination, but did not mind "a little competition." On returning to the same theme a few moments later, when Untermyer seemed about to use this view against him, Morgan admitted that he preferred competition. To Morgan's consternation, counsel seemed equally pleased with that answer, and the witness realized he faced an uncomfortable dilemma. If he spoke in favor of competition, Untermyer was prepared to prove that he opposed it in practice; if, on the other hand, he should praise cooperation and combination, then the money trust conspiracy was half proved.

Morgan admitted he had destroyed competition between two railroad lines when he had united them in forming the Northern Securities Company in 1901. Why, counsel wanted to know, had he done this? Torn between the choice of appearing malicious or stupid, Morgan elected the latter, and claimed he did not know. Later witnesses, like Morgan, chose ignorance, if indeed it was a choice. A very few, like George F. Baker, seemed genuinely sincere in their lack of knowledge.

When counsel had determined that marketing of securities was normally accomplished in a non-competitive manner, Morgan defended the practice with the rather irrelevant argument that the bank, as issuing agent, was ultimately responsible if the securities or bonds proved to be bad. Untermyer pointed out that the bank's responsibility had always been to itself first, rather than to the stockholders. Morgan claimed such a case would be the exception, not the rule. Untermyer replied if that were true, Morgan should cite some concrete examples concerning the securities of, say, railroad companies, but Morgan could not recall any:

"Can you not give us one?" Untermyer asked.

"I can not recall it at the moment," replied Morgan.

"In the whole history of railroading and railroad reorganization?"

"I have had a good deal of it."

"I know it; and that is the reason I am asking you to scan the whole history of it and give us a single instance in which the banker who advanced the interest on a defaulted security, or advanced any other money on a defaulted security, failed to get back his money in the reorganization."

"I can not recall it now, sir, but I am sure there are cases."

"If you find any of that sort—"

"I will give you the details of it."

"It would be quite a find, would it not?"

"Yes."

Although more at ease than on his first day of testimony, Morgan remained fidgety, chewing his lips and gums constantly, swinging about in his chair for signs of approval from his lawyers and family, and sometimes banging the table in front of him. His scale of values was particularly amusing; at one point Morgan insisted that he was not a large stockholder in the National City Bank, then admitted he owned "only about a million dollars' worth."

He seemed to enjoy denying his own power and the existence of a money trust. "What I say," he volunteered, "is that control is a thing, particularly in money, and you are talking about a money control—now, there is nothing in the world that you can make a trust on money [*sic*]." When asked if a man might "make a try at it," he replied, "No sir, he can not. He may have all the money in Christendom, but he can not do it." The rationale behind this strange conclusion was not deemed worth pursuing by counsel.

Similarly, Morgan maintained that character was the basis for credit—not money or property. "I have known a man to come into my office," he informed skeptical committee members, "and I have given him a check for a million dollars when I knew he had not a cent in the world." He continued, "A man I do not trust could not get money from me on all the bonds in Christendom." Morgan informed the committee that he always acted in the best interests of the country, since it was always good business to do so. Throughout his testimony, Morgan revealed himself as an exponent of individualism, with a firm belief in a harmony of interests and absolute natural laws. If a man abused his power, Morgan asserted, he would lose it forever. He did not explain how this amazing catharsis would occur, and was indeed unable to cite any actual examples when asked to do so.

Perhaps the most revealing part of Morgan's testimony concerned his purchase of the controlling stock of the Equitable Life Assurance Society. The company was capitalized at $100,000, dividends were fixed at seven percent, and a controlling interest of the stock, $51,000, had eventually been bought by Thomas Fortune Ryan and Edward H. Harriman for $2.5 million. In 1910 Morgan went to Ryan, who by then held sole control of the fifty-one percent, and offered him the original purchase price plus interest, or about $3 million in all. It seemed absurd that such a price would be paid for stock which returned only $3,750 per year (seven percent of $51,000), until it was realized that the Equitable owned half a million dollars' worth of stock in several important New York banks and trust companies, including the Mercantile Trust Company. Untermyer attempted to elicit Morgan's reason for this purchase. Morgan explained he "thought it was a desirable thing for the situation to do that."

"You care to make no other explanation about it?"

"No."

"The assets of the Equitable Life are a little over $500,000,000 are they not?"

"I do not know what they are."

"According to the charts and papers in evidence, on December 31, 1911, they were $504,465,802.01. Did Mr. Ryan offer this stock to you?"

"I asked him to sell it to me."

"You asked him to sell it to you?"

"Yes."

"Did you tell him why you wanted it?"

"No. I told him I thought it was a good thing for me to have."

"Did he tell you that he wanted to sell it?"

"No, but he sold it."

"He did not want to sell it, but when you said you wanted it, he sold it?"

"He did not say that he did not want to sell it."

"What did he say when you told him you would like to have it, and thought you ought to have it?"

"He hesitated about it, and finally sold it."

A more graphic demonstration of Morgan's power would be hard to find.

After testifying, Morgan again shook hands with committee members, and left immediately on a special train for New York. The press response to his testimony was mixed; a few newspapers accepted his denial of a money trust, but most editors concluded that the hearings proved that the financial resources of the country were dangerously concentrated. An anonymously published brochure entitled "J. P. Morgan's Testimony—The Justification of Wall Street," appeared before the month was out. Printed for free distribution, it was actually a carefully edited transcript, deleting Morgan's most revealing statements and embarrassing moments before the committee.

Some witnesses disagreed emphatically with Morgan's views. The most outspoken of these was George Reynolds, president of the Continental and Commercial National Bank of Chicago, and a former president of the American Bankers Association. He favored protection of minority stockholders' rights as well as the incorporation and regulation of clearing houses; he disapproved of interlocking directorates, and characterized the growing concentration of money and credit as a "menace to the country."

Jacob Schiff, senior partner in Kuhn, Loeb and Company of New York, admitted that a few men had gained control over the nation's largest financial transactions, but found this no cause for concern. A staunch individualist, he believed there should be no restraints placed on men, only on corporations. Schiff admitted that he had not competed with the House of Morgan for at least five years, but added that he usually split securities sales with Morgan, the First National Bank of New York, and the National City Bank of New York.

During the trial, Untermyer had asked most witnesses to name any securities transactions of more than $25 million not involving one of the largest six or eight banking houses in the country. Davison, Morgan's most prominent partner, came prepared for this question, and at the proper moment submitted a list of such transactions. Untermyer went through the list, pointing out one by one that each of the cases did indeed involve the biggest houses in the country, including the House of Morgan, through interlocking directorates and other means of control. Davison confessed that someone else at Morgan and Company had prepared the list, and that he himself was not familiar with the facts. He finally asked to withdraw the list from evidence.

Davison was also good enough to volunteer an explanation of banking ethics for the committee. This unusual moral code required polite refusal on the part of banks to compete with each other for any security issues. Francis L. Hine, president of the First National Bank of New York, substantiated Davison's testimony in this regard, but quickly added that each bank was ultimately free to do as it wished, and therefore a competitive system was maintained. He was, however, unable to recall any actual instances of such competition having ever occurred.

Untermyer's abilities as a cross-examiner were making a marked impression on witnesses and the public alike, and a hint of his technique was dramatically described by reporter Ida Tarbell:

> Much of the testimony held the spectator breathless. He strained his ear not to miss a word of question or answer, his eye not to miss a play of the mobile, gray countenance of the questioner. . . . And if [the witness] hid behind the technical "I do not know," a heavy silence clutched the listener until Mr. Untermyer broke it with his smooth and damning "You do not know" and passed on.

When one witness pleaded "Let me think; give me time to think," Untermyer replied, "You do the talking and let me do the thinking." Although criticized for his tenaciousness, Untermyer was invariably courteous and often smiling.

Once on the stand, some witnesses volunteered to submit written information and documents previously withheld. Early critics, such as Congressman James T. Lloyd of Missouri, and the editors of *Outlook* magazine, confessed at the conclusion of the hearings that Untermyer had done a good job. The most unusual compliment to Untermyer, a Jew, was paid by reporter Tarbell who, after marveling at his extraordinary skill, exclaimed, "It isn't Christian to be so able!"

George F. Baker, considered by many observers second only to Morgan in terms of power and influence, surprised the committee with his lack of knowledge of the businesses with which he was in daily contact. Faulty memories and outright ignorance were fairly endemic among many witnesses but Baker seemed to outdo them all, and did so with an alarming degree of sincerity and good-naturedness. He admitted being a director in many companies, but could not recall the names of all of them, nor could he recall how many directors certain of those companies had. As a director of several railroads, he was not sure which, if any, of a number of railroads named by Untermyer were his competitors. As a director of the New York, Susquehanna, and Western Railroad, he confessed he did not know where the line began or ended, nor the length of the road, nor even how long he had been a director. Finally throwing up his hands, he admitted he knew so little about the company he could "not answer intelligently any question regarding it." He was not even sure how he had become a director of so many companies, since he had not sought them, and believed he had too many.

The possibility that Baker was a pawn of the Morgan interests was never pursued, although evidence pointed to it. When asked how he had become a director in the Morgan-dominated United States Steel Corporation, he stated that while vacationing abroad he received a telegram from Morgan saying he had been unanimously elected a director. As a trustee of the Guaranty Trust Company, also a Morgan company, he admitted he periodically signed a proxy for the election of directors, although he did not know who the proxy was, and never questioned the persons who brought the document around for his signature. Morgan had earlier informed the committee that he and Baker had been good friends since at least as far back as 1873 when both were rapidly becoming important financial figures in New York—Morgan at the head of his private banking house and Baker at the head of the First National Bank. Baker freely acknowledged that Morgan was the dominant power on Wall Street. During the panic of 1907 and for some time thereafter, Baker, Morgan, and James Stillman of the National City Bank, frequently worked together. Moreover, Baker had not competed with Morgan for any security issues for at least the past five years—on the contrary, it was their custom, he said, to share in such transactions.

Competition, in fact, was not held in high regard by the seventy-two-year-old Baker, who confided he had always followed Jay Gould's personal advice that interlocking directorates were useful in overcoming certain problems. He had "never given any thought" to voting trusts such as he exercised in several of his companies, yet after having the implications of this arrangement explained by Untermyer, he admitted that it was not a good form of government for banks. He went on, however, to point out that since they were "working very well," he could "not care about it one way or the other." Indeed, the general business of the country was "first-rate just as it is," and, he added, as long as dividends were paid nobody cared what went on in Wall Street.

After the second day of Baker's testimony, Untermyer continued an informal conversation about money trusts. "What do you understand by a money trust?" counsel continued.

"I give it up. I don't know."

"Then you do not know whether there is one or not, do you?"

"No, I do not. I do not take much interest in that." This line of questioning led to Baker's admission that "there is a great amount of money that has come together here, more or less concentrated."

"I suppose you would see no harm," Untermyer went on, "in having the control of credit, as represented by the control of banks and trust companies, still further concentrated? Do you think that would be dangerous?"

"I think it has gone about far enough," Baker replied.

"You think it would be dangerous to go further?"

"It might not be dangerous, but still it has gone about far enough. In good hands, I do not see that it would do any harm. If it got into bad hands, it would be very bad. . . ."

"So that the safety, if you think there is safety in the situation, really lies in the personnel of the men?"

"Very much."

"Do you think that is a comfortable situation for a great country to be in?"

"Not entirely."

Baker's uncle, Fisher A. Baker, and John C. Spooner, both serving as the witness's counsel, sat by helplessly while these damaging admissions were being made. Untermyer, with his typical sense of the dramatic, realized this was a climax, and thereupon excused the witness. The spectators, reported the *New York Tribune*, "sat back with a sigh."

Baker's testimony forced even conservative newspapers to admit there was potential danger in the growing consolidation of money and credit, and that it was up to the government to do something about it. The testimony of the few remaining witnesses, with the exception of William Rockefeller, was anticlimactic.

Rockefeller was in many respects the most interesting witness. He was head of the Standard Oil operations in New York from 1865 until 1911. He retired after the 1911 United States Supreme Court decision to dissolve the company, when his post was filled by Henry Clay Folger. Rockefeller was expected to explain the 1907 copper market episode, when the great resources of Standard Oil had proved inadequate, and the big corporation's withdrawal had left thousands of investors ruined.

Attempts to serve a subpoena on Rockefeller began in June 1912. For seven months the elusive businessman could not be found at any of his several places of residence. Finally in January 1913 it was announced by Rockefeller's attorneys that their client was in Nassau, and would "accept service [of the subpoena] unconditionally." This statement was preceded by the news that the seventy-one-year-old Rockefeller would run a "great risk" to submit to any kind of oral examination, since, in the words of his physician, he was "suffering from chronic throat trouble." A year earlier the same doctor, Walter F. Chappell, had scoffed at rumors that his patient might have cancer of the throat. His own diagnosis had indicated gout of the throat, and although the patient could hardly speak above a whisper, he had laughed and joked with reporters, belittling his illness.

When it appeared that Rockefeller might not be able to testify, there were threats from the committee to have the erratic and unpredictable Thomas W. Lawson, another participant in the infamous copper syndicate, testify instead. This tactic proved effective, and Rockefeller agreed to submit to a medical examination by a physician appointed by the committee. This doctor reported that the patient seemed able to submit to a "brief examination without immediate serious results." Arrangements were made for Pujo and

Untermyer, after all other witnesses had testified, to visit the invalid at his suite of apartments on Jekyl Island, Georgia, the scene of the famous Aldrich duck hunt two years earlier. The examination was indeed brief. Although able to walk about freely, Rockefeller trembled so severely that he could only respond to questions by whispering in the stenographer's ear. Seated in a rocking chair, he coughed and wheezed through the preliminaries. When asked about the notorious Amalgamated Copper Company, the old man was seized by a fit of coughing, and fell back in his chair. His whole body shook, his head wagged back and forth, and the muscles of his face contracted into a painful grimace. Pujo and Untermyer quickly concurred with Dr. Chappell's advice to end the hearing at once, and the inquisitors were hurried back to the mainland.

That evening the doctor issued a statement to the effect that his patient had not fully recovered from the ordeal of the hearing, but that there was no cause for alarm concerning his condition. The newspapers flailed Pujo and Untermyer for their callousness even though Pujo had been the only committee member to vote against holding the examination. Rockefeller was well enough in six weeks (after the Pujo investigation was over) to return to New York where he had been so conspicuously absent for nearly a year.

With the Rockefeller testimony out of the way, Untermyer traveled to Palm Beach, Florida, where he spent ten days drafting a 173-page report. Its conclusions, preceded by a lengthy summary of the evidence, startled no one who had been following the testimony. In its major finding, the report admitted the evidence did not prove the existence of a money trust in the conspiratorial and illegal sense of that term. However, the report went on, "surprisingly many of the elements of such a combination exist," and, if allowed to continue unchecked, the consequences were "fraught with peril to the welfare of the country."

The House of Morgan, followed closely by George F. Baker of the First National Bank and James Stillman of the National City Bank, were the leaders, the report alleged, in a "rapidly growing concentration of the control of money and credit" in the country. Around this inner group, and cooperating closely with it, revolved a constellation of banking houses which included the firms of Kuhn, Loeb and Company, Lee Higginson, and Kidder Peabody. Their major source of income and capital came from the deposits of large corporations whose policies were often directed by these same men through interlocking directorates, capital control, and stock ownership. While admitting the leaders of these financial institutions had contributed to the development and prosperity of the nation, the report emphasized that, as competition had been gradually destroyed, the potential abuses and dangers inherent in the system grew accordingly.

One of the primary dangers was the ability of the inner group to keep large amounts of capital out of the hands of undesirable competitors, thereby hindering the economic development of the country. Not concerned with small businesses, none of the witnesses could name any security issues exceeding $10 million which were made without the participation of this group. This domination did not necessarily interfere with the growth of new industries, such as the automobile, but these were nonetheless apt to come under such influence as they matured and grew to significant size. This control and monopolizing of large security issues, through such noncompetitive devices as banking ethics, led to exorbitant fees and commissions. The issuing corporations could absorb these costs only through higher prices on their goods and services.

Dependent on the inner group and its satellites, the report continued, were smaller banking houses such as Kissel Kinnicut and Company; White, Weld and Company; and Harvey Fisk and Sons. Small banks around the country sought big business to underwrite the large security issues controlled by the inner group. For a share of this lucrative business these smaller banks were willing to follow whatever lead the dominant houses offered, and could not afford to criticize or defy their policies. Through this patronage system they became dependent on the good will of Morgan and his allies.

The report offered an extensive list of recommendations for remedial legislation. Most of these concerned national banks and amendments to the National Banking Act. Such banks were to be expressly prohibited from creating dummy security company affiliates to evade the existing law. Striking directly at the inner group, the report recommended that the stock of national banks should not be held by other banks, and that interlocking bank directorates be prohibited when one of the banks was a national bank. The report also urged that national banks require minority stockholders to be represented on boards of directors, and, recalling the recommendation of the Comptroller of the Currency in his 1911 report, advised that there should be a law against national bank directors and officers accepting rewards in exchange for promoting loans.

Interstate corporations, the committee suggested, should not be allowed to deposit funds with private unregulated banks, such as the House of Morgan, and the security issues of railroads should be supervised by the Interstate Commerce Commission. The reorganization of bankrupt railroads, a lucrative business for bankers but ruinous for stockholders, should be handled entirely by the courts, advised the report. To re-introduce competition to large security issues, the committee urged that these be open to competitive bidding by banks.

The committee struck at clearing houses through the medium of the national banks, recommending that such banks be prohibited from becoming members of any clearing house not meeting certain conditions severely limiting its powers. Similarly, the committee decided that the New York Stock Exchange could be controlled only through the interstate commerce clause, and advised Congress to deny the use of interstate communications services to stock exchanges not meeting certain specified requirements designed to eliminate gambling and price manipulation. Two bills were offered by the committee, one dealing with national banks and the other with stock exchanges. There was no time, the report lamented, to draft bills dealing with the other recommendations.

The recommendations and bills were designed to be weak so as to win unanimous approval among the committee members. Three of the four Republican members, however, submitted a brief minority report which, while agreeing with the general findings of the majority, insisted there was too little time left for the Sixty-Second Congress either to evaluate the great mass of evidence or to consider remedial legislation. Ranking Republican Henry

McMorran of Michigan submitted an independent report disagreeing with most of the conclusions and recommendations of the majority, and paying high tribute to Wall Street. All seven Democrats signed the majority report. There was no debate over the report in the House of Representatives since there was no time to act on the recommendations.

To allegations that their evidence was selective and slanted against Wall Street, the committee had only to show that the evidence was selected by the bankers. The Committee's subpoena power did not extend to written records, and literally thousands of banks had refused to turn over any evidence at all, while others, led by the House of Morgan, chose carefully what little information they did submit. Indeed, the case against the money trust, strong as it was, suffered from the committee's inability to obtain important information. Nor, for that matter, could it be charged that the committee had built a case on the testimony of witnesses hostile to Wall Street. On the contrary, those summoned were the great financial leaders of the time. Scarcely concealing their hostility toward the committee, they testified only reluctantly, while others remained out of the country so they would not have to appear before the committee.

Because the Sixty-Second Congress was almost finished, Untermyer could not hear the testimony of some forty scheduled witnesses. He optimistically termed the committee report an "intermediate" one and included an "urgent recommendation" that the "incoming Congress continue the inquiry." Furthermore, he hoped that the Pujo bill authorizing inspection of national bank records would be revived and passed by the new Congress.

On the day before the report appeared, the House of Morgan released a statement blaming all financial problems on the national banking system and urged Congress to take appropriate action. Morgan took credit for the enormous industrial growth of the United States. The Morgan "brief" went on to invoke the immutability of natural economic laws and the importance of public trust in the nation's leaders, including bankers. The lines were clearly drawn by this statement and the Pujo Committee report for the struggle over legislation expected in the new Congress.

The struggle was, in fact, already underway. Carter Glass, chairman of the other Banking and Currency Subcommittee, had been at work for some time drafting a substitute for the Aldrich bill, and during January and February, 1913, held hearings on the subject. He had the greatest disdain for the Pujo investigation and feuded continually with Untermyer. Ironically, these two protagonists both came from Lynchburg, Virginia, yet their differences over the money trust issue represented two opposing camps. The conservative Virginia congressman had fought Untermyer's appointment as counsel to the Pujo Committee from the beginning, and later accused him of trying to muscle in on drafting the new banking act. In 1912 when Pujo decided to run for the Senate instead of the House, his committee would normally have been taken over by Glass, who believed Untermyer was trying to block his accession to that post. Untermyer denied this charge, but nonetheless Glass's rise to the chairmanship did in fact kill the prospects for reviving the money trust investigation. The new chairman, backed by heavy lobbying from banking interests, succeeded in preventing the resumption of the inquiry in the

Sixty-Third Congress. Glass concentrated his efforts instead on the fight to pass his own bill creating a Federal Reserve Banking System.

Reform Democrats opposed the Glass bill, similar in many respects to the despised Aldrich bill, and a bitter controversy raged throughout 1913. With the active participation of Woodrow Wilson a compromise was finally worked out by the end of that year, and the Federal Reserve, or Glass-Owen, Act was passed. Untermyer supported the bill, but with serious reservations, though in later years he claimed "it was the design of the Federal Reserve Act to destroy" the money trust. Glass was much closer to the truth when he declared that "there is not a provision of the Federal Reserve Act that is grounded on any revelation made by the 'Money Trust' investigation—not one." The Federal Reserve System was in fact created in response to demands by bankers, and was drafted with their advice and consent, after six years of study and debate. The act contained none of the specific recommendations of the Pujo report, and probably would have been passed had the Pujo hearings never been held. Yet the hearings had generated a demand for reform which much of the public mistakenly believed was achieved with the passage of the act.

It could be said that publicity from the hearings strengthened the hand of Senator Robert Owen and other reformers in getting more government control written into the act than might otherwise have been possible. Yet the effectiveness of such control proved more illusory than real. The decentralization features of the act in particular promised to break the back of the money trust which was centered in New York. Yet even here, the dominant financial position of New York, far from being wrested away and parcelled out among the twelve Federal Reserve districts, was reinforced by the Glass-Owen Act. The New York Federal Reserve Bank quickly assumed control over most of the foreign transactions for the government and for the rest of the Federal Reserve System, handled most of the open market functions, and set the discount rates for the entire system. The greater dominance of New York over the nation's banking system was vouched for by none other than Carter Glass, who had favored the decentralized system so ostentatiously enacted by the Glass-Owen Bill. "The proponents of the Federal reserve act," Glass told a Jefferson Day audience in 1916, "had no idea of impairing the rightful prestige of New York as the financial metropolis of this hemisphere. They rather expected," he went on, "to confirm its distinction, and even hoped to assist powerfully in wresting the scepter from London and eventually making New York the financial center of the world. . . . We may point to the amazing contrast," he emphasized, "between New York under the old system in 1907, shaken to its very foundations because of two bank failures, and New York at the present time, under the new system, serenely secure in its domestic banking operations and confidently financing the great enterprises of European nations at war."

This was only one of many disappointments for reformers. Others were on their way. Even the sensational series of articles by Louis Brandeis for *Harper's Weekly*, simplifying and summarizing the Pujo hearings for the public, failed to spur any real reforms. Appearing between August 1913 and February 1914, the articles were written by Brandeis to help his good friend Norman Hapgood, new editor of *Harper's*. They were published in book form in 1914 under the title *Other People's Money and How the Bankers Use It*. An impressive indictment of Wall Street, the book made the Pujo Committee report seem tame by comparison. Indeed, Brandeis expressed his disappointment that the committee recommendations did not go far enough.

The Clayton antitrust bill seemed to meet many of the reformers' demands. But by the time the Senate had finished emasculating the House bill the resulting act was so weak that, according to one disillusioned progressive senator, it "did not have enough teeth to masticate milk toast." The Clayton Act, passed in October 1914, prohibited interlocking directorates in Federal Reserve member banks and large corporations, and provided that competing corporations could not own each other's stock. The House of Morgan, along with a few other giants, noisily shed their interlocking directorates, but lost none of their influence because they utilized other methods of control. The Morgan-dominated National Bank of Commerce, for example, quietly absorbed several financial institutions formerly controlled by Morgan through interlocking directorates. The magnitude of their success was graphically documented by the famous Pecora investigation twenty years later.

The Federal Trade Commission Act, passed a few weeks before the Clayton Act, is another measure occasionally tacked on to the list of achievements due to the Pujo hearings. It outlawed "unfair methods of competition," but specifically exempted banks from its provisions to avoid conflicts with the Federal Reserve Act. As a result, no Pujo Committee recommendations appear in this measure. The commissioners appointed by Wilson were, in any event, pro-business or incompetent—or both—and fought continually among themselves over the issue which Congress had so carefully sidestepped—the definition of "unfair methods of competition."

Representative Robert Lee Henry of Texas tried to revive the money trust investigation in the new Congress, but his bill to authorize inspection of national bank records was sent to the Banking and Currency Committee where it was rejected by Chairman Glass. Senator Owen introduced legislation to carry out the Pujo recommendations concerning stock exchanges, but the Senate balked, and the measure failed. The threat of regulation had already spurred the New York Stock Exchange to do some housecleaning shortly before the Pujo report appeared, and the New York Legislature, a few months later, outlawed some of the worst abuses. Incorporation of the Exchange, however, was defeated, as was a proposal to increase the margin from ten to twenty percent. The New York Stock Exchange escaped drastic reform for another twenty years. Clearing houses also eluded the reformers for the most part, although in 1916 their lucrative out-of-town check operation was undermined when the Federal Reserve System began performing this service without charge. One important Pujo recommendation, prohibiting national banks from setting up dummy security companies to evade the law, was blithely ignored by Congress. Risking deposits and banking instability, this practice continued to flourish, and contributed to the waves of bank failures in the early 1930s.

Had Pujo not left Congress at this critical time his recommendations may have met a better fate. He might have pushed through some of his major reforms, and possibly achieved the fame eventually won by Glass. Also, had J. P. Morgan, the personification of the money trust, not died a few weeks after the hearings concluded, there might have been a greater demand for meaningful reform. Accusations that the Pujo hearings had killed the old titan were denied by his family. In any event, a month after the committee report was submitted, Pujo and Morgan were no longer on the stage, and the whole investigation seemed strangely out of date. Yet the disappearance of these two figures did nothing to invalidate the committee report or recommendations.

The Pujo report was based on the fundamental assumption that competitive free enterprise was the best economic system for a free society. Although businessmen already believed that cooperation and combination were going to replace competition, they were apparently unable to overcome the ideologically embarrassing consequences of this heresy. In 1912 Wilson was elected President, supposedly to re-establish competition through the "New Freedom" of government regulation. But the confusion caused by the clash of traditional beliefs with modern economic developments, compounded by the rivalry between reformers and conservatives, conspired to make his modest program an exercise in futility. The cataclysm of the Great Depression a few years later would attest to this sad fact, but would also offer the country a fresh opportunity to come to grips with these baffling forces.

BIBLIOGRAPHY

Aside from the primary sources reproduced here in part, the most complete account of the Pujo investigation is found in the large urban newspapers of the period. The best summary of the committee findings is Louis Brandeis's *Other People's Money and How the Bankers Use It* (New York, 1914). A brief summary of the entire investigation, written at the same time, is Ida Tarbell's "The Hunt for a Money Trust," *American Magazine,* (May, June, and July 1913,) which includes many good pictures.

Nathaniel Stephenson's biography of Nelson Aldrich (New York, 1930) revealed to the public for the first time the secret meeting at Jekyl Island to draft the Aldrich bill. Henry Pringle, in *The Life and Times of William Howard Taft* (New York, 1939), takes his subject to task for not acting against security company affiliates, but ignores the President's role in the Pujo investigation. Among several biographies of J. P. Morgan the most useful, because of the first-hand observations, is the one by his son-in-law, Herbert L. Satterlee (New York, 1939). For information about Woodrow Wilson see Arthur S. Link's massive five-volume biography, *Wilson* (Princeton, 1947–1965). An interesting biographical sketch of Untermyer appears in Henry Pringle's *Big Frogs* (New York, 1928). There is as yet no biography of Pujo.

Nor is there a first-hand account of the investigation by any of the participants. But nearly everyone involved with the Federal Reserve Act has written a book about it. These include Robert Owen, *The Federal Reserve Act* (New York, 1919), Carter Glass, *An Adventure in Constructive Finance* (Garden City, 1927), Samuel Untermyer, *Who Is Entitled to the Credit for the Federal Reserve Act?* (a short pamphlet which appeared in response to Glass's book, but contains no publishing information), as well as several accounts by bankers and economists (J. Laurence Laughlin, Paul Warburg, and H. Parker Willis) involved in drafting the various bills.

The only scholarly accounts of the investigation have been those by Benjamin J. Klebaner, "The Money Trust Investigation in Retrospect," *National Banking Review,* III (March 1966), 393–403; and Vincent P. Carosso's account in his *Investment Banking in America—A History* (Cambridge, 1970). A condensation of Carosso's views appeared as "The Wall Street Money Trust from Pujo through Medina" *Business History Review,* XLVII (Winter 1973), 421–37. Both Klebaner and Carosso argue unconvincingly that the committee's conclusions were unfounded.

PERTINENT DOCUMENTS

Samuel Untermyer to Arsene P. Pujo, July 19, 1912

Speech of Woodrow Wilson Accepting Democratic Nomination for President, August 7, 1912

Samuel Untermyer to President William Howard Taft, September 24, 1912

Attorney General George W. Wickersham to President William Howard Taft, November 9, 1912

President William Howard Taft to Samuel Untermyer, November 21, 1912

Testimony of Frank K. Sturgis, December 13, 1912

President William Howard Taft to Samuel Untermyer, December 17, 1912

Testimony of J. Pierpont Morgan, December 19, 1912

"Memorandum for the President" and Refusal of Untermyer's Request, January 8, 1913

Testimony of George F. Baker, January 9 and 10, 1913

Testimony of George M. Reynolds, January 16, 1913

Testimony of Francis L. Hine, January 24, 1913

Testimony of William Rockefeller, February 7, 1913

J. P. Morgan & Co. to Arsene P. Pujo, February 24, 1913

Majority Report, February 28, 1913

Minority Report, February 28, 1913

Teapot Dome
1924

OH BOY!
WHAT AN
APPETITE
FAITH
PUBLIC CONFIDENCE
TEA POT DOME
INVESTIGATION
REPUTATIONS
PRESIDENTIAL
HOPES

Teapot Dome 1924

by Hasia Diner

Of the corruption-ridden Harding Administration, Frederick Lewis Allen, the popular chronicler of the 1920s, noted in *Only Yesterday*, "the oil cases were the aristocrats among the scandals." For the year and a half that the Senate's Committee on Public Lands and Surveys pondered the perplexities of the Teapot Dome scandal, hundreds of witnesses paraded through the Senate investigating chambers, either answering or refusing to answer questions. When Senator Thomas Walsh (D.-Montana) began to direct the hearing in the Senate on October 24, 1923, few newspapers gave it prominent coverage. Walsh's hearings were expected to be dull, tedious, and short-lived. As the months proceeded, however, and as the Montana senator and the committee attempted to unravel and expose the various strands of the explosive scandal, the inquiry generated intense interest.

The taint of oil and corruption was eventually to stain both parties, causing at least three cabinet-level resignations, inspiring several Supreme Court decisions, and making the name Teapot Dome synonymous with the seamy side of American politics. This scandal also caused political thinkers, constitutional theorists, and government officials to discuss the proper role of Congress in the investigatory procedure.

What was Teapot Dome and the scandal surrounding it, and why should it have engendered such controversy, shattering any number of political careers? Simply, Teapot Dome was a tract of oil-rich land in Wyoming which had been set aside by President Wilson, under the auspices of the Department of the Navy, to be used exclusively by the navy. There were similar tracts of land in California, and Teapot Dome was known as Naval Oil Reserve Number Three. For some time, however, oilmen and developers had hoped to lease parts of the naval oil reserves. Conservationists, both in and out of the government, angrily contested any move to remove oil which they felt should be held in reserve for national emergencies. After a protracted dispute within Wilson's cabinet over the leasing of the oil reserves, a special amendment was pushed through the Congress in 1920 which gave complete control of the naval oil reserves to the secretary of the navy, who was entrusted "to conserve, develop, use and operate the oil reserves . . . directly." Previous to this legislation, the Interior Department maintained control of the lands. Conservationists such as Gifford Pinchot praised this complete transfer of control to the navy because its secretary, Josephus Daniels, was recognized as an ardent supporter of the conservation movement.

The conservationists' celebration was, however, brief. The year 1921 saw not only the end of Wilson's Administration and the return to power of the Republican party, but also the ascension of a number of dubiously qualified individuals to positions of power in the Harding Administration. Of particular concern to conservationists were Albert Fall, secretary of the interior, and Edwin Denby, secretary of the navy. Fall had begun his career as a gold and silver prospector in the southwest and Mexico. Eventually he settled in New Mexico and acquired large mining and land-holding interests. His dealings went beyond amassing land and wealth, and he immersed himself in state politics—but he was a Democrat in Republican territory. Fall, however, switched party affiliations in 1906, anticipating New Mexico's statehood. He quickly became a figure of some importance in Republican circles and after serving in several lower offices, in 1912 he was elected to the Senate by the New Mexico legislature. In the Senate he befriended Warren Harding, then senator from Ohio.

Early in his tenure as secretary of the interior, Fall discussed the possibility of a change in naval oil land policy. Denby agreed with Fall that the Interior Department should have control of the lands rather than the navy, and on May 11, 1921, Fall wrote to Harding, requesting that change. On May 21, after consulting with Denby, Harding issued Executive Order 3474, formally transferring the reserves.

The transfer received little public attention, barely meriting press coverage, although some conservationists were immediately aware of the implications inherent in future land policy. One such person was Harry Slattery, a Washington lawyer and former secretary to Gifford Pinchot, who brought his concerns to Senator Robert La Follette. He confided to the senator his fear that Fall would lease the oil lands for private exploitation. While Slattery had no specific evidence, Fall did have the authority to lease the reserves according to the General Leasing Act of 1920. The legislation permitted the reserves to be leased to prevent drainage from them through private drillings on the peripheries of the government lands. Earlier, Secretary of the Navy Daniels had allowed isolated private leasings, but he had never leased an entire reserve.

Secretary of the Navy Denby had been concerned with the drainage problem. Accordingly, he had been amenable to Fall's suggestion that the oil lands be transferred to the Interior Department. Denby was also concerned with the problems of military security, for he feared that, if a war with Japan developed, the underground oil would be utterly useless: the oil could aid in mobilization only if it were refined and accessible. Fall agreed with Denby and both officials assumed that the transfer of authority was but a prelude to further private exploitation of the oil lands under the auspices of the General Leasing Act.

The first of the private leases granted by the Department of the Interior was to Edward Doheny, head of the Pan-American Petroleum and Transport Company. Doheny was awarded part of Naval Reserve Number One in Elk Hills, California; he won the right to the oil reserves through open, competitive bidding. However, in April 1922, rumors began to circulate that private deals had been made involving private leasing of the oil land, both in Elk Hills and at Teapot Dome. Senator John Kendrick of Wyoming had received numerous communications from constituents about the clandestine leasing of Teapot Dome; Kendrick duly asked for information from the Interior Department. On April 14, 1922, the *Wall Street Journal* carried an article announcing that all of the Teapot Dome had been leased to the business interests of Harry F. Sinclair, president of Mammoth Oil Company. According to the *Journal,* "the arrangement . . . marks one of the greatest petroleum undertakings of the age and signalizes a notable departure on the part of the government in seeking partnership with private capital for the working of government owned natural resources." The next day Kendrick introduced a resolution in the Senate calling for further information on the leasing of the Teapot Dome. Within three days the acting secretary of the interior, Edward Finney, responded, stating that Sinclair's company had been given the lease to develop all of the Teapot Dome and that the Pan-American Petroleum and Transport Company, owned by Doheny, was to get the rest of the rights to the Elk Hills reserve. Shortly thereafter, the Senate was given a copy of the Sinclair lease, accompanied by a frank statement explaining that, because of naval preparedness and national security, there had been no competitive bidding.

While there was still little public attention focused on the issue, conservationists remained concerned with the secrecy of the Sinclair lease—there had been no official announcement of it. La Follette introduced resolutions on April 21 and 28, calling for the Senate Committee on Public Lands and Surveys to look into all leases on naval lands. He then pleaded with Senator Walsh to assume the leadership of the investigation. Although the senator agreed, he was appalled by the drudgery which the task would involve and stunned by the amount of material he would have to examine. In June Fall had ordered a truckload of documents and material sent to the Senate. At the same time Walsh was also informed in a letter by President Harding that the oil policy pursued by Fall and Denby "was submitted to me prior to the adoption thereof, and the policy decided upon and the subsequent acts have at all times had my entire approval."

While Walsh had little reason to question Harding's faith in his appointees, several suspicious events caused him to continue plodding through the reams of documents. For example, shortly after La Follette introduced his resolutions calling for an investigation, La Follette's offices were ransacked. Then, Walsh discovered that someone had been investigating his own past, and he had reason to suspect that his phones were tapped and that his mail was being read. While this was occurring, Walsh was barraged with intriguing rumors, especially those which pointed to Albert Fall's obvious increase in wealth shortly after granting the oil leases. Walsh's curiosity was further triggered in early 1923 when it was announced that Fall was leaving the cabinet to work with the Sinclair oil interests. Later, in the spring, Fall traveled with Harry Sinclair to Russia to obtain oil concessions on the island of Sakhalin. At his final cabinet meeting Fall ironically told reporters that he had "tried to impress upon my friends and associates that my leaving Washington is not a case of saying goodbye, but until we meet again." Seven months later, on October 24, Fall was among the first witnesses to testify in Walsh's investigation of oil, politics, and corruption.

Before Fall appeared in front of the Public Lands Committee, two days of testimony by geologists indicated that the oil from the Teapot Dome reserve was draining out at an alarming rate. One geologist, K. C. Heald, noted: "There is no doubt that from the point of development of the property and recovery of oil from it, it will be much better to develop the property as a unit. . . ." Republican Senator Reed Smoot, one of the staunchest Administration supporters on the committee, observed: "If the reports of the experts are accepted the theory that the Government made a mistake in leasing this . . . reserve has been exploded." This was an ominous beginning for those Democrats who hoped that the hearings would expose unsavory Republican policies and practices. Even the conservationists who were eagerly casting about for a way to discredit Fall and Denby were taken aback by the early geological evidence.

Fall's testimony lasted for two days. He not only defended his oil leasing policy in terms of the problems of oil drainage but in terms of "national security." Claiming that his actions in leasing the lands to Sinclair were part of a campaign for greater energy preparedness if the United States was forced into a war with Japan, Fall emphasized that President Harding had endorsed the leasing policy in his letter to the Senate committee. Walsh could do nothing after the two days of testimony but dismiss Fall with the reminder that he would most likely be called back again. Fall's testimony was followed by that of Denby, who stood behind the secretary of the interior and doggedly maintained that no wrongdoing was involved in the decision to transfer authority to the Interior Department or to lease the various oil reserves.

While Walsh assumed the burden of examining witnesses and ploughing through voluminous pieces of evidence, the officials of the Democratic party, and especially Cordell Hull, the chairman of the Democratic National Committee, began to take an interest in the Teapot Dome hearings. Hull convinced conservationist Slattery to draw up a list of potential witnesses, including Josephus Daniels, Franklin Roosevelt, Attorney General Harry Daugherty, as well as officers of the Departments of the Navy, Justice, and the Interior. The remaining days of October and most of November were taken up with minor witnesses who added very little to Walsh's search for substantive information. However, Walsh began hearing numerous stories about Fall's land deals in New Mexico—deals which had netted him a tidy profit. This put Walsh on a new path. He summoned witnesses from New Mexico, including a newspaper editor from Albuquerque—Carl Magee. Magee informed the committee that after 1923 Fall's Three Rivers ranch had vastly improved in condition. As Magee described it to Senator Walsh: "There had been pillars built up to this road, and beautiful woven wire fence put along, and trees planted, and beautifully concreted gutters, and a very expensive road, as far as I could see, up to the ranch house. . . . The conditions were so changed I couldn't recognize it." Magee contrasted Fall's newly found opulence with his dire economic straits of several years before. This testimony and that of several subsequent witnesses caused committee members to wonder about a possible connection between Fall's economic prosperity and the leasing of the Teapot Dome reserves.

On the same day that Magee testified, Fall's ranch manager appeared before the committee, revealing that Sinclair had been a guest at the Three Rivers ranch in December 1921. At that time Fall received several well-bred hogs and cows from Sinclair, who owned a farm in New Jersey. While Walsh was not interested in Fall's livestock interests, he decided to pursue the reasons why Sinclair might want to thank Fall in some material way. When Republican Senator Irvine L. Lenroot asked Edward Doheny if Fall had profited "in any way, directly or indirectly," through contracts, Doheny tersely answered: "Not yet." Walsh's suspicions were further whetted when Sinclair appeared again, on December 4. At first Sinclair's secretary, G. D. Wahlberg, answered for him, stating that Fall had paid for "seven cows and two bulls." Sinclair admitted, however, that he had been down to Three Rivers, saw that Fall did not have any cows, and that Fall had agreed to accept them as a gift.

As the sessions of 1923 ended and those of 1924 began, Walsh had made little progress. He was bogged down in trivial and circumstantial evidence and there seemed to be no end to the possible number of witnesses. The *New York Times* noted, "Senator Walsh was up against a stone wall. The wise politicos of Washington believed that he had gone as far as he possibly could go."

Walsh's investigatory drive was, however, not dampened, and a major breakthrough occurred on January 8, 1924, when Edward McLean's lawyer, former Attorney General A. Mitchell Palmer, informed the committee that McLean, then living in Florida, would make a full disclosure of a $100,000 loan that he had made to Fall in 1921. Walsh wanted to examine McLean, the publisher of the *Washington Post,* more closely, but McLean, ill with a sinus infection, would not appear in Washington. He did agree, however, to testify from his bed in Florida. Walsh, who was skeptical about the seriousness of McLean's illness, was then appointed as a subcommittee of one and he went to Palm Beach to accept McLean's testimony. On January 12, McLean revealed, much to Walsh's surprise, that Fall never used the money McLean had lent to him and had returned the checks to him uncashed. Walsh suspected that the reason Fall did not accept the money was because he had found some other, more lucrative, source. Walsh immediately asked Fall, who was also in Palm Beach, for a statement about the money. Only under threat did Fall agree to answer Walsh's questions. In a letter he admitted that he had not accepted McLean's loan, "because I found other sources." The whole matter, he quickly added, "was in no way connected with Mr. Sinclair of . . . Teapot Dome or any oil concession." He refused to appear in person before Walsh in Palm Beach, partially because of ill health and more importantly because he thought that he was "right in believing that on his visit here he [Walsh] was empowered only to examine Mr. McLean's confidential secretary. . . . As to the question of where I got the money . . . that is my own private affair. I do not feel called upon to discuss it either with Senator Walsh or any other man."

Fall's refusal to cooperate invigorated the expiring inquiry; journalists suddenly began to demand answers from Fall; newspapers which had previously dismissed the hearings and the work of the Walsh Committee began to report that there was, indeed, some substance to the suspicions they raised. The first major witness to appear before the Senate committee in this revitalized atmosphere, Edward Doheny, told the committee on January 24, 1924, that he had been the one who lent Fall the $100,000. Doheny revealed that his son had carried the total amount in cash to Fall's office "in a little brown satchel." Doheny's statement made it clear that Fall had lied to the committee. While Doheny maintained that "there was no discussion between Mr. Fall and myself as to any contract whatever" and that the loan "had no relation to any of the subsequent transactions," Democrats began to publicly charge a high degree of collusion between the Harding Administration and the oil interests. The Democratic National Committee played up the Republican party's part in the oil frauds and released a pamphlet, *The Land Ye Possess,* chronicling how conservation thrived under the Democrats, while the Harding Administration had mercilessly "raped" Teapot Dome.

The Democrats continued to exploit the proceedings of the Walsh Committee when Archie Roosevelt, son of the late President, testified that he had resigned from his position with the Sinclair oil enterprises because his suspicions of wrongdoings had been substantially confirmed by the findings of the committee. Roosevelt informed the committee that Sinclair's private secretary, G. D. Wahlberg, had admitted to him that $68,000 had been given to Fall's ranch foreman, and that he, Wahlberg, had possession of the canceled checks. Wahlberg then testified that the President's son had misunderstood him. Wahlberg boldly stated that he had told Roosevelt about "six or eight cows, and [Roosevelt] probably understood that to mean $68,000 in some manner," inferring that "thous" had been heard instead of "cows." Walsh could not prod Wahlberg into changing his story.

Fall, questioned in New Orleans, denied ever receiving money from Sinclair. Few observers, however, took his denials seriously, and most newspapers spoke cynically about Fall's cries of innocence. January 1924 saw a dip in favorable public opinion towards the Republicans, and various members of Harding's former cabinet joined in a chorus denying any complicity or any knowledge of the affair. Charles Evans Hughes, secretary of state, publicly announced his shock and claimed that "the question of oil leases had never come up in the Cabinet." Herbert Hoover echoed Hughes's declaration, saying: "My recollection is exactly the same as expressed by Secretary Hughes. There may have been some discussions . . . but if there . . . [were] I don't remember it, and I . . . missed very few Cabinet meetings in the last three years."

Two days after Doheny's explosive testimony a group of Republican congressmen desperately appealed to Calvin Coolidge, who had succeeded to the presidency on Harding's death: "Believe situation demands vigorous action by President in oil lease matter. Public amazed by developments and nothing could increase confidence in administration like use of 'Big Stick' without delay. Think it important hit at once and hit hard." At the same time, at an executive session of the Public Lands Committee, Walsh announced that he intended to offer a resolution on the floor of the Senate authorizing Coolidge to annul the leases of Teapot Dome and Elk Hills, to stop all further removal of oil, and to appoint a special counsel to prosecute those involved in the wrongdoings. Walsh had obviously come to the conclusion that the committee had ploughed through enough material to warrant congressional action, and the time was ripe for criminal prosecution.

Even though Walsh had desired to keep secret the proceedings of the executive session of the committee for several days, news of the committee's decision leaked to President Coolidge. After spending the day consulting with various Republican senators and with various Justice Department officials who had been vigilant observers of the Public Lands Committee hearings, he issued the following statement on January 27, designed no doubt to steal the thunder and the prerogative from Walsh's committee:

> It is not for the President to determine criminal guilt or render judgment in civil causes; that is the function of the courts. It is not for him to prejudge. I shall do neither. But when the facts are revealed to me that require action for the purpose of insuring the enforcement of either civil or criminal liability such action will be taken. That is the province of the Executive.
>
> Acting under my direction, the Department of Justice has been observing the course of the evidence which has been revealed at the hearings . . . which I believe warrants action for the purpose of enforcing the law and protecting the rights of the public. This is confirmed by reports made to me from the committee.
>
> If there has been any crime, it must be prosecuted. If there has been any property of the United States illegally transferred or leased, it must be recovered.
>
> I feel the public is entitled to know that in the conduct of such action no one is shielded for any party, political or other reason. As I understand, men are involved who belong to both political parties, and having been advised by the Department of Justice that it is in accord with the former precedents, I propose to employ special counsel of high rank drawn from both political parties to bring such action for the enforcement of the law. Counsel will be instructed to prosecute these cases in the courts so that if there is any guilt it will be punished; if there is any civil liability it will be enforced; if there is any fraud it will be revealed; and if there are any contracts which are illegal they will be cancelled.
>
> Every law will be enforced. And every right of the people and the government will be protected.

While Coolidge's pronouncement was primarily a criticism of Attorney General Daugherty, Coolidge's move to take the investigation and prosecution of the cases out of the Justice Department was also an attempt to lessen the legislative role in the affair. He quite clearly stated: "That is the province of the Executive." The message to Walsh, the Democrats, and the Senate was explicit.

January ended with a combination of frustration and success for Walsh's efforts. The committee had once again summoned Albert Fall to appear before them, but the former secretary of the interior again used the issue of his health to avoid testifying. Fall presented the testimony of four physicians who stated that they had "carefully examined Hon. A. B. Fall. We find that it would be detrimental to Mr. Fall's health for him to leave his residence in his present condition." While Walsh's efforts to bring Fall to public testimony were thwarted, on the same day, January 29, the Senate began to debate Walsh's resolution. The only obstacle to his proposal was Senator Lenroot, who as a member of the Public Lands Committee praised Walsh's thorough investigation, but condemned the partisan motives behind it. He attempted to amend Walsh's resolution by asking the Senate to express their doubts about the legality of the oil contracts, rather than explicitly labeling them illegal. There was no support except among Republicans for Lenroot's attempt to soften the Walsh resolution. Thus, on January 31, it was unanimously passed by the Senate, who called on Coolidge to begin legal procedures to cancel the oil leases and engage a special prosecutor to examine the situation.

Up to this point, the taint of corruption and collusion had clearly fallen upon the Republicans. Republicans could only accuse the Democrats of crassly exploiting a national disaster for purely partisan motives. Yet by early 1924 Republicans began to use the forum of the Public Lands Committee to implicate Democrats in the oil leasings. The Democrat upon whom they seized and whose political fortunes were destroyed because of his testimony before the committee was William Gibbs McAdoo, son-in-law of the late Woodrow Wilson, and in 1924 a leading candidate for the Democratic nomination for President. It was a Democrat, Senator James A. Reed from Missouri, who publicly linked McAdoo to the Teapot Dome and fatally damaged the aspirations of the former secretary of the treasury. Reed's motivations were more personal than ideological; he wanted the nomination himself. On January 31, after the Senate had passed the Walsh resolution, Reed asked the Public Lands Committee to recall Doheny. Reed suggested that the committee ask Doheny if he had ever "given or contributed any money to any person at the time holding a public position . . . or whether any such official . . . contributed or given any money to him." This was clearly intended to publicize and expose some earlier dealings with McAdoo.

Lenroot, chairman of the committee, conducted most of the Doheny investigation. He asked if Doheny had ever employed any cabinet members after they had retired from the cabinet; Doheny answered affirmatively. He had employed Franklin K. Lane, Wilson's secretary of the interior. He had also employed former Attorney General Thomas Gregory as an attorney "to represent us before the President in regard to a lot of permits that we were trying to get in Mexico. . . ." Finally, Lenroot asked, "Now, have you employed any other ex-Cabinet officers?" "Yes," answered Doheny, "at the time when our properties were greatly menaced in Mexico by the hostile attitude of the Mexican Government I employed ex-Secretary McAdoo." Doheny admitted that he had paid McAdoo $250,000 to represent the interests of the Pan-

American Company in Washington, especially to then President Woodrow Wilson. Senator Holm Bursum of New Mexico then attempted to tie McAdoo's involvement with Doheny to that of Fall. He asked the oil speculator: "How do you compare the value of Mr. Fall's service in relation to Mexican oil interests in which you are interested with the service performed by Mr. McAdoo as to benefits?" The mere mention of McAdoo's name at the hearing and the linking of his name with that of Fall and the whole series of incidents regarding oil policy almost instantly damaged the base of his wide-spread support for the Democratic presidential nomination. One newspaper in South Carolina noted that it "threw McAdoo over immediately [after] the oil touched him. . . . It would be impossible for the Democrats to capitalize the oil scandals to anything like their productive value with McAdoo as leader."

Urged on by his friends and by loyal Democratic supporters, McAdoo attempted to salvage his reputation and his credibility as a presidential candidate. He issued a statement condemning Doheny and stating that Doheny had no reason to bring up his name in the oil lease hearings. McAdoo then asked Walsh for the chance to appear before the Public Lands Committee to clear his name. He had previously written to Lenroot justifying his activities:

> What I have done was within my rights as a lawyer. In my representation of the Doheny companies in Mexican matters I never dealt in political influence, nor did I ask, or promise, or give, or receive political favors or other favors. If my conduct in acting professionally in these matters is open to criticism, then no lawyer can take a Cabinet office unless he be rich enough to give up all professional employment in business when he comes out of office. I do not believe that any such standard is wise or proper. I believe that the spirit of fair play of the honest-minded American people will not misunderstand my course in this matter, nor take their minds off of those who are guilty of betraying their trust as disclosed in this investigation.

That individual who had betrayed the trust of the public was the "real culprit—an ex-member of the Cabinet of this administration who appears to have acted corruptly." McAdoo boldly stated that he was "not willing that the innocent shall be made to suffer in order that the guilty may be protected or shielded by this transparent effort to bring odium upon innocent men connected with a former administration."

On February 11 when McAdoo appeared before the committee, he was treated with respect by the committee members, Republicans as well as Democrats. They readily accepted his records of a straight business transaction with the Pan-American Company. He adamantly insisted that there had been no official collusion between him and Doheny and that he had not had any contact, in fact, had not even met Doheny, until after he had left public office. McAdoo's testimony presented fairly clear evidence that he was not involved in the seamy side of Doheny's activities; McAdoo had taken no part in the illegal aspects of the Teapot Dome. Yet many observers noted that after McAdoo appeared before the committee, his refusal to *offer* to step out of the presidential race ruined his political fortunes. Sadly, or cheerfully, some Democratic politicos contended that McAdoo was no longer a viable candidate since he had accepted fees from Doheny, and according to one party figure, the Democrats "would be on the defensive the moment they would nominate McAdoo."

In the interim between McAdoo's decision to appear before the committee and his actual testimony, new issues and incidents entered into the narrative of the Teapot Dome. One of the major events occurred in early February. A group of physicians appointed by the committee issued a report stating that Albert Fall was now well enough to testify in person. The press, eager for lively print, was gleeful. The *New York Times,* for example, believed that both parties "were awaiting his testimony with ill-concealed nervousness." The *Santa Fe New Mexican,* a major and early critic of Fall, noted that, "the oil lease probe is spreading. The deeper you get into it the more bottomless it appears." And the always liberal *Nation* asserted that the revelations about Teapot Dome were just coming to a head, and the American public was "getting a delightful picture of what a business government really is."

Political commentators and politicians were eager for Fall's testimony. They were, however, once again disappointed. Fall refused to answer any of the committee's questions. Although he eventually refused to respond on the grounds of the Fifth Amendment, he also questioned the legality of the hearings and the right of the Senate committee to conduct its investigation. Fall stated that he did "not consider that acting under those resolutions [Senate Resolutions 282, 294, 434] . . . which authoriz[e] the committee to sit after the expiration of the Sixty-seventh Congress . . . this committee has any authority to conduct the investigation now attempted to be conducted by the addressing of this question to me."

Fall also told the committee that according to its own resolution the President now had sole authority "to prosecute such proceedings, civil and criminal, as may be warranted by the facts in the making of the said leases." The claim that the Senate had no legal authority to compel testimony was also raised by Sinclair at a later date, but Sinclair's refusal brought him a contempt citation. The committee did not take Fall's criticism seriously, but his refusal to provide the senators with any information added to the general confusion. One writer for the Baltimore *Sun* on February 5 speculated: "Neither Republican, Democrat or insurgent leaders [has] the least idea which way the 'cat is going to jump. . . .' All over Washington there is a feeling that the worst is yet to come."

One of the most significant clashes between the Senate and the President in the Teapot Dome imbroglio also occurred in early February 1924. As a result of Fall's refusal to testify and the growing impatience with the endless maze of witnesses, the Senate on February 11, in a basically partisan vote, called upon President Coolidge to request Denby's resignation as secretary of the navy. Coolidge refused to comply, claiming that the proper time for action had not yet come. He was waiting for the special counsel to inform him of the legality of the leases and about the "pertinent facts in the various transactions." Coolidge felt, moreover, it was his prerogative as President to decide who should remain in or who should leave the cabinet. He asserted that the Executive had the final and exclusive authority to remove a cabinet officer, in all cases except impeachment. Coolidge cited various statements by former

Presidents on the rights of the Executive, and he charged that the Senate's wish was a blatant violation of the principle of separation of powers. Most Republicans praised Coolidge's steadfastness, describing his actions in glowing terms of his loyalty to an innocent man and his commitment to the historic role of the presidency. The President's loyalty, however, did not save Denby. On February 18 the secretary tendered his resignation.

Meanwhile, Coolidge was searching for special counsel to take charge of the investigation of the leases, an investigation he hoped would steal the publicity and impetus from the Walsh Committee. At one point in early 1924 Coolidge had suggested Silas Strawn, a Republican from Chicago. Lenroot, always trying to protect the Republican interests on the Public Lands Committee, informed Coolidge that the committee was going to report back negatively on Strawn and advised the President to withdraw his name. Coolidge complied, wishing to avoid further controversy with the Senate committee. He next suggested Owen J. Roberts, a Republican lawyer from Philadelphia, who had been endorsed by Senator George Pepper. Walsh opposed the nomination; for while he was convinced that Roberts was a good lawyer with impeccable credentials, he felt that "the country knows nothing of him." Walsh, at this point, was suspicous of almost anyone, especially a Republican suggested by Calvin Coolidge. After a fairly heated debate over both Roberts and Coolidge's other nominee, Atlee Pomerene, the Senate confirmed both special counsels. Pomerene was approved first, and two days later (when Walsh was absent), Roberts was also confirmed.

Although Coolidge and the Republicans had hoped that the confirmation of the special prosecutors would take much of the initiative and the publicity away from the Public Lands Committee, on February 25, after a two-week recess, the committee once again resumed its hearings. Of the half-dozen witnesses who appeared over the next few days, the most significant was C. Bascom Slemp, Calvin Coolidge's private secretary. Walsh requested Slemp's testimony because Slemp had been in Palm Beach at the same time that Walsh was there questioning Edward McLean. Slemp admitted that he had talked to McLean while in Florida, but that his exchange with McLean had been purely personal and in no way involved McLean's supposed $100,000 loan to Fall. In response to Walsh's question, "Did you have any communication at any time while you were down there with anyone in the city of Washington in relation to the subject?" Slemp stated emphatically that he "had no communications with anyone in Washington at all." He admitted some communication with the White House of a purely personal nature, but also stated that he felt that those "communications that I would make to the White House I would have to reserve as confidential."

In the subsequent week, however, Walsh located and made public a series of bizarre telegrams which had been passed from McLean in Palm Beach to numerous persons in Washington. The telegrams showed that McLean was frantically trying to avoid being questioned by Walsh. Most were written in a secret code which had once been used in the Justice Department. For example, one dated January 11, 1924, read:

Cravingly in dxewoux resurge ledgment aliment fastidious tuck

> skewered suckled scrag emerse vethousl punctators gob. Virgin lectionary jangler high lander kelder hobgoblin roguery sawbuck hosier bonka gob saline dismounted renominated torso.

Another of January 24, also from Palm Beach, from a William Wiley, continued this garbled line:

> Saw apples, and everything fine. Also saw cherries and they were very good. The peaches will be just what you want, and I am sure any change in weather will not affect them.

Buried among the hundred of telegrams which Walsh had taken from two Washington telegraph offices were two wires from Coolidge to McLean. Neither wire was particularly damning. In one, Coolidge told McLean: "Prescott is away. Advise Slemp with whom I shall confer. Acknowledge." The other was even less obvious: "Thank you for your message. You have always been most considerate. . . ." An employee of McLean's, however, told the committee that among those people receiving some of the coded telegrams was Slemp. This series of telegrams piqued the appetites of the Democrats who were hoping to find something to link Coolidge to the various aspects of the Teapot Dome scandal. The rumors which had been making their way out of the Senate investigating chambers were ambiguous and unfounded. To add some substance to these shadowy innuendos, McLean was asked to appear again before the committee in mid-March, but he offered no new material which tied the President to any aspect of Teapot Dome or suggested that the purpose of Slemp's trip to Florida was to directly communicate with Fall or McLean. At the same time, Coolidge felt compelled to clear himself and to justify the two telegrams which clearly bore his name. The first telegram had concerned a routine political appointment, he said, and the second acknowledged a note McLean had sent to Coolidge congratulating him on his refusal to dismiss Denby.

For several weeks anti-Administration newspapers reveled in the linkage. The *Washington Daily News* advised the Walsh Committee that it would be irrational for it not to investigate the implications of a telegram "ambiguous in text, sent by the Chief Executive to one of the most important figures" of the Teapot Dome scandal. A more balanced judgment was rendered by the *New York Times* which said in a March 7 editorial that it was "humiliating to think that we have come to the point where every idle talk and gratuitous suspicion about the President . . . must be given resounding publicity." Democrats in Congress continued to fill the *Congressional Record* with statements questioning the President's role. Senator Norris, an independent, claimed that the entire drift of the Walsh investigations had made him doubt Coolidge's ability to serve as President. Coolidge's association with McLean, "one of the most disreputable characters in . . . Washington—a man who has lived a life of continual debauchery," had convinced the Nebraska senator that Coolidge was the wrong person for the office. Throughout the crisis, Coolidge, true to his public image of the tight-lipped, reticent New Englander, remained publicly unruffled and silent.

But the taint of oil continued to plague the beleaguered President. After Democratic senators attacked Attorney General Daugherty in late February, the Senate on March 1 established a special committee under Senator Burton K. Wheeler to investigate Daugherty's failure to prosecute Fall, Sinclair, Doheny, and others. The investigation featured numerous charges of illegality, graft, and influence-peddling in the Justice Department. On March 28 Harry Daugherty resigned. The Teapot Dome morass had claimed another victim.

Throughout the spring Walsh made a concerted effort to direct the hearings toward the true story of the Teapot Dome, continuing his search for some key to the whole fiasco. On March 8 he began a new tack, which involved the recollections of Gifford Pinchot. Walsh had heard rumors that the collusion surrounding Teapot Dome had begun before the 1920 Republican convention. Originating in a statement that General Leonard Wood had supposedly made to Pinchot, the rumor was that Wood told Pinchot that he would have gotten the Republican nomination had he agreed to turn over to private exploitation the public natural resources. While Pinchot told Walsh explicitly that he could not remember Wood making such a remark to him, Walsh continued to probe the story. On March 8 a front-page article in the *New York Times* claimed that before the 1920 convention certain oil interests had sought to persuade General Wood to appoint Jake Hamon secretary of the interior. In return for the promise of appointing Hamon, Wood was to receive the support of oilmen in his own bid for the nomination.

While Walsh could not subpoena Hamon, who had died several years before, he did bring in a series of witnesses who had some knowledge of this tangent of the investigation. One of the most verbose of these witnesses was Al Jennings, a real estate dealer and former train robber from California, who had announced to the press that his testimony would burst open the whole affair. Jennings, who had accompanied Hamon to the 1920 convention in Chicago, testified that Hamon had told him that "Harding would be nominated the next day, and it had cost him a million dollars." According to Jennings's recollections of the manipulations at the convention, "it had been agreed upon that day by Mr. Daugherty, Will Hays [Republican national chairman], and he named somebody else from Ohio, that he was to be Secretary of the Interior. He said it had all been settled; that Mr. Daugherty at first was in favor of Senator Fall occupying that position, and they had a fight, but he put it all over them, and it cost him a lot of money to do it." Jennings implied that Hays had received part of Hamon's million dollars; the charge was immediately denied by Hays.

The air around the oil leases and the 1920 Republican convention was still clouded and in late March 1924 the *New York Times* published substantial evidence that 75,000 shares of Sinclair oil stock had been used to assist the Republican party with its campaign expenditures. Hays denied this allegation also. He branded the *Times* story, "false in content, as it is libelous in purpose." Hays did admit, however, that Harry Sinclair had made a personal loan of $75,000 to the Republican party, but the gift was not in the form of oil shares. Hays added that he knew nothing about the oil leases at Elk Hills and Teapot Dome until he had read about them in the papers. A steady stream of subsequent witnesses called by Walsh could not flesh out the allegations and innuendos, so by late spring the committee was at a dead end.

Not giving up the battle entirely, Walsh continued to call in geologists, petroleum specialists, and other technical experts. The committee ended the search for political scandal and began looking for more concrete answers about oil drainage and the productive capabilities of the reserves in question. The symbolic end of public interest in the hearings could be dated May 8, when not one spectator came to listen to testimony about the geological features of the Teapot Dome.

As Walsh was having a progressively more difficult time tracking through the web of Teapot Dome testimony, and as interest shifted away from the Senate investigation, most of the work on the scandal was handled by the President's special counsel, Owen Roberts and Atlee Pomerene. Some of the Teapot Dome drama had also moved to the courts. In March 1924 Sinclair was indicted for contempt of the Senate by a Washington, D.C., grand jury. He had refused to answer questions about his 1920 campaign contributions when he appeared before the Walsh Committee on March 23. He did not refuse to testify on the basis of the Fifth Amendment, but because he believed that the Senate committee had no "jurisdiction to question me further regarding . . . lease." Sinclair gave this same response on ten separate occasions, and on March 24 the Senate voted to bring grand jury action against him. The grand jury brought in its indictment on March 31, despite the fact that it had been several decades since a grand jury had indicted an individual on such charges. Sinclair pleaded not guilty. However, nearly three years later he was found guilty by the criminal branch of the Supreme Court in the District of Columbia. After a lengthy appeal to the United States Supreme Court, Sinclair's contempt sentence was upheld and the oilman served a three-month prison term. Sinclair also served a six-month term for a contempt of court citation stemming from his and Fall's conspiracy trial.

There was no doubt that the initiative for the investigation of the Teapot Dome began with Walsh and the Senate Public Lands Committee. Walsh, who had exerted more energy to get to the truth of the allegations and circumstances surrounding the leasing of the naval oil reserves than any other individual, had been the subject of criticism across the country. He had been accused by many of blatantly partisan behavior, of succumbing to rumor and innuendo, and of jumping to rash and unsubstantiated conclusions. Before Walsh and the Public Lands Committee issued their final report based on months of investigation, Walsh summarized his findings for *Outlook* magazine in May 1924. While the magazine did not fully agree with Walsh's "extreme claims," it felt that the public was entitled to hear the judgments of the Montana senator, the person who had inspected and analyzed more material on the subject than had any other public figure. According to Walsh's analysis, the most damning piece of evidence brought in against Fall was the fact that Doheny's lease on the Elk Hills reserve was secured without any kind of competitive bidding. This occurred simultaneously with his grant of $100,000 to Albert Fall. Fall's move from poverty to riches coincided with his awarding the lease of the Teapot Dome reserve to Sinclair. Walsh noted that the evidence of the technical experts, especially the later witnesses, had revealed that the government had been defrauded of its rightful portion of the oil when the reserves were leased out to private individuals. These points which Walsh touched upon in the *Outlook* article served as a synopsis of the majority report which emerged from the committee on June 6.

The report submitted to the Senate was signed by Senator Edwin Ladd of North Dakota, who had assumed the chairmanship of the committee from Lenroot, and the other Democrats and independent Republicans. The final report attacked Fall most severely for his lawlessness and his assumption of authority far beyond the limits of his position. The Senate committee found all the transactions surrounding the leasings to be corrupt, although it admitted that much of the evidence had been inconclusive and that there was no real proof that anyone had profited from advance knowledge about the leases. The committee report also failed to draw any real links between the machinations of the oilmen and the 1920 Republican campaign.

Not everyone was happy with the report. Naturally, the Republicans and the Administration supporters in the press were highly critical. A minority report was issued by Senator Spence of Missouri, claiming that the members had not had sufficient time to read the report and that it had been impossible for them to make any definite conclusions, given how much ephemeral material was presented to the committee. The *Boston Evening Transcript,* a staunch Administration organ, also criticized Walsh's report. Not only had Walsh usurped those powers which the Constitution had intended for the courts when he had declared the leases to be illegal, the *Transcript* declared, but he had been overtly partisan in his attack on the Harding Administration.

From the other end of the political spectrum, from the whole range of Democratic party spokespeople, there were also criticisms of the report. Harry Slattery, the ardent conservationist, thought that the report was much too mild in its complete exoneration of Archie Roosevelt and Secretary of the Navy Denby. Slattery was also convinced that certain aspects of Fall's behavior were not pointed out clearly enough by Walsh. The *Times* noted that the Walsh report was thorough and straight in its coverage of the facts, but "after the thunder and the earthquake, the still small voice. After the months of resounding inquiry . . . the report of Senator Walsh." Other commentators echoed the *Times's* disappointment: the Walsh report lacked drama; it lacked hard and fast conclusions about the web of collusion and conspiracy between government officials, party functionaries, and oil speculators. The official organ of the American Federation of Labor perhaps best summarized the liberal disappointment with the Walsh report: "The single, solemn truth is that the Walsh report is a flat fizzle. It doesn't sound like Walsh."

While Walsh was never able to produce indisputable data on the complex questions of Teapot Dome, Elk Hills, and the oil leasing policy of the Harding years, there was no question that he was able to point it in the right direction. The investigation of the oil scandals continued under the prosecution of Roberts and Pomerene, and indictments and guilty verdicts were handed down for conspiracy, bribery, and illegal transferral of the oil lands. On February 28, 1927, the Supreme Court unanimously decided that the lease upon the oil reserves had, indeed, been illegal. The Court later declared that the lease was a product of the Fall-Sinclair conspiracy, that Denby had purposely acquiesced, and in the process had allowed Fall to act without restraint.

The criminal proceedings against Harry Sinclair which eventually went to the Supreme Court and which centered on Sinclair's contempt of the Senate citation, were an important step in broadening the investigatory powers of the Congress. Sinclair had contended that the interrogations to which he had refused to respond "related to his private affairs and to matters cognizable only in the courts"; thus, the Senate had no jurisdiction. In April 1929 the Court refused to accept Sinclair's position and upheld the right of the Senate to investigate. This decision, *Sinclair* v. *United States,* stretched the purposes for which Congress could conduct its investigations. The Court first affirmed that Congress could dispose of and make all the necessary rules and regulations regarding the oil reserves. It further noted that

> the Senate had power to delegate authority to its committee to investigate and report what had been and was being done by executive departments under the Leasing Act, the Naval Oil Reserve Act, and the President's order in respect of the reserves, and to make any other inquiry concerning the public domain. . . . Congress, in addition to its general legislative power over the public domain, had all the powers of a proprietor and was authorized to deal with it as a private individual may deal with land owned by him. The committee's authority to investigate extended to matters affecting the interest of the United States as owner as well as to those having relation to the legislative function. . . . Moreover, it was pertinent for the Senate to ascertain the practical effect of recent changes that had been made in the laws relating to oil and other mineral lands in the public domain.

The *Sinclair* decision asserted that Congress may investigate in order to understand the effect of its own laws.

Two years before the *Sinclair* decision, in January 1927, the Supreme Court had decided in *McGrain* v. *Daugherty* that the Senate (or House of Representatives) "has power, through its own processes, to compel a private individual to appear before it or one of its committees and give testimony needed to enable it efficiently to exercise a legislative function belonging to it under the Constitution." This decision had also grown out of the Teapot Dome controversy, although it was not a result of the Walsh investigations. It was significant, however, that two of the most sweeping court decisions concerning the rights of Congress to act as an investigative body grew out of the same scandal and out of the efforts of Congress to get a thorough understanding of the activities within the Executive branch. The Walsh hearings cleared the way for a broader definition of the legislature as an investigatory body. While critics inveighed against Walsh and the other members of the Public Lands Committee for usurping the role of the judiciary, the Supreme Court, in two separate decisions, confirmed the growing role of Congress in the investigatory process. The Court resoundingly confirmed this growth by stating: "We are of opinion that the power of inquiry—with process to enforce it—is an essential and appropriate auxiliary to the legislative function." The importance of that growth was earlier asserted by one of the nation's outstanding legal scholars and a future Supreme Court justice. In a 1924 article in the *New Republic,* Felix Frankfurter replied to critics of the congressional investigation:

> The procedure of congressional investigation should remain as it is. No limitations should be imposed by congressional legislation or standing rules. The power of investigation should be left untram-

meled, and the methods and forms of each investigation should be left for the determination of Congress and its committees, as each situation arises. The safeguards against abuse and folly are to be looked for in the forces of responsibility which are operating from within Congress, and are generated from without.

BIBLIOGRAPHY

Congressional Record. 67th Cong., 2nd sess., 68th Cong., 1st sess.

Frankfurter, Felix. "Hands Off the Investigations." *The New Republic,* (May 21, 1924).

Hard, William. "The Tale of the Teapot." The Nation, November 21, 1923.

McGrain v. *Daugherty* 273 U.S. 135 (1927).

Noggle, Burl. *Teapot Dome: Oil and Politics in the 1920's.* (Baton Rouge, 1962).

Sinclair v. *United States* 279 U.S. 263 (1929).

U.S. Congress. Senate hearings. 68th Cong., 1st sess.

Walsh, Thomas. "What the Oil Inquiry Developed." *The Outlook,* (May 21, 1924).

Werner, Morris R. and Starr, John. *Teapot Dome.* (New York, 1959).

PERTINENT DOCUMENTS

Introduction of Kendrick Resolution, April 12, 1922

Senate Debate over La Follette Resolution, April 28 and 29, 1922

Testimony of Albert Fall, October 24, 1923

"The Tale of the Teapot" by William Hard, November 21, 1923

Testimony of Carl C. Magee, November 20, 1923

Testimony of Harry F. Sinclair, December 4, 1923

Albert B. Fall to Thomas B. Walsh, January 11, 1924

Testimony of Edward B. McLean, January 11, 1924

Testimony of Edward L. Doheny, January 24, 1924

Testimony of Archie Roosevelt, January 26, 1924

Refusal by Senator Albert Fall to Testify and Committee Debate, February 2 and 7, 1924

William G. McAdoo to Irvine L. Lenroot, February 7, 1924

Testimony of William G. McAdoo, February 11, 1924

Senate Debate over Demands for Denby Resignation, February 11, 1924

Testimony of Edward McLean, March 12, 1924

Testimony of Harry F. Sinclair, March 22, 1924

"Hands off the Investigations" by Felix Frankfurter, May 21, 1924

"What the Oil Inquiry Developed" by Thomas Walsh, May 21, 1924

Majority Report and Views of the Minority, June 6, 1924

Opinion in *McGrain* v. *Daugherty*, January 17, 1927

Opinion in *Sinclair* v. *United States*, April 8, 1929

The Pecora Wall Street Exposé 1934

Time magazine

Chief counsel Ferdinand Pecora so thoroughly dominated the 1934 investigation of Wall Street that the Senate committee came to be known by his name rather than its chairman's.

The Pecora Wall Street Exposé 1934

by Donald A. Ritchie

Suspicious, fearful, and frustrated, the Depression Congress of 1932 filled its hampers with a record number of resolutions for investigation. Most sought some explanation for the stock market crash, business liquidations, and bank failures. Unemployment paralyzed the nation, demanding exposure of the conditions and persons responsible. Few of these investigations ever materialized—only the Senate Banking and Currency Committee's examination of Wall Street captured the public's attention. After the committee had stumbled aimlessly through a maze of incomprehensible financial data under a series of inept counsels, the investigation at last succeeded when it gained the leadership of Ferdinand Pecora and his staff. So thoroughly did Counsel Pecora dominate the proceedings that *his* name, rather than the committee chairman's, became irrevocably identified with the hearings. The Pecora probe, with its careful documentation of banker and broker misdeeds, and its contributions to corrective legislation, set a worthy model for future congressional investigations.

In the twenty years since the Pujo Committee hearings on the "Money Trust," the American economic structure had grown disastrously worse. Of fifty billion dollars' worth of stocks sold in the United States during the 1920s the House Commerce Committee estimated, half had been "undesirable or worthless." Securities houses of the most reputable banks manifoldly increased their profits at the expense of their own clients. Powerful investment bankers continued to fill key corporations' boards of directors. Overly-optimistic loan programs threatened vast banking chains with domino-like collapse. Utility holding companies teetered precariously upon an intricate system of interlocking directorates with little regard for corporate efficiency or local requirements. Concurrently, the federal government remained willfully ignorant of stock exchange and private banking operations. "The business of America is business," Calvin Coolidge had noted with satisfaction during the 1920s; by 1932 that business verged on bankruptcy.

To a generation of liberals, the market crash and the subsequent Depression verified the prophesies of Louis Brandeis's economic tract, *Other People's Money*. Drawing from the Pujo Committee findings, first in a series of articles for *Harper's Weekly* and then in his book, Brandeis had warned that an amalgamation of investment bankers and insurance companies was using its control of "other people's money" to infiltrate American industry. These "banker-barons" were more concerned about the market value of a corporation's securities than for the value of its product. Worried that their combination of wealth and power had slowly stifled the competitive free market system, Brandeis sounded the alarm: "We must break the Money Trust or the Money Trust will break us." The government, he declared, must demand full publicity on all stock dealings, including bankers' commissions and the extent of the bankers' control over the issuing corporation. "Sunlight is said to be the best of disinfectants; electric light the most effective policeman," he concluded, so full financial disclosure would purify imperfections within the economic system.

Armed with the first new reprinting of the book in twenty years, old and young liberals alike carried its message to Washington with the new Roosevelt Administration. In congressional committee rooms the book became a familiar sight—many witnesses introduced it as proof of their arguments. Legislative drafts emerged verbatim from its pages. The book also provided a historical link between the two great financial investigations, for Brandeis and his followers viewed Pecora's work as the fulfillment of the Pujo investigation.

Economic conditions, political support, and public interest all gave Pecora advantages denied to his predecessor, Samuel Untermyer, counsel for Pujo. Where the Pujo hearings had commenced in a relatively prosperous period, Pecora began his hearings at the nadir of the Depression. Where President William Howard Taft had withheld cooperation from Untermyer, President Franklin D. Roosevelt personally encouraged Pecora, endorsed the hearings, and incorporated their recommendations into his legislative program. The press, hostile to the earlier inquiry, lavished extensive coverage on Pecora, filling columns with his photographs and accounts of his activities. Pecora also benefited from Untermyer's mistakes. Recalling his unsuccessful attempts to gain sufficient evidence, Pecora acquired far stronger subpoena powers than his predecessor. He marched his staff directly into the banks and brokerage houses rather than depend upon his witnesses to produce material voluntarily.

For more than a year Pecora called many of the nation's most prestigious financiers before the public. Repeatedly, he elicited from them such startling admissions of wrongdoing that he stole headlines from even the masterful Franklin Roosevelt. Nevertheless, Roosevelt cheerfully supported the hearings, for their publicity helped counteract business opposition to his financial reforms and aided passage of such controversial measures as the Securities Act of 1933, the Securities and Exchange Act of 1934, and the Public Utilities Holding Company Act of 1935. Constant revelations from the witness stand and revulsion against them distracted the attention of liberal elements within Roosevelt's loose political coalition. At the same time FDR more actively courted the business community through the National Recovery Administration.

In a small part, the Pecora investigations contributed to a reforming rather than a revolutionary spirit in the New Deal's program. At a time of considerable questioning of the capitalist system, the hearings personalized the causes of the Depression. By producing a string of villains, they translated complicated economic problems into moral terms. Bankers, Pecora demonstrated, had abandoned their fiduciary responsibilities. He expended his greatest wrath on the "incompetence, negligence, irresponsibility, or cupidity in the profession." The banking and securities systems, it followed, needed only a change in personnel and stricter governmental supervision so that such abuses might not reoccur. Government regulation of private finance, rather than nationalization or centralization, was the investigation's message and its legislative legacy.

The Banking Committee hearings could claim both the Hoover and Roosevelt Administrations as patrons, and as a result enjoyed unusual bipartisan support. Herbert Hoover, despite his philosophical aversion to government interference with the stock exchanges and other market machinery, took credit for initiating the investigation. These claims, however, deserved some qualification. Early in his presidential term, Hoover had summoned various stock exchange officials for talks on the economy. Worried over the dangers of unrestrained speculation and unrealistically high market prices, but also convinced he had no constitutional right or power to intervene, Hoover urged the exchange leaders to assume more self-discipline over the stock markets. For his efforts he received "profuse promises" but no action. Within months the market crashed, but Hoover clung to his narrow interpretation of government responsibility. To quiet congressional murmurs, the White House issued assurances that "in the long run the system of free selling is better." When a flurry of resolutions from both Republicans and Democrats made some action imminent, the President stepped up his campaign for stock exchange self-reform.

Continually declining markets in 1930 and 1931 led Hoover to lay blame for the economic collapse on the "bear raiding" tactics of professional stock manipulators. These "bears" made commitments to sell stock which they did not own, on the assumption that the stock's price would soon drop. Borrowing equal amounts of stock from cooperative underwriters to cover their sales, they waited until the market sank far enough to buy shares at a lower price than that at which they had agreed to sell. The difference, less a percentage for the underwriters, was pure profit. Frequently short sales like these first involved boosting the stock's price through calculated purchases on different exchanges, and then a sudden burst of sales to bring the price down: the bear raid. When organized pools of speculators abruptly unloaded stock, they often created panic selling among smaller investors, further depressing the market to the bears' financial advantage. Such profiteering on the Depression appeared particularly reprehensible to the Congress. Yet despite their threats of investigation and urgent presidential pleas, the governing boards of the major exchanges refused to outlaw short selling.

Richard Whitney, speaking for the New York Stock Exchange, which handled more than half the nation's stock transactions, expressed the belief that short selling provided badly needed liquidity in times of crisis. Short sellers eventually had to buy stocks to settle their sales, the exchange argued, and thereby provided purchasers during periods of heavy selling. The exchange preferred to retain the practice under limited controls and threaten its temporary suspension as a weapon in cases of emergency. As a concession, the New York Stock Exchange agreed only to prohibit its member firms from lending stocks to short sellers without the original stockholder's written consent, a rule which they predicted would reduce short selling by fifty percent. Hoover, however, considered this action totally insufficient. On February 19, 1932, the day after the exchange announced its new rules, the President met with Republican Senators Frederic Walcott and Peter Norbeck of the Senate Banking and Currency Committee, endorsed an investigation of short selling, and encouraged them to proceed vigorously.

Hoover's fears extended to his political future. Facing a hard reelection campaign that year, he imagined that the bear raiding represented secret Democratic attempts to embarrass his Administration. He reserved his deepest suspicions for such prominent Democratic financiers as Bernard Baruch and John J. Raskob, then chairman of the Democratic National Committee, and he hoped the investigation would reveal their stock dealings. Ironically, while none of these men was engaged in bear raiding, some of the most active bears, like "Sell 'Em" Ben Smith, did time their larger sales to correspond with Hoover's optimistic speeches. They had learned that whenever the President predicted recovery, the market invariably declined.

Acting for Hoover, Senator Walcott had already introduced a resolution allotting $3,000 for an investigation into the specific practice of short selling. Walcott made it clear he wanted no federal legislation to reform the exchanges. Instead, he planned to force the exchanges, through adverse publicity, to adopt stronger rules on their own. This measure proved too tepid for the majority in Congress. Sentiments against the exchanges had grown too powerful, and on March 4 the Senate endorsed an investigation into all stock market practices. To support this investigation they appropriated $50,000, an unexpectedly large sum, considering that the hearings were scheduled to end with the adjournment of Congress in June.

Even after the resolution passed, the Banking Committee made little effort to implement it. The committee had already voted to make Senator Carter Glass's banking reform bill its pending business, and unforeseen altercations and lengthy deliberations on that bill delayed any investigation planning for another month. Its sponsors soon began to fear that the session would close without having opened hearings into stock exchange abuses.

Then, on Friday, April 8, 1932, Hoover received private warnings that bear raiders planned heavy stock sales for the next day, to sabotage his recovery program. Senator Walcott rushed to the Republican cloakroom to gather majority members of the Banking Committee. Since Chairman Norbeck was absent, campaigning for reelection in South Dakota, Senator Smith W. Brookhart, an insurgent Republican from Iowa, stood as the acting chairman. But Brookhart allowed the conservative Walcott to take command in spreading word of the "great bear raid." From the cloakroom Walcott telephoned New York Stock Exchange President Richard Whitney and demanded that he provide the committee with a list of all short sellers on the exchange. When Whitney refused to comply voluntarily, Walcott won committee approval to subpoena him. The committee ordered the exchange president to appear on Monday with lists of all stocks sold short in excess of ten thousand shares, and all those who traded in the stocks. Senator Brookhart, long a supporter of a Wall Street investigation, rejoiced in the move. "We are going to look into Mr. Whitney's machine," he promised. "We are going to get the real facts, and we think he knows them."

Chairman Peter Norbeck hurried back from South Dakota to be present when Richard Whitney appeared before the committee's Monday morning session. The hastily called hearings quickly developed into a complete debacle for the committee. Walcott had appointed Claude R. Branch, a soft-spoken and unimpressive lawyer from Rhode Island, as the tentative counsel, but Branch pursued an ill-prepared and fruitless examination of Whitney. The stock exchange president had appeared without the data which the committee had requested, explaining that 175 exchange employees were busily compiling the voluminous records. Deprived of any hard evidence, neither Branch nor the committee could follow any intensive line of inquiry. Innocently, Whitney pleaded no knowledge of any bear raid, nor any widespread short selling. He could not explain "rigging" stock to them, and begged ignorance of "floor pools." The hearings that promised sensational disclosures produced nothing at all, and no bear raid took place that Saturday. Public interest in the hearings faded, the *New York Times* noted editorially, "because of the somewhat foolish anticlimax that has been reached."

Much chagrined at Whitney's easy success, Chairman Norbeck dismissed Branch and hired Philadelphia attorney William A. Gray to continue the examination. Gray had the added advantage of the lengthy short selling reports which the New York Stock Exchange had finally submitted. Since this material consisted entirely of raw data, and Gray had the aid of only one secretary and one financial advisor, he decided not to examine the report. "The exchange furnished information from which you could not get anything unless you studied it for a week," he explained as he reconvened the hearings. Relying on his skillful courtroom tactics to draw out information, Gray immediately recalled Whitney to the stand and led him through a repetition of much of the same questioning that Branch had already conducted. Again, Whitney easily avoided or deflated the questions.

Eventually, Gray realized the futility of his approach and adjourned the hearings to collect and analyze his data. The Banking Committee subpoenaed the general records of ten brokerage firms, and after reading through the material, published the names of 350 bear traders. To Hoover's disappointment, no leading Democrats appeared on the list. "These obviously are dummy names in many cases," Senator Walcott explained bitterly. Again

Gray called Whitney to testify on the exchange's attitude toward short selling, and Whitney continued to profess ignorance of any wrongdoing. "You make rules that are just paper rules," Chairman Norbeck exploded in exasperation. "I ask for proof of that," Whitney countered. "You attend these hearings for a while and you will see," Norbeck assured him. "I have been," Whitney responded wearily. "Yes," Norbeck thundered back, "but up to now you have been running them!" (Reported in the press, Norbeck's last statement does not appear in the official committee transcripts.)

Opponents of the hearings charged that they had done nothing to restore public confidence in the exchanges nor to drive out the bear raiders. Even the once militant Walcott hedged his support. "I am not sure now that short sales depress the market," he admitted. For the more progressive Norbeck, the humiliating hearings and growing public disenchantment with the investigation were infuriating. Storming out of an executive session of the committee, he shouted to reporters: "We are going to carry this investigation through to the end."

Seizing full control of the investigation, Norbeck established a five member steering committee, which he headed, and which noticeably omitted Walcott. The subcommittee then hired four special investigators and an accounting firm to assist Gray in sifting through the mountains of financial records they had accumulated. These new directions produced new witnesses. Percy Rockefeller, nephew of John D. Rockefeller, sr., appeared and confessed that he sold short to cover his losses of "many, many millions of dollars" in the stock market crash. One of his partners in these transactions, Ben Smith, also testified, admitting that he participated in a pooling of R.C.A. stock, along with John J. Raskob and Michael J. Meehan, a heavy contributor to the campaigns of Alfred E. Smith.

In early June, the committee called Raskob to testify. Prodding the Democratic national chairman on his trading of General Motors stocks, Counsel Gray attempted to paint him as a short seller deliberately undermining Hoover's programs. Raskob urbanely parried each question, maintaining that he had "always been a bull on America." Bluntly, Senator Carter Glass interjected that "it has been whispered for weeks around the Capitol that this investigation was initiated to involve several prominent Democrats." Gray's badgering of Raskob irritated even Republican Senator James Couzens, who complained, "I don't see where we are drifting." But Gray persisted. Excusing Raskob he subpoenaed Charles E. Mitchell, chairman of the National City Bank, to explain that bank's dealings in speculative Anaconda Copper stocks. Soon after, he launched into a brief examination of the Radio-Keith-Orpheum transactions. When Congress adjourned on July 16, the hearings had produced no significant revelations nor any report on possible further action. Despite rising criticism, Chairman Norbeck vowed to continue, "The bigger things are still to be done."

November's elections brought major political changes. Depression politics swept Hoover out of the White House and obliterated the tenuous Republican majority in the Senate. The Seventy-Third Congress would contain fifty-nine Democratic and thirty-six Republican senators. Florida Senator Duncan U. Fletcher would move to the chairmanship of the Banking Committee. However, the new President and Congress would not arrive until the following March and the Seventy-Second Congress which returned to Washington in December contained an unusually large flock of lame ducks. At first the Banking Committee busied itself with new banking legislation, revisions in the Reconstruction Finance Corporation Act, and numerous monetary proposals, but Norbeck had won a new resolution, increasing the investigation's appropriation and granting it power to examine income tax records in executive sessions. At the same time, he dismissed Gray and began the search for a Democratic counsel.

Early in January, the committee selected Irving Ben Cooper as its new counsel. Fresh from a successful investigation of corruption in New York City as Samuel Seabury's chief assistant, Cooper promised a burst of new enthusiasm. Unexpectedly, though, he demanded complete freedom to conduct his investigation, plus fifty blank subpoenas, and announced he would conduct most of his work in New York. Jealous of their prerogatives, and still sensitive over Gray's misguided tactics, the committee balked at losing control and refused this blank check request. Insulted, Cooper promptly resigned.

Since Norbeck had failed with three counsels, Senator Fletcher approached his longtime friend, former Secretary of State Bainbridge Colby, to offer the position. Colby declined but recommended an associate from the old Bull Moose Progressive party of 1912, who like himself had jointed the Democrats in 1916. His choice was Ferdinand Pecora.

Then fifty-one, Pecora had been born in Nicosia, Sicily, and came to the United States at the age of five, where he grew up in the Chelsea area of New York City. At first studying for the Episcopal ministry, Pecora had quit to help support his family. Working in a law office, he financed his own way through New York University Law School. From 1918 until 1930 he served as chief assistant district attorney for New York County. His former boss, District Attorney Jacob Banton, assured the senators that Pecora would conduct the hearings with a "lawyer-like, scholarly manner, without playing up to publicity." During Banton's long illnesses, Pecora had directed much of his office's work. He established an impressive record of convictions in eighty percent of the one thousand cases he handled. His investigations into small "bucket-shop" stock selling operations had introduced him to the murky practices of securities fraud, and he had helped to close 150 such shops through numerous prosecutions. He had also won the conviction of the New York State banking superintendent on bribery charges. Honest and diligent, with a sharp and retentive mind, Pecora would provide the shrewd stewardship missing so long from the investigation.

Offer of the job came as a surprise to Pecora, who thought the committee had already concluded its work. Senator Norbeck assured him that little business remained other than preparing the final report to the Senate, due before Congress adjourned on March 4. When Pecora arrived in Washington, he found the committee's records stuffed into a large file cabinet in Norbeck's office. As he sifted through the material, he was struck by its limited nature and lack of conclusive evidence. The original resolution, he decided, had called for a much broader investigation. Norbeck, who had always shared these opinions, gladly threw his support behind a resumption of the hearings during the few short weeks that remained.

Fully aware of the difficulties of his assignment, Pecora stopped first to build a staff that he could trust. He drew primarily from the bright and industrious young men who had worked with him in the D.A.'s office. Two young lawyers, David Saperstein and Julius Silver, became his chief assistants, while Frank J. Meehan, an accountant who had worked on the bucket-shop investigations, joined the team as chief statistician. Pecora added other lawyers and accountants, but the committee's tight budget limited his selection. The highest salary he could offer, and take himself, was $3,000 a year, much less than any earned in private practice, even during the Depression. Two old anti-Wall Street warhorses volunteered their services without compensation: Max Lowenthal, a former Harvard Law School student of Felix Frankfurter, who had made a fortune handling stockholder suits against corporations and had written a muckraking account of corporation reorganization in *The Investor Pays;* and John T. Flynn, a highly successful freelance writer, financial editor of *The New Republic,* and lecturer on contemporary economics at the New School. Both men eagerly sought the opportunity to expose business practices they abhorred. Fiery financial iconoclasts, they added a measure of experience and fearless disapproval of the bankers that the younger men might have lacked.

Pecora officially opened his probe in February 1933, a week after the governor of Michigan had declared a "bank holiday" to salvage his state's banking system. Nationwide, more than five thousand banks had suspended operations since the 1929 stock market crash. Now, state after state followed Michigan's example. For the bewildered thousands of depositors who waited in line to withdraw their savings, if possible, the Banking Committee hearings provided a timely financial education.

Aiming for the March 4 deadline, Pecora had hurriedly planned a tentative schedule of witnesses. By chance, Charles E. Mitchell, flamboyant chairman of the National City Bank, became the first target when Pecora read of his impending trip to Europe to discuss stabilization of the lira with Mussolini. Tracking down the banker to his Bermuda retreat, Pecora issued subpoenas for his appearance and for all minutes and records of the National City Bank and its investment affiliate, the National City Company, for the five years prior to October 1929. On Thursday, February 9, Pecora and his staff arrived at the bank's Wall Street headquarters. As they waited, a parade of bank clerks carried in massive volumes of records and piled them into high stacks. Privately, the counsel admitted he felt "appalled by their magnitude." From Thursday night until Saturday night, working almost around-the-clock, he and a corps of accountants combed through the records, photostating all documents they thought useful for the hearings. On Monday, Pecora returned to Washington to conduct a brief inquiry into the Samuel Insull utility company system, while his staff continued to collect and analyze National City data.

By February 21, when the National City hearings began, Pecora had acquired far more damaging information than the unsuspecting Mitchell imagined. With an air of obvious self-confidence, Mitchell swept into the Senate caucus room, with a crowd of lawyers and bank officials surrounding him. No stranger to Washington, the tall, well-tanned, gray-haired Mitchell had advised every Republican President since Warren Harding. A year before he had sat through Counsel Gray's quizzing with no damage to his reputation as a responsible banker. Pecora, the short, cigar-smoking Italian immigrant, did not worry him. Yet, within a day under Pecora's persistent questioning, Mitchell's self-confidence waned. He seemed perplexed at Pecora's detailed knowledge of his doings, and the counsel wondered if Mitchell understood how completely they had examined the bank's records. On his first day as a witness, Mitchell admitted he paid no income taxes in 1929 after selling 18,000 shares of stock to his wife to establish a $2,800,000 loss. "That sale was really just a sale of convenience to reduce your taxes?" asked Senator Brookhart. "Yes," Mitchell replied frankly. From 1927 until 1929, he confirmed, he had received bonuses of $3,500,000 from the National City Bank and its investment company, in addition to his annual salary of $25,000.

A large portion of these bountiful profits came from the speculative successes of the National City Company, which had distributed more stocks than any other investment firm during the 1920s. Mitchell, who originally rose to prominence as president of the National City Company and was the firm's greatest salesman, tried to rationalize its more questionable dealings with the bank. Early in the 1920s, for example, the bank had made several large loans to the Cuban sugar industry. In 1927, when these loans were in default, National City Bank issued $50,000,000 in new bank stocks. Without informing the stock purchasers, the bank then transferred this additional capital to the National City Company, which purchased controlling interest in the sugar industry, recently consolidated into the General Sugar Corporation. With this windfall, the sugar industry promptly repaid its debt to the National City Bank. Unweaving the story, Pecora asked: "Is this what is known in the vernacular as 'bailing out' of the bank of a bad loan?" Mitchell protested this implication, but did admit that the stockholders had no idea their money had enabled the investment company to assume the bank's "slow and doubtful" sugar loans. Such conflicting banking and investment interests had troubled the government as early as 1911 when Solicitor General Frederick Lehmann found the National City Company clearly in violation of federal laws for holding the stocks of its parent bank and for engaging in illegal investments. Lehmann's opinion, however, had gathered dust in government files, wholly ignored for the next twenty years.

When Mitchell stepped down, an investor who had placed his fortune in the trust of the National City Company succeeded him to the stand. Edgar Brown of Pottsville, Pennsylvania, explained to the committee how the National City Bank had recommended that he allow the investment company to convert his $225,000 savings in U.S. bonds into a portfolio of stocks. He accepted their advice. When the stocks did poorly, Brown nervously tried to sell, but the agents of the company talked him out of it. "I was placed in the position of one who was about to put his own mother out of the house," he recalled. As a final insult, when Brown's investments collapsed, leaving him bankrupt, the National City Bank refused his application for a loan. Yet, simultaneously, as Pecora's documentation revealed, the bank freely advanced loans on insufficient collateral to its own officers to meet their market commitments.

The National City investigations shocked Wall Street and made headlines across the country. President-elect Roosevelt congratulated Pecora and urged him to carry on the hearings into the next Congress. Chairman-designate

Fletcher introduced the resolution to make this possible. On February 27, Charles Mitchell offered his resignation as chairman of the National City Bank, which its board of directors hastily accepted. A week later, the bank's new chairman announced the severing of all connections between the bank and the investment company. The New York district attorney then filed a suit against Mitchell for tax evasion. On March 2, as the committee recessed for the inauguration, Pecora conferred with Senator Norbeck at his office. As the two men looked out of the window towards Union Station, they spied Mitchell, with shoulders stooped, carrying his own luggage across the plaza from his hotel to the railway station. The retinue of bank officials who had accompanied him at the start of the hearings were now nowhere in sight. Mitchell left quietly and alone.

"The money changers have fled from their high seats in the temple of our culture," Franklin Roosevelt proclaimed in his inaugural address two days later. Roosevelt's Administration took office in the midst of a nationwide banking chaos. When the President declared a national bank holiday, the Senate Banking Committee moved to devote its entire energies to banking reform legislation. A week later, when the banks reopened, one of those that remained closed was Joseph Harriman's National Bank and Trust Company. A year before, when the Banking Committee hearings had first begun, Harriman had taken out a newspaper advertisement to warn against them. "Washington is ill equipped to investigate important matters of commerce and finance affecting the public welfare," he warned ominously, "and in the present instance there is no certainty that it will not uncover things much better left sealed." Now, Harriman fled from federal agents before his eventual arrest and imprisonment for misappropriating funds and tampering with his bank's records.

As the senators rushed through the "first hundred days" of Roosevelt's legislative program, Pecora returned to New York and planned new strategy for the investigations. Having finished with the commercial National City Bank, he turned to the practices of the great private banks, and chose their most impressive figure, J. P. Morgan, jr., as his next subject for examination. Arriving in New York, Pecora telephoned Morgan to arrange a preliminary meeting before issuing the banker a subpoena. "Yes, I think I've heard of you, Mr. Pecora," Morgan acknowledged, and invited him down to his office at 23 Wall Street. But Pecora refused his request and insisted that Morgan come uptown and meet him at his own offices. He wanted to make it dramatically clear that the banker faced a representative of the United States government rather than Ferdinand Pecora, the individual.

Pecora's New York office was a small suite of rooms, rented on a monthly basis, in the same building as his private law firm. Filled with second-hand furniture, without rugs, draperies or any other ornamentation, it presented a starkly functional appearance. Morgan arrived with his silver-maned and stately lawyer, John W. Davis, the 1924 Democratic presidential nominee. As Pecora had hoped, the two seemed "impressed by the shabbiness of the room." Without excessive formalities, he proceeded forthrightly to tell them he wanted complete access to the files of J. P. Morgan & Company and any subsidiaries. Morgan, taken out of his baronial surroundings, cut a rather shy and deferential figure. Pecora found him exceedingly courteous and cooperative. Morgan's lawyer, on the other hand, strenuously objected to all his requests as an unconstitutional intrusion into a private citizen's business. A rigid conservative, John W. Davis held sacred the rights of privacy, economic liberty, and the sanctity of private banking. He dismissed most congressional investigations as publicity-seeking, and distrusted all sweeping reforms. Davis insisted that Pecora specify exactly what material the bank should prepare for the committee; he wanted no invasion of the bank's records by Pecora's staff of accountants. In response, Pecora submitted twenty-three specific requests for materials. Morgan & Company agreed to fifteen, took seven under consideration, and rejected one, a request to see the bank's articles of copartnership and distribution of profits.

Pecora would stand for no recalcitrance. Together with Senator Fletcher he prepared a new resolution to broaden his mandate to cover all phases of banking beyond the original securities objective. The resolution passed unanimously, and the Senate granted an additional $25,000 for further hearings.

Throughout April, Pecora's investigators sorted through the voluminous records at the Morgan bank on Wall Street. Davis and Pecora sparred frequently over the confidentiality of the bank's depositors and borrowers. Not quite as obliging as the National City Bank's counsel, Davis denied Pecora the right to work nights in the bank after closing hour. But by the end of May, Pecora had accumulated enough material to call J. P. Morgan, jr., as a witness.

Long lines of curiosity-seekers filled the corridors of the Senate Office Building as the Banking Committee inquiry resumed on May 23. A squad of telegraph operators stood ready to relay reporters' stories to newspapers across the country. Press photographers stationed themselves in the caucus room. All waited to see the head of the famed House of Morgan testify before Congress for the first time since 1912, when the elder J. P. Morgan faced the Pujo Committee; and many wondered if Pecora would again score as heavily as he had against Mitchell. Entering the great marble chamber, the ponderous Morgan perfectly fit his austere public image. On the stand, however, he palled in comparison with his father. Gone were the arrogant, self-assured responses with floor-thumping emphasis. Morgan, jr. was an affable, quiet-spoken witness. His voice, with its distinct British accent, fell so low that few spectators could hear him. Although he and his firm's other partners had studiously undergone Davis's coaching sessions before the hearings, Morgan still stumbled over names and events and frequently conferred with his counsel before answering.

After the sordid revelations on the National City Bank, Pecora found J. P. Morgan & Company a relatively conservative institution. Even so, he unveiled enough surprising evidence to fill headlines for the next two weeks, exposing the private dealings of a very private banker. In every instance, Morgan & Company could claim the technical legality of their policies, while Pecora could demonstrate how far they had gone to stretch their legal and ethical standards. Most shocking to the Depression-ridden public was the initial disclosure that the fabulously wealthy Morgan and his partners paid no income taxes during the years 1931 and 1932 in the United States, although Morgan had paid taxes in England during those years. This deficiency had resulted from the firm's net loss of twenty-one million dollars during 1930; and

Morgan put his office manager, Leonard Keyes, on the stand to verify the bank's substantial decline. Pecora rebutted these contentions by revealing that the bank had added a new partner two days after the New Year in 1931 in an intricate maneuver to extend their losses of 1930 for another year. "That sort of parlor magic may satisfy the courts and the moronic sycophants of big business," a columnist for *The Nation* wrote in undisguised anger, ". . . but it will neither soothe nor deceive any honest person of adult intelligence."

Bringing Morgan back to the stand on the second day, Pecora moved from taxes to stock distribution and created an even greater shock wave by disclosing a long list of dignitaries who had accepted favors from the Morgan bank. In 1929 these favors had taken the form of preferential invitations to buy stock in the Allegheny Corporation, a railroad holding company venture which the Morgan firm was handling. Since Morgan & Company generally dealt in bonds and did not sell common stock to the public, it decided to permit certain individuals to privately purchase the stock, offering it to them at twenty dollars a share, while the market value averaged thirty-five dollars a share. Invited purchasers included officials from banks, insurance companies, industry, railroads, and utilities, as well as editors, lawyers, and politicians. The names of Roosevelt's Secretary of the Treasury, William H. Woodin, Ambassador-at-Large Norman H. Davis, Senator William G. McAdoo, Charles A. Lindbergh, John W. Davis, former Vice President Charles G. Dawes, and Democratic National Chairman John J. Raskob peppered the Allegheny list. While the bank disclaimed any desires for favors in return, Pecora was able to produce an embarrassing note from Raskob, who assured the bank of his deep appreciation and sincerely hoped that "the future holds opportunities for me to reciprocate." Finding public officials from both parties on the list seriously damaged the bank's credibility. Few observers accepted it as a strictly business arrangement. Such conservative journals as the *New York Times* and *Business Week* editorially criticized the House of Morgan, while columnist Walter Lippmann denounced such practices as preferential lists as evidence "that no set of men, however honorable they may be and however good their traditions, can be trusted with so much power and the opportunity for personal gain which it carried with it."

Twenty years earlier, Brandeis had warned in *Other People's Money* that "the dominant element in our financial oligarchy is the investment banker." These bankers used their depositors' funds and their own profits from stock underwriting to move onto innumerable boards of directors, where they could heavily influence the course of American industry. In 1933, Pecora revealed that Morgan partners held 126 directorships in 89 different corporations, with total resources of nineteen billion dollars. Morgan's influence further spread through the loans his bank had made to select individuals, including many prominent bankers. "They are friends of ours, and we know that they are good, sound, straight fellows," Morgan insisted, denying any improprieties.

The banker objected most strenuously to Pecora's plans to make public J. P. Morgan & Company's articles of copartnership. These impressively engrossed parchments, hung from a metal bar with a new sheet for each partner, pinpointed Morgan as the exceedingly powerful lord of his own financial empire. Final decisions in all banking matters lay with Morgan. He approved all new partners and could fire any one of them at any time. Further, Morgan retained complete discretion over the distribution of half of the firm's annual profits. None of this information had been public knowledge. No bank examiner ever went through the bank's books. Morgan insisted that he would not have had the "slightest objection" to releasing the information, but that no one had ever asked, except for the Pujo Committee. "That investigation was the one held about twenty years ago?" Pecora asked. "That is the only public statement we have ever made about anything," Morgan responded.

On May 25, while Morgan was still on the stand, the Senate passed the Glass-Steagall banking reform bill. In the light of the Pecora inquiry, Congress had amended the bill to cut from two years to one the time in which all commercial banks, like National City, must divorce their investment affiliates, and private banks, like Morgan & Company, must abandon either their banking or investment functions. Passage of the bill also freed its sponsor, Senator Carter Glass of Virginia, to devote more time to the Wall Street hearings. Alternately ill and busy with his own bill, Glass had rarely attended the early committee meetings when Pecora had outlined the broad scope of his plans. Now, the senator insisted that the counsel should give preliminary briefings to the committee before each session. Beyond his concern for senatorial prerogatives, Glass felt personally involved in the Morgan inquiry. Two of Morgan's partners, Russell C. Leffingwell and S. Parker Gilbert, had served as Glass's assistants when he was secretary of the treasury in the Wilson Administration. Both now complained to him of the injustices in the committee's proceedings. At closed-door executive sessions Glass supported the Morgan contention that the committee should not make public such information as the preferential stock lists or the names of borrowers from the bank.

Glass's impatience finally burst into the public hearings during Pecora's examination of another Morgan-sponsored holding company, the United Corporation, and its preferential stock lists. Peevishly, the senator questioned the whole point of the hearing. Pecora responded by reading aloud the text of the resolution authorizing the hearings, but Glass remained unsatisfied. Pecora was wasting the committee's time, he argued, with highly technical questions of "no significance to a man of ordinary intelligence." Obviously irritated over Glass's heckling, Pecora described his plans to the committee, plans which had already been outlined during Glass's absence, and remarked that not a single committee member had requested further information. "I want to assure Senator Glass that the compensation of $255 a month which I am receiving for these services is no incentive to me to render these services or continue to render them," Pecora said heatedly. With these words, spectators in the chamber suddenly broke into loud and prolonged applause for the counsel, visibly startling many of the senators. "Oh yes," Glass grumbled as the cheering died down, "this is what it is all about. We are having a circus and the only thing lacking now are peanuts and colored lemonade."

Throughout these clashes, the committee's chairman, Duncan Fletcher, consistently came to Pecora's defense. A small, frail man of seventy-five, with a thin, quavering voice, Fletcher generally played a passive role in the hearings, rarely interrupting Pecora's questioning. When Senator Glass demanded a special executive session to discuss the counsel's techniques, Fletcher invited Pecora to attend and defend himself. "Our members have been drawn around a long table for nearly a week without one particle of knowledge beforehand about what counsel for the committee proposed to disclose," Glass complained. At the session on Thursday morning, June 1, Glass proposed that counsel should not introduce any testimony that he had not already explained in advance to the committee. Senators James Couzens and Fred Steiwer, both Republicans, and Democrat Edward Costigan, all spoke out against the proposal. Pecora, at Fletcher's request, added that the proposal would destroy the investigation's effectiveness by increasing chances of premature leaks to the press. "How dare you tell this committee what to do?" Glass interrupted indignantly. If the motion passed, Pecora continued, he would resign and tell the press the reasons why. "Now you're trying to intimidate us!" Glass stood up shouting. Fletcher and the majority of the committee, however, rallied to Pecora's support and solidly defeated the Glass proposal. On their way back to the hearings, Fletcher pointedly took hold of Pecora's arm as a physical gesture of support.

Passing through the crowd of reporters at the caucus room doorway, the senators sensed from the commotion that something unusual had happened in their absence. While the committee had met in executive session, an enterprising press agent had slipped into the hearing room and placed a circus midget in the lap of an unsuspecting J. P. Morgan. Thinking at first it was a child, Morgan put his arm protectively around her. "I've got a grandson bigger than you," he said. "But I'm older," replied the midget. "She's thirty-two," the press agent informed him, and Morgan slid the little woman off his lap while press photographers clamored around taking pictures. Thoroughly angered, Chairman Fletcher denounced the incident as a discourtesy and requested that newspapers refrain from printing any photos. But the next morning pictures of Morgan with the midget in his lap spread across the nation—ironically symbolizing the congressional humbling of the once Olympian bankers.

"Public opinion unquestionably is behind me," Pecora told the press after his confrontation with Glass, "and I will bring out all the facts regardless of whence they hit." Even Glass recognized the political liability in defending Morgan, and at the next week's session he pressed for a new resolution to give Pecora more power to delve into Morgan's taxes. The Internal Revenue Service, the committee felt, had treated such prominent bankers as Mitchell and Morgan far too gently. It had spent merely one day in examining tax returns from J. P. Morgan & Company and its investment house, Drexel & Company, for 1930; and a revenue agent had approved one statement with the notation: "Returned without examination for the reason that the return was prepared in the office of J. P. Morgan and Company and it has been our experience that any schedule made by that office is correct." J. P. Morgan, however, believed that Pecora had distorted his tax situation. He reminded the committee during his final day of testimony that his firm paid heavy taxes all during the 1920s until the stock market crash. "Income taxes are, after all, paid upon income and not upon deficits," he concluded. Not all of his partners could afford such indignation. Two Morgan associates, Thomas W. Lamont and his son, Thomas S. Lamont, paid back taxes and stiff delinquency fines as a result of Pecora's disclosures.

Additional power to examine and use income tax records assured an inescapably tight legal and financial web against any witness. The great success of Pecora's investigations came primarily from his skill at collecting, analyzing, and assimilating large quantities of data concerning his witnesses' activities. With the power of subpoena, his staff would descend upon a banker or broker and go through his records, file drawer after file drawer, page by page, selecting and photostating documents. Staff lawyers and accountants would assemble this material to reconstruct the motivations, discrepancies, delinquencies, and frauds involved. They drew a multitude of charts, tracing every event and statistic. After narrowing down the documentation, they outlined the subject's transactions in chronological narrative on letter-sized sheets, with citations in the margins to specific documents which could prove each assertion. The corresponding records filled two large trunks, which Pecora entrusted to his nephew, Louis Stephens, who made sure that the appropriate item was ready at each stage of the hearings. Armed FBI agents guarded these trunks day and night.

Such a mass of documentation, covering long and obscure financial dealings, presented a formidable challenge for any attorney to keep straight during his cross-examination. Here Pecora's photographic memory amazed even his own staff. Each night he would read rapidly through the thirty- or forty-page memorandum they had prepared for the next day, stopping to question only an occasional reference. After that he would rarely refer to the memorandum again. Yet he covered the material coherently and correctly during the next day's proceedings. "I looked with astonishment," wrote John T. Flynn," at this man who, through the intricate maze of banking syndicates, market deals, chicanery of all sorts, and in a field new to him, never forgot a name, never made an error in a figure, and never lost his temper."

Since Pecora already knew the answers he expected to elicit during testimony, and had the proof to challenge any witness who lied, he could proceed in a genial fashion, without badgering his witnesses. Politely, he would allow them to go off on their own stories until he felt they had registered a point, then he would return to his own line of questioning. He worked around the periphery of each problem. When a witness began to suspect his intentions and balked at answering, Pecora would start at another point on the periphery and work inwards from that direction, until finally his central objective became obvious to everyone. At the crucial moment in the testimony, Pecora's whole demeanor would change. Leaning forward in his chair he would rapidly recall all of the earlier admissions he had led the witness to make, pointing inexorably toward his guilt or complicity. Attuned to public relations, he also geared his questioning towards the daily press deadlines. As the hearings progressed he learned to make his most important points early at each session to ensure press attention and headlines in the afternoon papers. He saved some entirely new material for late in the day for the next morning's papers. Public dissemination of information always remained one of his fixed goals, as important as establishing corrective legislation.

Throughout the long hearings, Pecora depended heavily upon his staff and maintained a close working relationship with them. From Monday through Friday he shared a suite of rooms with them at the Mayflower Hotel, which the nearly bankrupt hotel provided at a reduced rate for them and other luminaries, in an attempt to attract more guests. At night, Pecora would return to the Mayflower, look over new material for the next day, and then relax with the staff, usually in long card-playing sessions. For the most part, the staff worked together smoothly. As the hearings wore on and pressures mounted, tensions did rise, but Pecora, an excellent raconteur, could lean back, light his cigar, and tell another long story to ease the situation. The staff of younger men called him "Chief," a moniker from his days as chief assistant D.A. He in turn called them "Boys." This paternalistic relationship brought him complete devotion from them, although he demanded the last word on all decisions and could summarily dismiss a subordinate whose loyalty he doubted.

The Congress of the New Deal's "first hundred days" recessed on June 16, 1933, but the Pecora hearings continued on into the summer. Oppressive heat and humidity, perennial afflictions of Washington summers, soon had an impact. By the end of the Morgan hearings, Fletcher had permitted gentlemen in the room to remove their jackets, J. P. Morgan dozed in his chair, and other witnesses appeared dazed and tired on the stand. Before adjourning, however, Pecora wanted to examine the second most prominent private banking house in the United States, Kuhn, Loeb & Company. Otto Kahn, senior partner in the firm, had already informed Pecora of his deep distress over the National City Bank revelations and his desire to cooperate fully with the committee to help end "improper practices." As a witness, the elderly banker, dapper and cosmopolitan, with a large handlebar mustache, condemned the "cutthroat competition of bankers in the 1920s," and he recounted tales of American bankers fighting each other for control over European and South American bonds. Kahn denounced the profit-and-loss provisions of tax laws which created artificial depressions each December when investors sold stocks to establish losses, and he called for government control of every organization that dealt with money. "I know a great deal must be changed," he admitted. "And I know the time is ripe to have it changed."

Out of deference to other members of the financial community, however, Kahn was less than candid, and reneged on his promise of complete honesty. Annoyed over Kahn's increasing hesitancy, Pecora pointed out that Kuhn, Loeb & Company had not been free from transgressions themselves. When he brought up the issue of ninety million dollars in loans that the company had arranged in Chile, Kahn winced. "You have touched on a sore spot," he admitted. "It is the only issue which my firm has made, the only foreign issue, which is in default." Kahn himself, Pecora revealed, had paid no income taxes for 1930, 1931, and 1932, although his firm reaped profits of more than twenty million dollars from pool operations between 1927 and 1931. For distributing the stocks of the Pennroad Corporation, a railroad holding company, Kuhn, Loeb & Company had earned a profit of $5,840,000, although investors in the stock had lost over $106,000,000 collectively when its price plunged in the crash. "We were all sinners," Kahn now repented. "If we indulge again in practices that are socially, economically and from the point of view of the country undesirable, I think the policeman ought to be ready to step in."

As Kahn stepped down, Pecora conceded to the heat and senatorial pressures to recess his investigation for the summer. During their vacation, he set his staff at examining the records of two other well-known banks: Dillon, Read & Company, a private bank influential in the stock markets; and the Chase National Bank, reputedly the largest commercial bank in the world.

Concentrating first on Dillon, Read, Pecora subpoenaed its officers to testify in early October. The bank actually specialized in selling securities and did a relatively small business in accepting deposits, but Dillon, Read & Company had shown much ingenuity in raising funds from other sources.

During the "Great Bull Market" of the 1920s, Dillon, Read had pioneered in developing the highly popular investment trust. Through this device they offered average investors an opportunity to buy shares of a corporation which did nothing but invest in stocks itself. Presumably, with its experienced management and skilled analysts, the investment trust would purchase only the most sound and productive stocks available. At the height of the speculative heyday of 1929, an average of one new investment trust appeared every day. Dillon, Read exhibited particular skill in organizing such trusts and managed to maintain control over them through the use of "nonvoting" stocks. Only a small portion of the investment trust's stocks which Dillon, Read retained carried voting privileges. The far greater number of stocks earned dividends, but their holders had no say in the trust's management.

In 1924 they formed the Foreign Securities Corporation, capitalized at $30,000,000, of which Dillon, Read purchased $5,000,000 in voting stocks, enough to totally control the organization. Later that same year, they formed the even larger United States and International Securities Corporation, capitalized at $60,000,000, of which Dillon, Read purchased $10,000,000 worth of controlling voting stock. This latter ten million, however, came not from Dillon, Read, but from the earnings of the Foreign Securities Corporation. The bank had thus used its voting privileges in one investment trust to divert its surplus funds into another, rather than distribute the money as dividends to the common stock holders. Furiously, Senator James Couzens called it "rotten ethics to take $10,000,000 out of an investment trust you own, or which you control . . . and put it into another investment to further augment your own profits. I think that is reprehensible." Furthermore, Pecora noted that eleven members of Dillon, Read & Company had made almost seven million dollars in profits on the common stock of these trusts, after an initial investment of only $24,110.

Greed and excessive profits also characterized the activities of the giant Chase National Bank, as Pecora unraveled that story. Earlier that year Chase had deflected public attention by adopting his own sweeping reforms. President Winthrop Aldrich endorsed the National City Bank plan to divorce banking and investment facilities, and Chase cut loose its own Chase Securities Corporation. At the same time, Aldrich called for stronger federal laws to regulate commercial and private banking. But Pecora was less interested in Aldrich than he was in the bank's recently retired chairman, Albert H. Wiggin, known as "the most popular banker in Wall Street." Wiggin had stepped down from the bank in December 1932 after twenty-eight years of service, shortly after Chase had merged with the Rockefeller-dominated Equitable Trust Company.

Still held in high esteem on Wall Street, Wiggin was a member of fifty-nine boards of directors and served on the executive committee of the Federal Reserve Bank of New York. In fact, stockholders of Chase National Bank had little idea of the complete extent of Wiggin's popularity until the investigations disclosed how the bank's executive board had secretly granted Wiggin a yearly retirement salary of $100,000 for life. During the last four years of his active service, the banker had also received $1,500,000 in salaries and bonuses from the bank and securities company. Wiggin protested that his associates from the bank had determined these generous emoluments. "And I helped to fix theirs," he added. "You helped to fix theirs and they helped to fix yours?" Pecora asked incredulously. "Yes," said Wiggin, "we all sat together." As a result of the hearings, an intensely negative reaction from Chase stockholders forced Wiggin to relinquish his $100,000 annual salary.

Unlike many of his predecessors on the stand, Wiggin had dutifully paid his income taxes throughout the panic and Depression. Indeed, Pecora found it interesting that Wiggin and his family paid $4,625,000 in taxes from 1928 to 1932, surprisingly excessive even considering Chase's bonus system. This evidence led Pecora into an examination of three Wiggin family corporations, the Shermar, Murlyn, and Clingston, named for Wiggin's daughters and their husbands, and three other family corporations in Canada. He discovered, as he had anticipated, that the banker had used these corporations for speculative purposes, engaging in a number of pool operations. But even Pecora had not suspected the chairman of the Chase National Bank of speculating in his own bank's stocks. From 1927 until 1931 the Chase Securities Corporation, with Wiggin's full knowledge, had manipulated Chase stocks by purchasing and selling over $860,000,000 in shares to exercise a "steadying effect" on its market value. Despite these efforts, the stock had fallen from a high of 575 in 1927 to 17¾ in 1933. During these same years the Wiggin corporations realized a net profit of $10,425,000, largely by selling short the bank's stocks.

Wiggin admitted his transgressions in a quiet voice, in short, simple answers, without the lengthy attempts at explanations that had so ensnarled other bankers on the stand. He made no attempt to accept personal blame for any actions, but attributed the banking abuses of the 1920s to simply "the time." During one discussion of pool operations, Pecora inquired: "Is that not a scheme for 'churning the market' and producing an activity that would stimulate prices?" "I think the market was a 'God-given' market," Wiggin replied. "Are you sure of the source?" one committee member interrupted.

In the audience, Chase President Winthrop Aldrich sat mortified over Wiggin's confessions. When Wiggin concluded his testimony, Aldrich stepped forward and asked permission to address the committee. "As long as I have anything to do with the management, the market in Chase stocks shall not be affected by the operation of trading accounts by affiliates of the bank," he swore. Later Aldrich approached Pecora privately. He had learned more about the operations of the Chase Bank during Pecora's interrogation, he admitted, than during his four years as the bank's president. The record of Wiggin's transactions, the *New York Times* bemoaned, "brought astonishment and pain to all his friends and former admirers. But this personal consequence is as nothing compared to the great shock to public confidence in our banking system."

On Wall Street, feelings ran contrary to these fears. Bankers and brokers at the securities exchanges questioned Pecora's purposes and his tactics. Although they had reached a consensus that some form of federal regulation would undoubtedly follow the investigation, many asked how the exposure of individual bankers' indiscretions could produce legislation for the stock markets. Some members of the Banking Committee agreed and anxiously counseled that the hearings return to a focus on stock manipulation. Pecora, too, was ready to shift emphasis. He had used the banking probe to examine banks' roles in stock distribution, syndicates, and the granting of loans for buying stocks on margin. Having boldly publicized the machinations of Mitchell, Morgan, and Wiggin, he turned his attention to the manipulative practices of brokers and floor traders at the mammoth New York Stock Exchange.

In this pursuit, Pecora had plenty of company. The Roosevelt Administration considered stock exchange reform among its first priorities. Because of his experiences with the Pujo Committee, the assignment for drafting an exchange reform bill fell to seventy-five-year-old Samuel Untermyer. Unfortunately, Untermyer devoted himself less to the bill than to his dream of returning to the spotlight as chief counsel for the Banking Committee. Months earlier he had rejected Senator Norbeck's pleas to accept the post under the then valid assumption that the original resolution granted insufficient powers for a complete investigation. Since then, Pecora had won new powers and considerable glory, and Untermyer realized his error. As a result of his preoccupation, he submitted a bill rehashing his earlier proposals that the Post Office Department regulate stock exchanges through control of their use of the mails. Roosevelt's advisors scoffed at this idea; it was twenty years out of date.

To ease Untermyer's disappointment, Roosevelt divided the responsibilities of the job in half. He granted Untermyer another year to devise a new exchange regulation formula, and he assigned former Federal Trade Commissioner Huston Thompson to prepare legislation for the more immediate problem of preventing fraudulent stock sales. The Senate Banking Committee, busy with the Glass bill and the Morgan inquiry, readily accepted Thompson's draft for securities regulation. But the House Interstate and Foreign Commerce Committee, under Chairman Sam Rayburn, found his version hopelessly inadequate and secured a more sophisticated bill from three young proteges of Felix Frankfurter: Thomas Corcoran, Benjamin Cohen, and James Landis. At the joint Senate-House conference committee, the wily Rayburn outmaneuvered Senator Fletcher to win adoption of the House bill. Since the Securities Act of 1933 contained no provisions for general exchange regulation, Pecora was determined to impress the findings of his investigation more fully upon the eventual exchange bill.

During the summer recess, Pecora informed Chairman Fletcher of his planned study of the New York Stock Exchange to see "the way the wheels turn around." Unexpectedly, the market mechanism gave him a spectacular show in mid-July when the "New Deal Market," a brief boom that had followed the creation of the NRA, suddenly burst. In one week thirty million shares changed hands in a downward spiral sickeningly reminiscent of 1929. Dragging the market down were the "wet" stocks of breweries and other post-Prohibition businesses that had soared in anticipation of final ratification of the Twenty-First Amendment. The pattern of short selling accompanying the decline convinced Pecora that manipulative pools were at work. Staff investigator John T. Flynn charged in his regular *New Republic* column that many of the stocks had obviously been "rigged." Commercial solvents stood at 16½ in May 1933, but during nineteen days in July almost all of its two and a half million shares were traded, running the price up to 57¼. Just as abruptly, the pool behind it unloaded the stock, which then slid to 36. Similarly, a pool had pushed National Distiller's Products up from 9 in May to 124¾ in July. During the week of July 17 the stock plunged 68 points.

Keenly interested in these developments, Pecora called upon President Richard Whitney of the New York Stock Exchange. Despite Whitney's assurances that the exchange would carefully investigate all pool operations, Pecora doubted the effectiveness or sincerity of exchange self-regulation. He intended to pursue public hearings on exchange practices, but found he faced an entirely different situation than with the banks. Rather than a single organization with a single set of books, the exchange actually performed as a trading post for thousands of brokers dealing with millions of corporate stocks. Finding it impossible to subpoena all these records, Pecora chose the method of a questionnaire centered on pool activities for the exchange and all of its members.

On September 30, 1933, Pecora sent two of his staff members, young David Schenker and the more experienced John T. Flynn, to present Whitney with the questionnaires. Whitney immediately recognized Flynn, whom he loathed for his caustic books and anti-Wall Street columns. Flushed with anger, the stock exchange president rushed from the room to compose himself before he could begin any conversation with them. When he returned, the two men requested that the exchange distribute their questionnaires. "You gentlemen are making a great mistake," Whitney said of their investigation. "The Exchange is a perfect institution." Two weeks later, he wrote to Pecora rejecting the request to send out the questionnaires. The cost of time and accountants to prepare answers would run into the millions of dollars, Whitney complained, and he did not feel he had the authority to make exchange members comply.

Pecora responded by subpoenaing records from the most active floor traders on the exchange. With this information, and the advice of the commission houses' brokers who generally opposed Whitney's domination of the exchange, Pecora fashioned a new questionnaire which he sent directly to the 1,375 exchange members, and a special questionnaire for the exchange itself. It then took months for the recipients to complete and return these questionnaires, and for Pecora's staff to wade through the accumulated data.

In the interim, the Banking Committee's hearings continued at a hectic pace and with a wide variety of witnesses. John J. Raskob appeared again to explain a large speculative loan that he and former Governor Alfred E. Smith had received from the Chase National Bank. Reconstruction Finance Corporation chief Jesse H. Jones testified on loans his agency had made to Texas banks with which he was associated. Harry Sinclair of Teapot Dome fame came under subpoena to discuss syndicate dealings in Sinclair Oil stock. The seeming unwieldiness of the hearings caused some dissension. "Pecora was like a police chief who rounds up all the suspicious characters in town to solve a jewel robbery," presidential-advisor Raymond Moley sniffed. But Pecora also bore much pressure not to miss any opportunities to expose financial ills. Banking Committee members each had areas of special concern they urged upon him. Michigan Senator James Couzens directed him towards the Detroit bank crisis. Ohio Senator Robert Bulkley was interested in the Cleveland bank situation. New Jersey Senator Hamilton Kean asked for an investigation of short selling in airline stocks. Eventually the long length and diversification of the hearings began to weigh upon their effectiveness. The three-ring-atmosphere of New Deal Washington came to dwarf Pecora's side show. His additional evidence disappeared into the financial pages, and only occasionally could he grab new headlines. Senator Fletcher finally concluded that the hearings had lasted long enough. He asked for completion by January 1, 1934, in time for the committee to draft legislative recommendations.

Competition from other quarters also hastened the committee's concern for a stock exchange bill. Although Untermyer had made little progress with his bill, a special committee under the chairmanship of Assistant Secretary of Commerce John Dickinson was also examining stock exchange regulation. Roosevelt had appointed the Dickinson Committee in response to both the July market crash and the growing hostility on Wall Street to the strict Securities Act. Characteristically, the President had filled the committee with a mixture of liberal reformers and arch-conservatives. As a result, they had produced a blandly moderate report. Racing against the Dickinson Committee, one of Pecora's staff investigators, Max Lowenthal, approached Securities Act drafters Corcoran, Cohen, and Landis and asked them to assist in preparing an exchange bill for the Banking Committee. Lowenthal, like the three young men, was a representative of Felix Frankfurter's large contingency of former law students working in the New Deal, and he knew he could count on their help. Landis, then an FTC commissioner, sent two young aides, I.N.P. Stokes and Telford Taylor, to draft the initial versions of the bill. Cohen and Corcoran revised their draft, working nights, weekends, and vacations, while holding other government positions. By January when the Dickinson report went to the White House and when Senator Fletcher was ready to ask Pecora for a bill, they had almost finished.

Fletcher's request caught Pecora in the middle of his investigation into the complicated Detroit banking collapse. Unwilling to break off the hearings, he accepted the Cohen and Corcoran draft and assigned several of his aides, including Schenker, Saperstein, Meehan, Lowenthal, and Flynn to help shape the bill into final form. After so many months of delving into Wall Street malpractice, these staff members found the Cohen-Corcoran draft far too lenient to suit their tastes. Rather than grant broad discretionary powers to any regulatory agency, they wanted the bill to specifically prohibit all forms of stock manipulation, such as short selling, pools, and wash sales. Furthermore, they insisted that the bill forbid brokers from buying and selling for their own accounts at the same time they transacted business for their clients. To prevent conflict of interest, they wanted brokers to choose either one function or the other, but not to practice both. John Flynn, who passionately distrusted all bankers and brokers, warned that any vague sections in the bill would permit shrewd Wall Street lawyers to circumvent its basic intent. Flynn's strong arguments accounted for much of the stringency in the final draft. Both Cohen and Corcoran recognized they were working for Pecora and must adhere to the wishes of his staff. In a final forty-eight hour session of continuous work, the combined group produced a bill which Pecora could wholeheartedly endorse.

As the legislative process took up the exchange bill, Pecora's role diminished. He concluded his investigations into the Detroit and Cleveland banking structures as the Senate Banking Committee prepared to open hearings on the bill. The whole focus of committee procedures shifted, with the center of attention moving from the counsel as prosecutor questioning unsuspecting witnesses to the witnesses as advocates, arriving with prepared speeches for or against the bill. Where the senators had previously permitted Pecora to conduct the questioning relatively unhindered, they now took the lead in quizzing the witnesses themselves. When Thomas Corcoran appeared to defend the exchange bill, the committee even permitted Roland Redmond, counsel for the New York Stock Exchange, to cross-examine him. Pecora fell increasingly into the background.

The New York Stock Exchange and its allies conducted a bitter lobbying and publicity campaign against the bill, convincing many congressmen of the need for compromises in the stern first draft. Whitney testified that the bill, by tampering with margin trading, might disrupt the nation's credit system, that its requirements for regular financial reports would be "absolutely prohibitive," and that it might drive stocks and investors to foreign exchanges. Instead, he proposed a program of exchange self-regulation through participation on a federal regulatory panel, similar to the Dickinson Committee recommendations. Conservative opposition in Congress, small but intense, followed this line. Republican representatives also attacked Cohen and Corcoran personally as the boys from "the little red house in Georgetown" who had prepared the bill to "Russianize everything worthwhile."

By the time the conference committee met to settle differences between House and Senate versions of the exchange bill, the original draft had undergone serious revision. The congressmen had reduced margin requirements and made them more flexible, authorized a new Securities and Exchange Commission, and delegated to it powers to oversee the activities of the nation's stock exchanges. Congress also avoided prohibiting several controversial practices and, instead, authorized the SEC to carry out further studies on segregation of broker-dealer functions, regulation of the vast "over-the-counter" market of unlisted securities, and revising exchange rules for more self-regulation. After it passed overwhelmingly in both houses, Cohen and Corcoran found genuine pleasure with the compromise bill. Both suspected that they would never have gained so much if the original draft had not been so demanding. But many of the Pecora staffers were bitterly disappointed with the enacted law. They especially blamed Treasury Department and Federal Reserve Board conservatives for weakening the measure and scorned the President for not endorsing their draft more vigorously. "One word from Franklin D. Roosevelt, and the dramatic first bill would have been passed with a whoop," Flynn concluded in disgust.

Passage of the Securities and Exchange Act of 1934 brought the Pecora investigations to a close, an event not entirely satisfying to the chief counsel. He still had numerous topics left which he had hoped to cover. Max Lowenthal and others begged him to reconsider demobilizing his staff and reminded him of the work remaining. Pecora himself had hoped to conduct an extensive survey into the abuses of protective committees which reorganized bankrupt corporations. But time had run out. Many of these unfinished examinations became the responsibility of the new SEC, including the protective committee study which two young Yale faculty members, William O. Douglas and Abe Fortas, ably conducted for the agency.

In his final report, drawn from the twenty-two volumes of committee transcripts and still unused evidence, Pecora strongly indicated the need for further study and additional legislation. The Glass-Steagall Banking Act, for instance, had made a first step in detaching investment houses from the powerful banks, but too often these divisions were more real on paper than in practice. J. P. Morgan & Company gave up its securities business to the newly created firm of Morgan, Stanley & Company, and Morgan placed his son Henry in charge of this "independent" house. Brown Brothers, Harriman & Company continued as a commercial bank, while it created Brown, Harriman & Company to assume its investment business; W. Averell Harriman and his family remained as major stockholders in both. The income tax laws also needed revision. Attorney General Homer Cummings was already conducting further investigations into tax evasions on the part of bankers and brokers, even delving into the tax returns of former Treasury Secretary Andrew Mellon. Pecora was especially pleased to note that the Internal Revenue Service had recovered several million dollars in back taxes as a result of the hearings, far more than the $225,000 which the investigation had cost the government.

Whatever Pecora's admiration for the frugality of the hearings, their low budget had placed serious financial burdens upon him. He had dropped his own private law practice and felt uneasy about resuming it. Fundamentally, he could not envision serving as counsel for the banking and brokerage houses he had so recently exposed, and yet he knew the pressures he would feel to take their cases. Nor had the meager $255-a-month salary he collected during the hearings helped his financial independence. When the hearings came to a close, the Banking Committee met in executive session with Pecora to discuss that very question. His persistent nemesis, Carter Glass, introduced a resolution to compensate Pecora for the true worth of his time and energy. Glass proposed that the Senate pass a special appropriation of not less than $125,000 for his services, "a drop in the bucket" compared with the retainers of the Wall Street lawyers appearing in adversary during the hearings. The full committee unanimously approved Glass's resolution, but Pecora asked them not to pass it. He had acted strictly out of public service, he explained. Furthermore, having received an outpouring of mail from across the country commending him for working on a small salary, he could not accept such a large reward now.

His refusal was altruistic, but Pecora also had political ambitions. In October 1933, for example, he had acquiesced to the urgings of James Farley and President Roosevelt to accept the reform Democratic nomination for New York district attorney, although he could campaign only on weekends so as not to interrupt his hearings. In the LaGuardia fusion sweep in that municipal election, Pecora lost badly. Many observers, however, felt that the President owed him a favor. Pecora dropped a hint to that effect at the White House ceremony when Roosevelt signed the Securities and Exchange Act. "Ferd, now that I have signed this bill and it has become law, what kind of a law will it be?" the President asked as he handed him one of the pens. "It will be a good bill or a bad bill, Mr. President," Pecora replied, "depending upon the men who administer it." Afterwards, Pecora let it become widely known in Washington that he expected the chairmanship of the new SEC.

It came as a definite shock to Pecora, therefore, when Roosevelt nominated him for a one-year post on the commission and gave the five-year post, with his implicit approval for chairman, to financier Joseph P. Kennedy. Only a few months earlier, Pecora had uncovered Kennedy's name as a participant in a pool of Libby-Owens-Ford Glass Company stocks during the July crash. Neither he nor his staff could believe that such a stock market operator could lead the commission they had helped create. "I did not in my wildest dreams imagine he would appoint a speculator as chairman of that body," John T. Flynn exclaimed. "I say it isn't true. It is impossible. It could not happen." Pecora thought first of refusing the appointment, but then he appeared for the swearing-in ceremony and delayed it for two hours while he privately negotiated with Kennedy over commission policies and personnel. Several of his assistants from the hearings, including Saperstein, Schenker, and Stephens, eventually followed him to the SEC. But after so long in the spotlight as the leader of the hearings, Pecora could not adjust to the bureaucratic routines of the new regulatory commissions. Within six months he resigned the post to take a seat on the New York Supreme Court, where he remained for the rest of his career, with the exception of an unsuccessful campaign for mayor of New York in 1950.

Nor were the years of aftermath totally rewarding for other participants in the Pecora hearings. Albert Wiggin returned to his retirement still wealthy, but with his reputation shattered. J. P. Morgan left the Pecora hearings only to face more congressional scrutiny before the Nye Committee. Increasingly, Morgan withdrew from his banking firm and spent his last ten years as far away from press photographers as he could. In 1940 the Morgan bank finally incorporated, and in 1942 it joined the Federal Reserve System, ending its aloof and private status. Richard Whitney, the aristocratic president of the New York Stock Exchange, lost his position with the help of new SEC-sponsored exchange rules. In 1938 he confessed to insolvency and admitted to embezzling funds entrusted to his investment company. As his property went on the auction block to pay his debts, Whitney left for imprisonment at Sing Sing. Of all the discredited witnesses, Charles E. Mitchell emerged the most honorably in later years. In 1938 the Supreme Court ruled he owed the government $1,100,000 in taxes and penalties. Refusing to declare bankruptcy because it was not the "square" thing to do, Mitchell worked for years to repay his taxes and debts.

The Pecora investigations and the creation of the Securities and Exchange Commission profoundly affected Wall Street. They transformed the New York Stock Exchange from an almost private club into a semi-public institution, and they made the federal government responsible for overseeing nationally vital banking and brokerage activities. The flagrant financial abuses that characterized the 1920s became less pronounced, although they did not disappear. Five years later, while writing his memoirs of the hearings, *Wall Street Under Oath,* Pecora predicted possible regression. "These laws are no panacea; nor are they self-executing," he warned. "More than ever we must maintain our vigilance. If we do not, Wall Street may yet prove to be not unlike that land, of which it has been said that no country is easier to overrun or harder to subdue."

BIBLIOGRAPHY

The twenty-odd volumes of Senate Banking Committee transcripts and reports provide the core of material on the Pecora investigations. Important supplementary information is also available in such contemporary sources as the *New York Times, New York Herald Tribune, New York American, Wall Street Journal, Washington Post, Literary Digest, Time, Business Week, The Nation,* and *The New Republic,* and in a series on "The Battle of the Market Place," by Joseph Alsop and Robert Kintner in *The Saturday Evening Post,* CCX (June 11, 1938 and June 25, 1938). I benefited from personal interviews with Benjamin V. Cohen, Thomas G. Corcoran, Telford Taylor, Louis Stephens, and Louis Pecora, as well as the oral histories of Ferdinand Pecora and James M. Landis at Columbia University. Pecora himself interpreted the hearings in *Wall Street Under Oath, The Story of Our Modern Money Changers* (New York, 1939, 1968). Other helpful sources include: Frederick Lewis Allen, *The Lords of Creation* (New York, 1935); Harry Barnard, *Independent Man: The Life of Senator James Couzens* (New York, 1958); Ralph F. DeBedts, *The New Deal's S.E.C., The Formative Years* (New York, 1964); John Kenneth Galbraith, *The Great Crash* (Boston, 1955); William H. Harbaugh, *Lawyer's Lawyer, The Life of John W. Davis* (New York, 1973); Matthew Josephson, *The Money Lords, The Great Finance Capitalists, 1925-1950* (New York, 1972); Raymond Moley, *After Seven Years, A Political Analysis of the New Deal* (New York, 1939); Michael E. Parrish, *Securities Regulation and the New Deal* (New Haven, 1970); and Arthur M. Schlesinger, jr., *The Coming of the New Deal* (Boston, 1959).

PERTINENT DOCUMENTS

Carter Glass–Ferdinand Pecora Exchange, May 26, 1933

Testimony of Otto H. Kahn, Kuhn, Loeb & Co., June 30, 1933

Article by Robert Winsmore, "Wall Street's Reply to the Senate Investigation," July 22, 1933

Testimony of Albert H. Wiggin, November 1, 1933

Franklin D. Roosevelt to Duncan U. Fletcher, March 26, 1934

Speech by Senator Duncan Fletcher Introducing the Stock Exchange Bill, May 7, 1934

Max Lowenthal to Ferdinand Pecora, May 12, 1934

Article by John T. Flynn, "The Marines Land in Wall Street," July 1934

The Nye Munitions Committee
1934

New York Public Library Picture Collection

top: *Irenee du Pont (with pipe), Pierre S. du Pont and Lammot du Pont before the Nye Committee.* bottom: *The Nye Committee (l. to r.)—Senators Vandenberg, Barbour, Nye; Alger Hiss, legal assistant; Senator Clark; Stephen Raushenbush, chief investigator, Senator Pope.*

The Nye Munitions Committee 1934

by John Edward Wiltz

If September 4, 1934, the Tuesday after Labor Day, seemed a typical late summer day in Washington—hot and humid—many individuals in the nation's capital were nevertheless astir. Representatives of the people, in the present instance a special committee of United States senators, after a fashion which had become (and would remain) a veritable ritual of American democracy, were about to begin the arduous business of exposing the awful merchants of death—greedy and conscienceless men, according to a popular view, who shamelessly took profit from the blood and misery of war. It mattered little that there was no air-conditioning in the white marble caucus room of the Senate Office Building, the scene of Teapot Dome hearings of recent memory, future site of such happenings as the Pearl Harbor, Army-McCarthy, and Watergate inquiries; and by mid-morning several hundred people had crowded through its doors. Some were lawyers, conservatively dressed, fidgeting with brief cases. About fifty were reporters, many in shirtsleeves, obviously enjoying the discomfort of certain of the distinguished principals in the spectacle about to unfold. Others were clerks, secretaries, security guards, photographers, cameramen, electricians. Still others were spectators, some of them tourists who rattled chairs and pointed out notable senators and titans of industry while preparing to witness a moment not apt to be lost in history.

The centers of activity in the caucus room that morning were several dark wooden tables—the altars about which the ritual of senatorial inquiry would be played out. The tables were littered with papers, pencils, cigarette packages, ash trays, flash bulb cartons, and four microphones stamped with the letters NBC. Taking a seat at the middle of the main table as 10:00 approached was the presiding official of the ritual, Senator Gerald Prentice Nye, chairman of the Special Senate Committee Investigating the Munitions Industry. Forty-two years old, Nye was a "progressive" Republican from North Dakota. Flanking the chairman were five older colleagues: W. Warren Barbour of New Jersey—a "regular" Republican, Walter F. George of Georgia, Bennett Champ Clark of Missouri, Homer T. Bone of Washington, and James P. Pope of Idaho—all Democrats of varying political colorations. Another Republican member of the committee, Arthur H. Vandenberg of Michigan, was absent. Facing the senators from a distance of barely fifteen feet, at the end of a short table which butted the middle of the main table, were officials of the Electric Boat Company, America's premier builder of submarines. Between the senators and industrialists, on opposite sides of the short table, were a committee investigator and thirty-eight-year-old Stephen Raushenbush, the investigative chief of the committee, who carried the unpretentious title of Secretary. (Senator Nye and his colleagues had no intention of letting Raushenbush, son of the well-known social gospeler Walter Raushenbusch, take the limelight as had Ferdinand Pecora in the investigation of financial malfeasance completed only a few weeks before.)

At 10:00 A.M. the chairman leaned forward and in a bell-like voice announced: "The Committee will come to order." The hum of electric fans became audible, movie cameras whirred. From Nye came no harangue, only a brief statement outlining procedures for the hearings. Still, the atmosphere was heavy with tension as senatorial inquisitors and the chieftains of Electric Boat peered at one another. For in the view of the senators and industrialists, not to mention uncounted millions of people across the world, the present affair, like many senatorial inquiries, seemed more than an investigation. It seemed a trial: *Peace-loving and Moral People* v. *Manufacturers and Salesmen of Implements of War.*

I

To borrow from Victor Hugo, the Senate's investigation of the munitions industry in the mid-1930s was an idea that had originated, for many Americans, in a time of peace, but had concluded in those years that businessmen of Europe and America were profiting from war. The logic seemed compelling. War or the threat of war offered a market for men who made and sold implements of death and destruction, hence it was in their interest to stir up tension and hostility among nations, and if war resulted, so much the better. Should the conclusion be valid, the time had come for Americans to do what they could about the munitions trade, perhaps by nationalizing their own armament industry. The obvious instrument for testing its validity and determining what if any action Congress should take was an inquiry by a committee of the United States Senate.

The idea that makers and salesmen of munitions were a cause of war had existed for many years. At The Hague, less than a hundred miles from the Western front, the First Congress of the Women's International League for Peace and Freedom in 1915 had found "in the private profits accruing from the great arms factories a powerful hindrance to the abolition of war." Delegates to the Paris Peace Conference of 1919 revealed a similar uneasiness about the munitions trade, and Article 8 of the Covenant of the League of Nations stated: "The Members of the League agree that the manufacture by private enterprise of munitions and implements of war is open to grave objections. The Council shall advise how the evil effects attendant upon such manufacture can be prevented, due regard being had to the necessities of those Members of the League which are not able to manufacture the munitions and implements of war necessary for their safety." Two years later a subcommittee of the League reported that munitions firms had fabricated war scares and bribed officials, organized international munitions combines, and exaggerated reports of military and naval programs. At the behest of the League an international conference in 1925 fashioned the Geneva Arms Traffic Convention, an innocuous document providing that each signatory government would regulate the munitions trade within its borders by a system of licenses.

The response in the United States? Americans had taken part in peace congresses which scored the munitions trade, helped write Article 8 of the League Covenant, and signed the Geneva Arms Traffic Convention. During the congressional debate over America's entry in the World War in 1917, Senator George W. Norris of Nebraska had charged that a vast propaganda effort was pressing the country to war to guarantee "the enormous profits of munition manufacturers, stockbrokers, and bond dealers." Appeals for regulations of the munitions trade, however, thus far created hardly a ripple in the United States. Even the piquant affair of William Baldwin Shearer in the latter 1920s aroused few Americans to the point of insisting on control of the builders and purveyors of armaments.

Brash and intolerant, Shearer in August 1929 filed suit against the three leading American shipbuilders, charging that they owed him more than $250,000 for advancing their interests over the past three years. Whereupon observers of the Geneva Naval Conference of 1927 recalled that Shearer, claiming to be a newsman, had attended the Conference, done what he could to stir discord, and received credit (or blame) in some quarters when delegates failed to agree on a naval disarmament treaty. For a few days Shearer commanded headlines, President Hoover expressed disbelief that shipbuilders might have tried to defeat the plans of the government, and a three-man subcommittee of the Senate undertook an investigation. Nine months later the chairman of the subcommittee, Samuel M. Shortridge of California, declared the affair closed. He reported that he and his colleagues had found no evidence that shipbuilders had dispatched Shearer to Geneva in 1927 to sabotage the naval conference. As for Shearer, Shortridge conceded that at Geneva he "may have been extravagant and assertive, but so far as I see it there is no reason for criticizing him."

Meanwhile another topic had caught the attention of many Americans: war profits. When talk turned to war profits in the 1920s and 1930s those discussing them were weighing a more pervasive, if less titillating, subject than the munitions trade, for in addition to the builder and seller of armaments, war profits touched all citizens—the manufacturer of nonmilitary commodities and Wall Street financier, farmer and worker—who stood to realize handsome returns, should the United States tumble into a new war, as in 1917–1918. People felt concern about war profits for two reasons. Applying logic similar to that used in sorting out the motives of munitions makers, Americans who were in rhythm with the assorted peace organizations which flourished at the time viewed potential war profits as a threat to peace. Not so lacking in conscience as dealers in munitions, general citizens who stood to profit in the event of American belligerency were not apt to wreck disarmament conferences or hatch conspiracies to move countries to war, so the argument went; but if it seemed that the United States was edging *toward* war they might be less than steadfast in the quest for peace and, on the contrary, might throw their influence toward the balance for hostilities.

Other Americans, particularly members of veterans' groups, thought it scandalous for citizens on the home front during wartime, as in 1917–1918, to realize bonanza returns while the men enduring the dangers and miseries of combat were drawing a dollar or two a day. So peace organizations and veterans' groups, which seldom agreed on anything, urged legislation to "equalize the burdens" should the United States again become a belligerent. The former thought such legislation would constitute a deterrent to war; the latter expected that the outcome would be justice for the fighting man.

Responding to appeals of pacifists and veterans, Congress in 1930 established the War Policies Commission comprising four members of President Hoover's cabinet, four senators, and four representatives. A few months later, in 1931, the commission in sixteen days of hearings took the testimony of a range of individuals who had thoughts about war profits. Few witnesses agreed with Richard Bartholdt, a former congressman from Missouri, that "war profits constitute a greater menace to peace than any other factor" and that "with the profits taken out of war, those who heretofore hugged war as their benefactor and friend, probably would not recognize it if they met it in the street." Most seemed to concur with Bernard M. Baruch who found it unthinkable "that any human could be persuaded by the prospect of personal gain, however magnificent, to invoke the horrors of modern war" and with General Douglas A. MacArthur, Army Chief of Staff, who believed that efficiency in war was desirable, effectiveness mandatory. (And effectiveness in his estimate required "normal" profits.) In its report, which Congress ignored, the commission recommended legislation for fixing prices and taxing "excessive" corporate profits in time of war.

The findings of the War Policies Commission faded quickly from the public consciousness. One need not search for an explanation for this. The new reality of life for Americans as they moved into the 1930s—the great overwhelming and bewildering problem commanding their attention—was the economic calamity known to history as the Great Depression. Still, as they sought a way out of their economic miseries, Americans of the early 1930s, if labeled "isolationist" by latter-day historians, were not oblivious to the undulations of politics and diplomacy across the world, and the threat of a new general war was never far from their thoughts. The threat seemed real enough, for it was manifest in those troubled years that the peace settlement worked out at Paris at the end of the "Great War" (as people continued to refer to the holocaust of 1914–1918) was coming apart. Seizing on an incident of their own manufacture, the Japanese in 1931–1933 swarmed over Manchuria and brought that sprawling territory, nominally a province of China, under the Rising Sun. Nobody could be sure where Japanese aggression might end.

The dictator, Benito Mussolini, meanwhile was haranguing throngs of Italians with talk about reviving the imperial grandeur of ancient Rome. And there was Adolf Hitler, an unimposing little man (in the American view, at any rate) who took power in Berlin in 1933 amid promises that he would restore the military might of Germany and right the wrongs which he claimed the victors in the Great War had inflicted on the Germans at Paris in 1919.

How should America respond in the event that the threat of general war became a reality? Anybody who has taken a freshman history course knows how Americans of the time answered that question. Disillusioned that their crusade of 1917–1918 had failed to accomplish its objective of making the world safe for democracy, touched by the assortment of books, plays, and movies depicting the horror of modern war which had appeared over the previous decade, moved by the pacifist contention that there was no such thing as a "just war," they began to insist that the United States should stay clear of any new hostilities. Let the peoples of Europe, Asia, and elsewhere strangle and mangle each other if they wished, but please excuse Americans from such insane, immoral, and fruitless enterprises.

As goings-on in Europe and Asia—and also in Latin America where Paraguayans and Bolivians were butchering one another for a trackless expanse of jungle called the Gran Chaco—strengthened the commitment of Americans to peace, such organizations as the National Council for Prevention of War; Women's International League for Peace and Freedom; and Stop Organized Slaughter (SOS, for short) stepped up their activities. For a variety of reasons they gave a fair part of their considerable energies to assailing manufacturers and salesmen of munitions. Like the slave traders of a century before, men who dealt in armaments offered unique opportunities for sensational disclosures. Whether these disclosures rested on evidence acceptable to lawyers or scholars was of no consequence. Consider the munitions merchant, slithering about the steaming Chaco peddling instruments of death to Paraguayans and Bolivians alike, and if the bloodletting and its profits seemed about to wane, spreading rumors in La Paz and then Asunción of new offensives by the other side. Or consider the dark-suited manufacturer of high explosives arriving at his skyscraper office building in a chauffeured limousine, secluding himself behind mahogany doors in a plush board room, and plotting destruction of a disarmament conference or arranging the secret sale of gunpowder to the enemy of his own government. Then many activists in the peace movement were political radicals, *i.e.*, socialists of one sort or another, and attacks on what they often referred to as "the private traffic in arms," certain to stir popular sentiment for nationalization of the munitions industry, fell in with larger objectives. Not that such activists were cynical people trying to advance socialism by spreading monstrous lies about the munitions business. Far from it. Given their perception of capitalist ethics, they believed what they said about men who made and sold armaments.

The effect of the attack on the munitions trade is hard to measure—before 1934, that is. In 1934 the attack escalated into a veritable barrage, and before the year was half over there was scarcely an American who did not know something about the misdeeds, real and alleged, of the men who trafficked in the paraphernalia of war.

An article entitled "Arms and the Men" appeared in March 1934, in *Fortune*, a magazine hardly reputed for anti-business pyrotechnics. It spun a sordid tale of intrigue and unconcern for human life by manufacturers and salesmen of munitions and reached millions of readers when Doubleday, Doran and Company published it as a pamphlet and *Reader's Digest* two months later brought it out in a condensed version. Asserted its unidentified authors, who were staff members of *Fortune:* "According to the best accountancy figures, it cost about $25,000 to kill a soldier during the World War. There is one class of Big Business Men in Europe that never rose up to denounce the extravagance of its governments in this regard—to point out that when death is left unhampered as an enterprise for the individual initiative of gangsters the cost of a single killing seldom exceeds $100. The reason for the silence of these Big Business Men is quite simple: killing is their business. Armaments are their stock in trade; governments are their customers; the ultimate consumers of their products are, historically, almost as often their compatriots as their enemies. That does not matter. The important point is that every time a burst shell fragment finds its way into the brain, the heart, or the intestines of a man in the front line, a great part of the $25,000, much of it profit, finds its way into the pocket of the armament maker."

The authors claimed that the "Armorers' Philosophy" was: "Publish periodical war scares. Impress governmental officials with the vital necessity of maintaining armaments against the 'aggressions' of neighbor states. Bribe as necessary. In every practical way create suspicion that security is threatened." They declared that "the armament leopards have never changed their spots. Detail upon detail, incident upon incident, illustrate how well the armament makers apply the two axioms of their business: When there are wars, prolong them; when there is peace, disturb it." The authors wrote that the Soviet Union "is today the only country in which there is no 'private' manufacture and sale of armaments." And a footnote observed: "Parenthetically it will be recalled by those who have followed the dreary course of disarmament conferences that Russia, in the mouth of Comrade Maxim Litvinov, has been the most consistent and the loudest advocate of disarmament."

At the same time that readers of *Fortune* were considering "Arms and the Men," booksellers began to advertise three key books: Otto Lehmann-Russbüldt, *War for Profit* (a new edition of a volume, originally published in Germany under the title *Die Blutige Internationale*, which had created a minor stir when first brought out in the United States in 1930); George Seldes, *Iron, Blood and Profits: An Exposure of the World-Wide Munitions Racket* (rated best of the three by the reviewer R. L. Duffus in the *New York Times*), and Helmuth C. Engelbrecht and Frank C. Hanighen's *Merchants of Death: A Study of the International Armament Industry* (perhaps as a consequence of its more imaginative title, the most influential of the three books).

In message and argument the books were indentical to "Arms and the Men." All essayed the evils associated with such names as Krupp and Skoda, Schneider-Creusot, and Vickers-Armstrong. All touched on the affair of William Shearer and presented chapters on Sir Basil Zaharoff, a shadowy munitions salesman *par excellence,* who for a half-century had moved about Europe's capitals peddling arms, and was variously labeled the "King of Armaments" (by Seldes), the "Supersalesman of Death" (by Engelbrecht and Hanighen), and the "Wickedest Man Alive," by a pamphleteer of 1934 who so designated Sir Basil because "he has given his life to an industry so vile and cruel, so fatal to the happiness and welfare of humankind, as to surpass the iniquity of the Inquisition, the slave trade, and the pogroms of the Jews." All three volumes devoted many pages to the alleged trading of strategic materials and munitions among corporations in the countries of opposing belligerents during the Great War. All found their sources in hearsay, tracts by assorted pacifist and socialist writers, and statistics and statements susceptible to varying interpretation.

Whatever their deficiencies, the effect of these articles and books was both immediate and dramatic. Remarks on the Senate floor by William E. Borah of Idaho denouncing munitions manufacturers ("international racketeers" in his phrase) received surprising publicity. The Foreign Policy Association and the American Academy of Political and Social Science invited Helmuth Engelbrecht to lecture their members on the evils of the munitions trade; the Book-of-the-Month Club made *Merchants of Death* a selection for April 1934. Rallies by peace organizations assailing armament makers attracted unprecedented attention. Editorials and cartoons on the arms trade blossomed in newspapers, new articles exposing the munitions business appeared in magazines: John Gunther's "Slaughter for Sale," in *Harper's* and Jonathan Mitchell's "The Armaments Scandal," in the *New Republic,* both appeared in May 1934. Even *Foreign Affairs,* a cautious—and in the view of some people, an almost stodgy—journal, offered an article, albeit a nonaccusative one, entitled "Arms Manufacturers and the Public" in its issue of July 1934. Most important, a resolution introduced by Senators Nye and Vandenberg providing for an investigation of the munitions industry and war profits won the consent of the Senate.

For the previous two years a congressional investigation of the munitions trade had been an object of one of the prominent peace organizations, the Women's International League for Peace and Freedom, and in 1933 the Executive Secretary of the American section of the WIL, Dorothy Detzer, had sought a senatorial sponsor of a resolution to bring about such an investigation. On the suggestion of Norris of Nebraska, too ill himself to get involved in a full-dress inquiry, she eventually turned to Nye of North Dakota.

A native of Wisconsin who found his way to North Dakota during the World War, Gerald Nye had drunk deeply of the ideas of Robert M. La Follette, and when he took on the editorship of a county newspaper in eastern North Dakota, he became an instant spokesman of those ideas. On appointment to the Senate in 1925 at the age of thirty-two, he slipped into alliance with such Republican progressives as Norris and Borah, and was one of those progressives whom Senator George H. Moses in the late 1920s labeled "sons of the wild jackass." His concerns in those early years in the Senate were not military affairs nor foreign policy. The great and overbearing problems of America in his view were monopoly and concentrated wealth—the oppressors, he was convinced, of farmers and small businessmen. As for his reputation as a senator, he had won minor acclaim before 1934 as the man who presided over the Continental Trading Company phase of the Teapot Dome investigation and played a part in sending Harry F. Sinclair to jail. He served as chairman of the special committee which had scrutinized tactics and expenditures in the senatorial elections of the 1930s (a precursor, of sorts, of the Watergate inquiry of 1973–1974), one aspect of which was exposure of the famous attempt to defeat Norris in Nebraska by placing on the same ballot the name of George W. Norris, a grocery clerk. At the time Detzer approached him Nye was attracting some attention, together with Borah, by attacking the National Recovery Administration, which he thought promoted monopoly and weakened small business.

Reluctant at first, Nye at length succumbed to Miss Detzer's appeal, and in the Senate chamber on February 8, 1934, snapped his fingers for a page and sent to the desk a resolution to investigate the munitions industry. At that moment he thought the resolution stood little chance of passage. But then came "Arms and the Men," which he inserted into the *Congressional Record* with the comment that "I think there has not been published in ages anything quite so enlightening as is this article appearing in *Fortune*." After that came Borah's remarks and the books purportedly exposing the munitions makers, particularly that by Engelbrecht and Hanighen. The Senate could not easily be oblivious to the increasing popular awareness of the alleged evils of the arms business.

Nye and Detzer meanwhile observed that earlier in the session Senator Vandenberg, urged on by the American Legion which continued to insist that the burdens of war be equalized, had introduced a resolution to review the findings of the War Policies Commission of 1930–1931. So they reasoned: Why not combine the Nye and Vandenberg Resolutions? By combining the resolutions, Detzer later recalled, "the measure would gain a double-barreled support from two diametrically opposed wings of public opinion—the peace movement and the Legion." Vandenberg was agreeable, and the outcome was S. Res. 206, authorizing the vice president to appoint a seven-member committee to investigate individuals, corporations, and agencies in the United States engaged in the munitions business; report on the adequacy of existing laws and treaties pertaining to the arms trade; review findings of the War Policies Commission; and submit recommendations on the desirability of nationalizing the country's armament industry. To carry out its mandate the special committee would have authority to subpoena witnesses and documents and would receive an appropriation of $15,000.

Without a word of dissent the Senate on April 12, 1934 approved S. Res. 206.

In view of the munitions inquiry's latter-day reputation as an exercise in demagoguery, the absence of criticism of S. Res. 206 in the spring of 1934, in retrospect, seems remarkable. No member of Congress or other individual of influence intimated that a munitions investigation might be inconsistent with the spirit of the general legislative power granted by the Federal Constitution, or that political considerations rather than legislative intent had moved Nye,

Vandenberg, and other proponents of the resolution. Nobody hinted that the special committee might infringe upon powers delegated to the judiciary, and from the White House came no laments that the special committee was about to embark on a fishing expedition which might weaken the national defense establishment or complicate the country's foreign relations.

Perhaps the mood of the moment received its most eloquent expression in a message to the Senate from President Franklin D. Roosevelt six days after the adoption of S. Res. 206. Even if not in complete agreement with all of his assertions (and there is no evidence to that effect), the fact that he felt constrained to make them testified to the national outrage over the munitions business. In his message the President expressed gratitude that the Senate was preparing to investigate the munitions industry, recommended that the Senate give generous support to the investigating committee, and charged the Executive branch to cooperate with the committee "to the fullest extent." Declared Roosevelt: "The private and uncontrolled manufacture of arms and munitions and the traffic therein has become a serious source of international discord and strife." He urged that the Senate consent to the Geneva Arms Traffic Convention of 1925, and appealed to the General Disarmament Conference, soon to reassemble in Geneva, to draft a more inclusive document regulating the munitions trade. He claimed that people in many countries were being taxed to the point of starvation to enable governments to engage in "a mad race in armaments" which if not stopped would result in war. "This grave menace to the peace of the world," he concluded, "is due in no small measure to the uncontrolled activities of the manufacturers and merchants of engines of destruction, and it must be met by the concerted action of the peoples of all nations."

The presidential message produced an instant response. Within an hour of its receipt Key Pittman of Nevada, chairman of the Senate Foreign Relations Committee, reported the Arms Traffic Convention of 1925 and introduced a joint resolution drawn up by the State Department prohibiting Americans to ship munitions to Paraguay and Bolivia; Senator Nye asked an additional $35,000 for the munitions investigation. In a matter of days the joint resolution had become law, and the munitions inquiry received the extra funds. Two months later the Arms Traffic Convention obtained the consent of the Senate—with the reservation that it would not bind the United States until approved by eight other nations and the British Empire.

Vice President John Nance Garner, meanwhile, had appointed Nye, Vandenberg, and five of their colleagues to the Special Committee Investigating the Munitions Industry, and on motion by Clark of Missouri the committee on April 23, 1934 named Nye chairman. For the senator from North Dakota the events of recent weeks had been exhilarating, and he found it impossible to await scrutiny of testimony and documents before deciding that the munitions makers were guilty, as Engelbrecht and others had charged. At New Haven on April 29 he declared, "I confidently predict that when the Senate investigation is over, we shall see that war and preparation for war is not a matter of national honor and national defense, but a matter of profit for few." Next day in New York he saw futility in trying to move out of the Great Depression when "we are preparing for new wars which will and ought to be the end of our whole civilization," and after castigating armament expenditures as insane, proclaimed the time was at hand when it would be understood "what monkeys the munitions makers can make of the otherwise intelligent people of America."

II

Not the product of a disciplined or ranging intellect, those words were spoken in a clear, unpretentious accent, and came from a resonant baritone voice. They also came from the heart, for Gerald Nye was an honest man who meant what he said about merchants of death.

If often viewed from the vantage point of the present day as a demagogue and a Neanderthal isolationist whose mark on history is best forgotten, Nye was nevertheless an interesting person. Of average height, he was strong and muscular. He also was handsome. And notwithstanding his reputation as a man who spoke out in shockingly crude language against industrialists and bankers and, after the onset of the Second World War in Europe, against so-called "interventionists," he was a genial man who got on well with his colleagues. His historical reputation as a bullwhip orator, relentless investigator, and crusader for peace via isolation, in truth, is misleading. Nye was not an angry man. He did not pace the corridors and cloakrooms of the Capitol haranguing fellow senators and newsmen. He did not have boundless confidence. Never having attended college, he stood in awe of university-educated colleagues. He was reserved, and even shy. In the estimate of some observers he presented the image of a rather ordinary Midwesterner. Comparing him with colleagues on the munitions investigating committee, one reporter wrote that "he looks less like a senator than any of them. . . . He has no flowing mane, but a recent haircut. He has no senatorial bay window, but the lean build of a second baseman." Fortunately Nye had assets: energy, zeal, determination—and that magnetic voice.

For obvious reasons the Special Committee Investigating the Munitions Industry, from the moment of Nye's election as chairman, came to be called the Nye Committee. That was unfortunate, inasmuch as entitling the committee with the name of its chairman tended to exaggerate the chairman's part in the munitions investigation. Nye's interest in the inquiry, to be sure, never flagged. He spent many hours with colleagues and members of the committee staff mapping the investigation and poring over documents. He attended nearly every hearing. But if in that period Rudolf Hess was telling Germans that "Hitler ist Deutschland und Deutschland Hitler ist," Senator Nye was not the Nye Committee. Bennett Clark, for example, was as dedicated to the inquiry as Nye, and almost as active. Clark, and to a lesser extent Vandenberg, exercised nearly as much influence as the chairman in determining the direction of the inquiry. Clark, Vandenberg, and Homer Bone were much more energetic in interrogating witnesses. And it was Raushenbush, the committee secretary and a veteran critic and investigator of big business, who, in addition to helping the senators plan the investigation, supervised the crucial business of the munitions inquiry, namely, the searching of the files of such corporations as Du Pont and J. P. Morgan for incriminating or provocative documents, sifting through the piles of documents brought in by investigators, and drafting questions to be asked of witnesses.

The gathering and scrutiny of documents by Raushenbush's staff may have been the crucial business of the munitions inquiry, but it was the hearings in the caucus room, presided over by Nye, that attracted attention. There were ninety-three such hearings, and they concentrated on four topics: manufacture and sale of munitions (with emphasis on the international aspects of the arms trade); activities of the major shipbuilders of the United States; plans for removing, or at least reducing, corporate and individual returns in the event of American involvement in a new war; and finally, the economic circumstances of America's entry in the World War in 1917.

The first hearing, as mentioned, took place on September 4, 1934, the last, on February 20, 1936. Manufacture and sale of munitions was the focus of twenty-nine hearings in September and December 1934, and in February 1936. The shipbuilding industry was the subject of thirty-six hearings from January to April 1935; and in December 1934 and March and April 1935 the Nye Committee devoted eighteen hearings to war profits. After April 26, 1935, there were no hearings until January 7, 1936, when the committee held the first of ten hearings on loans to the Allied powers, industrial expansion, and neutrality during the World War—an attempt to discern whether the prompting of Wall Street financiers and other economic considerations had nudged the United States into war in 1917.

It was no accident that the Nye Committee elected to take up the munitions trade in the opening hearings. The trade was on the popular mind in 1934. People were anxious for the committee to expose the "merchants of death," and they would have felt a sense of letdown had hearings begun with consideration of such prosaic topics as collusive bidding among shipbuilders and excess-profits taxes in time of war. The public wanted to watch witnesses—unctuous and overfed tycoons of industry and sleazy arms salesmen—squirm when confronted with incriminating documents and accusative questions. The committee of course was anxious to satisfy the popular will, for it wanted to prevent any weakening of interest in the inquiry. The reasons were transparent. All of the members shared the national disgust with the arms trade, all were interested in other topics to be taken up during the investigation, notably corporate and individual profits, should America be drawn into the inevitable "next war," and they understood that any erosion of interest in what the committee was about would reduce chances of approval of legislation to bring the munitions makers to heel and equalize the economic burdens of American involvement in war. Then, too, the Nye Committee was operating on a parsimonious budget, and feared an early end to the inquiry if popular interest did not compel new appropriations. The inquiry's survival, then, seemed to depend on keeping interest at a high level. Finally, the senators were politicians, and if they made no public utterances to the effect that the munitions inquiry was apt to be a marvelous carriage for advancing political reputations, they must have thought as much. Should popular interest in the inquiry diminish, it went without saying, their coach would turn into a pumpkin.

The calculus of the senators proved accurate, for hearings on the munitions business produced a spate of sensational, or at least highly quotable, documents and testimonies which received front-page publicity. The Senate appropriated the funds necessary to keep the investigation going, and Nye *et al.*, remained in the spotlight.

There were two letters by Frank S. Jonas, an agent for such firms as the Remington Arms Company, Curtiss-Wright Export Corporation, and Federal Laboratories, Incorporated, who operated in South America. Jonas had written in late 1933: "The Paraguay and Bolivia fracas appears to be coming to a termination, so business from that end is probably finished. We certainly are in one hell of a business, where a fellow has to wish for trouble so as to make a living, the only consolation being, however, that if we don't get the business someone else will. It would be a terrible state of affairs if my conscience started to bother me now." In 1932, on a happier occasion (for him), Jonas had reported: "The unsettled conditions in South America has [*sic*] been a great thing for me, as I sold a large order for bombs to Brazil and also a fair cartridge order. I also sold very large bomb orders for Colombia, Peru, Ecuador, Bolivia, and now have made up all my losses, and I am back on my feet. It is an ill wind that does not blow someone some good." The first of those letters inspired Helmuth Engelbrecht to write another book, entitled *One Hell of a Business.*

If Frank Jonas was a small-bore arms salesman, authors of other documents put in evidence by the Nye Committee to prove the unconscionable character of the munitions trade were leaders of business. Such an individual was Vice President Lawrence Y. Spear of the Electric Boat Company who in 1928 had lamented that "it is too bad that the pernicious activities of our State Department have put the brake on armament orders from Peru by forcing the resumption of formal diplomatic relations with Chile." Asked by Senator Clark in 1934 if he indeed had regarded efforts by the State Department to improve relations among South American countries as pernicious, Spear had replied, "That is the word I used." Then there was Clarence W. Webster, President of Curtiss-Wright Export, who in 1933 had told an agent in Peru, "For your confidential information you might diplomatically inform interested parties that your neighbor to the extreme north [Colombia] is still purchasing [military equipment] in large quantities. Do not overlook such items as bombs, ammunition, machine guns . . . etc." Moved also by the prospect of profits to be taken from the war in the Gran Chaco, Webster in that same year had advised another agent in South America: "If we are able to sell them [the Paraguayans] anything, we will have to work very carefully and quietly . . . as the Bolivian Government would naturally raise 'merry hell' if they believed that we were dealing with their enemies." Webster's letters and kindred documents prompted Raushenbush to comment that the munitions business was "one in which the absence of moral judgment is a primary essential to success."

Still, the Nye Committee's attempt to prove the indictment of the munitions business drawn up by peace organizations and such authors as Engelbrecht and Seldes came to little. Raushenbush's investigators spent perhaps a thousand hours rifling through letters, reports, and memoranda in the files of sixteen corporations (and a few subsidiaries) in the United States which manufactured and distributed arms, ammunition, and other materials of war. They examined records of the Departments of State and Commerce and such private organizations as the Army Ordinance Association and Navy League. They found scattered documents indicating that at one time or another munitions makers and salesmen had committed many of the sins attributed to them by their critics: ignored the morality of customers, sold arms illegally, opposed disarmament schemes and arms embargoes. In aggregate, however, the evidence was paltry, and regarding most articles of the "gospel according to Engelbrecht" failed to support general conclusions. Most notably, documents and testimony failed to provide even the scantiest proof of the central contention of Engelbrecht *et al.*, namely, that there existed an international munitions "ring" composed of the principal arms makers of Europe (Krupp, Skoda, Vickers-Armstrong, Schneider-Creusot, Hotchkiss, Bofors) and America (Du Pont and possibly others) which, like a ubiquitous monster spreading its tentacles across the world—as cartoonists of the 1930s sometimes portrayed "the ring"—used bribery and whatever else might be necessary to prevent governments from negotiating disarmament treaties and imposing other restrictions on the munitions trade. The Nye Committee, of course, had no access to records of arament companies and chancelleries in Europe, Asia, and Latin America, and one can only speculate whether such records would have provided the proof of the Engelbrecht-Seldes-Detzer thesis on the munitions trade which the American Senate's special committee sought in vain in files in the United States.

All the Nye Committee affirmed about the munitions industry was that its overseas business depended to a large extent on "greasing the palms" of public officials in Latin America, the Near East, and China. Files of nearly every company scrutinized by Raushenbush's investigators yielded documents reporting payments to this or that functionary in return for arranging sale of a few airplane engines or cases of cartridges. At one point Senator Nye asked Clarence Webster, formerly of Curtiss-Wright Export, if it was not true that such a payment was called a commission. Webster replied, "That would be a very polite word for it, Mr. Chairman." "In fact," Nye asked, "it would be bribery, would it not?" "It would," answered Webster. "It is a rather harsh word, but it would be, strictly speaking." Bribery, however, was not a preserve of the munitions trade, so documents disclosing its use provided marginal reinforcement for the view that makers and sellers of arms were marked by special qualities of corruption. When the committee exhibited evidence that Du Pont had paid commissions to officials in China, Felix Du Pont explained that bribery was used "in most of the countries of the Orient in all walks of commercial life." "It is no different in the munitions business than it is in any other commercial business," he went on. "It is accepted; not talked about very much; but people in competition in those countries simply could not possibly carry on their trade if the customs of the country were not adhered to."

Failure of the Nye Committee to provide much support for the devil view of the munitions trade, however, was not readily apparent. That is understandable. Before the munitions hearings began many Americans had accepted the contention that arms makers were merchants of death, and scattered evidence supporting this or that particular of the Engelbrecht-Seldes indictment, some of it quite sensational (*e.g.*, the Jonas letters), buttressed such belief. Then there was the committee's procedure during hearings. If the committee had taken up the so-called "international munitions ring," exhibited all documents purporting to indicate the existence of a ring, and summoned witnesses from Du Pont and Remington and Electric Boat to answer questions about the ring, the paucity of evidence would have become apparent. People, accordingly, might have understood that the ring possibly was the creation of excited imaginations and in any event did not include American corporations. If the committee had focused on the contention that a standard practice of arms dealers was to make sales to one party to a conflict or dispute and then quietly advise the other belligerent or disputant that it had better keep abreast of its opponent, people would have seen that the two or three letters exhibited to the point scarcely supported a general conclusion. Instead of moving from topic to topic, the committee unfortunately moved from corporation to corporation. Documents indicated that this company had committed one type of indiscretion, that company another. Only a perceptive observer under such circumstances was apt to discern that on few occasions, bribery excepted, did abuses reappear.

Perhaps the perception of Americans and others would have been clearer had they grasped a message implicit in testimony given during hearings and in the thousands of pages of documents eventually published by the Nye Committee, namely, that the munitions industry in the United States in the mid-1930s was in pretty sad shape. Markets for its wares were scarce, its capacity for mischief was sorely restricted. Of the dozen or so companies (not including shipbuilders) which comprised the industry, only Du Pont, one of three or four producers of gunpowder in the country, seemed reasonably prosperous, and a mere fraction of Du Pont's manufacturing profits—two percent over the previous ten years—had come from sale of military products. As for the others, several of them shoestring operations, the larger ones only marginally involved in the business of making and distributing military arms, they were closed out of sales to the powers of Europe and Japan and their empires were unable to secure many orders from the government of the United States, which was spending little money on armament, save warships. Thus such companies were reduced to scrounging for sales in a few meager markets, mainly in Latin America.

The committee, one must assume, did become aware of the poverty level of America's munitions industry. Its investigative staff certainly did. After his first day at the Winchester Repeating Arms Company, the investigator, Robert Wohlforth, reported to Raushenbush: "In Winchester yesterday as per schedule. It is even more dismal a plant than Remington—a cross between an old ladies' home and a prison factory. This bunch are surely down in the mouth since the Olins took over; every department has been cut to the bone and the whole place seems to be wheezing along on one cylinder. . . . As far as I can make out, they use the Ix-nay system of filing. The old crone in the central filing room takes a bunch of papers marked 'U.S. government,' turns around three times with her eyes shut, says 'Ix-nay' and files the papers under 'Venezuela—commercial business.' . . . Needless to say I camped in Mr. Beebe's department [H. F. Beebe, Director of the Foreign Department]. . . . We fell to talking about the 1925 business [a meeting between government and arms company officials]. With another stroke of luck we discover he has all the papers on that little business in a folder, unbeknownst to Apple Annie of the filing room."

Still, the committee, perhaps sensing that its inquiry would lose its *raison d'être* if it blemished the popular portrait of munitions corporations wallowing in the profits of blood and gore while the rest of the world languished, gave no hint of the depressed state of America's merchants of death. And the merchants? They did not seem anxious to publicize their actual condition.

But alas, the truth more or less won out in the end. Without saying much about it, Americans gradually came to the conclusion that makers and salesmen of munitions were not such dangerous fellows after all. Perhaps people subconsciously understood that the Nye Committee had failed to prove the case against the manufacturers and sellers of arms. Perhaps they simply tired of pondering heady notions about merchants of death. After all, happenings other than the munitions inquiry were commanding their attention. There was the World Series of 1934 between the Cardinals and Tigers, an exciting affair dominated by the Dean brothers. By the year 1935, in any event, fewer individuals were issuing broadsides on the threat to peace and humanity presented by the munitions trade. And if Senator Nye, on Independence Day 1935, could shout that the "next war" ought to be called "a war to make the world safe for Du Pontcracy" and proclaim that munitions makers—he called them racketeers—"go out over this world and build up the hates, fears, and suspicions that build wars, that drive people into war, and then getting them there, they keep them there as long as they can," fewer people seemed to be listening than had listened the year before.

The erosion of faith in the truisms of 1934 never abated. When the Nye Committee in the spring of 1936 issued its report, only four members (Bone, Clark, Nye, and Pope) favored nationalization of the munitions industry, that elixir which in one grand swallow so many Americans and surely every certified pacifist had believed would eliminate the evils of the arms business and dramatically strengthen the cause of peace. Agreeing with the majority on every other point, the committee minority (Barbour, George, and Vandenberg) did not think the ills of the munitions trade warranted such drastic and unsettling medicine, the more so in light of the darkening state of world politics. In 1937 Philip Noel-Baker's book entitled *The Private Manufacture of Armaments,* a refined reiteration of information and themes set out by Engelbrecht and Seldes in 1934, created hardly a ripple. (Noel-Baker, however, would continue to toil in the vineyard of peace, and in 1959 receive his reward, a Nobel Peace Prize.) By 1938 scarcely anyone in America appeared to care a hoot about the comings and goings of such shadowy characters as Frank Jonas or the tactics of United Aircraft Export in selling a few planes in South America. By that time, it was true, the Yankees had become so dominant in baseball that the World Series no longer was very interesting, either. Still, Mussolini's conquest of Ethiopia, Hitler's remilitarization of the Rhineland, and the aftermath of the incident at the Marco Polo Bridge near Peiping seemed sufficient to prevent people from dreaming up new chapters in yesteryear's awful saga of the merchants of death. Twenty years later, even Gerald Nye, a man in the twilight of life, his career in the Senate having terminated in 1945, could say that he never had accepted the idea that munitions makers were a principal cause of war.

At the same time the senators were interrogating men who manufactured and sold munitions and basking in the national spotlight, Raushenbush's investigators were assembling materials from the files of the country's private shipbuilding industries. As everyone knew—or so it seemed—the shipbuilders had dispatched William B. Shearer to the Geneva Naval Conference of 1927, and like other makers of implements of war were suspected of conniving with federal departments and spending vast sums of money to influence Congress. In the words of the National Council for Prevention of War: "Our shipbuilders are probably our most aggressive and sinister propagandists of competitive naval building even if it brings war. They have for years been ruthless in pursuit of profits."

The Nye Committee, however, treated shipbuilders apart from ordinary makers of guns and amunition, for, unlike so-called merchants of death whose prosperity depended on overseas markets, America's shipbuilding industry constructed nearly all of its war vessels for the government of the United States, and thus was not open to such accusations brought against the munitions trade as bribing foreign functionaries, stirring tensions in small countries, and violating arms embargoes. Some of the sins of which the committee suspected shipbuilders, in truth, had little relation to questions of war and peace. Most important, the senators thought, the "big three" of the shipbuilding industry—Bethlehem Shipbuilding Company, New York Shipbuilding Company, and Newport News Shipbuilding & Dry Dock Company—had come to dominate the industry, and that dominance had produced several evils: attempts to freeze out smaller competitors; organization of elaborate lobbies in Washington; and collusive bidding for naval contracts.

The Nye Committee's exhaustive study of the shipbuilding industry proved another exercise in frustration. The senators proved that two shipbuilding executives had lied to the Shortridge Subcommittee during its investigation of the Shearer Affair in 1929, and established that the industry had maintained an expensive lobby in Washington to influence legislation pertaining to merchant marine and naval construction. But they exhibited only circumstantial evidence, effectively countered by representatives of the industry, that shipbuilders had engaged in collusive bidding—the aspect of the study of the shipbuilding industry to which they gave the most time. And in its re-examination of the Shearer episode the committee added nothing to the findings of the Shortridge Inquiry of 1929–1930.

Equally frustrating no doubt, the lengthy examination of the shipbuilding industry, heavy with figures on cost estimates and bids, stirred little popular interest and only rarely prompted city editors to think that copy submitted by reporters deserved the front page. One of those rare instances came when the committee aired a bizarre and inconclusive account of a union official standing outside a hotel room while a representative of one of Washington's "most influential citizens" and a "fixer" allegedly promised to arrange a contract award to Gulf Industries, Incorporated, a small shipbuilder, in return for $250,000. Another titillation came when the committee interrogated the volatile Shearer about a pamphlet he had written in 1928, entitled *The Cloak of Benedict Arnold,* in which he had tagged several prominent Americans as "unpatriotic" because they did not share his Mahanian views about a big navy. Senator Bone asked Shearer if he still considered President Woodrow Wilson's Secretary of War, Newton D. Baker, as "unpatriotic." Shearer answered that he did. Bone asked about Harry A. Garfield, the son of the former President. Shearer explained that listing Garfield had been "a little bit of plagiarism on my part, taken from the Hearst papers." Bone told Shearer that "you ought not to admit plagiarism." Replied Shearer: "I am a plagiarist. I am in that case." What about former Attorney General George W. Wickersham? Claiming that he had served as an attorney for the Mitsubishi interests of Japan, Shearer said he still considered Wickersham "unpatriotic." Bone pointed out that Shearer had listed Franklin D. Roosevelt among the "unpatriotic." "Hearst," Shearer said. Retorted Bone: "Do you want to hide behind the skirts of a newspaper publisher?" "Let me tell you, Senator," Shearer exclaimed, "I do not hide behind anything, but Hearst published an article at that time that gave me the opportunity to use it, and I took it and put it in that pamphlet. I am opposed to all foreign entanglements and to being made an adjunct of the British." "Are you so cowardly," Bone asked a few moments later, "that you would not indict him [Roosevelt], if he required indictment, as a 'Benedict Arnold'? You told us you had lots of courage." "I have not mentioned my courage," Shearer spoke out, "and I do not like the implication about being a coward." "That is unfortunate," snapped Bone. Whereupon Shearer rose from his chair and began to move menacingly toward Bone. Nye pounded his gavel and shouted, "Go back to your seat as a witness and remain there." Shearer stopped short and returned to his chair.

III

In addition to the munitions trade and the shipbuilding industry the Nye Committee, as mentioned, took up war profits and economic influences on America's relations with Europe's belligerents in 1914–1917.

Abnormal returns in the form of dividends, wages, and bonuses when the United States was at war—all conveniently called war profits—were a subject which stirred popular emotions in the mid-1930s, as it had in some quarters as far back as 1920, the year the new veterans' organization, the American Legion, opened a campaign in behalf of legislation to curtail large civilian profits in time of national belligerency. In the view of many people it was manifestly unfair that a soldier at the front should be required to risk life and limb for a couple of dollars a day while workingmen, farmers, and industrialists (especially *industrialists*) at home realized bonanza returns, as in 1917–1918. Or as Senator Clark, an army officer in the World War, expressed it: "If a man is drafted . . . and is compelled to fight for the Old Flag for one-dollar-and-a-quarter a day [the wage of a private in the American Expeditionary Force in 1917–1918], why should not a man engaged in the industrial end of the game—which I agree is very essential, whether he be an executive or a laboring man—also make some sacrifice for the Old Flag?"

More than a spirit of fair play moved many Americans to deplore war profits. The prospect of huge returns in time of war, according to a popular belief, constituted a threat to peace. So the argument went, legions of Americans—workingmen, farmers, businessmen—recalling the returns of 1917–1918, might be tempted to view a new declaration of war by the government in Washington as a blessing, particularly in a time such as the present, *i.e.*, at a time of economic distress. Should large numbers of people—and especially captains of business who were assumed to have great influence in the councils of government—come to such a view, America's involvement in the next general war in Europe or Asia was inevitable. How might Americans be immunized against viewing war as a "positive good" (to borrow John C. Calhoun's famous estimate of slavery)? This was easy. Pass a law to "equalize the burdens of war," namely, a law which would guarantee that *no* American, workingman and industrialist as well as soldier and seaman, would realize large monetary returns during the period of hostilities. Such a law, the writer-economist John T. Flynn told the Nye Committee, would make war highly unpopular. Explained Flynn: "I rather think that the man who is disposed to be very sensitive, if some Japanese lieutenant fails to take his hat off in the presence of the American flag some place in Manchukuo, will not be so sensitive and will be more reasonable in his patriotism."

The Nye Committee shared popular emotions about war profits and determined to do something about them. The committee, in truth, viewed its investigation of war profits, if less apt to produce sensational documents and testimony, as more important than its scrutiny of the munitions trade. Its reasoning seemed logical. However shabby, the activities of a few arms companies in Peru and Paraguay were not likely to imperil America's peace. The profits to be taken in the aftermath of a new declaration of war appeared something else. These would touch virtually every citizen of a depression-weary republic, and if not foreclosed before eruption of that inevitable "next war" in Europe or Asia, the promise of such profits would dramatically reduce the chances of America staying clear of hostilities. The trick was to find a formula for restricting war profits which would pass muster with the national populace and its representatives in Washington.

This was a trick the Nye Committee failed to turn. Millions of Americans, it seemed evident when the committee began work in 1934, agreed that the prospect of untrammeled profits in time of war threatened America's peace. Thus, if the committee, then at the peak of its influence, had struck for a drastic war profits measure at that time the legislation might have passed. But it was apparent by the spring of 1935, when discussion of war profits came to a dramatic climax in Congress, that much of the citizenry was less fearful than the Nye Committee and its supporters in the peace movement that the expectation of abnormal returns would draw the country into war. Perhaps ordinary people, on reflection, had arrived at a "gut" feeling, beyond the comprehension of some men on Capitol Hill, not to mention quixotic crusaders of the peace organizations, that Americans would not betray their young men for uncounted pieces of silver. What bothered Americans by 1935 was the unfairness, and the scandal, of profiteering on the home front when American soldiers were facing death in the trenches. This meant that by that point the object of thoughtful citizens was, via price controls or excess profits taxes or both, to hold individual and corporate earnings in war to something approximating peacetime levels. Those same citizens, moreover, had come to sense that an extreme attack on the profit motive in time of hostilities might imperil the national war effort, and like General MacArthur, back in 1931, accepted the axiom that victory in *any* war in which the United States found itself must receive first priority. As for the Nye Committee, it remained intent on crushing any economic incentives Americans might have for going to war by making their involvement in war as economically unpalatable as possible.

More concerned with corporate than individual returns (large bonuses to corporate executives excepted), the Nye Committee began its public scrutiny of war profits by establishing what everybody already knew, namely, that American corporations had realized unprecedented returns in the time of the First World War. The picture was fuzzy, however, inasmuch as the committee made little distinction between the returns of corporations in 1914–1917, before America's entry into the conflict, and the year and a half following its declaration of war. Profits in the nearly three-year period before the Declaration of April 1917 of course hardly seemed germane to the committee's mandate to consider the matter of profits during national belligerency.

Whatever the confusion resulting from its approach to the subject, the Nye Committee made some unsettling disclosures during its hearings on war profits. There was the haggling between Du Pont and the government in 1917–1918 over construction of the Old Hickory smokeless powder plant near Nashville, Tennessee. The haggling had gone on for three months before the Du Pont corporation agreed to terms. As Lieutenant Colonel C. T. Harris, in the planning branch of the War Department in 1917–1918, told the committee, "three months were taken up in negotiations which finally led to the final agreement. . . . There were 3 months lost in the middle of the war by these negotiations. That had a very serious effect on the military effort. Fortunately it did not have a fatal effect, but it might have had." Evidence indicated that Du Pont, the only company in America capable of building and operating a smokeless powder plant of such dimensions, had delayed agreement in hopes of securing better terms. Or, as Pierre S. Du Pont had explained in a letter of November 1917, "We cannot assent to allowing our patriotism to interfere with our duties as trustees." Such reasoning seemed shocking in 1934, and Senator Clark expressed the Nye Committee's sentiments: "You take men to carry a gun and get jabbed up with bayonets without any consultation or negotiations or haggling." Then there was disclosure that during the war corporations had deferred tax payments when they disagreed with the government on the amounts to be paid. Evidence revealed that most such cases were not resolved until years later, and in nearly every instance the sum eventually paid was less than the liability originally calculated by the government. The Bureau of Internal Revenue, for example, had calculated the tax liability of the Phelps-Dodge Corporation for 1917–1918 at $16,378,000. The Corporation argued for $6,245,000, and deferred payment. When settlement of the case finally came in 1929 Phelps-Dodge had to pay only slightly more than $7,000,000.

In executing its mandate under S. Res. 206 to examine the findings of the War Policies Commission the Nye Committee, as indicated, hoped to provide a foundation for legislation that would restrict monetary gain and more or less equalize economic burdens when the United States went to war. Its views on what such legislation should entail were set out in a plan prepared by John T. Flynn and considered in hearings in March and April of 1935. The Flynn Plan was drastic. It urged that corporations in wartime be limited to annual profits of three percent of their real value. It called for confiscation of all annual individual earnings in excess of $10,000, a mind-boggling (and perhaps *mindless*) proposal which prompted Senator Pope to ask if such taxation would not be a serious matter. Replied Flynn: "It would not be a serious matter at all. It might be serious for them [persons whose life-style was geared to high incomes], but not for the Nation." Senator Clark interjected: "It is not as serious as being hit by a high-explosive shell, is it?" Flynn: "Not nearly." Flynn's plan also would require officials of industries declared essential by the President to register for the draft, whereupon the government could induct them into the industrial–management forces of the army at a rank no higher than colonel at pay appropriate to that rank, and then assign them to manage their own corporations. What about workers? Believing that there should be no exceptions, that the burdens of war must fall equally, Nye and Clark thought the plan should provide for conscription of labor as well as capital. But workers were too numerous and had too many friends on Capitol Hill, so the committee regretfully directed Flynn to make no recommendations for drafting labor.

Claiming that "the time has come to take the profit out of war," President Roosevelt meanwhile, in December 1934, had appointed a committee headed by Bernard M. Baruch and Hugh S. Johnson to draft legislation to eliminate excessive returns in time of war. The Baruch-Johnson Committee did not amount to much, and after cursory study reiterated the well-known views of Baruch. Then, in January 1935, Representative John McSwain of South Carolina, the author of many war profit resolutions over the years, introduced a new measure to curtail returns in wartime. An embodiment of Baruch's ideas, the McSwain Bill authorized the President, when the United States became a belligerent, to proclaim a ceiling on prices, rents, rates, commissions, and rewards, and granted the Chief Executive other powers over the economy intended to facilitate the national war effort.

The Nye Committee viewed the appointment of the Baruch-Johnson Committee and the introduction of the McSwain Bill as a crude maneuver by the White House to head off the drive for drastic legislation to eliminate war profits. Still, it felt compelled to invite Baruch to present his views at committee hearings. Baruch accepted the invitation. Of the McSwain Bill he exulted: "This is a great measure, not alone to prevent war, if there be people who desire profits in war, but to make certain this country will have the greatest war machine that we ever had, that the world has ever seen."

About the Flynn Plan Baruch held his peace during hearings, only to attack it a short time later in a statement filed with the committee: "I am not debating here whether the profit motive is right or wrong. I am only insisting that we recognize reality and what is here proposed. And I *am* saying that the advent of modern war and threatened national destruction, when the fate of the people, as at no other time, depends on the efficient operation at high-speed pressure, of its industrial system, is *not* the moment to select to switch from the fundamental base of our economic system to a new and wholly experimental system which was never adopted at any time in the world's history in peace or war without an immediate result of collapse and ruin."

If in the opinion of many people "Barney" Baruch was a "pompous ass," most Americans probably agreed with his estimate of the consequences of the sort of attack on war profits envisioned by the Nye Committee and its Flynn

Plan. In any event, when the issue of war profits came to a climax on Capitol Hill, in April 1935, the House of Representatives, returning to reality after a heady and tumultuous day during which it seemed to embrace the Nye Committee's ideas, approved the McSwain Bill by a vote of 367 to 19. Ignoring the obvious, *i.e.*, that legislation styled after Flynn's plan stood no chance of gaining consent of Congress or signature by the President, Nye determined to tilt against windmills and persuaded the Military Affairs Committee to accept Flynn–like amendments to the Senate's version of the McSwain Bill. This was to no avail. Only a handful of senators was interested in such an extreme remedy for the problem of profiteering in war, so the bill never came to a vote in the Upper Chamber, and by summer of 1935, in the face of concern over worsening relations between Ethiopia and Italy, the steam had gone out of the drive to enact war profits legislation.

Many months later, in January-February 1936, came the hearings on how economic considerations may have influenced the policy of the American government in 1914–1917.

To discern whether the munitions industry in any way was responsible for America's entry in the World War, the Nye Committee early in its inquiry determined to examine events of 1914–1917, whereupon investigators under the direction of Josephine Joan Burns began to assemble evidence from the State Department and other departments and agencies. Still, the Nye Committee, when it began its investigation in 1934, had no idea that it might become entangled in a great national debate over America's policy when other countries went to war—a debate over *neutrality*. At the time the Senate adopted S. Res. 206 the question of neutrality, in truth, did not seem urgent. The Far East was momentarily tranquil and the war in the Gran Chaco presented no threat to the United States. Congress, moreover, had considered neutrality the previous year, and the outcome had been an impasse which betrayed no sign of abating.

But then, in early 1935, the impending conflict in East Africa stirred new interest in neutrality, and in March of that year President Roosevelt, to the surprise of the senators and for reasons that remain unclear, suggested that the Nye Committee look into the matter of neutrality and draft relevant legislation. A few weeks later Nye and Clark, by then absorbed with the neutrality issue, introduced joint resolutions prohibiting loans to belligerent governments and their nationals, denying passports to Americans wishing to enter war zones, and prohibiting shipment of arms to belligerents, victims and aggressors alike—measures calculated to preclude activities and incidents of the sort which the senators believed had drawn the United States to war in 1914–1917. "Isolationists" (so-called) who wanted America to stay clear of foreign embroilments at almost any price, Nye and Clark agreed with a sentiment expressed in that period by the historian Charles A. Beard: "We tried once to right European wrongs, to make the world safe for democracy. Even in the rosiest view the experiment was not a great success. Mandatory neutrality may be no better, for aught anyone actually knows. But we nearly burnt our house down with one experiment; so it seems not wholly irrational to try another line."

The Nye Committee meanwhile announced plans for examining files and interrogating officers of J. P. Morgan & Company, the financial angel of the

Allied governments in 1914–1917. That announcement brought a thunderclap from across the Atlantic, particularly from Great Britain, whose ambassador in Washington expressed fear that the committee would treat the British Government as a circus animal performing for spectators and deplored the consequences of such a spectacle on relations between Britain and the United States. The committee, as a result, did not gain access to Morgan's records until mid-August 1935, and it was not until January 1936 that Raushenbush's investigative staff had prepared the essential foundation for hearings. Too late to influence the debate which had culminated in the Neutrality Act of 1935, those hearings seemed certain to bear on discussion of what kind of legislation if any should be enacted upon expiration on February 29, 1936, of the neutrality measure of 1935.

If it put the Nye Committee back on "Page One" for a few days, the interrogation of J. P. Morgan and his partners on the subject of finance and foreign policy in 1914–1917 proved still another exercise in frustration. Equally distressing from the vantage of the committee—or, more accurately, the committee majority—an utterance by Senator Nye in the course of that interrogation brought an end to the entire munitions investigation.

Frustration and distress did not seem a probable outcome when on January 7, 1936, the Nye Committee faced the Morgan witnesses in the high-ceilinged Senate caucus room. Not since the first days of the munitions hearings had the committee attracted so much attention, the room being filled to capacity long before Nye called for order. The scene, if tense, was informal, almost unruly. Huddled at the witness table were J. P. Morgan (the younger), his pipe billowing smoke, and his partners, Thomas W. Lamont and George Whitney. Behind them was a corps of accountants, clerks, and publicists. Unlike during the Pecora Inquiry nearly three years before, the Morgan witnesses seemed anxious to submit their case to the public. Whenever the committee exhibited a document a Morgan functionary would extract a sheaf of copies from a brief case and distribute them to the forty or so reporters seated at two, long, flanking tables. And Morgan, wearing a high starched collar which made him appear a relic of another generation, talked with reporters and posed patiently for photographers.

When the hearings got underway the committee permitted Morgan to read a statement in which he conceded that, notwithstanding President Wilson's appeal of August 1914 urging Americans to be impartial in thought as well as action, the Morgan partners had found it "quite impossible to be impartial as between right and wrong." He explained that from the moment the war started "we, in common with many others, realized that if the Germans should obtain a quick and easy victory the freedom of the rest of the world would be lost." The Morgan partners therefore had "agreed that we should do all that was lawfully in our power to help the Allies win the war as soon as possible." That thought, he said, was "the fundamental idea underlying everything that we did from the beginning of the struggle till the Armistice of November 1918." Why did the United States eventually become a belligerent? "Germany drove the United States into the war by a series of insults and injuries, resulting in the loss of many American lives, any one of which injuries might have proved a cause of war had the United States not been so desirous of maintaining peace."

Morgan's statement did not satisfy the committee, for the senators wanted to know if his company out of affinity for the Allies or for its own advantage had prompted changes in President Wilson's policies which they suspected had drawn the United States closer to the war. Two happenings in particular, one in 1914 and another in 1915, sparked their interest. After letting investment bankers know in August 1914 that they should arrange neither loans nor credits to belligerents, Wilson two months later had given his consent to an extension of credits to the warring governments. Did Wall Street have a hand in persuading Wilson to make that change in his loan-credit policy? Conceding that there was no essential difference between loans and credits, only a technical one, J. P. Morgan denied any part in bringing the change, and the committee could produce no documents to contradict him. The second happening had occurred in August 1915 when the Morgan firm, which over the previous six months had supported the pound sterling in the international monetary market, withdrew support. The price of sterling plunged, and British purchases of American munitions, materials, and foodstuffs—purchases which in the past year had touched off an economic boom in the United States—seemed threatened. Whereupon Wilson revised his policy and sanctioned loans to belligerents (*i.e.*, allowed bankers to float Allied securities in the United States), the pound recovered, and America's prosperity bounded forward. Did Morgan withdraw its support of sterling in August 1915 for the purpose of compelling the President to permit loans? No, the Morgan partners insisted. And again the committee had no documents with which to counter their denial.

If Morgan and other investment bankers had not conspired to persuade Wilson to pursue policies which in the Nye Committee's view had compromised America's neutrality and tended to draw the country in the war on the side of Britain and France, did not extensive trade with the Allies produce that result? In the words of Senator Vandenberg, "everybody that worked in one of these munitions plants was monetized, directly or indirectly, and all of these people [who] . . . had come to a realization of the tremendously important factor that this war trade was upon our economy had a sense of monetization."

In support of the view that trade with the Allies in 1914–1917 had weakened the determination of Americans and their leaders to stay neutral, the committee cited statements by a string of participants in the events of 1914–1917. After a conversation with Wilson's adviser, Edward M. House, in 1916, the German ambassador had reported House as saying that the President had lost the power to coerce the British because "American commerce was so completely tied up with the interests of the Entente that it was impossible for Wilson to disturb these commercial relations without calling forth such a storm of protest on the part of the public that he would not be able to carry out his intention." Britain's wartime Prime Minister David Lloyd George had recalled after the war that trade with the Allies "had its influence in holding back the hand of the American Government whenever excited to intense irritation by some new incident of the [British] blockade, it contemplated retaliatory measures." In his book *France and America,* Andre Tardieu, French High Commissioner in the United States in 1917–1918 and later the Premier of France, had written that on becoming economically bound with

Britain and France "the victory of the Allies became essential to the United States." More interesting was a cable to the State Department from the American ambassador in London, Walter Hines Page, dated March 5, 1917, claiming that the Allied financial situation was so desperate that termination of purchases in America was imminent. "This will, of course, cause a panic in the United States." Believing the crisis to be "too great and urgent for any private agency to meet," Page reported that only assistance by the government in Washington could save the situation. But such assistance presented a problem, inasmuch as the American government, as a neutral, could not legally aid belligerents, or as Page put it: "Unless we go to war with Germany, our Government, of course, cannot make such a direct grant of credit." He concluded that "perhaps our going to war is the only way in which our present prominent trade position can be maintained and a panic averted." Alas, there was no proof that President Wilson had read the Page cable, and the Nye Committee found not a shred of evidence indicating that Wilson had given even passing thought to economic considerations in taking the United States to war on the side of the Allies.

With its frequent suggestions that Wilson in 1914–1917 had fashioned policy for the benefit of the Allied powers while proclaiming neutrality, the Nye Committee meanwhile was stirring the anger of many Democrats for whom the wartime President remained a symbol of forthrightness and integrity. Indeed two Democratic members of the committee, George and Pope, had made themselves conspicuously absent during most of the interrogation of the Morgan partners. Then, on January 15, 1936, the committee considered evidence, circumstantial but persuasive, that before America's entry in the war Wilson had known of the secret treaties by which the Allies had agreed to a division of spoils, should they win the war. It also showed that Wilson and Secretary of State Robert Lansing in 1919 had told the Senate Foreign Relations Committee that they had not learned of the secret treaties until after the war. That discrepancy prompted Nye to remark that "both the President and Secretary Lansing falsified concerning this matter."

Wilsonians erupted. Tom Connally of Texas told the Senate: "I do not care how the charges were made; they are infamous. Some checker–playing, beer–drinking, back room of some low house is the only place fit for the kind of language which the Senator from North Dakota, the Chairman of the Committee, this Senator who is going to lead us out toward peace, puts into the *Record* about a dead man, a great man, a good man, a man who when alive had the courage to meet his enemies face to face and eye to eye." On January 17 Carter Glass of Virginia spoke out. Every seat on the Democratic side of the aisle in the Senate chamber was occupied, a large delegation of House Democrats was on hand, the galleries were filled. "From time to time," he rasped, "it has been suggested in the newspapers that the members of this committee were going to present the country shocking revelations. It remained until day before yesterday to present anything of a shocking nature; and that was the unspeakable accusation against a dead President—dirtdaubing the sepulcher of Woodrow Wilson." Of the committee's suspicion that Wall Street had influenced the wartime President, he shouted: "Oh, the miserable demagogy, the miserable and mendacious suggestion, that the house of Morgan altered the neutrality course of Woodrow Wilson." Pounding his desk until blood appeared on his knuckles, Glass concluded: "Now, Mr. President, lest I should infringe those rules which I always obey, perhaps I should better desist, because what I feel like saying here or anywhere else to the man who thus insults the memory of Woodrow Wilson is something which may not be spoken here, or printed in the newspapers, or uttered by a gentleman." Democrats were jubilant. They cheered and whistled and clapped, although one commentator later reported that it had been unclear whether Glass, a long-time friend of banking interests, was "more wroth for Morgan alive or Wilson dead."

Whatever his motives, Glass had signaled the sentiment of most Democrats when he promised that he would not vote another dollar to a committee whose members were "so insensible to every consideration of decency" that they would "bitterly assail two dead men who are honored by this entire Nation." And that was bad news for the Nye Committee, which was out of money and could not continue its inquiry without a new appropriation. To enable it to complete investigations in progress and prepare a report the Democratic majority in the Senate relented to the extent of voting a final $7,369, but the committee had to abandon long-range plans, and at 4:00 P.M. on the afternoon of February 20, 1936, Chairman Nye let his gavel fall and adjourned the munitions hearings for the last time.

From the vantage point of the writer of history it is too bad that the hearings did not end on February 5, the day the committee concluded its interrogation of the Morgan partners. When that interrogation had begun a month before, it seemed that the Nye Committee, out of the public eye for the better part of a year, was back on the main track and operating under a full head of steam. The outcome, the committee obviously anticipated, would be such popular support that the Senate, however grudgingly, would appropriate funds to enable it to continue and enlarge its investigation. But the documents and testimony did not prove sufficient to keep the steam pressure up; Connally and Glass threw obstacles on the track. And so it was that newsmen and photographers recorded the scene of February 5. There was Senator Nye, tired and discouraged if managing a weak smile, admitting forthrightly (and Nye was a forthright man) that his committee had proved nothing to the discredit of Morgan and his banking house in ten days of hearings on the firm's wartime and postwar operations. Then there was J. P. Morgan, jr., his briar pipe billowing smoke, his face beaming. Shaking hands with Nye, the titan of Wall Street said: "I have had a fine time; I would not have missed this investigation for the world."

IV

Investigations by committees of the United States Congress in the twentieth century have achieved varying historical reputations. Such inquires as those managed by Ferdinand Pecora in 1933–1934 and Harry S. Truman in 1941–1944 have received high marks as investigations conducted with a high sense of responsibility and in the best interests of the republic. Other inquiries, *e.g.*, the search for subversives by committees and subcommittees headed by the likes of Martin Dies and Joseph R. McCarthy, are generally viewed as deplorable exercises in demagoguery—or latter-day witch hunts

—fueled by popular hysteria resulting from frustration and warped understandings of national problems and ailments.

The Nye Committee inquiry of 1934–1936 has tended to fall in the second category. The historian Arthur S. Link has written that the committee did not conduct "a restrained inquiry but rather a ruthless investigation." In the view of Dexter Perkins the munitions inquiry reinforced "the thesis that American entry into the [World] War was the work of wicked Wall Street bankers, aided and abetted by sinister arms barons." According to Thomas A. Bailey, the Nye Committee aroused Americans "over the wrong things, and this state of mind contributed powerfully to the passage of the heads-in-the-sands neutrality legislation of the 1930s." Richard W. Leopold has written that "with an astonishing display of oversimplification and a remarkable disregard for causality, the committee argued that the United States had entered the Great War to protect the arms traffic and save the bankers." In Leopold's estimate the result "was to stimulate the resurgence of isolationism." In his memoirs former Secretary of State Cordell Hull wrote that "the Nye Committee aroused an isolationist sentiment that was to tie the hands of the [Roosevelt] Administration just at the very time when our hands should have been free to place the weight of our influence in the scales where it would count." Former Senator and President Harry S. Truman recalled that "the Nye Committee, which was backed by isolationists and 'America Firsters,' was pure demagoguery in the guise of a congressional investigating committee." And America's first Secretary of Defense, James V. Forrestal, recorded in his diary in 1947 that "the Nye Committee . . . was staffed by Communist attorneys and . . . had much to do with the curtailment of our own armaments industry in the period 1936 to 1939."

According to the prevailing historical estimate then—or historical indictment—the Nye Committee, encouraged by political leftists who despised the capitalist economic system, set about to prove that munitions makers were merchants of death and that greedy titans of Wall Street, to save their huge investments in an Allied victory, had maneuvered the United States into the World War. On proving its central assumptions, the estimate continues, the committee expected to give America a leftward push toward socialism and secure passage of legislation to assure America's isolation in the event of a new general war. To achieve its grand purpose, the committee, under the relentless leadership of Chairman Nye, intimidated witnesses and ran roughshod over the rules of evidence, *i.e.*, conducted "a ruthless investigation." What was worse, the Nye Committee, if failing to move the country to the left, succeeded in its purpose of stirring isolationist impulses and encouraging anti-militarism in the United States at a time when the American republic should have been standing forthrightly against the aggression of Italy, Japan, and Germany.

Like other historical estimates, that pertaining to the Nye Committee contains a measure of truth. But the estimate is faulty on several counts, and the image of the munitions inquiry which results from it is transparently distorted.

It is true that Engelbrecht and Seldes and the spokesmen (and spokeswomen) of those peace organizations who roused Americans against the munitions industry were decidedly leftist in political orientation and viewed the alleged evils of the arms trade as proof of the rottenness of capitalism. Still, the munitions investigation, particularly in its early stages, received support from quarters not usually considered radical. The *Wall Street Journal,* in September 1934, while defending the work of the Nye Committee, declared of the international munitions trade: "It is a vicious system which both admits and tempts men to the commercial development of bad blood among neighboring peoples." Several months later the *Chicago Journal of Commerce* contended that "history has shown that the activities of munitions makers in times of peace are an important cause of war."

As for the committee, Stephen Raushenbush and some members of the investigative staff, including Alger Hiss, were opponents of big business and probably viewed the munitions inquiry as an instrument for moving the American republic in the general direction of socialism. Then observers of the Washington political scene often labeled Nye as an agrarian radical, and Senator Bone had an obvious affinity for socialist ideas. But Senator Pope was nothing more leftist than a faithful adherent of the New Deal (and few historians of the present day are inclined to view the New Deal as particularly radical). Clark's views were rather ill-defined. Suspicious of big business, he nonetheless looked on economic change with misgiving. In the main, Clark was a caustic man still consumed with bitterness because Woodrow Wilson had snatched the presidential nomination from his father, Beauchamp "Champ" Clark, at the Democratic National Convention in 1912. The other three members of the Nye Committee—Barbour, George, and Vandenberg—were well to the right of the center of the American political spectrum.

What of the committee's recommendations and hearing room behavior? Did they betray a leftist bias? The Nye Committee made only two recommendations which one might consider radical or leftist—and in both instances the obvious goal was advancement of the cause of peace, not socialism. Over the dissent of three of its seven members the committee recommended nationalization of the munitions industry (as did legions of non-radical Americans in the 1930s) and supported the drastic Flynn Plan for eliminating large economic returns in time of war. Otherwise the questions asked and statements made by senators and staff members during hearings were remarkably free of anti-capitalist overtones. Even Alger Hiss, about whose "dad-bum" questions Carter Glass later complained, was a model of restraint and propriety on the two or three occasions when he interrogated witnesses, and asked nothing which seemed intended to discredit America's economic and social system.

The contention that the Nye Committee sought to bind the United States to an isolationist foreign policy by proving that J. P. Morgan & Company had maneuvered the United States to war in 1917—and that it succeeded—is a more difficult proposition.

Certainly there is nothing to indicate that when the munitions investigation got underway in 1934 the senators or staff members viewed it as an instrument for prompting legislation committing the American republic to noninvolvement—or isolation—when other countries went to war. At that time, as mentioned, America's policy vis-à-vis belligerents was not a pressing issue. That Senator Pope, one of Capitol Hill's most outspoken proponents of collective security via cooperation with the League of Nations, was an active and enthusiastic member of the committee in the inquiry's early stages is illustrative of the fact that few if any people thought exposure of the merchants of death might have large implications regarding America's relations with belligerents. But then, in early 1935, such relations commanded new attention, and the Nye Committee at Roosevelt's curious behest set about to examine the question of neutrality. To that end it announced its intention to investigate economic influences on America's policies toward Europe's belligerents in 1914–1917. Before the committee could conduct those hearings, so matters turned out, Congress in August 1935 passed the Neutrality Act, an isolationist measure providing for a mandatory embargo on arms shipments to belligerents, authorizing the President to prohibit Americans to sail on belligerent ships, restricting use of American ports by belligerent submarines, and establishing the National Munitions Control Board to license exporters and importers of munitions. When interrogation of J. P. Morgan and his partners finally took place, in January–February 1936, neutrality again was front and center as an issue—because of the imminent expiration of the Neutrality Act of 1935—and it was apparent that the Nye Committee's majority (Bone, Clark, Nye, and Vandenberg) was counting on those hearings to strengthen arguments for a more stringent neutrality law when the existing act expired.

And so one comes to the question: In what measure was the munitions investigation responsible for the impulses which resulted in the isolationist neutrality legislation of the mid-1930s? A precise answer of course is impossible, but it is difficult to escape the conclusion that historians and other observers have exaggerated the Nye Committee's responsibility for the neutrality laws of 1935–1937.

The overbearing commitment of Americans to peace—the veritable obsession of many Americans with the idea of peace at almost any price—surely antedated the Nye Committee. The committee held no hearings and issued no manifestoes on the subject of neutrality before passage of the first Neutrality Act of the period, that of 1935, and it was news in August 1935 that war in East Africa was imminent, not any revelations or appeals by the Nye Committee, that triggered the activity on Capitol Hill which resulted in that neutrality legislation. Then the Neutrality Act of 1936, enacted after the committee's hearings on economic influences on foreign policy in 1914–1917—hearings which one might have expected to exert large influence on subsequent legislation—fell so far short of the goals of the so-called Nye-Clark Neutrality Bloc that for a time Nye and his cohorts considered a filibuster to prevent its passage. Still, the Nye Committee, when doing nothing at all with the question of neutrality and concentrating only on munitions makers, shipbuilders, and war profits, was stirring America's will to peace, and it was the will to peace which produced the neutrality legislation of 1935–1937. The publicity which they received in connection with the munitions inquiry, moreover, probably strengthened the appeals of Bone, Clark, Nye, and Vandenberg when they spoke out in behalf of the legislation of 1935 (although that publicity did not prove sufficient to carry their ideas in 1936).

Fortunately the "ruthless investigation" charge against the Nye Committee is more easily disposed of: it is categorically untrue. In the opening hearings in September 1934 the committee showed a lack of sensitivity for the requirements of diplomacy when it exhibited documents implicating several Latin American dignitaries and King George V of Great Britain in assorted munitions dealings. In December 1934 it irresponsibly intimated that Du Pont had taken a profit of 39,321 percent in connection with construction and operation of the Old Hickory smokeless powder plant in 1918. In February 1935 Senator Clark, in a moment of pique, exhibited an unauthorized State Department document, and in January 1936 Nye and Clark referred to a sensitive British memorandum of 1917 (which memorandum, more embarrassing to admirers of President Wilson than to the British, then found its way into the press, probably by way of a member of the committee staff).

Otherwise, the committee in its handling of documents displayed a surprising sense of responsibility and admirable restraint, the more so in view of the high emotional state of Americans at the time when they pondered munitions makers, war profiteering, and neutrality. Chastened by its indiscretions of September 1934, particularly that of bringing the name of the King of England into the hearings, the committee worked out an arrangement with the State Department when setting about to scour the files of J. P. Morgan & Company for evidence pertaining to Wall Street's relations with the Allied governments in 1914–1917 and any attempts by investment bankers to influence American policy: The Department would maintain custody of Morgan's files during their scrutiny by committee investigators and the committee would publish no document without a State Department stamp and release. When the committee, in January 1936, found interesting wartime correspondence in the files of the National City Bank, whose records were not covered by the foregoing agreement, Chairman Nye thought it appropriate to secure the State Department's approval before using the material. He behaved in similar fashion a short time later when investigators turned up sensitive documents in the files of Colt's Patent Fire Arms Company.

As for treatment of witnesses, the Nye Committee's behavior was generally exemplary. On occasion a question or comment by Senator Clark, who had a reputation for public rudeness, contained a barb, and occasionally Senator Bone's temper seemed to rise, as during the aforementioned exchange with William Shearer. But there were no personal attacks after the fashion of "Joe" McCarthy's denunciation of Brigadier General Ralph Zwicker in 1954, when McCarthy accused Zwicker of being ignorant and a disgrace to the military uniform, or Senator John McClellan's badgering of union officials in hearings a few years later. Queried by the author in the latter 1950s, such Nye Committee witnesses as Charles W. Deeds of Pratt & Whitney, William S. Carpenter of Du Pont, George Whitney and Russell C. Leffingwell of J. P. Morgan, and William Flook of New York Ship, writing in a latter-day climate of opinion hostile to the committee when it would have been credible to claim intimidation, were surprisingly uncritical of the committee's behavior in commenting on their appearances at the munitions hearings. Flook said simply that "my treatment by the Committee was entirely courteous and unobjectionable." During interrogation of J. P. Morgan and his partners the *Wall Street Journal* observed that "on the whole, the Committee has not been too flagrantly unfair to any of them, the senatorial point of view being what it is." The committee allowed witnesses to make statements and exhibit documents even faintly relevant to the inquiry, and gave them ample opportunity to defend or explain their actions. Indeed it tended to treat representatives of such corporate giants as Du Pont and Morgan with considerable deference.

Contrary to an impression implicit in most commentaries on the munitions investigation, Senator Nye, moreover, was a model chairman—in the hearing room and during the committee's executive sessions. As the Du Pont public relations department reported in a memorandum to the author in 1958, "the Senator did not carry his platform eloquence over into the hearing room, at least during du Pont's appearance. By comparison, his conduct of the hearings was restrained. . . ." In the hearing room Nye spoke infrequently. Sometimes he interjected a question or opinion, or made a statement, but only rarely did he cross-examine. On occasion he cautioned that the committee must defer judgment until all evidence was in. During a dispute between Raushenbush and Thomas W. Lamont over the cause of American entry in the World War he interrupted: "Let us have a little agreement here that before we undertake, as members of the committee, spokesmen for the committee, or as witnesses, to declare whether or not it was the submarine which got us into the war, or industry and business and banking, that we will take the record of the documents on the subject into consideration, and then after that record has been completed, we can all have our say as to what the real cause was." When J. P. Morgan insisted on presenting a statement at the start of his appearance before the committee, Nye permitted him to do so, then interjected: "Mr. Morgan, thus far I fail to see that this is in anywise responsive to the question that was asked. However we will not quibble about this. Proceed with your statement."

But alas, the Nye of the hearing room was not the Nye of the speaker's rostrum. In the hearing room the senator was a gentleman, courteous and restrained, cognizant of his responsibilities. When he sat down before a radio microphone or, better still, stood face-to-face before a throng of admiring partisans, he cast restraint and responsibility to the winds and became a raving demagogue. An audience in truth seemed to do for him what the magical potion did to Doctor Jekyll. To make matters worse, he repeatedly intimated in 1934–1936 that the munitions investigation had substantiated his heady and extravagant assertions about arms makers, war profits, and neutrality. In most instances that simply was not true. Thus Nye, the model chairman in the hearing room, sorely abused his responsibility as chairman of the committee by rhetorical pyrotechnics. More than that, he contributed to the Nye Committee's latter-day reputation for ruthlessness. At least that was the estimate of Raushenbush, who many years later proposed to this author that historians and other observers, not inclined to work their way through 13,750 pages of testimony and exhibits published by the committee, had taken note of the chairman's speeches and concluded that they were indicative of the way the committee functioned. What prompted Nye to Jekyll-Hyde behavior? Perhaps one of the new psycho–historians now coming into vogue can answer that question. Raushenbush found an explanation in a mixture of Nye's feelings of personal inadequacy and his love of the roar of the crowd. By launching oratorical broadsides against the Du Ponts and Morgans the senator could generate roars from his audiences which crowded out feelings of inadequacy and persuaded him that he was a man of importance and courage leading people in the good fight for peace.

Whatever its investigative restraint and hearing room demeanor, did the Nye Committee stay within the bounds of its authority as a legislative investigating committee?

As shown elsewhere in the present series of books, the investigative authority of Congress was established in the first years of the Republic, and received reinforcement six years before the Nye Committee began its investigation when the Supreme Court in a unanimous opinion ruled that "the power of inquiry—with process to enforce it—is an essential and appropriate auxiliary to the legislative function." According to the justices, "a legislative body cannot legislate wisely or effectively in the absence of information respecting the conditions which the legislation is intended to affect or change; and where the legislative body does not itself possess the requisite information—which not infrequently is true—recourse must be had to others who do possess it." In the view of Woodrow Wilson, writing in the 1880s, enlightenment in the interest of wise and effective legislation was not the only justification for congressional investigations: "It is the proper duty of a representative body to look diligently into every affair of government and to talk much about what it sees. It is meant to be the eyes and the voice, and to embody the wisdom and will of its constituents. Unless Congress have and use every means of acquainting itself with the acts and the disposition of the administrative agents of the government, the country must be helpless to learn how it is being served; and unless Congress both scrutinize these things and sift them by every form of discussion, the country must remain in embarrassing, crippling ignorance of the very affairs which it is most important that it should understand and direct."

At the time of the Nye Committee's investigation, then, nobody seemed to doubt that committees of Congress had authority to conduct inquiries—and had authority to subpoena witnesses and documents—to gather information required for legislative discussion, serve as a brake on the Executive branch of the government, and alert the country to abuses and dangers.

When the munitions investigation got underway in 1934, as mentioned, no political figure or other observer of national affairs spoke out that the Nye Committee might abuse its authority. Nor did the committee later come under criticism on the ground that it had violated that authority. Even Senators Connally and Glass, in their crude assault on Senator Nye in January 1936 for his remarks about former President Wilson, did not charge the committee with ignoring constitutional restraints on congressional investigations. In those frenzied times of New Deal activity, of course, committees of Congress were continually investigating this or that aspect of national affairs, and in light of the work of the assorted committees and subcommittees which had exposed Teapot Dome and Pecora's uncovering of the manipulations of Wall Street, congressional investigating committees stood in high repute as instruments for promoting the public good. Unlike in the 1950s, in the aftermath of the nefarious activities of "Joe" McCarthy, there was no large opinion that the activities of congressional committees ought to be curtailed.

In retrospect it seems fair to say that the Nye Committee functioned in accord with the constitutional prerogatives of congressional investigating committees, and one might add parenthetically that Senator Nye and his colleagues never trampled on the constitutional rights of witnesses as subsequent congressional investigating committees were accused of doing. As if guided by the Supreme Court's opinion of 1927, the committee in every aspect of its investigation sought to prepare a foundation for possible legislation. In its study of the munitions industry it hoped to determine the desirability of nationalizing the munitions industry, and if a majority of the committee was persuaded in advance of the desirability and was seeking reinforcement of arguments in favor of nationalization, the committee in no way obstructed evidence and testimony supporting arguments against nationalization. In its inquiry of the shipbuilding industry the committee tried to determine if shipbuilders, in addition to being guilty of a variety of sins attributed to other producers of armament, required stricter control, via legislation, to prevent such abuses as collusive bidding for naval contracts. In its study of war profits the committee sought to determine what—if any—legislation should be enacted to restrict economic returns when America was at war, and to that end accepted arguments which opposed as well as supported its own views. In its investigation of economic circumstances surrounding America's entry in the World War in 1917 the committee contributed to the current congressional debate over neutrality legislation. One may add that the Nye Committee seldom if ever strayed from its legislative purpose. Documents exhibited and questions asked consistently seemed intended to enlighten Congress and the public about conditions which might require legislative attention, and in many instances sought to elicit information and ideas on the specifics of possible congressional enactments.

The Nye Committee, however, may have stretched its mandate under S. Res. 206.

The resolution clearly authorized investigation of the munitions industry and war profits, and it would seem that the authority to study the munitions industry gave the senators latitude to examine all aspects of naval shipbuilding. Whether it sanctioned the study of financial relationships and neutrality is questionable. Chairman Key Pittman of the Foreign Relations Committee certainly thought neutrality outside the Nye Committee's authority, and early in 1935 Senator Vandenberg, a sort of Midwestern windbag in the view of some people, but a man who during the munitions inquiry distinguished himself by judicious comments and questions, said that war profits were the only part of the neutrality question within the committee's jurisdiction. But the committee majority, citing Roosevelt's suggestion that the committee consider neutrality, determined to press on; and, on beginning the interrogation of the Morgan partners in January 1936, Chairman Nye quoted from S. Res. 206, including that passage authorizing the committee to investigate "the methods used in promoting or effecting the sale of arms, munitions, or other implements of war." He explained that "our investigations have shown us that, prior to our entry into the World War, a great deal of the sale, distribution, export, and also financing of arms and munitions of war was put into the hands of a few of our banking organizations." Thus it was "in accordance with this duty laid upon us that we propose during the course of the next days to examine into and secure information from witnesses regarding the matters which we were directed to investigate in this paragraph which I have just read." Whatever the merits of Nye's logic, nobody challenged the committee's authority to conduct that aspect of its inquiry, perhaps because there was so much interest in the question of the investment bankers and neutrality in 1914–1917, the more so in light of the debate on neutrality legislation then underway on Capitol Hill.

V

How does one, finally, assess the work of the Nye Committee? From its own perspective the committee must have viewed the munitions investigation as having come to little. Congress did not even consider, much less vote, nationalization of the arms industry, passed no legislation to restrict profits in time of war, and ignored two bills urged by the committee to prevent collusive bidding and limit profits by private shipbuilders on naval contracts. If Congress approved isolationist neutrality legislation, it turned aside the committee's contention that, when a neutral country becomes "an auxiliary arsenal" for foodstuffs and other nonmilitary supplies as well as arms for one set of belligerents (as the United States had become for the Allies in 1914–1917), it inevitably becomes an object of the military and naval strategy of the other belligerents—and when this happens any "neutral's" eventual involvement in the war becomes a virtual certainty. The neutrality laws passed during the period, as a result, were not as inclusive (or isolationist) as the committee majority thought they should be. About all the Nye Committee could show for its efforts, so the senators must have thought, was establishment of the National Munitions Control Board, an innocuous agency to watch over the arms trade (included in a provision tacked on to the Neutrality Act of 1935); a provision in the Neutrality Act of 1936 prohibiting loans to belligerents (already prohibited for most practical purposes under the Johnson Debt Default Act of 1934); and a provision in the Relief Appropriation Bill of 1935 that "no part of the appropriation shall be expended for munitions, warships, or military or naval matériel."

As matters turned out, however, the Nye Committee may have registered some achievements not readily apparent at the time. It inadvertently debunked a couple of notions which were distracting Americans in the mid-1930s: the proposition that American arms makers were part of an international munitions conspiracy, and that Wall Street had engineered America's entry in the World War. If Americans still faced the agonizing question of their place in world affairs—particularly their responsibilities when aggressor states went on rampages—they could face that question without having their thoughts muddled by arguments about merchants of death and Wall Street manipulations. It may then be that the committee's study of war profits, which touched the larger issue of wartime mobilization, saved the American people a great deal of money in the Second World War. The first federal price administrator during the War, Leon Henderson, at any rate thought it did. Henderson wrote the author in 1962 that "undoubtedly the Nye Committee findings helped us at OPA [the Office of Price Administration]. . . . I cannot put a dollar value on them—tho it was *high*."

Against its achievements or credits one of course must balance the Nye Committee's debits, notably its contribution to America's isolationist mood of the 1930s—assuming that isolationism was bad for the country and for the world at *that* time. Whether the committee's credits outweigh its debits will remain a matter of individual judgment.

BIBLIOGRAPHY

The reader who wishes to go beyond the present essay in examining the Nye Committee investigation might begin with my book *In Search of Peace: The Senate Munitions Inquiry, 1934–36* (Baton Rouge, 1963). The volume remains the only book-length study of the munitions investigation. For a somewhat different perspective, *e.g.*, the author believes the Nye Committee had larger responsibility for prompting isolationism in America in the 1930s than I do, there are the two chapters on the munitions inquiry in Wayne S. Cole's excellent book, *Senator Gerald P. Nye and American Foreign Relations* (Minneapolis, 1962). Cole's book has the additional advantage of placing the munitions investigation in the larger context of Nye's entire career in the Senate.

The more enterprising reader might wish to look at the committee hearings and report. When published the Nye Committee hearings and exhibits, in forty parts, filled 13,750 pages. Part 40, in a single volume, is an index of hearings, exhibits, and documents. More manageable is the report. Published in stages during 1935 and 1936, the report comprises seven thin volumes, and much of it consists of hearings and documents which the committee considered especially important. One might also examine the accounts of hearings which appeared in the *New York Times*. Unfortunately the reporters of the *Times* as well as other newsmen, if they caught the drama of the hearing room, seemed more intent on securing headlines than were the senators, and as a result their accounts sometimes emphasized documents and testimony to which the committee attached little importance.

There are of course some special books which might be of interest, notably Helmuth C. Engelbrecht and Frank C. Hanighen, *Merchants of Death* (New York, 1934), George Seldes, *Iron, Blood and Profits* (New York and London, 1934), and Philip Noel-Baker, *Private Manufacture of Armaments* (London, 1937). Then there is Dorothy Detzer's memoir *Appointment on the Hill* (New York, 1948) in which the author set out her recollections of the Nye inquiry.

PERTINENT DOCUMENTS

"The Marine Follies: Glorifying the Dance of Death Inspired by Fanatics Who Worship Self-Inflicted Torture" by William B. Shearer, 1935

Statement of Bernard M. Baruch before War Policies Commission, March 6, 1931

Sir Charles Craven to Henry R. Carse, October 30, 1932 and January 6, 1933

"Arms and the Men," March 1934

"The Profits of War and Preparedness," Radio Address by Senator Gerald P. Nye, April 10, 1934

Message of Franklin D. Roosevelt to the Senate, May 18, 1934

"Arms Manufacturers and the Public" by "F." July 1934

Senate Resolution 206, September 4, 1934

New York Times Report, September 2, 1934

Testimony on "Cooky Pushers" of the State Department, September 13, 1934

Memorandum of Lammot Du Pont to Gerald P. Nye, November 14, 1934

The McSwain Bill, January 3, 1935

"The Crusading Mr. Nye" by E. Francis Brown, February 1935

Report of War Policies Commission, March 5, 1935

Extract of Testimony of William B. Shearer on Shipbuilding Industry, March 12, 1935

Explanation by Bernard M. Baruch of "Price Ceiling Plan," March 27, 1935

Memoranda of Joseph C. Green, Division of Western European Affairs, March 30, April 10, and 12, 1935

New York Times Report, April 16, 1935

New York Times Report, April 17, 1935

Summary Findings and Recommendations of Nye Committee on Shipbuilding Industry, June 1935

Statement of J. P. Morgan on Financial Operations at the Outbreak of War, January 7, 1936

Senate Debate over Nye Committee's Work, January 18, 1936

Summary Findings and Recommendations of Nye Committee on Munitions Industry, February 24, 1936

W. C. Carpenter, E. I. DuPont De Nemours and Co., to John Edward Wiltz, December 24, 1958

Dorothy Detzer Denny to John Edward Wiltz, September 26, 1960

The Dies Committee
1938

Life magazine

Life magazine

top: *Martin Dies, founding chairman of the House Committee on Un-American Activities, developed exposure-by-committee into a profession.* bottom: *Anti-Nazi, anti-church Red propaganda exhibit at a Dies Committee hearing.*

The Dies Committee 1938

by Michael Wreszin

From the passage of the Alien and Sedition laws in 1789 to the mid-twentieth century attempt to outlaw the Communist party, House and Senate committees have sporadically turned their attention to the activities of individuals and organizations charged with subversion. In 1919, during what is popularly known as the "Red Scare," a Senate committee was created to investigate the alleged propaganda activities of the brewery industry. Known as the Overman Committee, it quickly turned the main focus of its attention from German to Bolshevik propaganda. This shift from concern with the danger from the Right to that from the Left previewed the circumstances surrounding the creation of the Dies Committee, which was presumably fathered to expose Nazi and anti-Semitic propaganda, but quickly turned its attention to Communist and leftist activities. The Overman Committee was the first congressional committee to investigate alleged Communist activity, for even at that time it was customary for many Americans to link Bolshevism with "pro-Germanism" and to see both as alien, authoritarian ideologies.

Official concern with the Bolshevik menace died quickly in the 1920s and was replaced by a virulent racist xenophobia. Catholics, Jews, and blacks were lumped together with immigrants as a growing threat to the nation's Anglo-Saxon heritage. Demand for immigration restriction and the continued deportation of alien radicals occupied the minds of congressional defenders of Americanism. With the beginning of the Depression these racist and nativist anxieties were stimulated by a search for a scapegoat to explain the failures of the American system.

In May 1930 the House of Representatives was suddenly alarmed by New York Police Commissioner Grover Whalen's charge that the Russian Armtorg Trading Corporation was engaged in Communist propaganda. New York's aristocratic Republican representative, Hamilton Fish, was quickly appointed to chair the Special Committee to Investigate Communism in the United States. Fish, with an impeccable genealogy, was an appropriate choice to defend America against imported ideologies, but his direction of the committee revealed his scant knowledge of the subject. Although astonished by the very existence of avowed Communists in America, he treated the witnesses with the courtesy expected of a gentleman with his credentials. Congressman Carl Bachmann of West Virginia, on the other hand, played a role that became standard on such committees. Described by the hostile literary critic, Edmund Wilson, as the perfect caricature of the "lower type of Congressman . . . pot gutted . . . greasy looking . . . pig eyes . . . ," Bachmann's questions were designed to prove that communism was a weird belief held primarily by immigrants and other outcasts with no capacity to grasp the virtues of Americanism. His solution was to deport alien radicals and increase restrictions on immigration.

The findings of the Fish Committee were a potpourri of conflicting assertions and drastic recommendations. While it discovered that there were only 12,000 registered Communist party members in the United States, the committee estimated that there were also between 500,000 and 600,000 Communists and Communist sympathizers here. The American Civil Liberties Union was declared a bulwark of communism, passing itself off as a defender of the Bill of Rights. American labor unions, it charged, were Communist-infiltrated and in New York alone Communist youth camps were said to turn out 15,000 party members each year.

What should be done? The committee recommended outlawing the Communist party, registering all aliens determined to be radicals, and censoring the mail service to thwart publication of Communist propaganda. It also requested that the State Department obtain permission for Treasury agents to go to Russia to investigate their use of forced labor—a peculiarly quixotic proposal given America's continued resistance to recognition of the Soviet government.

The report and its recommendations were ridiculed by even the relatively conservative *Outlook* as both "stupid and dangerous." One critic charged that the "proposals of the Fish Committee may be far more dangerous to liberty and freedom than the pitiful handful of Communists in the United States have ever been." Fish warned about Communist promotion of class hatred and race mixing, and issued a proclamation asserting that America, with the fairest, most honorable government in the world, must stand ever vigilant against this alien menace.

This was the national atmosphere when Martin Dies came to Congress from Orange County, Texas, in 1931. He was to make it his mission each year to present bills labeled "Aliens, for the deportation of certain," or "Immigration, to further restrict." He soon gained a seat on the Committee on Immigration and Naturalization, a hotbed of nativist and anti-radical sentiment. In May 1932 Dies's bill, HR 12044, for the expulsion and exclusion of alien Communists, passed in the House over the vigorous opposition of Congressman Fiorello LaGuardia. It was, however, tabled in the Senate under the leadership of Robert La Follette, jr.

In these initial years Dies was not taken seriously. He was known for his leadership of the House "Demagogues Club," which was made up of younger members like himself who sarcastically pledged to vote for any appropriation bill and against any tax measure. Making a great display at roll call, they would dash into the chamber and register their votes to the accompaniment of loud guffaws and clowning antics. This "good ole boy" contingent of aspiring Dixie Demagogues was tolerated with general good humor. Dies appeared to be a simple country lawyer from Texas who was glad to be on the federal payroll and was quick to admit that it was "better than working." Marquis Childs, an astute observer of the congressional beat, recalled that he had never encountered a more cynical man who, despite his display of good humor, seemed to have nothing but "utter scorn for the whole institution of Congress."

How Dies became obsessively devoted to the issue of subversive activities is open to speculation. Childs suggests it may simply have been the developing political climate of the 1930s, the "frustration of obscurity and neglect," or some "gnawing force beneath the outer surface of cynicism" that awakened a latent zealotry which fed on itself and was encouraged by others. Allan Michie and Frank Ryhlick, in their study *Dixie Demagogues,* attribute it to a self-serving ambition aimed at pleasing Texas oil and utility interests opposed to all New Deal regulatory measures.

As a member of the Committee on Immigration and Naturalization, Dies soon encountered Samuel Dickstein, who represented a largely Jewish immigrant constituency on New York's lower East Side. Dickstein was devoted to the fight against anti-Semitism in extremist organizations which were encouraged by the rise of Hitler. If Martin Dies was to become an authority on Trojan horses designed to deceive God-fearing Americans, he found the right man for his purpose in this rabbi's son. He used Dickstein's concern with right wing propaganda groups as a cover to launch an assault on the entire spectrum of the Left in America and to smear the New Deal with a red brush. It was a shrewd political manipulation which was aided by the increasingly conservative congressional leadership.

In January 1934 Dickstein offered a resolution calling for an investigation of Nazi activities in the United States. After a rousing debate, during which opponents of the bill charged Dickstein with tarnishing the image of decent German Americans, the bill passed. Congressman John McCormack of Massachusetts was appointed chairman and Dickstein vice chairman of the investigating committee.

In light of subsequent investigations of subversive activity, the work of the McCormack-Dickstein Committee was relatively sane and judicious. It concentrated on such organizations as the German American Bund and the Friends of New Germany, but it also reviewed the evidence on communism gathered by the Fish Committee. It heard testimony from Earl Browder and

James Ford, two high officials of the American Communist party, and concluded that both Fascist organizations and the Communist party served the interests of foreign governments. Neither, however, presented an immediate threat, but both were potential dangers to the country.

The committee's procedures were unique in that all witnesses were interviewed first in executive sessions before undergoing public hearings, thereby eliminating wild charges and acrimonious debate. The committee retained the services of Thomas Hardwick, who had previously defended Communists during the Gastonia strike litigation, as its counsel. Later committees would have hardly found such a man acceptable.

The most significant legislation to emerge from the committee's recommendations were the McCormack Foreign Agents Registration Act of 1938 and a bill which permitted congressional committees investigating subversive activity to subpoena witnesses when conducting hearings outside of the District of Columbia. But before this legislation had been passed, McCormack, whose committee had been charged with having produced no legislation, presented a forceful argument that became the predominant justification for many subsequent investigating committees. McCormack asserted that legislation should not be the cardinal criterion for measuring the accomplishments of such committees. Their major purpose was to alert the public to an important problem and aid in the formation of public opinion. Dies was later to argue that "simple exposure was the most effective weapon" against subversive activities. "When the light of day is brought to bear we can trust public sentiment to do the rest." This was indeed a prophetic analysis.

Historically, there were three purposes for congressional investigating committees: to obtain information that would assist Congress in designing wise legislation; to supervise the Executive branch to see that the laws were faithfully executed; and, finally, to serve as a national forum—that is, to inform as well as shape public opinion. While the Supreme Court had only affirmed the first of these three purposes, it had generally agreed that the second and third were legitimate functions. The third, over the years, had broadened to mean the influencing of public opinion by the circulation of certain facts and ideas. This often became the sole defense of a committee's *raison d'être*.

In a defense of congressional investigations Woodrow Wilson pointed to the dire need for "instruction and guidance in political affairs" which the people might receive from a body which kept "all national concerns suffused in a broad light of discussion." He insisted that the "informing function of Congress should be preferred to its legislative function." The potential to abuse this "informing function" was quickly realized by astute politicians, sundry demagogues, and their victims.

During the twenties and thirties liberal reformers supported a host of congressional investigating committees which served to mobilize support for progressive social and economic legislation. In 1924 when Congress was investigating the moneyed interests and the Harding scandals, Felix Frankfurter, a champion of civil liberties, insisted that "the power of the investigative process should be left untrammeled." When conservatives attacked the committees as star chamber proceedings, liberals insisted on the "peoples' right to know."

It is not without significance, however, that the first hearings of the Dies Committee began in August 1938, just one day after what appeared to be the final hearings of the La Follette Committee, which concentrated on the violation of civil liberties by union-busting corporations. New Dealers were soon to discover that their effective weapon of securing favorable public opinion could also be used by a belligerent Congress to attack the New Deal Administration. Telford Taylor observes, in his fine history of investigating committees, that during the late thirties the "chickens came home to roost."

Throughout the Depression there had been a preoccupation with what Alistair Cooke called the "universal hobby of looking for a scapegoat." Conspiracy theories have not been the eminent domain of paranoid rural populists, as some recent historians have suggested. The liberal supporters of the New Deal, in their search for a simple explanation for the breakdown of the economy, had been delighted with the exposure of the "money changers," the "merchants of death" in the munitions industry, and the "economic royalists" of the corporate hierarchy. But despite the exposure of these villains, the Depression continued and soon the sophisticated "brain trusters" and social engineers of the New Deal bureaucracy found themselves in the rogue's gallery of scapegoats that marked the decade.

Southern Democrats, in league with vengeful Republicans, began to publicly voice their contempt for the wild schemes of the "lunatic professors." Others suggested a Machiavellian power play under the guise of fraudulent humanitarian rhetoric. From there it was only a short step to the old conservative charge that the New Deal program was a simple masquerade covering an alien and un-American conspiracy.

The Communist party line in the late thirties lent weight to this argument. During the earlier hard-line period, the party had reviled Roosevelt as a "social fascist" and the New Deal as a sugarcoated pill of reaction. This had guaranteed the party's isolation from the main thrust of American reform. But with the rise of powerful Fascist forces in Italy and Germany, the party had somersaulted and embraced democratic reform in its enthusiasm for a popular front against fascism. Now communism was defined by party spokesmen as nothing but twentieth century Americanism, and Communists as the "sons and daughters of the American Revolution." Many American reformers had been fascinated by the "Soviet experiment" and saw in Russia a unity of purpose and collective social consciousness lacking in the United States. It was not difficult to accept the Soviet Union or even American Communists as crusaders against Hitler and fascism abroad and bigotry and reaction at home. This apparent agreement between New Deal reformers and Communists on a program of social and economic reforms gave sustenance to the growing anti-New Deal coalition bent upon exposing the New Deal as the vehicle for an alien radical ideology.

By 1937 Martin Dies was on his way to becoming a leader in the anti-New Deal coalition. He had opposed the wages and hours legislation and had repeatedly called for an investigation of the "Communist instigated" sit-down strikes. Vice President Garner, who was beginning to make a sharp distinction between traditional Democrats and New Dealers, encouraged the young congressman. Big, boyish—an American to the core—Dies would make a perfect standard-bearer in defense of purity. He had all the qualifications—a fine-honed contempt for big city sophistication, a hatred for big labor lawlessness, and a suspicion of foreigners of any kind. In frequent speeches he recalled the example of his congressman father, who had bolted the party during the fight against the League of Nations because Wilson had been corrupted by "foreign advisors." Dies announced that he would always place the country before the party in a battle for true Americanism.

By the spring of 1938 the fortunes of the Roosevelt Administration were approaching their lowest point. The abortive attempt at court reform had seriously strained liberal loyalties and the sit-down strikes which accompanied a downturn in the economy had undercut the President's authority in Congress. Democratic ranks were bitterly divided and Roosevelt had let it be known that he planned a purge of backsliding party members in the upcoming congressional election campaign. "Nothing," wrote the historian William Leuchtenburg, "divulged the sourish spirit of 1938 more than the creation of the House Committee on Un-American Activities."

Dies's bill (HR 282) had been in the works for nearly a year when it came up for debate again on May 26, 1938. It contained almost the same wording and provisons as the previous Dickstein resolutions for the investigation of subversive activities which had failed to pass. But Dies, according to Robert Strippling, had, unlike Dickstein, the tacit support of the House leadership and had been requested by the vice president to gather support for an Un-American Activities Committee that would have "substance and specific duties."

Contrary to the assumption of Walter Goodman, who labeled the Dies Committee "Dickstein's Monster," there is little irony in the bill initially proposed by Dickstein that resulted in the Dies Committee. That appears to have been the plan from the start, and partisans on both sides were aware of it. The son of a Russian rabbi would hardly be a fit leader for champions of American nativism. Nor is it likely that the Administration spokesmen in Congress had been caught napping as another analyst suggests. In the past, Roosevelt had been able to inspire friendly congressional committees and thwart hostile probes, but those days were gone. The Administration had lost much of its control of congressional leadership, and this had encouraged the ambitions of Martin Dies. New Dealers may have underestimated the subsequent power and popularity of the committee, but the debate of May 26 must have warned them of the ultimate designs held by the bill's supporters. Dickstein's initial anti-Nazi preoccupations had only served as a shallow cover for a committee with much broader political ambitions.

Necessary support had been mustered well in advance, so Dies was able to assume a moderate and diplomatic role during the debate. To the charge that such a committee might endanger individual civil liberties, Dies eloquently voiced his own fears. He warned that any "legislative attempt to prevent un-American activities . . . might jeopardize fundamental rights far more important than the objectives we seek." But that danger could be avoided simply by the way such a committee was chaired. Publicity-seeking politicians or sensation-mongers must, of course, be barred from serving on such a committee. This was a reference to Samuel Dickstein, who had been labeled as such by opponents of his anti-Nazi assaults.

In an indirect way, the public debate made several things clear to the politicians. Dies was assuring his colleagues that Dickstein would have no place on his committee. The exchange between Dies and John Cochran over appropriations for the committee revealed that Cochran understood that Dies was to be the chairman of the committee. And, as both John Rankin and J. Parnell Thomas had made it clear that no committee with Dickstein on it would receive their support, Dies was more than conciliatory on that point. He assured skeptical critics that the committee could achieve its modest goals during the remainder of the year and that it would not need a lavish appropriation. Evidence of Dies's calculated dissembling clearly supports Marquis Childs's opinion that the case history of Martin Dies is a story of "ambition, by Shakespeare, out of True Story Magazine."

If Dies took on the mantle of judicious statesmanship, a far cry from the earlier demagogue jeering at House protocol, the more flamboyant rhetoric demanded in such rituals was supplied by the traditional New Deal haters. Congressman Taylor of Tennessee was allotted an inordinate amount of time to defend the resolution, most of which he used to wrap himself in the flag, embrace red-blooded Americanism, and denounce the defilers of virtue who had only recently painted Plymouth Rock an unholy red. Scoundrels of this stripe, he shouted, should be "hunted down like rattlesnakes and kicked out of the country." Continuing on, he attacked Francis Perkins and the Department of Labor for their coddling of immigrants who "cared nothing about America."

J. Parnell Thomas pointed out that the Communist party was a greater threat than Nazi organizations since, according to his research, Communists outnumbered Nazis by more than five to one. Worse than both were the Communist-influenced agencies of the federal government; these were the real sources of un-Americanism and *they* must indeed be investigated.

It was left to F. Maury Maverick (D.–Texas), Gerald Boileau (D.–Wisconsin), and John Main Coffee (D.–Washington) to defend civil liberties and the integrity of the New Deal. They ridiculed the "pompous patriotism" of the bill's supporters and the potential spectacle of congressmen "swaggering around the country like inquisitors." The proposed committee was not designed to deal with fundamental problems facing the nation, but was a plot to dismantle the New Deal and harass liberal organizations. What constituted un-Americanism was a question which remained vague and ill defined. Dies argued that un-Americanism was simply the understanding that Americans derived their fundamental and inherent rights not from society or government but "from Almighty God." Maverick retorted that if one were for the wages and hours laws, for free speech, and for a living wage, he was apparently un-American, since these rights came from the determination of the courts and not from God. "Un-American is simply something that somebody else doesn't agree to," he concluded. Representative Harold Knutson (R.–Minnesota) won the prize for brevity. He repeatedly answered the question "What is un-American?" with the single word, "Goosestepping." What his colleagues thought about that is not recorded, but he did know the purpose of the committee. It was just another machination improvised to provide hard-pressed congressmen with "room and board during the summer months."

For all the "ballyhoo and bunk" the tally was an overwhelming 191 to 41 in favor of the resolution. Representative Cochran explained the lop-sided vote for an anti-New Deal measure in a House dominated by Democrats. Newspapers, he observed, would make it clear, if the resolution failed to pass, that the House had declined to investigate subversion. "I do not want to be accused of refusing to vote for legislation to investigate un-American activities." Eugene Lyons's later assertion that the Dies Committee grew out of a tiny congressional faction is simply erroneous. It was not a victory for the "Dies-Dickstein strategy" as Walter Goodman has observed. On the contrary, Dies had used Dickstein as his own Trojan horse upon which to ride the plains of anti-New Deal discontent. Dickstein, the reputed father of the committee, was not even permitted three minutes to address his colleagues at the end of the debate and was denied membership on the committee.

On June 6 Dies was predictably appointed chairman; the committee members, to no one's surprise, were five to two and often six to one against the Roosevelt Administration. Conservative Democrats Dies, Joe Starnes of Alabama, and Harold G. Mosier of Ohio were allied with the two Republicans, J. Parnell Thomas of New Jersey, and Noah Mason of Illinois. Only John J. Dempsey of New Mexico could be described as a New Deal Democrat, albeit a wavering one. The seventh member, Arthur Healey of Massachusetts, was a will o' the wisp Democrat who voted one way and then another but was usually absent at crucial junctures. Jerry Voorhis, the most dependable of New Deal liberals and a constant critic of the committee's conduct, was appointed to replace Mosier when he was defeated in the 1938 elections. Dies would later point to Voorhis's membership on the committee to counter charges of political partisanship.

While some observers persisted in believing the committee's main target was Nazi propaganda, ideologues on the Right and the Left were aware of the reality. Father Coughlin's *Social Justice* assured its readers that the anti-Communist block had backed the committee. The *New Republic* cited Dies's record against the New Deal and concluded that "if the principal energies of Mr. Dies are not given over to hounding Communists, it would be a miracle." But Dies was a knowledgeable performer and, as Walter Goodman has observed, he called upon anti-Nazi testimony intermittently during the investigations "like the comic who pops out between . . . skits with a broom and sets diligently to sweeping the stage until he is kicked off so the show may proceed."

During the months between the creation of the committee and its initial hearings in August 1938 Dies continued in his role with statesmanlike decorum. The committee, he informed the press, would conduct no "three ring circus." As chairman he would not permit "any individual or organization to use the Committee as a sounding board to obtain publicity." Dies's opening statement on August 12, 1938, was perhaps his most magnificent performance; it was as though it had been composed by the American Civil Liberties Union. The committee would conduct all hearings on a "dignified plane" and maintain a "judicial attitude." To the merriment of cynics, he insisted that the committee members held no preconceived views and that their single goal was to discover the truth. All witnesses would be treated with courtesy, fairness, and impartiality. There would be no "character assassination" nor "smearing of innocent people." Reckless charges would not be condoned, as the gathering of facts, not opinions, was the prime objective. "Charges unsupported by facts" were of no value. "It is easy," he warned, "to smear someone's name or reputation and very difficult to repair the damage that has been done." In the investigation of un-American activities it must be kept in mind that "because we do not agree with opinions or philosophies of others does not necessarily make such opinions or philosophies un-American." Too often partisans branded their opponents with a pejorative label rather than engaging in argument with "facts and logic." Conservatives were inclined to call all liberals Communists and "so-called liberals" stigmatized all conservative ideas as fascistic. The committee would take the utmost care to distinguish between what was "un-American and what was no more or less than an honest difference of opinion" on economic, political, or social questions.

Walter Goodman, after a study of subsequent hearings, wondered if "the lady of breeding" who had made such "a dignified entrance into town" had not in fact established "a bawdy house." But the charade was maintained by the first witness, John C. Metcalf, a German-American who had infiltrated the Bund and had gathered a file on their bizarre activities. The stage seemingly set for a thorough investigation of Nazi propaganda, Dies dropped the curtain the following day and introduced John P. Frey, president of the metal trades department of the American Federation of Labor, who immediately launched a sustained attack, charging Communist domination of the rival Congress of Industrial Organization. Here was the committee's response to the Senate's La Follette Committee, which had just ended its hearings on anti-union activities.

In three days, Frey provided 186 pages of testimony and accompanying documentation to support the A. F. of L. allegations. Frey was encouraged to make charges, and few CIO unions of any consequence escaped his condemnation. He named 210 union officials as "Communistic," but supplied little documentation to prove his allegations. He received no challenge from the committee, however. He also charged that the La Follette Committee investigators had close contacts with members of the Communist party; that charge proved to have some substance.

Frey's testimony received much attention in the press. *Communists Rule The CIO, La Follette Committee Linked to Communism* read the bold, black headlines. With roughly eighty-five percent of the press in opposition to the New Deal in 1938, Dies had little trouble monopolizing the front pages. Kenneth Crawford, a seasoned journalist, later declared that it was the "amazing success of the Frey testimony as an experiment in publicity that awakened Dies and his associates to a full realization of the . . . political gold mine they had struck. From Frey on it was catch as catch can with no holds barred."

The committee did not simply depend upon the hearings to produce publicity. It became standard practice for members and the staff to make statements outside of the public hearings; unfortunately, these often appeared in the press as part of the committee's findings. While Frey was testifying on August 14, Edward Sullivan, a committee investigator with a long history of labor spying and anti-Semitic associations, charged Harry Bridges, the longshoreman leader, with responsibility for sixty percent of the labor strife on the West Coast. In spite of his Communistic connections and inclination,

Sullivan continued, Bridges was being protected by an "outstanding official" in the Department of Labor.

Dies did not vouch for the authenticity of the charge. However, he soon joined with those calling for the impeachment of Frances Perkins, who refused to deport Bridges as an alien Communist organizer because the Bridges case was already being litigated in the courts and the Department of Labor had no legal grounds upon which to initiate deportation proceedings. Bridges was hounded by the Dies Committee and later by the whole House, which eventually passed a bill for his deportation on the grounds that it was "in the best interests of the United States." In 1945 Justice Murphy closed the case in Bridges's favor, with the observation that "seldom . . . in the history of the Nation has there been such a concentrated and relentless crusade to deport an individual because he dared exercise the freedom that belongs to him as a human being and that is guaranteed him by the Constitution."

Following Frey the committee offered a platform, in direct contradiction to Dies's opening day statement, to Walter S. Steele, a professional patriot and professional witness who made a career of testifying before subversive activities committees. Steele, claiming to represent 114 patriotic organizations and some 20 million Americans, named 640 organizations as Communistic and claimed that six and a half million Americans were engaged in some form of foreign propagandistic activity. Even the Boy Scouts and Campfire Girls were suspect for their pacifist inclinations and their faith in internationalism.

Dies anticipated the response of critics to such absurd testimony and occasionally interrupted to suggest that the testimony would not be admissible in a court, and thus the committee should be wary of causing injury to innocent persons. Dies's duty done, the witness would then be allowed to continue the harangue, urged on by friendly and leading questions from the committee members.

Day after day it went on. A legionnaire attacked the League for Peace and Freedom as Communist-dominated and committee member Noah Mason, picking up the cue, named eight government officials as members of the organization. J. Parnell Thomas initiated his crusade against the WPA with an assault on the Federal Theatre Project. The committee exposed its racist underpinnings by boldly pursuing the lurid story of a black project worker who had the temerity to ask a woman fellow worker for a date. Sally Saunders, the witness, disclosed that Communist workers "hob-nobbed indiscriminately" with blacks and "threw parties with them left and right." In answer to a question from Joe Starnes, she agreed that "social equality and race merging" were part of the Communist program.

The Frey and Steele testimonies established the general conduct and atmosphere of the hearings for the committee's first year. After the first month Dies violated nearly every code of conduct that he had initially announced. The committee was used as a platform by partisan witnesses, who, with few exceptions, were given free reign to make damaging accusations unsupported by corroborative evidence. If they were friendly witnesses, there was virtually no cross-examination. Committee members would put words into their mouths and urge them on with provocative and leading questions. Testimony which attacked organizations and reputations and offered no effective opportunity for rebuttal was constantly released to the press. Individuals were named and condemned on the basis of simple associations with organizations described as "Communistic." Paul Douglas, John Dewey, Reinhold Niebuhr, even H. L. Mencken, were referred to derogatorily, as the reporters scribbled on. If the hearings themselves failed to produce immediate headlines on any given day, members were free to take to the public podium to make further charges and to capture attention.

The witnesses were either "experts" who filed long, unexamined briefs, or rabid partisans. Particularly acceptable to the committee were disgruntled bureaucrats who had failed to find a home in some New Deal agency and sought an outlet for their animosity. D. A. Saunders of the *Public Opinion Quarterly* concluded in April 1939 that the witnesses had hardly inspired confidence in the investigation. A large number seemed "to have been professed patriots, vigilantes, political stool-pigeons, labor spies, anti-Semites, Nazi sympathizers and even criminals." One grieving member of the press covering the hearing complained that "the mixture of plausible testimony with fantasy, the practice of Committee members putting words in the witnesses' mouths, their almost universal failure to seek development of proof of startling accusations or to develop the backgrounds of possible animus of the accusers, makes covering the inquiry a headache of major proportions." Unfortunately, his conscientious concern was hardly typical.

If ignorance of the field of investigation and vagueness of direction characterized the initial hearings, they were saved, so to speak, by the evangelical proselytiser, J. B. Matthews. Shortly after a lengthy testimony on Communist-front organizations, Matthews was made an investigator for the committee, a job he held through the Hiss-Chambers hearings in 1949. He later served briefly as a staff director on the McCarthy Committee. Matthews was the classic American "seeker." He had traveled from evangelical fundamentalism to the humanitarianism of the Social Gospel, on down the road to the progressivism of the elder La Follette, through the pacifism of the Fellowship of Reconciliation, to the left wing of the Socialist party, into the Popular Front and militant consumerism, and, finally, back to the fundamentalism practiced by anti-Communist converts. There is some humor in the fact that Matthews's conversion to anti-communism occurred when, as an executive of Consumer's Research, he was outraged by a strike of its employees, charging that it was a Communist plot to take over the organization. Benjamin Gitlow saw him as a lightweight on Marxist social and economic theory, but Matthews could chart every twist and turn in the tortured history of fellow traveling.

This was the man for Dies. He lent respectability to the committee and was deferentially referred to as "Doctor" by some of its members. Whether he analyzed any situation as a witness or as an interrogator, his testimony was filled with the most minute details of popular front organizational structure, lists, names, dates, and places. He was a master archivist and his exhaustive knowledge made him invaluable to the committee because he could make connections between liberals, fellow travelers, and the hidden Communist conspiracy. Dies was out to slander the New Deal, and Matthews served his purpose well.

Matthews first appeared as a witness on August 22, 1938. He listed at least twenty Communist fronts with which he had been affiliated and recalled the most inconsequential episodes down to the last detail. Like so many anti-Communist witnesses, he inflated the Communist attributions of power and influence to organizations which were more accurately described by Murray Kempton as "structures of enormous pretension and pathetic foundation." But it was the meat and gristle of his life, and he did not believe that he had been on a feckless journey. He had heard the roar of the crowd in Madison Square Garden, as well as the mumblings in storefront temples.

It was Matthews who made the gaffe that the committee never lived down. In explaining how innocent, well-meaning people could be used by Communists, he noted that several movie stars such as Clark Gable, James Cagney, and Shirley Temple had been persuaded to send congratulations to a French Communist newspaper on its first anniversary. Matthews made a point of not saying they were Communists or Communist sympathizers but rather that their reputations had been exploited in the interest of Communist propaganda. But it was too late. Every critic of the committee leaped to the advantage. Harold Ickes conjured up visions of burly congressmen leading posses of investigators into Shirley Temple's nursery to gather evidence of Communist conspiracy. Frances Perkins thanked God that Shirley was a citizen and could not be deported.

By October 1938 the congressional election campaign was underway, and the political potential of the committee was apparent both to its chairman and to the Administration. Heated election struggles were already going on in the crucial swing states of Minnesota, Michigan, and California. On October 17, after protesting that the committee was only interested in communism and not political disputes, Dies produced Steve Gadler of St. Paul who testified that the Democratic candidate for governor of Minnesota, Elmer A. Benson, had been endorsed by Browder and the candidate had not repudiated the endorsement. Gadler went on to charge that the Farmer Labor party had been captured by the Communists, and six other nondescript witnesses testified to the same general information.

From Minnesota on to Michigan—the committee went to work on a Roosevelt favorite, Governor Frank Murphy, who was running for reelection. Returning to the sit-down strikes of two previous years, the committee recruited Paul V. Gadola, a Republican judge, to testify that the timid negotiating policy of Governor Murphy had contributed to the breakdown of law and order in that state. Murphy, Gadola charged, had become nothing more than a pawn in the hands of a crew of Communist lawyers and had refused to support the judge's injunction against lawless seizures of private property. After further damaging testimony from American Legionnaires and some local police officers, the committee heard from John M. Barringer, a former city manager and director of public safety in Flint, Michigan. Dies played on Barringer's testimony as though it were a musical instrument, leading the questions all the way. ". . . Would you say that [the sit-down strikes] would not have occurred if it had not been for the investigation and active leadership of the Communists?" Barringer obligingly replied, "No, it would not have occurred. And I can further answer that question—it would not have developed . . . if it had not been for the attitude of the members of the La Follette Committee, and Governor Murphy's treasonable action in not giving us help when we should have had it." Dies hit a bull's-eye which gained him headline dividends that surpassed even his wildest hopes.

Ignored during the questioning was the great potential for violence inherent in the organizing drive for industrial unionism. Murphy, under terrible pressure, had chosen the tactics of delay and negotiation over armed force, and the strike ended with no loss of life. From Murphy's perspective the situation had come close to civil war, with the American Legion at the head of assorted vigilante groups confronting a tough core of determined union militants.

Roosevelt, smarting under the steady attack on members of his Administration and angered by the blatant political partisanship of the committee's conduct, issued a public condemnation. The President described the witnesses as a "coterie of disgruntled Republican office holders," led by a "disgruntled Republican judge," a "discharged city manager," and a group of "officious" policemen who had been recruited to make "lurid" and unjustified charges that could not be verified. He eloquently defended Murphy as a "profoundly religious, able and law-abiding Governor" whose handling of the strike was such that "all peace loving Americans should praise him." The President indicted the committee for allowing itself to be used in a "flagrantly unfair and un-American attempt to influence an election." He hoped that the committee would abandon the practice of providing a forum for those who sought headlines.

Undaunted, Dies immediately reaffirmed all of the charges, insisting that despite the President's anger and opposition, he would continue to do his duty "undeterred and unafraid." Next to appear were two Californians who accused the Democratic candidate for governor, Culbert Olsen, of owing his nomination to Communist support. It was later asserted that these witnesses represented the interests of the Associated Farmers, a West Coast anti-union organization of fruit growers and packers which supported Republican candidates.

The Administration blamed the Dies Committee for the defeat of Murphy in Michigan, and Dies was delighted to accept the credit. Arthur Krock in the *New York Times* acknowledged the influence of the committee when he asserted that the election returns had emphatically rebuked the sit-down strikes and the Democratic-CIO alliance.

Dies and his committee were the beneficiaries of a growing disenchantment with the New Deal program and a fearful anxiety over what lay ahead. He had no intention of losing momentum, so he and his colleagues kept up a running assault on officials in the Executive bureaucracy. In an Armistice Day speech Dies accused Secretaries Ickes and Perkins of being purveyors of class hatred. Almost no agency or department head was immune from criticism as a collaborator or dupe of Communist design.

Harold Ickes was the only one to return the fire with any enthusiasm. In a press release he said that "anyone who wanted to get anything out of his system against any New Dealer" should apply to the accommodating Dies Committee. Dies, Ickes quipped, was the "outstanding zany of American political history." The following day Dies called for the resignation of Ickes and Perkins because no American could feel secure with an Administration staffed by Communists, Socialists, and the "ordinary garden variety of crackpots."

While this extracurricular activity went on, the committee conducted its final hearings in December 1938. They were designed to expose the criminal mismanagement of the Works Progress Administration (WPA) and particularly, the writer and theatre projects. With unerring instinct Dies and J. Parnell Thomas recognized that these projects constituted "the soft underbelly" of the WPA. Many Americans were indifferent or unsympathetic to a federal program providing employment for writers and actors whom they felt were, at best, loafers and, at worst, troublemakers. It was true, as Thomas repeatedly charged, that many Communists and fellow travelers of varying radical persuasions had found a home in the projects. This was notoriously true of the New York projects, which were frequently in a state of upheaval resulting from factional political struggles. In the eyes of middle-class respectability, the projects were composed of a motley crew of wild-eyed and frequently drunken poets, writers, and assorted bohemians whose life-style was an affront to all that was pure and decent. Imagine what the suffering, self-reliant taxpayer thought of a mystical raconteur like the legendary Joe Gould who, when not writing his mythical "Oral History of the World," rambled around his Greenwich Village turf flapping his arms like a seagull and disrobing at parties. Nor is it likely that the general populace could appreciate the genius of the Village bohemian-turned-Communist, Maxwell Bodenheim, who actually rose to the position of a supervisor in the writer's project until his penchant for spirits made it impossible for him to show up for work—even once a week.

This "gallery of grotesques," combined with the sectarian warfare between Stalinists and Trotskyites in the New York projects, gave the entire program a bad reputation and was a constant embarrassment to the Administration. As the hearings proceeded it was obvious that no major Administration official would exert much effort to protect this experiment in federal sponsorship of the arts, despite its many fine achievements.

The thrust of the attack on the projects rested on the testimony of disgruntled former employees. They charged that Communists controlled the employees' union, the Workers' Alliance, and used their power to intimidate and harass non-Communists. The editorial staff, they accused, was dominated by Communists who insidiously introduced propaganda into literary and theatrical productions. Critics complained that the famous state guidebooks invariably employed Communist phraseology, stressed the struggle between capital and labor, referred to blacks as the downtrodden, and championed the virtues and nobility of the "underprivileged." It was noted that the Massachusetts guide devoted more pages to the Sacco-Vanzetti case than it did to the Boston Tea Party.

Committee members followed their all too familiar practice of putting words into the mouths of witnesses.

> Congressman Mason: Would you say that the federal Writers Project is being used by a group of radicals to propagandize the states through the use of these guides?
>
> Witness: I do; and that is just the beginning.
>
> Chairman Dies: Do you think Mr. Alsberg (director of Writers Project) is bringing into the department as many radicals as he can?
>
> Witness: I don't know whether he is doing it under orders or voluntarily.
>
> Dies: But he is doing it?

Witness: It has seemed to us for a long while that he has been bringing in such persons.

Friendly witnesses were seldom cross-examined. However, when Ellen Woodward, the assistant administrator, testified in defense of the project, her testimony was challenged at every point, proof demanded of any generalizations, and her fitness as a witness discussed at length.

After a score of accusatory witnesses were heard, Mrs. Hallie Flanagan was finally permitted to defend the theatre projects. She was a spirited witness not intimidated by the committee. When asked what her duties were, she remarked that she worked to combat un-American activities by providing jobs for professional men and women. Dies refused to allow her to testify to anything she had not personally witnessed and no hearsay evidence was permitted. This was an astonishing switch from the usual procedure which had encouraged reams of unsupported hearsay evidence.

During her testimony, an old article by Mrs. Flanagan was dug up in which she referred to the "Marlowesque madness" of worker's theatres taking root in America. Congressman Starnes wanted to know who this Marlowe was. "Is he a Communist?" he asked. Mrs. Flanagan respectfully replied that she had been referring to Christopher Marlowe, but Starnes, unsatisfied, pressed on. "Tell us who Marlowe is. . . ." To this Mrs. Flanagan responded with delight: "Put in the record that he was the greatest dramatist in the period of Shakespeare, immediately preceding Shakespeare." A shout of laughter echoed through the chamber and out across the nation and every opponent of the committee was comforted by the knowledge that the rednecked Starnes knew as little about drama as he did about communism.

The theatre and writers projects had produced an amazing variety of material, some first rate and much of it little more than crude and inept political propaganda. But to the committee it was not so much Communist literary banality, as it was the abominable association of the government with these disreputable figures. It is a toss up as to who should be credited for ultimately killing these projects. The New Deal Administration found the experiment a political liability and gave it little support once under attack. The Dies Committee exploited every sensational facet of political and social nonconformity, thus damaging the reputation of the entire experiment, and the Communists' continuous, disruptive bickering and crude attempts at politicization made them vulnerable to ridicule.

The WPA hearings were a rehearsal for the first debate over the renewal of the committee. Dies had good reason to be optimistic, for despite the fact that a poll of journalists, solicited by Roosevelt, had declared the committee's conduct unfair and the Administration had hired Paul Anderson, a journalist, to attack it on a national network, a Gallup poll showed that it had wide popular support.

Harold Ickes insisted that the only way to deal with Dies was to confront him directly. He planned a nationwide speech entitled "Playing with Loaded Dies," which would inform the public of the outrageous conduct of the hearings. But the President, increasingly wary of Dies's political influence, especially after the decisive defeat in the congressional elections, was persuaded to cancel Ickes's speech. He continued to entertain the hope that congressional leadership could either curb the committee's longevity or the size of its appropriation through careful political maneuvering. He was advised that an Ickes attack would simply rally anti-New Deal support for Dies.

Ickes replied that Dies was making gains because the President and his Administration had refused to take the offensive. A number of cabinet sessions were turned over to a discussion of Ickes's strategy. He urged the Administration to encourage an additional appropriation for the La Follette Committee to counterbalance Dies's investigation, or to pack the Dies Committee with loyal New Dealers.

The President vacillated between these two proposals but refused to allow administrative officials to lobby on the Hill. The degree to which Roosevelt feared Dies may be seen in his request that Frank Murphy, whom he had only recently appointed attorney general, begin an investigation of the organizations that the committee daily attacked as subversive. This, however, gave substance and respectability to the charges of the committee.

Ickes was disconsolate when the committee was renewed in February and received a sizable increase in its appropriation, while the La Follette Committee's appropriation was cut in half in the Senate. He recorded in his diary that it was another example of "a complete falling down of Democratic leadership." They had "abjectly surrendered" to the demagogues. Sam Rayburn remarked: "Martin Dies could beat me right now in my own district."

When Congress convened in January 1939, Dies submitted the 125-page committee report. A considerable portion of the report was allotted to a defense of the investigation and an assault on the lack of cooperation from Roosevelt's Administration. Reflecting the opinion of its chairman, the committee report emphasized the notion that Americanism was the recognition that a citizen's fundamental rights came from God. The preaching of class conflict was un-American. The real danger of communism was not overt conspiracy, but the infiltration of organizations and the government itself. In its survey of the hearings, what evidence the committee chose to include was highly selective. It carefully detailed the testimony covering Communist influence in the WPA, but the hostile testimony of Hallie Flanagan was entirely omitted. Frey's charges of Communist domination of the National Labor Relations Board and the CIO were reasserted, as was the testimony attributing treasonous action to Governor Murphy during the sit-down strikes. Walter Steele's rambling testimony was constantly quoted to support charges against alleged Communist-front organizations. The American League for Peace and Freedom was cited as a prime example of a Communist front, and it obviously was. The Workers' Alliance, the American Student Union, and the National Negro Congress were all castigated as suspect organizations willingly serving the ends of Communist propaganda.

The general reception of the report in Congress and in the press was favorable. All agreed that the menace of un-American activities was a real threat to national security and that the committee's purpose had been justified. The problem was that the frequently shoddy conduct of the committee violated the American sense of fair play. Here was the beginning of that haunting refrain, "I believe in the objectives but I deplore the methods," which later became the basis of anti-Communist apologia during the next two decades.

The position of the *New York Times* was a classic of the genre. The committee, the newspaper asserted, had performed a useful service. It had exposed the deceit and hypocrisy of the so-called front organizations, the insidious nature of Communist tactics, and had correctly linked communism with nazism and fascism as another form of undemocratic authoritarianism. It was important that the public be alerted to propagandistic and subversive activities. On the other hand, the Dies Committee was not the perfect instrument to achieve these ends, the *Times* said. It had entertained "hysterical tosh," arrived at conclusions in advance of evidence, and was guilty of "red-baiting." Despite these failings, the newspaper endorsed the committee, felt it should be continued, and hoped for some reform of its personnel.

The *New Republic,* a strong supporter of the popular front, condemned the committee and its works. But the depth of their civil libertarian principles seemed to depend on certain conditions. They urged support for the La Follette Committee on the grounds that "nothing holds the forces of darkness in check like a Senatorial searchlight always in readiness to be turned upon their activities." Supporters of the Dies Committee held the same view with respect to a congressional searchlight on alleged subversive activities. One might agree that the power of union-busting corporations presented a greater threat to genuine democracy than that of the Communist Left during these years and that the conduct, research, and documentation of the La Follette investigation far surpassed the unfair and slip-shod methods of the Dies Committee, but this double vision, which accepted the political motivation of one committee while rejecting the other, set an example for the wavering integrity of some liberals who grew to accept the work of the un-American activities committees as a necessary evil in the fight against international communism.

While partisans of both sides discussed the needs, failings, and implications of the committee, *Colliers* magazine captured the popular attitude. In spite of some obvious theatrical flaws, phony witnesses, and fantastic stories, the public wished the show to go on, hoped for some improvement in the proceedings, and advocated a larger appropriation.

Dies was confident. In the congressional debate over renewal of the committee, the war horses of the opposition retreated. They no longer repudiated the committee's existence but simply demanded reform of committee conduct. Only one representative, Adolph Sabath, still angered over their neglect of anti-Semitic and Fascist groups, voted against renewal in the Rules Committee. After an hour of debate on the floor, Dies won an overwhelming vote of confidence, 344 to 35. Republicans supported the committee to a man; Democrats, reading public sentiment and noting the feeble opposition of the Administration, went along. The committee was awarded $100,000 and another year's tenure.

Dies was jubilant. "We've proved the job should be done." To conciliate critics and prove nonpartisanship, the liberal Californian, Jerry Voorhis, replaced Mosier, who had been defeated in the last election. For the next four years Voorhis played the role of the committee's conscience, invariably condemning its conduct while defending its continued existence.

In the spring of 1939 as the European horizon darkened, there was a lull in the headline accounts of the committee's activities. In the House, Dies continued to push for legislation to exclude and expel alien Communists, require registration of suspect, "Communist" organizations, and bar federal employment of known Fascists and Communists. The latter became law in August 1939, and it was not long before Dies would follow his triumph by exciting the House to attach riders demanding the dismissal of bureaucrats investigated by the committee to many appropriations bills.

The committee's first headlines of 1939 occurred on May 18. Committee investigators, a shadowy and elusive crew, had uncovered a Fascist, anti-Semitic plot allegedly threatening the entire nation. The plot involved the most bizarre of the right-wing fringe and a group of unknown red Jews. The story was shrouded in mystery, with secret sessions of the committee and unknown witnesses hidden from one another and the press. As details were leaked, it was learned that the anti-Semite, Dudley Pierrepont Gilbert, had discovered, through a waiter in a restaurant frequented by wealthy Jews, that there was a conspiracy afoot to take over the country. Gilbert had passed the information on to right-wing patriots who, in turn, planned a counterplot to rid the country of the Jewish menace.

As the story unfolded in the press the emphasis shifted from an exposure of anti-Semitism to an account of the Communist-Jewish plot. Anti-Semitic right-wing leaders, testifying before the committee, expounded upon the nature of the worldwide Communist-Jewish conspiracy. The effect was the revival of the flagging careers of those fringe groups who insisted that their main purpose was to protect the country from communism, a disease invariably carried by Jews. General George Van Horn Moseley, a retired army officer and leader of anti-Semitic groups, and George E. Deatherage, the national commander of the anti-Semitic, nativist Knights of the White Camelia, gave lengthy dissertations on the attempts his group had made to mobilize a counterforce against this conspiracy. Moseley's "astute" scholarship was summed up in his observation that "over two thousand years of recorded history shows very clearly that those traits which have made the Jew unwelcome every place he has domiciled cannot be bred out."

One is tempted to equate the fears of the Communist and Fascist menace as equally bizarre manifestations in American life during a period of hysteria. But if respectable institutions did not support the likes of Moseley and Deatherage, their tolerance of anti-Semitism was overt. Only a year later the genteel aristocrat Albert Jay Nock was commissioned to write an essay for the *Atlantic* on the "Jewish problem." In it he refined Moseley's message to assert that the Jew and the Gentile could never live amiably side by side and that some form of apartheid was necessary if the country was to survive. Neither could the press be excused for twisting this story and others so as to hang its headlines on the spectacle of an ancient Jewish conspiracy while playing down the anti-Semitic aspects of the affair. More than one historian of the committee has wondered why, with so much evidence of anti-Semitism, it failed to utilize its information to develop a full-scaled investigation of the native Fascist movement.

As was his practice, Dies delayed formal public hearings on this matter until the late summer and fall when Congress had adjourned. In August the approach of war in Europe brought the real menace of Hitler home to the American people. Dies obligingly investigated the German-American Bund and its national leader, Fritz Kuhn. The historian of nativist Fascist movements, Sandor Diamond, notes that in a "strange but understandable way"

Kuhn owed much to Martin Dies. Because "Dies was more concerned with the Communist threat to America than with the Nazi menace," Kuhn's only hope of reviving his waning movement was by "converting it into a militant anti-Communist and isolationist group." The Dies hearings on the Bund provided his platform but could not help but mobilize anti-Fascist feelings. It was not the Dies Committee, however, that was responsible for Kuhn's subsequent conviction on a tax evasion charge; it was the liberal Congressman La Guardia of New York.

The diverse and rambling hearings of the summer of 1939 simply could not sustain attention. The Nazi-Stalin Pact of August 24, 1939, was a lifesaver to the committee and its chairman, for they now had the documentation for their long-held contention that there was no difference between fascism and communism. Both were Godless forms of totalitarianism which would stop at no form of deceit. The subsequent invasions of Poland and Finland only confirmed the charge, which was immeasurably strengthened by the slavish servility of American Communists and fellow travelers who went to absurd lengths to defend these events. The apologetics of the Communist party, which involved the abandonment of their call for resistance to fascism and an espousal of pacifism and isolationism, proved to the committee and to most Americans that the party was nothing more than a vehicle of Soviet foreign policy. The stupidity of party spokesmen was more than many fellow travelers and former sympathizers could take. Granville Hicks, a literary critic who had eloquently defended the nobility of the popular front, submitted his farewell to the party to the *New Masses,* which refused to publish it; but the *New Republic,* still reeling from the shock of the Pact, did. Hicks lamented that the party had abandoned all pretense of independence from the Kremlin with its shameful claim that the Pact was a contribution to peace and democracy. He was chagrined that the party had not even bothered to defend the agreement as an act of political expediency necessary to gain time to prepare a defense against future Nazi aggression (which did become the rationale of many). He charged that since they were ill-equipped "to defend the Soviet Union intelligently, they would defend it stupidly."

For the less ideological and more romantic supporters of Communist goals, the Pact dealt a devastating blow to their idealistic commitments and principles. Irwin Edman's reaction is perhaps the most representative of many of the left-wing partisans who had marched with the Communists in worthy causes. There could be no rational reason for the Pact. The fact that there were such rationalizations, Edman wrote, "had eaten like a canker into the bloom of every value we enjoy and every ideal we cherish." It had made "a mockery of all their former hopes and knowledge." Even the "private joys" of former comradeship were made "shamefaced and precarious." Edman lamented that men in the nineteenth century had been saddened because they could no longer believe in God. But he and his friends were "more deeply saddened because they could no longer believe in man."

Such a lament tells more about the Communist menace than anything ever alleged by an un-American activities committee. The betrayal of political decency by the party struck a blow against the foundations of liberal optimism and soured a generation of well-meaning men and women on all forms of social commitment, encouraging many to retreat into private visions or a resigned acceptance of the irrational. Others enthusiastically embraced the status quo as the best of all possible worlds. Adopting a sophisticated Niebuhrian pessimism, they proclaimed a cynicism tantamount to political maturity. *This* was the most devastating legacy of the American flirtation with communism in the 1930s. It may also help to account for the conduct of jaded liberals during the cold war and in the 1960s when they, too, resorted to duplicity to justify actions beyond the understanding of reasonable men.

The undermining of liberal confidence and commitment was one of the goals of the Dies Committee and its chairman did not let the advantage offered by the Pact slip by. It provided an opportunity for the committee to exploit the more ludicrous dimensions of Communist logic. Earl Browder shamelessly declared that world peace would be the consequence of the agreement of Germany and Russia to refrain from mutual attack. William Z. Foster continued to insist that the American Communist party was independent of the Soviet Union. There were, he claimed, "tens of thousands" of times when the party had taken a stand independent of the Comintern. When pressed, however, he could think of no particular instance. He admitted that after a party member had been educated to a particular position but continued to oppose it, he would be expelled. None of this was startling information, but the committee presented it in such a way as to provide sardonic anti-Communists with unsurpassed examples of Communist sophistry.

At one point during Browder's hearing the Communist official broadened the definition of "transmission belt," a term used in Communist jargon to mean independent organizations used by the party to transmit their words to the masses, to include the A. F. of L. J. Parnell Thomas, right on cue, read off a list of liberal organizations to which high officials in the New Deal, including the President and his wife, had given addresses and asked if they were not also part of the transmission belt. When Browder conceded, Thomas commented with smug satisfaction that it seemed that the New Deal was working "hand in glove with the Communist Party."

During this period of daily revelations by Communist functionaries, Dies was shaping the strategy that would become his principal method of maligning the Roosevelt Administration. As early as 1938 Harold Ickes had confided in his diary that Dies had sent to the Department of State a long list of organizations which he insisted were "agents of a foreign government." Ickes had concluded then that Dies's strategy was "to put it up to the executive departments to take action." If they failed to respond, then Dies could go to the country urging the need for greater support and appropriations for his committee as the only defense against alien subversion.

In October 1939 the committee heard the testimony of the Reverend Harry Ward, one of the social gospelers who had found twentieth century Christianity in left-wing causes and was currently president of the American League for Peace and Democracy. During the Ward hearings committee investigators broke into the files of the Washington, D.C., chapter of the league. After some bickering with committee members Dempsey and Voorhis, the committee released to the press what was either a mailing or membership list. Major newspapers across the country gave their readers 563 names of citizens who were allegedly members of the league and at the same time government employees. Since the committee had already informed the public of the Communist-front nature of the organization, it concluded that these were defiant Communists or fellow travelers who had no business in the United States Government. When errors were corrected and names of people included who had no connection with the league or any knowledge of its activities, the committee blandly replied that the error was not theirs, but the league's. When others objected that many people named had long since left the league, committee members pointed out that they had had a full year to see that their names had been expunged from the list.

Through mass exposure, the Dies Committee investigations illustrated the power of publicity in punishing American citizens who were guilty of no crime but that of holding opinions contrary to those of the committee. The committee did not have to assert that the people listed were Communists, only that the league was a Communist-front organization. With publicity, the committee applied effective "moral suasion" forcing their resignations. It became clear that Dies was not interested in the Communist menace or the Fascist menaçe so much as he was in what he frankly described as the "left-wingers and radicals who do not believe in our system of private enterprise." This was a sweeping category encompassing all dissenters from the mildest liberal critics of *laissez-faire* orthodoxy to genuine revolutionaries. It obliterated all distinctions in opinion and victimized citizens guilty of nothing more than an association with unpopular causes.

Committee member Dempsey denounced the release of information as a damnable un-American act. Voorhis presented an eloquent but ambivalent appraisal of the situation: He denounced the committee for publishing the names but defended the sincere, if mistaken, motives of his colleagues. He argued that there were two real dangers to American democracy—"honest to goodness" subversive activities that had to be exposed at both extremes of the political spectrum, and the kind of political demagoguery of the moderate right and left, who branded their opponents with Fascist and Communist labels. He supported continued publicity concerning true subversives and defended the committee on the whole as having conducted itself "in a proper and fair way."

The President described the committee's action as a "sordid procedure," and Dies responded by denouncing the "sordid" policy of an administration which continued to hire and harbor Communist sympathizers. It was almost like a dress rehearsal for the McCarthy era, replete with lists, names, and an increasingly vulnerable administration.

Four days following the publication of the league's list of names the *St. Louis Post Dispatch* and the *Washington Sunday Star* printed an article based on an interview with Dies in which he boasted about the accomplishments of his committee thus far. Among a long list of achievements were the following: The committee had succeeded in "paralyzing the left-wing influence in the Administration," discredited the CIO, defeated Murphy for governor of Michigan, brought about an investigation of the National Labor Relations Board, encouraged the congressional abandonment of the federal writers and theatre projects, and stimulated the movement to cut the appropriation of the La Follette Committee. Dies never repudiated this article and later repeated most of the claims.

The last controversial event of the committee's activities in 1939 was the publication of J. B. Matthews's report on the Communist domination of the consumer movement. Matthews had been an executive official of Consumer's Research until its staff went on strike in 1935, when he abruptly lost his taste for Socialist militancy. Bent on personal revenge against his former associates, he founded the rival Consumer's Union. Matthews, now working with business interests, warned the country that many consumer organizations were determined to undermine the noble services of American advertising and manufacturing in order to support the Communist critique of decadent capitalism. Apart from fulfilling Matthews's vendetta against his former associates the report served to further Dies's growing political ambitions by encouraging the support of businessmen delighted with any attack on the consumer movement.

The Matthews report, released under the imprint of the committee, had never been discussed by its members. There had been no hearings, no witnesses called, and no vote taken. Matthews had simply aired his antagonism, courtesy of the official facilities of the committee.

It is astonishing that after a detailed account of such scurrilous violations of judicious procedure an historian of the committee, August R. Ogden, could still find praise for the "uniformly high plane" of the committee's performance during its second year. The conduct of the hearings had improved and now compared "favorably with the average run of investigations and exhibit[ed] only the faults common to this method of legislative procedure."

This tolerance reflected the apologetics of the time. With the exception of the leftist critique, no act of the committee seemed so nefarious as to suggest that the committee should be abolished. Walter Lippmann's appraisal of January 11, 1940, is a masterpiece of rhetorical ambivalence. The committee, he observed, was not "really a legislative committee at all." It was, on the contrary, a "committee of public safety" designed to repress activities condemned by the majority of the people, but which "are in themselves either not unlawful, or even if they were . . . could not be dealt with by the ordinary procedure of the law." In short, the Dies Committee, Lippmann conceded, was nothing more than a form of "official" vigilantism. Since its members operated in the absence of much needed legislation, they were, by necessity, often "lawless in spirit and disorderly in their methods."

But Lippmann was quick to insist that "only the very innocent and self-deluding have any doubt that the Dies Committee have been attacking a formidable evil in modern society. The menace is real. It is not imaginary," he warned. This posed the "ancient moral question of whether the end justifies the means." It was clear that Lippmann felt the seriousness of the problem simply had to be met and, while he went on almost routinely to indict the methods of the committee for their flagrant violations of "American morality," he conceded that the end, "which is to protect the American system," was being maintained by means which, "if used for some other end would be deplored by everyone . . . except . . . the revolutionists Mr. Dies is stalking."

According to Lippmann, the committee could not be abolished because the end did justify the means; it needed only to be reformed. He suggested the idea of adding "one or two learned lawyers" to the committee who "would make it their business to reform the procedure." He advocated a larger appropriation to insure the hiring of competent investigators so that the committee would cease to rely upon "dubious informers and crackpots who always gather about an inquiry of this sort."

This argument was repeated in one way or another by liberal and conservative politicians and commentators, and it has remained the basis for many subsequent evaluations of the committee. It goes a long way toward explaining how a committee whose means were its ends became an integral part of the American political process for the next three decades. It remains one of the curiosities of historical analysis that Lippmann's article was cited years later as "the soundest criticism . . . voiced at the time."

By late November 1939, Dies was preparing for the renewal debate coming up in January. A Gallup poll published in mid-December indicated strong popular support, but within the committee there was a deepening factional struggle. Voorhis, Dempsey, and Joseph E. Casey, a New Deal Democrat from Massachusetts who replaced Healey, were still furious over the publication of the ALPF list and the discovery that Dies and Matthews had already drafted the second annual report without consulting them. Stunned by the belligerent flamboyance of the report, largely the work of Matthews, they threatened to destroy the bipartisan image of the committee by issuing a minority report. Dies, ill and apparently fearful that a break in the ranks of House support was a possibility, agreed to support a new report prepared by Voorhis and unanimously signed by the other members.

The second annual report of the committee was published on January 3, 1940. It was described by the *New York Times* as an "astonishingly able and balanced document . . . a model of sound democratic reasoning." Even some of the committee's most persistent critics found it a judicious statement on the problem of subversive activities and the achievements of the committee in combating these forces. Others on the left, while conceding the change in tone, suspected that it was designed to weaken the resolve of the opposition.

The report was a classic liberal defense of the need for the committee. It began with the observation that the preservation of constitutional liberties and an adjustment of the nation's economic life were the two major problems facing America. It then offered a more precise definition of un-American activities, describing them as the work of organizations or groups "subsidized, directed or controlled by a foreign government" for the purpose of changing the American form of government in accordance with the "wishes of a foreign government." While it still left plenty of latitude for a broad interpretation, it was an improvement on the vague religiosity of earlier definitions.

The report outlined a solid case against the Communist party, U.S.A., proving that it was simply a branch of the Comintern, and associated with eleven front organizations serving Soviet propaganda interests. Noticeably lacking was a mention of the American Civil Liberties Union which Dies and Matthews had repeatedly charged with Communist infiltration.

In a section devoted to Communist influence in the union movement the report asserted that an overwhelming majority of CIO members and officers were neither Communists nor sympathizers and that at most the leadership of ten or twelve unions out of forty-eight were "more than tinged with Communism." But there was also encouraging evidence that the "leadership" of the CIO was making every effort to purge all Communist influence.

In marked contrast to the hysterical tone of its previous reports, the committee now argued that neither Communist nor Fascist organizations constituted much in the way of a direct threat to American institutions. The real danger was the possibility that totalitarian groups through deception might persuade a substantial number of citizens that their only defense lay in some form of violence against their opponents.

In its conclusion the committee listed the conviction of Earl Browder for traveling on a forged passport and the conviction of Fritz Kuhn for the mishandling of Bund funds among its achievements. However, in both cases, federal and state law enforcement agencies had begun investigations before the committee had held hearings, and it is dubious that the committee played any substantial role in their arrests and convictions. Defenders of congressional committees invariably make these kinds of claims, but Telford Taylor has observed that few congressional investigations have ever turned up evidence contributing to criminal prosecution that was not well known and acted upon by state and federal agencies.

Equal space in the report was given to summaries of Communist and Fascist propaganda, suggesting that a broad American consensus believed it was faced with a threat equal from the left as from the right. This illusion of balance, used to refute the charge that the committee's primary purpose was to harass the left, distorted the real political struggle of the 1930s, however. That conflict was not so much a confrontation between political extremists and the center as it was between the forces of reform and the defenders of the status quo. And it was not a struggle between equals. It is difficult to equate the power and influence of reform and leftist movements, even during this so called "red decade," with that of the conservative institutional forces opposed to fundamental changes in the American system. Surely the CIO, supported by the militant activism of many Communists and encouraged by members of the New Deal Administration, never had the strength of America's corporate hierarchy. It is unlikely that the liberal and leftist press had anything comparable to the power, influence, and circulation of the nation's conservative newspapers. The allegedly dangerous and subversive front organizations like the League for Peace and Freedom or the American Student Union, both weakened, had nowhere near the influence of the patriotic organizations—the veterans' associations, the Chambers of Commerce, the National Association of Manufacturers, or even the American Medical Association. Too often commentators, embroiled in what Telford Taylor calls the "Cold Civil War," have attributed far too much influence to the power of militant reform in this decade. Thus, even Voorhis's widely praised report hardly informed the people of the real issues at hand.

Once again, their report formed the basis for the defense of the committee's renewal during the debate in January 1940. That debate received a charge when Congressman Frank E. Hook, an ardent New Dealer from Michigan, fell victim to a clever hoax perpetrated by conservative supporters of the committee. Hook rose dramatically to offer documented evidence linking Dies with William Dudley Pelley of the anti-Semitic "Silver Shirts." The evidence consisted of an exchange of correspondence between Pelley and David Mayne, another official of the Silver Shirts, and confirmed charges made repeatedly by the radical press. However, within a week the letters proved to be forgeries sold to Gardiner Jackson, an agent of liberal opponents of the committee. The letters had then been turned over to Congressman Hook, who had been, in the words of Mayne, "played for a sucker." Hook was forced to make a humiliating apology to the entire House, which exonerated Dies from any connection with the extreme right. However, the leftist press, which had taken the bait, continued to make the charge, claiming that the hoax failed to repudiate other solid evidence of Dies's warm associations with right-wing extremist organizations.

With the exception of this bizarre incident, in itself revealing of the atmosphere surrounding the committee's activities, the debate over renewal had become little more than a formality. Defenders championed the committee as the lone bulwark against all threats to the American way of life. Opponents damned it as an un-American violation of unpopular opinion. Representatives of labor remained silent, hoping that the committee would leave them alone. Liberal congressmen feared for their careers if they participated in an attack on Dies or the committee, but of course, Voorhis and Coffee played their standard roles; they continued to rebuke the committee for its conduct in certain particulars while eloquently insisting on the necessity for its continued existence. There was the usual talk of reform of committee procedure, but it was nothing more than talk. The committee had its own procedure.

The vote, 344 to 23, was another triumph for Dies. Voorhis's reasoned and moderate report had weakened what at one point looked like a faintly promising attack on the committee. Crawford, in the *Nation*, described the vote as Dies 344, Decency 23. Opponents of the committee feared that a vote against the committee would be widely interpreted as a vote for communism.

Dies started off the new year by announcing that there were seven million aliens in American industry who deserved serious investigation and exposure; Communist subversion in Hollywood was rampant; and there was a far flung Soviet secret police operation in the United States. It soon became apparent that his real attention this year was directed to middle-rung Communist party functionaries who, he announced, would be subpoenaed and requested to supply names, under threat of congressional contempt citations.

In March and April 1940 committee investigators, with the aid of local law officers, raided several party headquarters in various cities and absconded with party records. A federal judge in Pennsylvania, George A. Welsh, ordered the arrest of the raiders and enjoined Dies not to make use of the stolen documents, and in May the judge ruled the raid an illegal violation of the Fourteenth Amendment. Communists were an unpopular minority, but their rights had been violated, rights, the judge declared, that are sacred to all Americans regardless of their political persuasions. Dies, in response, fumed over the state of a society that would extend fundamental rights to "agents of a foreign dictator."

Apparently the documents proved worthless because the committee, when it did subpoena a number of Communists to demand membership lists and the names of friends and associates, for the first time, was defied by the Communists, who refused to answer questions. The committee, they charged, was establishing an illegal black list, their questions were prompted by the unlawful seizure of private property, and, more to the point, the committee was invading personal privacy by seeking information irrelevant to its stated investigative purpose.

Sol Cohn, the attorney for one of the witnesses, cited *Sinclair* v. *United States* (1929) as a defense of his client's right to refuse to answer questions regarding the Communist affiliations of members of his family. The limits of congressional inquiry had been raised in *McGrain* v. *Daugherty* as early as 1927, when the Court upheld the right of congressional investigations to demand information for the purpose of legislating, but also asserted that a witness "rightfully may refuse to answer questions . . . not relevant to the matter under inquiry." The *Sinclair* case was an elaboration on the *McGrain* case. The Court issued a ringing defense of civil liberties when it asserted in the majority decision that it had always been recognized that fewer rights were of greater importance than exemption from unauthorized, arbitrary, or unreasonable disclosures, in respect of "the citizens' personal and private affairs."

The committee's counsel insisted, however, that the only established grounds for refusal to respond to questions was "self-incrimination" under the Fifth Amendment. The committee preferred that plea because of the automatic inference of guilt it carried with it, the inference obviously serving the committee's purposes.

Dies did manage to have a number of witnesses cited for contempt, but only a few were ever convicted, and they received suspended sentences. The process involved court litigation and did not serve the publicity aims of the committee. Silent witnesses seldom produced headlines.

The first half of 1940 was chaotic, with the committee's seizure of worthless Communist records, hostile and unresponsive witnesses, and a rebuke by the courts for high-handed and illegal activities. In addition, the world's attention had become rooted on the German *blitzkrieg* of the low countries in May. The latter event gave strength to Dies's warnings against the threat of a fifth column and his case was further aided when the Smith Alien Registration Act was passed in July, making it a crime to "teach and advocate the overthrow of the United States Government by force and violence." There were only four votes against that measure, further evidence of the solid ground upon which Dies was now working.

Dies naturally understood these events as support for the committee's work and requested additional funds, which he received in September ($35,000). Dies was riding high; the committee had become synonymous with his name. It became the rule to conduct one-man hearings out of which information was released to the press. He, or one of his colleagues, seemed to be everywhere, holding closed meetings and releasing sensational disclosures concerning sabotage and fifth column conspiracies.

Dies had promised not to conduct hearings during the presidential election campaign in 1940, but on the eve of the election his first book, *The Trojan Horse in America*, was published. It proved to be little more than a lengthy polemic indicting the Administration: Public officials had deliberately harbored Communists; the President, Ickes, Wallace, Perkins, and countless lesser figures had served the evil designs of the "Trojan horse." Stalin, he charged, had "baited his hook with a 'progressive worm,'" and the New Deal suckers had "swallowed the bait—hook, line, and sinker." Mrs. Roosevelt had proved to be "one of the most valuable assets of the Trojan horse" because she had addressed countless subversive organizations, giving them prestige and respectability.

With Roosevelt's reelection in November 1940, Dies believed it was essential to transform the committee from a congressional investigative unit into a law enforcement body coequal with the Department of Justice and the Federal Bureau of Investigation. Such a grandiose ambition was sure to promote a direct confrontation with both and it was not long in coming.

Dies charged that the FBI's methods of fighting sabotage were not sufficient to cope with the present menacing situation. In October he claimed to have a list of over 300,000 active fifth columnists employed by the government, or by defense industries under contract to the government. He threatened to publish the list if the Administration did not initiate a more aggressive policy of screening suspected subversives.

On November 20, 1940, Dies's challenge to the Executive, the Department of Justice, and the FBI came to a head. The committee released a special report, the "White Paper," on alleged Nazi espionage and sabotage activities. Advertised weeks in advance, it proved to be an anticlimax; the information was widely known. The *Times* remarked that the report seemed to expose the "little schemes of little men" whose techniques hardly justified the extravagant claims made by the committee's chairman.

Two days after the publication of the White Paper Attorney General Robert H. Jackson publicly accused Dies and his committee of interfering with the work of the FBI. Jackson lectured the committee on the distinction between the responsibilities of an investigative committee and those of a law enforcement agency, a distinction which Dies was bent on ignoring. He charged that the publicity of the Dies Committee had jeopardized the department's attempt at apprehension and prosecution in several cases.

Jackson's criticism of the committee was a shrewd ploy not only because it pitted Dies against J. Edgar Hoover, but in choosing to fight over Nazis rather than Communists, the Administration also shifted the battlefield away from Dies's familiar stamping grounds. In late November the committee balanced its "White Paper" with the "Red Book" on Communist plans for sabotaging American industry. This was followed by a report from Hoover refuting Dies's claims to having exposed an extensive sabotage network in America. Hoover, while conceding the good work of the committee, insisted that it should not set itself up in competition with the FBI, thereby endangering the bureau's ongoing work.

Dies was aware that there was no political advantage in a dispute with Hoover. He requested a meeting with the President to work out a means of cooperation between his committee and the Executive departments. Roosevelt agreed, but pointed out that the administration of justice was an Executive responsibility and that "hasty seizure of evidence" and "premature disclosure of facts" were injurious to the Administration's pursuit of real subversives.

Dies met with the President on November 29. His account of the meeting suggests that Roosevelt lightheartedly belittled Dies's crusade. He reported later that the President had jocularly boasted that some of his "best friends were Communists." However, if Roosevelt treated Dies lightheartedly before the public, it is clear that he continued to view the chairman and his committee as a powerful threat that must be handled with kid gloves. Roosevelt supported a firm agreement among the committee, the Department of Justice, and the FBI. The committee agreed to cease publication of information until it had been cleared by the Department of Justice, which checked to see that it did not interfere with secret investigations which might lead to prosecution. The Department of Justice agreed to furnish the committee with all of its information on cases which it felt could not be successfully prosecuted in a court of law.

The effect of this conciliation was to enhance the committee's reputation as an integral branch of the law enforcement apparatus. In addition it amounted to an official recognition and a sanction of the committee's tactic of punishing people by proscriptive publicity, even if their actions were not unlawful. Roosevelt belittled Dies publicly, but the Administration accepted the committee and its methods as an established part of the system.

The committee's third annual report to Congress, published on January 3, 1942, defended the committee's existence by claiming to have been the "decisive force" in shaping the attitudes of the American people toward fifth column activity. The committee's work, it boasted, had been in the form of "public education," the importance of which could not be exaggerated. It noted that not a single country overrun by Hitler had had the protection of a similar committee preceding its downfall.

For the first time the annual report offered recommendations for legislation. The list was a veritable grab bag of restrictive prohibitions necessary to protect the nation. The committee called for the deportation of alien spies and saboteurs and all aliens who advocated "any basic change in the form of our government." (This supported Dies's assertion that attacks on capitalism were inherently un-American.) It insisted that the government withdraw all financial aid to educational institutions that permitted advocates of communism to remain on the faculty. It called for legislation barring immigration from countries refusing to accept the return of deported nationals. It called for new postal restrictions against "totalitarian propaganda," and asked for an extension of the statutory period during which citizenship might be revoked.

As a parting shot the committee closed its report with a hint as to its next major challenge to the Administration. It recommended that it become official policy to deny employment in the government or in national defense to any "person who has been and is now active in any political organizations found to be under the control and guidance of a foreign government." Since the committee would make that determination, it was clear that Dies intended to mount a legislative assault on the Executive by dictating his selection of Executive personnel. It was also, indirectly, an attack on the judiciary because the committee would be free to determine guilt outside of due process of law and, by mobilizing public opinion, they could punish the accused. This technique of exposure would become one of the most effective strategies of the committee in later years. Jerry Voorhis signed this report, objecting only to the proposed withdrawal of federal funds to educational institutions charged with harboring Communist faculty members. He felt such legislation would be impossible to administer fairly, but Voorhis's complaint was hardly a ringing defense of civil liberties.

The subsequent debate over renewal was a simple matter for the committee. Even Representative Coffee abandoned the opposition. Indeed, he had run for reelection in 1940 proudly endorsing the Dies Committee. Congressman Sabath, usually a critic, lavishly praised the committee's work when he reported the resolution for extension out of the Rules Committee. Only the hapless Samuel Dickstein and the eternally belligerent Vito Marcantonio vigorously fought against renewal. When Dickstein charged that Fascists had a key to the back door of the committee, the House, spurred on by Mississippi's John Rankin, ordered Dickstein's remark expunged from the record. Rankin made it clear that Dickstein did not speak for "the old line Americans." The vote was 354 to 6 and the committee was awarded its highest appropriation—$150,000.

The activities of the committee after 1941 are difficult to trace because it had become a one-man investigation that seldom held public hearings; Dies had transformed the committee into a one-man "denunciatory agency." From the summer of 1940 to the end of his tenure as chairman in 1944 Dies never appeared at a public hearing. His activities and those of most of the committee's members were reduced to speeches, articles, and the constant barrage of press releases informing the people of the committee's constant vigilance against subversion.

The German invasion of the Soviet Union on June 22, 1941, hardly served the interests of Chairman Dies, however. Once again the Communists' policy reversed itself and they presented themselves as comrades-in-arms against the Fascist menace. Although Dies never gave up the battle, he was driven to despair at the sight of Communists and their sympathizers masquerading as ardent patriots supporting the war effort. But, as the Administration mobilized for war, the Executive bureaucracy expanded and it hired men and women whose names were found in Dr. Matthews's encyclopedic files as members or supporters of suspicious organizations operating in the thirties.

Periodically, Dies released lists of names and renewed his demand that the Administration dismiss all persons remotely associated with alleged front organizations. Leon Henderson, head of the Office of Price Administration, was charged with membership in the Friends of Spanish Democracy. Robert Brady, Henderson's head consultant, had written a book critical of capitalism and was accused of being a Socialist and a destroyer of the church. Goodwin Watson, a broadcast analyst for the FCC, had been associated with a number of front organizations indicted by the committee and had supported Vito Marcantonio, a brazen and defiant fellow traveler who never lost an opportunity to denounce and ridicule Dies and his committee. Invariably, these charges were made without committee hearings or consultations. In fact, Voorhis and other members learned of these official findings in their daily papers.

When James L. Fly, chairman of the FCC, defended Watson and released a story revealing that Congressman Dies was repeatedly praised for his attack on to an FCC appropriation bill stipulating that Watson's salary be withheld. Malcolm Cowley, a former popular front literary critic, resigned his position as an analyst for the Office of Facts and Figures after Dies charged him with connections to seventy-two front organizations.

In March 1942 Dies accused Vice President Wallace of shoddy administration of the Board of Economic Warfare. Dies charged that thirty-five officials on the board had front affiliations, and, despite Wallace's outrage, he promised to see that the FBI checked all of the names on the list.

As ridiculous as Dies's activities appear, he was having a genuine impact on administrative policy. In the spring of 1941 Congress appropriated $100,000 to enable a willing Department of Justice to investigate federal employees accused by Dies. Attorney General Francis Biddle received a list of

1,121 names of suspects to investigate and indict if the sedition charges proved true. Biddle was under pressure from the President to follow through quickly in order to placate Dies's adherents. In September 1942 Biddle announced the results of his investigation. Only two persons were discharged as a result of information gathered by the Dies Committee, but Biddle took the occasion to censure the reckless methods of the committee. A large proportion of the complaints, he charged, were unfounded and never should have been submitted in the first place. He denounced the inquisitorial behavior of the committee for having sapped the time and energy of FBI investigators. Dies responded by accusing Biddle of hamstringing the FBI and insisting that the committee should see the reports, not the department heads.

In January 1943 when the committee published its fourth annual report, Voorhis refused to sign it, submitting a minority report critical of the unilateral action of the chairman. Dies's report was the product of no hearings and had been presented to committee members for signature on a "take it or leave it basis." Voorhis's complaint was of the chairman's autocratic conduct. He continued to insist that the committee, with proper leadership, could serve a useful purpose by stiffening American resistance to Nazi propaganda. When Voorhis finally resigned from the committee in 1943, he admitted that his efforts to reform the committee had been "one hundred per cent unsuccessful" and arrived at the "novel" notion that the committee had become "more and more a political instrument of definite conservative bias" and less and less a "dignified, important and effective congressional committee." Many observers might have wondered when it had ever served in a dignified manner.

Dies cared little about this dissent for he had discovered the old congressional weapon, the power of the purse. The attachment of riders to appropriation bills, insisting that suspected employees found guilty by verdict of the committee, i.e., Martin Dies, be dismissed or the department be denied its appropriation became a potent tool. This was perhaps the boldest attack on the Executive branch during the entire history of the committee.

On February 1, 1943, Dies rose in the House to defend himself against repeated charges that he was aiding the Axis powers by his unrelenting attacks on the Administration. The wartime alliance with the Soviet Union had made him and his committee vulnerable to criticism for hindering the war effort. In the course of his defense he came up with another list of names; this time it was thirty-nine government employees who were, according to Dies, irresponsible, unrepresentative, radical, and crackpots. He threatened the Administration: "If you do not get rid of these people, we will refuse to appropriate money for their salaries." It was no idle threat. The House, in the Goodwin Watson affair, had excluded his salary from an FCC appropriation, but the Senate had killed the bill.

The House, intent on pursuing the Dies strategy, created on February 9 a special subcommittee of the Committee on Appropriations to review the charges. It was an extraordinary situation. Dies would be the prosecuting agent, the new House committee would serve as a jury, and the whole House would constitute "the Lord's High Executioners." The obvious encroachments on the prerogatives of the Executive branch were ignored. Although the subcommittee dismissed the charges against most of the thirty-nine suspects, it did vote, after a heated debate, to demand that three be denied salaries before their respective departments received appropriations. The three victims were Goodwin Watson, William E. Dodd, jr., also of the FCC, and Robert Morss Lovett, formerly an eminent professor of English at the University of Chicago, a veteran of popular front causes, and presently the government secretary to the Virgin Islands. A House vote of 317 to 62 was unanimously rejected by the Senate, but during ensuing weeks Senate opposition weakened as the departments became pressed to meet their financial obligations.

The Administration and even conservative supporters of the Dies Committee denounced the act as a modern bill of attainder. The Administration kept the accused at work, but they were deprived of their salaries. Finally, the Supreme Court, in *Lovett* v. *United States,* rebuked the House for its illegal action. Justice Black, speaking for the majority, reminded the Congress that "when the Bill of Rights were written, our ancestors had ample reason to know that legislative trials and punishments were too dangerous to liberty to exist in the nation of free men they envisioned. And so they proscribed bills of attainder."

The last significant public hearings of the Dies Committee came in June and July of 1943 and, fittingly, were related to one of the most shoddy episodes in American history. In 1942 the Roosevelt Administration, bending before the hysteria following the attack on Pearl Harbor, inaugurated the evacuation of all persons of Japanese ancestry, citizens and aliens alike, from the West Coast. Hundreds of thousands of Japanese were transported to "relocation centers" under "protective custody," that is to say, concentration camps situated in the mountain and desert regions of Arizona and Wyoming. The reason for this flagrant violation of justice—military necessity.

There were other forces at work. For nearly fifty years prejudice against the Japanese had been prevalent on the coast. Nativist and racist sentiment was supported by hard economic interests. The efficient and hard-working Japanese farmers posed a constant threat of competition to Western growers and producers. Such organizations as the Sons of the Golden West and Legionnaires allied with the Chambers of Commerce and growers associations to pressure West Coast politicians to support evacuation. Among those supporting this movement was the attorney general of California, Earl Warren.

The camps were directed by the War Relocation Authority and staffed by men of good will who attempted to make the best of a bad situation. By 1943 they had mapped out a plan for the release of those evacuees whose "loyalty tests" showed they were of no danger to the nation. Those groups who had most enthusiastically championed evacuation, however, had never contemplated the return of the Japanese before the end of the war. Many had seen the program as the first step toward ultimate deportation. They immediately launched an attack on the WRA for faulty security, coddling of internees, failure to separate the loyal from the disloyal, and an ineffective Americanization program.

At this juncture the Dies Committee was called in to serve a purely political purpose. Dies had claimed shortly after Pearl Harbor that the Administration had thwarted a committee investigation of Japanese subversion by preventing the release of information that could have averted the sneak attack. The committee now leaped at the opportunity to further slander the Administration. For tactical reasons it was decided to create a subcommittee chaired by a native Californian, John Costello. Congressman Costello was a member in good standing of the nativist Sons of the Golden West, with close ties to the Los Angeles Chamber of Commerce. The old tactic of advance publicity was again employed to promote the hearings, and J. Parnell Thomas went to Los Angeles in May, a full month before the hearings were to begin. He bombarded the local press with inflammatory press releases which accommodating local editors turned into sensational headlines: *Rep. Thomas Reveals Jap Army in L.A.; Dies Prober Charges Relocation Plan is a Farce.* Thomas lamented the deplorable spectacle of "fat-waisted Japs" being released while "American boys" on Guadalcanal "were barely receiving enough food to keep alive"; but Thomas had yet to go near a relocation center. Robert Strippling, the chief investigator for the committee, authorized a statement from Washington asserting that the WRA was releasing "spies and saboteurs."

When the hearings began in early June, Costello had recruited a motley crew of nativists, Legionnaires, and a disgruntled former employee of the WRA to smear the program and its administrators. They raised the old saw, "once a Jap always a Jap," and ridiculed the notion that Orientals could ever be assimilated into a Caucasian society. These racist ruminations went unchallenged by the committee. Only Representative Herman P. Eberharter attempted to keep the hearings within the minimal bounds of judicious behavior. As was standard practice, the committee entertained accusatory witnesses before it would permit supporters of the program to rebut the charges, thus allowing the press to spread abroad the damaging testimony. Later rebuttals seldom attracted headlines.

Carey McWilliams observed that the committee conducted an inquisition rather than a hearing. It had deliberately encouraged scare stories about "dynamite caches" in the desert to inflame the local populace and to serve the racist, nativist, and economic interests determined to prevent the Japanese citizens from returning to their homes in California. It was an inexcusable performance, playing upon every tactic the committee had used throughout its career to exploit the worst instincts in the body politic and to serve the most reactionary political interests, while at the same time impugning the competence and loyalty of the Administration.

Despite the fanfare, the committee's final report was a relatively mild document calling for a more effective means of segregating the loyal from the disloyal prisoners, a more rapid Americanization program which did not bow to the ethnic eccentricities of the Japanese, and a review board that would investigate each evacuee who applied for release. Eberharter, in a minority statement, concluded that the report was marked by prejudice, and that its charges against the WRA were unsubstantiated.

It is no mitigation of the deplorable conduct of the committee to recall that many of its liberal critics supported the evacuation program. Few challenged the right of the government to imprison American citizens guilty of no crime. Thus, it is difficult to conclude that this latest travesty of the committee was the sole work of extremists. On the contrary, the conduct of the committee was simply the last episode in an act of injustice initiated and condoned by the established liberal community.

Despite the contemptuous performance of the committee, the House in January 1944 again renewed its contract and appropriated another $75,000 to facilitate its work, bringing the total appropriation to $625,000. Nevertheless, its activities and its dignity had been severely tarnished. Dies, who had abandoned public appearances before the committee, continued to use its files to launch attacks on the Administration, the labor movement, and organizations and individuals he deemed subversive. In the spring he engaged in a degrading public debate with Walter Winchell, a former ally. Winchell accused Dies, the committee, and other congressmen of hurting the war effort. So, even breast-beating patriots of Winchell's calibre came to the belated conclusion that the committee and its supporters no longer served the best interests of the nation. Dies, of course, demanded equal network time to call Winchell a liar.

By that time Martin Dies's days as chairman were numbered. He had lost a bid for a Senate seat in 1941 and faced stiff opposition for reelection in the fall of 1944. Militant labor groups in the Texas oil refineries had denounced him as a demagogue and were organizing to campaign against his reelection. Dies was tired and ill. He announced on May 12 that he would not seek reelection because he had "always had a dread of becoming a professional politician dependent upon the public" for his livelihood. One can fault his sincerity and integrity, but not his sense of humor.

Only a few weeks before the 1944 elections the committee published a report denouncing the Political Action Committee of the CIO and Dies promised to reveal more sensational documentation indicting the New Deal for disloyal collaboration with Communist forces. Dies ended his career as he had begun it, by using the committee's facilities for political purposes during an election campaign. The beneficial work of the Dies Committee was quickly recognized when Congressman Rankin, by careful political maneuvering, persuaded the House to make the Un-American Activities Committee a permanent standing committee. Even without Dies the committee would go on to bigger battles in the days ahead, until it was finally eliminated by the Ninety-Fourth Congress in January 1975.

August Ogden, author of the committee's most detailed history, leaves the reader with an ambivalent judgment about its performance. He laments that the committee failed to take advantage "of a wonderful opportunity to render real service to the country." He concludes that while the committee's work was not a total failure, it "stands in the history of the House of Representatives as an example of what an investigating committee should not be." Ogden's conclusion proceeds upon the assumption that the committee was created to render responsible service to the American people, and the evidence fails to support that notion.

If the Dies Committee and its successors were designed to serve such lofty ends, surely the House would not have appointed the likes of Fish, Dies, Thomas, Rankin, Velde, or Pool to chair such investigations. It is more reasonable to believe that the committees were designed to pander to popular fears during times of anxiety and to serve partisan political ends. Decent and responsible men were seldom persuaded to serve on these committees because they understood that the committee's conduct was rooted in the purpose for which it was created.

Too often commentators have presented the distorted notion that the liberal community constituted a united front against the committee. Evidence does not support such a self-serving interpretation. Liberals condemned the committee's questionable conduct but bowed before its political clout, justifying its continued existence. On occasion they tried to restrain the impact of the committee by supporting slightly weaker measures against the threat of subversion, as happened during the Truman Administration. At other times they tried to prove they were tougher on communism by increasing the penalties advocated by the committee, hoping to counteract the "soft on communism" charge made by their political opponents.

During the cold war the established liberal community seldom challenged the existence of the committee in any effective way. While tolerating its excesses, they shifted the blame for its existence on to rural reactionary elements in American life. When that was insufficient, they apologized for the committee's undemocratic methods by stressing the disreputable character of its victims. At times some suggested that the results of the committee's activities were not so horrendous since the targets of its wrath were kooks, Stalinist hacks, and people of no account. By denouncing the character of the victim, one could mitigate the iniquity of the committee's criminal conduct.

The basic argument which justified the committee's existence proceeded upon assumptions which, from the advantage of hindsight, seem dubious at best. It was widely accepted that the Communist menace constituted a genuine internal threat to the republic. This notion came to be held as sacred orthodoxy—to be challenged only at the price of self-incrimination. It was asserted that Communist influence and power pervaded the intellectual community, infiltrated the government, and controlled unions and the communications industry, thereby constituting a force equal to the country's established conservative institutions. This assumption appears more and more to have been a form of self-delusion. By such rationalizations the liberal community helped to inhibit sincere dissent and genuine reform, which is the lifeblood of a democratic society.

But self-delusion lived on. In 1953, after Dies had returned to the House, a Senate subcommittee investigating possible ways of reforming the conduct of congressional inquiries called on Dies for his expertise. He advised the senators: "Primarily, if you get a good chairman and a good committee you will have a good investigation. Outside of that all you need is a few general rules to see that the witness and the public get a fair break."

BIBLIOGRAPHY

Auerbach, Jerold S. *Labor and Liberty: The LaFollette Committee and the New Deal.* New York, 1966.

Barth, Alan. *Government by Investigation.* New York, 1955.

———. *The Loyalty of Free Men.* New York, 1951.

Bentley, Eric. *Thirty Years of Treason.* New York, 1971.

Buckley, William, and the editors of *The National Review. The Committee and its Critics: A Calm Review of the House Committee on Un-American Activities.* New York, 1962.

Burns, James M. *Roosevelt: The Lion and the Fox.* New York, 1956.

Carr, Robert K. *The Constitution and Congressional Investigating Committees.* New York, 1954.

———. *The House Committee on Un-American Activities, 1945–1950.* Ithaca, 1952.

Cooke, Alistair. *A Generation on Trial.* New York, 1950.

Dies, Martin. *The Trojan Horse in America.* New York, 1940.

Goodman, Walter. *The Committee: The Extraordinary Career of the House Committee on Un-American Activities.* New York, 1964.

Gurke, Leo. *The Angry Decade.* New York, 1947.

Ickes, Harold. *The Secret Diary of Harold Ickes.* New York, 1954.

Kempton, Murray. *Part of Our Time: Some Ruins and Monuments of the Thirties.* New York, 1955.

Latham, Earl. *The Communist Controversy in Washington.* Cambridge, Mass., 1966.

Leuchtenburg, William. *Franklin D. Roosevelt and the New Deal.* New York, 1963.

Lyons, Eugene. *The Red Decade: The Stalinist Penetration of America.* New York, 1941.

McGeary, M. Nelson. *The Development of Congressional Investigative Power.* New York, 1940.

McWilliams, Carey. *Prejudice: Japanese-Americans, Symbol of Racial Intolerance,* New York, 1944.

Mangione, Jerry. *The Dream and The Deal: The Federal Writers Project, 1935.* Boston, 1943.

Michie, Allan A., and Ryhlick, Frank. *Dixie Demagogues.* New York, 1939.

Ogden, August Raymond. *The Dies Committee: A Study of the Special House Committee for the Investigation of Un-American Activities, 1938–1944.* Washington, D.C., 1945.

Seldes, George. *Witch Hunt: The Technique and Profits of Redbaiting.* New York, 1940.

Taylor, Telford. *Grand Inquest: The Story of Congressional Investigations.* New York, 1955.

Voorhis, Jerry. *Confessions of a Congressman.* New York, 1947.

Wilson, Edmund. *American Jitters.* New York, 1932.

PERTINENT DOCUMENTS

Opening Debate over House Resolution to Establish Un-American Activities Committee, May 26, 1938

Opening Statement of Martin Dies, August 12, 1938

Testimony of Walter Steele, August 16, 1938

Testimony of Miss Sallie Saunders, August 20, 1938

New York Times Report on Roosevelt Critique of Committee, October 25, 1938

Dies Response to Roosevelt Statement, October 26, 1938

Testimony of Mrs. Hallie Flanagan, December 6, 1938

Committee Discussion on Methods and Rules of Evidence, December 14, 1938

First Annual Report of Dies Committee, January 4, 1939

House Debate over Committee Renewal, February 3, 1939

Time Article, May 29, 1939

Testimony of Earl Browder, September 6, 1939

Attack on Committee by John J. Dempsey, November 1939

New York Times Report of Roosevelt Attack on Dies Committee, October 27, 1939

New York Times Report of Dies Response to Roosevelt Attack, October 28, 1939

Second Annual Report, January 3, 1940

Critique of Committee by Walter Lippmann, January 11, 1940

Sol Cohn's Defense of Witness's Refusal to Answer, April 3, 1940

Speech of Martin Dies, "Trojan Horse," May 17, 1940

New York Times Report, December 11, 1940

New York Times Report, December 17, 1940

Third Annual Report, January 3, 1941

Fifth Annual Report, January 2, 1943

Critique of Committee by Jerry Voorhis, February 8 and 10, 1943

The Truman Committee
1941

Time magazine

The Truman Committee set a precedent for careful and discriminating methods of congressional investigation.

The Truman Committee 1941

by Theodore Wilson

The Senate Special Committee to Investigate the National Defense Program (popularly known as the Truman Committee) is often characterized as the most successful congressional investigative effort in United States history. Whether or not this is correct, this committee certainly played an important role in the ebb and flow of Executive-Legislative relations which shaped the mobilization effort of the United States during the Second World War. The Truman Committee, created to satisfy a junior senator's pique regarding the allocation of defense contracts, evolved into the dominant congressional body scrutinizing the defense program. As such, it became enmeshed in numerous critical questions—constitutional, political, economic, and ethical—regarding the organization and administration of America's wartime mobilization efforts. Although the committee and its chairman did not resolve certain of these questions (and, indeed, refused to confront certain of them), its record of responsible, restrained investigation established an admirable standard.

In times of national crisis, especially in time of war, the constitutional demarcations of authority between the Legislative and Executive branches of government have wavered and shifted dramatically. During the nineteenth century and into the twentieth, Congress and the President struggled periodically for supreme control over the process of war-making and its attendant responsibilities. This struggle was a result of the ambiguous language of the Constitution regarding Executive and Legislative responsibilities for declaring, prosecuting, and concluding wars. Each branch possessed strong claims to primacy. Certainly, the Constitution's grant of authority was great: "The executive power shall be vested in a President of the United States of America"; he shall recommend "such measures to Congress as he shall judge necessary and expedient"; and, most important, "the President shall be Commander-in-Chief of the Army and Navy." On the other hand, the Constitution empowered Congress "to provide for the common defense and general welfare of the United States, . . . to declare war, . . . to raise and support armies," and "to provide and maintain a navy." Further, Congress was given authority "to make all laws which shall be necessary and proper for carrying into execution the foregoing powers, and all other powers vested by this Constitution in the government of the United States, or in any department or officer thereof." These phrases, ambiguous in content, would appear to make possible a titanic struggle for domination should the two branches find themselves disagreeing about the necessity for military action or the manner of conducting a war.

On the basis of explicit constitutional authority, Congress would appear to have the upper hand in any such conflict. It possessed power over both the purse and the sword, it guarded the sole authority to declare war, and the Executive's war power was but rhetoric unless Congress bestowed its approval via appropriations and other legislation. That the President, by virtue of his role as supreme military commander and other powers which have accrued to him, has come to dominate almost all phases of the nation's activities in time of war was the result of Executive aggrandizement and, equally, of Legislative ineptitude and abdication. It is, nevertheless, the central fact in any analysis of Executive-Legislative relations during wartime.

Before the Civil War, Congress held the upper hand in both constitutional theory and practice. The Commander in Chief clause, upon which expansion of Executive authority was later based, was viewed only as stating the obvious fact that the President was "top general and top admiral" of the armed forces. As Chief Justice Taney observed of the President in 1850:

> His duty and his power are purely military. As commander-in-chief, he is authorized to direct the movements of the naval and military forces placed by law at his command, and to employ them in the manner he may deem most effectual to harass and conquer and subdue the enemy. . . . But his conquests do not enlarge the boundaries of this Union, nor extend the operation of our institutions and laws beyond the limits before assigned to them by the legislative power.

President Abraham Lincoln interpreted his role as Commander in Chief as authorizing Executive intervention in areas previously reserved to Congress. On his own, during the period after Fort Sumter, Lincoln created an enormous army, paid it out of Treasury funds without authorization or appropriation, proclaimed a blockade of Southern ports, suspended the writ of habeas corpus, and undertook various other actions without statutory authorization. He justified these measures by claiming that his position as Commander in Chief, combined with the President's duty "to take care that the laws be faithfully executed," produced a war power sufficient to carry out all necessary steps. Taken together, these acts amounted to an assertion that the President has, as Edward S. Corwin wrote, "for the first time in our history, an initiative of indefinite scope and legislative in effect in meeting the domestic aspects of a war emergency." President Lincoln "had laid hold upon vast emergency powers not describable in the usual terms of military command, the results of which, nevertheless, Congress had accepted, willy-nilly; and in these regards the Civil War was the prototype of both the First World War and the Second." But Congress did not accede to the President's actions without a struggle.

Indeed, the Joint Committee on the Conduct of the War, an intensely partisan investigatory committee which harassed the President throughout the war, did assert a powerful check on presidential authority. The committee was established on December 9, 1861, following the Union defeats at Bull Run and Balls Bluff, to "inquire into the conduct of the present war." Dominated by Radical Republicans and chaired by a leading radical senator, Benjamin F. Wade, the Joint Committee claimed the right not only to investigate Executive acts and advise the President, but attempted to take over direction of the war effort. Hearings were convened in late December 1861 and continued until early 1865. At these sessions, the committee discussed past and future battles and strategic plans, disloyal employees, and war supplies and contracts. In this effort the committee was partly successful, for the Confederate leader Robert E. Lee commented that "the Committee was worth about two divisions of Confederate troops." The committee repeatedly questioned the strategy and tactics of the Union, establishing a standard for meddling to which later congressional investigations might aspire, though the more responsible ones, such as the Truman Committee, consciously rejected the presumptions and behavior of the Joint Committee on the Conduct of the War. Senator Truman and his colleagues would have agreed with one later writer who shuddered at the War Committee's "undocumented insinuations, loud publicity against the reputations of men who were not permitted to defend themselves, its suppression of testimony which did not support the official thesis about the war, its star chamber atmosphere, and its general disregard of the rules of fair procedure." The Joint Committee played a powerful role in the conduct of the Civil War, but its power derived from political not constitutional sources. Thus, its influence was of brief duration and, by any estimate, the presidency emerged the victor.

The experience of the First World War further strengthened the hand of the President, though Congress also acquired enormous, hitherto unimagined, authority over personal and property rights. Edward S. Corwin has written: "First and foremost of the constitutional problems that confronted the President and Congress in 1917 . . . was that of adapting legislative power to the needs of 'total war.' Congress was suddenly called on to extend its power to a vast new range of complex subject matter that had hitherto existed outside the national orbit, and at the same time to give its legislation a form capable of keeping it easily responsive to the ever changing requirements of a fluid war situation. The problem was solved by the delegation to the President of the broadest discretion." The President received and, in some cases, merely took authority over a wide range of activities. While Congress might have originally bestowed these powers, the active role of the President in implementing them, and the pattern of delegating powers to persons and agencies acting solely in his name tended to exclude Congress from any meaningful part in directing the war effort.

To meet the challenge of rearmament during the Second World War, as early as 1938 President Franklin D. Roosevelt began to establish Executive offices responsible for the nation's defense. Shortly after the bombing of Pearl Harbor, a White House organization chart listed forty-two Executive agencies, of which thirty-five had been created by Executive order rather than by statute. The agencies which were given congressional authorization, such as Selective Service and the Office of Lend-Lease Administration, were staffed and operated with little regard for the sensibilities of Congress.

Despite the broad latitude permitted the President, the nation's defense mobilization moved forward slowly because of inadequate planning. The War and Navy Departments assumed, that prior to a declaration of war, "it was unlikely that an appreciable mobilization, either in manpower or materials, could be expected." There was no provision for gradual mobilization, and the Industrial Mobilization Plan, a sketchy document drafted without consultation of civilian leaders, would go into effect only when war was imminent. Because of congressional indifference, as late as March 1940, the House Appropriations Committee reduced a War Department request for replacement airplanes from 496 to 57, denied funds for an air base in Alaska, and discouraged any rapid expansion of the armed services.

The German blitzkrieg in the Low Countries and France during May 1940 reversed congressional opposition to rearmament and opened the floodgates for extensive defense expenditures. On May 16, 1940 the President requested an urgent appropriation of $1.2 billion for the armed services; two weeks later he requested another billion. Congress quickly authorized these sums. On July 10 Roosevelt proposed further authorizations and appropriations totaling almost five billion dollars which were approved in less than two months. Altogether, between June 1 and December 1, almost $10.5 billion in defense-related contracts were awarded.

At this point, however, the lack of careful preparation and the peculiar administrative philosophy of President Roosevelt became critically important. The President could request billions for defense and Congress could appropriate funds, but production of weapons and munitions remained largely beyond their control in a country that was officially at peace. Factory production capacity, still at depression levels, could be quickly increased, but the nation's resources were not unlimited, and priorities had to be established.

The Roosevelt Administration's penchant for overlapping organization, the growth of competing bureaucracies, and the President's inability to delegate authority realistically produced conflicts between existing defense agencies and the President's newly-created organizations. No organization had complete control of any defense program; instead, each agency had partial control of many operations. On May 26 FDR created a National Defense Advisory Commission, with members drawn from business, labor, and government. Though the NDAC acquired a staff and assorted responsibilities (including approval of defense contracts), it never overcame its administrative deficiencies. Individual members acquired considerable power (in 1940 Donald Nelson became administrator of priorities; William S. Knudsen, industrial production; and Sidney Hillman, manpower), but coordination proved impossible. In December 1940 FDR responded to the clamor for unified direction of the defense program by establishing another new agency, the Office of Production Management. Although OPM had only two chairmen, Knudsen and Hillman, their ability to coordinate the war effort was impaired as they were not given the authority to establish priorities, place orders, or allocate resources.

Despite the Administration's failure to achieve internal cohesion, once the United States entered the war, the President and his subordinates accepted responsibility for the conduct of the war. Indeed, President Roosevelt, in an address to Congress on September 7, 1942, asserted his right to ignore an act of Congress if necessary to win the war.

By 1941, Congress had accepted (and by its acceptance given tacit approval to) the Executive's claim to major authority in conducting the war effort. Given the political situation of 1941–1945, an inordinately skilled politician occupying the White House and his party dominating both houses of Congress, it appeared that the wartime role of Congress would be passive. Executive predominance was based on claims of superior knowledge; since this knowledge was derived from the Executive's accessibility to vital elements of information and organization which were denied to Congress, Congress could only acquiesce, thus excluding itself from meaningful participation in directing the war effort.

Executive control of America's participation in the Second World War was not questioned until March 1941, when the Senate Special Committee to Investigate the National Defense Program was created. Indeed, the investigatory power of Congress, hallowed by a great tradition of Legislative practice in English and American history, appeared to offer Congress an effective means of challenging claims of Executive preeminence: "We are called the Grand Inquest of the Nation, and as such it is our duty to inquire into every step of publick management, either Abroad or at Home, in order to see that nothing has been done amiss," William Pitt had informed the House of Commons in 1742. No one seriously questioned the right of Congress to conduct investigations for, as Donald H. Riddle has noted, "the purpose of informing itself, controlling the executive branch, or informing the public."

Senator Truman and his colleagues could not match the President's domination of the mechanisms of government, especially his control over information vital to a public challenge to his authority. Also, Truman did not intend to duplicate the shoddy work of the Civil War investigation. Therefore, much of the potential for Legislative-Executive conflict, embodied in the Truman Committee's charge to make a full and complete study of the national defense program, was siphoned off at the outset.

The creation of the Senate Special Committee to Investigate the National Defense Program is an undramatic story, perhaps befitting the sober mien of its chief sponsor and first chairman. In early 1941, Harry S. Truman, newly reelected junior senator from Missouri, was returning to work after an exhausting campaign. As a strong supporter of the Roosevelt Administration, Senator Truman was naturally interested in the measures then underway to achieve the President's "arsenal of democracy" program. Truman, a member of the Military Affairs Committee and the Military Subcommittee of the Appropriations Committee, possessed a life-long interest in military issues. He had visited a number of army installations and had become alarmed about the waste, favoritism, and lack of direction which he found in the defense program. Letters from constituents made him aware of the enormous economic benefits to be gained from the assignment of defense plants and military installations, and he was determined that Missouri communities should receive a fair share of this lucrative defense business.

On August 15, 1940, Senator Truman wrote confidently to his friend, Lou E. Holland, president of the Mid-Central War Resources Board in Kansas City, that Missouri possessed a great opportunity to obtain defense plants and defense-related contracts. "I have been interviewing the people here who are at the source of the fountain, and I believe that with proper organization Missouri can get its proper place in the set-up," Truman told his friend. He went on to describe the mobilization program, as army and administration officials had explained it to him: The key was decentralization. "The program, as outlined, contemplates the location of Government plants and key industries in five different sections between the Appalachians and the Rocky Mountains. . . . We are in Area C, which consists of southern Indiana and southern Illinois, Missouri and Kansas. The plan is to make each area a complete unit, with every sort of set-up needed in the National Defense program. Powder plants, loading plants, small arms factories, and so forth will be in each one of these areas. They are urging factories to decentralize all over the whole area. . . . This is our opportunity, if we ever had it." Within a few months, however, Truman recognized the favoritism given to Eastern states. "I think they are working with a little private clique of their own and not giving the local people a chance to do the work," he charged the War Department. Although Missouri had received fifty-five percent of all defense expenditures between the Mississippi River and Rocky Mountains by mid-1941, Truman decided that he had to defend the interests of the mid-West and the little businessman.

On February 10, 1941, after weeks of preparation, Truman rose in the Senate to address the problems he had identified in the defense program. This speech, a rare event for Truman, was given before a small but increasingly interested audience of colleagues, journalists, and professional gallery-sitters. Truman had previously stated that his purpose was "heading off scandals before they started." This speech dealt mainly with possibilities for corruption and the geographical and economic injustices which the present system of letting war contracts perpetrated. "There seems to be a policy in the national-defense set-up to concentrate all contracts and nearly all manufacturing that has to do with the national defense in a very small area," he observed indignantly. "I am reliably informed that from 70 to 90 percent of the contracts let have been concentrated in an area smaller than England." Such concentration was militarily unwise and also unfair to those regions which were being denied an opportunity to participate in the defense program, a result of the federal bureaucracy's preference for dealing with large corporations located in a few heavily industrialized areas. "The little manufacturer, the little contractor, and the little machine shop have been left entirely out in the cold. The policy seems to be to make the big man bigger and to put the little man completely out of business."

Personal favoritism, the sort of palm-greasing, "do a favor for a friend" attitude that had produced so much waste and graft during the First World War was wide-spread. For example, a Detroit company had won an ammunition plant contract from equally qualified construction firms in Missouri. Was it accidental that a partner in the Detroit firm was a good friend of a member of the War Department's Construction Advisory Board? Similarly, non-local companies had obtained contracts for the St. Louis Ordnance Plant and Ft. Leonard Wood and, in the latter case, the firm awarded this huge contract possessed no construction experience. This was simply not fair, Truman concluded, especially since the War Department was blatantly ignoring suggestions from members of Congress. "It is considered a sin for a United States Senator from a State to make a recommendation for contractors, although he may be more familiar with the efficiency and ability of our contractors than is anybody in the War Department," he said.

One means of correcting this deplorable situation, Senator Truman proposed, was to establish a committee to investigate the manner in which defense contracts were being awarded. Since tax money was being spent, the Senate should make use of "every safeguard possible to prevent their being misused and mishandled." Such a committee, empowered to ascertain the facts, would perform an important service in maintaining public confidence in the defense program. To that end, Truman announced his intention to introduce a resolution calling for such an investigation: "I am merely stating what I believe to be conditions that deserve investigation. If nothing is wrong, there will be no harm done. If something is wrong, it ought to be brought to light." He introduced Senate Resolution 71 three days later and had it referred immediately to the Committee on Military Affairs. On February 22, the committee unanimously reported the resolution to the Senate. At this point, however, Truman's proposal was frozen, being referred back to another committee, the Senate Committee to Audit and Control the Contingent Expenses of the Senate, chaired by James F. Byrnes, a confidant of President Roosevelt.

The Administration naturally was concerned about any proposal for a congressional investigation of the defense program. Congressional snooping into such sensitive matters as contracts and the progress of the mobilization effort might produce unwelcome publicity, thus upsetting the President's carefully orchestrated campaign to swing public opinion in favor of America's support of Great Britain. A call for such a committee in May 1940 by Republican Senator Arthur H. Vandenberg had been immediately scotched, but by early 1941 pressures for a congressional inquiry were mounting. In January two such resolutions had been introduced in the

House of Representatives. One, by Representative Eugene Cox, a conservative Georgian hostile to organized labor, called for a joint committee "to investigate and keep itself currently informed on all activities of the Federal Government in connection with the national defense." As well, a young Republican congressman, Henry Cabot Lodge, jr., had introduced a resolution that proposed a congressional committee with authority "to formulate and develop a consistent and complete defense policy for the United States." Lodge's proposal "amounted to a committee to conduct the war." No one in the Administration wanted either of these probes, and the only other alternative appeared to be the comparatively mild investigation proposed by Senator Truman. When the Cox resolution was discussed at a White House meeting, Byrnes informed the President: "I can fix that by putting the investigation into friendly hands." Truman later implied that he had given such assurances to the White House; "I couldn't get Jimmy Byrnes to act. Everybody thought I wanted to set up a headline business like the Dies Committee. . . . After much haggling and delay he recommended that I be given the magnificent sum of $15,000 with which I started the activities of that committee." Byrnes permitted Senate Resolution 71 to be reported on March 1, 1941. It was unanimously adopted the same day, with two alterations: an increase in the size of the committee from five to seven members, and, as noted above, a reduction of Truman's funds from $25,000 to $15,000.

Senator Truman, sponsor of the resolution, became committee chairman. His proposal had been authorized by the Senate (and tacitly, at least, by the Administration); he had $15,000 to spend, and, if he and the committee proved themselves worthy of the Senate's trust, the prospect of additional funds and a renewed authorization at some point in the near future.

Although initially it proved difficult to persuade senatorial colleagues to serve on the committee, within a week all seven had been selected. On March 8, the committee's membership was officially appointed: Truman as chairman; Joseph H. Ball (R.–Minn.); Owen Brewster (R.–Me.); Tom Connally (D.–Az.); Carl Hayden, James M. Mead (D.–N.Y.); and Monrad C. Wallgren (D.–Wash.). Carl A. Hatch (D.–N.M.) soon replaced Hayden, who resigned on April 15, 1941, and perhaps should be considered an original member. The committee was comprised of five Democrats and two Republicans, probably a reflection of the Administration's anxiety that it not spawn a political vendetta. The membership reflected impressive geographical balance and considerable diversity of background and political outlook. Notably, however, all save Connally, Hatch, and Truman were serving their first terms in the Senate.

At the time he became chairman of the Special Committee, Harry S. Truman was fifty-seven years old. The junior senator from Missouri had been in the Senate since 1934, but was virtually unknown outside his home state and the Senate chambers. A quiet, hardworking, physically unprepossessing man, Truman had served a long political apprenticeship. When he first came to Washington, he was identified with the political organization of Kansas City boss Thomas Pendergast; he gradually made a name for himself by supporting the New Deal. In 1941, Truman was just coming into his own, having won a tight battle for reelection with almost no assistance from the Administration. Intelligent, pragmatic, and deeply conscious of the historical dimension of the committee's work, Truman was determined to make a success of this assignment, the most important he had been given during his tenure. Nevertheless, no one would have predicted that he would demonstrate great ability, and that his dedicated and crusty leadership of the investigation would make his name a household word within a few months.

Ball had been appointed to the Senate in 1940 and won reelection in 1942. An ardent internationalist, Ball strongly supported FDR's program in foreign affairs (he would co-author the B_2H_2 resolution), and accepted the Administration's conduct of the war. The committee's senior Republican, Brewster, had also entered the Senate in 1940. Connally was the ranking Democrat on the committee. Connally had enjoyed a long career in Texas and national politics and was by 1941 one of the most powerful men in the Senate. Hatch did not attend committee sessions regularly, but he had served in the Senate since 1933 and could be counted an Administration loyalist. One of the most active members of the committee, Mead had served nineteen years in the House, was then appointed to the Senate in 1938, and elected in his own right in 1940. Mead was an Administration regular and perhaps the most liberal among the committee members. Elected in 1940, Wallgren was a little-known Democrat interested primarily in problems affecting his home state, such as lumber, light metals, and aircraft.

The membership of the committee was remarkably stable and these seven members served throughout Truman's chairmanship. The group was enlarged to ten members in November 1941, when Styles Bridges (R.–N.H.), Harley M. Kilgore (D.–W.Va.), and Clyde L. Herring (D.–Ia.) were appointed. Bridges resigned from the committee, pleading other responsibilities, in March 1942. He was replaced by Harold H. Burton (R.–Oh.), who took an active part in the committee's inquiries until he was appointed to the Supreme Court in 1945. Becuase Herring was defeated in the 1942 elections, Homer Ferguson (R.–Mich.) was appointed and became an aggressive critic of the military, particularly interested in the administration of the defense program.

Senator Truman once said of his colleagues on the committee: "I have . . . been extremely lucky in having associates who are sound thinkers and honest men." From small towns and middle class in background, the committee members appeared to share Truman's pragmatic approach to their job, viewing it as a vehicle for exposure and correction of abuses (especially where big business was concerned) rather than a platform for ideological disputation. Although every member had at least six committee assignments (Truman served on seven committees), the seven freshman senators were less heavily burdened than their elders and, undoubtedly, considered the Truman Committee a superb opportunity to gain quick recognition. As a whole, the committee established a standard of participation and knowledgability considerably above the norm.

The committee's second urgent chore was to obtain a qualified staff. On the recommendation of Attorney General Robert Jackson, Truman appointed Hugh Fulton, a young lawyer who had served as a United States attorney, as chief counsel. After a second appropriation in August 1941, Truman and Fulton then recruited the remainder of the staff, consisting of an associate counsel, an assistant counsel, a chief investigator, twelve to eighteen investigators, and various clerical persons. Matthew Connelly, who later became President Truman's appointment secretary, was the first chief investigator, and he recommended many of the other investigators, mostly young lawyers or accountants. For a time the committee, following a tradition of some years, co-opted employees from various Executive agencies (such as the Justice Department, Labor, the U.S. Housing Authority, Federal Power Commission, and the Office of Price Administration) as investigators.

In all, between 1941 and 1948, the Truman Committee held 432 public hearings at which 1,798 witnesses appeared (giving 27,568 pages of testimony), and another 300 Executive sessions that produced 25,000 additional pages of transcript. Fifty-one reports totaling 1,946 pages were published; and, as a result of the committee's careful attention to relations with the media, thousands of press releases were issued. All this was the end product of uncounted hours of research, hundreds of field trips, and thousands of interviews. Throughout its existence, the committee was almost never embarrassed by sloppy or inaccurate staff work. Indeed, the Truman Committee's thoroughness soon became so highly regarded that other congressional committees which became involved with defense issues often borrowed the committee's documentation, tacking on their own conclusions.

Together, Truman and Fulton decided upon guidelines for staff investigations and committee sessions. The Truman Committee asked only for the right to subpoena witnesses, as they normally dealt with readily available information and cooperative witnesses. The committee received thousands of letters during its existence, many describing alleged graft or waste; but it usually made independent decisions to launch investigations. Hearings were but a small part of the committee's activities; Truman and the staff often arranged numerous private meetings before deciding whether to schedule a hearing on a particular topic.

These public hearings (and the Executive sessions which were convened if issues directly affecting the national security or the individuals' reputations were involved) were conducted by explicit though unwritten rules. Although Truman was not always able to control the conduct of his colleagues, he insisted upon a modicum of fairness and objectivity. The committee decided not to act as a court of law and witnesses were accorded an impressive range of legal protections. They were permitted to submit prepared statements, to be attended by counsel, to place in the record documents supporting their views, and to review the pertinent hearing transcripts. The committee stated that it recognized, without prejudice, recourse to the Fifth Amendment, though a careful search of the record suggests that no witness ever invoked this provision. In sum, the Truman Committee followed a code of procedures that was rational, fair, and efficient; perhaps as objective as such an agency—which, after all, was created and conducted by politicians for political purposes—can be.

Overlapping jurisdiction greatly worried Truman, for the committee faced potential friction from standing committees and other investigatory groups. Fortunately, the Truman Committee encountered little hostility from the Senate establishment. Neither Naval Affairs nor Military Affairs evinced any interest in procurement and contract procedures, the Small Business Committee did have certain interests in common, but Truman and its chairman worked out a compromise. Truman kept his colleagues informed of the committee's work senators were welcome at committee hearings and were invited to take part in examination of witnesses. Further, the members of the Truman Committee, via service on other committees, strengthened the committee's position.

Two House committees, Naval Affairs and Military Affairs, occasionally grumbled about the Truman Committee's intrusions into their spheres. Their dissatisfaction may have been caused by the favorable headlines earned by Truman and his colleagues. An army officer stated as much in September 1941: "Confidentially I sat in on a meeting . . . where the House Naval Affairs Committee were bemoaning the fact that the Truman Committee has grabbed all the glory, has received the maximum of publicity, and has dampened the efforts of the other investigatory committees." Fortunately, relations with the House Select Committee to Investigate Defense Migration, which under the leadership of Representative John Tolan looked at a variety of defense-related problems, were quite friendly. The Tolan Committee might be termed the House equivalent of Truman's inquiry, though it never received the public recognition accorded its Senate counterpart.

The resolution that created the committee bestowed it with a remarkably broad grant of authority. Empowered to investigate all phases of the national defense program, the committee was specifically requested to study the following:

1. the types and terms of contracts awarded by the government;
2. methods by which such contracts are awarded and grantees selected;
3. use of small business facilities, through subcontracts or otherwise;
4. geographic distribution of contracts and location of plants and facilities;
5. effects of the defense program on labor and the migration of labor;
6. the performance of contracts and the accountings required of contractors;
7. benefits accruing to contractors;
8. practices of management or labor, and prices, fees, and charges which interfere with the defense program or unduly increase its cost;
9. such other matters as the committee deems appropriate.

Again and again, Truman and other members stated that their aim was to serve as a watchdog, a "benevolent policeman," to dig out the facts and present them to the American people. Originally, the Truman Committee was concerned with possible corruption and waste stemming from the rapid and enormous expansion of the defense production program. "I have had considerable experience in letting public contracts," Truman observed in an early speech, "and I have never yet found a contractor who, if not watched, would not leave the Government holding the bag. We are not doing him a favor if we do not watch him." The deplorable experiences of the aftermath of the First World War, during which numerous investigations uncovered widespread corruption and waste in the government's war production activities, was a powerful argument for careful scrutiny while contracts were being awarded and weapons manufactured.

The Truman Committee fulfilled this assignment with admirable efficiency and fairness. During the most active period of its existence—from summer 1941 to spring 1944—the committee investigated an incredible list of problems alleged to be retarding progress of the nation's domestic war effort and hundreds of cases of supposed graft and corruption. They maintained close scrutiny over the government's policies with regard to the award of contracts, labor-management relations, the geographical distribution of war plants, and the treatment of small business (Truman's pet concern). The committee held hearings and issued reports on such diverse problems as the aluminum shortage, camp and cantonment construction, light metals, aircraft, rubber, the conversion program of the War Production Board, Senator Albert B. Chandler's swimming pool, manpower, gasoline rationing, barges, farm machinery and equipment, renegotiation of war contracts, fake inspections of steel plate by Carnegie-Illinois Steel Corporation, shipbuilding and shipping, the comparative merits of rayon and cotton tire cord, magnesium, Ream General Hospital, conditions at Curtiss-Wright Corporation, and transactions between Senator Theodore G. Bilbo and various contractors. Its watchfulness certainly resulted in diminished graft, since potential wheeler-dealers were deterred from engaging in shady activities. One estimate of the actual monetary savings for which the Truman Committee was responsible is fifteen billion dollars. More important, perhaps, thousands of lives were saved as a result of the committee's success in ferreting out cases of production of defective weapons, aircraft, and other war supplies.

Nevertheless, the work of the Truman Committee, judged in historical perspective, was to prove not entirely successful. Increasingly, as mobilization picked up speed, it became apparent that the greatest threat to full production and to efficient and equitable use of the nation's resources was the chaotic administrative situation in Washington. The Truman Committee, as with previous investigatory committees in similar circumstances, found itself in a quandary regarding the issue of governmental waste and inefficiency. Should the committee have wished to do so, it might have found a justification in its grant of authority (especially its charge to investigate "such other matters as the Committee deems appropriate") to undertake a full inquiry into the Roosevelt Administration's conduct of the war. Such a step was repugnant to Truman, the other Democrats on the committee, and even to their Republican colleagues, for they sincerely desired to "help the President to win the war." They feared that public exposure of the full dimensions of bureaucratic confusion and conflict in Washington—and of its effects on the defense effort—would weaken and, perhaps, destroy public confidence in the Administration. That, in turn, might have caused the United States to lose the war.

Senator Truman clearly was aware of this conflict and of the dangers it posed. During a Senate debate in August 1941, he was pressed by Senator Vandenberg to admit that the President was culpable.

> "In other words," Vandenberg challenged Truman, "the Senator is now saying that the chief bottleneck which the defense program confronts is the lack of adequate organization and coordination in the administration of defense. . . . Who is responsible for that situation?"
>
> Truman: "There is only one place where the responsibility can be put."
>
> Vandenberg: "Where is that—the White House?"
>
> Truman: "Yes, sir."
>
> Vandenberg: "I thank the Senator."

To face this problem squarely, however, would be to open a Pandora's box. Truman and his Democratic colleagues certainly wished to avoid doing political injury to the President. At the same time, no one on the committee wanted to risk charges of whitewash because they ducked legitimate questions. Even if the committee had raised the issue of presidential responsibility directly, Truman must have doubted whether his committee—or even Congress as a whole—possessed sufficient clout to force the sort of changes that were necessary. Above all, Truman wished to avoid the kind of disgusting spectacle evoked by the internecine warfare carried on between 1861 and 1865 by the Joint Committee on the Conduct of the War. The Truman Committee stated repeatedly that it would not concern itself with matters of strategy and tactics. Whenever Truman was informed that a committee inquiry threatened to enter this realm (as defined by the Executive branch), he abandoned that line of investigation. This, of course, proved a source of continuing frustration, for strategy and even tactics were even more intimately connected with matters of production and the allocation of resources during the Second World War than they had been during the Civil War.

At almost every turn, the Truman Committee, pursuing legitimate and seemingly innocuous inquiries, found itself in potential conflict with Executive prerogatives and policies. It may be that the value of tracing the committee's route is not so much in measuring their boldness under fire, not even in discovering how far they traveled; rather, any benefit may derive from recognition of the dangers they faced and being better prepared to avoid or defuse them if ever the nation again undertakes such a journey.

At its first meeting on March 12, 1941, the Truman Committee decided that it should not undertake the investigation of any controversial subjects until it had established its legitimacy before the Senate and the American people. For the time being, Truman eschewed study of such sensitive topics as the location of defense facilities and racial discrimination in hiring at these plants. Public relations, the members correctly recognized, was of foremost importance for any congressional investigatory committee; without popular acceptance, its efforts would be worthless. Thus, the committee agreed that "its first duty would be to give to Congress and the public a clear picture of the present state of the program." On April 15, the committee convened hearings on this subject and sat back to hear Secretary of War Henry L. Stimson, Under Secretary of War Robert P. Patterson (soon to be a familiar visitor), Secretary of the Navy Frank Knox, and OPM's Hillman and Knudsen discourse on how smoothly the program was proceeding. The session gained favorable publicity for the committee and introduced it to certain of the complex issues to be dealt with in the next few years.

The committee's next target in this preliminary phase was the camp and cantonment construction program, a matter of great interest to the public. Some 229 projects had been started at an estimated cost of slightly over 500 million dollars; thus, the likelihood of waste and chicanery was large. Investigators of the Truman Committee failed to uncover corruption, but they did raise further questions about the concentration of contracts and they discovered that the construction program was far in excess of its original estimated cost. Ultimately, the cost was $828,424,000, over $300 million above the original estimates. General Brehon Somervell, the arrogant chief of the army's Services of Supply, bitterly complained about the Truman Committee's meddling, a forewarning of other clashes. Somervell admitted increased expenditures of over 100 million dollars but justified them on grounds of the urgency of the situation. This, too, would become a familiar refrain. The committee gave the army a fair opportunity to rebut its findings, sending Somervell a copy of its draft report and expressing willingness to reevaluate its conclusions. The report, released on August 14, 1941, placed blame for the enormous cost of the construction program on the cost-plus contract scheme (whereby a contractor received all costs incurred in fulfilling a contract, plus a percentage profit) and the inability of the Quartermaster Corps (which was responsible for all construction) to administer efficiently such projects. The committee did not recommend outright abolition of cost-plus contracts. It did, however, suggest that responsibility for construction be shifted to the Engineers Corps. Some months later the War Department accepted this recommendation, a decision which greatly enhanced the Truman Committee's reputation.

Two other investigations in the committee's first months of operation—a one-day session on labor problems in the coal industry and a careful look at aluminum shortages—were typical of the watchdog dimension of its activities. In April the committee decided reluctantly that it should take a hand in the bitter dispute between the United Mine Workers and the coal operators. Concerned about the effects of the coal strike on steel production, Truman convened a one-day hearing which accomplished little aside from giving UMW chief John L. Lewis a forum for some flamboyant oratory. However, a settlement was reached a few hours after the committee adjourned.

A study of the critical shortages of aluminum which had come to light during the spring was much more serious. The Aluminum Company of America, which possessed a virtual monopoly over production of aluminum, had repeatedly given assurances that it could supply the needs of both the defense program and the private sector. However, in recent months demand had outstripped Alcoa's production by more than one hundred percent. The Truman Committee held hearings during May-June 1941, responding with impressive speed once the bottleneck was brought to its attention. In the June 26 report the committee criticized Alcoa for acting selfishly to protect its monopoly and blasted the Office of Production Management's handling of the situation. Faulting OPM for underestimating aluminum requirements and for indecision once the problem had been discovered, the Truman Committee pressed for better coordination of the defense program. Truman commented: "We rapped some knuckles to be sure, but we tried to do it in a constructive way. We didn't take the easy course and blame the President. We want aluminum, not excuses." Unfortunately, the only way to obtain more aluminum immediately was to let Alcoa off the hook. This would not be the last time the Truman Committee would encounter this sort of genteel blackmail: the necessity to ignore principle in order to obtain immediate production.

The Truman Committee, particularly its inexperienced chairman and staff, performed with the skill of veterans. Truman was greatly encouraged, believing that "we have justified the existence of the Committee." He wrote a friend: "I don't believe there will be any serious difficulty for us to get the necessary funds from now on to carry out our work." His confidence was justified, for in August 1941 the Senate increased the committee's budget and authorized use of facilities and personnel drawn from the Executive branch. Thereafter, the Truman Committee's position never was seriously challenged, and its mandate was routinely renewed each year.

Senator Truman, as committee chairman, was receiving favorable recognition as well, as he was eager to dig into what he believed to be glaring inequities regarding the location of defense plants and the treatment of small business. In part, this resulted from an emotional distrust of "bigness" in any form. Writing in a populist vein to a Missouri friend, Truman stated:

> I am trying my best to carry on my investigation of the . . . contract racket as fairly as I possibly can. It is a most difficult job to perform but I believe we are getting some results. . . . It has been the policy of the Army and Navy to let contracts to big contractors and to big business because it is the easiest way out. A half a dozen big construction companies and manufacturers have more than seventy-five per cent of all the contracts. They obtained all the priorities on basic metal, and the little manufacturers like Chapman Brothers there in Independence are simply being put out of business.

Bringing every sort of pressure at the committee's command to bear on this problem, Truman and his colleagues obtained a measure of improvement. However, the War Department, concerned with getting as much production as quickly as possible, persisted in dealing mainly with large firms. All through the war, unhappy constituents deluged Congress with complaints. Truman himself admitted: "If you should see my correspondence, you would think that every little businessman in the country is going out of business." Frustrated by its inability to correct the problem, the Truman Committee gradually realized that the government's method of awarding contracts was not solely responsible, but that the total approach to defense production, including such problems as cost-plus contracts, allocation of scarce materials, reliance on dollar-a-year men, and the stubborn impassivity of the War Department, was also involved. Exerting pressure on OPM to correct these inequities was futile, since OPM was helpless to bring into line the agencies which it supposedly managed.

This realization caused the Truman Committee to confront the most important issues it would deal with during the war. Fearful for the defense program if the current state of administrative chaos in Washington was permitted to continue, the committee faced awkward alternatives: it could blow the whistle and subject OPM and the entire Administration—including, if necessary, the President—to indictment and trial in the forum of public opinion; or the committee could work behind the scenes, hoping to force the administrative *apparat* to pull together for the common good. Neither strategy was very appealing, and either course entailed considerable risk for the committee's members and for the nation. Not surprisingly, the committee adopted a compromise strategy, borrowing from both of the above alternatives as the situation warranted. None of its members wanted to run the war, a possible outcome if a publicity barrage attacking the Administration had been totally effective. "The Committee," its first annual report affirmed, "has not and does not intend to substitute or attempt to substitute its judgment . . . for the judgment of the executive agencies involved." Its proper role, Senator Truman stressed again and again, was "auditor of the national defense program," not dictator. But, at the very least, OPM must be replaced by a new agency with real power over the assorted satrapies that had sprung up. If that were done, the committee could provide powerful support for the Administration, using its publicity leverage against recalcitrant bureaucrats instead of the President.

Senator Truman unveiled the committee's plan in his presentation of the first annual report to the Senate on January 15, 1942, just five weeks after Pearl Harbor had propelled the United States into war. There was little drama in Truman's awkward summary of the committee's findings; but the conclusions he diffidently offered had a dramatic effect on his audience. The report was, clearly, a devastating indictment of the Office of Production Management. "Its record has not been impressive," the report began. "Its mistakes of commission have been legion; and its mistakes of omission have been even greater. It has all too often done nothing when it should have realized that problems cannot be avoided by refusing to admit that they exist." The report criticized the practice of using dollar-a-year men and lambasted OPM for ignoring the tremendous contribution which small companies could make. "Fundamentally," Truman observed, "the disappointing record of the Office of Production Management is not so much due to its lack of power as to its failure to perform the functions for which it was created." Cynically, one might view this as an attempt to absolve the President of blame by placing that blame on ineffective subordinates. Nonetheless, Truman sincerely believed in this explanation. The report also blasted selfish interests, especially organized labor, concerned solely with their own aggrandizement; but it returned repeatedly to OPM as the chief bottleneck in the defense program. The report recommended that a single person be appointed to direct the production and supply program, and that OPM be abolished and a new agency be created.

The Truman Committee's major proposal already had been implemented when Truman spoke. Two days before, on January 13, President Roosevelt had announced the creation of a new super agency, the War Production Board, which would "exercise general direction over the war procurement and production program." He appointed as its head Donald Nelson, the experienced and highly regarded former Sears Roebuck executive.

While the President was being pressed from all quarters to straighten out the administration of the domestic war effort, Truman's submission, some days before its formal release, of the committee report to FDR may well have prodded him into a decision. Certainly, the press credited the Truman Committee with a major role in this reorganization of defense programs.

It appeared that the committee's efforts to obtain central direction of the war production program had been amply rewarded. Nelson, who had been permitted to draft the Executive order that set up the War Production Board, had inscribed therein sweeping powers for himself. The chairman's authority over other agencies was explicitly stated: "Federal departments, establishments, and agencies shall comply with the policies, plans, methods, and procedures in respect to war production and procurement as determined by the Chairman." However, Nelson's authority was seriously circumscribed, for it depended, as did all such administrative arrangements under the New Deal, on his personal relationship with FDR and the coterie of presidential intimates surrounding the President. Nelson did not possess the complete confidence of the White House. Lacking this, officials of agencies theoretically subordinate to Nelson's authority could (and did) go over his head, taking their objections to Roosevelt or one of his advisers. Further, Nelson was no "production czar" but rather a super-coordinator. His decisions had to be enforced on those agencies which negotiated procurement contracts and supervised the production of war supplies. As the Truman Committee was soon to learn, Nelson simply was not aggressive enough to protect and extend his authority. Preferring persuasion to coercion, Nelson avoided confrontations with imperious representatives of other government departments. This defect was obvious in his relations with General Somervell, chief of the Army Services Forces. Somervell's procurement activities clearly placed him under Nelson's authority, but he operated the agency with almost total private freedom. "Nelson was not aggressive about his jurisdiction and his powers," the historian of WPB admitted. "He allowed [the Army-Navy Munitions Board] to elude his group, although it was subordinate to him, and he permitted the War Department's Services of Supply, over which he said he had control, to become something decidedly other than what he thought it ought to be." In Nelson's favor were his flexibility, openness, and enthusiasm.

These latter qualities favorably impressed the Truman Committee. Nelson quickly gained good relations with committee members and, in particular, with Truman. The WPB was careful to keep the committee fully informed and normally dealt with Congress through Truman. In response, the committee adopted a proprietary attitude toward WPB. At Nelson's first appearance before the committee in late January, Truman stated: "Mr. Nelson, this Committee has been working for seven months to get the responsibility for the war effort centered in one man, with the power to act. . . . We have fought to get you this job. We are going to fight to support you now in carrying it out." Nelson had come to discuss the dollar-a-year men issue, and the committee objected vehemently to his statements in support of the practice. However, Senator Truman's comments revealed the situation in which the committee found itself following Nelson's appointment. Truman first remarked:

> We want you to understand . . . that we want the war won as quickly as possible. If you have to have dollar-a-year men to win the war, this Committee is not going to interfere with that procedure on your part, because we want the war won, but we still have some ideas on dollar-a-year men and the ethics and things that are brought to bear on that subject. But this committee does not want to hamper you in carrying out your job. That comes first. . . . Here is the situation. Whether you are right or wrong under the present circumstances, this Committee feels . . . that your idea ought to prevail, because we have to win the war.

Arranging Truman's emotional statement in a roughly logical sequence demonstrates the committee's helplessness. Although the committee believed that reliance on dollar-a-year men, favoritism of big business, *et al* were ethically wrong and boded ill for the future, they had to be accepted if they contributed to the war effort. The committee accepted the sole competence of the Executive branch to judge whether something did or did not contribute to winning the war. The Truman Committee certainly never gave automatic approval of WPB decisions. During the next twelve months, the committee objected strenuously to a number of WPB policies and decisions, and relations between Nelson and Truman were at times decidedly strained. The possibility of a total break was minimal, for Nelson recognized that the Truman Committee was his strongest ally and the committee believed WPB was its best hope for centralized control and, thus, protection of civilian interests.

The fatal defect in this strategy was that the Truman Committee could not force Nelson to use the powers he had been given. It could only offer encouragement, as Truman stressed during Nelson's first appearance before the committee: "If you meet any obstacles . . . where this committee can turn the light of publicity on the subject or call attention to legislation that should be enacted to give you the necessary means to carry the job out, we want to be informed, and we are at your service"; but what if Nelson refused to fight, what if the process of bureaucratic imperialism continued unabated, what if the President permitted these quarrels to persist? Truman and his colleagues were obligated by their own definition of the proper role of an investigatory committee in wartime not to mutiny. Notably, the Truman Committee first opposed proposals that were introduced to Congress in mid-1942 for the creation of a top-level liaison committee between Congress and the Executive branch. Many congressmen were unhappy about their lack of knowledge of the defense program. "All is not well with us. . . . We do not always have the information which we should have," lamented one senator in October 1942. FDR rejected the liaison proposal, and the Truman Committee at this time also opposed it, largely because its members believed the committee served this function.

Of course, Harry Truman was psychologically incapable of restraining his irritation and repressing frustration with WPB's failures. Throughout 1942 and into early 1943, the Truman Committee held hearings on critical areas where production bottlenecks had developed. The rubber program (which proved a source of great embarrassment for Nelson), defense housing, steel shortages, and gasoline rationing were some of the topics it examined. The committee criticized the greedy actions of both large corporations and the unions, and gained enormous support for this position. Truman's outspoken statements regarding those who used the war as an opportunity for private profit made him one of the most popular figures in America.

Increasingly, however, Truman and the committee zeroed in on the War Department as the greatest source of difficulties in the war effort. This resulted from the committee's bitterness about the army and navy procurement agencies' role in destroying the effectiveness of Nelson and the War Production Board. It certainly was possible to date the downfall of WPB to March 12, 1942, when an agreement setting forth the relationship between WPB and War Department purchasing agencies was signed by Nelson and Under Secretary of War Robert Patterson. In effect, WPB abdicated to the armed services full responsibility for military procurement and, given shortages, tight production schedules, and conflicting priorities regarding military and civilian needs, that inevitably produced further conflict.

The Truman Committee remained steadfastly loyal to Nelson; but it could not tolerate the erosion of his authority. Other agencies asserted their independence, leading eventually to a reorganization of WPB in September. Further rebellions during the fall culminated in February 1943 in a decision by FDR to replace Nelson with the World War I "czar," Bernard Baruch. The Truman Committee regretfully abandoned Nelson and began to speak in favor of a legislative solution to the need for centralized authority. A bill to establish a Department of Supply, long advocated by Senator Kilgore, a committee member, was introduced and received Truman's support. In April the committee scheduled hearings on "conflicting war programs" and its report on this subject, released on May 6, stated forcefully: "Today discussion of the overall legal authority of the War Production Board is mere pedantry. Although the authority may exist it has not been exercised." Four days later, the Senate enthusiastically approved a bill to establish an independent, civilian-dominated supply agency. White House alarm at this threatened congressional revolt led to FDR's appointment of his "assistant president," James Byrnes, to the post of director of an Office of War Mobilization. Byrnes was given essentially the powers to coordinate the procurement and production programs that WPB had possessed.

This decision ended the struggle for primacy over war production. The Truman Committee applauded Byrnes's appointment and justifiably claimed that the congressional and popular pressure it had mobilized was a major cause of FDR's decision. Certainly, the committee had played an important role throughout the struggle, although the objectives for which it originally had entered the fray—favoritism toward big business, wasteful procedures regarding contracts, over-emphasis on military needs, and so forth—had not been achieved. Nor would they receive significant attention in the future, for Byrnes, a conservative Southerner who was sympathetic to the military's viewpoint, had no need to look for support to the Truman Committee.

The committee's involvement in overall control of the domestic war effort did, however, continue, though its emphasis shifted. As the battle for domination of the domestic war effort progressed, Truman and several other members began referring to the critical issue not as centralized administration but in terms of a struggle for civilian control of the war effort. This concern emerged quite early though it was largely obscured by other problems until WPB's disintegration. On November 26, 1942, for example, Truman took part in a "March of Time" interview. Responding to a question about the problem of civil-military relations, Truman bluntly stated:

> That is the most important question of the day. The function of generals and admirals is to fight battles, and to tell us what they need to fight battles with. They have no experience in business and industry, and the job of producing what they ask for should be left to business men under the direction of experienced civilians. I am firmly convinced that any attempt on the part of these ambitious generals and admirals to take complete control over the nation's economy would not only place vital functions in inexperienced hands, but would present a definite threat to our postwar political and economic structure.

He was referring specifically to the conflict then raging over utilization of manpower but the threat, as perceived by Truman and others, involved every phase of American economic and social life. The generals and admirals in no way pursued a calculated plan to take over the country, though they might have succeeded had they made a serious effort. They were interested solely in obtaining everything necessary to win the war, and they approached the wartime economy from this narrow perspective. Military bureaucrats such as General Somervell, who once described the Truman Committee as "formed in iniquity for political purposes," had no patience with arguments that the people at home required a fair share of rubber, aluminum, gasoline, and other scarce materials. Civilians had to make do; military requirements—which often reflected an assessment of actual needs and all possible contingencies—came first.

The Truman Committee cooperated with other groups to resist the War Department's efforts to impose its priorities on the nation. Where the military's challenge of civilian control was blatant—the manpower issue, stockpiling of truck tires, or the conflict between the army program and legitimate domestic requirements—resistance was remarkably effective. The principle of civilian authority was maintained, though the pervasiveness of the military in domestic matters continued to increase until the end of the war.

As noted previously, the Truman Committee repeatedly renounced any desire to meddle in strategy or tactics. But that did not resolve the problem of civil-military relations, for what was a legitimate military program and what represented an illegitimate military effort to overturn civilian rule? There were no clear guidelines, and the committee did not possess sufficient information—or the power to compel the military to make such information available—to devise effective rules. Access to information was crucial: With junior officers, the committee believed that it possessed the power to force military representatives to testify. Writing to Patterson in March 1943, Truman strongly objected to a War Department claim that Executive privilege excused Colonel John H. Amen from responding to the committee's questions. "Since the Committee obtained from other officers of the Army the information which it expected to obtain from Colonel Amen," Truman informed Patterson, "it will not take the necessary steps to cite him for contempt. But the Committee desires to make it clear that in so doing it does not in any sense acquiesce in your contention that any officer in the Army has the right to refuse to divulge to the Committee within the scope of its powers of investigation." However, when principal officers of the War Department refused information on the ground of military necessity, the committee willingly complied. Undoubtedly the most significant case of this sort arose when committee investigators ran across enormous and unexplained expenditures for something identified only as the Manhattan Project. Truman telephoned Secretary of War Henry L. Stimson, who told him: "Now that's a matter which I know all about personally, and I am only one of the group of two or three men in the whole world who know about it."

> Truman: "I see."
> Stimson: "It's part of a very important secret development."
> Truman: "Well, all right then &"
> Stimson: "And I—"
> Truman: "I herewith see the situation, Mr. Secretary, and you won't have to say another word to me. Whenever you say that to me that's all I want to hear."

Truman was not to learn the Manhattan Project's purpose until the day he became President.

More typical of the information imbroglio was the ill-starred Canol Project, a scheme to supply high-octane gasoline, using locally-produced and refined petroleum, for the Alcan Highway and U.S. airfields in the region. The project was clearly impractical and required enormous expenditures of manpower and scarce goods. Nevertheless, the War Department and, specifically, General Somervell, forged ahead, ignoring the question of cost-effectiveness and practicality. "Military necessity requires that the Canol Project be completed as rapidly as possible," was Somervell's stock answer when objections were raised by civilian agencies.

The Truman Committee launched an investigation of the Canol Project in summer 1943 and in September a subcommittee looked at the site and convened hearings. Gathering a huge amount of evidence, the committee soon decided that the scheme was indefensible, and should be closed down. WPB, the Department of Interior, and various other civilian agencies supported this recommendation. Although $100 million already had been spent, an immediate shutdown would save $30 million already authorized but not expended. The War Department flatly ignored the committee's judgment, stating without elaboration that Canol was "necessary to the war effort." Since no Executive agency was able to overrule the army, the Truman Committee's only recourse was to place the facts in the record. This was done via public hearings in late 1943 and a report by Truman to the Senate. Despite continued pressure from members of the committee, the army obtained a further appropriation from Congress and completed all phases of the project in October 1944. The fifth annual report of the Truman Committee, released in September 1946, reported that Canol had cost $134 million and had produced about as much fuel as could have been transported by one medium tanker in a period of three months. The Canol Project, though certainly not typical of wartime development programs, showed the limits of the Truman Committee's influence.

The committee performed splendidly in its principal role as production watchdog. Perhaps the greatest of the committee's accomplishments was the high level of public confidence in the Roosevelt Administration's conduct of the war. The committee served as an important source of information on what the government was doing to win the war, and most Americans accepted its assurances that the domestic war effort, despite administrative tangles and bureaucrative incompetence, was going well. Notably, the public seemed little concerned about the committee's reluctance to investigate charges of congressional graft and influence-peddling. Only three such inquiries took place (only one, involving Senator "Happy" Chandler's swimming pool, during Truman's tenure) in almost seven years.

In April 1942 Truman wrote his friend, Lou Holland: "We have the political campaign coming on, and with the Republican Committee endorsing the war program the campaign will be made of course on the efficiency of the conduct of that program. So unless the Democrats whole-heartedly endorse what my Committee is trying to do I fear very much I will become a political issue, and then the fat will be in the fire sure enough." Truman's anxieties proved unwarranted, for the committee attained such recognition and public acceptance that it became virtually invulnerable to political attack. Ironically, the committee's unique status largely stemmed from Truman's request that the committee's deliberations be conducted as impartially and reasonably as possible.

It may be said that Truman's resignation on August 4, 1944, to accept the Democratic Party's vice presidential nomination, was a watershed in the history of the committee. Although it was to continue in existence until April 1948, after Truman's departure there occurred a large turnover in the committee's membership, erosion of its prestige, and growth of partisan bickering. The committee, headed by James M. Mead, Harley Kilgore, and then Owen Brewster, conducted some forty-five public hearings. It issued reports on such important topics as reconversion, disposal of surplus property, the proposed loan to Great Britain, and the renegotiations of war contracts. However, if "congressional investigations are essentially exercises in the creation of public opinion," the heyday of the Senate Special Committee to Investigate the National Defense Program ended with Truman's resignation. Indeed, recognition of the feisty Missourian's centrality to all that the committee accomplished—and failed to do—perhaps is the most useful insight to be gained from study of its activities.

BIBLIOGRAPHY

The official records of the Special Committee to Investigate the National Defense Program, approximately 400 linear feet, are located in the National Archives. An almost equally valuable source is Truman's senatorial files, which fully document his role on the committee. These papers are at the Truman Library, Independence, Missouri. The published hearings and reports of the Truman Committee are also essential. Publications of various war agencies, especially the Budget Bureau's *The United States at War* (Washington, D.C., 1946), are informative. Also see the relevant volumes of the Department of the Army's history of the war.

Surprisingly, few historians have tapped this store of information. Donald Riddle, *The Truman Committee: A Study in Congressional Responsibility* (New Brunswick, 1963), remains the most helpful analysis. Roger Willson has written an impressively researched study, "The Truman Committee" (unpublished Ph.D. dissertation, Cambridge, 1966). See also Harry A. Toulmin, jr., *Diary of Democracy: The Senate War Investigating Committee* (New York, 1947), an uncritical account. Herman M. Somers, *Presidential Agency: OWMR, Office of War Mobilization and Reconversion* (Cambridge, Mass., 1950), Harry Lever and Joseph Young, *Wartime Racketeers* (New York, 1945), and Leslie R. Groves, *Now It Can Be Told: The Story of the Manhattan Project* (New York, 1962) treat important issues. Studies of the larger context in which the Truman Committee operated include Elias Huzar, *The Purse and the Sword* (Ithaca, 1950), Walter Millis, et al, *Arms and the State* (New York, 1958), Edward S. Corwin, *The President: Office and Powers* (New York, 1958), Roland Young, *Congressional Politics in the Second World War* (New York, 1956), and Alan Barth's excellent *Government By Investigation* (New York, 1955). Also useful are *War and Society: The United States, 1941–1945* (New York, 1972), by Richard Polenberg, and the prejudiced but insightful work by Eliot Janeway, *The Struggle for Survival: A Chronicle of Economic Mobilization in World War II* (New Haven, 1951).

Books by and about the personalities who struggled for power in wartime Washington include Harry S. Truman, *Memoirs: Year of Decisions* (Garden city, 1955), Margaret Truman, *Harry S. Truman* (New York, 1973), Merle Miller, *Plain Speaking: An Oral Biography of Harry S. Truman* (New York, 1973), Jonathan Daniels, *The Man of Independence* (Philadelphia, 1950), James McGregor Burns, *Roosevelt: The Soldier of Freedom,* 1940–1945 (New York, 1970), Donald Nelson, *Arsenal of Democracy* (New York, 1946), and James M. Mead, *Tell the Folks Back Home* (New York, 1944). Additionally, men such as Harold Ickes, Henry Wallace, Jesse Jones, Harry Hopkins, and James Byrnes are described in numerous biographies and memoirs. Bruce Catton, *The War Lords of Washington* (New York, 1948) effectively captures the atmosphere of those times.

PERTINENT DOCUMENTS

Senator Harry S. Truman to Lou Holland, President, Mid-Central War Resources Board, August 15, 1940

Speech of Senator Truman to the Senate, February 10, 1941

Senate Resolution 71, March 1, 1941

Truman Committee News Release, April 18, 1941

Truman Committee News Release, May 13, 1941

Senator Truman to Brigadier General L. E. Campbell, jr., Ordnance Department, June 18, 1941

Transcript of C.B.S. Radio Program, "The Congressional Mailbag," July 22, 1941

Truman Committee Statement of Policy, December 10, 1941

Senate Debate over Truman Committee Report, January 15, 1942

U.S. District Judge Lewis B. Schwellenbach to Senator Truman, January 23, 1942

Testimony of Donald M. Nelson, Chairman, War Production Board, on Dollar-a-Year Men, January 28, 1942

Senator Truman to Judge Schwellenbach, April 21, 1942

Truman Committee Report on Senator Albert B. Chandler's Swimming Pool, July 16, 1942

Senator Truman to Judge Schwellenbach, July 29, 1942

"We Can Lose the War in Washington," by Senator Truman, November 1942

Truman Committee Report on Gasoline Rationing, December 11, 1942

Donald M. Nelson to Senator Truman, January 4, 1943

Truman Committee Memorandum on Executive Session, January 20, 1943

Time Magazine Article, "Billion-Dollar Watchdog," March 8, 1943

Truman Committee Report on Conflicting War Programs, May 6, 1943

Radio Address by Senator Truman, Shenandoah, Iowa, October 4, 1943

Testimony of Lt. Gen. Brehon B. Somervell on Canol Project, December 20, 1943

Memorandum of Hugh Fulton, Chief Counsel, Truman Committee, May 26, 1944

Truman Committee News Release, June 15, 1944

Harper's Magazine Article, "The Job That Made Truman President" by Wesley McCune and John R. Beal, June 1945

The Kefauver Committee
1950

New York Public Library Picture Collection

Estes Kefauver focused national attention on the thriving world of bookies, pimps, gangland enforcers, and crime bosses, and the law enforcement systems which allowed them to prosper.

The Kefauver Committee
1950

by Theodore Wilson

The Senate Special Committee to Investigate Organized Crime in Interstate Commerce, popularly known as the Kefauver Committee, is one of the most famous congressional investigations of recent times, despite its failure to prove conclusively its principal thesis or to obtain legislative approval for its major recommendations. One factor, television, was largely responsible for fixing the public consciousness upon this one investigation from among the dozens of important congressional inquiries in the decade after the Second World War. For the first time millions of Americans (some twenty million by one estimate) observed the periodic bouts of drama and boredom which comprised a congressional hearing as it unfolded. Americans gaped as the denizens of other worlds–bookies, pimps, and gangland enforcers, crime bosses and their slippery lawyers–marched across their television screens. They watched and were impressed by the schoolmasterish Estes Kefauver, the dignified Tennessean who was the committee's first chairman, as he condemned criminals and the system of ineffective law enforcement, graft, and popular apathy which permitted them to thrive. Most important, they turned away from this spectacle persuaded that Senator Kefauver and his colleagues had uncovered the "true" causes of crime in America and that the crime committee had the problem under control. Certainly, the credibility and public support extended to the Kefauver Committee, a litmus test of the success of any congressional investigation, suggest that this inquiry deserved its impressive reputation.

Nonetheless, one is nagged by the thought that something more than television (and the fact that the committee's endeavors made Estes Kefauver a presidential contender) explains the Kefauver Committee's powerful impact. A partial explanation may be found, perhaps, by studying the Kefauver Committee within the context of those frantic years, 1949–1952—a time of bitter partisanship and of deep divisions within American society. Looked at in this way, as an example of oracular utterances to a people desperately clamoring for reassurance, the Kefauver Committee's popularity makes considerable sense. A cynic might assert that the Kefauver Committee was the social counterpart of Senator Joseph McCarthy's pursuit of a domestic political conspiracy aimed at the destruction of the United States. According to reputable sources, McCarthy and Kefauver competed for the authority to mount a crusade against organized crime during the period when McCarthy was thrashing around in search of an issue to further his twisted ambition. Kefauver's inquiry and McCarthy's assorted "investigations" had almost nothing in common in terms of procedures, purposes, and achievements; but they did reflect the yearning of Congress—and the American people—in these parlous times for easy solutions, for scapegoats upon which to dump the frustration of accepting less than had been promised and of having apparently simple problems reach levels of complexity beyond their understanding. Both reflected and exemplified a general feeling of dissatisfaction and insecurity that was only hazily expressed but was no less ominous because of its vagueness.

The nation's affairs had seemed to collapse into an unending downward spiral since the glorious days of mid-1948—when the Marshall Plan and tremendous prosperity confirmed the innate superiority of American institutions—and since Harry Truman's come-from-behind victory in the presidential sweepstakes of that year. Soon after Truman's reelection, serious national and international problems and difficulties within the Truman Administration arose, challenging the optimism with which the President and most of his countrymen had looked to the future. Less than a year after Truman's triumphal inauguration, the country faced growing external problems, a serious economic recession, and debilitating political scandals. In particular, the humiliating flight of Chiang Kai-shek's Chinese Nationalist regime to Formosa, the revelation in September 1949 that Russia had exploded an atomic bomb, the sensational trial of Alger Hiss, and mushrooming suspicions that the federal government harbored numerous traitors eroded public confidence in Truman's leadership. In part, Truman's conduct of the presidency was also responsible. One of his closest advisers later confessed:

> Something happened between Truman's first and second terms that is hard to pin down. There was a change of atmosphere around the White House. . . . During the first term, we were all playing it pretty much by ear—sensing what had to be done and getting on with it. There wasn't much pressure from the outside, from the lobbies and the special interest pleaders or the big politicians. . . . And then came the 1948 election, and

> —my God—how cocky he was after that. . . . Now he was all bustle and decisiveness and full of big plans, and to hell with the details. . . . But now the outside pressures began to close in on him and on us. . . . The people who wanted things now knew they had to deal with him or not deal at all. So now they began to scheme and to ponder and to sort of feel around to see what was the best way of getting to him. . . . There was nothing sinister about this you could put your finger on. But it was a new mood and a new climate, and in a way Mr. Truman was a captive of it.

The discovery of "Commies" in high places weakened President Truman's credibility, but he could not be held personally responsible. However, the disclosures of shady dealings by Administration officials threatened to reach inside the doors of the White House itself.

In August 1949 a special Senate committee was investigating "influence-peddlers," lobbyists, and others who arranged, for fat fees, favors for businessmen eager to obtain lucrative government contracts. Investigators found evidence that General Harry Vaughan, Truman's military aide and an old and close friend from Missouri, had permitted his office to be used by lobbyists to exert pressure on various government officials. This had been going on for some years in fact. Vaughan, it appeared, was friendly with several "five-percenters," men who helped businessmen gain preferential treatment from government agencies for a five percent fee. It was learned that Vaughan had assisted one friend in obtaining an allocation of structural steel for the construction of a race track and had used his influence to open doors for various others. "Evidence before the Senate subcommittee showed," Cabell Phillips has noted, "that he poked his nose into the fields of public housing and surplus property disposal, into Federal trade regulations, and even into the Department of Agriculture, where the legitimate interests of the military aide to the President would seem to be minimal." Vaughan appears to have been more a victim of his desire to be a "good guy" than a man on the take. He apparently did not accept cash payoffs for these favors, and he believed that his actions, taken to assist the President and the Democratic party, were entirely proper. The Senate investigation did dredge up evidence that Vaughan had received numerous large contributions for the party, and that he also had accepted a deep freeze, a scarce item because of lingering controls, from the client of one of his lobbyist buddies.

The practice of influence-peddling had a long and venerable history in Washington. People who "knew the ropes"—often ex-congressmen, retired military men, or civil servants—had been functioning as middle men since the Jackson Administration and even before. The activities of this particular group of five-percenters were hardly in the same class as Teapot Dome and other instances of corruption; however, heightened public awareness, partly the result of Harry Truman's determined pursuit of "wheelerdealers" as chairman of the wartime Special Committee to Investigate the National Defense Program, produced an enormous outcry against Vaughan and the "mess in Washington." Newspapers were still carrying cartoons that caricatured Vaughan and his deep freeze when a serious scandal involving the

Reconstruction Finance Corporation broke in early 1950. Here again, one of Truman's principal assistants was charged with improper conduct.

The Reconstruction Finance Corporation, a Depression agency created to assist businesses which could not obtain loans from commercial sources, had expanded into other fields during the Second World War and continued after the war's end as a bulwark against economic difficulties and a source of development capital. By the late 1940s the RFC was issuing loans for a variety of speculative enterprises and had gained a reputation as being one of the most "political" of federal agencies. Responding to charges of political deals, influence-peddling, and financial irregularities supposedly rife in this sprawling, semi-autonomous organization, the Senate Banking and Currency Committee launched an investigation of the RFC in February 1950. A subcommittee, headed by Senator J. William Fulbright (whom President Truman violently disliked), eventually reported that the RFC was suffering from mismanagement and found numerous instances of loans awarded in return for political favors. Truman's personnel director, fellow Missourian Donald Dawson, was singled out by the Fulbright subcommittee as "the man to see" where pressure on the RFC was concerned. The Democratic National Committee and its chairman, William M. Boyle, another Missourian, were accused of imposing political conditions on RFC loans and of extracting large contributions from applicants.

Before Truman left office, corrupt practices by Internal Revenue Service officials had been uncovered, and charges of a vast network of influence-peddling in the nation's capital were under investigation by Congress. The President was forced to submit proposals for the reorganization of the RFC and the IRS. After much debate he also established a special White House commission to investigate the whole issue of governmental corruption. These decisions were made under strong public and congressional pressure and further intensified tension between the Executive and Legislative branches. The President's impassioned defense of his friends did not help his cause. Indeed, by insisting, "My people are honorable—all of them are," Truman subjected himself to ridicule and suspicion regarding his own possible involvement.

The significance of these unfortunate episodes—which by no means can be compared with Teapot Dome or Watergate—derives largely from their crippling effects on Truman's authority and public image. For a variety of reasons, Truman's second term degenerated into political bickering and ineptitude. One cause, certainly, was the "mess" in Washington. In addition, the bipartisan coalition that had sustained Truman's bold initiatives in foreign affairs fell apart under the strain of widespread dissatisfaction with the Administration's China policy and parallel unhappiness about the demonstrable effects of economic and military assistance to Europe. Assorted explanations for the perilous position in which America found itself were offered. The most popular one, that Communist agents strategically located in the government bureaucracy were distorting and delaying the achievement of American foreign policy goals, produced a witch hunt that further crippled the authority of Truman and his Administration. To a considerable degree Congress was the temporary beneficiary of this reversal in presidential fortunes. By early 1950 eager congressmen were charging off in all directions, using the investigatory power of Congress to dig into the Truman Administration's handling of various domestic and international problems. Investigations were undertaken of such previously sacrosanct issues as the giving of economic assistance to Socialist governments abroad, East-West trade, and United States policy toward Spain, Yugoslavia, and, of course, China. Other probes dealt with domestic subversion (within and outside the federal bureaucracy), housing, the motion picture industry, civil rights, shipping problems, and organized crime, to name but a few.

Of these, the crime investigation is among the most interesting—on its own merits and because it reflected so many aspects of the confused, unhappy public mood. There is little doubt that an investigation of "organized crime," which implicitly questioned existing federal law enforcement programs and which focused on criminal operations in cities almost exclusively dominated by Democratic political machines, would not have taken place in normal circumstances. Even so, despite the Truman Administration's siege mentality and the widespread belief that America confronted a moral crisis of apocalyptic dimensions, the decision of a Democratic Senate to appoint a committee controlled by Democrats to investigate a problem involving and likely to embarrass powerful Democratic leaders was astounding. One may argue that the Kefauver crime investigation was intended to head off a dangerous, Republican-initiated study; but even if Kefauver's original purpose was to protect the Administration —which was highly doubtful—the Senate Special Committee to Investigate Crime in Interstate Commerce soon was caught up in the fervent moral absolutism that swept the nation. Sidney Shalett began the introduction to *Crime in America,* Senator Kefauver's "personal account" of the crime investigation, by observing:

> In the spring of 1951 the American people were a little sick of politicians. Some of the contemporary exhibitions of what passed for political morality didn't sit well against the gnawing heartache of the Korean War and the awful feeling that here we go again. Rising taxes and the return of economic restrictions the people could take, though they didn't like it. But when they saw their children being drilled from kindergarten up to lie down on the dirt and cover their heads with their hands as protection against the atom bomb that the Russians were supposed to drop on us, the people were heartsore and angry—and, Americanlike, they started looking around for a whipping boy. Rightly or wrongly, the politicians filled the bill.

In such a climate, it was perhaps inevitable that the Kefauver Committee's investigation of organized crime would also become an inquest into the state of America's moral health.

I

The involvement of Congress in efforts to combat criminal activities stretched back into the nineteenth century. Although the dominant tradition in the United States supported local rather than national law enforcement programs, the federal government had always been responsible for prevention of certain crimes (counterfeiting, smuggling, tax evasion, and so forth). State governments, of course, exercised most "police powers" either directly or by delegation to county or municipal law enforcement agencies. Until the progressive period crimes against person and property remained the exclusive domain of state and local government, as did immoral activities such as gambling, and prostitution. There existed, however, one exception to the general pattern of decentralized responsibility for law enforcement: federal authority over interstate commerce. By the late nineteenth century certain problems arising from industrialization and the centralization of American business grew beyond the regulatory power of individual states. "Americans had seen nothing quite like the industrial sabotage, collusion, stock manipulation, use of private armies, and public corruption that accompanied the development of Big Business in the United States," William H. Moore has written. Responding to popular clamor for control of labor violence, financial manipulations, and corruption, the federal government attempted—by means of its taxing authority and powers over interstate commerce—to dampen the fires through regulation. In addition, Congress enacted legislation to eradicate certain illegal (or immoral) activities: interstate lotteries, and the "white slave trade," transportation of women across state lines. Congressional investigations were conducted on several of these problems.

The most notable action of Congress in the crusade against vice and the criminal operations it supposedly spawned was Prohibition, making it illegal to manufacture and distribute alcoholic beverages. The Eighteenth Amendment, which made liquor illegal, produced the Volstead Act, a federal effort to assure its enforcement. Since little provision was made for implementation of the Prohibition concept, the Volstead Act and the Eighteenth Amendment itself soon became a mockery. Sociologists and historians are still debating whether Prohibition spawned the well-organized criminal gangs that typified the "roaring twenties," or whether the presence of Dutch Schultz, Al Capone, and their brethren prevented the "noble experiment" from achieving complete acceptance by the American people. Certainly, the era of Prohibition focused public attention for the first time on the problem of *organized* criminal elements and the threat they posed to public safety and the nation's morals. Gangland murders, gleefully reported in big city newspapers, appeared an almost everyday occurrence; and gangsters such as "Scarface" Al Capone, head of a Chicago mob that at times seemed to exert total control over the city's police and political leadership, were portrayed as glamorous if also frightening figures.

Partly as a result of the enormous publicity given criminal leaders and their murderous jousts for supremacy, the federal government moved more aggressively to control crimes that had some interstate dimension. The Justice Department received expanded authority and manpower, and the Federal Bureau of Investigation was reorganized under the control of a tough young lawyer, J. Edgar Hoover. The view of federal law enforcement agencies and of the numerous crime commissions (such as the Wickersham Commission created by President Herbert Hoover in 1929) was that crime was somehow inherent in certain groups and classes of Americans. Thus, it could be eradicated only by tough, swift, and determined enforcement of the law. Actually, the FBI and other police agencies paid little attention to organized crime, for they were forced by public opinion to concentrate their meager resources on dramatic but isolated criminal acts such as the Lindbergh kidnapping, and bankrobbers such as Pretty Boy Floyd, Bonnie and Clyde, and John Dillinger.

A subcommittee of the Senate Commerce Committee held hearings on "racketeering" for two years beginning in 1933; however, its vague conclusions regarding the potential threats of organized, deeply entrenched criminal operations were ignored. The phenomenon of racketeering, which implied the existence of a nationwide criminal conspiracy, was "discovered in the early 1930s, though organized extortion, comprising a private tax on the exchange of goods and services" by extralegal agencies, had long been a familiar practice in urban life. Also during the 1930s ambitious efforts to control prostitution and gambling rackets were launched. Once again, however, federal and state law enforcement programs dealt largely with a few "big fish," leaving undisturbed the substructure of illegal activities and linkages between criminal bosses and political leaders. Concern about "crime syndicates" did increase, but mostly as a result of such inflammatory books as *Crime Incorporated* and its bestselling successor, *Murder, Inc.* Notably, the criminal geniuses portrayed in books and journalistic exposés increasingly were Italian-Americans, and the public came to accept the thesis, which the Kefauver Committee later propounded vigorously, that, "behind the local mobs which make up the national crime syndicate is a shadowy, international criminal organization known as the Mafia, so fantastic that most Americans find it hard to believe it really exists." Regrettably, little was done by Congress or the Executive branch to prove whether a "Mafia" did control crime in America—or to explore the causes and implications of this complicated issue.

The Second World War shifted government's and the public's attention to external threats, and few efforts, except for certain investigations of the Truman Committee, were given to expose organized criminal activities. This was doubly unfortunate, because the tremendous opportunities for vice, racketeering, and graft, and because the equally tremendous powers assumed by the federal government during the war provided impressive means by which it might have carried through an effective crime control program. The years immediately after the war witnessed an even greater growth of crimes against people and property. Sociologists might argue with civil servants that the causes of this new "crime wave" were wartime pressures on family life leading to juvenile delinquency, the widespread violations of rationing, price control measures, and the draft system that made Americans tolerant of the "black market" and other devices to avoid government regulations, or simply the complexity of life, with its attendant frustration and alienation, in postwar America. Most people, however, blamed organized crime.

That a frightening increase in crime of all types had occurred was beyond question. A memorandum prepared in May 1949 for President Truman by the office of the attorney general observed: "It is shocking to realize that in the United States in 1948 a serious crime was committed at the rate of one every 18.7 seconds. Moreover, the increase in the number of crimes involving violence and brutality has been too great to pass unnoticed. In 1948, aggravated assaults and rape, to mention only a few, increased 68.7 per cent and 49.9 per cent, respectively, over prewar averages (1938–1941). The crimes of burglary, murder and robbery all are on the increase." The Justice Department, which for a time supported the position that juvenile delinquency was a major cause of the problem, did launch several efforts to stem the tide. It convened a National Conference on Prevention and Control of Juvenile Delinquency in November 1946, and some months later it supported increased FBI programs and created a "racket squad" to work with federal grand juries in various big cities. In mid-1949 Attorney General J. Howard McGrath, on the advice of the FBI and in response to vocal pressures from state and municipal leaders, proposed a National Conference on Crime and Law Enforcement. This group was supposed to "discover, study, and analyze the causes of this dangerous crime trend in the United States and . . . devise methods to improve and remedy the situation." At this point municipal officials and crime fighting reporters, unhappy with Attorney General McGrath's "lackadaisical" approach to crime, especially national crime operations such as slot machines and the racing news wire service, decided to go directly to Congress with their tale of an organized criminal conspiracy bent on taking over America.

In September 1949 Mayor deLesseps Morrison of New Orleans, then president of the American Municipal Association, had requested that the federal government investigate the political influence of criminal elements (which he believed to be organized on a national scale) in numerous cities throughout the country. Three months later the AMA itself asked that the Justice Department give extraordinary assistance to embattled state and municipal agencies, asserting that "the matter is too big to be handled by local officials alone; the organized criminal element operates across state boundaries on a national scale." It appeared to activists that the Truman Administration's sole response was to revive the idea of a national conference on crime, to meet in February 1950 in conjunction with the annual convention of United States attorneys. Assisted by powerful journalists such as Drew Pearson, Mayor Morrison and his colleagues pressed for congressional action. Among the congressmen most sympathetic to the anti-crime forces was Estes Kefauver, freshman senator from Tennessee.

Kefauver later said that his interest in an investigation of organized crime derived from several factors, an important one being his participation some years before in a House Judiciary Committee inquiry into the activities of a Pennsylvania federal district judge. "In the process of gathering the evidence that subsequently resulted in the retirement of this man who disgraced his robes," Kefauver recalled, "the full import of what rottenness in public life can do to our country came home to me. From then on the subject never was far from my mind." After Kefauver moved to the Senate, having won a bitterly fought election from the Crump political machine in 1948, he became somewhat obsessed with "the phenomenon of politico-criminal corruption and what it was doing to the country." Also, of course, the Tennessee senator, who possessed a driving ambition, was anxious to find some means of obtaining national recognition. While he perceived risks in the "crime problem," involving as it did possible laxity of federal agencies, collusion between criminal forces and politicians in Democratic strongholds, and uncertain political alignments in Congress, Kefauver decided that the risks were acceptable and the potential benefits unlimited. Perhaps only in the confused atmosphere of 1949–1950 could a very junior senator have so boldly thrust aside the constraints of party loyalty, Executive primacy, and the procedures of that exclusive club, the United States Senate.

Senator Kefauver was not alone in his desire to head a congressional investigation of organized crime, however. As noted previously, the aggressive and ambitious junior senator from Wisconsin, Joseph McCarthy, was wavering between crime and communism as sure-fire reelection issues. Also, soon after the attorney general's conference on crime concluded (with a great deal of publicity but almost nothing in the way of positive recommendations), Representative Kingsland Macy, a New York Republican, stepped forward to propose a sweeping congressional investigation of organized crime, especially its evil influence over local, state, and federal governments. However, Kefauver was first in the field, and, though he faced deep and continuing opposition from many in the Senate to his proposal, the Tennessean eventually emerged with authorization for an investigation and approval of himself as the investigatory committee's chairman.

It should be noted that Kefauver, despite his junior standing, possessed impressive credentials. First, he already owned a considerable reputation as a political comer on the strength of his surprising victory over the powerful political machine of "Boss" Crump in 1948. He had accomplished this with almost no support from the Democratic national organization, and thus was not tied in any way to the embarrassing situation which the Democratic party faced in 1949–1950. Although Kefauver's victory was not so remarkable as a sympathetic press claimed (Crump's power was already declining and Kefauver won by a rather narrow margin in a three-man race), the public remembered him as the shyly articulate Southerner who wore a coonskin cap and who was, nonetheless, praised as one of the most promising and effective liberals to enter the Senate in decades. In addition, Kefauver had made himself knowledgeable about the crime issue. From close contacts with crime reporters and Justice Department investigators he received information about their fascination with the threat of organized crime. In particular, he was made aware of the findings of the California Crime Commission, which had dredged up an enormous store of evidence about criminal activities in that state and elsewhere. Kefauver was already at work on bills to deal with specific abuses, such as a curb on the racing news wire service and the slot machine distribution question, when the opportunity arose to conduct a full-scale investigation of crime and political corruption.

On January 5, 1959, Senator Kefauver introduced Senate Resolution 202 calling for "a full and complete study and investigation of interstate gambling and racketeering activities and of the manner in which the facilities of interstate commerce are made a vehicle of organized crime." He proposed that this investigation be conducted by the Judiciary Committee (of which he was a member), or by a subcommittee thereof. In justification of the resolution, Kefauver offered the following statement:

> Responsible and nationally known reporters and magazine writers have for the past several years been writing of a national

> crime syndicate which they allege is slowly but surely through corruption gaining control of, or improper influence in, many cities throughout the United States.
>
> On September 14, 1949, Mayor deLesseps S. Morrison as President of the American Municipal Association, and speaking for that association, asked the Federal government to investigate the encroachment by organized national racketeers on municipal governments throughout the United States with the intent to control their law enforcement agencies.
>
> The Chicago and California Crime Commissions in 1949 reported the insidious influence wielded by this crime syndicate through corruption of public officials and its political and financial control.
>
> Also, . . . the mayors of several large cities, such as Los Angeles, New Orleans, and Portland, and many others, have complained in the past year of attempts being made by national crime syndicates to control and corrupt the local political affairs of their respective cities, and that they do not have adequate means to cope with this well organized and powerful criminal organization, and have asked the Federal government for assistance in coping with this alleged criminal aggression.
>
> There appears to be no adequate Federal statute which can be invoked against the activities of this organized syndicate. The Resolution I am filing today would authorize and direct the Committee on the Judiciary of the Senate to make investigation to determine whether there is an organized syndicate operating in interstate commerce which is menacing the independence of free municipal governments, for the benefit of the criminal activities of the syndicate, and determine and report to the Senate their findings on whether the states and municipalities can, without Federal assistance, adequately cope with this organized crime movement. The Committee would also be directed to investigate the jurisdiction of the Federal government over the activities of any criminal syndicate, and make recommendations for any necessary legislation.

Senator Kefauver clearly was reflecting the contention of the AMA, the crime-fighting journalists, and others that a nationwide criminal conspiracy did exist and that it already possessed sufficient strength to threaten democratic control of American life in various places. Further, the statement implied that the "Federal government"—by which he meant the Truman Administration—was negligent in meeting this threat and must be forced to take action. Kefauver's commitment to these preconceived views never wavered. Perhaps the most remarkable achievement of his investigation was that these assumptions were accepted as correct by the general public and by a majority of Congress.

The path of Senate Resolution 202 from its introduction to ultimate approval by the full Senate comprises an excellent case study in the complex issues affecting a congressional investigation. Tracing the course of Kefauver's proposal through the halls and committee rooms of Congress would demand far more space than is possible here; however, a brief description is essential, for the treatment accorded Senate Resolution 202 made obvious the problems and pressures which confronted any investigation—and especially one involving such a sensitive issue as "politico-criminal corruption"—during a difficult period.

It has been stated that numerous similarities exist between the Kefauver Committee and the Truman Committee, especially regarding the problems each encountered in obtaining support and funding from the Senate leadership; however, the traumatic early history of Kefauver's project makes Harry Truman's problems with his attempt to carry out a study of the defense program appear mild by comparison. There were three potential roadblocks: the attitude of President Truman and federal law enforcement agency heads, the issues of jurisdiction and propriety raised by the Senate leadership, and the vulnerability of any such inquiry to partisan political maneuvering. Kefauver was required, of course, to drag his proposal over all three of these obstacles simultaneously; but in order to comprehend the scope of the problems they posed, each will be analyzed separately.

In some ways, the danger of an attempt by the President or his advisers to squelch the proposed investigation was least worrisome. By early 1950 the Truman Administration simply did not have sufficient strength to oppose a congressional study of organized crime, for any such act would lead to charges that the Administration had something to hide. Attorney General McGrath and, undoubtedly, President Truman were concerned about the baneful effects of Kefauver's investigation. They feared that the inquiry might get out of control and they specifically worried about the embarrassment it might cause Democratic candidates in the 1950 elections. There was, however, little they could do to stop Kefauver, though a number of the President's supporters in the Senate were pressed to cool down the impudent Tennessean.

Kefauver seems to have been so little concerned about White House reaction that he neglected to consult either the President or the attorney general before filing his resolution. (He did send a copy of the proposal to McGrath on January 9 with the comment: "I tried to reach you before filing this resolution, but was unable to do so, and circumstances were such that it was necessary to go ahead with it, at the time I did.") There were certainly no conditions imposed by the Executive comparable to those Truman had had to swallow ten years earlier. It appears that the Administration sought only to restrain Kefauver from going overboard (as was happening with McCarthy's investigation of internal subversion) and to use delaying tactics whenever possible. Kefauver did meet with the attorney general in mid-January and as a concession to the Administration agreed to take part in the upcoming crime conference and to postpone formal presentation of his resolution until the conference had ended. For his part, McGrath blocked an effort to have the crime conference issue a resolution of support for a congressional investigation and the Justice Department and other Executive agencies offered only formal assistance for some months after the committee launched its inquiries.

Possible countermoves by the Administration undoubtedly worried supporters of the Kefauver project; but they had their hands full warding off friendly enemies and competitors in Congress. Kefauver had planned that the Judiciary Committee would oversee any investigation of organized crime. That idea was immediately caught up in a jurisdictional squabble between the Judiciary Committee and the Interstate and Foreign Commerce Committee, neither of which was especially enthusiastic about Kefauver's proposal. At the same time, Senator McCarthy made an abortive effort to have the Special Investigations Committee, which had examined the "five-percenters" scandal the previous year, and on which he served, assume principal responsibility for any crime investigation. Suggestions were also made that the investigation be converted into a joint House-Senate affair. Because the resolution focused on criminal operations which crossed state lines, the Commerce Committee, which had conducted similar inquiries in the past, appeared to have clear title to control an investigation that, in Kefauver's own words, would study "the manner in which the facilities of interstate commerce are made a vehicle of organized crime." Objections by Kefauver and his supporters were simple: Kefauver was not a member of the Commerce Committee and thus could not have taken part in any investigation sponsored by it. On the other hand, the Judiciary Committee, according to the Senate Democratic leadership, was hardly a wise choice. It was chaired by Senator Pat McCarran, an old-line conservative who despised the Truman Administration and, being from Nevada, was certainly not sympathetic to an investigation of organized crime. Further, the Judiciary Committee contained Republicans Homer Ferguson of Michigan and Forrest Donnell of Missouri, both of whom were eager to seize upon an investigation of crime and corruption in urban centers for partisan political advantage.

A wild melee of cloakroom discussions and parliamentary maneuvers, lasting for some four months, ensued. Kefauver later admitted: "As I look back on the struggle to set up the committee I sometimes wonder that we were ever able to bring it into existence." First, McCarran blocked progress of Senate Resolution 202 for two months by assigning it to a study group which he dominated, and then tacked on impossible amendments when the full committee did consider it. Eventually, the favorable publicity Kefauver's idea was receiving forced McCarran to release the resolution. However, at this point a further effort was made to assign the crime investigation to the Commerce Committee. Belligerent Republicans attempted to put over a *fait accompli* by having a commerce subcommittee undertake a study of the race wire service question and later to extend the scope of its activities. The only notable result of this short-lived probe was a statement by Attorney General McGrath that the Justice Department had no persuasive evidence that a "national crime syndicate" did exist.

The stalemate was broken in mid-April 1950 when the Democratic Policy Committee, composed of the Democratic leadership of Congress, recommended that a special investigatory committee, with members from both the Judiciary and Commerce Committees and with Estes Kefauver as its chairman, be created. It has been suggested that this compromise was the result of the discovery on April 6, 1950, of two murdered Kansas City gangsters and political figures, their crumpled bodies found in a Democratic club, sprawled under a huge photograph of President Truman. The publicity from this incident certainly had its effect, but the Democratic leadership probably acted because of the threat of a Republican takeover of the crime investigation. Certainly partisan politics played a large role in the final chapter of Senate Resolution 202's hegira. Republicans, outraged by the blatant move to avoid Commerce Committee (and thus, Republican) sponsorship of the investigation, worked furiously to defeat authorization by the full Senate. Amid shouts of "whitewash" and "cover-up" the Senate voted and found itself deadlocked. Vice President Alben Barkley, acting as a faithful Democrat, cast the tie-breaking vote, and the Senate Special Committee to Investigate Organized Crime in Interstate Commerce came into existence.

It is perhaps unnecessary to reiterate that the Kefauver Committee was born amid political antagonisms and would be involved in partisan politics for its duration. Democrats assumed that the investigation would tread lightly past questionable relationships between gangsters and big city Democratic organizations. Republicans were equally sure that the purpose behind the inquiry, which after all had been proposed and organized by Democrats, was to whitewash the iniquities perpetrated by Democratic political machines. Such assessments ignored the personality and outlook of Estes Kefauver. He had always gone his own way and kept his own counsel, refusing to give blind allegiance to a political party or its leaders. One writer was to comment later: "Kefauver's handling of the crime hearings was a very special feat. To a lesser man, such an assignment could have been political suicide." Kefauver was permitted to assume a comparatively independent position not because he was trusted, but because few people in either party believed that his investigation would receive much attention. Probably no one was more surprised than Kefauver when his dream of winning national recognition as a crime-fighting congressman came true.

II

Senate Resolution 202, as amended, was approved by the Senate on May 2, 1950. It established the Special Committee to Investigate Organized Crime in Interstate Commerce, with all the scope that its title suggested. It was given authority to conduct its study of crime until March 1, 1951 (later extended until September 1, 1951), a budget of $150,000, and the usual subpoena and other powers. The committee was charged with three tasks: "to determine whether organized crime utilizes the facilities of interstate commerce" to carry on illegal activities; to investigate the "manner and extent of such criminal operations," identifying the guilty parties; and to discover if the activities of organized crime "were developing corrupting influence in violation of the Federal law or the laws of any state." This was an impressively broad mandate.

Senator Kefauver, who naturally assumed he would be chairman of the committee, began immediately to press for office space and staff; but for a time he found himself without authority or even colleagues. Vice President Barkley deliberated for a week over the appointment of the committee's members, but finally announced his selections on May 10, 1950. He chose the ranking Republican members of the Commerce and Judiciary Committees—Charles W. Tobey of New Hampshire and Alexander Wiley of Wisconsin—as the minority representation. Then, from a large list the Vice President appointed Kefauver, Lester C. Hunt of Wyoming, and Herbert R. O'Conor of Maryland as the Democratic members. At its first meeting the next day, May 11, the committee formally elected Kefauver as their chairman.

In his impressive biography of Kefauver, Joseph B. Gorman has observed: "All five [committee members] were known as relatively quiet, mild-mannered, and fair men, and the attention the committee was to attract stood in sharp contrast to the personalities of the senators serving on it." Despite his aggressive efforts in behalf of the investigation, Kefauver was determined that the probe proceed cautiously and with a minimum of sensationalism. "The temptation to become a publicity-grabber, a table-thumper, a modern Torquemada was great," one of Kefauver's associates has noted; but the scholarly Tennessean abjured McCarthy-style tactics. Such tactics were risky and, more important, flamboyance and inquisitorial pressures made Kefauver uncomfortable. His colleagues on the committee agreed with this view of the investigation, though on more than one occasion members were to violate the spirit if not the letter of the agreement.

In 1951 Estes Kefauver was forty-six years old. Born in Madisonville, Tennessee, in 1903 to a socially prominent and wealthy family, Kefauver attended the University of Tennessee and Yale Law School, obtaining great popularity for his athletic and academic exploits. He practiced law in Chattanooga for a decade, joining "everything in town," and then won a seat in the House of Representatives in 1939. For the next ten years he worked steadily at this job, earning a reputation as one of the brightest and most effective of the southern liberal bloc in Congress. He also became known as something of a political maverick, challenging the House leadership on such issues as TVA and civil rights. By personal inclination and experience, Kefauver was a single-minded student of each issue that claimed his attention. He clearly was determined to put all else aside to conduct the crime investigation, though, of course, having just been elected to a six-year term, he could afford to ignore his constituents. Kefauver, like Harry S. Truman before him, was the moving force in the investigation he headed.

Kefauver's Democratic colleagues on the committee were both experienced politicians but relative newcomers to Washington. Lester C. Hunt had been elected to the Senate in 1948, after holding various state offices in Wyoming and serving as governor for three terms. Hunt, a former dentist, was considered an Administration "regular" and had already obtained two prestigious committee assignments: Armed Services and Commerce. Although he had been initially reluctant to serve on the crime committee, Hunt soon recognized its potential, and he became a fairly active member. Herbert R. O'Conor, one of three lawyers on the committee, was a onetime reporter who had served as governor of Maryland during the Second World War. O'Conor came to the Senate in 1947, and had been a member of the Special Committee to Investigate the National Defense Program, then tottering toward dissolution, and of the Internal Security Sub-committee. He was close to Senator McCarran and was known as a conservative, opposed to much of Truman's domestic program. O'Conor was always doubtful about the wisdom of Kefauver's investigation of organized crime and took only an occasional interest in the committee's hearings.

Despite the fact that the two Republicans, Tobey and Wiley, were running for reelection in 1950 and that both faced serious challenges, they took an active part in the committee's deliberations. Clearly, both were eager to seize any political (or partisan) advantage that service on the crime committee might offer; but the two senators, especially Tobey, became deeply interested in the outcome of the investigation. Charles W. Tobey, a veteran of New Hampshire and national politics, had been in the Senate since 1939. Entering political life as a Bull Moose Republican, Tobey was counted among the liberal Republicans, though perhaps more for his eccentric personality than for substantive reasons. One writer has described his participation as follows: "Tobey used his appointment to the Kefauver Committee to his political advantage in New Hampshire and made it into a forum for his intense showmanship, but he also genuinely enjoyed the sleuthing, energetically pursuing leads from taxicab drivers and porters, and continually referring rumormongers to an indulgent Committee staff." Alexander Wiley, also a colorful, veteran campaigner, had entered the Senate in 1938. Though Wiley was a member of several powerful committees, including Foreign Relations, he had *sought* an appointment to the Kefauver crime probe. His participation was limited by the other demands on his time, but he did take part when topics with vote getting potential, such as the Chicago crime situation and Democratic corruption, were raised.

In sum, the membership of the special crime committee was typical of such inquiries but perhaps reflected better qualifications and greater involvement than most. The committee was less important in some ways than the staff which served it. Kefauver recognized this fact. He insisted that the committee hire the best qualified staff to be found and that their selection be on a non-partisan basis. He later expressed his viewpoint on this crucial issue:

> Before choosing anyone for the staff, we had several committee meetings at which I stated my position to my fellow members. I told them I felt we had a great challenge to prove that we really were going to carry out our promise of a sincere, thorough, and non-partisan investigation. . . . My colleagues all agreed with me that the way to confound . . . critics was for us to forget that we were Democrats or Republicans, to select a non-partisan staff, and to investigate without regard as to whom we might benefit or hurt. I told my colleagues firmly that I never did believe in committees being divided into majority and minority factions; that if we were to do any good at all we had to work as a team. I told them that I had no favorite lawyers or investigators from my home state of Tennessee to place on the committee . . . and that I would like to see all personnel chosen without regard for patronage or politics. Competence rather than influence was to be the yardstick for choosing the staff. The committee, I believe, faithfully utilized that yardstick.

Given the difficult political climate in which the crime investigation was launched, Kefauver's desires were carried out with surprisingly few difficulties. A major factor was the appointment of Rudolph Halley as chief counsel to the committee. Halley had impressive experience with congressional investigations, having served on the staff of the Truman Committee and later as chief counsel for its successor, the Mead Committee. A brilliant and aggressive lawyer, Halley left a lucrative New York law practice to work for the crime committee. He quickly assumed responsibility for planning the committee's schedule and, recognizing the tremendous publicity to be gained from public hearings, pointed Kefauver toward the "grand finale" confrontation with the "big shots" of organized crime in New York.

Both Kefauver and Halley agreed that the crime committee should rely primarily on information dredged up by other inquiries, especially state crime commissions, and that this should be supplemented by interviews and testimony. Thus, the staff should be composed of persons with solid contacts with law enforcement agencies and study groups. The investigative component was headed by Harold Robinson, who had worked for the Truman Committee and was then chief investigator on the California Crime Commission, and included several newspapermen, former FBI agents and race track investigators, police officers on leave from various urban police departments, and narcotics, gambling, and wiretapping experts. The legal staff in Washington possessed equally diverse and intensive backgrounds in law enforcement and related fields. In addition, investigators were hired or borrowed from cooperating agencies in each city through which Kefauver's "crime show" moved on its journey across the country. At times this caused confusion and tension within the committee staff and between the staff and disgruntled outsiders. But the staff did manage to schedule and complete preparatory work on over six hundred witnesses in less than one year.

The course to be followed by the Kefauver Committee was written during the weeks prior to its first hearings, held in Miami on May 26, 1950. As mentioned previously, Kefauver did not intend that the committee would undertake a comprehensive study of crime in America. His concern was whether a nationwide crime organization existed, where the sources of its power lay, and the degree to which criminal elements had purchased the cooperation and acquiescence of local governments in their activities. The principal means of uncovering information about these three issues was through a probe of gambling, "the life blood of organized crime"; that meant that Kefauver and his colleagues first focused on urban areas, the strongholds of both gangsters and Democrats. During the fifteen months of its existence, the crime committee convened hearings in fourteen major cities: Miami, Kansas City, St. Louis, Philadelphia, Chicago, Tampa, Cleveland, Detroit, New Orleans, Las Vegas, San Francisco, Los Angeles, New York, and Washington. Of course, investigators visited numerous other areas, but the committee itself confined its activities to these cities, with the exception of a brief foray into Saratoga County, New York, the location of a famed gambling spa and race track.

Kefauver's conception of the committee's task was that it should reveal and dramatize to the American people the extent to which organized crime had infiltrated the nation's economic and political life. Therefore, he was much more interested in confrontations with known bosses and corrupt politicians than in the tedious job of uncovering all others involved in criminal activities. Thus, the committee could rely heavily on information garnered from previous investigations at the local level. J. Edgar Hoover once asserted, in fact, that local authorities already knew enough about criminal operations that they could "clean up organized gambling in forty-eight hours if they wanted to." Kefauver readily admitted that the crime committee was turning up little that was new; but, he said, "the fact that certain information is known to some people and the assembly of that information in such a way that a legislative program can be based on it are two quite different things." The investigators did uncover fascinating and significant details about criminal activities. Further, the decision of President Truman in June 1950 to order appropriate agencies of the federal government to open their files to the committee produced some important breakthroughs. Information from income tax files controlled by the Treasury Department and the Internal Revenue Service was especially helpful, though this source was closed off as the investigation proceeded.

The critical procedural issue faced by the crime committee was not accessibility of records, but availability of witnesses. Since the public impact of the investigation was based upon face-to-face interrogations of "real live criminals" (as well as assorted police chiefs, district attorneys, and federal officials), the ability of the committee to compel witnesses to appear and, then, to have them respond to direct questioning was basic. The committee made enormous use of the subpoena power, but it encountered considerable difficulty in enforcing its subpoenas because of the archaic procedures imposed upon it by the Senate's rules.

Kefauver recalled this problem: "As soon as we served subpoenas on certain hoodlums many of their partners in crime, whose testimony was vital, went into hiding—some even fleeing the country. We felt it was urgently necessary for us to be able to go directly to the full Senate and obtain immediate warrants of arrest for subpoena-dodgers. . . . We found ourselves saddled with a time-wasting procedure which required us to go through the formality of requesting the Senate sergeant-at-arms to search for the missing witnesses before the arrest warrants were issued. The estimable Senate sergeant-at-arms, of course, is a parliamentary officer rather than a policeman and simply has no facilities of his own for tracking down fugitive gangsters." This difficulty was never resolved.

Secondly, there arose the thorny problem of compelling witnesses to answer questions once they did appear before the committee. Kefauver and Halley decided at the beginning to follow rules regarding the rights of witnesses established by the Truman Committee. Witnesses were permitted the aid of counsel and could submit prior statements to the committee. Kefauver insisted that persons accused in testimony be given an opportunity to refute charges against them and instituted other safeguards. The American Civil Liberties Union later commented: "The hearings were conducted, with one or two exceptions, in an atmosphere of fairness and sober fact-finding, without resort to the hysteria and wild accusations which have marked other Congressional probes." Nevertheless, there arose serious questions regarding the committee's procedures: with regard to the effect of television (a problem that will be discussed later), and the right of witnesses to plead the Fifth Amendment.

At the time the Kefauver Committee conducted hearings, the use of the Fifth Amendment safeguard was under attack from various quarters. Although Kefauver and chairmen of other investigatory committees admitted that congressional hearings were not judicial proceedings and that they were held to obtain information and not to ascertain guilt or innocence, the temptation to assume the position of a prosecutor was often irresistible. When witness after witness answered even the most innocuous questions with the bland phrase, "I refuse to answer on the ground that it may tend to incriminate or degrade me," Kefauver and his colleagues sought to force compliance by issuing contempt of Congress citations. The committee's view was that the Fifth Amendment did not excuse witnesses from answering "legitimate" (non-self-incriminating) questions or from answering questions relating to state or local offenses. Voting contempt citations in such circumstances clearly represented an attempt to punish hostile witnesses, and federal courts, recognizing that fact, overturned the first twenty-two contempt cases stemming from the crime committee hearings; after two years the courts had upheld only three such citations. In the court of public opinion, however, the committee won a smashing victory. Each time a Frank Costello, Joe Adonis, or some other sullen-faced gangster uttered the fateful words, he was found guilty by the public.

III

Many of the above questions had still to be faced when the crime committee convened its first hearings in Miami. The "Miami story" did not prove especially noteworthy or unique, but as the first of many visits to urban centers it focused public attention on the committee and provided a powerful impetus for continuation of the crime committee's activities. Kefauver's purpose in going to Miami was to look into the gambling situation—and he found evidence of gambling everywhere. "Card games, dice games, numbers games, roulette and other gambling wheels operated in establishments varying from the well-appointed air-conditioned casinos set up for the purpose, to night clubs and restaurants and private rooms in various hotels. Bookmaking operated out of newsstands, cigar stands or elaborate horse rooms, in most hotels, and even from specially fitted cabanas on the beach." The most shocking information dramatized by the committee was an apparent connection between persons close to Florida's Democratic governor, Fuller Warren, and a bookmaking syndicate controlled by the Capone mob in Chicago. Until 1949, most bookmaking in Miami had been conducted by the "S. and G. Syndicate," a local organization which operated betting shops in some 200 hotels and had grossed $26,500,000 in 1948 alone. Then, in January 1949, Governor Warren appointed W. O. Crosby as a special investigator to control gambling; Crosby was later found to have been involved with the Capone organization, but he did lead some gambling raids in Dade County, though only against S. and G. establishments. S. and G. suffered further difficulties when the Continental Press Service, a racing news organization also controlled by Capone people, cut off the flow of information about horse and dog races to S. and G. About this time a Capone associate, Harry Russell, was made a full partner in the S. and G. Syndicate. The Kefauver Committee later learned that Russell had paid $20,000 for half of a $26,000,000 business. Shortly thereafter, raids on S. and G. bookies ceased and the racing news service was restored. The committee also learned that another Capone representative had given $100,000 to Governor Warren's campaign fund. Further, when it was disclosed that the sheriff of Dade County had become a wealthy man after five years in office and had tried to block a crime study by the Greater Miami Crime Commission, only to be upheld by Governor Warren, the Kefauver Committee had uncovered a real case with which to dramatize gangsterism and political corruption.

Unfortunately, pursuit of the mess in Miami forced the committee to attack the state Democratic organization—from Governor Warren down. The committee limited its criticism to a summary statement in its report, but the damage was done. Governor Warren began a bitter vendetta against Kefauver and other committee members, but his attacks served only to hasten his own demise and to generate favorable publicity for the committee. However, the episode also produced some nervous foreboding in the headquarters of the Democratic National Committee—and anger in the White House. Soon thereafter, cooperation from the Truman Administration noticeably cooled down.

The committee's next stop was Kansas City, the place from which Harry Truman had emerged to national prominence and in which the President still retained close ties with the local Democratic organization. The crime committee's findings regarding criminal activities in Kansas City were not particularly shocking, but they may be viewed as typical of the developing emphases of the investigation. As Kefauver observed in *Crime in America*: "Between Miami Beach and Kansas City, we had been assembling small pieces of the national crime mosaic which would fit later into the big picture. We had not been overwhelmed yet by the repetitious mass of evidence we were to accumulate all over the country, pointing to raw and brutal rule by criminals and utter prostitution of their oaths of office by some officials who were supposed to serve the public. Hence the Kansas City situation hit us with doubly powerful impact. . . . I shall never forget my first impression of the city as a place that was struggling out from under the rule of the law of the jungle." What the committee found (or believed it found) there "was a staggering example of a prosperous city . . . which, through indifference and civil inertia, had fallen under the influence of as vicious a bunch of criminals as existed anywhere." In particular, the committee considered Kansas City to be dominated by the Mafia.

The Kansas City example completely justified the crime committee's investigations, for it possessed all those ominous developments which the committee had dedicated itself to exposing. First, there was clear proof of a nationally organized criminal conspiracy operating within the city. Second, Kansas City offered abundant information and clues as to who led this conspiracy and their motives. Third, the committee's study also revealed the connection between these criminal leaders and state and local elected officials. Hearings were held in Washington and in Kansas City, and forty-eight witnesses, including Governor Forrest Smith, various law enforcement representatives, and "a number of the city's known gamblers and racketeers," were questioned.

Kefauver decided that information obtained in Kansas City provided indisputable proof that the racing wire services represented the principal vehicle by which organized crime was spreading its influence across state lines and throughout the nation. This conviction, a basic support of the committee's assertion that an organized criminal conspiracy did exist, received constant reiteration. Kefauver termed the racing news service (particularly the Continental Press, the nation's largest racing wire operation) "America's Public Enemy Number One." Continental Press, which leased 23,000 miles of telegraph circuits from Western Union for the purpose of distributing racing information, was supposedly an independent, lawfully operated business. In fact, the Kefauver Committee concluded, it was "a powerful and indispensable ally of the underworld," and was totally controlled by the Capone organization. Kansas City was a vital distribution center for the CNS racing news operation.

Of note was the observation that the persons behind CNS and almost every other gambling-vice activity in Kansas City were Italian-American. The list of witnesses called before the Kefauver Committee in Kansas City included Joseph Di Giovanni, James Balestere, Tony Gizzo, and Tano Lococo. The committee was convinced that this was not coincidental, that the domination of Kansas City crime as elsewhere by Italian-Americans was further proof that the Mafia, an international criminal conspiracy, controlled crime throughout the United States. "In past years," the committee's *Third Interim Report* proclaimed, "Kansas City was known as a center for the activities of the Mafia, or Unione Siciliano, which is said to be a secret organization operating throughout the country and internationally." Though witnesses claimed total ignorance of any such organization, the committee refused to credit their testimony. It listed sixteen unsolved murders as Mafia-arranged, and suggested that the killings of Charles Binaggio, a gambler and Kansas City Democratic leader, and his henchman, Charles Gargotta, in April 1950 were masterminded by the Mafia leadership after Binaggio failed to fulfill a promise to use his political influence to "open up Kansas City."

The Binaggio case led the committee into an ugly case of political corruption and influence-peddling that stretched from the headquarters of the First Ward Democratic Club possibly as far as the statehouse in Jefferson City. "The Committee heard considerable testimony," its *Report* cautiously admitted, "relating to attempts by Binaggio to exert political influence to open up for gambling and other illegal operations the State of Missouri, and particularly St. Louis and Kansas City." Rumors of enormous contributions by Binaggio to Governor Smith's campaign fund were discussed, but no solid evidence was presented. It was clear that Smith and Binaggio were friendly, and that the governor had appointed police commissioners "who were at least acceptable to Binaggio"; however, the committee refused to accuse Governor Smith of willful wrongdoing.

By its very presence, nonetheless, the Kefauver Committee was calling attention to an awkward, politically embarrassing mess in President Truman's backyard. Kefauver could say, as he did in a concluding statement in Kansas City on September 30, "We haven't been out here with the intention of protecting anyone, of harming anyone, but of carrying out the mission that we were given by the United States Senate." Even so, Democrats were being harmed, some badly, by the committee's disclosures. The committee itself might struggle mightily not to take sides, but others inevitably drew politically-motivated conclusions from the crime committee's reports. An example of this phenomenon was the Chicago hearings, hurriedly arranged by Kefauver after the killings of two men who were at work gathering evidence on ties between organized crime and the Cook County Democratic organization. Senator Scott Lucas, then fighting an uphill battle for reelection, had been assured that the crime committee would not come into Chicago until after the election. Having agreed reluctantly to support Kefauver's proposed investigation the previous spring, Lucas was furious when the committee convened hearings in Chicago in late October. On November 1 Police Captain Dan Gilbert admitted to permitting widespread violations of gambling laws and other irregularities. This testimony, given in closed session, found its way to Chicago newspapers and was published just days before the election. Senator Lucas and numerous other Democrats were defeated, an occurrence Lucas attributed completely to the Kefauver Committee's inopportune appearance in Chicago.

As the crime committee travelled from city to city during the fall and early winter of 1950, it seemed that Kefauver had accomplished—though at what cost no one then knew—his aim of conducting a fair, nonpartisan inquiry in order to bring the staggering dimensions of organized crime before the American people. Joseph B. Gorman has effectively summed up this first phase of the committee's endeavors. "The pattern was the same everywhere the committee went. Local crime commissions, grand juries, crusading newspapers, and sympathetic law enforcement officers all made available everything that might be of interest to the committee, and the staff had all it could handle just organizing the information supplied to it. Even though almost all the local evidence had been made public before, there was nevertheless a shock on reviewing the accumulated evidence of years, and the Kefauver Committee made headlines wherever it went." Favorable publicity, combined with the stance of absolute impartiality assumed by the committee (despite internal conflict and external attacks), made the crime committee, for a time, almost invulnerable to attack. By the end of the year Senator Kefauver had been transformed into a modern Sir Galahad, crisscrossing the country in search of evildoers upon whom to wield the fatal sword of public exposure. Of course, Kefauver was protected not by some magic talisman but rather by the continuing decline of popular support for President Truman and the partisan bickering of Congress. In the unhappy days of early 1951, with the Korean "police action" grinding on and the country caught in a spiral of inflation and shortages, any hero, even such an unlikely one as Estes Kefauver, was welcomed.

Opposition to the crime committtee was growing in Congress, however, and was led by the vengeful Scott Lucas, Pat McCarran (who had been outraged by Kefauver's report on organized crime's domination of Las Vegas), and others. Little could be done, though, while the committee enjoyed such enormous popularity. "Let's face it," a Democratic stalwart admitted, "the Kefauver committee hurts the party and the longer it keeps going, the more we'll be hurt. But we can't stop it, not while it possesses glamour. Any effort to block it would be a political blunder, maybe suicide." The Democratic leadership's helplessness was reflected in the Senate's quick approval of Kefauver's request that the committee's authorization be extended in order to conduct hearings already planned for New York City. Senators could grumble but they dared not oppose the request. Not even a protest emerged from the White House, where an embattled President kept his own counsel. Possibly, leaders of both the Legislative and Executive branches hoped that the crime committee's claim on popular attention was about exhausted and that after the hearings in New York it would fade away into oblivion. If so, they were soon disabused. The New York hearings, which introduced television audiences to numerous "Mr. Bigs" in the underworld, proved to be the high point of the entire investigation.

That the Kefauver Committee in one day of televised hearings became a "national phenomenon" was totally unexpected, for the decision to permit a New York station to televise the proceedings was made only a day or so before the first session. It must be emphasized, however, that Kefauver and the committee staff had been pointing toward New York as a perfect final act for their travelling show since the beginning. The committee stated: "The New York hearings were vital . . . for a number of reasons. New York City, because of its size, location, dominance in the country, complexity of its population and governmental problems, is one of the major centers of organized crime." Rudolph Halley, the committee's ambitious chief counsel, was particularly determined that the New York hearings be a smashing success. In fact, Halley seems to have considered the other city investigations as something like out-of-town rehearsals. They certainly had that effect, for the New York hearings featured impressive performances by the committee, the staff, and their totally believable supporting cast of gangsters and their mouthpieces.

The Kefauver Committee was the fifth congressional committee to allow television cameras into a hearing room. The most notable use of television previously had been at the House Committee on Un-American Activities interrogation of Alger Hiss. Of course, congressional investigations had authorized the presence of film crews for some two decades, and newsreels had given most Americans some familiarity with the setting and procedures of a congressional hearing. Thus, no one apparently considered television to be in a different category. The committee's hearings in New Orleans already had been televised live. The favorable response to that experiment persuaded Kefauver to allow television in New York; but neither he nor anyone else grasped clearly the essential difference between television and film: that viewers were observing events as they happened. The tremendous power of television derived from this fact, and its discovery made Kefauver a presidential contender and perhaps did even more for the fledgling television industry.

When the committee opened hearings in New York on March 12, 1951, only New York and a few other stations carried the broadcast, but stations in twenty cities blanketing the eastern seaboard and much of the midwest quickly picked up the hearings. *Time* agreed to sponsor New York coverage; the response astonished everyone. Kefauver's personal assessment was most revealing: "The hour-by-hour television coverage of the proceedings . . . reached an estimated audience of between 20,000,000 and 30,000,000, and the effect was unbelievable. In New York City itself . . . businesses were paralyzed; many movie houses became 'ghost' halls . . . ; and housewives did their ironing and mending in front of their TV sets. Throughout the country the Crime Committee became . . . a national crusade, a great debating forum, an arouser of public opinion on the state of the nation's morals."

A statistical-demographic analysis suggests certain obvious explanations for the popularity accorded the crime hearings. First, the percentage of homes with television sets in the New York metropolitan area had jumped from 29 to 51 percent during the previous year. At that time the typical daytime programming was so poor that only 1.5 percent of those sets were in use on an average morning. The incredible rise in viewing (seventeen times normal) and equally rapid growth in the viewing audience could be easily explained. At certain times 86.2 percent of those watching television in the New York area were tuned to the crime committee hearings.

Still, statistics cannot convey the incredible impact of the hearings upon their audience. For eight days Americans watched spellbound as some forty witnesses marched confidently forward to be sworn in (eight days of public hearings and five private sessions were held; the committee heard eighty-nine witnesses and conferred with approximately five hundred others), only to be reduced to an incoherence of belligerent silence by Halley's devastating questioning and the calm, confident behavior of Kefauver and his colleagues. "It was as if everything . . . had been designed to reinforce the simplistic concepts of American politics conveyed through thousands of high school government classes and textbooks," one scholar has written. "Good and evil, heroes and villains, black and white categorization made each specific encounter between committee and witness easy to follow. All five senators played their roles perfectly." The committee was eager to explore such topics as the links between crime and politics in New York, criminal operations on the waterfront, bookmaking and gambling activities, especially at Roosevelt Raceway, and the narcotics situation. However, the hearings pivoted upon the presentation of the argument that one criminal organization, a syndicate headed by gangsters Joe Adonis, Frank Costello, and Meyer Lansky, dominated New York crime. Both personal conviction and popular fascination with these underworld tycoons prompted the committee to zero in on the Costello-Adonis-Lansky operation and its influence over local government.

Frank Costello's appearance on March 13, and repeat performances later, proved the dramatic high point of the hearings. In part this was the result of both the man's reputation and the manipulative effects of television. Costello objected violently to the television cameras, and the committee decided that only his hands would be shown. Those hands twisted and clenched, revealing Costello's inner fears and confusion as Halley fired question after question at this "elder statesman" of crime. Increasingly frustrated by the committee's interrogation, Costello lapsed into incoherence and refused to answer many questions on grounds of self-incrimination. During the hearings on March 15 Costello abruptly claimed he was too ill to testify and walked out, pursued by Kefauver's ringing indictment. He returned the next day but proved so uncooperative that the committee cited him for contempt. This episode was significant because Frank

Costello came to symbolize organized crime for millions of Americans, and they greeted his condemnation by the crime committee with unreserved approval, despite the committee's inability to substantiate many of its assertions about the New York situation.

Other interesting witnesses presented themselves before Kefauver, his colleagues, and the omniscient television camera before the hearings closed on March 21, 1951. Joe Adonis, his pomaded hair and tailored clothes a gangster caricature, bombastically described himself a law-abiding citizen, but then had to resort to the Fifth Amendment when his involvement in gambling, extortion, and gang warfare was explored. Then came Virginia Hill, a stereotypical gangster moll, who told an incredible story of her relationships with Adonis, Costello, and Bugsy Siegel. Perhaps most disturbing of all was the painful exploration of former New York mayor William O'Dwyer's association with Costello and other gang leaders. O'Dwyer, who was currently serving as ambassador to Mexico, was asked to answer charges of influence-peddling and corrupt practices. His responses proved so unsatisfactory that the committee recommended perjury action be initiated and that his income tax returns be investigated. His testimony, however, did raise the matter of the committee's integrity for the first and only time (aside from Governor Warren's persistent but unsubstantiated sniping). O'Dwyer claimed he possessed evidence that Senator Tobey had received underworld money for political campaigns. Tobey made an emotional denial of the charge, and it turned out that O'Dwyer's "evidence" was worthless. The ambassador soon resigned his position, but the episode caused much embarrassment to the Administration. As elsewhere, the New York hearings left the local Democratic organization in difficult circumstances.

The Kefauver Committee returned to Washington, persuaded, as *Life* magazine proclaimed, that "the week of March 12, 1951 will occupy a special place in history." Scheduled hearings were conducted in Washington but then, though public interest in the investigation continued to be high, Kefauver decided that the committee had accomplished its principal goals and should be dissolved. "I do not think that the kind of investigative committee that we have had . . . is justified any longer, because we've found out what we were supposed to determine," he told *U.S. News and World Report* in April 1951. "Now that we have determined that, I think it's time to recommend legislation and see what we can get passed in the Congress." Kefauver's reasons for recommending an end to the inquiry were personal, pragmatic, and political. He had travelled over 50,000 miles on committee business and had conducted hearings on ninety-two days; thus, he was desperately eager to return home again. As well, Kefauver sincerely believed that the committee had proved its case and that its task now was to prepare a comprehensive legislative crime control program on the basis of the information it had acquired. Thirdly, Kefauver may have sensed that the committee could not continue on its independent course much longer without risking violent retaliation from the White House. Immediately after the conclusion of the New York hearings, the Truman Administration began to formulate new initiatives on the "crime front" and to publicize the efforts of federal law enforcement agencies. At a press conference on March

29, for example, President Truman said: "We have been studying quietly but consistently the problems of adult crime, particularly organized crime which spills over state boundaries." Joseph McCarthy might have ignored these signals, given the comparative powerlessness of the Truman Administration; but Kefauver was not prepared to risk an open break with the Administration. In addition, he was advised to begin immediately the consolidation of the national reputation he had gained by a coordinated schedule of lectures, interviews, and writing.

Other members of the committee, more interested in the direct exposure from further hearings, demanded that an extension of the committee's mandate until at least September 1, 1951, be requested. Kefauver finally agreed to the extension but insisted on resigning as chairman. Senator O'Conor replaced him and the crime committee conducted a few desultory inquiries, largely following up leads uncovered earlier in the summer of 1951. Its effective end came, however, when Kefauver resigned as chairman and after the *Third Interim Report,* containing the crime committee's basic findings and recommendations, was released in May 1951.

IV

It must be said that the Kefauver Committee left as many questions unanswered as had the most reticent of the hundreds of witnesses who appeared before it. Even today the real purposes of Senator Kefauver and the crime committee remain something of a mystery. Equally uncertain is any full assessment of the committee's accomplishments. One recent study of the committee, William Moore's impressively researched *The Kefauver Committee and the Politics of Crime, 1950–1952,* concludes that Kefauver launched the investigation almost entirely for political gain and, further, that the committee's basic thesis—that an organized, national crime conspiracy was at work—was erroneous. This is not the place to debate the existence of the Mafia, though it is clear that Kefauver and his colleagues, responding to public pressures, were determined from the beginning to find a scapegoat, some type of conspiratorial group with responsibility for much of America's crime.

Whether or not the Mafia or the syndicate or the mob was central, one must point to the almost total lack of success the committee experienced in getting crime control laws through Congress. Kefauver agreed with other law enforcement experts that crime control remained essentially a local responsibility. A federal police force or any of the other alarmist reactions to the crime committee's disclosures were, he believed, impractical and possibly dangerous. The committee's recommendations included the following:

> Creation of a Federal Crime Commission "to coordinate and bring together and avoid duplication in the investigative services of the Federal Government."
>
> Establishment of a "racket squad" in the Justice Department.
>
> Establishment of a mechanism for maintaining "a list of known

gangsters, racketeers, gamblers, and criminals whose income tax returns should receive special attention by a squad of trained experts."

Effective enforcement by the Internal Revenue Bureau of existing laws requiring adequate records of income and expenses by all taxpayers.

Strict controls over the records of gambling casinos.

"The law and the regulations of the Bureau of Internal Revenue should be amended so that no wagering losses, expenses, or disbursements of any kind . . . incurred in or as a result of illegal gambling shall be deductible for income-tax purposes."

Regulation of the transmission of gambling information across state lines by telegraph, telephone, television, radio, or other means "so as to outlaw any service devoted to a substantial extent to providing information used in illegal gambling."

Prohibition of the transmission of bets or wagers across state lines via the methods described above.

Prohibition of the transportation of slot machines in interstate commerce should be extended to include other gambling devices, such as punchboards, roulette wheels, and so forth.

Substantial increase in the penalties against illegal sale of narcotic drugs.

Amendment of the immigration laws to facilitate deportation of "criminal and other undesirable aliens." Other changes were also proposed.

Substantial expansion in the numbers of federal law enforcement personnel.

Clarification of the existing federal statute with respect to perjury.

The attorney general of the United States should be given authority to grant immunity from prosecution to witnesses whose testimony may be essential to an inquiry conducted by a grand jury, or in the course of a trial or of a congressional investigation.

Passage of legislation to compel the presence of evasive witnesses before a congressional investigation.

Legislation to prevent racketeers from entering the liquor industry and to eliminate any criminal elements presently involved in the production or distribution of liquor.

Recommendation that the Interstate Commerce Commission "be required by law to consider the moral fitness of applications" for certificates of necessity.

In one sense this list of recommendations comprised a comprehensive program for effective control of organized crime. Unfortunately, very few of the committee's proposals were enacted into law. Of some 221 legislative recommendations submitted to Congress as a result of the committee's activities, only a handful obtained a full hearing by standing committees of Congress. But the pressure generated by the crime committee and by an alarmed public did produce stronger enforcement of existing laws, and this must be considered a positive achievement.

In general, any assessment of the Kefauver Committee must deal with the tremendous effect it had on public awareness of the problem of organized crime. For better or for worse, the "publicity function" is basic to the work of any congressional investigation. There can be no doubt about the success of the crime committee in this field. As a result of the committee's dramatization of the problem, public concern about organized crime and instances of local corruption attained a level of awareness heretofore unimagined. More than seventy local commissions were created, and those already in existence received fresh support. There existed the danger of vigilantism and, even more worrisome, the possibility that local groups would conclude that the crime committee had shown the problem was beyond their capabilities or that such groups would rely solely on the federal government for solutions to the threat of organized crime. Something like this did occur over the next decade, but Senator Kefauver and the crime committee did not intentionally foster vigilante sentiment or the belief that a "man on horseback" would appear to save America from organized crime. Yet the nature of the investigation and the manner in which the committee presented its case led inevitably to such judgments. The "times were out of joint," and it would have demanded men of extraordinary courage and vision to resist the yearning for simple, easy solutions to problems and concerns then sweeping the nation.

Indeed, placed against this backdrop of popular tensions and political turmoil, the procedures followed by the Kefauver Committee were remarkably enlightened and objective. Kefauver and his colleagues were essentially fair-minded men, and their investigation, though limited by preconceptions regarding the problem of organized crime, did reflect concern for fair play. The committee faced certain difficult procedural questions: applicability of the Fifth Amendment, the punitive nature of contempt citations, and the provision of immunity from prosecution. It may be stated that the committee sincerely believed that its position was correct and that the rights of witnesses would be safeguarded. In any event, the courts would be compelled to clarify these questions because of the activities of other congressional investigations then being conducted.

Only with regard to the status of television did the Kefauver Committee introduce a new element into the structure of congressional investigations. The committee did not recognize any important difference between filming hearings for theater showings and the use of live television. However, it soon became clear that television posed serious issues. Lawyers feared that television would distort the legal process, giving the aura of truth to unsubstantiated testimony and influencing prospective jurors. The Federal Bar Association of New Jersey asserted that the "glaring melodrama" created by the presence of television apparatus would produce a warped atmosphere. Somewhat later the federal courts, in *United States* v. *Kleinman et al,* adopted a similar position with regard to the atmosphere created by television. Others worried about the effects of commercial sponsorship of government hearings and the danger that investigators, conscious of the enormous audiences watching their every move, might "play to the galleries." Thurman Arnold warned of what might happen if Joe McCarthy or someone like him were given a television spot. "When the Senator does put on his show," Arnold commented soon after the Kefauver Committee's hearings in New York, "I'll lay a substantial wager with my bookie . . . that McCarthy will make the efforts of the present committee look like the work of inept amateurs." However, the House of Representatives ruled out televised coverage of hearings in February 1952. The Senate Rules Committee recommended in January 1955 that witnesses have the right to request that television or other cameras not be directed at them during testimony. The precise effects of televising congressional hearings is still being disputed, though the advocates of the "Congress as classroom" viewpoint would seem to have the upper hand.

Had Estes Kefauver been successful in converting the popular approbation he received for his "crime-busting" exploits into a successful campaign for the presidency, as he attempted to do in 1952, historical evaluations of the crime committee might have been quite different. As President, Kefauver would have been in a position to throw the full weight of the federal government into the fight against organized crime, and there might have occurred a test of the thesis that chopping off the heads of the criminal hydra would destroy the beast itself. However, Kefauver discovered that the investigation which made him a presidential contender also served to deny him the prize.

Not an excited public but professional politicians selected the Democratic candidate for the presidency, and at the 1952 convention Kefauver, despite successes in the primaries, faced a hostile array of urban bosses, vengeful congressmen, and an outgoing President who violently opposed his candidacy. Kefauver had sought to reach the White House via the same route carved out by Harry Truman; but instead of following the markers of party loyalty and obeisance to the President's leadership, as had Truman, he set his own course. Perhaps an independent stance could not have been avoided in the difficult circumstances of 1950–1951, but so long as the system endured, retribution was sure to be visited on violators of the political code, no matter how powerful or secure their positions might appear to be. Then, too, circumstances changed, and people soon forgot yesterday's heroes.

BIBLIOGRAPHY

Essential primary sources for any study of the Kefauver Committee are the papers of Senator Kefauver at the University of Tennessee, Knoxville, Tennessee; the Charles Tobey papers, Dartmouth College, Hanover, New Hampshire; the Alexander Wiley papers in the Wisconsin State Historical Society, Madison, Wisconsin; and the Lester Hunt papers at the University of Wyoming, Laramie, Wyoming. Senator O'Conor's papers were destroyed. Also informative are various collections in the Harry S. Truman Library, Independence, Missouri, especially the papers of Truman, George Elsey, and J. Howard McGrath. At last report, the records of the Kefauver Committee, now under the control of the Commerce Committee, were not available to scholars.

The Crime Committee issued four reports. These, especially the *Third Interim Report* (Washington, D.C., 1951), are extremely useful summaries but should be supplemented by the nineteen volumes of committee hearings, which include some twelve thousand pages of testimony. Reports of the Communications Subcommittee of the Commerce Committee, the Special Investigations Committee, and other congressional bodies involved with government operations during the Truman era offer useful comparisons.

Estes Kefauver, *Crime in America* (Garden City, 1951), is laced with colorful anecdotes but contains little not available in the committee's reports. Two recent books, *Kefauver: A Political Biography* (New York, 1971), by Joseph B. Gorman, and William H. Moore's *The Kefauver Committee and the Politics of Crime, 1950–1952* (Columbia, Mo., 1974), are indispensable. Both are solidly researched but reach quite different conclusions regarding Kefauver's motives and the committee's achievements. See also Harvey Swados, *Standing Up for the People: the Life and Work of Estes Kefauver* (New York, 1952), Jack Anderson and Fred Blumenthal, *The Kefauver Story* (New York, 1956), Charles Tobey, *The Return to Morality* (Garden City, 1952), and Harry Kirwan, *O'Conor: The Inevitable Success* (Westminster, Md., 1962). Interesting perspectives on the "mess in Washington" are found in Cabell Phillips, *The Truman Presidency* (New York, 1966), Jules Abels, *The Truman Scandals* (Chicago, 1956), and Eric F. Goldman, *The Crucial Decade—And After* (New York, 1960).

The literature on crime, criminals, and the efforts to stop them in twentieth century America is enormous. A few of the more helpful works are: Fred J. Cook, *The F.B.I. Nobody Knows* (New York, 1964), Donald R. Cressey, *Theft of the Nation: The Structure and Operations of Organized Crime in America* (New York, 1969), Rufus King, *Gambling and Organized Crime* (Washington, D.C., 1969), Hank Messick, *John Edgar Hoover* (New York, 1972) and his earlier works, Ralph Salerno, *The Crime Confederation* (New York, 1969), and the muckraking *Murder, Inc.: The Story of the "Syndicate"* (London, 1953), by Burton B. Turkus. For arguments regarding the Mafia, see Peter Maas, *The Valachi Papers* (New York, 1968), Francis A. J. Ianni, *A Family Business: Kinship and Social Control in Organized Crime* (New York, 1972),

Joseph L. Albini, *The American Mafia: Genesis of a Legend* (New York, 1971), and Fred J. Cook, *Mafia!* (Greenwich, Conn., 1973). Daniel Bell's brilliant analysis, *The End of Ideology* (New York, 1962) also deserves special mention.

PERTINENT DOCUMENTS

Summary by J. Edgar Hoover on Crime Conditions, May 11, 1949

Introduction of Senate Resolution 202, January 5, 1950

Senate Debate over Resolution to Establish Crime Committee, May 2 and 3, 1950

Closing Statement of Estes Kefauver, Kansas City Hearings, September 30, 1950

Testimony of Captain Daniel A. Gilbert, October 17, 1950

Testimony of Joseph Doto, also Known as Joe Adonis, December 12, 1950

Kefauver Committee Second Interim Report, February 28, 1951

Testimony of Frank Costello, March 13, 1951

Testimony of Virginia Hill Hauser, March 15, 1951

Testimony of Frank Costello, March 15, 1951

Statement by President Harry S. Truman at News Conference, March 29, 1951

Kefauver Committee Third Interim Report, May 1, 1951

Kefauver Committee Final Report, August 31, 1951

"Responses to the Televised Kefauver Hearings: Some Social Psychological Implications" by G. D. Wiebe, 1952

The MacArthur Inquiry
1951

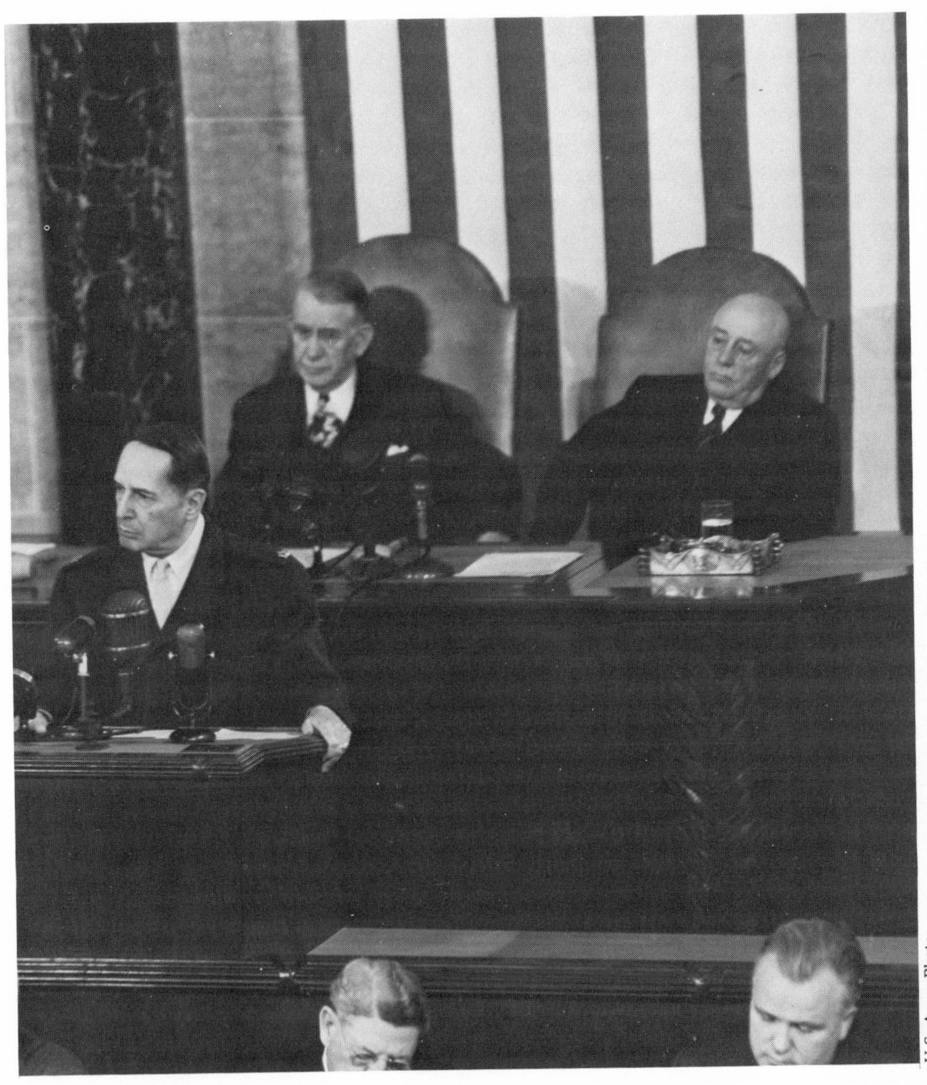

U.S. Army Photo

General Douglas MacArthur addresses Congress after being out of the country for fourteen years. Behind MacArthur are Vice President Alben Barkley and Speaker of the House Sam Rayburn.

The MacArthur Inquiry 1951

by John Edward Wiltz

On the morning of Friday, August 17, 1951, the twenty-six members of the Senate's Armed Services and Foreign Relations Committees assembled in Room 212 of the Senate Office Building in Washington for their last meeting in connection with their "inquiry into the military situation in the Far East and the facts surrounding the relief of General of the Army Douglas MacArthur from his assignments in that area." The inquiry had been triggered by President Harry S. Truman's dismissal the previous April of MacArthur as commander in chief, United Nations Command; supreme commander for the Allied powers in Japan; commander in chief, Far East Command; and commander in chief, army forces in the Pacific. The main issue to be resolved that morning was whether the committees, which in their joint inquiry had taken two million words of testimony from thirteen witnesses during forty-two days of hearings in May and June 1951, should prepare a report. After more than an hour of discussion the senators resolved that there should be no report but that members of the two committees could file their views and conclusions with the chairman, who would see that they were printed in an appendix. A fortnight later, in accord with that resolution, eight Republican members—Owen Brewster (Maine), Styles Bridges (New Hampshire), Harry P. Cain (Washington),

Ralph E. Flanders (Vermont), Bourke B. Hickenlooper (Iowa), William F. Knowland (California), H. Alexander Smith (New Jersey), and Alexander Wiley (Wisconsin)—submitted their "individual views."

Those views make interesting reading in the 1970s. They betray none of the euphoria about differences between Communist countries and the so-called free world which, in light of President Richard M. Nixon's pilgrimages to Peking and Moscow and optimistic talk about détente and peaceful coexistence, later captivated large numbers of Americans. They reveal instead disillusion and frustration over the failure of America's military crusade of 1941–1945 to make the world safe for the principles of liberty and justice—as Americans of the time perceived those principles.

Nearly all Americans in 1951, whether admirers of Douglas MacArthur or Harry Truman, shared the conviction that "international communism," under the disciplined control of the Kremlin, had ruthlessly enslaved millions of people in the aftermath of the Second World War. In that grim catalogue of tragedies the greatest catastrophe had been communism's conquest of China, the most populous country on earth, one that the United States, so the senators asserted and most Americans seemed to believe, had befriended and protected and whose people felt special esteem for America. Not satisfied by the swallowing of China, the appetite of international communism—and here was an article of faith even of people considered Socialists by the right-wing of American politics—proved to be nothing short of subjugation of the entire world.

If nearly all Americans in 1951 seemed to share this estimate of the evil character and global ambitions of communism, they differed in their views of why communism in recent years had dramatically enlarged its influence and power. Some credited Communist successes to a combination of ruthlessness, postwar chaos, and the failure of non-Communist leaders (notably in China) to meet the problems of grinding poverty. Others, including the eight senators, contended that the key to communism's triumphs had been the unwitting (or witless) and treasonable assistance which it had received from Americans; that had been the case most notably and tragically in China. By pursuing policies of expediency and appeasement, they wrote, particularly at the Yalta Conference in February 1945 and during General George C. Marshall's famous mission to China, December 1945 through January 1947, in failing to consult General MacArthur or follow the counsel of Lieutenant General Albert C. Wedemeyer regarding China, and in refusing to provide adequate support for the Nationalist regime of Generalissimo Chiang Kai-shek, "the victory won by our Armed Forces in the Pacific [in 1941–1945] has been squandered by our diplomats." The eight senators, all identified with the Republican party's "Old Guard" and in general agreement with Senator Joseph R. McCarthy's contention that the federal bureaucracy had been penetrated by Communists or Communist-sympathizers, also argued that what they termed vicious propaganda against Chiang Kai-shek and Communist subversion in the State Department had contributed to communism's triumph in China.

Americans in 1951 likewise differed on how the presumed threat of international communism should be met. Many favored a policy whereby the United States, working closely with allies, would try to contain communism within its existing territory, thus guarding against Communist expansion in Europe. Others, including the eight senators, took a suspicious view of America's allies, particularly Great Britain, and thought the United States never should pull its punches for the sake of maintaining harmony with foreigners. Feeling a particular attachment to Chiang Kai-shek, Americans of the latter persuasion also contended that communism in East Asia was as much a menace to America's security and interests as in Europe. In many respects, the world view of such individuals seemed a maze of vague and conflicting ideas. On the one hand, they looked with some contempt upon the outer world and exalted Americans and their institutions, sometimes betraying a yearning to retreat from world responsibilities to something approximating a "Fortress America." On the other hand, they often deplored the containment policy of the Truman Administration and spoke of rolling back the Iron Curtain in Europe and Asia. While urging a reduction of American strength in Europe, which hardly squared with the rollback conception, some were willing to risk World War III to rescue China from the clutches of communism.

What prompted the thinking of the eight senators and their political and intellectual companions? A simple answer might be that it resulted in part from misgivings over the government's departure, via the Truman Doctrine, Marshall Plan, and North Atlantic Treaty, from the historic peacetime policy of nonentanglement, relative aloofness, or national reserve (as it had been variously called)—or isolation (a popular if inadequate and misleading label). Such misgivings certainly seem to explain the flirtation of neo-isolationists (as the eight senators and other critics of Truman's foreign policies frequently were referred to) or nationalists (as they preferred to be called) with the Fortress America conception. In seeking an answer to this question one might also note the vision of communism held by neo-isolationists. While it was true that nearly all Americans of 1951 despised and feared communism, the hatred and fear of the neo-isolationists exceeded that of many of their countrymen. Neo-isolationists accordingly rejected the idea of peaceful coexistence with the Communists and inclined to the view that America had two choices in foreign affairs: conceding most of the world to international communism while building Fortress America as a bastion of liberty and democracy, or acting aggressively to bring about the collapse of communism.

There was more to neo-isolationism, however, than concern over new departures in foreign policy and aggravated anti-communism. Most neo-isolationists, including the eight senators, were attached to the conservative wing of the Republican party, and nearly all had been noninterventionists or isolationists in the period before America's entry in the Second World War. For such individuals the psychic burden of recent history had been almost unbearable. The ascendency of the principles of the Democratic welfare state brought about by President Franklin D. Roosevelt's New Deal in the 1930s, the universal repudiation of the central assumption of prewar isolationism, namely, that Axis aggression presented no threat to the United States, and five consecutive defeats in presidential elections had brought the conservative wing or Old Guard of the Republican party to the depth of frustration. As the cold war unfolded and seemed to go from bad to worse; the Old Guard saw an opportunity to refurbish its reputation, recapture the White House, and turn back the clock of history to those revered days before Roosevelt and the welfare staters had taken the American republic on a radical binge. This opportunity appeared in the national disillusionment over the failure of the Second World War to bring forth the kind of world envisioned by the Atlantic Charter and the Charter of the United Nations, the great victories of communism in Eastern Europe and China, and the alleged infiltration of legions of Communist traitors into the federal bureaucracy. Since Democratic welfare staters had been the managers of the republic's affairs during this time, it followed in accord with the iron law of American politics that blame for the great tragedy rested with them.

Encouraged by the stunning reelection victory of their acknowledged leader, Senator Robert A. Taft of Ohio in November 1950, and already deploying for a grand effort to put Taft in the White House in January 1953, Old Guard Republicans in late autumn 1950 touched off what news commentators were soon referring to as a Great Debate over American foreign policy. The debate reached the floor of Congress in early 1951 when the Old Guard made a strenuous effort to prevent President Truman from sending two army divisions to Europe to bolster America's commitment to NATO. They succeeded in persuading the Senate to pass a resolution declaring that the President should not send additional troops to Europe without congressional consent. When Truman dismissed MacArthur, a Republican who shared the conservative political and social philosophy of the Old Guard and a renowned national hero who had clashed with their sworn enemy, "Give 'em Hell Harry" Truman, the Old Guard inevitably embraced MacArthur and made him a symbol of their views (although in truth MacArthur's ideas about world affairs in some ways varied with their own). MacArthur returned the embrace.

So began the MacArthur inquiry of 1951, for by the time the inquiry got underway nobody was questioning the President's authority to dismiss the general. The brainchild of Old Guardsmen (but not managed by them, inasmuch as Democrats were in control of Congress), the inquiry was a new and climactic chapter in the Great Debate over American foreign policy. By presenting MacArthur as the champion of their views and concentrating on the Far East, where communism had registered its most staggering postwar triumphs (and hence American policy under the Democrats had suffered its most staggering defeat), the Old Guard hoped to demolish its opponents, force a dramatic revision of American foreign policy, and, most important of all, prepare the way for the capture of the White House a year and a half later by "Mr. Republican," Senator Taft.

I

Whatever their views about the origin of the cold war and how it should be prosecuted, most Americans had acquiesced in President Truman's decision at the end of June 1950 to throw American armed forces into the battle to resist Communist North Korea's invasion of South Korea. They agreed with the Truman logic that failure to stop this first overt act of aggression by "international communism" since 1945 would only encourage further aggression and, ultimately, result in a new world war. They were pleased, even reassured, when the President placed the seventy-year-old General MacArthur in command of American forces in Korea and, when the United Nations assumed responsibility for resisting North Korea's attack, it asked the United States and MacArthur to assume command of UN operations in Korea.

After stopping the North Korean offensive along the Pusan perimeter at the southeastern corner of Korea, American forces, in one of MacArthur's most celebrated maneuvers, struck the North Korean flank and rear at Inchon, the Eighth Army broke out of the Pusan perimeter, and by the end of September 1950 South Korea (Korea below the thirty-eighth parallel) had been cleared of Communist forces. Then came a fateful decision, sanctioned by the UN but made in Washington, that directed UN troops to cross the thirty-eighth parallel and sweep communism from the northern half of Korea. Leaders in the United States were anxious, however, lest the Chinese enter the war, particularly if UN troops advanced toward the Yalu River, the border between North Korea and China. During a dramatic meeting on Wake Island in mid-October the President raised this possibility with MacArthur. The general either speculated or expressed reasonable certainty, depending on whose account of the discussion one accepts, that the Chinese would not intervene.

UN forces then pressed forward, and in an offhand remark MacArthur expressed hope that American troops would be home by Christmas. Even as the commanding general uttered those words, however, Chinese soldiers were streaming across the Yalu into the rugged territory between MacArthur's separated contingents, and at the end of November they struck out savagely against the outnumbered UN infantrymen. When the UN retreat ended in January 1951, the Communists had recrossed the thirty-eighth parallel and driven UN forces, then under the field command of Lieutenant General Matthew B. Ridgway, to a line fifty miles below Seoul, South Korea's battered capital city. For MacArthur, a proud and sometimes brilliant soldier, defeat came as a bitter pill, and to salvage the victory which had seemed within his grasp the previous November, he requested authority to send UN bombing planes against Communist supply depots, staging areas, and railroads in Manchuria, to impose a naval blockade against China's coastal cities, and introduce Chinese Nationalist troops from Formosa into the Korean combat. Determined to keep the war limited to Korea, Truman turned aside MacArthur's increasingly public appeals and finally, on April 11, 1951, dismissed the five-star general from his commands.

In retrospect, one is tempted to wonder why Truman put up with MacArthur as long as he did. The previous July, while UN troops were dug in along the Pusan perimeter, the general had flown to Formosa to check on the defenses of Chiang Kai-shek's island, and while there he expressed subtle disapproval of Washington's policy of preventing Nationalist attacks on China's Communist-ruled mainland. (When America intervened in the Korea conflict, Truman had ordered the Seventh Fleet to the Formosa Strait to protect Formosa and also to prevent Chiang from attempting an attack against his adversaries on the mainland.) In the last days of August 1950 MacArthur's public relations office in Tokyo handed reporters a copy of a statement by the general which was scheduled to be read in America on August 28 at the annual encampment of the Veterans of Foreign Wars. Although its theme was that Formosa should not be permitted to fall into hostile hands, the statement emphasized the importance of Formosa to the defense of American interests in the Pacific and seemed inconsistent with Truman's statement of June 27 in which he stated his policy was to neutralize Formosa until such time as "restoration of security in the Pacific, a peace settlement with Japan, or consideration by the United Nations" was secured. Infuriated and concerned that the world might begin to wonder what America's policy regarding Formosa was, the President, as he later recorded in his *Memoirs,* considered relieving MacArthur of his command in Korea, but settled for an order directing him to withdraw the statement.

Truman's pique with MacArthur seemed to evaporate a few weeks later in the aftermath of the operation at Inchon and the subsequent rush of UN forces up the Korean peninsula. It appeared in those euphoric days of September–October 1950 that the American-inspired action of the UN in Korea was going to achieve its original objective and a good deal more besides; that is, it would succeed in repelling the North Korean invaders from South Korea and in addition bring a non-Communist reunification of the Korean nation, all without turning the so-called limited war of "police action" into a general war. But then came China's intervention and the heartbreaking UN retreat of November–January.

As exhausted UN units fell back across the thirty-eighth parallel in early December 1950, MacArthur advised the Joint Chiefs of Staff that China's entry into the war "calls for political decisions and strategic plans in implementation thereof adequate fully to meet the realities involved." Unable or unwilling to accept the logic of his superiors for keeping the war limited to Korea, he made a transparent appeal for authority to enlarge the war by carrying hostilities to the Chinese territory. Unfortunately, MacArthur was not content to keep his thoughts in military channels. In response to questions by *U.S. News and World Report* the first week in December, he maintained that orders preventing UN attacks beyond the Yalu were "an enormous handicap, without precedent in military history." More pointed were comments given about the same time in a statement to the president of the United Press. After explaining the advantage the "privileged sanctuary" in Manchuria gave the Communists, he scolded European proponents of limited war in Korea—and by implication American proponents, including the President—for failing to comprehend the importance of the conflict in East Asia: "If the fight is not waged with courage and invincible determination to meet the challenge here, it will indeed be fought, and possibly lost, on the battlefields of Europe." The general's broadsides irritated Truman, who wrote in his *Memoirs,* "I should have relieved General MacArthur then and there." But, Truman recalled, he did not want it to appear that the general was being made a scapegoat for the debacle in Korea. Instead, the President, on December 5, issued an order directing that no civil or military official (namely MacArthur) was to make any public statement on foreign or military policy without first getting a clearance from the Department of State or Department of Defense.

In the last days of December 1950 MacArthur composed a communication to the Joint Chiefs of Staff urging a dramatic expansion of the war in East Asia: a naval blockade of China, unrestricted air and naval attacks against Chinese industry, employment of Chiang Kai-shek's Nationalist troops in Korea, and removal of restrictions preventing the Nationalists on Formosa from attacking the Communists on China's mainland. On receiving a message from Washington turning aside his appeal, MacArthur, as he later recalled, "shot a query back" in which he advised the Joint Chiefs that his forces, weary and pinned down in Korea, no longer could guarantee the safety of Japan, the centerpiece of America's interests in the Far East; he requested substantial reinforcements or authority to evacuate Korea. In the words of Truman's secretary of state, Dean Acheson, recorded nearly two decades later in his memoirs, "here was a posterity paper if there ever was one, with the purpose not only of clearing MacArthur of blame if things went wrong but also of putting the maximum pressure on Washington to reverse itself and adopt his proposals for widening the war against China." Under heavy pressure from the UN and allies in Europe to keep the war in East Asia limited to Korea, which they were committed to do in any case, civil and military leaders in Washington were much annoyed. Finally, they dispatched a message to Tokyo which offered no reinforcements and directed MacArthur to stay in Korea "unless actually forced by military considerations." To provide any clarification that might be required, and also to discuss with MacArthur what might be done in the event matters got worse in Korea, two members of the Joint Chiefs of Staff, Generals J. Lawton Collins of the army and Hoyt S. Vandenberg of the air force, flew to Tokyo. A few days later Truman sent a long personal message to MacArthur explaining with uncharacteristic tact the global considerations underlying American policy.

Meanwhile the Communist offensive in Korea was running out of steam, and in late January 1951 UN troops under Ridgway, strung across the peninsula from a point fifty miles below Seoul, began to edge forward once more. In mid-March UN forces recaptured the remnants of the South Korean capital (the fourth time the city had changed hands in nine months), and within a few days were approaching the thirty-eighth parallel. Thereupon MacArthur rekindled his campaign for widening the war. In a public statement on March 7 he observed that "as our battle lines shift north the supply position of the enemy will progressively improve, just as inversely the effectiveness of our air potential will progressively diminish, thus in turn causing his numerical ground superiority to become of increasing battlefield significance." He concluded: "Vital decisions have yet to be made—decisions far beyond the scope of the authority vested in me as the military commander, decisions which are neither solely political nor solely military, but which must provide on the highest international levels an answer to the obscurities which now becloud the unsolved problems raised by Red China's undeclared war in Korea." If couched in subtleties, the statement left little doubt about what MacArthur wanted to do. On March 15, in clear violation of Truman's order regarding public statements on high policy, the commanding general issued another communication to the president of the United Press. In it he expressed his opposition to stopping the UN advance at the thirty-eighth parallel or short of "accomplishment of our mission in the unification of Korea." As Acheson later recalled, "he had been told over and over again that this was not his mission."

From the UN and NATO allies, leaders in Washington were receiving different signals, namely, urgent appeals that they seek a cease-fire in Korea. The conditions for a battlefield truce certainly seemed opportune. The battle line was roughly where it had been when the war broke out and neither side could advance without incurring devastating losses. A cease-fire along the present line, moreover, would not result in any substantial loss of face for either side, for if neither had achieved total victory in the war, the United States and UN could claim that they had saved South Korea from the Communist aggressors and the Chinese could boast that they had prevented destruction of a Communist sister-state, North Korea. Weary of the war and unwilling to incur the expense in blood and treasure that further offensive action would require—and also concerned about reports that the Soviets were assembling troops in Siberia for possible commitment in Korea if the UN pushed ahead—the Truman Administration needed no prodding. On March 20 the White House completed the draft of a statement to be issued by the President indicating that because the aggressors had been cleared from South Korea the UN would consider a cease-fire and peace negotiations. Copies of the draft statement went to fourteen other governments which had furnished troops for the UN effort, and General MacArthur was advised by radio that the President was about to make a peace overture. Leaders in Washington summarily dismissed MacArthur's response, an urgent request that "no further military restrictions be imposed upon the United Nations Command in Korea."

Then came a bombshell—labeled a routine communiqué a few years later by MacArthur in his reminiscences, but in Washington's eyes, an act of open defiance of the President's December 5 order. In a statement dated March 24, 1951, the commanding general made his own offer to negotiate with the enemy! MacArthur declared that despite inhibitions restricting its operations, his command had thwarted aggression in Korea and that the enemy "must be painfully aware that a decision of the United Nations to depart from its tolerant effort to contain the war to the area of Korea, through an expansion of our military operations to his coastal areas and interior bases would doom Red China to the risk of imminent military collapse." Seeing no reason why the Communists should continue the struggle, MacArthur stood ready to confer with the enemy commander in chief.

Officials at the UN and in the capitals of America's allies were aghast; leaders in Washington furious. In addition to committing what his superiors considered an arrogant act of insubordination, MacArthur had cut the ground from under Truman's proposed peace overture. Clearly the general had to go. But Harry Truman, often impulsive in personal matters, was surprisingly cautious in matters of state. Before recalling MacArthur, he was determined to weigh the military and political consequences of such a dramatic move.

On April 5, 1951, the Republican leader in the House of Representatives, Joseph W. Martin, jr., of Massachusetts, stood in the House chamber and reported that several weeks before he had written MacArthur soliciting his views on the use of Chiang Kai-shek's Nationalist forces "in the opening of a second Asiatic front to relieve the pressure on our forces in Korea." He explained that he had asked the general to express himself either on or off the record, and since MacArthur's reply had not stipulated confidentiality, "I owe it to the American people to tell them the information I have from a great and reliable source." He then read MacArthur's letter. After supporting the idea of a Nationalist attack on the Chinese mainland MacArthur asserted: "It seems strangely difficult for some to realize that here in Asia is where the Communist conspirators have elected to make their play for global conquest, and that we have joined the issue thus raised on the battlefield; that here we fight Europe's war with arms while the diplomats there still fight it with words; that if we lost the war to Communism in Asia the fall of Europe is inevitable; win it and Europe most probably would avoid war and yet preserve freedom. . . . There is no substitute for victory." From London that same day came a news dispatch quoting MacArthur as having told a reporter that a web of artificial conditions was circumscribing UN forces in Korea, that the war had no definite objective, that it was not the soldier who had encroached on the realm of the politician. The general also allegedly said that the true object of a commander in war was to destroy the forces that opposed him, that such was not the case in Korea, and that the situation would be ludicrous if men's lives were not in the balance.

After consulting with diplomatic advisers and the Joint Chiefs, the President on April 10 signed the orders relieving MacArthur of all commands in the Far East. It was intended that the orders would be cabled to Secretary of the Army Frank Pace, who was on an inspection mission in Korea, and that he would deliver them personally to MacArthur, before their release to the news media. At approximately seven o'clock in the evening, however, the presidential press secretary, Joseph Short, reported that the *Chicago Tribune* had learned of MacArthur's dismissal and would print the story the next morning. Hurrying to Blair House where Truman was having dinner (because the renovation of the White House living quarters was then in progress), General Omar N. Bradley, chairman of the Joint Chiefs, advised the President that if MacArthur learned of his dismissal via the *Tribune* story, he probably would try to resign. The President was purported to have snapped: "He's not going to be allowed to quit on me. He's going to be fired!" Unable to contact Pace to have him deliver the dismissal orders at once, Bradley, after another conference with Truman, dispatched the dismissal message directly to MacArthur's headquarters. It was a few minutes before midnight, Washington time; a few moments later Short summoned reporters to the White House and at 1:00 A.M. read the dismissal message. Before Bradley's communication got through to MacArthur, however, the embassy in Tokyo picked up a report of the dismissal in a commercial broadcast; an aide of the general at the embassy then telephoned MacArthur's residence, relayed the news to Jean Faircloth MacArthur, who in turn informed her husband. The general replied: "Jeannie, we're going home at last." It had been nearly fifteen years since the MacArthurs had last been in the United States.

What followed must seem, in retrospect, almost unreal to Americans whose memories do not reach back to 1951. Across the republic expressions of outrage over the dismissal of the imperious MacArthur, the architect of victory in the southwest Pacific in World War II and the bearer of democracy to conquered Japan, drowned out the few voices raised on behalf of the President, whose reputation had recently been tarnished by disclosures that some of his subordinates had been peddling influence. When MacArthur, his wife, and young son arrived a few days later in San Francisco it seemed, so the general later recalled, "that every man, woman, and child . . . turned out to cheer us." On April 19 came perhaps the climax of MacArthur's long career—an address to both houses of Congress and the national television and radio audience. In his speech he restated his views on foreign policy and the Korean War and concluded by quoting the familiar refrain of an old barracks ballad—"Old Soldiers never die, they just fade away." From the capital MacArthur moved on to tumultuous receptions in New York, Chicago, and Milwaukee, the city of his childhood.

Old Guard Republicans, meanwhile, had been discussing the idea of a congressional investigation into MacArthur's dismissal and America's Far Eastern policy. Democrats, including Truman, also spoke out in favor of such an inquiry, and on April 25 the Senate unanimously approved a resolution offered by Richard B. Russell, Democrat of Georgia, providing for a joint investigation by the Armed Services and Foreign Relations Committees. On the suggestion of Tom Connally of Texas, chairman of the Foreign Relations Committee, the honor of presiding over the joint inquiry went to Russell, chairman of the Armed Services Committee and a lanky and baldish bachelor of fifty-three. An eighteen-year veteran of the Senate, by 1951 he was one of the most respected (and powerful) men on Capitol Hill. The two committees agreed to commence hearings on May 3 by interrogating MacArthur himself, but before the interrogation could get underway Republicans and Democrats brawled over the question of whether the hearings should be open to the public or conducted behind closed doors. Counting on MacArthur's Olympian manner and polished phrases to strengthen support for their views, especially if the hearings were televised, Republicans demanded open hearings. Democrats countered that the inquiry would be dealing with secret documents and sensitive subjects, hence national security required closed hearings and censorship of transcripts of testimony before their release to the news media. Because Democrats had a majority of the votes, their view carried.

II

The MacArthurs had taken up residence in a $130-a-day suite in the Waldorf-Astoria in New York, and on the three days he testified before the Armed Services and Foreign Relations Committees the general commuted between New York and Washington by plane. On his arrival at the Senate Office Building the first day, May 3, two hundred reporters and photographers scrambled about as he made his way through the corridors. Wearing his famous khaki campaign cap and accompanied by his long-time aide, Major General Courtney Whitney (who had quit the army in the aftermath of MacArthur's dismissal), he waved and half-smiled. When he entered the caucus room, site of the early hearings, the newsmen followed, and in the words of one reporter "cameramen clambered on chairs to capture the firm jaw, the still-dark hair and serious mien, for the afternoon editions." While reporters and photographers milled about, MacArthur shook hands with the twenty-six members of the two committees and other senators who were also present. At length the journalists were ushered out of the room, the doors closed, and at 10:15 the interrogation began.

Hour after hour over the next three days the general, dressed in a ribbonless "Eisenhower jacket" and khaki necktie, slouched in a padded swivel-chair behind a table, puffing on a briar pipe as he answered questions, occasionally consulting Whitney who was seated to his left. Democrats as well as Republicans treated him with elaborate courtesy, and only Senators Brien McMahon of Connecticut and J. W. Fulbright of Arkansas displayed enthusiasm for barbed or embarrassing questions. The general never seemed to tire or show any strain; he never appeared irritated. It was clear nonetheless that he was anxious to get on with other things, and to hasten the proceedings he persuaded the senators on the second and third days to lunch on sandwiches and coffee in the hearing room and continue the interrogation until seven o'clock each evening.

As was the case with all witnesses, the interrogation of MacArthur was confusing. Instead of moving logically from topic to topic, the questioning moved from senator to senator—from a member of the Armed Services Committee to a member of the Foreign Relations Committee, back and forth in accord with seniority—and when not asking questions, those senators in attendance often wandered in and out of the hearing room. The interrogation, as a result, touched on an incredible array of topics, some only remotely connected with the central purpose of the inquiry. The hearings were plagued by endless repetition of questions and answers (Secretary of State Acheson having to give an almost identical answer on six different occasions when queried about the use of the veto to keep China's Communist government out of the United Nations) and only with great effort could one ascertain the points being explored in the hearing room.

Among the points developed during the three days of MacArthur's appearance was that the general, in his judgment, had made no errors in his conduct of military operations in Korea.

It was inevitable that MacArthur's management of the Korean campaign would come under scrutiny, for the general received considerable criticism for having divided his forces as they advanced toward the Yalu in October-November 1950, thus leaving vacant a vast corridor through which the Chinese had entered and lashed out against the flanks of the Eighth Army and Tenth Corps. It was just as inevitable that MacArthur would give no quarter to his critics. The five-star general insisted that the first American troops dispatched to Korea from his command in Japan in July 1950, contrary to reports of nearly every observer, had been intensively trained and brought to a high state of professional efficiency. MacArthur explained that he had divided his forces because the northern extremity of Korea was so wide that he did not have the manpower to maintain a continuous line across the peninsula in that area. But was it not true that there had been virtually no liaison between the Eighth Army and the Tenth Corps? he was asked. "All that sort of stuff . . . is scuttlebutt written 10,000 miles away from the scene by these skillful propagandists who were trying to destroy the confidence of the American people in their own institutions." What about MacArthur's attack toward the Yalu in late November 1950 that was supposed to have ended the war by Christmas? It had not been an attack, the general maintained; it had been a reconnaissance in force to determine the strength of the Chinese in North Korea. As for the subsequent withdrawal from the Yalu by UN forces, "the concept that our forces withdrew in disorder or were badly defeated is one of the most violent prevarications of the truth that ever was made." The withdrawal, MacArthur contended, had been planned from the beginning, was orderly, and resulted in minimal losses. The entire action would have been obviated, of course—and victory assured—had he been permitted to destroy the Yalu bridges and attack supply bases and lines of communication in Manchuria as soon as it became apparent that the Chinese were entering Korea.

On the matter of his dismissal, MacArthur professed not to know why he had been relieved of his commands in the Far East. Never in his long career, he insisted, had he ever been insubordinate, nor would he do anything to undermine the principle of civilian control of the military: "Any idea that a military commander in any position would possess authority over the civil functions of this Government is a treasonable concept in my mind." Hence, he did not question the President's right to relieve him, explaining that Truman had acted "within his complete authority, and his responsibility, and I don't challenge either, in any way, shape, or manner." Reiterating a theme set out in his address to Congress and widely trumpeted by his supporters, MacArthur intimated that his quarrel with the Administration had resulted from the failure of officials in Washington to issue clear directives defining his mission in Korea. His own recommendations for expanding the war, he testified, had been intended to secure policy directives, for "I could not go on ordering men to their deaths by the thousands, in such a complete vacuum of policy decision." Had Truman been forthcoming with such policy directives "I would, to the best of my ability, have carried them out completely and absolutely."

Regarding his statement of March 24 in which he offered to negotiate a truce with the enemy commander, MacArthur testified that "the notice I put out was merely that which every commander at any time can put out." The message from Washington of March 20 advising him that the President was about to make a peace announcement "hadn't the slightest bearing" on his own statement, and he could not imagine that his statement might have embarrassed the President or influenced what he and the UN were trying to do. As for his letter to Congressman Martin, he said he always had felt that any member of Congress was entitled, within the limits of security requirements, to any information he might ask for: "That is what I visualize is the proper courtesy and respect that is due to the legislative leaders of the country." Otherwise, the letter "was merely a routine communication such as I turn out by the hundreds" and "made so little impression upon me . . . that later on when somebody said a great deal of commotion had been raised by that letter, I had to consult my files to see what the letter was."

General MacArthur was nothing if not forthright, and in commenting on the larger aspects of American foreign policy he must have sent chills down the spines of such Old Guardsmen as former President Herbert C. Hoover who had recently been championing a retreat to "Fortress America"; the general, it seemed, was an unreconstructed globalist. He portrayed himself as a more confirmed globalist than were those leaders of the Truman Administration who had recently completed America's emancipation from the shackles of isolationism. According to the general, "You can't let one-half of the world slide into slavery and just confine yourself to defending the other. You have got to hold every place." As for Europe, its first line of defense was in Korea, and if the Communists succeeded in breaching that line, the fighting "will roll around to Europe as sure as the sun rolls around."

All this meant that MacArthur had no patience with the idea of waging a limited war in Korea for the limited goal of securing South Korea from communism. The war in Korea, he insisted, had to be conducted without restriction until the Chinese, and with them communism, were driven north of the Yalu and the entire Korean nation united under a non-Communist regime—this had been the UN objective, he maintained with dubious accuracy, from the onset of the Korean War. As he had said in his address to Congress on April 19: "War's very object is victory, not prolonged indecision. In war there is no substitute for victory." Restricting the use of one's forces in war, the general thought, was a form of appeasement, and "if you hit soft, if you practice appeasement in the use of force, you are doomed to disaster." Such a disaster, he reasoned, already was taking shape in Korea, where the opposing armies at dreadful expense had pushed one another up and down the Korean Peninsula in "an accordion war" and now seemed headed toward a bloody and inconclusive stalemate. MacArthur urged "that some plan be carried out that will bring this dreadful slaughter to a definite end." What he wanted, of course, was expansion of the war by lifting restrictions on bombing Chinese territory, imposing a naval blockade against the China coast, and putting the troops of Chiang Kai-shek in the battle against the "Red Chinese." Guessing that between five and ten million Chinese died of starvation every year, he contended that the economic disruption resulting from the execution of his proposals would turn great segments of China's population to disorder and discontent, and "the internal strains would help to blow up her potential for war."

But might not expansion of the war in Korea provoke the Soviets and raise the risk of World War III? That, as Senator Wiley noted, was "the most serious question, and probably the most speculative one, and the one that most concerns our associates in the United Nations" regarding MacArthur's proposals.

The general's answer to the question was negative. In his view the Soviets had a timetable for world conquest and could be diverted from it only if it was transparently advantageous for them to do so. A small provocation in East Asia, in a word, was not apt to bring a Soviet response. MacArthur believed the Soviets would be more tempted to act if the war in Korea dragged on inconclusively; hence "I believe that the program I have suggested will tend to not precipitate a world war, but to prevent it." To reinforce his contention that the Soviets would not intervene if the UN expanded the war in Korea, the general minimized the Soviet Union's current involvement in the conflict: "It has been quite apparent to me . . . that the linking of the Soviets to this Korean War has paled out as the events have progressed." The interests and prestige of the Soviet Union, therefore, would not be imperiled by an expansion of the war, since the only objective of such an expansion would be to drive the Chinese from Korea. As a matter of fact, the Soviets might consider it to their advantage to have the UN administer a setback to "this new Frankenstein that is being gradually congealed and coalesced in China." Asked MacArthur: "Would the Soviet desire to have China become so powerful that it might even challenge the Soviet? Would it be the desire, would it be possible for the Soviet to retain a maximum degree of control if China became too powerful?"

Some senators remained unconvinced. McMahon observed that MacArthur's speculations on the probable course of events had been wrong in the past—notable was the case of China's entry in the Korean War. The general countered that in that instance the secretary of state and the CIA had made the same mistake. Senators Estes Kefauver of Tennessee and Wayne Morse of Oregon raised the question of whether the Sino-Soviet Pact of 1950 might require a Soviet response if the UN carried the war into Chinese territory. MacArthur dismissed the question as speculative. Morse wondered about the Soviet response to the bombing of the rail lines in Manchuria which the Soviets jointly owned and operated with the Chinese and which served Soviet interests in Siberia. Replied MacArthur: "In my opinion, it is a minor point." Morse also wondered about the Soviet response to a naval blockade, inasmuch as the blockade proposed by the general would include the Soviet naval base in Manchuria, Port Arthur. MacArthur retorted: "I do not believe the small incident involved would materially affect in any way the great decisions that would be involved in bringing the Soviet into a global war."

Even if one accepted the contention that expansion of the war would not trigger a Soviet response, questions nonetheless remained. How much of a build-up of UN, principally United States, forces would be required to execute MacArthur's proposals? The general could give no precise figures but was confident that expansion of the war would require the commitment of only a few more ground troops and several additional naval and air units to the East Asian conflict. Could not China match such an enlargement of UN forces? MacArthur did not think so: "I believe that practically the maximum effort that she is militarily capable of is being exerted in Korea at the present time." What about the so-called American sanctuaries in South Korea and Japan? If the United States carried the war into Chinese territory might not they retaliate by turning their air and naval forces loose against South Korea, America's bases in Japan, and the American navy off the Korean coast? "I don't believe that Red China has the potential to bomb any of those places," MacArthur told the senators. "I don't believe she has got the air or the navy to make any threat." Well, what about America's European allies? They seemed adamantly opposed to expansion of the war in Korea. "My hope would be of course that the United Nations would see the wisdom and utility of that course [expansion of the war], but if they did not,

I still believe that the interest of the United States being the predominant one in Korea, would require our action." "Alone?" Senator Theodore Green of Rhode Island asked. MacArthur replied: "Alone, if necessary. If the other nations of the world haven't got enough sense to see where appeasement leads after the appeasement which led to the Second World War in Europe, if they can't see exactly the road that they are following in Asia, why then we had better protect ourselves and go it alone." But what if the MacArthur plan failed in its objective of driving the Chinese from North Korea? "I believe that the methods I have proposed will be completely effective. . . . I believe I wouldn't attempt to predict the exact time that that would be accomplished but, applied long enough, I believe its results would be a certainty." What if after being pushed out of Korea the Chinese remained in large formations in Manchuria along the Yalu? Might they present a continuing threat to Korea? "Such a contingency is a very hypothetical query," MacArthur countered. "I can't quite see the possibility of the enemy being driven back across the Yalu and still being in a posture for offensive action."

Whether to deploy Chiang Kai-shek's Nationalist forces against the Communists had been an aspect of MacArthur's controversy with his superiors in Washington, and during the general's appearance in the witness chair the question came up repeatedly. Less interested in the prospect of introducing Nationalist troops in Korea than he had been several months before, MacArthur now seemed consumed with the idea of helping Chiang return to China's mainland. A first step in executing such a return would be the removal of the Seventh Fleet from the Formosa Strait, a step which he considered long overdue inasmuch as the mere threat of a Nationalist foray across the strait, he thought, would have taken pressure off UN forces in Korea after China's intervention across the Yalu and saved many thousands of UN lives. As for the danger of a Communist invasion of Formosa if the Seventh Fleet was withdrawn, MacArthur reverted to his contention that the Chinese Communists were already fully committed in Korea and thus did not have the capacity to make an amphibious assault across the Formosa Strait. What sort of operation by the Nationalists against the mainland did the general have in mind? Well, that would be up to the generalissimo but it probably would be "an infiltrative effort at various points" rather than a large-scale amphibious movement. Citing alleged reports that there were a million and a half anti-Communist guerrillas in China, MacArthur expected that Nationalist troops would coordinate their operations with those guerrillas. Because of their experience with the ways of the Communists he also thought "most sincerely" that great numbers of ordinary Chinese would rally to the Nationalist banner when Chiang's troops returned to the mainland.

The senators inevitably raised more questions. In view of the widespread belief that Chiang Kai-shek was not well respected by other non-Communist Asians, would the United States risk losing its remaining friends in East Asia if it helped him return to the mainland? MacArthur replied that to the average Asian the generalissimo stood out as a great symbol of anti-communism and that those who favored communism opposed him "completely and absolutely." Moreover, supporting Chiang, the general testified, did not mean that the United States was required to endorse everything he did or said. The overriding consideration was that Chiang's interests paralleled those of America. About the alleged corruption in Chiang's regime, MacArthur said: "In great international decisions, if they are to be based upon the details of corruption in government, Senator, there would be few countries that would pass unscathed." In any event, Chiang apparently had his administrative problems under control, for during his visit to Formosa the previous year MacArthur had found contentment and prosperity and evidence that Chiang was establishing a standard of government that compared favorably with many of the world's democracies.

The senators wondered about the quality of Nationalist forces and their capacity to get across the Formosa Strait and secure themselves on the mainland. MacArthur conceded that Chiang's soldiers were short of artillery and trucks and that his navy amounted to little. Of the Nationalist air force he said it had only a couple of hundred planes, but the pilots were capable "and for such a jerk-water group, they make a pretty brave showing." Accordingly, the Nationalists would require large-scale assistance by the United States. In the MacArthur scenario the American navy would transport the Nationalists to the mainland and with the American air force cover their operations. Perhaps five hundred American technicians and military advisers would accompany the Nationalists, and the burden of supplying the operation would be assumed by the United States. Under no circumstances, however, would American combat units be introduced into the ensuing struggle. Said MacArthur: "No man in his proper senses would advocate throwing our troops in on the Chinese mainland." Well, what if the Nationalists went to the mainland and were wiped out? "I am unable to answer a hypothetical question," MacArthur replied, "in which you put up a suggestion that the forces of the Generalissimo would be destroyed. I do not believe that they are going to be destroyed; and, if we gave him the proper support, they would not be destroyed."

As he continued to respond to this question raised by Senator Henry Cabot Lodge of Massachusetts, MacArthur reiterated a point that he had been making over the past year and during the hearings: "I would insure that Formosa shall not fall into Red hands." The general's vision of the strategic importance of Formosa, in truth, seems incredible in retrospect—and seemed so to some Americans in 1951. Declaring that the "loss" of Formosa would make Japan and the Philippines indefensible, he said: "I believe that from our standpoint we practically lose the Pacific Ocean if we give up or lose Formosa. . . . If the enemy secured Formosa and secured thereby the Pacific Ocean, that would immeasurably increase the dangers of that ocean being used as an avenue of advance by any potential enemy. And Alaska is on that ocean; it would unquestionably increase the dangers to Alaska as well as it would be to the State of California, the State of Washington, and Oregon, Central and South America." When Senator Russell Long of Louisiana doubted that Formosa had so much strategic importance, the general repeated his contention with uncompromising vehemence.

The immediate effect of the MacArthur testimony, printed in its entirety by some newspapers, was hard to measure. If some of his ideas seemed outlandish and others not clearly formed, the general nonetheless remained a magnetic personality who in spite of his arrogance and vanity had touched many Americans, just as he had nine years before when, as he left the island of Corregidor, he uttered those memorable words: "I shall return."

MacArthur's simplistic declaration that there was no substitute for victory appealed to the large segment of the American populace which always had sought simplistic solutions to complicated problems and which presently felt demoralized by cold war setbacks and frustrated by the vagaries of the limited conflict in Korea. Then, there was a top secret memorandum dated January 12, 1951, to which MacArthur had referred over and over during his three days in the witness chair and which seemed to strengthen his position. The general claimed the document proved that three months before his dismissal the Joint Chiefs of Staff had supported most of his proposals for expanding the war in East Asia. Because the memorandum was classified as top secret it had remained unpublished, but if what the general said was true, it would appear that he had not been alone in calling for dramatic action against the enemy. If his interpretation of the memorandum was correct, moreover, the stature of the Joint Chiefs, who had concurred in his dismissal and whose alleged opposition to his ideas was central to the case against MacArthur, would be seriously diminished. It would appear that they had been persuaded by political leaders to support the dismissal of a distinguished fellow officer, even though they shared his view of what should be done in Korea.

As for the general's detractors, they must have found some reason for cautious encouragement in his testimony. MacArthur's case for expanding the war in East Asia was full of holes, his statements on the strategic importance of Formosa had been ludicrous, and most important, the senators on several occasions had forced him to admit that as a theater commander he had not had access to the requisite information for making high policy decisions and that his perspective on the East Asian war accordingly was limited.

III

Following MacArthur into the witness chair during the next month were spokesmen for the anti-MacArthur view, or the view of President Truman's Administration: General of the Army George C. Marshall, the secretary of defense; General of the Army Omar N. Bradley, chairman of the Joint Chiefs of Staff; General J. Lawton Collins, chief of staff of the army; General Hoyt S. Vandenberg, chief of staff of the air force; Admiral Forrest P. Sherman, chief of naval operations; and Dean G. Acheson, the secretary of state.

Marshall, the seventy-year-old chieftain of the Department of Defense who conceded that he answered more readily to the title of general than to that of Mr. Secretary, proved a patient and effective witness, and by the time he completed his seven days of testimony it was evident that he had considerably weakened the convictions of those senators who espoused General MacArthur's cause. In his first minutes in the witness chair Marshall just about demolished MacArthur's argument that the Joint Chiefs of

Staff's memorandum of January 12, 1951, proved that military leaders in Washington had agreed with his prescription for expanding the Korean War. At the time the memorandum was prepared, Marshall explained, officials in Washington faced the possibility that UN forces might be compelled to evacuate Korea, and the proposals put forward by the JCS in the memorandum, which included preparations for a naval blockade of China and logistical support for operations by Chiang Kai-shek's Nationalists against China's Communists, were offered as tentative actions if an evacuation of Korea appeared imminent. But then, over the next week, came a dramatic improvement in the military situation in Korea. Clearly the Communists were not going to drive UN armies off the peninsula, so it was unnecessary to put into effect all of the actions outlined in the memorandum.

In his testimony Marshall observed that the American objective in Korea was to defeat aggression and restore peace, and to that end the United States had sought to confine the conflict to Korea and prevent it from escalating into World War III. "General MacArthur, on the other hand, would have us, on our own initiative, carry the conflict beyond Korea against the mainland of Communist China, both from the sea and from the air. He would have us . . . risk involvement not only in an extension of the war with Red China, but in an all-out war with the Soviet Union. He would have us do this even at the expense of losing our allies and wrecking the coalition of free peoples throughout the world. He would have us do this even though the effect of such action might expose Western Europe to attack by the millions of Soviet troops poised in Middle and Eastern Europe." He said that the differences in judgment between officials in Washington and MacArthur had arisen "from the inherent difference between the position of a field commander, whose mission is limited to a particular area and a particular antagonist, and the position of the Joint Chiefs of Staff, the Secretary of Defense, and the President, who are responsible for the total security of the United States, and who, to achieve and maintain this security, must weigh our interests and objectives in one part of the globe with those in other areas of the world so as to attain the best over-all balance." Conceding that it was both understandable and commendable for a field commander to become so wrapped up in his own operations and responsibilities that he would find some directives from higher authorities not to his liking, Marshall explained that "what is new, and what has brought about the necessity for General MacArthur's removal, is the wholly unprecedented situation of a local theater commander publicly expressing his displeasure at and his disagreement with the foreign and military policy of the United States." Marshall also inferred, for he dared not attack MacArthur's soldierly integrity, that because MacArthur was so critical of established policies, there had been some doubt about his ability to execute those policies, if not in the letter at least in their spirit.

Old Guardsmen tried with little success to chip away at Marshall's case for MacArthur's dismissal. "Do you mean to say," Senator Alexander Wiley of Wisconsin asked, "that a man in General MacArthur's position, who was the Chief of Staff when you were a colonel, had no right to discuss or advise or recommend to you leaders in Washington?" Marshall said: "There was no limit whatever on his representations of his views to the officials in Washington. There is a great difference between that and the public announcements." What if Marshall, during the Second World War when he was chief of staff of the army, had differed very strongly with the Roosevelt Administration over military policy? "I would have done my best directed to the President to have it changed, and I might say I had some very difficult scenes with Mr. Roosevelt over certain phases of the matter . . . ; but I didn't make any public speeches," he replied. Still, was not a member of Congress, like Congressman Martin, entitled to a frank reply when writing to a military leader? "No, sir;" Marshall said, "I don't think from the senior commander, when he knows he is advocating something to the leader of the opposition party to the administration that he as the commander is in total disagreement with his own people." As for the contention that in the weeks before his dismissal MacArthur had operated virtually without instructions from Washington on official policy and thus somehow was justified in setting out his own policy views, Marshall testified that "he was given full information [regarding policy] right along the line."

As expected, Marshall gave short shrift to MacArthur's proposals for expanding the war in East Asia. Execution of the general's proposals, he maintained, might have drastic consequences: a falling out between America and its allies, a Soviet strike westward in Europe, or a nuclear confrontation between the Soviet Union and the United States. There was no way, he told the senators, that the gains which might be realized from an expanded war in Korea could justify such risks. But, MacArthur's supporters demanded to know, had the United States not risked a Soviet response when it organized the Berlin airlift in 1948 and set about arming the countries of Western Europe in accord with the North Atlantic Treaty of 1949? The situation in Europe in 1948–1949 had not been parallel with the present one in Korea, Marshall countered. Failure to act decisively in Europe in 1948–1949 would have left the way open for a Communist conquest of Western Europe. Failure to take the risks implicit in the MacArthur plan for Korea would leave exposed no American interest in East Asia.

In testimony deleted from the public transcript by the censor Marshall went further in his critique of MacArthur's proposals. He told the senators that the United States plainly did not have the armed strength which would be required to conduct an expanded war in East Asia. More intriguing, he observed that just as the United States was keeping its air and naval forces in check in East Asia, so were the Communists. The advantage of mutual restraint, he said, rested with the United States and its allies. Bombing targets in Manchuria, for example, were widely scattered, while those of the UN forces in Korea were concentrated. Particularly vulnerable to a large-scale Communist attack was Pusan, the UN command's major port and logistical center. Marshall intimated that military leaders in Washington were concerned over the vulnerability of UN troops, communications, and installations if the Communists suddenly unleashed their air and naval forces known to be in the Far East. Marshall took a low view of MacArthur's proposal for employing Chiang Kai-shek's Nationalist troops either in Korea or in an assault on China's mainland. Putting the Nationalists in

Korea or on the mainland would weaken the defenses of Formosa, might provoke an escalation of the war by the Communists, and was certain to cause friction between America and its allies. In addition, the Nationalists, he made clear in testimony later excised by the censor, were not nearly as strong as was commonly thought; they did not even have the capacity to hold Formosa without external help. "The record of the Chinese Nationalist troops for losing equipment furnished them," he also observed, "increases the reluctance of the Joint Chiefs of Staff to equip them and employ them in battle."

Since it was clear that Washington had no intention of ordering an expansion of the war or of trying to expel the Communists from North Korea by pushing the war much beyond the thirty-eighth parallel, pro-MacArthur senators demanded to know how Marshall and the Joint Chiefs of Staff proposed to terminate the conflict in East Asia. If the combat in Korea remained on its present course, they contended, the probable outcome would be a long and costly battlefield stalemate. Surely an expansion of the war in accord with MacArthur's ideas would be preferable to that. Marshall conceded that he and the Joint Chiefs looked with trepidation on the prospect of an extended stalemate in Korea. But in testimony deleted by the censor he expressed hope that the war might soon be brought to an end along the present battle line. The idea was to use the UN's firepower superiority to extract such a toll of soldiers and equipment from the Communists that within a short time they would consent to an armistice. Marshall hoped that the Communists would keep up the offensive they had opened in recent weeks: "The best possibility that we see at the present time is immediately a continuation of the attack by the Communists, with the hope that we get fair weather, and inflict such tremendous losses on them in proportion to what has occurred in the past two weeks that we have broken the power of their trained armies."

In accord with their mandate, the senators grilled Marshall on the larger aspects of America's Far Eastern policies in recent years as well as on the dismissal of MacArthur. There was the matter of Marshall's "mission" to China in 1945–1947 during which the general had pressed the Nationalists of Chiang Kai-shek and the Communists of Mao Tse-tung to terminate their civil war. Marshall insisted that his purpose had not been to urge the disputants to accept a coalition government; the Nationalists and Communists had agreed to a coalition government a short time before he left for China. His purpose had been to work out an armistice and a program for demobilization, although he eventually became involved in political affairs to the extent that he sought to help the opposing sides execute agreements they had made previously. Marshall pointed out that the operating document for the coalition gave Chiang a veto over government action and, more importantly, provided that China's army would comprise fifty Nationalist divisions and only ten Communist.

Another facet of this controversy was the celebrated report on China and Korea drafted by Lieutenant General Albert C. Wedemeyer following his own mission to East Asia in 1947. Marshall, as secretary of state, had prevented its publication or, in the parlance of the Old Guard, suppressed it. The senators wondered why. According to Marshall, Wedemeyer had proposed putting the China problem before the UN and placing Manchuria and Korea under a UN trusteeship, but that would have complicated discussions in Congress and at the UN concerning current affairs in Greece. "I know that they [people in the State Department] did go through it to see how we could delete, and it seemed to be so woven into the report, that part of the United Nations phase, that it would excite more speculation and more complications than would be desirable."

The chairman of the Joint Chiefs of Staff, Omar Bradley, followed Marshall to the witness chair, and in the early minutes of his interrogation Senator Wiley asked him to tell the committee what had been said in a meeting on April 6, 1951, involving Bradley, Marshall, Secretary Acheson, W. Averell Harriman, and President Truman. Bradley responded: "Senator, at that time I was in a position of a confidential adviser to the President. I do not feel at liberty to publicize what any of us said at that time." That response touched off a sometimes angry debate among the senators over the relationship of advisers to a President. The debate consumed nearly two days of the hearings and occupied more than a hundred pages in the printed transcript. At length, by a vote of 18-8, the two committees sustained Bradley's refusal to divulge presidential conversations.

Otherwise, Bradley reinforced the points made by Marshall, and in a prepared statement before his interrogation began made the most publicized utterance of the inquiry, saying that in the estimate of the Joint Chiefs the MacArthur strategy "would involve us in the wrong war, at the wrong place, at the wrong time, and with the wrong enemy." To execute the MacArthur program, he told the senators, the United States would have to strip its defenses in other areas of the world, and having done that he doubted that expansion of the war would bring victory in Korea. On the contrary, he suspected that expansion might result in a new world war—a war which the United States simply was not prepared to fight. If careful to avoid offending the proponents of air power, he expressed limited faith in MacArthur's view that bombing planes striking targets in Manchuria and elsewhere in China with non-nuclear bombs would cripple the Communist military effort in Korea. He observed that UN bombers presently had two hundred miles of Communist supply lines in North Korea to patrol and were unable to stop the movement of men and matériel to the battlefront. As for an attempt to destroy the source of the enemy's military production by sending strategic bombing planes against China's cities, Bradley pointed out that the sources of production for the Communist war effort in Korea were in the Soviet Union, not China.

Of MacArthur's dismissal, Bradley explained that the Joint Chiefs had concurred in the decision to relieve MacArthur because he had violated Truman's directive of December 5, 1950, regarding public statements on high policy, undermined the President's proposed peace overture of March 1951, and because in their view "General MacArthur's actions were continuing to jeopardize the civilian control over military authorities." His only concession to MacArthur supporters was that the dismissal might have been executed more adroitly. About MacArthur's failure in November 1950 to act on a warning by the Joint Chiefs in Washington that the flank of the Tenth Corps in North Korea was exposed Senator Fulbright asked if that action had influenced the Joint Chiefs in their decision to support MacArthur's dismissal. Bradley was not sure. It might have had some relevance, but they had not discussed it at the time they made the decision.

The three service chiefs, Generals Collins and Vandenberg and Admiral Sherman, were next to testify in the MacArthur inquiry. Each man spent two days in the witness chair in the last days of May 1951.

Although posing Collins the same questions about the expansion of the war in Korea and receiving answers similar to those offered by Marshall and Bradley, the senators seemed particularly interested in eliciting more comments on MacArthur's dismissal. Why, they asked, had the Joint Chiefs endorsed the decision? Because of an accumulation of incidents, Collins testified, "and a growing conviction that General MacArthur was not in sympathy with the basic policies under which he was operating; and that the President of the United States, as the Commander in Chief, was entitled to a field commander who was in consonance with the basic policies of his Government." Was it not a fair assumption, Senator Bourke Hickenlooper of Iowa asked, that the Joint Chiefs merely contrived to justify a decision already made at the White House? Reiterating that the Joint Chiefs had sought to give the President an honest opinion, Collins said: "You can ask me it in 10 different ways and I am going to give you the same answer." If the reasons for the dismissal had been cumulative and existed before April 1951, why had the Joint Chiefs not recommended MacArthur's relief at an earlier date? Collins replied that it had not been known before April that the President was becoming, in Collins's words, "fed up" with MacArthur. That was a lame answer, and, indeed, senators who were critical of MacArthur's ideas and behavior, notably Morse and Fulbright, suspected that the Joint Chiefs were vulnerable to criticism for having kept silent in the face of those accumulating incidents.

If he was intimidated by MacArthur's reputation before April 1951, Collins was not reluctant to fault the general's behavior in testimony to the two committees. MacArthur's response to an attempt by Old Guard senators to justify his statement of March 24, 1951, by citing two appeals by MacArthur in autumn 1950 that the enemy in Korea stop fighting, was called into question. Collins explained that the autumn appeals had been made with the concurrence of leaders in Washington and on the basis of detailed instructions regarding surrender terms. MacArthur had received no similar sanction in March 1951 and was, in fact, operating at that time under a clear directive (Truman's December 5, 1950, proclamation), that he make no such statement without clearance from higher authorities. More significant was his response when asked by Senator Alexander Smith of New Jersey if MacArthur ever had violated a military directive by the Joint Chiefs of Staff—a question touching on MacArthur's military integrity, to which Smith obviously expected a negative answer. Collins replied that as a matter of fact MacArthur had violated a directive by the Joint Chiefs in November 1950, when he sent American troops to the banks of the Yalu. To reassure the Chinese that UN armies had no aggressive designs on Manchuria, Washington had wanted no American troops visible along the river and had given MacArthur notification to that effect, but he ignored the directive and dispatched GI's to the Yalu. Collins did not back down when Senator

Harry Cain of Washington charged that, unintentionally perhaps, he had done "a first-rate hatchet job" on a man whose "splendid reputation . . . has been the pride of our Nation for many years." Far from backing down, Collins testified that the incident of late November had raised fears among the Joint Chiefs about MacArthur's obedience to orders; this ultimately contributed to the decision to dismiss him: "I think this was one indication among others . . . that General MacArthur was not in consonance with the basic policies that led us gradually to fear that just as he violated a policy in this case without consulting us, perhaps the thing might be done in some other instance of a more serious nature."

A man who radiated much confidence, General Vandenberg did not dwell on MacArthur's alleged violation of the directive of autumn 1950 but testified—several times for the benefit of senators who increasingly were absent from the hearing room when colleagues were interrogating witnesses—that it was difficult for a field commander to carry out the spirit and intent of orders which conflicted with his own views: "You had broad policies that you had to give to a commander, and in those broad policies, he had to have considerable latitude; in the use of that latitude, if he felt strongly in opposition to the policy that the Chiefs had felt necessary, there was a danger." It had seemed prudent, therefore, that someone else should be put in command in the Far East.

Vandenberg's testimony in response to questions relating to MacArthur's ideas about expanding the air war in the Far East was highly significant. Although MacArthur had bestowed lavish praise on the air force and the effectiveness of air power (which must have gladdened the hearts of all disciples of Billy Mitchell), Vandenberg stood unalterably opposed to MacArthur's proposals for carrying the air war to Chinese territory. In view of the fact that Vandenberg was an airman and MacArthur was not, his arguments were not easy to refute, especially since they did not rest primarily on the supposition that an expanded bombing campaign might trigger World War III, but on a realistic appraisal of the strength and global responsibilities of the United States Air Force. Execution of the MacArthur plan, Vandenberg told the senators, would require double the strategic power which the air force could muster, and in testimony deleted from the public transcript he said that if compelled to operate over the expanse of China, an air force four times the size of the existing USAF would be "a drop in the bucket." He observed that Communist bases in Manchuria were defended by anti-aircraft batteries controlled by radar and that in combat around the Yalu the air force had learned that such batteries could be very effective. Accordingly, he advised the senators that an expanded bombing campaign in the Far East would result in such serious losses of planes and pilots that the defenses of the United States and its allies would be imperiled: "In my opinion the shoestring United States Air Force that we are operating today, in view of our global commitments, must not be utilized until it is larger for anything except holding it intact as nearly as possible against a major threat, against a major power, because in my opinion again it is the sole deterrent to war up to this time; and if we emasculate it, that sole deterrent will be gone."

If the testimony of Vandenberg was devastating to MacArthur's plan to expand the air war in the Far East, that of Admiral Sherman was equally destructive of MacArthur's proposal that the United States subject the Chinese ports to a naval blockade. Sherman viewed blockades as more effective than aerial bombardment in hostilities with countries such as China and told the senators that a blockade of China's ports in late 1950 would have compelled the Chinese to turn to the Soviet Union for many of the necessities of their existence. The Trans-Siberian Railroad, he thought, could not have handled the increased traffic. A blockade in 1950 would have opened the way for plagues and epidemics which would have sapped the strength of the Chinese people. Sherman also indicated that the American navy had the ships and personnel to manage a blockade of China without jeopardizing its ability to meet commitments elsewhere, and said that he would favor a blockade if it had the sanction and support of the United Nations. But, he explained, there was no possibility that the UN would approve a blockade, and unlike MacArthur who was willing to "go it alone," Sherman wanted no part of a unilateral blockade. Such a blockade, according to Sherman, would not be effective unless applied to Hong Kong and a blockade of Hong Kong would strain relations with the British. More serious, the blockade would also have to be applied to the Soviet leaseholds of Dairen and Port Arthur, thus inviting a war with the Soviet Union. The goal of the United States, for the time being, should be to achieve results similar to those which might be expected from a blockade by persuading UN members to honor a recent resolution calling for an economic boycott of China.

IV

With the testimony of Vandenberg and Sherman, the Old Guard senators lost much of their enthusiasm for MacArthur's proposals for expanding the war in Korea. That did not mean, however, that they were ready to urge an adjournment of the inquiry. On the contrary, they determined to press on, concentrating on America's policies in East Asia over the past six or seven years. Their object was transparent: establishment of their thesis that since about 1944 the Democratic Administrations of Roosevelt and Truman had taken a "soft" stance on Communist expansions in East Asia, that resultant policies had virtually delivered China to the Communists and invited Communist aggression in Korea, and that if not checked by an aroused citizenry and vigilant Congress, the Democratic leadership was apt to continue the discredited policies of the past with equally disastrous consequences. To that end they subjected the last of the so-called Administration witnesses, Secretary Acheson, to an intensive interrogation and then pursued the matter with several other prominent individuals who had been involved in East Asian affairs.

The atmosphere in the hearing room was charged on June 1, 1950, when Dean Acheson, dressed in a gray tropical suit, made his first appearance before the committees. Twenty-three of the twenty-six members were in their places. But interest in the tedious and repetitious questioning quickly faded, and during much of the interrogation of the secretary of state only a few senators were present. Inasmuch as such administration stalwarts as

Connally, Fulbright, Green, Johnson, Kefauver, and McMahon were among the most frequent absentees, Acheson spent most of his time in the witness chair responding to the queries of Old Guardsmen: Brewster, Bridges, Cain, Hickenlooper, Knowland, Smith, and Wiley. Like Acheson, who had spent many hours going over testimony already given in the inquiry and preparing answers to probable questions, the Old Guardsmen had done their homework and entered the hearing room with brief cases bulging with notes and documents upon which they would base their interrogation.

With his patrician accent and Ivy League manners and dress, appearing suspiciously British in the minds of the Anglophobic Old Guardsmen, the secretary of state represented everything that they despised about the management of America's foreign relations. Old Guardsmen, in truth, already had made Acheson the scapegoat for frustrations which they and other Americans felt over the way international affairs had unfolded in the recent past, particularly those frustrations emanating from the Communist takeover in China. Acheson had been under continuous attack for many months. Demands that he resign or be fired were a daily occurrence, and by spring 1951 most observers in Washington doubted that he would last out the year in the State Department. Even Democrats who endorsed his views about international affairs, but considered him a political liability, had begun to express the hope that he would step aside.

For his part, Acheson clearly had the unwavering confidence and support of the combative man in the White House, had lost none of his own self-assurance (interpreted as arrogance by his critics), and gave no hint that he might quit. Still, it was manifest throughout his eight days in the witness chair—the longest stint of any witness—that the incessant attacks upon him and the policies of the Truman Administration had not been without effect. Acheson, for example, betrayed none of the contempt for repetitious questions that sometimes had surfaced in previous testimonies, and instead displayed such tact and patience that Old Guardsmen treated him with a larger measure of courtesy and restraint than anyone expected. (Acheson himself must have felt confounded when near the end of his ordeal Senator Wiley, one of the most volatile of the Old Guardsmen, said: "You have had a long chore, sir, and you have done a grand job for yourself, I would say, with that mind of yours. Keeping everything in mind it is a remarkable accomplishment.") Much of the civility which prevailed during his interrogation may be attributable to the fact that Acheson seemed bent on establishing that he yielded to no Old Guardsmen in his determination to resist Communist expansion in East Asia and sustain Chiang Kai-shek on Formosa, a position not entirely consistent with that which he had taken a year and a half before.

Civility notwithstanding, the Old Guardsmen never lost sight of their goals for the inquiry; thus, they were constantly maneuvering and probing in an effort to find weak points in Acheson's defense of recent East Asian policy. Inevitably, they dwelled on the famous speech the secretary had delivered to the National Press Club in Washington on January 15, 1950, in which Acheson had sketched America's defensive perimeter in the Far Pacific, indicating that both South Korea and Formosa were outside it. Had not that speech been a veritable invitation to the Communists in North Korea, six months later, to make their lunge across the thirty-eighth parallel? In what must have sounded to his critics like a tortured explanation, and perhaps to some of his friends as well, Acheson explained that the United States in early 1950 had felt committed to defend only those areas in which American troops were on station, and at that time no GI's were in South Korea or Formosa. But whatever the location of the American defensive perimeter, the Communists were given no reason to believe that the United States had no interest in such areas as South Korea and Formosa and would not respond to Communist aggression against them, for, Acheson went on, the United Nations, of which the United States was a member, was obliged to respond to aggression and the UN thus far had held its ground on that point.

During Acheson's appearance before the committees many senators pressed a point which for many months had been a source of irritation to many Americans, namely, the behavior of America's allies with respect to the Korean War. Why had such allies as Britain and France made only token contributions to the UN military effort? Why had those allies, notably the British, continued to ship strategic materials to China at a time when the Chinese were killing UN soldiers in Korea? As had the Joint Chiefs of Staff before him, Acheson reminded the senators that the British were fighting Communists in Malaya and the French were doing the same in Indochina—and indeed, the combined Anglo-French military effort in Southeast Asia was roughly equivalent to that of the United States in Korea. The United States, however, was continuing to urge UN members who had made no contribution at all in Korea to make some; Acheson, of course, was hopeful that some governments would respond. On the matter of the shipment of strategic materials to China, the secretary of state was decidedly upbeat. Despite some differences of opinion over what constituted strategic materials (for example, the British were not inclined to consider rubber a strategic item), governments allied with the United States had tightened controls over what they shipped to China, and as member states had responded to the UN resolution of May 18, 1951, urging an embargo on shipments of strategic commodities to China, there was hope that the supplies which the Chinese military mechanism in Korea was receiving from America's allies might soon be terminated.

As important as the prosecution of the Korean War, or so it seemed to the senators, was how the United States proposed to deal with the rival claimants to authority in China. In particular, the senators wanted to know whether the United States one day might extend diplomatic recognition to the Communist government in Peking, tolerate the admission of "Red China" to the United Nations, and permit Formosa to pass to the control of the Communists. On the matter of diplomatic recognition of the Peking regime, Acheson testified: "We are not recognizing the Communist authorities in China. We are not contemplating doing it. We are opposed to it." He denied that the United States ever had indicated conditions under which it might recognize Mao's government and emphasized that the United States recognized Chiang Kai-shek's regime in Taipei as the legitimate government of China. Regarding a UN seat for the Communist Chinese, Acheson reiterated (several times) the opposition of the Truman Administration to that proposal. To date, he said, there had been seventy-seven attempts to seat representatives of the Peking government in the UN or on one of the world organization's many special agencies or associated bodies. The United States, he said, had led the fight against seating the Communist Chinese on each occasion and had been successful in every instance save one. As for Formosa, Acheson believed that MacArthur had exaggerated its strategic importance. Still, the United States, he told the senators, had every intention of preventing the island from falling into hostile, Communist hands.

Old Guardsmen were only partially reassured. They called attention to a secret document of December 1949 in which the State Department had professed Formosa to be of no strategic importance and intimated that its takeover by the Communists would threaten no American interests in East Asia, a position which hardly squared with the current one. The secretary of state testified that there had been no change in the State Department's view of Formosa; the Old Guardsmen simply did not understand the circumstances which had prompted the so-called Formosa document. Even in December 1949, Acheson explained, leaders in Washington looked on Formosa as a territory of importance and hoped that it might be saved from the Communists. At that time, however, there seemed no way to prevent a Communist takeover of the island short of armed intervention by the United States; indeed it was generally assumed that the Communists would conquer Formosa sometime in 1950. In order to make the best out of a bad situation and to minimize the damage to American prestige when Formosa passed to the Communists, the State Department prepared the document of December 1949 for use by the Voice of America in its broadcasts. Six months later, of course, the Communist aggression in Korea afforded the United States the opportunity to put a naval force between Formosa and the Communists.

Then what about America's support of a UN resolution in January 1951 in which the world organization promised to consider the disposition of Formosa and the question of China's representation in the UN in exchange for an armistice in Korea? the senators asked. Had not that promise been a veritable offer of Formosa and a seat in the UN to the Communist Chinese if they would agree to a cease-fire? Not at all, Acheson told the senators. The resolution had provided that upon termination of hostilities in Korea the future of Formosa and China's representation in the UN would be discussed. If the Communists had accepted the resolution—and American leaders had felt certain they would not—the United States would have continued to oppose both the transfer of Formosa to the Communists and a UN seat for the Peking regime, and given America's influence within the world organization, leaders in Washington had been confident that their arguments would prevail. As it turned out, Acheson said, America's support of the cease-fire resolution, coupled with its rejection by the Chinese, had prepared the way for adoption by the UN a month later of a resolution branding the government in Peking as an aggressor in Korea.

As expected, Old Guardsmen consumed many hours grilling Acheson about the China policy of the Democratic Administrations of Roosevelt and Truman in the time before Chiang Kai-shek's expulsion from the mainland.

But the interrogation brought few surprises, for the Old Guardsmen presented questions and Acheson recited answers which had been explored many times in recent years. Why had American leaders at the Yalta Conference of February 1945 supported concessions to the Soviets in Manchuria in return for a Soviet pledge to enter the war against Japan? To save American lives during the anticipated invasion of the Japanese home islands. Why had Chiang Kai-shek not been immediately informed of the Yalta concessions? Because his regime was notorious for leaking information to the Japanese, and the Yalta conferees did not want to risk a sudden strike by the Japanese against the Soviets in Siberia. Why had the United States in 1945–1946 encouraged China's Nationalists to form a coalition government with the Communists? Because every Chinese expert in Washington considered a political arrangement the best solution to the problem of China—as did Chiang Kai-shek, who had first proposed that solution in 1937. When had the State Department begun to view the Chinese Communists as agrarian reformers? The State Department never had viewed China's Communists as anything other than rigid Marxists. Why had the United States been so miserly in its support of Chiang Kai-shek in the years after the Second World War? On the contrary, the United States had provided more than two billion dollars to Chiang from the end of the war to the time of his flight to Formosa.

More interesting were the recitations of Senators Sparkman and (during a couple of rare appearances in the hearing room) McMahon, who cited a range of documents showing that down to 1949 Republicans had not taken a particularly hard line against China's Communists or viewed the preservation of Chiang Kai-shek as an overbearing American interest. For example, Congressman Walter H. Judd of Minnesota, by 1951 one of the Old Guard's most vocal proponents of Chiang, had issued a statement at the end of 1945 in which he announced support for the idea of including Communists in China's government. Congressman George H. Bender of Ohio, the floor manager of Senator Taft's presidential bid at the Republican national convention of 1948, had delivered a speech to the House of Representatives in spring 1947 in which he referred to Chiang's regime as the "present Fascist Chinese Government." Congressman Howard H. Buffett of Nebraska in that same period had made a blistering attack on Chiang's government and deplored the prospect of any further American aid to it. In 1948 Senator Arthur J. Vandenberg of Michigan had declared that the United States could not underwrite the destiny of China, whereupon the Republican-controlled Eightieth Congress pared down President Truman's request for five hundred and seventy million dollars in aid to China and voted four hundred million, instead.

The interrogation of Acheson finally droned to a conclusion late in the afternoon of June 9, 1951, a Saturday; the following Monday morning, promptly at 10:15 A.M., Lieutenant General Albert C. Wedemeyer was seated in the witness chair. Presently the commander of the Sixth Army in the western part of the United States, Wedemeyer in 1943–1944 had served as deputy chief of staff of the Southeast Asia Command and in 1944–1946 commanded American forces in China, where he was chief of staff to Generalissimo Chiang Kai-shek. A year after his departure from China, in summer 1947, he was again in the Far East, this time appraising the political, economic, and military situation in China and Korea as the personal representative of President Truman. After less than eight weeks of moving about the principal cities and countrysides of China and Korea, he had returned to Washington and submitted the so-called Wedemeyer Report, which the State Department declined to publish. Later, in the aftermath of Chiang Kai-shek's defeat on the mainland of China, "suppression" of the Wedemeyer Report had become a rallying point in the national controversy over East Asian policy. According to critics of Democratic management of affairs in the Far East, non-publication of the report was the result of the fact that Wedemeyer's views and recommendations ran counter to the prevailing notion in the State Department that Chiang's days of power in China were numbered and that new outlays of aid to his Nationalist regime could not prevent a Communist takeover of the country. Inasmuch as Wedemeyer had been out of step with official policy in 1947, it was taken for granted in 1951 that he still was out of step—and anybody who was out of step with official policy in the Far East was assumed to be an advocate of the ideas of General MacArthur. Wedemeyer, in truth, owed his summons to testify at the inquiry to the insistence of Old Guardsmen who expected that he would counter the testimony of "administration" witnesses like Marshall, the Joint Chiefs, and Acheson.

The expectations of Old Guardsmen were only partially fulfilled. During his three-day interrogation Wedemeyer spoke out in favor of MacArthur's proposal for bombing Manchuria, even at the risk of provoking the Soviets, and announced his support of a unilateral naval blockade of the China coast. If America's European allies refused to go along with expansion of the war in Korea, the United States, as MacArthur had urged, should "go it alone," or as Wedemeyer expressed it, "their alternative is enslavement of mind and body; and we ought to make it crystal clear to them that our way is a selfless, Christian approach to international problems; and if they don't follow us, they have the alternative of enslavement." He told the senators that a field commander ought to be allowed to conduct a military campaign without restriction, and he endorsed MacArthur's plan for "taking the wraps" off Chiang Kai-shek's Nationalist forces. But Wedemeyer disagreed with MacArthur's contention that Formosa was a territory of critical importance, and in one astonishing statement declared that China "is not a critical, decisive, strategic area insofar as I am concerned." Regarding MacArthur's controversial peace overture of March 24, 1951, Wedemeyer felt that a field commander never should take such action without clearance from higher authority, and when Senator Sparkman asked to whom the people and Congress should look for guidance in the event of a disagreement between a field commander and the Joint Chiefs, Wedemeyer answered: "The Joint Chiefs of Staff, without question, sir."

Wedemeyer was an exasperating witness. He often obscured his points in rambling, almost incoherent discourses. At other times he strayed far off the points of questions put to him by senators, and on occasion appeared to take positions different from those expressed in earlier testimony. In addition, there was his proposal, so preposterous that even Old Guardsmen blinked, that South Korea be abandoned to the Communists. Although UN forces in Korea were at or beyond the thirty-eighth parallel and seemed in no danger of being shoved back, he urged an immediate withdrawal of UN armies from the Korean peninsula. Since there was no likelihood of expanding the war to achieve total victory, he argued, the only alternative was a long and expensive stalemate in a peripheral area, namely Korea, which in his judgment had no strategic importance. Moreover, Wedemeyer, who had a veritable obsession with psychological warfare, thought the United States was suffering from a psychic defeat in Korea because of its inability to liquidate the armies of a third-rate power. In his words, America's first team had been unable to defeat communism's third team. The best course, therefore, was for America to cut its losses, both military and psychological, and leave the South Koreans to the mercies of the Communists.

If sometimes casting an image of confused innocence, Wedemeyer nonetheless seemed a man of candor and integrity. At the start of his interrogation he pointed out that as soon as it had become apparent that he might be called to testify he determined to have no conversations with MacArthur or anyone else connected with the inquiry. He wanted to be able to offer unvarnished opinions. When discussing Chiang Kai-shek and the reasons for the generalissimo's defeat in China's civil war, he made no concessions to the fantasies of Old Guardsmen. He emphasized that corruption had been pervasive in Chiang's government, and he categorically refuted the Old Guard contention that Chiang had lost the mainland for want of greater support by the United States. The Nationalists had gone down to defeat, he told the senators, because the Communists effectively employed the tactics of psychological warfare. Communist propagandists had exploited the corruption and maladministration in Chiang's regime, capitalized on the national war weariness, and persuaded Nationalist soldiers and civilians that life might be better under a Communist regime. Dean Acheson and men in the State Department, of course, had been saying the same thing for at least two years.

Wedemeyer's successor on the stand was Louis A. Johnson, the secretary of defense in the Truman Administration from January 1949 until September 1950, when he resigned as a result of pressure by the White House. Because of the circumstances of his resignation, it was widely thought that Johnson might speak out against the Administration's position in the MacArthur controversy and thus buttress the contentions of Old Guardsmen. That did not prove to be the case. If resentful of the criticism that his economy-minded management of the Defense Department had been responsible for the weakened state of the military establishment at the outbreak of the Korean War, Johnson claimed no bitterness over his dismissal. In his two days of testimony he betrayed no inclination to even any scores with the President and his top advisers. On the contrary, he told the senators that Truman was a man who did not seek to hurt people unnecessarily, and he said that if the President had lost confidence in MacArthur, he certainly should have dismissed him. As for MacArthur's proposals for prosecuting the war in East Asia, he favored a blockade of the China coast provided it did not include the Soviet leaseholds of Dairen and Port Arthur, but opposed the bombing of Manchuria, felt no enthusiasm for using Chiang Kai-shek's Nationalists in Korea or putting them on the mainland,

and testified that for the time being the present policy, not MacArthur's, was the best one for Korea. About the only satisfaction he gave Old Guardsmen was expression of the view that during his time in the Truman cabinet the State Department had shown little enthusiasm for Chiang Kai-shek and his regime.

By the time of Johnson's appearance the MacArthur inquiry no longer was commanding the front page of newspapers and even Old Guard senators were finding it increasingly convenient to absent themselves from the hearing room. The sentiment among members of the Armed Services and Foreign Relations Committees was unanimous that it was about time to bring the hearings to an end. The two committees, therefore, drastically pruned their list of possible witnesses (which at one time had numbered more than a hundred) and set about concluding the hearings. The last witnesses would be Vice Admiral Oscar C. Badger (one day of testimony), Major General Patrick J. Hurley (two days), Major General David C. Barr (one day), and Major General Emmett O'Donnell, jr. (one day).

The navy's current Eastern Sea Frontier commander, Admiral Badger had been in charge of America's demobilization in the Pacific after the Second World War, and in that capacity had made frequent visits to China to arrange shipment of surplus war matériel from islands in the western Pacific to Chiang Kai-shek. In the witness chair he expressed little support for expansion of the war in Korea, and on the matter of the conflict of views between the Joint Chiefs and the theater commander, he testified: "There is no question in my mind but that the Joint Chiefs of Staff are the senior of the two, and are fully informed as to world conditions and circumstances which a theater commander may not be familiar with." Noting that the island's harbors were too small and its facilities too restricted, he dismissed MacArthur's notions about the strategic importance of Formosa. Formosa's principal value, he thought, was psychological, inasmuch as economic and political progress on the island provided material for propaganda aimed against the Chinese mainland. Other remarks by Badger afforded more comfort to Old Guardsmen, however. The admiral said that the people of South China were sick of communism, and by dispatching bands of Nationalist soldiers to stir up guerrillas it might be possible to wrest China south of the Yangtze from Communist control. He conceded, nonetheless, that he was "a little inclined to accept China as being gone," and thus believed the United States ought to concentrate on saving Southeast Asia from communism. As for American aid to the Nationalists during the struggle for control of the mainland, Badger told the senators that considerable amounts of American equipment from the South Pacific had gone to the Nationalists without spare parts or technicians to supervise their use. More interesting, he said that if American aid intended for General Fu Tso-yi in summer 1948 had arrived in time the entire civil war in China might have been turned around. At that time, he explained, Fu was in command of armies fighting against the Communists along the Great Wall.

Following Badger into the witness chair was General Hurley, a volatile Republican from Oklahoma who had served as secretary of war in President Hoover's cabinet and been ambassador to China from November 1944 until November 1945. Hurley had become a churlish critic of the China policies of the Democratic leadership, and was summoned to testify at the behest of the Old Guardsmen. It is doubtful that he did much to advance the interests of the Old Guard, however. His oratorical broadsides against Secretary Acheson, the State Department, and the Yalta agreements appeared unreasonable, and his unstinting praise of President Roosevelt, who he insisted had been a sick man in early 1945 and thus was without blame for the alleged disasters at Yalta, must have caused Old Guardsmen to cringe. Otherwise Hurley's principal concern appeared to be to defend his record as ambassador and counter the Democratic contention that he had been a good deal less than a stalwart anti-Maoist in 1944–1945 and, indeed, had favored a coalition government in China. Countering the Democratic contention proved difficult, especially when Senator McMahon read into the record a string of documents quoting Hurley in 1944–1945 as asserting that there were no essential differences between China's Communists and the Nationalists, that the Chinese Communists favored government by and for the people, and that the Soviets did not consider the Maoists bona fide Communists and thus were not supporting them.

A more articulate witness was General Barr, chief of the American military advisory group in China in the period of January 1948–January 1949 and commander of the Seventh Infantry Division in Korea from September 1950 to February 1951. He expressed his opposition to MacArthur's proposal for expanding the Korean War, saying that expansion could trigger a global clash with the Soviets. If one ignored political considerations, was there not a compelling military argument for expanding the war? he was asked. As a trained military man, Barr told the senators, he could make no clear distinction between political and military considerations. Did Barr favor the introduction of Chiang Kai-shek's Nationalist troops in Korea? He did not. "Knowing the Chinese as I do, they would be entirely dependent upon us" if dispatched to the Korean battlefront. Besides, the Nationalists were needed to defend Formosa. What did Barr think of the idea of putting the Nationalists back on the mainland? He thought poorly of it; so far as he knew—and the observation was deleted by the censor—there were no organized anti-Communist resistance groups anywhere in China with whom the Nationalists could link up, hence a commitment of American troops would be a requisite if a Nationalist invasion of the mainland was to stand any chance of susccess.

If Barr's testimony on the Korean War offered little comfort to Old Guardsmen, that pertaining to the Nationalist defeat in China's civil war brought still less. Denying that the Yalta concessions to the Soviets had any important bearing on the disasters which eventually befell the Nationalists, Barr explained that at the end of the Second World War the Nationalists had been stronger than the Communists, but "the Communists were smart and the Nationalists were not." The Communists, for example, looked out for the welfare of their soldiers. In the Nationalist army the officers expropriated much of the pay of the enlisted men—if a soldier got breakfast, it was by his own initiative; dependents of soldiers were ignored. The outcome showed a great disparity in the fighting spirits of the combatants. Leadership in the Nationalist army, moreover, had been atrocious. While Communist commanders maneuvered their armies about the countryside, the

Nationalists preferred to draw up behind the walls of cities where they were easily besieged. Barr denied that the Nationalists had suffered serious shortages of equipment and ammunition, although breakdowns in the supply system often prevented equipment and ammunition from reaching troops in the field. In addition to quantities of American ordnance, most of which he said ended up in Communist hands, the Nationalists had received more than half of the war matériel left behind in China by the departing Japanese. As for the renowned General Fu, who Admiral Badger thought might have saved the situation for Chiang along the Great Wall, Barr recalled telling Chiang that Fu could not hold the line in North China and thus should be ordered southward. When Chiang ignored the advice, Fu surrendered without a fight and joined up with the Communists.

The MacArthur hearings finally played themselves out on June 25, 1951, with the interrogation of "Rosy" O'Donnell. In command of the Fifteenth Air Force headquartered in California at the time of the investigation, O'Donnell, in the days after the outbreak of the Korean War, had organized the Far East Bomber Command and stayed on as its commander for six months. On June 25 he was in the witness chair for less than four hours, the shortest stint of any witness, and apart from testifying that Formosa was of no importance to the air force, he contributed little of substance to the discussion at hand. He told the senators that the United States had made a terrible mistake at the end of the Second World War when it failed to issue an ultimatum, presumably one packing a nuclear threat, directing the Soviets to give up their conquests and go home. Although he now opposed a bombing campaign against Manchuria (for like Vandenberg he feared that resultant losses of bombers and crews would weaken the Strategic Air Command as a deterrent to global war), he believed the bombers should have been loosed against Manchuria when the Chinese entered the Korean War in late 1950. Inasmuch as air defenses in Manchuria at that time were not menacing, the air force could have struck Manchurian targets without risking its ability to deliver a "Sunday punch" (O'Donnell's term) against the Soviets if they got out of line. Ignoring the fact that America's bombers in recent months had been unable to stop the flow of soldiers and supplies from Manchuria to the battlefront in Korea two hundred miles below the Yalu, he declared that bombing raids against Manchuria in late 1950 might have proved decisive. Exalting the destructive capacity of the bombing plane, he said: "I would say that the entire, almost the entire Korean Peninsula is just a terrible mess. Everything is destroyed. There is nothing standing worthy of the name." Why Communist soldiers and supplies were continuing to make their way down from the Yalu, nobody bothered to ask.

V

It is not an easy task to sort out impressions from conclusions after surveying the many sides and confusing events of the MacArthur inquiry, but one might begin by offering a few comments on the event's management. In truth, the inquiry was hardly managed at all. The attorneys for the Armed Services and Foreign Relations Committees played no discernible part in determining who should be called to testify or in the nature of the questions to be presented to witnesses. It was the senators who nominated prospective witnesses, who then were summoned after a majority vote by the combined committees, and it was the senators who fashioned the questions which were asked in the hearing room. Presiding over the entire affair, of course, was Senator Russell, an indefatigable committee chairman if there ever was one. After much pontificating that the MacArthur inquiry was one of the most important congressional exercises in the history of the republic, a majority of the members of the two committees, as already mentioned, found it convenient to absent themselves from the hearing room most of the time. Russell did not; he remained anchored in his chair throughout.

Russell merits further comment, for during the MacArthur inquiry he acted as an almost model chairman. In addition to maintaining an exemplary attendance record, introducing witnesses and interrupting the interrogation upon expiration of the time (eventually fifteen minutes) allotted to each senator during a round of questioning, he went to extreme lengths to appear fair and nonpartisan. He refused to discuss the MacArthur controversy with any representative of the White House. He was unfailingly courteous and evenhanded in his treatment of witnesses and senators—so much so that he won plaudits from Old Guardsmen and spokesmen of the Truman Administration alike. He tolerated the endless rounds of interrogation of each witness, however repetitious or off the subject the questions might be, and when his own turn to query witnesses came around, his questions contained no barbs and were calculated to do nothing more than elicit pertinent information. (So nonpartisan was Russell's behavior, so noncontroversial were his questions, that newsmen were forced to speculate on where he actually stood on the issues raised by the MacArthur imbroglio.) Apart from an occasional lament about the absenteeism of his colleagues, he seldom betrayed any irritation, even when senators pressed witnesses with questions that had been asked and answered, often several times, while they were away from the hearing room.

It is transparent, of course, that the hearings would have proceeded more expeditiously and certainly been more enlightening if the chairman and counsellors, with the approval of the full membership of the two committees, had prepared an agenda of topics to be explored with each witness and then adhered to the agenda in the hearing room; for example, if the interrogation had moved from topic to topic or from issue to issue instead of from senator to senator. But neither expedition nor enlightenment appeared to be Chairman Russell's principal purpose. His object seemed to be to use the inquiry as a vehicle for calming the passions which the MacArthur controversy had stirred across the republic, and he clearly understood that achievement of that goal required that he, as presiding officer, protect himself against charges of partisanship or unfairness and that he permit the senators, particularly the Old Guardsmen, to press on until they exhausted their arguments or were exhausted themselves.

If Chairman Russell was its most dedicated participant, General MacArthur in his three days in the witness chair established himself as the inquiry's central personality. Apart from his displays of humility, his flattery of senators, or his assertions that he had no idea that his statement of

March 24, 1951, might upset Truman's peace initiative or why the President had relieved him of his Far Eastern commands, MacArthur's Olympian manner and finely turned phrases utterly dazzled most of the senators (a notable exception being Senator McMahon). Most awestruck, of course, were the Old Guardsmen, who seemed to be competing to see who could heap the most extravagant praise upon the general. Even Senator Morse, the maverick from Oregon who already was renowned as a hard-nosed independent, seemed star-struck in the presence of the imperious MacArthur, and when presenting him with provocative questions, he virtually apologized and explained that he merely was trying to get certain points in the record. The contrast in their behavior towards General Marshall, who followed MacArthur into the witness chair, but whose military reputation at least rivaled that of MacArthur, was striking. Perhaps the senators had seen so much of Marshall in recent years that, in the proverbial phrase, familiarity had bred a measure of contempt. Marshall's interrogation brought little flattery, a good deal of sharp questioning, and occasional flashes of animosity.

MacArthur's mesmerization of the senators prevented any serious scrutiny of the proposition that underpinned many of the arguments in behalf of his proposals, namely, that the general was America's premier expert on the military and political affairs of East Asia—including China. Accepted as an article of faith by Old Guardsmen, the proposition was expressed in the early minutes of the inquiry when Senator Wiley asked MacArthur: "Do you know of any man in America that has had the vast experience that you have had in the Orient, getting acquainted with various nations in the Orient? Do you know of any other man that has lived there so long, or known the various factors and various backgrounds of the peoples, and their philosophy, as yourself?" Flattered, and conceding that "it is something else again" as to whether he had profited in terms of knowledge and wisdom from his long tenure in the Far East, the general allowed that "the scope of my duties were complete and enveloping, as far as the Far East was concerned and, to some extent, involved the entire world." Numerous references testifying to MacArthur's expertise regarding the Far East, by Democrats as well as Republicans, found their way into the record during the general's three days in the witness chair. Later suggestions by General Marshall and Secretary Acheson that the general might not have been well-informed about China, the country at the center of the controversy, seemed to make no impression.

On the basis of the hearings, it appeared beyond dispute that MacArthur's reputation as a Far Eastern expert was exaggerated and probably rested largely on myth. The general had been in the Far East, or more accurately, in the Far Pacific (Philippines, Australia, and Japan), for many years. As for the East Asian mainland, MacArthur acknowledged that he had not been in China since 1937, and it was apparent that before the Korean War he rarely had visited Korea. Then in the closing minutes of his interrogation Senator Fulbright casually asked a question which any expert on East Asia should have been able to answer in an instant: "We have been told that Mao Tse-tung was trained in Moscow and had close personal relations in Moscow. Is that not true?" Blurted MacArthur: "How would I know, senator?" An observer of the inquiry might even have wondered about the extent of the general's knowledge of Japan—whether he had often strayed far from the Dai Ichi Building in Tokyo. There was no evidence that he knew anything about the Japanese language, no mention of contacts with ordinary Japanese, and he admitted that he never had visited Hiroshima, but had merely flown over it. MacArthur's reputation as a Far Eastern expert remained intact, nonetheless. By comparison, General Marshall, who had spent three years in China in the 1920s and the better part of a year during his postwar mission to China, was not conceded to have any special understanding of China or the Chinese. And when Senator Cain became nettled by General Barr's assessment of probable Communist strength in South China in 1951, he dismissed his testimony on the ground that Barr had not been in China for two years.

Yet, the interrogation of MacArthur and other witnesses did establish the point that, however expert he may have been on affairs of the Far East, the general had been a theater commander. As such he had not been privy to the spectrum of political and military intelligence that would enable him to speak with authority on global strategy or grasp the larger ramifications of recommendations he might make—for instance, the effect on the deterrent capacity of the Strategic Air Command resulting from a bombing campaign against Manchuria. Thus a resounding "no" was given to one of the central questions raised by the MacArthur controversy: Was it conceivable that a theater commander, particularly one of such an illustrious reputation as MacArthur, might have a clearer vision of the requirements of world strategy than that of political leaders and the Joint Chiefs of Staff in Washington? If the MacArthur inquiry did nothing more than provide that answer, the arduous exercise probably was worthwhile. After a few feeble attempts at presenting himself as one who had sufficient global expertise to view the situation in the Far East in a larger perspective, even MacArthur was compelled to concede that officials in Washington alone had the requisite information and viewpoint to fashion world policy. Similarly, when Vandenberg demonstrated that MacArthur simply did not understand the military ramifications of his proposal for expanding the air war in the Far East, nothing substantial remained of the case for MacArthur in the controversy which had triggered his dismissal. Henceforth, the general's Old Guard defenders, when not pressing the argument that the Democrats had made possible a Communist victory in China, were more or less reduced to insisting that MacArthur had not been insubordinate and that Truman and his Administration had treated him with unpardonable shabbiness in the manner of his dismissal.

If captivated by the myth that General MacArthur had unmatched expertise regarding the Far East, most participants in the MacArthur inquiry also seemed persuaded by the myth of the unlimited capacity of air power in modern war. In the words of General Wedemeyer: "We must have undisputed control of the air. It isn't on the ground that the future wars are going to be settled, sir, it is in the air." And nobody, it appeared, had more faith in the aerial weapon than did General MacArthur. Like "Rosy" O'Donnell, MacArthur believed that if he had been allowed to hurl the big bombers against Chinese bases and lines of communication in Manchuria in late 1950, the UN would have been spared the monstrous defeat it suffered when the Chinese entered the Korean War. Nobody pressed the point that since early 1951, in addition to the usual supply depots and staging areas, the air force had had two hundred miles of communications lines in North Korea to pulverize but had been unable to stop or even seriously impede the southward movement of Communist soldiers and supplies. In the climate of 1951, of course, it was perhaps understandable that such old soldiers as Wedemeyer and MacArthur and such senators as Russell and Knowland would be taken in by the proponents of air power. The sight of one of the new F-86 Sabrejets streaking across the sky or one of SAC's giant B-36 bombers approaching a landing field was awesome, and the self-assurance and bravado of the men who flew them was hard to resist. One wonders, however, if the air enthusiasts of 1951 might have exhibited greater humility about the capacity of the aerial weapon had they been able to look ahead to 1952, and see the failure of a concerted air force campaign to do little more than sever the rail lines reaching down from the Yalu to the thirty-eighth parallel, or if they could have peered a decade and a half into the future and witnessed the limits of incredibly more powerful and sophisticated aircraft in the war in Vietnam.

Another myth that remained throughout the MacArthur inquiry was that China had been a victim of Soviet conquest and presently functioned as a subservient appendage of the Kremlin's monolithic empire. In truth, the way in which witnesses and senators interpreted the relationship between the Soviet Union and "Red" China—so as to buttress their own arguments—was one of the more arresting aspects of the MacArthur inquiry.

Skirting the question of whether the Soviets via Chinese stooges had actually conquered China, MacArthur gave surprisingly little credence to the idea of the Soviet domination of the Communist government in Peking. He testified: "I believe there is an interlocking of interests between Communist China and the Kremlin. The degree of control and influence that the Kremlin may have in China is quite problematical." At another point, in a statement that appears almost clairvoyant in retrospect, he said that "there is a point that might well be reached where the interests of Red China and the interests of the Red Soviet did not run parallel, that they started to traverse and become antagonistic." Adherence to the proposition that the connection between the Soviet Union and China was tenuous was almost imperative, if one was to accept MacArthur's contention that bombardment of Manchuria and a naval blockade of the China coast was not apt to provoke the Soviets and plunge America into World War III.

But Old Guard supporters blandly ignored the logic of his position. While they endorsed MacArthur's proposals for expanding the war in the Far East, they continued to insist that China was a docile satellite of the Soviet Union. They also clung to the notion that the Soviets, not Mao Tse-tung and his followers, had managed to defeat Chiang Kai-shek and his Nationalist regime in the civil war and thus, they could be legitimately styled as the conquerors of China. As with MacArthur's perception of the relationship between the governments in Moscow and Peking, the view of the Old Guardsmen seemed self-serving. The proposition that Mao's regime was an arm of the Kremlin justified continued recognition of Chiang's government on Formosa as the legitimate government of China and hence the legitimate representative of China in the United Nations. The proposition that the Soviets had conquered China, in addition to strengthening the argument for continuing to recognize and support the Nationalists, reinforced the Old Guard contention that the Democrats had grossly misunderstood the civil war in China and this misunderstanding had provoked policy decisions which had opened the way for the Communist takeover of the country.

Equally self-serving seemed statements on the relationship between China and the Soviet Union by witnesses who spoke for President Truman's Administration, particularly Secretaries Marshall and Acheson, although those statements were consistent with positions taken by Acheson in July 1949 in his letter of transmittal accompanying the celebrated White Paper on China. Whatever his purpose (and the purpose may have been to tell the truth as he saw it), Marshall told the senators: "I have gone on the assumption that she [China] was operating not only in conjunction with but literally under the direction of the Soviet Union." Acheson agreed with MacArthur on the possibility of an eventual fissure between China and the Soviet Union, but testified that he thought the connection between the two countries was greater than the general had indicated. (In the White Paper he had asserted that "the Communist leaders have foresworn their Chinese heritage and have publicly announced their subservience to a foreign power, Russia.") Such a view certainly reinforced the argument that expansion of the war in Korea in accord with the MacArthur conception was likely to provoke the Soviets and perhaps bring about a global confrontation. At the same time, the view also justified the current policy of nonrecognition of the government in Peking and support of Chiang Kai-shek's regime on Formosa. On the other hand, Marshall and Acheson conceded nothing to the Old Guard argument that in the civil war in China the principal weight in the balance had been Soviet power, nor did the two men, notably Acheson, retreat from the position taken in the White Paper, that the Communist victory in China had resulted largely from Nationalist corruption and ineptitude, not from any lack of support by a confused United States.

Other myths intruded upon the MacArthur inquiry, especially that which blamed America's alleged misunderstanding of the realities of the civil war in China on those Communist subversives whom many Americans, thanks to the rantings of Senator Joseph R. McCarthy and others, thought were slithering about the State Department. To their discredit, the Old Guard senators made certain that the stench of McCarthyism never entirely subsided in the hearing room. They demanded to know the extent of the influence on America's Far Eastern policies of Professor Owen Lattimore of Johns Hopkins University, described by Senator McCarthy only a year before as the premier agent of the Soviet conspiracy in the United States. Acheson's statement that he never had met Lattimore and that the professor had never been an official of the State Department made no impression, and Lattimore's name continued to surface intermittently. The Old Guardsmen also wanted to know more about the activities of John

Stewart Service, John Carter Vincent, John Paton Davies, and Raymond Ludden, foreign service officers who had been in China in the 1940s and were subsequently tarred as pro-Communists. General Wedemeyer, under whom the four men had functioned while he was commander of American forces in China, vouched for their integrity and intelligence and observed that their criticisms of Chiang Kai-shek, a centerpiece of the charges made against them by the Red-hunters, had been no more severe than his own. It did not seem to matter; their names continued to be injected into the interrogation. Old Guard senators, meanwhile, asked when it was that the State Department had begun to view China's Communists as "agrarian reformers," wondered if Alger Hiss and others in Washington had been largely responsible for America's reverses in foreign affairs in recent years, and demanded the name of an obscure public information officer whom General Marshall had ordered home shortly after his arrrival in China in late 1945, on the ground that the man's press releases had seemed unduly sympathetic with the Maoists.

Turning away from the omnipresent myths, one may ask: Did the MacArthur inquiry fall within the bounds of the investigative authority of the Armed Services and Foreign Relations Committees? It is questionable whether a sanction for the inquiry could be found in the Supreme Court's opinion of 1928 which said that the legislative responsibilities of Congress justify congressional investigations. No legislation pertaining directly to the military and diplomatic affairs scrutinized by the two committees in May–June 1951 was pending, although the senators could have made a strong argument that matters taken up in the MacArthur inquiry doubtless would have a bearing on a range of legislative decisions which Congress would have to make in the near future. If, of course, one accepted the proposition set out by Woodrow Wilson in the 1880s that every affair of government is a legitimate subject of scrutiny by committees of Congress, in order that both Congress and the national populace receive maximum enlightenment, he could not easily dispute the legitimacy of the MacArthur investigation.

A more important question, however, is whether the MacArthur inquiry served any useful purpose. The answer is an unqualified yes. Reinforced by UN military successes in Korea and rumors that the Communists were about to consent to armistice negotiations, the inquiry defused the MacArthur controversy, if not the related controversy over why the so-called free world had "lost" China. After the testimony of General Marshall and the Joint Chiefs of Staff, particularly that of General Vandenberg, few Americans retained much enthusiasm for expanding the war in Korea. The MacArthur inquiry, indeed, was a veritable national seminar on foreign affairs. In their interrogations the senators ranged across the spectrum of issues which were troubling and dividing Americans in the area of foreign policy and their endeavors received unprecedented media coverage. Accordingly, as Richard H. Rovere and Arthur M. Schlesinger, jr., wrote in their book *The General and the President*, published a few months after the inquiry: "One clear result of the MacArthur hearings was to improve popular understanding, not alone of the complexities of Far Eastern policy, but of the whole precise and delicate course to which the United States had committed itself." Most important, perhaps, Americans began to shed that obsession with total victory in diplomacy and war which had afflicted them at least since that memorable night in 1862 when the telegraph tapped out the news that U. S. Grant had insisted on unconditional surrender of the Confederate garrison at Fort Donelson. This notion had received further reinforcement by MacArthur's dramatic pronouncement that there was no substitute for victory. However belatedly and even reluctantly, Americans began to grasp the truth of the words set out more than a century before by the great Prussian military philosopher, Von Clausewitz: "As war is no act of blind passion, but is dominated by the political object, therefore the value of that object determines the measure of the sacrifices by which it is to be purchased."

The MacArthur inquiry must have reassured allies of the United States, not to mention many Americans who shuddered at the prospect of a nuclear confrontation with the Soviet Union, that America's leaders would not rashly risk global war. The leaders of the republic, on the contrary, appeared cautious and prudent and even courageous in their resisting of the firestorm touched off by the dismissal of MacArthur. Then, too, the inquiry generated renewed reflection on the principle of civilian control of the military, and established beyond dispute that political and military leaders in Washington alone, not theater commanders in Asia or Europe, even if the latter had such names as MacArthur and Eisenhower, had access to the necessary intelligence and had the requisite perspective from which to formulate global policy for the United States.

The MacArthur inquiry possibly had at least one unfortunate consequence: it may have contributed to the prolongation of the Korean War. So adamant were such witnesses as Marshall and Bradley against expansion of hostilities in East Asia that they announced a virtual commitment by the Truman Administration to keep the war confined to the Korean peninsula so long as the Communists did likewise. (In testimony deleted from the public record by the censor, Bradley, at one point did indicate that after the military build-up then underway had strengthened the armed forces the United States might consider a MacArthur-style expansion of the war in East Asia should the present policy fail to bring satisfactory results. But there was no indication that such a possibility had been communicated to the Communists.) They also made it clear that UN forces in Korea would not press the war much beyond the thirty-eighth parallel. In so doing they conveyed an unmistakable signal to the Communists that they need be in no hurry to reach a cease-fire agreement. So long as they were willing to bear the cost of a stalemated conflict, the Communists could prolong the armistice negotiations with every expectation of wringing concessions from the war-weary Americans and their allies. The outcome was that truce talks dragged on intermittently at Kaesong and later Panmunjom for many months in 1951 and 1952. But then, in early 1953, Dwight D. Eisenhower took over the White House. Not wedded to the existing policy in Korea, the new President shortly threatened the Communists with expansion of the war and implied that he might order the use of nuclear weapons if the hostilities did not come to an early termination. Perhaps the Communists took him at his word; perhaps they assumed that as a professional military man he did not share his predecessor's inhibitions about expanding the war. A few months later, however, they agreed to a cease-fire. (One must acknowledge, of course, that other circumstances and events, for example, the uncertainties in the Communist world resulting from the death of Joseph Stalin in March 1953, may have had as much influence as Eisenhower's threats in persuading the Communists to accept a cease-fire in Korea.) Could the leaders in Washington in 1951–1952 have threatened the Communists with equal effect? We shall never know; at the time of the MacArthur inquiry they virtually foreswore such threats as a possible tactic for ending the nightmare in Korea.

In retrospect, one is left with the suspicion that at the time of the MacArthur inquiry Marshall and other military men may have exaggerated the danger of World War III inherent in an expansion of the conflict in East Asia along the lines recommended by General MacArthur if the Communists rejected an ultimatum to make peace in Korea. Although testimony deleted from the public record indicated that the Soviets had the means of delivering enough nuclear warheads to the United States to render great damage to American cities, it was apparent that the Strategic Air Command, notwithstanding Vandenberg's lament that it was a shoestring instrument, was capable of inflicting far greater devastation on the Soviet Union. Thus it seems doubtful that leaders in the Kremlin might have risked a global confrontation with the United States following a limited expansion of the war involving a bombing campaign against Manchuria and a blockade of China's ports. Also, one wonders if America's allies, as Marshall and others intimated, might have seriously considered severing their connections with the United States had leaders in Washington acted upon MacArthur's proposals. In view of their dependence on the United States for defense and economic assistance, what alternative did the allies have than to acquiesce in whatever America elected to do in East Asia?

The foregoing observation is not intended as a criticism of President Truman and his advisers for turning aside MacArthur's appeal for an expansion of the East Asian war in the spring of 1951. In light of the military situation in Korea and the signals emanating from Communist capitals that the Chinese and North Koreans were ready to consider a battlefield armistice, expansion of the war at that time would have been totally irresponsible. What is intended as a criticism of the Truman Administration is that they virtually threw away their trump card in the diplomatic game in East Asia; specifically, the threat that a Communist refusal to accept a reasonable cease-fire agreement at an early date might have very serious consequences was compromised.

This does not imply that a belated endorsement of General MacArthur is due, for the general never suggested that his object in urging an expansion of the war in East Asia was to force the Communists into early armistice negotiations and acceptance of a cease-fire line near the thirty-eighth parallel. A truce at the parallel, he insisted, would be appeasement of the Communists and would mean a defeat for America and its allies. Rather, his purpose was to expel the Communists from the entire Korean peninsula and implant the Stars and Stripes along the Yalu—where that banner had been implanted by soldiers under his command in November 1950. Incredible as it may seem in retrospect, nobody during the MacArthur inquiry demanded an answer to the question which logically derived from MacArthur's purpose: Would the conquest of North Korea for President Syngman Rhee of South Korea and the non-Communist world, the resultant enlargement of America's reputation as an inconquerable foe of communism, and the corresponding decline in prestige of the government in Peking justify the human and material sacrifices required to execute MacArthur's strategic ideas? The only answer that prudent men could make to that question in 1951 was an unqualified no, and nothing has transpired in the ensuing two decades which might persuade the student of history to answer otherwise.

Other questions which begged answers in the spring of 1951 went largely unanswered during the MacArthur inquiry. One question had to do with relations between MacArthur and his superiors in Washington in the months before his dismissal: Why had Truman, Marshall, and the Joint Chiefs not made a more concerted effort to harness the five-star general? The answer was obvious: they were awed by his reputation and intimidated by the strength of his personality. Still, it seemed that leaders in the capital had almost encouraged MacArthur to commit acts such as the issuance of the peace statement of March 24, 1951, and the posting of the letter to Congressman Martin—acts which they considered insubordinate and certainly injurious to what the United States was trying to accomplish in the Far East. When MacArthur dispatched his letter to the VFW in August 1950 Truman gave him no dressing down; he merely required him to withdraw the letter. When in the aftermath of the disaster along the Yalu in December 1950 the general made public his dissatisfaction with restrictions on his management of the war, the President again declined to reprimand MacArthur and instead confined himself to a general directive requiring *all* officials to refrain from public statements on high policy. Later, in February and early March 1951, when MacArthur made fresh comments indicating continued displeasure over Far Eastern policy, there was no response from Washington. One can only speculate as to the effect on the conduct of the war and the search for peace of an early and more forthright stance vis-à-vis the general.

Then there was the question of America's relations with China: Was it in the United States' best interest to align itself so uncompromisingly with Chiang Kai-shek and his regime in Taipei and virtually proclaim perpetual enmity toward the Maoists in Peking? Granted, a calm and more searching discussion of America's interests in East Asia and the best policy to pursue in dealing with the Chinese was not possible in the spring of 1951, for passions in the United States were too inflamed in light of events in China and Korea in recent years, not to mention news stories cascading out of the Far East at the time of the MacArthur inquiry that a massive and bloody purge of non-Communists was taking place on the Chinese mainland. Yet, a time or two during the MacArthur hearings Senator Fulbright clearly was edging toward the proposition that the chief threat to American interests was the Soviet Union, not communism, and that perhaps the United States should think in terms of separating such Communist states as the People's Republic of China from their bonds with the Kremlin—that is, it should abandon its crusade against "international communism" and actively encourage other communist leaders outside the Soviet Union to emulate the example of President Tito of Yugoslavia. Americans of the 1970s can only lament that Fulbright did not press the question and nobody else took it up—that the Tito heresy, as testimony during the MacArthur inquiry made manifest, had touched no chord in the breasts of most Americans.

* * *

In July 1961 Douglas MacArthur made a final return to the Philippines to participate in that republic's celebration of fifteen years of independence. MacArthur seemed increasingly a relic of a bygone era, the more so as the Korean War passed farther into history. He had not lost his old charisma and rhetorical skill; far from it. In 1962 the general, a tottering old man, traveled to West Point to accept the Sylvanus Thayer Award for distinguished service to the United States. In the peroration of his remarks to the corps of cadets, supposedly extemporaneous, he said:

> The shadows are lengthening for me. The twilight is here. My days of old have vanished—tone and tint. They have gone glimmering through the dreams of things that were. Their memory is one of wondrous beauty, watered by tears and coaxed and caressed by the smiles of yesterday. I listen vainly, but with thirsty ear, for the witching melody of faint bugles blowing reveille, of far drums beating the long roll.
>
> In my dreams I hear again the crash of guns, the rattle of musketry, the strange, mournful mutter of the battlefield. But in the evening of my memory always I come back to West Point. Always there echoes and re-echoes: Duty, honor, country.
>
> Today marks my final roll call with you. But I want you to know that when I cross the river, my last conscious thoughts will be of the corps, and the corps, and the corps.
>
> I bid you farewell.

A short time later the general had lunch at the White House and exchanged pleasantries with President John F. Kennedy, the first Democrat since his nemesis, Harry Truman, to command the Oval Office. The event seemed to demonstrate that the wounds wrought by the bitter controversy of spring 1951 had about healed. Still, as MacArthur had told the cadets at West Point, the shadows were lengthening. A few months after his eighty-fourth birthday, in spring 1962, he underwent surgery at Walter Reed Hospital in Washington for a malfunctioning gall bladder, was visited by and photographed with (his last photograph) a man who was to become another Democratic President, Lyndon B. Johnson, who had interrogated him during the MacArthur inquiry of 1951. Then, on April 5, 1964, the old soldier died, and six days later, as a bugler sounded taps, his body was placed in a crypt in the MacArthur Memorial in Norfolk.

BIBLIOGRAPHY

The principal source for the foregoing essay on the MacArthur inquiry was the printed hearings, published by the Government Printing Office in 1951 under the title of *Military Situation in the Far East.* In five parts, *Military Situation,* including the "individual views" of the Old Guard senators, an appendix of documents, and the index, runs to 3691 pages. The interrogation of witnesses consumes 3133 of those pages. The printed hearings, however, do not include testimony that was deleted by the censors at the time of the inquiry. Fortunately, the deleted material was declassified in 1973 and is now available to scholars. Likewise the Joint Chiefs of Staff in spring 1974 declassified the memorandum drafted by the Joint Chiefs and circulated to top political and military officials in January 1951 which became a source of controversy during the subsequent MacArthur imbroglio. The Joint Chiefs at the same time declassified—save for a couple of entries emanating from the State Department whose declassification must await publication of the *Foreign Relations* volumes for 1950 and 1951—a lengthy document containing paraphrases (to protect ciphers) of much of the communication between General MacArthur and the Joint Chiefs in the period June 1950–April 1951. Prepared by the Joint Chiefs for use by the senators, the latter document was frequently cited during the MacArthur inquiry. Materials recently declassified were examined by the present author, as were newspapers, news magazines, and journals of thought and opinion which in 1951, of course, abounded with reports and commentaries and pictures relating to the MacArthur affair.

Of considerable interest to the student of the MacArthur inquiry are the recollections of individuals who in one way or another participated in the drama of 1951. There is the second volume of Harry Truman, *Memoirs, Years of Trial and Hope* (Garden City, 1956), the pages of which are dotted with references to MacArthur and the MacArthur controversy. Like most memoirists, Truman was careful to set out all of the arguments tending to establish the correctness of his position in the quarrel with the general. Still, the Truman recollections have a ring of truth, the more so when put alongside the available documentary evidence. Unfortunately the thirty-third President seemed to lose all sense of balance during interviews on the subject for Merle Miller's *Plain Speaking: An Oral Biography of Harry S. Truman* (New York, 1974), and the resultant account is next to worthless so far as shedding light on the MacArthur affair. Not much better are Douglas MacArthur's *Reminiscences,* (New York, 1964). MacArthur's attempt to justify his behavior and establish himself as a veritable Solomon in matters relating to military and diplomatic affairs led him to countless distortions of fact. The book, moreover, does not have the literary charm and dramatic impact of MacArthur's better public addresses. The principal value of the *Reminiscences* lies in what they tell the reader about MacArthur's personality and character. Of equal value—that is, very little—are the memoir-biographies of MacArthur: Charles A. Willoughby and John Chamberlain, *MacArthur, 1941–1951* (New York, 1954), and Courtney

Whitney, *MacArthur: His Rendezvous with History* (New York, 1956). In a quite different category are the chapters on the MacArthur controversy in Matthew B. Ridgway, *The Korean War* (Garden City, 1967), and J. Lawton Collins, *War in Peacetime* (Boston, 1969). Both of those principals in the Korean conflict, Ridgway and Collins, composed balanced and thoughtful chapters on MacArthur's dismissal and the problem of the relationship between field commanders and superiors in Washington. Then there is Dean Acheson's memoir, *Present at the Creation* (New York, 1969). If sometimes betraying his well-known disdain for mortals of lesser intellect than he, *i.e.*, all Old Guardsmen and anybody else who had the audacity to disagree with him, the former-secretary's long segments on the Korean War and MacArthur controversy seem to square with available documents and hence, like Truman's recollections (in his memoirs), have the ring of truth.

A somewhat breezy summary of the controversy, but one having the virtue of fitting it in neatly with the battlefield events in Korea, appears in Robert Leckie, *Conflict: The History of the Korean War* (New York, 1962). More scholarly, and certainly more satisfactory on the Senate hearings, are the appropriate passages and sections in David Rees, *Korea: The Limited War* (New York, 1964). Although the author is unabashedly pro-Truman, perhaps the most satisfying summary account of the MacArthur affair is that in a chapter entitled "The President and the General" in Cabell Phillips, *The Truman Presidency* (New York, 1966). As did Rees, Phillips deftly presented the MacArthur controversy against the larger backdrop of diplomacy and domestic politics, *e.g.*, the so-called Great Debate over American foreign policy which commanded headlines from November 1950 down to the time of MacArthur's dismissal. Unfortunately, all three of the aforementioned authors, like most writers who have considered the controversy of 1951, concentrated almost exclusively on the matter of MacArthur's dismissal and his proposals for expanding the war in Korea, and thus virtually ignored consideration by the Senate committees of America's policy towards China.

Of the three books dealing with the MacArthur affair, that by Richard H. Rovere and Arthur M. Schlesinger, jr., *The General and the President and the Future of American Foreign Policy* (New York, 1951), appeared in autumn 1951, only a few months after completion of the MacArthur inquiry, and reveals both the pitfalls and virtues of "instant history": the book lacks that perspective on which historians tend to place so much value but also captures the mood and tensions of the moment more effectively than do pieces by authors who have recalled the affair vicariously through printed hearings and news reports. A more cogent criticism of Rovere-Schlesinger is that the book is transparently polemical, *i.e.*, is a vigorous defense of President Truman's position in the controversy. Whatever its shortcomings, the book, reissued under the title of *The MacArthur Controversy and American Foreign Policy* (New York, 1965), is beautifully written and, unlike most authors and memoirists who have written about the controversy of 1951, Rovere and Schlesinger did not concentrate on MacArthur's dismissal and his proposals for expanding the Korean War to the virtual exclusion of any consideration of exchanges between senators and witnesses during the Senate hearings on the larger question of America's Far Eastern policy.

The other book-length treatments of the MacArthur affair are John W.

Spanier, *The Truman-MacArthur Controversy and the Korean War* (Cambridge, Mass., 1959), and Trumbull Higgins, *Korea and the Fall of MacArthur* (New York, 1960). The Spanier book is excellent. It was thoroughly researched and properly footnoted, conclusions are thoughtful and balanced, and the prose is bright and clear. For the student of the MacArthur inquiry of 1951 it has only two shortcomings. Like all authors who have written on the controversy save Rovere-Schlesinger, Spanier did not go into the scrutiny of Far Eastern policy by the Armed Services and Foreign Relations Committees, and instead stayed with MacArthur's quarrel with his superiors in Washington. Then Spanier, like everyone else writing on the subject before 1974, did not have access to classified materials which recently have become available to scholars. Nor did he have the benefit of such sources as the recollections of MacArthur, Acheson, and Collins. As for the Higgins book, it too concentrates on MacArthur and his relations with his superiors. More to the point, the book is a study of the problem of waging limited war in the nuclear age. As such, it is provocative and tightly argued.

PERTINENT DOCUMENTS

The McCarthy Era
1954

U.S. Information Agency Photo

Senator Joseph McCarthy, in his heyday as discoverer of alleged Communists in and out of government, reads from the Daily Worker.

The McCarthy Era 1954

by H. Lew Wallace

It was a heterogeneous group dining at the Colony Restaurant in Washington, D.C. on January 7, 1950. The four men who met were a priest, a teacher, an attorney, and a U.S. senator. The priest was Father Edmund Walsh, dean of the Georgetown School of Foreign Service; Charles H. Kraus taught political science at Georgetown University; William A. Roberts was a lawyer and businessman in Washington; the senator was Joseph R. McCarthy, the Republican junior senator from Wisconsin. The meeting was arranged by Kraus, for in addition to his teaching, Kraus served as a member of McCarthy's staff. The reasons for the meeting, from the perspective of twenty-five years later, are somewhat obscure. It is fairly clear that McCarthy, up for reelection in 1952, was looking for one large issue for his campaign. It was obvious to McCarthy that "past performance" would net him little.

In 1946 McCarthy had made a spectacular entrance into national politics by defeating Robert M. La Follette, jr. for the Republican senatorial nomination, thereby ending nearly forty years of distinguished, liberal representation by the La Follettes, senior and junior. Although a combination of personal and political factors undermined La Follette, McCarthy, whose slogan was "Congress Needs a Tail Gunner," came to represent the warrior hero, fresh from battles to save the world for democracy, now ready to ply those great energies that saved America to serving America. Unfortunately for McCarthy the proof was in the fact, not the assertion of the fact, that he could serve as well as he once "fought." ("He fought on LAND and the AIR all through the Pacific. He and millions of other guys kept you from talking Japanese." So ran two lines from a McCarthy flyer. It is hard to imagine now, an "anti-hero" generation or so from the emotional climate of the war era, that such lines could be interpreted as anything more than high camp.) For McCarthy, the beginning of his national career (until the heady wine and roses years of McCarthyism) was also the highpoint. McCarthy coasted to an easy victory over his Democratic opponent, Howard MacMurray; McCarthy went to Washington, an "interesting" figure for a short while. However, he became less interesting. By 1950 he was thought of as an aggressive, pugnacious, somewhat colorful, but basically directionless junior senator from the midwest.

McCarthy, then, was a man in search of an idea, a hard, central armature around which could be coiled all the threads of doubts, fears, troubles, hopes, and fantasies of his constituents. Kraus thought Roberts and Father Walsh could help McCarthy. Whether the idea of communism as that issue was already half-formed before the meeting is hard to determine, but both Kraus and Roberts admired Father Walsh and had read his books, particularly *Total Power*, the theme of which was the urgent need to resist the global menace of communism and in particular its subtle power for subverting democracies. McCarthy had not read Father Walsh's books, though Kraus had urged him to do so. The next best thing seemed to be a meeting between the senator and the priest; that the subject of communism in some form or another would come up was almost to be taken for granted.

After a few pleasantries, McCarthy brought the conversation around to the low state of his political situation. He asked for ideas on a campaign issue. Roberts proposed that McCarthy become spokesman for the St. Lawrence seaway. McCarthy was not taken with the idea, perhaps because he had one to which he had given some thought, one which had potential mass appeal—a refurbishing of the old Townsend plan. McCarthy's plan was quickly vetoed, however. First, because any new plan would carry with it the same economic weakness that marred the original; second, because the idea was too demagogic. (After all, Townsend and his idea had been rather loosely relegated to the "rise of the demagogues" chapter in the history of the New Deal period.)

Later, in Roberts's office, the subject of communism, which may have been touched upon at the Colony, became the central proposition of the evening. Father Walsh gave a lengthy discourse on the need for democracies to be particularly vigilant against the Communists' power to infiltrate and subvert governmental structures. Not only was the issue important in its own right, Father Walsh suggested, but it was an issue that any foresighted, anticipatory politician should make use of. McCarthy liked the idea, maybe a bit too much. "The government is full of Communists," he said, adding that someone ought to "hammer at them."

McCarthy's reaction struck the first discordant note of the night. Among his other characteristics, McCarthy had a rough though not unappealing affability and coarse, ingratiating geniality about him. Kraus and Roberts, like McCarthy, were marine veterans, and the camaraderie of that time could yet tie men in common cause. Then, too, the idea of a possible Armageddon, communism on one side, freedom on the other, was a particular fixation of the fifties, and particularly strong among Catholics. That Kraus, Roberts, and Father Walsh, all Catholics, should desire to encourage, as Richard Rovere wrote in *Senator Joe McCarthy*, "in a young Catholic Senator a serious approach to serious matters," was natural enough. But Father Walsh, an impassioned believer in the menace of communism, did his research and arrived at premises less through emotion than through thought and global perspective. Kraus, too, had reached his conclusions through thoughtful processes. Roberts, for his part, though a profound admirer of Father Walsh and a foe of communism, was a liberal, and a Democrat at that.

For these three men, McCarthy's remark indicated too quick a leap from premise to conclusion, though in essence the remark showed McCarthy's spendid, frightening ability to distill complex matters into simple, albeit perverted, basics. In words which were ironic in retrospect, Roberts quickly warned against trying to campaign on the revival of the "Red" scare. The other two men sided with Roberts, emphasizing the idea of a responsible approach. Only on the facts, said McCarthy casually, would he base any campaign. Though all three men, in a short time, would feel compelled to repudiate McCarthy, none realized at the moment the furies they unleashed that winter's night in 1950.

If they did not realize the import of the moment, the same could be said of McCarthy. Looking back, it is too easy to believe that communism as an issue sprang full-grown out of the head of McCarthy. But, soon after the night of the meeting, McCarthy asked the Senate Republican Campaign Committee to arrange a Lincoln Day speaking schedule; his suggested subject—"Communism in the State Department." That he had perhaps found an issue was important for McCarthy, but that he never gave much thought to the issue, to the significance of his subject, seems equally clear. McCarthy had read nothing serious about communism, could not define it, never felt it necessary to do so, and had stumbled on the issue like a child over a new toy. The campaign committee booked McCarthy for speeches in Wheeling, West Virginia, Salt Lake City, Utah, and Reno, Nevada, a tour that was the closest thing to political exile. (This schedule was slightly reminiscent of the Yucca cactus-Gila monster circuit that James Farley laid out for Huey Long in 1932.) But McCarthy did not object.

McCarthy did a bit of casual preparation for his Lincoln's Birthday speeches. (When they shovelled Abraham Lincoln into the tomb, he forgot about the Confederates, and the Carpetbaggers, and the Scalawags, wrote Sandburg. Fortunately Lincoln was also forever spared specious allusions and false parallels.) When finally aware of communism as a subject of concern, McCarthy realized that it had been a subject of concern for some years, and that there were materials about the land to be learned from. McCarthy, with some help, put some of these materials together in rough outline.

I

In a glancing sort of way, McCarthy was, of course, aware of the growth of communism as a political issue since 1948. Perhaps the best example of the "Communist issue," a vague, nebulous term, powerful in part because of its vague and highly suggestive quality, as a factor in American politics, was the part the issue played in the 1948 campaign of Henry A. Wallace. Fired from the Truman cabinet in 1946, Wallace became involved as a speaker, although not a member, in the Progressive Citizens of America, an organization formed just prior to the 1946 congressional elections. It was an amalgamation of smaller groups from the ranks of labor, the arts, the academic community, and other professional groups whose various organizations, dedicated to revitalizing politics, dated back to 1940. In 1947 the PCA, the nucleus of the 1948 Progressive party, already disenchanted with the Administration's foreign policy, broke sharply with the Democrats over the Truman Doctrine.

Since foreign policy was considered bipartisan, the PCA saw no alternative in the Republican party and thus began organization for a third party. While Wallace was making his speeches—and thus showing his receptiveness to heading a third party—the executive vice president of the PCA, C. B. Baldwin, was quietly working with the executive board of the PCA, urging members to vote for an endorsement of Wallace as an independent candidate for the presidency. This endorsement was received in mid-December, and Wallace declared his candidacy on December 29, 1947.

After endorsing Wallace, the executive board submitted its decision to the second annual convention of the PCA, which met in Chicago in 1948. The convention ratified the executive board's action in a resolution that also provided for delegates from the PCA to attend an April founding convention for their third party. The national board of the PCA would determine at that time (subject to ratification by two-thirds of the state chapters) whether the organization would become the nucleus for a third party or retain its identity by merely affiliating with that party.

The third party was formed officially at the April meeting in Chicago. The organization that evolved out of the meeting was the antithesis to Wallace's desire for a party with a broad "peoples' " base. At that meeting a 700-member Wallace-for-President Committee, representing various local and state groups supporting Wallace, merged with the PCA. The machinery of the latter group formed the basis on which was built an elaborate and complex superstructure, so cumbersome that it ultimately proved to be a deciding factor in the poor showing of Wallace's campaign.

It proved almost impossible to mesh together gears of such odd and diverse sizes into an effective working apparatus. Consequently, the task of organization became more and more the work of fewer and fewer persons. The real power structure of the third party revolved around the campaign manager, C. B. Baldwin, who, when the New Dealers and liberals, doubtful about Wallace and his policies, failed to respond in adequate numbers, found himself turning to those groups that were willing to act—the political Left, including Communists. Hence, though their numbers were small and though they held no important offices, Communists did wield real power in the third party. This posed a dilemma for Wallace. Accepting their support meant losing the broad base on which he had planned; forcing them out meant a total reorganization of the party and an enormous expenditure of precious campaign time. Wallace tried to ignore the nagging problem of communism in the third party, but he found it increasingly difficult to do, since the press, the Democrats, the southerners, and the Communists themselves refused to let the issue be ignored.

From a political point of view Wallace's dilemma was the salvation of the Democratic party. Once the press established that the third party was the Communist party in disguise—a debatable premise, for certainly Wallace and his running mate, Glen H. Taylor, were not Communists, nor were the purposes of the party communistic—there was a twofold benefit for the Democrats. First, the charge not only discouraged those previously inclined toward Wallace's political philosophy, but caused major defections by early supporters. Secondly, the Democrats channeled charges by the Republicans of communism in high places (a thesis that predated McCarthy) into the third party. And so, for short-term pragmatic political gains, the Democratic party contributed its share to the Communist shadow world.

What was most unfortunate about the specter of communism, as raised by the press (including the Communist press, which was obviously not modest about taking far more credit than was due), was the opportunity it provided for vicious, vituperative attacks on Wallace. Particularly in the South, Wallace and Taylor were assaulted, sometimes with chilling acts of physical violence. However one might then or now disagree with Wallace's ideas as realistic solutions to international relations in 1948, there is a haunting irony in the fact that Wallace and Taylor, campaigning on a platform of peace and the equality of men, should find themselves ridiculed and abused by those who justified ridicule and abuse as legitimate weapons for upholding the traditional American freedoms of liberty and justice against the threat of communism. Worse, groups such as the militant segregationists, whose real vendetta with Wallace and Taylor was their challenge to racial bigotry, were allowed to vent their rage against the third party candidates without having to admit that prejudice and bigotry were their standards. In all, it pointed out the rare quality of Lincoln, who could disagree with, or even hate, the ideas of another man, without hating the man. Further, it pointed out the timelessness of Roosevelt's magnificent words: "Let me assert my firm belief that the only thing we have to fear is fear itself—nameless, unreasoning, unjustifying terror which paralyzes needed efforts to convert retreat into advance." It was not a good year for dissenters; it would not be a good decade for them. Soon McCarthy would inherit this kingdom of shadows, would mold and shape the ridicule, abuse, hate, fear, oblique attack, and character attack into the art of paralyzing terror.

Arthur M. Schlesinger, jr., discussing the relief felt by Democrats when they learned that Huey Long's death removed a proposed third party threat in 1936, once summed up the history of third parties in American politics by saying, "it may be put down as an axiom of politics that third parties are more formidable in May than November." This was true of the Progressives in 1948, for the party started early and strongly, but was limping by the July convention and had lapsed into oblivion by November. Perhaps part of the reason for the third party axiom is that the short-run advantage of an early start, which third parties usually take, is a long-run disadvantage. First, Americans are short-run crusaders, tiring easily of abstract politics of morality. Second, a candidate who stays too long begins to speak his hopes rather than his beliefs and can find himself entangled in events over which he has little or no control, and which seemingly refute everything he has said for public record. He is thus made to appear a charlatan, a hypocrite, or a fool. There were three such events in the early campaign of Wallace and Taylor. All were related to the decline of the Progressive party as a force in the 1948 campaign and all contributed to the context of fear and confusion which McCarthy diabolically exploited.

The first of these events, in late February 1948, was the Communist coup in Czechoslovakia. Under President Edward Benes and Foreign Minister Jan Masaryk, Czechoslovakia had maintained a tenuous but hopeful position as a neutral nation—a "bridge between East and West"—through a coalition government of Communists and non-Communists. But in February, the Communist party took over the government. The coup was a shock to all men who had hoped that despite growing differences the United States and Russia would extend into peacetime their wartime alliances. The Czechoslovakian coup was interpreted as a power move by Russia and it struck a particularly damaging blow to Wallace's campaign, since it seemed to refute his argument that the Russians would peacefully coexist with the United States if allowed to. Worse for Wallace (and ultimately for his case of deferred judgments and rational approaches as means for coping with crises) was the fact that shortly after the Communists took over Czechoslovakia, Masaryk committed suicide. Thus, the episode became a "horror" event, reacted to on an emotional, rather than on a rational, level.

Wallace at first tried to explain the Communist move as a reaction America could expect anywhere if the government continued its "get tough" approach to Russia. The "get tough" policy, Wallace stated, was a two-way street. Given his basic premise, Wallace had taken a logically defensible position, but, unfortunately, he did not stop there. As reporters continued to question him, Wallace suggested that the Communists had had to move to stave off a rightist coup. Under pressure, his argument veered perilously close to the inverted logic of the "preventive coup," the time-honored device of groups who seek justification for their own aggression.

The damage to Wallace's "crusade for freedom" was sizable. A few weeks later came the second incident which weakened the Progressives's spring campaign. Wallace "wrote" an open letter to Stalin, which he delivered in a Madison Square Garden speech on the night of May 11. Stalin answered it. Earlier in the day the newspapers had carried the story of an exchange of notes between Foreign Minister Vyacheslav Molotov and Ambassador Walter Bedell Smith, the tone of which, it was thought, was moderate. On May 18 the *New York Times* carried the rather surprising story of Stalin's answer to Wallace's letter. In his speech Wallace had set forth general areas in which he suggested Russian-American cooperation was necessary, and Stalin's reply implied he agreed, again generally, with Wallace's proposals, calling them a step forward from the Molotov-Smith notes. Reaction to the letters was considerable. Wallace was at first elated; the Truman Administration was considerably less enchanted, and several members of Congress felt that Wallace's dabbling in foreign affairs was a violation of the Logan Act of 1799.

Matters changed little until June, when the Berlin blockade by the Russians irrevocably severed the admittedly vague and undiplomatic "peaceful coexistence probe" by Stalin. Since Russia's conciliatory words often preceded some hard action, the appearance given was that the soft words were only cynical diversionary tactics for some preconceived power move. Even today it is barely possible to suggest that Wallace's argument, while not the whole truth, had some truth to it. But it is possible to suggest that a greater fear, a more deeply-rooted sense of inferiority, rested in Russia than the West believed in the early postwar period. Ravaged in two world wars, nearly conquered in the second, misinterpreting and mistrusting the West as much as Wallace suggested the West did Russia, it is quite possible that Russia reacted to situations quite as often as it initiated them. Still, it is not necessarily what is true that counts, but what men believe is true. Overestimating the Russians, looking at them, as Eisenhower once said, as if "they were all eight feet tall," connecting events in a "this, then this" relationship, many Americans saw Wallace a dupe of the Communists, a perpetual Chamberlain to Stalin's perpetual Munich.

The third event of the troubled spring concerned Taylor; it was a prelude to the greater troubles of the third party, but more, a portent of the tumult and frustration of the McCarthy period generally. Taylor went to Birmingham, Alabama, to address the Southern Negro Youth Congress. The group, finding considerable opposition to its meeting, had trouble locating a site. Finally a small Negro church was selected. City officials allowed the meeting; separate (but presumably equal) entrances were provided for whites and blacks. It was as inevitable that Taylor would try to enter through the Negro entrance as it was that he would be arrested for the attempt. Taylor's court hearing reflected the cool contempt the South felt towards the Progressive candidates. Convicted of disorderly conduct (although he had been roughed up by the police and given a suspended jail sentence), Taylor also received a stern lecture by the presiding judge on the evils wrought by outsiders who interjected race issues into politics.

There were other similar and related events in early 1948, but these epitomized and indeed electrified the atmosphere in which the candidates moved. The shadow of the "Communist issue," the fear of communism, especially the fear that Wallace and Taylor, though not stricken themselves, were carriers of that plague, thus enveloped the political party, the party *Time* magazine called "the pink facade," a party with a platform that "in chapter and verse . . . was a faithful reflection of a lengthy resolution prepared for the Communist's own convention. . . ."

Of these matters, McCarthy had nothing to say. Nor was he much concerned with the startling events of the summer of 1948, when Elizabeth Bentley and Whittaker Chambers testified before the House Committee on Un-American Activities that their activities in the Communist party had brought them into contact with former government officials. Miss Bentley, who testified that she had been a courier for a spy system for five years, gave the committee the names of thirty ex-employees, including former assistant secretary of the treasury, Harry Dexter White. Chambers accused nine former government employees of being Communist party members, including Alger Hiss, who had once been the State Department's director of special political affairs.

For the next two years, until Hiss's conviction for perjury, the Bentley-Chambers-White-Hiss affair, compounded by a myriad of other Communist "issues," created an American milieu in which tale, truth, distortion, fact, and fancy released into American politics the twin furies of fear and hysteria. Although McCarthy rode these furies into a unique kind of power, he was, until after the Wheeling speech, a dabbler, not a devotee, of Republican charges of communism in high places. He was a casual admirer of the House Committee on Un-American Activities. In 1946 he had suggested that Howard MacMurray, his opponent in Wisconsin, tended towards communism, and in 1947 he proposed his "anti-Communist" amendment (never seriously considered) to the Taft-Hartley bill. In an offhanded way McCarthy observed the mounting anti-Communist pressure in the country as the Hiss case evolved, but he was not, except in the most incidental way, a source of that pressure. McCarthy did not create the ambiguous, confusing, contradictory shadowland of anti-communism, although, once he inherited it, he shrewdly extended its boundaries and masterfully ruled it for a short time. Above all, he gave it a myth and mythology that would long outlive his brief incumbency.

McCarthy's rather haphazard preparation for the Wheeling speech showed that he hoped he had an idea but had no inkling that he had embarked upon a great cause. Gathering his materials with some help, McCarthy put together a piecemeal speech which outlined, probably unwittingly, the fears and charges of the postwar years. He flew to Wheeling, a relatively obscure senator on a relatively obscure speaking junket. He delivered his speech to a Republican Women's Club, then flew to Salt Lake City for his second endeavor.

II

McCarthy changed planes in Denver. To his surprise, he was met by a crowd of reporters. He was suddenly well known. When he arrived in Salt Lake City, he was again surrounded by reporters; he was famous. It was a few lines in the Wheeling speech that started McCarthy on his great crusade and the country on its something less than greatest era. From the beginning there was a murky, zany quality about the McCarthy period. In his speech McCarthy said he had in his hand a list of Communists in the State Department and he mentioned a number. What that number was, and what list he had in his hand, were questions around which controversy would revolve for years. It is perhaps symbolic of the era that the hunt for the exact number mentioned received more attention and concern than the meaning and magnitude of the charges. Perhaps nothing more reveals the essential hollowness of McCarthy, however, than the fact that he was never able to recall, or to find out, exactly what he said. He wanted to know, and he spent some time trying to document, after the fact and like an interested outside observer, his exact words. The beginning and the end of the McCarthy era reflected the symmetry of emptiness. What did I say, asked McCarthy at the beginning. Near the end of the Army-McCarthy hearings, when Army Counsel Joseph H. Welch delivered his celebrated denunciation of McCarthy's methods, McCarthy seemed genuinely surprised, wondering what he had done to incur Welsh's wrath.

But he did know, like the hedgehog of the Greek fable, one important thing—that he had that dramatic, all-encompassing issue for his campaign. The furor told McCarthy he had struck a nerve, and that was all that mattered. The Truman Administration responded to the Wheeling speech almost immediately. Deputy Undersecretary of State John E. Peurifoy sent McCarthy a telegram demanding proof of his accusations. He was not disturbed by the call nor the fact that he could not at the moment account for his accusation. McCarthy's was a career built on froth, not substance, thus luck and chance were his main stocks. Never having much to lose, McCarthy plunged for his big chance with boldness and audacity. He wrote a letter to Truman, demanding that Truman revoke the policy of closing the security files to Congress. Neatly turning the request for "proof of the pudding," McCarthy had countered that he could not supply information because he was denied access to records. He also implied that by his diligent efforts he had been able to obtain information on Communists in the State Department, but that information could be judged only if security files were opened. In one of his more imaginative touches, McCarthy added that Truman's failure to match information would "label the Democratic Party of being the bedfellow of international communism."

McCarthy's statement was a fair example of what Richard Rovere called "his most formidable weapon, the multiple untruth," a statement so complicated, flexible, and grandiose in its mendacity as almost to defy rational refutation. He had, however, other weapons in his arsenal, one of which was his ability to obscure issues with numbers, which all too often pass as facts. Numbers played a large part in the McCarthy period. Some examples are the number of Communists in the State Department he gave at Wheeling, variously reported as 205 and 81 and 57; the number of investigations of McCarthy himself, 7; the number of investigations he was part of before 1953, 5; the investigations of his subcommittee of the Committee on Government Operations, 445 preliminary investigations and 157 investigations; and the number of anti-American books on the shelves of the State Department's Information Centers, "large numbers."

McCarthy's talent for tying ideas into Gordian knots with numbers evolved out of necessity. McCarthy had to document his statements to keep the machine of his Wheeling speech in motion. On February 20 he documented, in his own way, his Wheeling statements on the floor of the Senate. In 1947, after the Republicans had gained majority control of Congress, the House had acted on its version of a general "get-tough-with-Communism" scheme, largely by concentrating on what some suspected was the Communists' favorite nesting place, the State Department. A House committee, headed by investigator Robert E. Lee, examined materials in the State Department's security files, files which contained information gathered by several government agencies, including the FBI. (Truman's directive, closing security files to congressional investigations, came on March 13, 1948.) The House committee security file, often referred to as the "Lee list," went to several congressional committees, and copies of the files were used and referred to many times before McCarthy brought his version to the Senate floor. This version contained two new twists: first, he implied that he was reading materials gained by his own efforts, not from a nearly three-year-old file; second, he changed the numbering system, adding further to the illusion that his evidence was menacingly fresh and new. Having only numbered cases (he later got the references matching names with case numbers), stringing together numbers, pronouns, and suggestive phrases and references out of context, McCarthy gave a masterfully confusing performance. Though it was apparent in the questioning following his speech that bluff and bluster were sometimes his only defense, he avoided all traps. He had help, however, for most of the Republican senators, if not friendly to McCarthy, were nonetheless partial to undermining the Democrats. The Democrats hurt themselves by trying to pin down McCarthy on the number of card-carrying Communists in the State Department. Their sarcastic reference to numbers played into McCarthy's hands; he cited numbers back in answer. And Truman's directive helped, since there was no objective way of cross-checking McCarthy's "documents" without access to the files. Finally, McCarthy's charges carried so much weight in the Senate and in the country that the result was a Senate resolution to investigate "whether persons who are disloyal to the United States are, or have been employed by the Department of State."

To investigate the thesis of the State Department as the politburo in residence, a special subcommittee of the Senate Foreign Relations Committee was set up under the chairmanship of Senator Millard E. Tydings, Democrat from Maryland. Between March 8 and June 28 the subcommittee held thirty-one days of hearings. In the interim between his Senate speech and the start of the hearings, McCarthy worked diligently at strengthening his case. Though he had gained time, publicity, support, and new materials by the time the hearings opened, the first sessions did not go well for him. Tydings, whom Roosevelt had tried to purge unsuccessfully in 1938, subjected McCarthy to close and sharp examination. From the first, he moved in on McCarthy, focusing particularly on "case 14," the case of a Communist who had been shielded by a high-ranking member of the State Department, which McCarthy had cited in his Senate speech. Tydings wanted names but McCarthy could not, would not, and did not give them. Several sharp exchanges followed. McCarthy seemed very much on the defensive; Tydings was confident, formidable, a slight smile showing his contempt of the senator from Wisconsin. (But, as in the case of the lady from Niger and the tiger, the smile changed faces before the ride was over.)

As the hearing proceeded, McCarthy began naming his cases. At first—at least within the confines of the hearings—the names he gave and the materials he cited seemed pallid support for his sensational charges. Many of the names and much of his material were fairly generally known. Yet, in telling his twice-told tales, McCarthy revealed yet another of his not inconsiderable talents for "making bricks without straw." Perhaps not since

Samuel Adams had edited the letters of Thomas Hutchinson had anyone revealed old, already worked material in such startlingly new ways as had McCarthy.

In his four days of testimony McCarthy gave the names of ten people whom he accused of being Communists, Communist sympathizers, or Communistically inclined. His first case involved charges against Dorothy Kenyon, a New York lawyer. A committed liberal, her name had appeared in a number of suspect organizations that various anti-Communist committees, including the Dies Committee, had assembled. She was not a member of the State Department, however, so her ties with the theme of McCarthy's charges were nearly as questionable as the case McCarthy made against her.

McCarthy was off to a wobbly start, but he got better. Particularly did McCarthy strengthen his case when he named Philip C. Jessup, United States ambassador at large, Haldore Hanson, an official in the (then) new Point Four program, and John Stewart Service. His cases against these men were as vague, rambling, and scattered as always, but he found a common denominator in their careers. In different ways and in varying degrees, each had been associated with China policy. In the context of the times, the term "China policy" was one that evoked a reaction as demonstrable, particularly within the Republican party, as that of Pavlov's dog's to the bell.

One has only to remember the long love affair of the Republicans with China, or the myth of China; the fact that Republicans had traditionally looked to the Pacific, the Republican province, with a fond and paternalistic gaze; the fact that, during the most ardent periods of Republican "isolationism," isolationism meant only keeping a safe distance from decadent Europe and did not necessarily apply to points west of San Francisco. Particularly galling was the fact that in 1947 the Republican Eightieth Congress (the no-good, do-nothing Eightieth Congress of Truman's 1948 campaign) had not only acquiesced, but concurred, in the Truman Administration's decision to emphasize European recovery, with only token military and economic support going to Chiang Kai-shek. When, in 1949, the Communists gained control of mainland China, it was tempting to forget the realities underlying the China coup, to forget that Republicans had deluded themselves into thinking that China was safe under Chiang Kai-shek, to forget the realism of the Eightieth Congress, and revert to the thesis of a Democratic sellout in China, a sellout engineered by conspirators within the State Department.

In naming Jessup, Hanson, and Service, McCarthy was rubbing salt into raw and open wounds. McCarthy then presented the name of Professor Owen Lattimore of Johns Hopkins University, an Asian scholar who had served for a short time in the State Department as an expert on the Far East, particularly China. Though Lattimore's name is the one that can still strike a responsive chord in the minds of people who recall the McCarthy days, and though his was to be the controversial case in the McCarthy charges, McCarthy's first mention of him was casual, and, given the context, relatively innocuous. McCarthy had a hard time categorizing Lattimore, at various times labeling him a Communist spy, a fellow traveler, and then, finally, "the architect of our Far Eastern policy." The latter label, though borrowed (perhaps from Richard M. Nixon, who had earlier bestowed the title on Philip C. Jessup), was a happy choice for McCarthy. It was general; it connoted much, and much of it evil; yet, it could not be refuted in any point-by-point approach.

The long-range effects of McCarthy's charges were not, however, immediately apparent. Indeed, as the hearings proceeded, the case seemed to incline against McCarthy. The defendants, particularly Lattimore, on whose case McCarthy settled as the one that would crack the State Department wide open, were particularly sharp and peppery. Lattimore was seemingly unawed by McCarthy's charge that he had somehow manipulated the United States to the very edge of the door leading into the world of communism. By contrast, the pro-McCarthy witnesses seemed harried and indecisive.

Within the sessions, McCarthy's charges too often seemed to be fabrications spun from bombast and empty rhetoric. But he gained strength as he fabricated. The hearings were widely covered and McCarthy netted publicity, some notoriety, and also support. The so-called "China lobby" saw him as their new spokesman. Such powerful Republican senators as Robert A. Taft (Ohio) and Kenneth S. Wherry (Nebraska) among others, as aware as McCarthy of the coming elections, encouraged, supported, and defended McCarthy. Indeed, as the hearings proceeded the investigations themselves seemed subordinate to the high-pitched battle between the Democrats and Republicans, focusing on the long, Democratic tenure in the presidency and Republican attacks on that tenure. Then, too, McCarthy drew growing support from millions of Americans who saw in him not a man seizing his moment, but as someone who was at long last making sense out of the complex and bewildering changes that had taken place in American society following World War II.

One of McCarthy's greatest assets was his particular talent for imposing on issues what Edward Hallett Carr, in *What Is History*, called "the bad King John" interpretation of events. This interpretation seems particularly attractive to Americans, since it appeals to a persistent pattern of belief that the world is divided into good and evil, that evil has a tangible and recognizable form, which once identified, can be overcome by a proper mixture of faith, good work, and righteous wrath.

What McCarthy's campaigns revealed was the tenacity with which people hold on to old ideas and old approaches to problems in the face of all evidence that they are no longer relevant. The McCarthy era, with its maze of investigations and hearings, emphasized the strong pull sectionalism exerts over nationalism, nationalism exerts over internationalism and personality exerts over intellect. The American, as so much of the McCarthy days seems to indicate, is basically conservative, if by that word one means he wishes to continue making changes, but changes which take place within familiar patterns. He wants to believe that all problems can be quickly resolved, possibly because he sees the source of all problems in a simplistic way, focusing on one person or combination of persons whose removal brings about an uncomplicated solution. Perhaps, too, because the country's national history has been so brief, its accomplishments many and varied, the "glory road" interpretation of the American experience is a reality for many. Americans have been able to escape having to take a tough-minded, realistic look at the darker traditions which also flow through the American experience—its capacity for violence, the stereotyping of both people and ideas, the manufacturing of single scapegoats for complex, deeply-rooted problems, the holding of racial and conspiratorial interpretations of history.

Even in his worst moments before the Tydings Committee, when forced to shift the grounds and evidence for his charges, when forced to evade sharp questions, when forced to generalize to the point of absurdity, McCarthy was on solid ground, both historically and psychologically, with his fear and crisis approach. Americans do respond to a crisis, sometimes magnificently, but seldom do they patiently cope with problems before they reach a crisis, or thoughtfully listen to an explanation of those problems as the result of complex, involved, many-faceted, and often impersonal processes. If there are problems, local, state, regional, or national, Americans prefer to believe that the source of the problems is outside the immediate society with which they identify themselves. Further, they prefer the source to be concrete, tangible, recognizable. Thus, if the source of all problems, the cause of a crisis, immediate or imminent, can be identified as an individual or a group of people, then its solution is simple: Remove the person or the group and the problem will subside.

McCarthy, with intuitive cleverness, was plucking a dark thread which runs through American history when he appealed to the emotion of fear and offered the State Department (and by implication the Democratic party) as the target for that fear. On that dark thread—which might be identified as the conspiratorial theory of history—dangled witches, Indians, chancellors of the exchequer, King George, the Federalists, John Quincy Adams, slaveowners, carpetbaggers, Abraham Lincoln, gold-money men, Kaiser Wilhelm, Reds, Catholics, Jews, and Adolf Hitler. All at one time or another had been portrayed as the simple and single causes for crisis or catastrophe; their elimination was supposed to have ushered in the beginning of a bright, new day.

Equally troubling in the hearings of the Tydings Committee was that very delicate legal and philosophical issues were raised in their course. With so many of McCarthy's charges beyond refutation unless countered with evidence, and with so much of that evidence closed in the files of the State Department, the omnipresent problems of a free and democratic society operating in the harsh and real world were bound to arise. At what point does national security take precedence over the public's right to know? How is it possible to differentiate between fact and opinion in a security clearance dossier? What is fact and what is opinion? At what point does a man depart from his party, or his President, for the public weal? To whom does one owe his greatest allegiance, to the least of society's members, to friends and compatriots, to party, to nation, to the brotherhood of man, to conscience, or to "truth" ? These questions are disturbing ones to which there are no final answers, but only tentative solutions arrived at for the tenuous moment, to be agonized over by men who realize their own limitations and the ambiguity of what Andre Malraux called the human condition.

McCarthy's great but ignoble contribution to the history of congressional investigations, once and future, was his ability to personify events, to subordinate and vulgarize the questions which are at the heart of any investigation. That he had help has already been suggested, help from supporters, help from his opposition, help from "the flow of events," which often gave his case an uncanny "plausibility."

As the hearings progressed, and as McCarthy proved to be a master of creating a Mad Hatter and March Hare tea party atmosphere, Tydings appealed to Truman to allow the committee to examine the files. When Truman agreed, McCarthy promptly veered from his argument that the files would support his case to the argument that the files had been altered to support those he had been accusing. What gave McCarthy's argument a plausible underpinning was the fact that his charges could have been true. Certainly enough time had passed for it to happen. But further, the members of the subcommittee, pulling apart along party lines, were engaging in some of the most bitter controversy that had ever marked a congressional investigation. As a lone voice crying out in the wilderness, McCarthy might have been rightly suspect, but with strong, partisan support he was given the aura of a prophet and a truthsayer. When McCarthy, the man, the Republican, became a rallying-point, so, by extension, did his pathetically reasoned, pathetically documented, scattered charges.

Luck and chance, those two ingredients that Charles Pierce, one of the great contributors to the pragmatic philosophy, said should be calculated in the human process, proved prime ingredients in the process called McCarthyism. On July 14, 1950 the Tydings Subcommittee issued its majority report; it was an utter refutation of McCarthy and McCarthy's charges. The gist was that McCarthy had lied, that his charges were fabrications. Perhaps as damning as any issued in Senate history, the report was nonetheless parried by the counteraccusations of Republican supporters of McCarthy, most notably Senator William E. Jenner (Indiana) and Senator Homer Ferguson (Michigan). But the event that took most of the sting from the report was the Korean War. When, on June 25, 1950, the North Koreans invaded South Korea, the investigations of the McCarthy charges were no longer headline stories. And in July, when the majority report was forthcoming, it no longer had that immediate and dramatic effect that it would have had had not the Korean war swept away the "Communist issue" in the face of the "Communist confrontation."

III

In the long run, of course, nothing helped McCarthy more than the events in Korea, though they drove his name from the headlines for several months. Nothing could have been more generously calculated to prove McCarthy's charges, had he been allowed to write the script himself. After the first shock and the immediate rally behind Truman's actions, the war evolved into a dreary, dispiriting, limited, "no-win police action," a conflict that was seemingly so far removed from the American tradition that the very tradition itself was being sold out somewhere along the line. Perhaps that "somewhere along the line" was where McCarthy said it was—a point identified as the State Department, which was aided and abetted by those who "were soft on communism." Thus, the Communist issue became a political issue in the 1950 campaign. In the campaign, those who were "soft on communism" were often Democrats, coincidentally, Democrats who had opposed McCarthy.

McCarthy played a vigorous role in the later months of the 1950 senatorial campaigns. He now was on the main circuit, and he relished his role. In many ways he relied on the too familiar strategies of American politics: carry out a fighting campaign, leading the attack to the opponent; separate the candidate from his party when his party's record is clearly good; tie him to his party's record if the record is poor; use that particular brand of humor that relies on ridicule and denunciation for its effectiveness; reduce issues to a current crisis. Campaigns relying on those strategies which forge a reciprocity with the worst features of American public opinion practically insure that the election contest will never be what it has been hailed as in myth—an educational and rational process. McCarthy did not create the process, but he did exploit it with vigor and impudence, as he had done in every Senate hearing with which he was associated. And, perhaps more than any one man, as a veritable Dr. Samuel Johnson of the loaded sally, he added a new dimension to the political process, inspiring a whole new lexicon of terms which included parlor pinks, Communists, dupes, and fellow-travelers, Commiecrats, whitewash of communism, green light to communism, and soft on communism to name just a few.

Many of McCarthy's targets, and they were this, not simply opponents of the Republican party, had some reason to be surprised to find themselves active agents of the Communist conspiracy. One of the most improbable "international conspirators" was Millard E. Tydings. Tyding's credentials in aiding and abetting communism were, from McCarthy's point of view, impeccable. He had opposed McCarthy and had been the chief architect of the stinging majority report, so McCarthy went after Tydings, as he did Scott Lucas of Illinois and Brien McMahon of Connecticut, in the 1950 campaign.

Tydings, at first, appeared invulnerable, promising to be as much of a stonewall to McCarthy as he had been to Roosevelt. McCarthy's surface attack was forceful, but not overwhelming; he gave three major speeches outlining Tydings's attempts to protect traitors in the government, but Tydings's defenses appeared unassailable. He had four terms in the Senate behind him. He was a conservative Democrat from a state which supported both his position and his party. Tydings could have withstood the frontal attack, but the frontal attack was only a part of McCarthy's arsenal. Into the camp of Tydings's opponent, John Marshall Butler, a Baltimore lawyer, came McCarthy and his staff. They met with Butler, planned their strategy, and, later supplied Butler with funds, much of which went into a slick, well-orchestrated newspaper and radio campaign against Tydings.

Meantime, Tydings was purportedly going about with such friends as Earl Browder, leader of the American Communist party. This, of course, was not true, but McCarthy forces produced a composite photograph of Tydings and Browder, subtly altered to give the impression of the two men in deep and serious conversation.

When the election was over, Tydings was out; so was Scott Lucas; and so, it appeared, with few exceptions like McMahon of Connecticut, were all the Democrats that McCarthy had singled out for political death. As in the case of La Follette, jr., in Wisconsin, there were a number of complex issues which determined the general Democratic defeat in the 1950 elections. McCarthy and his cause were only a part. Yet, because McCarthy was able to translate the appearance of power into real and present political power, his role was perhaps the most crucial.

There was a noticeable, and understandable, swagger to McCarthy's gait after his victory. He reveled in apocalyptic terms, the language of Armeggedon. It was all surface, however, for in spite of the aggressive tone and the things that he did to people and said about them, and in spite of the fact that he would hit back and seek revenge, McCarthy never really seemed to hate anyone. Perhaps his hollowness was most revealed by the fact that in the most heated battles McCarthy never felt very deeply about his victories, his defeats, or his issues. He lived superficially, subordinated the tangled, complex plurality of problems and events to the kind of rhetoric which seems to focus on deep issues and complexities, but which, in fact, forms an almost impenetrable crust over these issues and complexities. That he had a talent for making the zany seem logical, the logical seem zany, is undeniable. McCarthy was a living metaphor of the humorous fear and the fearful humor that marks the works of Franz Kafka and Lewis Carroll.

The confusing contradictions of McCarthy continued after the defeat of Tydings. With power and vigor, he pursued his "enemies." Yet, now at one of the peaks of his power and influence, at a time when he elicited emotions that ranged from fear, at worst, to grudging respect, at best, when his was perhaps the dominant name in the mass media, when general approval for his activities was reflected in public opinion polls, McCarthy became the subject of yet another investigation—an investigation evolving out of the Maryland campaign. Tydings, though not conceding to McCarthy credit for his defeat, nonetheless questioned the methods used against him and filed a formal complaint.

On February 3, 1951, the Subcommittee on Privileges and Elections voted to hold public hearings on the campaign. For a time the subcommittee dealt with the issues in the Maryland campaign. Chaired by Guy M. Gillette (D.-Iowa), the subcommittee was a balanced, efficient group. In addition to Gillette, the other Democratic members were A. S. Monroney of Oklahoma and Thomas A. Hennings of Missouri. The Republicans were represented by Margaret Chase Smith of Maine, a critic of McCarthy, and Robert C. Hendrickson of New Jersey, a "sometimes" critic. The subcommittee focused its investigations on three major points—funding for the campaign, campaign materials, and unethical interference. Most of the principals in the campaign—with the exception of McCarthy himself—appeared before the subcommittee, whose hearings ended in April. The subcommittee, which had done such a commendable job of confining the issues and structuring the hearings, then began to wobble a bit. There was a long period of wrangle and delay over the report, a confusion in no small part due to the presence of McCarthy and the fact that the defeat of Tydings in the first place seemingly had its genesis in such a report. Also, at the same time the subcommittee was struggling with the problems of the report, the Republicans made McCarthy a member of the full Committee on Rules and Administration.

In spite of the hovering presence of McCarthy, the subcommittee report, once written, was, like the Tydings report, a scathing criticism of McCarthy and his "back street" methods of outside interference. The Rules Committee accepted the report and had it printed.

The report brought quick and varied responses. McCarthy, predictably, denounced it as the handiwork of politicians who would go to any length to "ignore or whitewash" communism in the government. An equally strong but opposite reaction came from Senator William Benton, a Democrat from Connecticut. While the report did an excellent job of condemning the unethical behavior of McCarthy, it contained, Benton charged, no specific recommendations of what should be done about "back street" politicians. Benton had a specific recommendation; he introduced a resolution in the Senate requesting that the Rules Committee conduct an investigation to determine whether McCarthy should be expelled from the Senate.

Immediate hell broke loose. McCarthy took the offensive and countered that he was the victim of a plot to conceal a plot. In short, he argued that Benton, a Democrat, was working with the Truman Administration to foil McCarthy's efforts to unravel the Communist conspiracy within the State Department. But fortunately for McCarthy's foes and critics, his greatest strengths and greatest weaknesses were inextricably intertwined. The problem of expulsion was complicated and vague; it was a process seldom resorted to in the history of the Senate. In fact, though there had been earlier proceedings, the Senate had never actually expelled anyone. Had he confined himself to a rather general attack, McCarthy could have carried the day. The Subcommittee on Privileges and Elections had been through a bruising battle with McCarthy over the Maryland campaign and no one, then, would be particularly anxious to pick up the gauntlet again—at least so soon. Further, Benton hoped to arouse more public chastisement of McCarthy, rather than entertaining any real hope that his resolution would pass.

For McCarthy, however, there were no fine points of departure. He continued to defend himself, and in the process he managed to offend the sensibilities of Senate Majority Leader Ernest W. McFarland, Democrat of Arizona, and impugn the honor of the two Republican members of the subcommittee who had conducted the Maryland hearings, Senators Smith and Hendrickson. In short, McCarthy unwittingly forged a bipartisan opposition out of his own personal pride and hurt feelings. Further, he assured himself of the subcommittee hearing by attacking still another member of the subcommittee, Senator Tom Henning, in a letter on September 18, 1951, in which he questioned Henning's integrity, associations (pro-Communist), and general qualifications for a place on the subcommittee. The press received the letter before Hennings did.

The senator from Missouri was quietly outraged. He responded to McCarthy's charges in a Senate speech, ably arguing that McCarthy's attacks were affronts not just to individual senators, but the Senate itself. Caught up in the challenge to their integrity, the subcommittee, initially reluctant to cross swords with McCarthy, decided to pursue Benton's resolution. On September 28, 1951 Benton began his testimony. Benton's charges were strong ones; he accused the Wisconsin senator of lying, character assassination, deception, and deceit. Further, said Benton, McCarthy had used the Senate as a hiding place, confining any specific charges he had ever made to the Senate floor, resorting to general inferences when off the floor. Benton cited examples which he said showed conduct unbecoming a member of the Senate.

McCarthy did not stand idly by to wait his turn in the subcommittee arena. As the subcommittee staff moved slowly in its investigation of Benton's charges, McCarthy moved rapidly, using the public forum to advance his usual thesis—that the subcommittee was conducting not an investigation, but a smear campaign against a senator whose only motive for action was his desire to fight communism and Communist subversion. Now and then he would depart from this rather lofty position to remind the subcommittee of what happened to Tydings, and his barrage was not without effect. The heat of righteous indignation within the subcommittee was cooling a bit, perhaps as some members did indeed remember what had happened to Tydings. In theory, congressional investigations proceed in atmospheres of calm, reason, detachment, and impartiality toward their "informing function." In practice they proceed in the buffeting winds of fears and fancies, the ethnic, religious, and political pressures that mark a society at a particular time. Too often they reflect opinion rather than present information necessary for the legislative process. Too often they are clearly vulnerable to partisan exploitation.

The subcommittee, which had started so strong, began to show restraint. Republicans began to have partisan doubts and political second thoughts, particularly as the investigation moved into the election year of 1952. McCarthy's fortunes took an upswing in April 1952 when following the death of Senator Kenneth Wherry, the Republicans changed committee assignments. McCarthy left the Rules Committee, replaced by Senator Herman Welker, a McCarthy supporter. When Welker replaced Margaret Chase Smith on the subcommittee, it appeared that the Benton charges were destined to be killed.

That they did not die is testimony that partisan politics is a negotiable street. Political pressures forced both McCarthy and Benton farther afield from their initial positions than either cared to go. Though McCarthy, always so visible and vocal, seemed to exploit every situation, he was in truth, exploited by men who saw in him the expression of their extreme views while at the same time retaining their own images as "moderates."

On April 10, 1952 McCarthy, who had hoped to grind the Benton charges to a halt, found himself introducing a resolution asking for an investigation into Benton's conduct as a member of the Senate. In July McCarthy brought his charges against Benton before the Subcommittee on Privileges and Election. Like Benton, McCarthy made serious charges, though, unlike Benton, he presented no point-by-point particulars. He accused Benton of following the Communist party line throughout his career and documented his case less with specific items than colorful, cascading terms.

With the subcommittee investigating both senators, the events set in motion by Benton's resolution, which had become complicated over time, became further complicated with a change in the membership of the subcommittee. The chairmanship of the subcommittee went from Senator Guy Gillette to Senator Tom Hennings. To further complicate matters, by the time the subcommittee had prepared its report, Benton had been defeated in the 1952 elections (by McCarthy's hand, many felt) and McCarthy, victorious in Wisconsin, was at the height of his power.

As happened with any investigation that involved McCarthy, the Benton-McCarthy investigations changed directions, issues, and personalities so many times that the initial reasons for the investigations seemed to have gotten lost. McCarthy proved a formidable figure, at times unbelievably reckless, utterly contemptuous of the subtle and balanced rights and powers that had evolved as the basis for congressional investigations, yet always adroit at forcing the opposition onto the defensive, pressuring witnesses and subcommittee members to be cautious and often tempted to settle on tangential rather than central issues. At one point both Benton and he were invited to appear before the subcommittee. Benton appeared; McCarthy declined the invitation. That the invitation was, ostensibly, politely offered and just as politely declined, did not mask the fact that the invitation was a summons which McCarthy ignored. The authority to summon witnesses, clearly the authority of the subcommittee, was deliberately flaunted, causing the subcommittee to consider a subpoena for McCarthy.

Though the lines of procedure and authority were clearly outlined, the members of the subcommittee hesitated to issue McCarthy a subpoena, fearing that he would not respond to it. Uncertain of the outcome of that kind of fight, the subcommittee decided against a subpoena. In forcing doubt and hesitation into the process of the subcommittee, McCarthy was issuing a serious challenge, not only to that particular subcommittee, but to the congressional investigative process itself. The strongly worded reports that McCarthy received and the Senate's ultimate censure of him notwithstanding, McCarthy forced political pressures and partisan ill-will onto the congressional investigations and into the public arena. In so doing, the mark he left long outlived the man.

The Benton-McCarthy investigation was the best example of his worst efforts. The legislative process, of which congressional investigations were to be an integral, supplemental part, is supposed to reflect the struggle to extract right principles and practices from the unwieldy and contradictory realm of ideas and meanings. As the investigations of McCarthy and Benton proceeded, the confusions over issues and principles forced a narrowing of the investigation from the issues of conduct and ethics, loyalty and freedom, to the question of McCarthy and Benton's finances. The switch from ideas to "things" and personalities, which seems, of course, easier to weigh and measure and which can give the illusion of coping with hard problems, has probably affected all subsequent hearings and investigations.

The subcommittee's report on January 2, 1953, while unfavorable to

McCarthy, was not as much a challenge to McCarthy as to the Senate. It stated that McCarthy had "deliberately set out to thwart any investigation of him by obscuring the real issue and the responsibility of the Subcommittee by charges of lack of jurisdiction, smear, and communist-inspired persecution." Further, the report posed a series of questions about McCarthy's finances, particularly about whether he was misusing money collected to finance the fight against communism. Though the report raised serious questions about McCarthy's activities, it never quite answered any of the questions or suggested recommendations. In short, it was a challenge to the Senate to confront the man and the issues.

The Senate declined, at least for a long moment, to take on Senator McCarthy. Perhaps this was understandable. McCarthy, in 1953, had tremendous power, a power that went beyond his victory in Wisconsin, his credit for Benton's defeat, the support for his anti-Communist crusade, and the Republican victory in the election. McCarthy had great power because people thought he had great power; and one of the foremost believers in the power of McCarthy was McCarthy. He dismissed the subcommittee report as further evidence of smear tactics and never seriously considered a Senate challenge.

McCarthy probably should have been more worried about his future. For nearly two years he had talked about communism in high places in the government, focusing his attack on the Democratic Administration which harbored and protected Communists. On this single issue he had built his reputation. Theoretically, the Republican victory in 1952 should have ended McCarthy's fears—and thus his career as a Communist fighter. Theoretically, the Republicans, once in power, had only to remove the Communists who had been located and identified by McCarthy, leaving him free of his awful burden. But McCarthy was, of course, not about to be freed of his burden. In 1951 McCarthy initiated an attack on General George C. Marshall, in which he accused Marshall of being part of an immense, worldwide web of conspiracy. Such a conspiracy had, by definition, to transcend particular circumstances, and particular parties. McCarthy clearly saw the need to pursue his battle even through the Republican years.

While conceding that McCarthy had been useful, or at least necessary in the Democratic years, Republicans generally anticipated that he would take a back seat after 1952. There was relief when, in early 1953, McCarthy became chairman of the Senate Committee on Government Operations and chairman of the committee's Permanent Investigations' Subcommittee. But the relief was short-lived. McCarthy chose to interpret "Permanent Investigations" to mean permanent investigations of communism. "McCarthy to Share Red Investigations," the *New York Times* reported on January 8. Perhaps the debatable part of the heading was the word "share," for what McCarthy meant by share was that the Eisenhower Administration would share the same treatment to which the Truman Administration had so wearily become accustomed. From 1953 to 1954 McCarthy's subcommittee, by its own account, undertook 445 preliminary hearings and 157 investigations. Out of this number came 17 public hearings. Few areas of the government escaped McCarthy's scrutiny, though his primary focus continued to be the State Department.

Busy as he was with his own investigations, McCarthy took time to share his thoughts with Eisenhower on certain ambassadorial appointments. In particular, McCarthy commented on Eisenhower's nomination of Charles E. ("Chip") Bohlen as ambassador to the Soviet Union. McCarthy, however, was not the only Republican with doubts about Bohlen, who had the taint of Yalta, where he had served as Roosevelt's interpreter. Anticipating some hard moments in the Senate's confirmation of Bohlen, Eisenhower persuaded Senator Taft to use his considerable talents on Bohlen's behalf. In a speech against Bohlen, McCarthy connected him with the same international conspiracy that had ensnared General Marshall. He generously forgave Secretary of State John Foster Dulles for supporting Bohlen, excusing Dulles for being too busy with the new job to understand Bohlen's record. "We want no part of this 'chip' off the old block of Yalta," he said.

Bohlen's nomination was confirmed, despite McCarthy's efforts, in no small measure due to Taft's able, if not enthusiastic, support. There was notable irony in seeing Taft, who had so often encouraged McCarthy when it seemed expedient to do so, on the other side of McCarthy charges. McCarthy, with his sense of the ridiculous, quite understood Taft and was aware of his discomfort.

McCarthy, however, was not successful in stopping Bohlen, nor was he ever successful in any of his efforts, if by that one means that he brought any matter into a conclusion consistent with professed aims. McCarthy's kind of success depended on his ability to seize an issue, drain it of its publicity value, saturate it with doubt and confusion, and then move on to another issue.

As chairman of the Permanent Investigations Subcommittee McCarthy was a master of the quick summons, calling to his hearing room at his caprice and convenience anyone he wanted. Most came, although many had but the barest notice that they were to be witnesses at all. McCarthy's high-handed, contemptuous handling of witnesses was to cast a long shadow over the already tenuous area of congressional authority and individual rights.

Directionless, the McCarthy investigations passed over the lines separating the traditional powers of government. Once trespassed, once merged, the lines became hard to draw again, half-hidden as they were behind a professed specific issue—Communists in the government.

The deep shading of lines of separation began early in McCarthy's career as an investigator. In February 1953, he turned considerable attention to the State Department by his investigation of "The Voice of America." Spawned by the State Department, itself filled with Communists and Communist sympathizers, reasoned McCarthy, it was natural to assume the Voice was a haven for fellow Communists. An operation that conjured suspicions without anything specific ever emerging to confirm them, the Voice had been questioned by the Eisenhower Administration, as well. On the other hand, Senator Bourke B. Hickenlooper, a Republican from Iowa, who had often supported McCarthy, gave the Voice generally favorable support at the very time McCarthy was investigating the agency.

With the power of pressure as opposed to authority, McCarthy forced the State Department to direct employees of the Voice to cooperate fully with subcommittee investigators. The result was predictable—a parade of witnesses, some of whom sincerely believing the Voice was pro-Communist, others who had petty grievances to settle against superiors, and some who were quite aware of what the subcommittee designated as Communist. As a result, McCarthy persuaded the State Department to forbid the Voice from quoting Communists under any circumstances.

Like so many of the McCarthy investigations the Voice investigation ended with a whimper. Even the most ardent McCarthy supporter would have been pressed to explain how the investigation furthered the legislative process or informed the public. The investigations merely evaporated without conclusion. What remained, though perhaps more subtly hidden than even the purpose of the investigation, was the fact that the separation between the Executive and Legislative branches of government had been seriously, albeit almost imperceptibly, narrowed.

McCarthy's next investigation was of the State Department's overseas information centers, another oblique attack on the State Department itself. This investigation featured the two men who were most closely associated with the worst of McCarthy's times, Roy M. Cohn, chief counsel for the subcommittee, and G. David Schine, a friend of Cohn and a consultant for the subcommittee. McCarthy gave considerable attention to the State Department's 150 overseas libraries, most of which, he felt, contained not Communists, but large numbers of Communist books. The investigation, like a Greek mask, had both elements of farce and overtones of tragedy.

The comic relief for the public evolved from the tour of overseas centers taken by Cohn and Schine in April 1953. According to Cohn the hours were ample—forty in Paris, sixteen in Bonn, nineteen in Frankfort. Schine thought the trip interesting and purposeful, promising material for future hearings. The press, with venomous humor, variously categorized the touring twosome as the quiz kids, junketeering gumshoes, and the Rover boys abroad. Although Cohn gave the tour a low key, explaining it as an inspection and question junket, there was a tendency to portray Cohn and Schine as tearing through information libraries, identifying Communist literature for future burning. This was exaggeration, but McCarthy, who built a career on exaggeration, often elicited counter-exaggeration from frustrated critics. There was, however, some truth to the book-burning charge.

In his book *McCarthy*, Cohn, in retrospect, makes a "come-let-us-reason-together" argument for the investigation, pointing out the concern President Eisenhower had about the purpose of the information centers. Cohn suggests the subsequent investigations proceeded along parallel lines with Eisenhower's attempt to define the delicate balance between free expression of ideas and the purpose of the information centers as agencies disseminating materials generally favorable to the United States, if sometimes critical. But the McCarthy investigations hardly seemed concerned with this delicate balance.

McCarthy brought before the subcommittee a number of Communist writers. Under his instigation the State Department sent out secret directives to its information centers which directed hundreds of books by some forty authors banned. In some centers the books were burned by overzealous employees, prompting a frustrated Eisenhower to denounce book-burners. Yet, for the moment, McCarthy, not Eisenhower, seemed to have the say over the policies and practices of that facet of the State Department.

More menacing were the premises upon which McCarthy defined a Communist author. Not at all awed by the reaction to his attacks, McCarthy, as a member of the Senate Appropriations Committee in 1954, revealed he was quite as capable of being a one-man supreme court for ideas and definitions as he was at directing the Executive branch. In a hearing on the State Department budget, he questioned Dr. James B. Conant, former president of Harvard University and then U. S. High Commissioner for Germany, about Conant's views on Communist books. Conant's views were qualified. He tried to determine definitions for a Communist author and what was meant by a Communist point of view, but McCarthy was not troubled by nuances and fine points of view. "The Communist is under Communist Party discipline, and the point of view is furthering the Communist conspiracy," said McCarthy. Further on, he defined a Communist author as "either a man who has been proved to be a Communist, or a man who says 'I won't tell, because if I told the truth I might to go jail!' " Legal and philosophical definitions, and even the Bill of Rights, had little place in McCarthy's crusade against communism.

Earlier, in the summer of 1953, McCarthy had announced proposed investigations of the military, the CIA, and the Atomic Energy Commission. McCarthy found a starting place by focusing on subversion and espionage in defense plants and among civilian workers in the Army Signal Corps at Fort Monmouth. In his first foray against the army, it seemed McCarthy had once more gained the high ground. In the course of the hearings to determine the extent of current espionage in the Signal Corps, McCarthy again demonstrated his ability to weave fact and fantasy, past history and present charges, suspicion and fear, into power ploys. Though the investigations and hearings netted little tangible evidence of a vast conspiracy, they gained for McCarthy further confidence in his ability to make institutions quail before him, since his investigations had prompted the suspension of a number of security risks.

The Monmouth investigations would trail over into the 1954 Army-McCarthy confrontation and would aid in the beginning of his decline; yet, there seemed, through 1953 into early 1954, to be little evidence that McCarthy would not continue on his unrelenting way. Although McCarthy had formidable critics—Senators Margaret Chase Smith, J. William Fulbright, William Benton, Herbert Lehman and Presidents Truman and Eisenhower, to name a few, he generally proved to be a frustrating opponent. His critics tried disdain, public lectures on his "fear and denunciation" approach to politics, and lofty exhortations of public censure of the man and the method. But the criticism that might have weakened any other senator glanced off McCarthy. Further, the criticism did not begin to deal with the deep and complicated fears and frustrations that had created McCarthy and "McCarthyism," and he was its most important and sustaining part. Proving his strength a strength built on myth denied the fact that myth is the greatest strength.

By 1954 McCarthy was at the height of his success. In actuality as well as mythology, the sources of greatest success carry with them the seeds of defeat. The circumstances which brought McCarthy to bay were as complicated and mysterious as those which had elevated him in the first place. McCarthy, as surprised as anyone at his rise to power, was equally surprised by his decline (which he never quite accepted).

Still on the trail of subversive elements in the Fort Monmouth operation, McCarthy's investigation brought him into opposition with Secretary of the Army Robert T. Stevens. This did not bother McCarthy, for he had confronted departmental secretaries before. He had pushed and they had given ground. But McCarthy pushed Stevens harder, perhaps harder than even he realized. The reason was that he felt that his Fort Monmouth investigations would be his best undertaking, promising to net him, at long last, evidence for his Communist conspiracy thesis. McCarthy's challenges to Stevens brought him closer to a direct confrontation than he seemed to realize. When John G. Adams, army counsel, became a liaison man between the Administration and Republican leaders, the Republican leaders and the Republican party began to stiffen against McCarthy for the first time in any concerted effort. McCarthy noticed this subtle change for the very understandable reason that Stevens continued a wavering course in his attempt to defend the army, yet he was careful not to give credence to McCarthy's thesis that the army, like the State Department, coddled Communists.

McCarthy, meantime, moved his investigation into wider areas, and his efforts netted him a "subversive" at long last, Captain Irving Peress, an army dentist. Peress had once refused to answer a questionnaire about possible subversive affiliations, basing his refusal on constitutional grounds. Here was a splendid example of McCarthy's "I won't tell, because if I told the truth I might go to jail" type of Communist. The army decided on an expedient answer to the question of Peress, issuing him an honorable discharge. Before the discharge came, McCarthy brought Peress before his subcommittee. The trail from Peress led, so McCarthy deduced, to his commanding officer, Brigadier General Ralph Zwicker.

General Zwicker was summoned before the subcommittee and was subjected to the usual bruising, aggressive questioning and accusation that McCarthy gave witnesses as a matter of routine. The difference was that this was a high-ranking army officer. While McCarthy might have considered his tactics routine, to the President (and former General) Eisenhower, McCarthy's open contempt for Zwicker revealed implicit contempt for Eisenhower himself. Eisenhower's ire, though not publicly displayed, contributed to the army's growing resistance to McCarthy.

While McCarthy had busied himself with the trail of subversives leading into the army, he had failed to notice or worry much about a trail from the army back to him, a trail around which the battlelines would be drawn. The trail was blazed by David Schine and, as the army later charged, Roy Cohn. Schine was drafted into the army in July 1953. Coincidental with his induction, so the army would later charge, Cohn attempted to secure preferential treatment for the famous private. He had, indeed, seemingly been successful in netting preferential treatment before, but Cohn, the army would charge, attempted to intimidate the service with the threat of continued investigations from the subcommittee.

With Stevens stiffening as he perceived Eisenhower's impatience with

McCarthy, the army issued a counter-challenge to McCarthy, drawing up a thirty-four-page report to chronicle its charges against McCarthy, Cohn, and Francis P. Carr, subcommittee staff director. When the charges became public, McCarthy tried to dispel any sympathies with the military, still popular despite divided emotions over the Korean conflict, by accusing the army of the old always effective charge of attempting to thwart his investigation of communism. The subcommittee made formal charges against Secretary of the Army Stevens, army counsel John G. Adams, and Assistant Defense Secretary H. Struve Hensel.

The charges and counter-charges, tangled as they already were, were further complicated by the question of whether the chairman of the subcommittee and his staff were witnesses or interrogators, accused or accusers. The subcommittee investigating the subcommittee forced changes in procedure. McCarthy stepped aside temporarily as chairman, with Senator Karl E. Mundt, a South Dakota Democrat, as acting chairman.

The hearings began on April 22, 1954, and continued until June 17, 1954. The thirty-five days of hearings were televised, and the drama drew an audience estimated at times to be twenty million people. The issues, both the narrow ones of interference and obstruction of purpose of which each side accused the other, and the larger issues of national security, Communist conspiracy, and democratic rights, were often subordinated to the personalities of the principals. In the center of the hearings were Special Army Counsel Joseph H. Welch and Special Subcommittee Counsel Ray H. Jenkins. Well-known senators and high-ranking army officers had special moments in the spotlight and featured, too, were Cohn and Adams. But the dominant figure was McCarthy. His role in the hearings was somewhat confusing—accused, accuser, and cross-examiner—but there was no confusion about the fact that he intended to conduct the hearings as he had in the past.

He frequently crossed swords with the minority Democrats, Senators John L. McClellan of Arkansas, Henry M. Jackson of Washington, and W. Stuart Symington of Missouri. Particularly heated were the exchanges with Symington, who finally decided that with McCarthy, one had better forget the rules—another example of McCarthy's use of extremes forcing more thoughtful men to retaliate in like manner.

Another of McCarthy's antagonists in the investigations was one who never appeared at the hearings—President Eisenhower. Trying to stay above direct conflict with McCarthy, Eisenhower was nonetheless pulled into McCarthy's realm. He was exasperated by McCarthy's attempts to gain the details behind the army's "list of particulars" from John Adams, army counsel, a list supposedly dictated by Sherman Adams, Eisenhower's chief of staff. In attempting to check McCarthy, the President extended the exercise of Executive privilege farther than he may have wished, directing that no testimonies on discussions and confidences within the Executive department be permitted in the hearings. The issue never became a central issue, yet, again, it was a telling example of how the exaggerations of McCarthy begot dangerous exaggerations of governmental powers. McCarthy, in the course of his "investigations," forced both Presidents Truman and Eisenhower farther behind the defensive lines of national security and

Executive privilege than anyone quite realized. (Thus, McCarthy forced an ironic foreshadowing of the future trials, tribulations, and defenses of the then Vice President Nixon.)

Important as the charges were, both for the moment and for the course of McCarthy's case, the most dramatic (and remembered) confrontation of the hearing involved McCarthy and Special Counsel Welch. It was the high-point of the hearings and, at least in retrospect, marked the abrupt decline for McCarthy. In the course of Welch's cross-examination of Roy Cohn, McCarthy interrupted, and Senator Mundt asked him if he had a point of order. Said McCarthy, "Not exactly, Mr. Chairman, but in view of Mr. Welch's request that the information be given once we know of anyone who might be performing any work for the Communist party, I think we should tell him that he has in his law firm a young man named [Frederick G.] Fisher whom he recommended, incidentally, to do work on this committee, who has been for a number of years a member of an organization which was named, oh, years and years, as the legal bulwark of the Communist Party, an organization which always swings to the defense of anyone who dares expose Communists." McCarthy's attack on Fisher invoked the famous "Have you no sense of decency?" rebuke from Welch. McCarthy sat bemused in the face of Welch's remarks.

Things had gone well for McCarthy for a long time, but now the center began falling apart. On March 9, 1953, while McCarthy was moving into the great Army-McCarthy conflict, Senator Ralph Flanders–(R–Vermont), gave a speech sharply denouncing McCarthy and "McCarthyism." The speech signaled a gathering of forces from without, a gathering that paralleled the subcommittee hearings. Events now seemed to break nearly as quickly against him as they had for him. On July 11, 1954 Flanders again took up the cudgels, asking that the Senate remove McCarthy from his committee and subcommittee chairmanships permanently, unless he satisfactorily answered questions raised against him in the course of the Benton controversy. After Senator William F. Knowland–(R–California), the Senate majority leader, raised objections, Flanders changed direction. In a speech on June 30, 1954 Flanders asked that McCarthy's conduct as a member of the Senate be "hereby condemned."

Following Flanders's lead, the Senate referred this and other resolutions to the Select Committee to Study Censor Charges. Hearings were held from August 31 to September 13 and focused on two issues: McCarthy's contempt of the Senate, and his abuse of the army, in particular his abrasive personal attack on General Ralph W. Zwicker.

The charges against McCarthy posed a dilemma for the Senate: how to draw the fine distinction between the abuse of senatorial power, while maintaining a clear-cut position on the investigative power of the Senate. The committee had less trouble with McCarthy's abuse of General Zwicker; it concluded that his conduct was "reprehensible" and grounds for condemnation of McCarthy. Also recommended was condemnation for his refusal to appear before the Subcommittee on Privileges and Elections in 1952. McCarthy reacted by doing precisely what he had done in the past —attack. "When the Watkins committee announced its recommendations, the Communists made no attempt to conceal their joy," said McCarthy in one of his most vituperative speeches. McCarthy, trying once more to conjure up fearful spirits from the depths, called the committee the "unwitting handmaiden" of communism. This time, however, it was to no avail. The spirits did not come. On December 2, 1954 the Senate, by a vote of 67 to 22, censured him.

McCarthy did not exactly go gentle into that good night, nor did he exactly quail before the censure. He continued, very nearly to the end, to say what he had always said and in much the same manner. It was just that no one seemed to hear anymore. Senator McCarthy died on May 2, 1957 at the age of 49.

IV

McCarthy did not fade into oblivion simply because of Joseph Welch's melodramatics, from his exposure to the nation on television, from the Senate's reaction to his assault on the Select Committee, or even because of the Senate's censure—though these were all contributing forces. McCarthy was a unique man, with unusual talents, but he was also an embodiment of power because he exemplified the fears, doubts, and particular conspiracy theories of the period following World War II, when certain events appeared to bear out the validity of these fears, doubts, and theories. In 1948 there seemed to be a noticeable pattern and direction to events. The Wallace campaign was an indication of the direction in which the currents of fear were moving; they were moving into politics.

Wallace's 1948 campaign was a minor version and a foreshadowing of the impact of the Communist issue in national politics on the two major parties. Some of the fears of communism were real; some were assumed for their obvious political potential; both parties contributed to the rise of the specter of conspiracy. In unleashing the furies on the third party, Democrats and Republicans would pay long-range consequences for short-term benefits. McCarthy, partly by chance, was both a creation and perpetuator of the politics of the "Communist issue." He helped enlarge its dimensions by making it a part of Senate investigations. The Korean War was the larger conveyor for "Communist issue" politics. It was the visible evidence and the symbol of the frustrations that McCarthy so ably exploited. McCarthy's power years paralleled the Korean War. When the visible proof ended in 1953, the frustrations and passions, the basis of McCarthy's strength, subsided, at least for the moment and McCarthy, too, subsided.

But McCarthy left his imprint on events. His shade, however dim, still stalks Senate investigations. One of his legacies was subtle, but very real. There were so many bewildering investigations and hearings associated with him (though there was only one investigation for McCarthy, the investigation of communism) that the words hearings and investigations were used so often and so interchangeably that both lost their meaning. "McCarthyism," a thoughtful summation of the maze of hearings and investigations at the time, also became, through overuse, a word that implied much but explained little.

McCarthy left his mark on Senate investigative processes in other ways—in the elevation of personalities over issues, the exaggerations which forced the institutions into frustrated counterexaggerations, and the consequential imbalance of the checks and balances and separations of government departments. Last of all, he forced the worst features of public opinion to prevail upon the legislative process, confusing public opinion so thoroughly with the public's right to be informed that the lines have yet to be clearly reestablished.

BIBLIOGRAPHY

Agar, Herbert. *The Price of Power: America since 1945.* Chicago, 1957.

Anderson, Jack and May, Ronald B. *McCarthy: The Man, the Senator, and the "Ism."* Boston, 1952.

Barth, Alan. *Government by Investigation.* New York, 1955.

Bell, Daniel, ed. *The Radical Right.* Garden City, 1963.

Buckley, William F., jr., and Bozell, L. Brent. *McCarthy and his Enemies: The Fight for America.* Chicago, 1954.

Caridi, Ronald J. *The Korean War and American Politics: The Republican Party as a Case Study.* Philadelphia, 1968.

Caughey, John W. *In Clear and Present Danger: The Crucial State of Our Freedom.* Chicago, 1958.

Cohn, Roy. *McCarthy.* New York, 1968.

Commager, Henry S. *Freedom, Loyalty, and Dissent.* New York, 1954.

Eisenhower, Dwight D. *The White House Years: Mandate for Change, 1953–1956.* Garden City, 1963.

Fenton, John. *In Your Opinion.* Boston, 1960.

Goldman, Eric F. *The Crucial Decade—And After: America, 1945–1960.* New York, 1961.

Griffith, Robert. *The Politics of Fear: Joseph R. McCarthy and the Senate.* Lexington, 1970.

Harper, Alan D. *The Politics of Loyalty: The White House and the Communist Issue, 1946–1952.* New York, 1969.

Kemper, Donald J. *Decade of Fear: Senator Hennings and Civil Liberties.* Columbia, Mo., 1965.

Latham, Earl. *The Communist Controversy in Washington: From the New Deal to McCarthy.* Cambridge, Mass., 1966.

Lattimore, Owen. *Ordeal by Slander.* Boston, 1950.

McCarthy, Joseph R. *McCarthyism: The Fight for America.* New York, 1952.

Merson, Martin. *The Private Diary of a Public Servant.* New York, 1955.

O'Brian, John Lord. *National Security and Individual Freedom.* Cambridge, Mass., 1955.

Patterson, James T. *Mr. Republican: A Biography of Robert A. Taft.* Boston, 1972.

Phillips, Cabel. *The Truman Presidency: The History of a Triumphant Succession.* New York, 1966.

Potter, Charles E. *Days of Shame.* New York, 1965.

Reeves, Thomas C. *Freedom and the Foundation: The Fund for the Republic in the Era of McCarthyism.* New York, 1969.

Rogin, Michael P. *The Intellectuals and McCarthy.* Cambridge, Mass., 1967.

Rovere, Richard. *Senator Joe McCarthy.* New York, 1959.

Schmidt, Karl A. *Henry A. Wallace: Quixotic Crusade, 1948.* Syracuse, 1960.

Straight, Michael. *Trial by Television.* Boston, 1954.

Taylor, Telford. *Grand Inquest: The Story of Congressional Investigations.* New York, 1955.

Westerfield, Bradford H. *Foreign Policy and Party Politics.* New Haven, 1955.

PERTINENT DOCUMENTS

Speech of Joseph McCarthy, Wheeling, West Virginia, February 9, 1950

Joseph McCarthy to President Harry Truman, February 11, 1950

Speech of Joseph McCarthy, February 20, 1950

Opening Remarks of Joseph McCarthy before "Tydings Committee," March 8, 1950

Joseph McCarthy's Charges against Owen Lattimore, March 1950

Reaction of President Harry Truman to Loyalty Investigation, "News Conference at Key West," March 30, 1950

"Declaration of Conscience" by Senator Margaret Chase Smith and Statement of Seven Senators, June 1, 1950

New York Times Report of Tydings's Investigating Committee Report and Senator McCarthy's Reply, July 18, 1950

Speech of Joseph McCarthy Attacking George C. Marshall, June 14, 1951

Speech by William Benton Calling for Investigation of McCarthy, August 6, 1951

Newsweek Article on McCarthy, August 20, 1951

Report on Investigation of Senator McCarthy

New York Times Report, January 8, 1953

Speech of Joseph McCarthy Attacking Charles Bohlen, March 25, 1953

Report on Voice of America Controversy, January 25, 1954

Testimony of Brigadier General Ralph W. Zwicker, February 18, 1954

Speech of Senator Ralph Flanders, March 9, 1954

Minutes of Executive Session of Senate Permanent Subcommittee on Investigations, March 16, 1954

Testimony of Secretary of the Army Robert T. Stevens, April 22, 1954

Joseph McCarthy–Joseph H. Welch Exchange, June 9, 1954

Opening of Watkins Committee to Study Censure Charges and McCarthy Statement, August 31, 1954

Statement by Senator Joseph McCarthy, November 10, 1954

Vote on Senate Resolution 301, December 2, 1954

The Watergate Inquiry
1973

THE WHITE HOUSE

WASHINGTON

August 9, 1974

Dear Mr. Secretary:

I hereby resign the Office of President of the United States.

Sincerely,

Richard Nixon

11.35 AM

HK

The Honorable Henry A. Kissinger
The Secretary of State
Washington, D. C. 20520

The Watergate Inquiry 1973

by Philip B. Kurland

Politics, as a practice, whatever its profession, had always been the systematic organization of hatreds.

The Education of Henry Adams

There is no novelty in a congressional inquisition to determine defalcations of power by Executive branch officials. This congressional power to oversee the various activities of government was termed its most important function by Woodrow Wilson, even before the turn of the century. It is safe to say, however, that despite its traditional origins, there never was an investigation like that which delved into the "Watergate affair." Its unique qualities are proved over and over again. That the two-year period covered by the Watergate investigation was one in which the Executive branch of the government of the United States was all but paralyzed in domestic affairs is irrefutable. And, that the investigation culminated in the resignation of the President certainly was a phenomenon unique in American constitutional history.

Unfortunately, it may also be said that in many ways the Watergate investigation was not unlike others that preceded it because, if the evils exposed were terminated, reform was not effected and all of the relevant facts did not come out. In fact, some pertinent information will continue to be obscured, perhaps forever, because of another event peculiar to Watergate—President Gerald Ford's premature pardon of President Richard M. Nixon for whatever crimes he committed or may have committed during his tenure of office. Indeed, as a result of Ford's action, the shadow of Watergate has not been lifted from the White House and may be seen there still.

The great American political tragedy—and "Watergate" was certainly that—was played not only over a period of years, but on a series of stages. For most, the main arena was in the mass media—newspapers, magazines, radio, and television—with the latter covering the congressional hearings both in the Senate and the House, saturating the public air waves while the newspapers and the magazines were uncovering important facts through superb investigative reporting. A second theater was afforded the investigation by the United States courts, with some emphasis on the courts in the District of Columbia, including the Supreme Court of the United States and other proceedings in New York and California. Two central features of the Watergate investigation were to be found in the hearings of the Senate Select Committee on Presidential Campaign Activities, better known as the "Ervin Committee" or the "Watergate Committee," and in the hearings of the House Judiciary Committee devoted to the impeachment question. The Senate Judiciary Committee also played an important part, and even the beleaguered "White House," not the building at 1600 Pennsylvania Avenue, but, the fourth branch of government neither established nor condoned by the American Constitution, produced major scenes for the enactment of the drama.

The events occurring in these different places were disorderly, overlapping each other, but always building toward a climax. To shift the metaphor, the theaters might better be designated as theaters of war, with battles occurring simultaneously, some waning while others waxed and some, of course, of greater significance than others. Eventually, all conflicts were resolved against the incumbent President, except that he secured the pardon that immunized him from all further legitimate demands that he, too, account for his stewardship.

If there was a hero of the Watergate era, it was Senator Sam J. Ervin, jr., whose commitment and that of his colleagues was, above all, to the primacy of the American Constitution and to the moral principles which it represents. Senator Ervin, mild-mannered but tough, folksy but sophisticated, was a country lawyer not afflicted with "Potomac fever," but with a knowledge of American constitutional law and Holy Writ that could be matched by few if any, in the Senate or out. Senator Ervin began his career in the Senate as a member of the special committee that censured Senator McCarthy and brought an end to the "McCarthy era." He concluded his career as chairman of the committee that, hopefully, will have brought an end to the equally infamous "Watergate era."

In a valedictory column George Will wrote: "Ervin has [always] been better than the Senate he ennobled . . . . Now, as he takes leave of us, let us praise this rare man whose fame, though great, does not match his great virtues. Washington will be diminished by his departure."

I

Although Watergate is a great American tragedy, it began as a farce that might have been written by George S. Kaufman and played by the Marx brothers. In fact, it was written by the higher echelons of the Committee to Re-elect the President (CREEP), persons who seemed totally without a sense of humor or a sense of morality. It was acted out by would-be James Bonds who were White House consultants and former CIA agents, including some who had earned their stripes in the Bay of Pigs fiasco during the Kennedy Administration.

The Watergate affair began on June 17, 1972, when five intruders were arrested in the offices of the Democratic National Committee in the Watergate complex, a plush office-condominium apartment building adjacent to the Kennedy Center, overlooking the Potomac. The five invaders were caught in the act, fully equipped with spy paraphernalia ranging from cameras to bugging devices. What they had hoped to discover in opened file drawers and behind ceiling tiles is an unanswered question. On arrest, they were appropriately charged with "second-degree" burglary.

They were caught because, having once placed a tape over a door lock to assure their entry and exit from the building, they replaced it after it had already been once removed by a building guard. The second time, the guard sent for the police. And the police, instead of arriving in formal array, came to the scene, purely by happenstance, in plain clothes and an unmarked vehicle, thus foiling the extensive early warning system that had been set up in true 007-fashion at the motel across the road.

Among those arrested at the scene, all of whom gave aliases, were James McCord, a security expert whose nineteen-year CIA career had ended in 1970, and Bernard L. Barker, leader of the burglary squad, who had previously worked under E. Howard Hunt when Hunt was a CIA official involved in the Bay of Pigs invasion, and for whom Barker was still working at the time of his arrest. The other three were Cuban refugees, two of whom had CIA attachments in their past, if not in their present. McCord was chief of security for the Republican National Committee as well as CREEP, and Hunt had been a consultant to Charles Colson, who was a special adviser to President Nixon. Hunt maintained an office safe in the White House itself, but the White House said that Hunt's connections there had been severed on March 29, two and one-half months earlier.

Perhaps if CREEP and its boss, former Attorney General John Mitchell, and the White House, through chief of staff H. R. Haldeman, had entered a public plea of confession and apology for the bungled burglary incident, the small fire would have been quickly doused. Instead, with a self-righteousness that was believed by very few, Mitchell announced on the day of the arrests that none of the accused was "operating on our behalf or with our consent." With equal disingenuousness, on June 22 President

Nixon volunteered a statement to the press—an unusual step for him—saying that the "White House had no involvement whatsoever." Then, however, the attempts to extricate the presidency and the Administration from liability for the illegality, stupidity, and foolishness of the break-in began in earnest. The effort was heroic, but it was doomed.

Police reporters on the *Washington Post*, Bob Woodward and Carl Bernstein, and political reporters on the national dailies and weeklies, such as Seymour M. Hersh of the *New York Times*, accepted the challenge implicit in the Administration's denials of complicity. The press, radio, and television, so long the whipping posts for the Nixon Administration, eagerly took up the chase and, like dogs at a hunt, eventually cornered their prey.

There was no doubt that members of the press desired to prove the guilt of the Administration, and it was only their obvious enthusiasm for their task that raised any questions about their credibility. Certainly the press had, from time to time, cried "Wolf!" without ever citing a sign of the beast. But this time they did uncover and publish facts concerning the machinations of CREEP officials with regard to huge campaign funds for which no accounting had been made, large cash payments delivered to one or more of the burglary defendants, about political espionage, agents, provocateurs, and sabotage, about huge contributions which had been followed by favorable governmental action, about campaign funds dispensed for the personal needs of or use by the President—and all were shown to be linked to CREEP and the White House staff, from the lowest to the highest.

The press served the American people well, although not all were pleased to receive the truth. Moreover, the disclosures of the press were not sufficient to convince everyone, especially since they were always met with official denials and denunciations. It remained for the Legislative and Judicial branches of the government to unearth and dispose of the quarry.

II

On January 11, 1973, when the Ninety-Third Congress was being organized, the Senate Democratic caucus voted in favor of a Watergate investigation. Senator Mike Mansfield, the majority leader, announced that Senator Sam J. Ervin, jr., of North Carolina, then chairman of the Senate Committee on Government Operations as well as the Senate Judiciary Subcommittees on Constitutional Rights and Separation of Powers, among others, would head that investigation. Earlier, in the waning days of the Ninety-Second Congress, Mansfield had requested Senators Ervin and Eastland to press for an investigation by a Judiciary subcommittee, saying: "The question is not political, it is constitutional. . . . At stake is the continued vitality of the electoral process."

On February 7, 1973, by a unanimous vote of 70 to 0, the Senate adopted a resolution for the appointment of a select committee to investigate charges of corruption in the 1972 elections. This vote had been preceded by a floor fight in which some Republicans called for equal representation on the committee by Republicans and Democrats and for an expansion of the investigation to include the 1968 campaign as well. The resolution, which had been well prepared by Ervin, made sure that the committee would have all the authority that could be conferred upon it by the Senate.

In addition to its chairman, the Senate committee had six members. Only Ervin was from the top echelon. Senators who had been or were likely to be presidential candidates did not qualify. Chairmen of the major committees and members of the majority and minority leadership were also not selected. The vice-chairman and senior Republican member was Howard Baker of Tennessee, boyish in appearance but well schooled in politics. The son of a long-time congressman and son-in-law of the redoubtable Senator Everett Dirksen, Baker's apparent openness concealed his inward nature as a tough and wily competitor, shrewd and manipulative. He was the only member of the committee capable of standing up to Ervin in the event of a conflict; but, in fact, they worked well together, complementing each other's talents.

The other Democrats chosen for the committee were Joseph M. Montoya from New Mexico, who brought few special credentials except his national origins; Herman E. Talmadge of Georgia, a scion of one of Georgia's political dynasties, tough-minded and sharp, but parochial; and Daniel K. Inouye of Hawaii, a Nisei, World War II hero, a middle-of-the-roader whose star could yet rise.

Edward J. Gurney and Lowell P. Weicker were the remaining Republican members chosen, and they afforded the greatest contrast of interests on the committee. Gurney from Florida, a rock-ribbed reactionary, was the President's man on the committee. Weicker was a liberal from Connecticut, wealthy and independent, who gave the appearance of a modern New-England abolitionist, "angry as a wasp," self-righteous as an Adams.

Professor Sam Dash of Georgetown Law School, a former district attorney for Philadelphia and author of a book on electronic surveillance, was appointed as the committee's counsel and staff director. As minority counsel Baker appointed a former campaign manager, Fred Thompson, who, though only thirty, had experience as a United States attorney specializing in the prosecution of federal bank robbers and illicit whiskey distillers.

The committee was not politically partisan. Each party had named senators representing a diversity of interests and viewpoints, and the committee, if anything, tilted more to right-wing elements than to the Left. Nor could members of the committee be considered witch-hunters. None of the committee members had ever been guilty of abuses of the investigatory processes of the Senate, although there certainly were senators available whose past behavior demonstrated their schooling at the knee of the late Joseph McCarthy.

Nonetheless, from the outset the White House treated the committee as its adversary, not its judge. The White House was convinced, and with good reason, that the greatest threat to any disclosure of malfeasance was to be found in the committee. And so President Nixon and his staff made every effort to frustrate and undermine the committee's activities. They might have succeeded in this had the committee and the television and radio networks not fully aired the committee processes, allowing the American public to see and hear what was happening and to judge for themselves which of the antagonists was more right.

Once the investigation was underway, a major bone of contention was the question of whether members of the White House staff could be called to testify before congressional committees. The question was first raised in the Watergate context in the hearings on the confirmation of L. Patrick Gray, 3d, to be appointed director of the FBI. On March 2, 1973, Nixon announced that he would not permit John W. Dean, 3d, counsel to the President, to testify at those hearings; on March 12 Nixon issued a statement on Executive privilege that he hoped would foreclose testimony by any White House staff member. The Judiciary Committee had, nevertheless, insisted on Dean's testimony, and when it was refused the committee indicated that Gray would not be confirmed. The threat of nonconfirmation was not a sufficient enough weapon to cause the White House to surrender its key members to public interrogation; as John Ehrlichman later testified before the Senate select committee, Gray was dispensable. Ehrlichman's own words to Dean were: "I think we ought to let him hang there. Let him twist slowly, slowly in the wind." No longer useful to the White House in its cover-up efforts, Gray could be thrown to the wolves.

Throughout the unraveling of the Watergate episode, the President "waffled" on the question of the committee's access to testimony of White House personnel. His dilemma was to try to prevent the revelation of incriminating data without giving the appearance of hiding relevant information—a true and, ultimately, insoluble dilemma.

The beginning of the committee investigatory process was not auspicious. When James McCord decided to turn "state's evidence," he wrote first (in March 1973) to Judge John Sirica, who had presided over the Watergate burglary trial where McCord and six other defendants were convicted, and he then turned to the grand jury that was continuing its Watergate investigation. After McCord talked to the committee staff on March 26, the staff briefed the committee and on March 28 McCord appeared before a closed session of the committee.

In his first discussions with the committee, McCord incriminated both Dean and Jeb Stuart Magruder, a former White House staff member, former deputy director of CREEP, and then a Commerce Department official. The story leaked to the press and was later confirmed by McCord. Appearing on March 28, McCord also implicated John Mitchell in hearsay evidence confided to him by G. Gordon Liddy, one of the burglary trial defendants. Liddy had been on Ehrlichman's staff at the White House Domestic Council in 1971, had left to become general counsel to CREEP, and after some internal conflicts had become counsel to the finance committee of CREEP. Liddy was the "master spy" and played the role to the hilt. A former FBI agent, he was as suave and ruthless as any fictional secret agent. Again, however, the story about Mitchell was leaked to the press.

The White House indicated its righteous anger at the information leaks and issued vigorous denials of their validity. The ire of the White House was further exacerbated by Ervin's refusal to allow White House staff to testify informally and without oath in a closed session. The committee's response to the leaks and to the suggestion of special treatment for the White House staff came on April 18, 1973, with Ervin's issuance of the procedural rules under which the committee would operate. These rules put an end to the closed hearings, left the investigatory process to the committee staff, and included an agreement not to subpoena White House staff members unless they had first refused less formal invitations to appear. Moreover, the committee rules were a response to the fact that Nixon had, on August 29, 1972, categorically denied White House participation. This he repeated on March 2, 1973. However, on April 17 he had announced that further investigation had been undertaken and his press secretary, Ronald Ziegler, said that prior statements about White House connections with Watergate were "inoperative."

The conspiracy had sprung holes and was leaking badly. Dean and Magruder, anxious for their own skins and unwilling to be "scapegoats," were talking to the grand jury and negotiating deals with the prosecutor. The press was uncovering more and more evidences of misbehavior that were confirmed by proofs and not dependent on the credibility of "reliable sources." The dam broke on April 30 when Nixon announced the resignations of H. R. Haldeman, John D. Ehrlichman, Attorney General Richard Kleindienst, and John Dean. The last did not jump, he was shoved.

Haldeman and Ehrlichman, known inter alia as "the Krauts," "the Katzenjammer Kids," and "the German mafia," were the most powerful and most hated men in American government. Obsessively dedicated to the maintenance of Nixon in office and themselves in power, they ruled the White House and attempted to rule the Executive, Legislative, and Judicial branches of the government with an iron fist not even concealed by a velvet glove. Only Henry Kissinger and John Mitchell in the Executive branch escaped their hegemony.

Elliot L. Richardson was appointed attorney general vice Kleindienst and General Alexander Haig was appointed to replace Haldeman as chief of staff. Richardson had been the jack of all trades for the Nixon Administration. He had served as undersecretary of state, as secretary of health, education, and welfare, and as secretary of defense. Richardson had a deserved reputation for integrity that distinguished him from most of the Nixon hierarchy, but had the chilly aspect of a Boston Brahmin, which he was, that permitted him both to condemn and ignore the gaucheries of the adventurers who bulked large in the Administration's offices. General Haig, a former deputy to Henry Kissinger and *Wünderkind* of the army general staff, never established a personal proximity to Nixon. However much power he came to wield as Nixon withdrew more and more into himself, refusing to attend to business, Haig never tried to play Bismarck to Nixon's Kaiser, as had Haldeman and Ehrlichman before him.

By May 1973 Watergate bombs were bursting everywhere—the "Pentagon Papers" trial of Daniel Ellsberg and the Gray nonconfirmation; the Richardson confirmation and the indictments of John Mitchell and Maurice Stans in New York for receiving illegal campaign contributions from the absconding stock manipulator Robert Vesco; confessions and accusations rang throughout the news—and the committee staff ploddingly and carefully prepared its case for presentation to the Senate select committee. The public hearings convened on May 17 in the historic Caucus Room of the Old Senate Office Building under the glare and heat of television lights, in the abundance of microphones and an outpouring of press and bystanders.

Senator Ervin opened the hearings with statements by each of the committee members attesting to the seriousness of the issues, the dedication of the committee to fairness and openness, and its commitment to revealing the truth to the American public. Senator Ervin's own statement, emphasizing the fact that the process was investigatory and not adjudicative, set out the issues and problems to be explored. He said, in part:

> If the allegations that have been made in the wake of the Watergate affair are substantiated, there has been a very serious subversion of the integrity of the electoral process, and the committee will be obliged to consider the manner in which such a subversion affects the continued existence of this Nation as a representative democracy, and how, if we are to survive, such subversions may be prevented in the future.
>
> It has been asserted that the 1972 campaign was influenced by a wide variety of illegal or unethical activities, including the widespread tapping of telephones, political headquarters, and even the residences of candidates and their campaign staffs and of members of the press; by the publication of forged documents designed to defame certain candidates or enhance others through fraudulent means; the infiltration and disruption of opponents' political organizations and gatherings; the raising and handling of campaign contributions through means designed to circumvent, either in letter or in spirit, the provisions of the campaign disclosure acts; and even the acceptance of campaign contributions based upon promises of illegal interference in governmental processes on behalf of the contributors.
>
> Finally, and perhaps most disturbingly, it has been alleged that, following the Watergate break-in, there has been a massive attempt to cover up all the improper activities, extending even so far as to pay off potential witnesses and, in particular, the seven defendants in the Watergate trial in exchange for their promise to remain silent—activities which, if true, represent interference in the integrity of the prosecutorial and judicial processes of this Nation. Moreover, there has been evidence of the use of governmental instrumentalities in efforts to exercise political surveillance over candidates in the 1972 campaign.

It is interesting to note that, unlike a criminal trial where the prosecution has the burden of proving its essential facts by proof beyond a reasonable doubt, a congressional investigation may arrive at a judgment that is based on the preponderance of the evidence. Each of the elements mentioned by Ervin in his opening remarks was definitely proved against the incumbent Administration and particularly against the top staff in the White House and those in charge of the Committee to Re-elect the President. It remained to other forums to impose sanctions on the wrongdoers. It remained for Congress, however, to enact legislation that might prevent the repetition of the evils and abuses uncovered by the Senate Watergate hearings.

Statements in Senator Baker's opening remarks were also worthy of note. For if others were worried about the adverse effects of the hearings on the power of the presidency, Baker was concerned about the preservation of the two-party system that had developed so early in our political history and had served so well for most of that time. He concluded:

> I would like to close, Mr. Chairman, with a few thoughts on the political process in this country. There has been a great deal of discussion across the country in recent weeks about the impact that Watergate might have on the President, the office of the Presidency, the Congress, on our ability to carry on relations with other countries, and so on. The constitutional institutions of this Republic are so strong and so resilient that I have never doubted for a moment their ability to function without interruption. On the contrary, it seems clear to me the very fact that we are now involved in the public process of cleaning our house, before the eyes of the world, is a mark of the greatest strength. I do not believe that any other political system could endure the thoroughness and the ferocity of the various inquiries now underway within the branches of Government and in our courageous, tenacious free press.
>
> No mention is made in our Constitution of political parties. But the two-party system, in my judgment, is as integral and important to our form of government as the three formal branches of the central government themselves. Millions of Americans participated actively, on one level or another, and with great enthusiasm, in the Presidential election of 1972. This involvement in the political process by citizens across the land is essential to participatory democracy. If one of the effects of Watergate is public disillusionment with partisan politics, if people are turned off and drop out of the political system, this will be the greatest Watergate casualty of all. If, on the other hand, this national catharsis in which we are now engaged should result in a new and better way of doing political business, if Watergate produces changes in laws and campaign procedures, then Watergate may prove to be a great national opportunity to revitalize the political process and to involve even more Americans in the day-to-day work of our two political parties. I am deeply encouraged by the fact that I find no evidence at this point in time to indicate that either the Democratic National Committee or the Republican National Committee played any role in whatever may have gone wrong in 1972. The hundreds of seasoned political professionals across this country, and the millions of people who devoted their time and energies to the campaigns, should not feel implicated or let down by what has taken place.

This effort by Baker to place the blame for Watergate on the amateurs seems to be a separation only by labels rather than facts. To say that the national committees were professionals, but that the staff of the White House, the President himself, and the leadership of CREEP (which included

Mitchell, Stans, and Magruder) were not professional politicians, is to draw lines so gossamer as to be invisible. Politicians are those persons engaged in the task of securing office for themselves or their principals; they are not divisible into categories denoting professionals and amateurs, except perhaps where you can find some who spend all their time—before, during, and after elections—as staff members of a political organization and do not themselves aspire to governmental office.

After the opening remarks, the business of the committee began. The proceedings were carried on from May 17 through August 7, 1973, in front of television cameras, thus affording the American public the opportunity to be present every minute. A huge part of the nation became television addicts during this time, but by the time the committee returned to its hearings of September 24 to November 15, the bloom was off the rose. Neither the committee nor the public was as engrossed as it had been. In part, this was so because other arenas claimed greater attention; in part, because the public had all the evidence it needed to reach a judgment on the questions that Ervin had outlined in his opening remarks.

The committee developed an unfortunate method of proceeding. Instead of having a chief inquisitor who might be followed by committee members who had questions to put to the witness, the rules called for the allocation of ten-minute question periods to each senator, with the round robin continuing as long as necessary to exhaust the questions that each had in mind. This system had the advantage of variety and of precluding the monopolization of prime television time by any one senator. But as any experienced trial lawyer knows, cross-examination cannot be successfully conducted where the continuity of the questions is so arbitrarily broken into time segments. It often takes more time than that to lead a witness through the preliminary questions necessary to establish the base for the more crucial questions.

Nevertheless, the hearings were both highly informative and dramatic. Some witnesses provided only background information, but even this was spiced with interest, as when Robert C. Odle, a baby-faced innocent who had been a director of administration for CREEP, revealed the total control exercised over the selection of the CREEP staff by Messrs. Haldeman and Mitchell.

The first major witness was James McCord, who sang a loud song on May 18. He testified about cloak-and-dagger discussions between himself and White House agents concerning the possibility of Executive clemency and supplying funds to the burglars. He also repeated his contention that Liddy had told him that Mitchell and Magruder had been involved in the planning and financing of the bugging and espionage activities undertaken by CREEP. Ervin and Baker noted that although hearsay evidence was not admissible in a court of law, it was acceptable for whatever evidentiary value it might have at a congressional hearing. When McCord resumed his testimony on May 22, he spent a large portion of his time explaining that he was testifying in no small part to prevent the Administration from placing blame for the Watergate fiasco on the CIA, to which he owed his supreme loyalty. Unfortunately, this dedication to his former employer was more frightening than it was praiseworthy.

The next witness that day was John J. Caulfield, a former White House staff member who had been implicated by McCord as the go-between on clemency and compensation operations. Caulfield, a former New York City policeman, was at the time of the hearing an official in the Treasury Department. Caulfield did not contradict McCord's proposition that his [Caulfield's] offer of clemency was purported to have come "from the very highest levels of the White House." He testified that on the basis of his White House experience, it was Dean who was the source of the offer, and he "rarely made decisions on matters of consequence without speaking to Mr. Ehrlichman, my guess was that when Mr. Dean referred to 'high White House officials' he at least meant Mr. Ehrlichman." Caulfield denied pressuring McCord to maintain silence.

It was on May 22, too, that the President issued a statement admitting implications of White House involvement but denied his own participation in the Watergate affair. He detailed at length the illegal activities indulged in to protect the national security, as he put it. He was, as it turned out, less than candid—and far from persuasive. Summarizing his position, he stated:

> Recent news accounts growing out of testimony in the Watergate investigations have given grossly misleading impressions of many of the facts, as they relate both to my own role and to certain unrelated activities involving national security.
>
> Already, on the basis of second and third-hand testimony by persons either convicted or themselves under investigation in the case, I have found myself accused of involvement in activities I never heard of until I read about them in news accounts.
>
> These impressions could also lead to a serious misunderstanding of those national security activities which, though totally unrelated to Watergate, have become entangled in the case. They could lead to further compromise of sensitive national security information.
>
> I will not abandon my responsibilities. I will continue to do the job I was elected to do. In the accompanying statement, I have set forth the facts as I know them as they relate to my own role.
>
> With regard to the specific allegations that have been made, I can and do state categorically:
>
> 1) I had no prior knowledge of the Watergate operation.
>
> 2) I took no part in, nor was I aware of, any subsequent efforts that may have been made to cover up Watergate.
>
> 3) At no time did I authorize any offer of Executive clemency for the Watergate defendants, nor did I know of any such offer.
>
> 4) I did not know, until the time of my own investigation, of any effort to provide the Watergate defendants with funds.
>
> 5) At no time did I attempt, or did I authorize others to attempt, to implicate the CIA in the Watergate matter.

6) It was not until the time of my own investigation that I learned of the break-in at the office of Mr. Ellsberg's psychiatrist, and I specifically authorized the furnishing of this information to Judge Byrne.

7) I neither authorized nor encouraged subordinates to engage in illegal or improper campaign tactics.

The facts which contradicted these propositions were ultimately revealed in the President's own tape recordings, but even without them, the presidential explanation sounded hollow. As the *Wall Street Journal* put it: "The context can only add to the impression that the President is acting like a man with something to hide." Similar reactions were reported by Republican senators as far apart in ideology as Senators Percy of Illinois and Goldwater of Arizona, who still called on the President to make a clean breast of the whole thing.

Back on the stand the following day, Caulfield testified that he adhered to his belief that the President knew of the offer of clemency. "I know what the relationships are [and] in my mind, I felt the President probably did know about [it]."

It was on May 23, 1973, that after lengthy hearings Elliot Richardson was finally confirmed as attorney general. This came only after the Judiciary Committee was satisfied that he would appoint an independent special prosecutor to conduct criminal prosecutions relating to Watergate. On May 17, after failing to convince others to take the job because they felt that he could not guarantee the necessary independence, Richardson offered the post to Professor Archibald Cox of the Harvard Law School, who had previously been solicitor general of the United States. On May 19 Richardson went ahead and fixed guidelines on the duties and responsibilities of the special prosecutor. Finally, on May 21, both Richardson and Cox appeared before the Judiciary Committee to give their assurances of rigorous execution of Watergate prosecutions.

Conflict between the committee and Cox developed almost immediately. The committee had asked for a court order, as required by statute, to grant immunity against prosecution to Dean and Magruder in order to secure their testimony for the hearings. The Department of Justice had authority to delay this grant for thirty days and they exercised this option; then on June 1 Cox conferred with committee counsel and sought to get the Senate hearings canceled. Cox was not short on talent, nor was he lacking in ego. The combination gave him the notion that it should be left to the Watergate special prosecutor to take over the investigation. It was reported that Cox threatened to go to court to get an injunction against the continuance of the hearings, but Cox later denied this. On June 4 Cox called on the committee to postpone its hearings from one to three months, but the committee took umbrage at the suggestion and unanimously rejected it.

On June 6 Cox asked the district court to impose a condition on its grant of immunity. He felt that the immunity should be granted only if the committee did not televise or broadcast its examination of Dean and Magruder. The committee, of course, opposed this motion, asserting that the court lacked the jurisdiction to put such restraints on the committee. Judge

Sirica granted the immunity without condition on June 12, agreeing that it was beyond the judicial power to impose such restraints.

Committee hearings had, in the meantime, been resumed on June 5 with the former secretary to Liddy and the former administrative assistant to Magruder appearing. The latter, Robert Reisner, testified that Mitchell regularly received reports of illegal wiretaps and that immediately after the Watergate break-in he received orders to destroy CREEP files: "Anything that would have concerned the opposition." Liddy's secretary testified to having seen photographs of Lawrence O'Brien's papers and to making out a false entry pass into McGovern headquarters.

Hugh Sloan was the next witness and his tale was an important one. Sloan had been the treasurer of CREEP and he testified that he had been pressured to cover up large cash payments that he had made to Watergate defendants. When he tried to tell White House officials that something was amiss, he was rebuffed. In his testimony he asserted that Mitchell, even while attorney general, had exercised direct control over CREEP funds. Calling the influx of money immediately before the effective date of the campaign contributions reporting law "a nightmare," Sloan revealed that he received five to six million dollars in a two-day period.

Sloan had a chart showing that he had disbursed $1.8 million, including $250,000 to Herbert Kalmbach, Nixon's personal lawyer, $350,000 to Gordon Strachan, Haldeman's assistant, and $199,000 to Liddy. Payments to Liddy seemed to concern the Nixon people most. When Liddy's request for $83,000 came to him, Sloan checked its validity with Stans, who told him: "I do not want to know and you do not want to know" what the money was for.

Magruder tried to convince Sloan to report a smaller expenditure to Liddy. When Sloan said that he would not perjure himself, Magruder informed him that he "may have to." Frederick LaRue, Mitchell's assistant, and Mitchell both worked on him to cover the amount paid to Liddy. Finally, when he met with Dwight C. Chapin, the President's appointment secretary, and Ehrlichman, they suggested that he take a vacation, which he did. Describing their discussion, Sloan stated:

> In the Ehrlichman meeting . . . I believe I expressed my concern, my personal concern with regard to the money. I believe that he interpreted my being there as personal fear and he indicated to me that I had a special relationship with the White House, if I needed help getting a lawyer, he would be glad to do that, but do not tell me any details; I do not want to know. My position would have to be until after the election that I would have to take executive privilege.

But Magruder again sought to get Sloan to falsify the amount given to Liddy. LaRue suggested that Sloan take the Fifth Amendment and Dean made the same suggestion to Sloan's lawyer; all to no avail.

Senator Baker's concern over Sloan's testimony related to the failure of the FBI to ask Sloan any questions about Liddy or the break-in, thus suggesting doubts about the integrity of the Department of Justice's investigation. Sloan reported, however, that his testimony before the grand jury was concerned with the same issues as those raised by the committee.

The next witness, Herbert Porter, conceded that he had in fact perjured himself about the payments to Liddy at the trial of the Watergate burglars. Porter was the scheduling director of CREEP and, at the behest of Magruder, he had lied to the grand jury and at the trial. Porter's testimony ended the list of lesser figures to come before the committee. The long-awaited principals—the President excepted—were then called. Most seemed out of character or, at least, they were different from what the public had a right to expect.

Maurice H. Stans, former secretary of commerce and former chairman of the finance committee of the re-election campaign, which he sought carefully to distinguish from CREEP itself, was the first of the high government witnesses to appear. At the time of his testimony, Stans, along with Mitchell, was under indictment in a federal court in New York in connection with the acceptance of an allegedly illegal contribution of $200,000 from Robert Vesco. Stans sought to postpone his appearance before the committee because of the pending trial. Although he was refused, the committee ruled that questions touching on the Vesco matter would be improper; and the senators and their counsel scrupulously adhered to this limitation.

Stans was the essence of incredulity. He could not believe that the Senate had the temerity to call him as a witness; nor could he believe that his own credibility and character were at issue. According to him, he had nothing to do with the disbursement of funds, but only with their collection. He did concede, however, that he had given $75,000 to Herbert Kalmbach, who asked for it on the authority of the White House for a "special mission," but he did not know that the money was to be used to pay off Watergate burglary defendants. The $75,000 did not come from committee funds, however. Forty-five thousand had come from Stans's safety deposit box and represented the balance of $50,000 given to Stans by Kalmbach when Stans became finance chairman, and was apparently left over from earlier campaign efforts. The other $30,000 came from three Filipino businessmen who were later reimbursed, because foreigners cannot make legal campaign contributions.

Stans admitted that technical violations of the new campaign expenditures act might have occurred, but there were certainly no intentional or major ones. The American contributions, washed through Mexican banks and ending up in Barker's account in Miami, were not illegal; "laundering" of campaign contributions was a legitimate means of protecting the privacy of donors. Even if some of Liddy's money had arrived at the committee after the law required records of contributors to be kept, the intention had been to make the contribution before April 7 and the contribution was treated as if it had.

Stans also did not question the $350,000 paid to Strachan, Haldeman's aide. He assumed that it was to be used for polling. Moreover, it was just a coincidence, he maintained, that the committee records of pre-April 7 contributors were destroyed immediately after the break-in was made public. Stans had no knowledge of what the committee did with the $1,777,000 paid out in cash before April 7, 1972.

During Stans's questioning, Senator Gurney attacked Senator Ervin for his "harassment of this witness." Ervin's response was soft but hardly calculated to turn away wrath: "I'm just an old country lawyer and I don't know the finer ways to do it. I just have to do it my way." This was as clear a pronouncement as necessary that the status of a witness, present or former, did not relieve him of a straightforward and hard-hitting examination calculated to get at the truth. Yet truth seemed at a premium. At one point, Senator Talmadge told his witness who was again protesting ignorance: "That strikes me as unbelievable." It is fair to say that such a characterization could have been made of most of Stans's testimony, whether justifiably or not. But it should be noted that the jury in the New York case against Stans and Mitchell brought in a verdict of not guilty. One will never know whether this was attributable to the judge's charge that the jury discount John Dean's testimony because of Dean's self-interest, but the Senate committee soon found Dean a far more believable witness than it thought Stans had been.

Stans was a colorless old Babbitt; his immediate successors on the stand were young men in grey flannel suits. It seemed that Nixon surrounded himself not so much with individuals as with clichés.

Of all the Watergate principals, two at the second echelon of authority, John Dean and Jeb Stuart Magruder, decided earliest that there was no point in fighting the inevitable. It was not so much a moral conversion of the kind Charles Colson later claimed, as the realization that there would not be enough places in the lifeboat when the ship ultimately went down, as it seemed sure to do. The press continued to be untiring in its pursuit of the facts. Moreover, these two were the most likely sacrificial candidates for their superiors if some sacrifice was necessary to save the Administration. They foiled any such "offering" by agreeing to testify, but not before they saw that others like Porter and Sloan would tell the truth anyway.

John W. Dean, 3d—young, smooth, bright, lacking only in experience and good judgment—held the prestigious title of counsel to the President. It was an office that dated back to Franklin D. Roosevelt's appointment of Judge Samuel Rosenman in 1942. Since then it had frequently been filled by a confidante and influential adviser to the President; it was the post held by Ehrlichman before he became assistant to the President for domestic affairs. But it is the man who makes the job; Dean succeeded to Ehrlichman's title but not to his authority. Nevertheless, to outsiders Dean was a powerful figure, quite capable of throwing around the weight of the White House in trying to assert his influence. Inside, he was more like an associate in a large law firm, responding to the needs of the senior partners and, as Caulfield had said, not taking important steps without guidance and approval from superiors. It was in this role, however, that he was a full participant in the Watergate affair. Indeed, Dean turned out to be the key figure in the unwinding of the Watergate mystery as it took place in Congress and the courts. He did not totally escape imprisonment through his aid to the prosecution, but he considerably reduced the sanctions against him with his cooperation.

Jeb Stuart Magruder also went to jail, but for a shorter term than would have been the case had he not spoken up. Magruder had worked for

Haldeman in the White House and then became deputy director of CREEP. His autobiography unwittingly reveals him as a slick young man on the make, selfish, arrogant to those below him and kowtowing to those above him—all but amoral. He had ability but few principles. And he epitomized the "bright young men" attracted to the Nixon campaign forces and the Nixon staff. Although Magruder was more closely linked to the Watergate escapades, he was almost never in direct contact with the President and so played second fiddle to Dean, who fingered the President as a prime culprit.

In the middle of June 1973 the committee adjourned for a week, so that Soviet Premier Leonid Brezhnev's visit with the President would not be confounded by the revelations at the hearings. The request for the delay came not from the White House, but from Senator Mike Mansfield, the Democratic leader, who was joined in the request by Minority Leader Hugh Scott. Only Senator Weicker objected; he thought that the hearings might be a good form of education in democracy for the Soviet leader.

John Dean was the next witness when the hearings resumed, and he occupied the witness chair for a full week. His was a tale of pervasive paranoia, of cover-up conspiracy, of payoffs and confessions. If his story were believed—corroboration was not forthcoming for some weeks and months—the guilt belonged not only to Magruder and Dean, but to Mitchell, Haldeman, and Ehrlichman, so far as the break-in was concerned, and to the President as well with reference to the cover-up.

For the first time the committee lost its aura of nonpartisan objectivity. Senator Gurney (himself soon to be indicted for election frauds) and Minority Counsel Fred Thompson viciously attacked Dean's character in hopes of destroying his credibility. But, on the whole, Dean came through as a sincere and repentant sinner finally prepared to tell the truth, if only to save his own skin.

Dean's 245-page prepared statement was read and took a full day to relate. It was supported by 47 documents. It said, in part:

> The Watergate matter was an inevitable outgrowth of a climate of excessive concern over the political impact of demonstrators, excessive concern over leaks, an insatiable appetite for political intelligence, all coupled with a do-it-yourself White House staff, regardless of the law. However, the fact that many elements of this climate culminated with the creation of a covert intelligence operation as part of the President's re-election committee was not by conscious design, rather an accident of fate.
>
> The White House was continually seeking intelligence information about demonstration leaders and their supporters that would either discredit them personally or indicate that the demonstration was in fact sponsored by some foreign enemies. There were also White House requests for information regarding ties between major political figures who opposed the President's war policies and the demonstration leaders.

The failure to produce proof of ties of this nature did not convince the White House that there were none. They attributed the failure rather to the inefficacy of the intelligence operations, including the FBI and the CIA. Dean testified that he heard complaints of this from the President himself. In fact, the White House supported "the presidentially approved plan that called for bugging, burglarizing, mail covers and the like." Haldeman, said Dean, told him "to see what I could do to get the plan implemented." When Dean complained to Mitchell, he rejected the plan, but he agreed to establish an "interagency evaluation committee." It was founded in 1971 with Caulfield as White House liaison and regular reports being made to Haldeman and Ehrlichman. Dean's office also received regular reports from the FBI and more sporadic reports from the CIA on demonstrations and radical groups.

There was concern, too, about news leaks, and Ehrlichman directed John Caulfield to put a tap on Joseph Kraft, a syndicated columnist, when FBI Director Hoover had refused to do so. After the Pentagon Papers were leaked to the *New York Times* and the *Washington Post,* the paranoia reached new heights and Colson suggested that the Brookings Institution be burglarized to recover "stolen documents." Dean said he told Ehrlichman that the scheme was "insane" and it was cancelled.

Dean was charged by Haldeman with the task of "improving our intelligence" with reference to demonstrators, and it was then that Liddy was retained by Dean, after his clearance from Ehrlichman, Mitchell, and Magruder. Dean was present at the first meeting at which Liddy presented his million-dollar plan to Mitchell and Magruder. The plan called for "mugging squads, kidnapping teams, prostitutes, and electronic surveillance." Mitchell quickly said it "was not quite what he had in mind" and indicated that the cost was prohibitive. Dean also objected at the second meeting and reported its substance to Haldeman, who instructed him to have nothing more to do with it.

Dean had been out of the country for a few days when the Watergate burglary took place. On his return, he was called by Colson, who told him that he had nothing to do with it, but that he was concerned over the contents of Howard Hunt's White House safe. Colson and Haldeman then charged Dean with custody of the contents of the safe. In discussion Liddy told Dean that Magruder had forced him to commit the burglary and Strachan reported that he had instructions from Haldeman to go through the files and "destroy damaging materials." Dean was also ordered to talk with Attorney General Kleindienst about limiting the scope of the investigation. At their meeting Kleindienst called in Assistant Attorney General Petersen, who was in charge of the criminal division, and Dean reported back that Petersen "would handle the matter fairly and would not pursue a wide inquiry into everything the White House had been doing for four years."

The contents of Hunt's safe included a briefcase full of documents: memoranda to Colson about "the plumbers unit," a number of papers relating to Daniel Ellsberg, a forged cable to show President Kennedy's involvement in President Diem's removal from power in South Vietnam, and reports of Hunt's investigations into the Edward Kennedy-Chappaquiddick incident. Ehrlichman instructed Dean to shred the papers and "deep six" the briefcase.

Dean reported that Robert Mardian had been worrying about acting

FBI Director Gray's extensive investigation into Watergate in June and July 1972. Mardian's inclination was to use the CIA to stifle the investigation. He testified that "Mitchell suggested I explore with Ehrlichman and Haldeman having the White House contact the CIA for assistance. Ehrlichman thought it was a good idea." Dean talked to the CIA assistant director, General Walters, but Walters said the director of the CIA would not take any such action except on the instructions of the President.

The contents of the Hunt briefcase were turned over to the FBI by Dean, except for "politically sensitive documents" that were given into the custody of Gray himself. Gray was not instructed to destroy the documents, but he did nonetheless.

Dean reported that on June 28 a discussion took place in Mitchell's office about the need for money to pay off the burglary defendants. Mitchell instructed Dean to get approval from Haldeman and Ehrlichman to have Kalmbach, the President's personal attorney, raise the money. It was at this point in Dean's testimony that he reported on his meetings with the President. In a September 15, 1972, meeting, Dean was complimented by the President on the handling of the Watergate case. There was conversation about the use of the Internal Revenue Service "to get" presidential adversaries and there was also talk about blocking the House investigation and stalling the trial of the burglary case until after the election. Both goals were accomplished.

In late November Mitchell had said that $350,000 in White House custody would have to be used for paying the defendants. The money was reluctantly delivered by Strachan to LaRue, who refused the receipt that was requested. Hunt had also made it clear that he wanted a promise of clemency before he pleaded guilty and Colson met with Ehrlichman in Dean's presence to put the proposition. Ehrlichman said that he would have to take it up with the President and later told Dean that he had given Colson an affirmative reply. Colson also said that he had raised the question with the President and the President had then conferred with Dean on two occasions.

The threat to uncovering the entire complexity was the newly created Senate investigating committee. Ehrlichman was particularly worried about Senate access to the grand jury data and thought that the attorney general should be instructed to fight any such disclosures. At the same time the President arranged a meeting with Senator Baker, and he was reported to have come away from the meeting with "the impression that [Baker] might be helpful." The President then arranged for Kleindienst to be Baker's "contact point." Whatever benefits the President sought, or thought he had secured, Baker proved "uncooperative." He appointed the minority counsel without consulting the White House as had been expected of him, and throughout the hearings Baker centered his questions on what the President knew and when he acquired the knowledge.

It was at a mid-February meeting, according to Dean, that Magruder told Paul L. O'Brien, a CREEP attorney, that he had had "his final authorization" for the Liddy operation from Gordon Strachan and Strachan "reported that Haldeman had cleared the matter with the President."

Dean testified that his next meeting with the President, after the September 15 meeting, was on February 27, at which time the President told Dean to report directly to him about Watergate matters. "He told me that Haldeman and Ehrlichman were principals in the matter, and I, therefore, could be more objective than they." The President also said that "he would never let Haldeman and Ehrlichman go to the Hill to testify." Dean said that the President should know that he, too, was involved in the post-break-in activities. This, said Dean, was brushed off by the President.

On March 13 Dean and the President discussed litigating the Executive privilege question to prevent anyone from going before the Senate committee. At this meeting, too, they discussed the question of payments to the Watergate defendants. The President asked Dean "how much it would cost. I told him that I could only make an estimate that it might be as high as a million dollars or more. He told me that was no problem." Dean explained that the demand was coming principally from Hunt and the President agreed that Hunt had been promised Executive clemency and that he had discussed the matter with Ehrlichman and Colson.

According to Dean, when he received still another demand for money from Hunt, he "had about reached the end of the line and was now in a position to deal with the President to end the coverup." On March 20 he had a telephone conversation with the President and told him: "I did not think he [Hunt] fully realized all the facts and the implications of those facts for the people at the White House as well as himself. He said that I should meet with him the next morning."

The famous March 21 meeting was the one in which Dean said he told the President "that there is a cancer growing on the Presidency and that if the cancer was not removed that the President himself would be killed by it." He said he spilled the whole story of the involvement of Mitchell, Haldeman, Ehrlichman, and Magruder, including his own suborning of Magruder's perjury at the burglary proceedings. He said that he, Dean, was under great pressure to provide more money for payment and that he "didn't know how to deal" with the demands.

Dean also told the President that if he were called to testify before the grand jury or the Senate committee, he would tell what he knew. It was impossible to continue the cover-up, but he thought that the President did not really understand the import of his message. After the meeting there was further talk among Haldeman, Ehrlichman, and Dean about getting Mitchell to "step forward" to take the whole rap. At the presidential meeting Dean had explained that he thought he, Haldeman, and Ehrlichman were subject to prosecution for obstruction of justice. In any event, Mitchell proved uncooperative.

At the March 22 meeting of the President, Haldeman, Ehrlichman, and Dean, the question was still how to forestall the Senate inquiry. By this time it appeared to Dean that the proposed "patsy" was no longer Mitchell but he himself, and when Dean was sent to Camp David to prepare a report on the Watergate affair, he was convinced he was being set up. At this point Dean retained counsel and repeated to Haldeman, Ehrlichman, and Magruder that if called to testify he would tell the truth. On April 2 Dean's lawyer told the prosecutor that he was prepared to talk to him.

Dean sent the President a note saying that he hoped that his talking to the prosecutor would not be regarded by Nixon "as an act of disloyalty" and he offered to meet again with him. A meeting was held on April 15. He admitted that he had the notion "that the conversation was being taped and that a record was being made to protect" Nixon. Nonetheless, on the following day Dean was called to the President's office to sign a prepared letter of resignation. He refused to do so, because the letters were virtual "confessions" to anything regarding Watergate. Later Dean said he would not resign unless Haldeman and Ehrlichman also did so.

On April 17 Dean received a call from the President to say that he was issuing a Watergate statement. Dean decided that he "would not be a scapegoat," and he announced this publicly on April 19. Strangely, the President called on Dean on April 22 to wish him a happy Easter; then on April 30 the President fired Dean and issued a further statement on Watergate.

Dean stood up well under cross-examination. He added telling details about presidential and White House "enemy lists," and he conceded that his case depended on his word against that of the President. "I can only speak what I know to be the facts, and that's what I'm providing the Committee."

The Dean testimony evoked another wrangle between Gurney and Ervin, with the former objecting to the chairman's admission of hearsay testimony. Ervin insisted that hearsay evidence was not barred at investigative hearings and cited Felix Frankfurter's comment at the time of the Teapot Dome scandal to support his position.

Nevertheless, the week of Dean's testimony was devastating to the President's case. Although it was Dean's word against the President's, the President declined repeated invitations by the committee to present his side of the story. Ervin seemed prepared to rely on the default of Nixon's testimony to suggest corroboration of Dean's story.

After this, the Senate Watergate hearings coasted. They reconvened on July 12, with John Mitchell testifying. He had decided to deny everything and engage in distasteful mocking, but he was neither a believable nor a likable witness; he contributed nothing to the revelation of facts on one side or the other. His manner convinced almost everyone of his guilt and complicity.

Mitchell was followed by Richard Moore, a special counsel to the President. He was a soft, sweet, grandfatherly type, who could not believe that the events described by Dean could have ever come to the attention of the President.

It was Alexander Butterfield, a former White House aide, who revealed what proved to be the essential evidence corroborating Dean's story. He reported that Nixon maintained a bugging system within the White House. A voice-activated tape recorder had recorded all conversations in the Oval Office and in the presidential office in the Executive Office building. In addition, four of the President's telephone lines had been tapped and recorded in the same manner. Only the President, Haldeman, Lawrence Higby, Haldeman's assistant, Butterfield, and the Secret Service staff who maintained the system, which had been functioning since the spring of 1971, knew about it.

After this, the hearings took second-place to the question of what was on the tapes and how they could be secured. It was ultimately the content of the tapes that indicted and convicted the President, causing his removal from office. But it was left to others to effectuate their publication, which took place in installments over a period of several months, during which time the presidency was paralyzed.

The committee's hearings did not come to an end after this revelation. Among others, there were still the testimonies of Haldeman and Ehrlichman to be heard. But, even had they had something to say, their statements would have been anticlimactic.

Ehrlichman claimed to know nothing. For him it was as if Watergate was a figment of Dean's imagination. He had nothing but disdain for the Watergate burglars and their bumbling efforts, although he exhibited the same disdain for everyone, including the committee members themselves. Throughout his testimony, his sneering, biting commentary and the manner in which he delivered it reminded many in the audience of the Hollywood version of a Nazi SS officer. As Mary McCarthy wrote: "In the Caucus Room people were arguing whether he or Mitchell was more purely evil." For Ehrlichman, anyone who believed that there was a Watergate conspiracy or cover-up was ignorant of how government and the very few important people who ran it really operated.

Haldeman, on the other hand, testified in so sweet a manner as to make Washington observers think that he and Ehrlichman had confused the Jekyll and Hyde roles that they had played throughout their stay in the White House. And he developed a convenient forgetfulness that was equally inconsistent with his reputation for efficiency and intellect. He, too, had nothing to do with Watergate, he said. After all, he was only the office manager for a very large enterprise.

Few believed Haldeman or Ehrlichman. Herbert Kalmbach then testified that he was an errand boy who had been assured by his superiors that he was doing nothing illegal. There was little doubt that he was only a tool, however willing, of his client.

The committee made numerous efforts to secure the all-important White House tapes. Their subpoena was rejected by the White House and the judiciary refused to enforce it, confident that their role was preeminent, and that the role of the Congress in uncovering the misdeeds of Executive Department officials was merely secondary.

Still, the Senate Watergate hearings did not end. Just before the appearances of the principal witnesses, the committee had heard from Anthony Ulasewicz, LaRue, Mardian, and Strachan. Ulasewicz, a former New York policeman and then a narcotics official in the Treasury Department, returned to the stand to testify about cloak-and-dagger arrangements for delivery of payments to the Watergate burglars. LaRue also testified about his role in making such payments, as well as to his memory of what occurred when he was present at Mitchell's meetings with Liddy about developing the "intelligence program" that culminated in the burglary. Mardian denied participation in any of the wrongdoing, except for his service as counsel to CREEP on its legal problems deriving from the criminal and civil suits. Gordan Strachan, testifying under a grant of immunity, told of his role as liaison between CREEP and the White House and particularly of Haldeman's link to Liddy's activities and the payoffs. Strachan gave credence to Dean's story.

After Ehrlichman left the stand, the committee took testimony from three former and present CIA officials who told a rather garbled story about being implored to shut off the FBI investigation by claiming it endangered CIA activities. They all denied accepting the role proferred them. Former acting director of the FBI, L. Patrick Gray, 3d, told a woeful story that contradicted the CIA story in particulars but not on the question of whether the CIA took the bait. Gray was a sorry picture as he revealed his destruction of Hunt's files in his Connecticut fireplace at Christmas. Obviously an underling regarded by Ehrlichman and others as wholly dispensable, Gray gave the impression of being an ex-military man, not overly bright, wanting to please his superiors, but not highly regarded by them. He evoked sympathy, an emotion not frequently stirred at the hearings.

Former Attorney General Kleindienst testified that he had undertaken a complete investigation and brooked no suggestion of restraint. He denied any knowledge that the FBI files on the case had been made available to Dean, and he withdrew entirely from the investigation when charges were made by Dean against Mardian and Mitchell, two of Kleindienst's close friends. He resigned on April 30, the coincidental date of the resignations of Haldeman, Ehrlichman, and Dean.

The assistant attorney general in charge of the criminal division was the next witness. Henry Petersen, a career official in the Department of Justice, had little doubt in his own mind that he had played the investigation straight and he resented his displacement by a special prosecutor. Subsequent tapes of his conversations with Nixon would have given the committee more material for their cross-examination, but the tapes were not available when Petersen was a witness. He conceded that he was trying to avoid turning the Watergate investigation into a wide-open political fishing expedition with the inhabitants of the White House as its catch.

The hearings recessed on August 7, 1973. Television's show of the century was losing its high Nielsen ratings. A Gallup poll revealed that while 52 percent of the population thought that the televised hearings had been good for the country, 41 percent felt otherwise. And while 57 percent credited the committee with the sole intent of uncovering the facts, 28 percent regarded it as a political effort to discredit the Nixon Administration.

Hearings were resumed on September 24, however, when Hunt recalled his part in the plumbers' operation, including the break-in at Dr. Daniel Ellsberg's psychiatrist's office. Hunt testified that he worked closely with Colson in matters of demands and receipts of large sums of money. He denied that he had ever asked for or received a promise of clemency, and he rejected the proposition that the money he received was the result of blackmail threats that he might talk.

On September 26 the emphasis of the hearings shifted from Watergate to problems of political sabotage and campaign contributions and their expenditures. But these activities, even when concerned with such personalities as Howard Hughes and Bebe Rebozo, did not have enough fascination to revive a flagging interest not only on the part of the public but even on the part of the committee members. These hearings lasted through November 1973.

In June 1974 the committee's most important work appeared in the form of a 1250-page report, with extensive evidence of wrongdoings by White House staff and associates, including the President. In filing the report, the committee had access to that portion of the presidential tapes that had been available to the House Judiciary Committee and the special prosecutor, but not to those that came to light only after the Supreme Court rejected President Nixon's claim of Executive privilege.

The report not only documented the Watergate misconducts and other electoral and White House malfeasances, but made a series of recommendations for legislation aimed at curing the structural deficiencies that gave rise to the usurpations and liberties taken by the Executive and his staff, in contradiction to the Constitution. Little came of the recommendations in the report, although, as a parting gesture in the last days of the Ninety-Third Congress, Senator Ervin introduced a bill to effect some of the recommendations of the special committee. It would remain for later Congresses to consider, if not enact, those Ervin proposals.

III

The denouement of Watergate came many months after the select committee concluded its hearings. Leon Jaworski, who had succeeded to the task of the special prosecutor, persevered in his pursuit of the Nixon tapes. As each new revelation of the content of those tapes was made, the public was informed of and supplied with additional proof of the culpability of the President of the United States and those who surrounded him in the White House. These revelations became the principal basis for the House Judiciary Committee's considerations of bills of impeachment.

On July 24, 1974, the Supreme Court of the United States, in the case of *United States* v. *Nixon,* unanimously ruled—with eight justices participating—that "Executive privilege" did not justify the refusal of the President to turn over the tapes demanded of him by the special prosecutor for use in pending criminal trials against the President's chief henchmen. On the evening of the same day, the Judiciary Committee began its debates on articles of impeachment—once again in the full light of television coverage. On July 30 a divided committee approved three articles of impeachment. The same day the White House turned over the tapes, in accordance with the Supreme Court's mandate. Their contents were deadly. Congressmen who had held back on impeachment now committed themselves to it. Impeachment by the House became a certainty.

On August 5, 1974, President Nixon confessed to his efforts to cover up the Watergate affair, while continuing to adhere to the position that he would not resign. The pressure from his own supporters within the legislature and outside, however, became irresistible. On August 8 Nixon announced that he intended to resign on the following day, thus becoming the first President in United States history to do so. On August 9 Gerald Ford, vice president by virtue of Spiro Agnew's earlier resignation after confessing to his own criminal activities, succeeded to the presidency. He succeeded, too, to the stigma of Watergate.

At a press conference on August 28, President Ford announced that he would not consider the question of a pardon for Nixon until after legal proceedings had run their course. On September 8, 1974, Ford announced to a disbelieving American public that he had pardoned the ex-President for "all offenses against the United States which he, Richard Nixon, had committed or may have committed."

The anticlimax of the criminal proceedings against Haldeman, Ehrlichman, Mitchell, *et al.* remained. But, after a short period of national furor over the pardon, Watergate receded into the background of history. Nixon had left not only a heritage of corruption, but a state of economic chaos that threatened another "Great Depression," with all the political and constitutional dangers inherent in such a catastrophe. The President and the nation then turned to the task of preventing the new dangers, leaving the country still exposed to the dangers inherent in the uncured corruption of the Constitution.

BIBLIOGRAPHY

Chester, Lewis, et al. *Watergate.* New York, 1973.

McCarthy, Mary. *The Mask of State: Watergate Portraits.* New York, 1974.

Magruder, Jeb Stuart. *An American Life: One Man's Road to Watergate.* New York, 1974.

New York Times. *The White House Transcripts.* New York, 1974.

Rather, Dan and Gates, Gary Paul. *The Palace Guard.* New York, 1974.

Schlesinger, Arthur, jr. *The Imperial Presidency.* Boston, 1973.

Sussman, Barry. *The Great Cover-up: Nixon and the Scandal of Watergate.* New York, 1974.

Tretick, Stanley and Shannan, William V. *They Could Not Trust the King.* New York, 1974.

United States House of Representatives. *Impeachment of Richard M. Nixon, President of the United States, Report of the Committee on the Judiciary.* 93rd Cong., 1st sess., 1973.

——. *Special Prosecutor and Watergate Grand Jury Legislation,* Hearings Before the Subcommittee on Criminal Justice of the Committee on the Judiciary. 93rd Cong., 1st sess., 1973.

United States Senate Hearings Before the Select Committee on Presidential Campaign Activities. 93rd Cong., 1st sess., 1974.

——. *Final Report of the Select Committee on Presidential Campaign Activities.* 93rd Cong., 2nd sess., S. Rep. No. 93–981, 1974.

Washington Post. *The Presidential Transcripts.* New York, 1974.

——. *The Fall of a President.* New York, 1974.

PERTINENT DOCUMENTS

Statement by President Richard M. Nixon on Executive Privilege, March 12, 1973

Rules of Procedure for the Senate Select Committee on Presidential Campaign Activities with Guidelines, April 1973

Statement by President Richard M. Nixon, April 17, 1973

Address by President Richard M. Nixon, April 30, 1973

Duties and Responsibilities of the Special Prosecutor, May 19, 1973

Testimony of Maurice Stans, June 12 and 13, 1973

Testimony of John Dean, June 25–29, 1973

Testimony of John Mitchell, July 10–11, 1973

Testimony of Alexander P. Butterfield, July 16, 1973

Testimony of John Ehrlichman, July 24–30, 1973

Opening Statement of Harry Robins Haldeman, July 30, 1973

Excerpts from the Final Report of the Senate Select Committee on Presidential Campaign Activities, June 1974

United States v. *Richard M. Nixon, Richard M. Nixon* v. *United States,* July 24, 1974

The Articles of Impeachment, August 4, 1974

Statement by President Richard M. Nixon on the Release of Additional Transcripts of Presidential Conversations, August 5, 1974

Resignation Address by President Richard M. Nixon, August 8, 1974

Remarks by President Gerald R. Ford on a Pardon for Former President Nixon, September 8, 1974

Proclamation 4311 Granting a Pardon to Richard M. Nixon, September 8, 1974

Index

C

D

E

F

I

J

K

L

M

N

O

P

Y

Z